L. E. Threlkeld

An Australian Language as Spoken by the Awabakal,

the people of Awaba, or lake Macquarie (near Newcastle, New South Wales) being

an account of their language, traditions, and customs

L. E. Threlkeld

An Australian Language as Spoken by the Awabakal,
the people of Awaba, or lake Macquarie (near Newcastle, New South Wales) being an account of their language, traditions, and customs

ISBN/EAN: 9783337318963

Printed in Europe, USA, Canada, Australia, Japan

Cover: Foto ©Paul-Georg Meister /pixelio.de

More available books at **www.hansebooks.com**

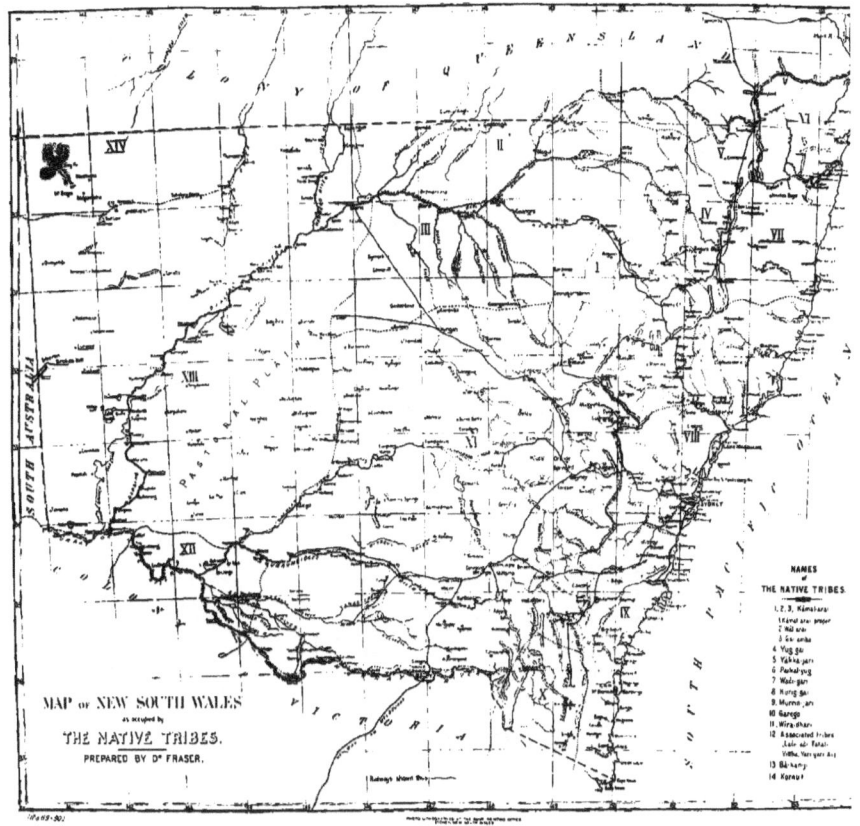

AN
AUSTRALIAN LANGUAGE

AS SPOKEN BY THE

AWABAKAL

THE PEOPLE OF

AWABA or LAKE MACQUARIE

(NEAR NEWCASTLE, NEW SOUTH WALES)

BEING AN ACCOUNT OF

THEIR LANGUAGE, TRADITIONS, AND CUSTOMS:

BY

L. E. THRELKELD.

Re-arranged, condensed, and edited,

WITH AN APPENDIX,

BY

JOHN FRASER, B.A., LL.D.,

Fellow of the Royal Society of New South Wales;
Associate of the Victoria Institute of Great Britain;
Délégué Général (pour l'Océanie) de l'Alliance Scientifique de Paris;
Hon. Corr. Member of the Celtic Society of Montreal;

Author of

THE ETRUSCANS: WERE THEY CELTS?
THE ABORIGINES OF AUSTRALIA: THEIR ETHNIC POSITION AND RELATIONS.

Sydney:
CHARLES POTTER, GOVERNMENT PRINTER.

1892.

THE EDITOR'S PREFACE.

This volume is issued by the Government of New South Wales, as a record of the language of native tribes that are rapidly disappearing from the coasts of Eastern Australia. Presentation copies will be sent to the chief learned societies at home and abroad. The indigenes of the Sydney district are gone long ago, and some of the inland tribes are represented now only by a few families of wanderers. In all New South Wales, there are only five thousand full-blood blacks; only four or five hundred in Victoria; and in Tasmania the native race became extinct in 1876. They have decayed and are decaying in spite of the fostering care of our Colonial Governments.

A considerable portion of this volume consists of Mr. Threlkeld's acquisitions in the dialect which I have called the Awabakal, from Awaba, the native name for Lake Macquarie—his sphere of labour. But we have now come to know that this dialect was essentially the same as that spoken by the sub-tribes occupying the land where Sydney now stands, and that they all formed parts of one great tribe, the Kŭriggai.

In an Appendix I have collected several Grammars and Vocabularies as a contribution to a comparative knowledge of the dialects. The map and other illustrations are new, and were prepared for this work.

The Gospel by St. Luke herein is now of no practical value, except to a linguist; but it is unique, and it shows the structural system of the language.

JOHN FRASER.

Sydney,
May, 1892.

CONTENTS.

	PAGES.
INTRODUCTION	xi—lxiv

PART I.—THE GRAMMAR AND THE KEY 1–120
    Grammar of the Awabakal Dialect ... 1—46
    Vocabulary of the Awabakal Dialect ... 47—82
    The Key to the Structure of the Awabakal
        Dialect 90–120

PART II.—TRANSLATION OF THE GOSPEL BY ST. LUKE 128-196

PART III.—THE LEXICON TO THE GOSPEL BY ST.
    LUKE 201–227

PART IV.—THE APPENDIX 1–148
    (A.) Grammar and Vocabulary of the
        Minyung Dialect ... ... 3—27
    (B.) Grammar of the Narrinyeri and other
        Dialects of South Australia ... ... 28—47
    (C.) Grammar of a Dialect in Western
        Australia ... ... 48—56
    (D.) Grammar and Vocabulary of the
        Wiradhari Dialect in New South Wales 56–120
    (E.) Prayers in the Awabakal Dialect ... 120–127
    (F.) Sentences in the Kamalarai Dialect 127–131
    (G.) The Earliest Specimen of an Australian Language 131–148

ERRATA.

Page 6, line 28. *For* 'sine' *read* 'shine.'
  ,, 11, ,, 25. *For* ġatoa *read* baġ.
  ,, 17, ,, 4. *Let* Nom. 1 and Nom. 2 change places, so that baġ and its line shall be Nom. 1.
  ,, 18, ,, 33. *Let* Nom. 1 and Nom. 2 change places, so that baġ and its line shall be Nom. 1.
  ,, 19, ,, 26. *Let* Nom. 1 and Nom. 2 change places, so that unni and its line shall be Nom. 1.
  ,, 37, ,, 16. *For* baġ (*bis*) *read* baġ †(*bis*).
  ,, 137, ,, 29. *The word* ġatun seems to have dropped out of the manuscript at * * *

APPENDIX.

Page 4, *ad finem*, *This*† recurs in the same sense on pp. 13, 14, 16.
  ,, 30,   ,,   *For* appendix *read* volume.

THE ILLUSTRATIONS.

1. MAP OF NEW SOUTH WALES AS OCCUPIED BY THE NATIVE
   TRIBES ... ... *Frontispiece*

This map is the issue of ten years' thought and inquiry on the location of our native tribes; nothing of the kind has been attempted before. The basis of the whole is the boundaries of the Kamalarai tribe, which were marked out for me by a friend who knew the tribe well fifty years ago; his information I have tested and extended by answers I got from others, who also knew the tribe about that time. The Walarai dialect differs only a little from the Kamalarai proper; so also the Wailwun, spoken by the Ngaiamba blacks; for this reason, and because they have the classification of the Kamalarai, these are regarded as only subdivisions of the great Kamalarai tribe. The Walarai dialect extends into Queensland.

The next great tribe is the Kuringgai on the sea coast. Their 'taurai' (hunting ground *or* territory) is known to extend north to the Macleay River, and I found that southwards it reached the Hawkesbury. Then, by examining the remains of the language of the natives about Sydney and southwards, and by other tests, I assured myself that the country thereabout was occupied by sub-tribes of the Kurringgai.

In a similar manner, I determined the territory of the Murrinjari on the south-east coast.

The boundaries of the Wiradhari tribe have long been known. Probably they did not extend quite to the Murray, but that river is their natural limit on the south.

From Moulamein westwards, as shown on the map, or from a line drawn from the Murrumbidgee to the Murray somewhat farther east than that, and on both sides of the Murray, there is a patch of associated tribes whose dialects are called Yerry-yerry, Marrawarra, Yuyu, Tataty, Watty-watty, &c., all from the local words for 'no.' Their position in fragments there is curious, and may be the result of some displacement from above by the incoming of stronger tribes, such as the Wiradhari.

The Bakanji is another strong tribe whose locality is well defined on the east by the Wiradhari. A sub-tribe of it is the Berriait, bordering on the Lachlan River and the Wiradhari frontier. A small portion of the north-west of New South Wales and much more of the adjoining territory in Queensland and South Australia has a tribe which some call the Kornu, but I am not sure that that is the correct name for it.

The boundaries of the Paikalyung tribe were given me by the Rev. H. Livingstone, who knows it well. Its territory runs along the coast up nearly to Brisbane.

The next tribe (I have called it Wachigari) has it's 'taurai' limited by the Paikalyung on the north and the Kuringgai on the south.

The Yakkajari speak the Pikambal dialect, and extend across our border some distance into Queensland.

The New England tribe, the Yunggai, has caused me much perplexity. There are scarcely any blacks of that territory now surviving; but the tribal language is quite different in its words from those around it; I also know for certain that the table-land of New England did not belong either to the Kamalarai or the Walarai. I have, therefore, called this tribe the Yung-gai, from Yung—the name which the coast tribes give to New England.

The Ngarego tribe belongs rather to Victoria than to New South Wales.

Of these tribes, the Kamalarai, Walarai, Ngaiamba, Bakanji, Wiradhari, the Associated Tribes, the Ngarego, the Kuringgai, are names already established and in use; and most of them are formed from the local word for 'no,' and thus describe more the speech than the people. The names, Murrinjari, Wachigari, Paikalyung, Yakkajari, I have made; for these tribes have no general name for themselves. Wachi-gari and Yakka-jari are legitimate formations from the local words for 'no'; Murrin-jari and Paikal-yung mean the 'men,' which also is the meaning of the native tribe-name Kuringgai—all from their distinctive tribal-words for 'man.' Tribes of aborigines, in many parts of the world, call themselves 'the men.'

2. PORTRAIT OF BIRABAN ... ... *Page* 88

This is the intelligent aboriginal who was so useful to Mr. Threlkeld. The illustration is reproduced from the pencil sketch which was made by Mr. Agate.

3. PORTRAIT OF "OLD MARGARET"—an 'Awabakalin,' or woman of the Lake Macquarie sub-tribe ... *Page* 196

'Old Margaret' is the last survivor of the Awabakal. She is now living in her slab-hut on a piece of land near Lake Macquarie Heads, and supports herself by her own industry. She had the advantage of early training in an English home in the district; she is respectable and respected.

Her features, as compared with those of other natives, show how much the type varies; and yet she is an Australian of pure origin. She was born at Waiong, near the Hawkesbury River, and is now about 65 years of age.

4. BUNTIMAI—'A MESSENGER' ... ... *Page* 212

This blackfellow is evidently on an errand which requires despatch. The 'possum cloak, the hair, and the general cast of the figure are true to nature, but the calves of the legs are stouter than usual.

INTRODUCTION.

I. The Grammars.

No large effort has yet been made to master the difficulties that present themselves in the study of the comparative grammar of the Australian languages. The only thing in this direction, that is known to me, is a paper on the "Position of the Australian Languages, by W. H. J. Bleek, Esq., Ph.D.," published in 1871. Dr. Bleek was a philologist who, in 1858, assisted in cataloguing the Library of His Excellency Sir Geo. Grey, K.C.B., then Governor of Cape Colony. Twenty years previously, Sir George (then Captain Grey), as leader of an expedition into the interior of our continent, had excellent opportunities of seeing the native tribes in their original condition; and the knowledge thus gained was enlarged by him and matured, while he was Governor of South Australia. The records of the knowledge of so intelligent an observer as Sir George Grey are sure to be valuable. These records are now in the South African Public Library, Cape Town, having been presented to that Library by him, along with his collection of books and other manuscripts.

The catalogue of Sir George Grey's Library was published by Trübner & Co., London, and Dr. Bleek devotes a portion of the second volume to the philology of the Australian languages.*

The earliest of individual efforts to deal with any single language of the Australian group was made by the Rev. L. E. Threlkeld, who, for many years, was engaged as a missionary among the blacks of the Lake Macquarie district, near Newcastle, New South Wales. His Grammar of their language was printed in Sydney in 1834, at the "*Herald* Office, Lower George Street." A few years previously, Mr. Threlkeld had translated the Gospel by St. Luke into the same language. This translation remained in manuscript and had disappeared; recently I discovered that it still exists, and is now in the Public Library of Auckland. This "Grammar" and the "Key" and the "Gospel," and some smaller fruits of Mr. Threlkeld's labours on that language, are now published in a collected form in the present volume. But Threlkeld's Grammar deals with only one dialect, and, for the purposes of comparative grammar, more languages than one are required.

---

* Throughout this Introduction I say "languages," although, in fact, there is but one Australian language with many dialects; I also use the word "language" instead of dialect, wherever the meaning is clear.

In looking about for another Grammar, I remembered that Mr. Horatio Hale, the philologist of the United States' Exploring Expedition, had, in his volume on the Ethnography and Philology of the Expedition*, made a short synopsis of two of our dialects. When in this colony, he got access to the Rev. William Watson, then missionary to the aborigines at "Wellington Valley," who drew up for him "an account of the most important peculiarities of the Wiraduri language, modelled as nearly as possible on the Grammar of Mr. Threlkeld, for the purpose of comparison." Further search disclosed the fact that, as early as 1835, a Dictionary and a Grammar had been prepared there, and the Gospel by St. Luke had been translated. How valuable these materials would now be, to illustrate the Awabakal of Lake Macquarie! but Mr. Watson had no relatives in this colony, and on his death his manuscripts were sold as waste paper; so I am told. Fortunately, the late Archdeacon Günther, of Mudgee, wrote a Grammar of the Wiradhari and collected a copious Vocabulary about the year 1838. The Vocabulary I found to be in the hands of his son, the present Archdeacon of Camden, and it is here published, along with a short introductory Grammar which forms part of the manuscript Vocabulary. A longer Grammar was, many years ago, sent to the home country, and I fear that it cannot now be recovered.

The next labourers in the field of Australian grammar were the Lutheran Missionaries, Messrs. Teichelmann (E. G.) and Schürmann (C. W.) In 1840 they published a "Grammar, Vocabulary, and Phrase-book" of the aboriginal language of the Adelaide tribe. Then, in 1856, appeared the primer, "Gurre Kamilaroi," by the Rev. W. Ridley. Mr. Ridley, who was a man of rare devotedness and self-denial, went among the aborigines of Liverpool Plains and shared the privations of their wandering life, in order that he might learn their language, and so be able to tell them the message of the Gospel. In 1866 (2nd edition, 1875), our Government Printing Office issued his book on the "Kamilaroi, Dippil, and Turrubul languages."

A Grammar of some of the dialects spoken in South Australia is contained in Taplin's "Folk Lore," which was published in 1879. This Grammar is given here in a condensed form.

II. Mr. Threlkeld.

Lancelot Edward Threlkeld, the pioneer in the field of Australian language, died in Sydney on the morning of the 10th October, 1859, having on the previous day preached twice in his own church—the church of the Bethel Union there.

---

* *See pp.* 479-531 of "United States' Exploring Expedition during the years 1838-42, under the command of Charles Wilkes, U.S.N.—Vol. VI., Ethnography and Ethnology; By Horatio Hale, philologist of the Expedition. *Philadelphia:* Lea and Blanchard. 1846."

Mr. Threlkeld's birthplace was Hatherleigh, in Devon, but the family belonged originally to the county of Cumberland, and there to the village of Threlkeld, which either had its name from them or gave its name to them. In "Burke's Peerage," we read of Threlkeld of Threlkeld in the time of Edward I. That family became extinct in the male line in the reign of Edward IV, but the name was continued through a younger branch, Threlkeld· of Melmerly, in the same county.

A romantic story from the Wars of the Roses connects itself with a Sir Lancelot Threlkeld by his marriage with the widow of Lord Clifford. Clifford had much power in Yorkshire, where his estates were, but, although related to the House of York, he was a keen supporter of the Lancastrians, and with his own hand he killed the youngest son of the Duke of York in cold blood after the battle of Sandal, in revenge for an injury he had received The sanguinary conduct of Lord Clifford on this occasion is commemorated by our poet, Drayton, in his 'Polyolbion,' in the lines beginning :—

"Where York himself before his castle gate,
Mangled with wounds, on his own earth lay dead,
Upon whose body Clifford down him sate,
Stabbing the corpse, and, cutting off his head,
Crowned it with paper, and, to wreak his teene,
Presents it so to his victorious Queene."

Three months after this, Clifford was himself shot through with an arrow in the battle of Towton, and the Yorkists, being now victorious, stripped the Clifford family of all their estates and possessions ; this happened in the year 1470. The heir to Lord Clifford's name and fame was a little boy then six years old. His mother feared that the House of York would seek to avenge on him the murder of their own boy, the young Earl of Rutland ; she had now no powerful friends to protect her and her son, and she knew that her movements were watched ; in these circumstances she resolved, for safety, to commit her boy to the care of her faithful retainers, and have him brought up as a shepherd on his own estates. Meanwhile, the report was spread that he had been sent to Holland and had died there. When he had reached the age of twelve years, his widowed mother married Sir Lancelot Threlkeld. This was a fortunate thing for the lad, for it led to his removal from the neighbourhood of his own home to places of greater security among the mountains of Cumberland ; and his new father, being entrusted with the secret, faithfully assisted in watching over the life of the orphan heir. To avert suspicion, it was still found necessary to continue his disguise ; but, although he was thus left without education, and could neither read nor write till happier days had come, yet the culture of his race showed itself in his natural intelligence and his personal demeanour. He grew up a tall and handsome youth, with the features and commanding mien of his grandfather, who had been much loved and regretted. While still living in obscurity as a shepherd, he gained such a knowledge of astronomy as made him a wonder to many in later years, and his gentle manners so shone through rustic attire that he secured the affection of a lady of rank, well known at that time as the "nut-brown maid"—the daughter of Sir John St. John; her he married. When the "Wars of the Roses" were ended by the accession of Henry VII., and peace was again come, the young Lord Clifford, now 32 years of age, asserted his right to the Londesborough estates, and, on petition to the King, was restored to his title and his lands. The men of the time called him the "Shepherd Earl." In addition to Londesborough, the place of his birth, he was owner of Brougham and Skipton, but he usually resided near Bolton, and there, after many years, he died, and was buried in the choir of the Abbey. His son was created Earl of Cumberland; and a grandson was a naval commander in Elizabeth's reign. In 1742 the heiress of the Cliffords married an ancestor of the present Duke of Devonshire, and with her the estates in Yorkshire passed over to that family.

This incident has only a remote connection with the Threlkeld family, but I have given it here as an interesting glimpse into the private history of noble families in those troublous times.

Our author was born in 1788 at the village of Hatherleigh, and, while still a boy, he experienced deep religious convictions under the ministry of the vicar of the parish. This ultimately led to his offering himself to the London Missionary Society for work in the foreign field, and so, after several years of instruction and training at Gosport under Mr. Bogue, he was ordained, along with Mr. Ellis, on the 8th November, 1815, and appointed to labour at Rai-atéa, in the 'Society' group of the South Seas. Towards the end of that month he embarked in a government vessel, the "Atlas," which was about to proceed to Sydney. At Rio de Janeiro, his wife fell ill, and for nearly a year he had to remain there, all the while acting as the first Protestant minister whom the English residents at Rio ever had. On 22nd January, 1817, he sailed again, along with Messrs. John Williams, Darling, Bourne, and Platt, all bound for missionary work in the islands of the South Seas.

After a short stay at Hobart, they reached Sydney on the 11th May, 1817, and Mr. Threlkeld proceeded to Raiatea soon after. The death of his wife led him to return to Sydney in 1824. Next year, the London Missionary Society established a mission to our native blacks at Lake Macquarie under the care of Threlkeld, and there, with assistance subsequently from the

Government of the Colony of New South Wales, the mission was maintained till December 31, 1841, when the number of the natives there had so declined that it had to be abandoned. It was during those seventeen years of labour that Mr. Threlkeld acquired so much experience in the use of the native dialect of the tribe, that he was enabled to prepare the works which form the bulk of this volume. The year 1842 and the surrounding years were a time of terrible commercial distress in the colony, and, when the mission station was abandoned, Mr. Threlkeld lost all his property there. But, in 1845, he was appointed minister of the Mariners' Church, Sydney, and in that office he continued till his death. By his first wife he had one son and three daughters; by his second wife—a daughter of Dr. Arndell, the Colonial surgeon of the time—he had two sons and three daughters. Those of his children who still survive occupy honourable positions in this colony.

The following is believed to be a complete list of Mr. Threlkeld's labours in the dialect which I have called the 'Awabakal':—

1827.—"Specimens of the Aboriginal Language"; printed then.

1829.—First draft of the Translation of the Gospel by St. Luke.

1832.—Translation of Prayers for Morning and Evening Service from the Ritual of the Church of England; these were selected by Archdeacon Broughton.

1834.—"The Australian Grammar" published. Mr. Threlkeld's memoranda show that at the beginning of this year the following subjects were occupying his attention :—

   1. Specimens of the Language.

   2. The Australian Grammar.

   3. The Gospel by St. Luke, under revisal.

   5. The Gospel by St. Mark, in preparation. The first rough translation was completed in 1837.

   5. The Gospel by St. Matthew, just commenced.

   6. The instruction of two native youths in writing and reading their own language.

   7. Reading lessons selected from the Old Testament.

   8. An Australian Spelling Book.

1836.—"The Spelling Book" printed.

1850.—"The Key to the Aboriginal Language" published.

1859.—At the time of his death he was engaged in completing the translation of the four Gospels; and was proceeding with the "Lexicon to the Gospel by St. Luke." Thus our author's life closed in the midst of 'labours many.'

III. Influences affecting the Language.

The position of our Australian dialects in their relation to the great families of language has not yet been determined. That task demands leisure, labour, and skill. A collection of carefully prepared Grammars and Vocabularies would make the task much easier; but where are these to be had? With the exception of those that I have named, I know of none. Australian Vocabularies have been collected in abundance, but, for the most part, these are quite useless to the philologist; they consist of dialect-names for native customs and weapons, for the birds of the air, the beasts of the field, and the trees of the forest. All this is mistaken labour which yields no fruit. What we want is to get from each dialect a sufficient number of words expressing the ideas essential to a language, in the form of substantive, adjective or verb, and a sufficient number of simple sentences; this would enable the philologist to ascertain what is the structure of its grammar and its vocables.

The Australian languages are subject to a principle of change which it is worth our pains to consider here. The native tribes name their children from any ordinary occurrence, which may have taken place at the birth or soon after it. For instance, if a kangaroo-rat were seen to run into a hollow log at that time, the child would be named by some modification of the word for kangaroo-rat. At a later period of the boy's life, that name might be changed for another, taken from some trivial circumstance in his experience; just as our own boys get by-names at school. When a man or woman dies, his family and the other members of the tribe, as far as possible, never mention his name again, and discontinue the use of those ordinary words which formed part of his name; other words are substituted for those common ones, and become permanently established in the daily language of the clan or sub-tribe to which the deceased belonged.* In this way new words arise to designate those familiar objects, the previous names for which have been cast aside; and these new words are formed regularly from other root-words, that describe probably another quality inherent in the thing in question. Let me illustrate this matter by examples. A man or a woman may get a name from some peculiar physical feature, such as a large mouth, or chin, or head; or a name taken from an animal or tree, or any similar object, animate or inanimate, which had some relation to his birth. A Tasmanian woman was called Ramanalu, 'little gull,' because a gull flew by at the time of the child's birth. After her death, the word rama would never be used again for 'a gull'; a new name for 'gull' would be invented, formed, it

---

* It is possible that the discarded word resumes its place in the language after a while; this point I have not ascertained; at all events, the adopted word remains.

may be, from a root-word meaning 'white,' because of the whiteness of the bird. This new word would be used by all the kindred and acquaintances of the deceased, and would ere long establish itself in the language of that portion of the tribe as the right name for 'gull.' Again, a boy of the Dungog tribe of blacks, in our own colony, was receiving instruction from the old men of the tribe; he was required to make a spear, and was sent into the bush to select a suitable piece of wood; he cut off and brought to them a piece of the 'cockspur' tree; this choice was so absurd, that forthwith his instructors dubbed him Bobinkat, and that was his name ever after. When he died, the word bobin would disappear, and some other name be found for the cockspur tree. And the operation of this principle is not confined to Australia; it is found also in Polynesia; but there it has respect to the living, not the dead. High chiefs there are regarded as so exalted personages, that common people must not make use of any portion of their names in ordinary talk, for fear of giving offence. If, for example, a chief's name contains the word pe'a, 'bat,' the tribe calls the 'bat,' not pe'a, but manu-o-le-lagi, 'bird of the sky.' In languages which are not subject to these influences, the derivation of such a word is usually very plain; the Latin vespertilio, 'bat,' for instance, bears its origin on its very face; but if a philologist, not knowing the history of the word manu-o-le-lagi, were to find it to mean a 'bat' in a Polynesian tongue, he would be puzzled to explain how it is that a creature so peculiar as the 'bat,' should have been named by a word having so indefinite a meaning as the 'bird of the sky.' Any one who may have had the curiosity to look into lists of names for common things in Australian vocabularies, must have been surprised to see how diverse are these names in the various tribes, but your wonder ceases to be wonder when the cause is known. In fact, we do find that among conterminous tribes, and even in the sub-sections of the same tribe, these words vary greatly; for the presence of death from time to time in the encampments kept up a frequent lapse of words.

To show how much a native language may be effected by this cause of change, I quote here a few sentences from Taplin, who, for many years, was in daily contact with the black natives of South Australia. In his Vocabulary he says:—

"Therto, 'head'; obsolete on account of death. Koninto, 'stomach'; obsolete on account of death. Muna, 'hand'; not used on account of the death of a native of that name. When any one dies, named after anything, the name of that thing is at once changed. For instance, the name for 'water' was changed *nine times* in about five years on account of the death of eight men who bore the name of 'water.' The reason of this is that the name of the departed is never mentioned because of a superstitious notion that his spirit would immediately appear, if mentioned in any way."

[B]

It may possibly be asked why our blackfellows had so strong a disinclination to mention the name of a friend who had died. We ourselves have a feeling of the same kind. We speak of our friend as 'the deceased,' 'the departed,' 'him who has gone'; and if we must mention his name, we apologise for it by saying 'poor' Mr. So-and-so, and seem afraid to use the simple word 'dead.' But our indigenes have a stronger reason than that. They believe that the spirit of a man, especially if he is killed by violence, is excessively uncomfortable after death, and malicious, and in its fretfulness ready to take offence at anything, and so pour out its wrath on the living. Even the mention of the dead man's name would offend, and bring vengeance on them in the night time. Our blacks seem also to have the idea that the deceased, for a certain number of days after death, has not yet got his spiritual body, which slowly grows upon him, and that, while in this undeveloped state, he is like a child, and is specially querulous and vengeful.

IV. Tests in Examining Languages.

I now proceed to show some results which may be obtained even from our Australian words, by comparing them with others elsewhere. It is agreed among philologists, that there is no surer test of the affinity of different languages than that which comes through the identification of their pronouns, numerals*, and, to a less extent, their prepositions. To this I would add, in our present inquiry, the identity of such common words as 'eye, foot, hand, fire, sun, moon,' and the like; for these words cannot have been used much in the names of individuals, and are therefore not likely to have suffered from the fluctuations which I have already explained. It is true that, in all languages, the pronouns and the numerals are subject to abrasion and decay, from the frequency and rapidity with which they are pronounced, and from a natural tendency everywhere to shorten the words which are most in use. But it is the function of the philologist, not only to understand these causes of decay, but to show the process by which the words fell away, and to restore them to their original forms for the purpose of identification.

It is agreed, then, that the numerals, the pronouns, and, to some extent, the prepositions, are a strong test of the affinity of languages. On this principle, such languages as the Sanskrit, the Greek, the Latin, the German and Gothic, the Lithuanian, the Keltic, have been tested and proved to be so much akin that they are grouped as a well-defined family of languages—the Aryan. Some anthropologists, especially when they are not linguists themselves, sneer at the labours of philology as deceptive and liable to

---

* Bopp says that the lowest numerals can never be introduced into any country by foreigners.

serious error; so are all sciences, if not managed with care and ability. A student in chemical analysis and synthesis may get results which are clearly erroneous; instead of declaring the prescribed methods to be faulty or his materials to be bad, he ought to blame only his own want of skill in manipulation. As to the utility of philology, I would only remark that it was by the study of languages that the place of Sanskrit (and consequently of the Hindu race) was determined in its relation to the other members of the family I have named, and it was philology alone that settled the claim of the Keltic, and consequently of the Kelts, to be regarded as one of the most ancient members of the Aryan family. In the case of the cuneiform inscriptions, the services which philology has rendered are inestimable. And it is quite possible that, amid the conflicting opinions as to the origin of our Australian race, the *via prima salutis*, the first dawn of a sure daylight, may in the future arise from a careful examination of their language.

As is well known, the Australian numeral system is very limited in its range; our natives say 'one,' 'two'; sometimes 'three'; occasionally 'hand' for 'five'; all else is 'many,' 'a great number.' It was alleged by Sir John Lubbock, and has since been repeated by everybody, that their having separate words only for 'one' and 'two' is a proof that Australians possess very limited mental powers, since they cannot count higher than 'two.' Every colonist, who has been much in contact with the blacks, can adduce proofs to show that their mental powers are not so limited, and that, when our indigenes are taken out of their adverse environment and encouraged to cultivate their intellectual faculties, they readily develope a decided capacity for improvement. A friend of mine, fifty years ago, taught two young black boys to play chess; they soon acquired a liking for the game, and learned to play with caution and skill, and even with success. If it were possible to surround the blacks with favourable influences continued from generation to generation, I have no doubt that their whole position would be altered; but any final separation from their ancestral habits would lead to their speedy extinction as a race; this was the issue that was rapidly approaching after the last remnants of the Tasmanians were removed to Flinders' Island. But, for many hundreds of years, no one can tell how many, the Australian race has lived in the midst of adverse surroundings, tribe warring against tribe, each tribe restricted to its own boundaries, the supply of food in our precarious climate often scanty, the paralysing terror produced by their strong belief in the supernatural power of demons and of their own wizards, the ravages of waves of disease and death sweeping over them from time to time; all these and other causes compelled them to think only of their daily subsistence and the preservation of their lives, fixed and deepened their degradation, and prevented even the possibility of amelioration and elevation. The natives of the South Sea islands, whose lot has been a fairer one, have had many yams and cocoa-nuts and bananas and other things to count, and so have developed a wide system of numbers; but our poor blackfellows, whose only personal property is a few spears or so, have not felt it necessary to speak of more than 'one,' 'two,' or 'three' objects at once. Then, as to the linguistic question on which Sir John Lubbock builds his charge, I think it could be shown that even the Aryan system of numbers—the most highly developed system of any—is founded on the words for 'one,' 'two,' 'three,' and no more, all the rest being combinations of these by addition or by multiplication. Further, the Aryans have singular and dual forms for nouns and pronouns, that is, they have number-forms for 'one' and 'two,' but all the rest beyond that is included in the general name of plural, that is 'more'; indeed the Sanskrit uses its word for 'four' in a general way to mean a considerable number, exactly as to our blackfellows all else beyond two or three is bula, 'many.' For these reasons I think that this charge against our blackfellows ought to be laid on better ground than that afforded by their numerals.

V. The Australian Numerals.

If Bopp's dictum is well founded, the numerals 'one,' 'two,' 'three,' when tested, may tell us something about the origin of our Australian blacks. I, therefore, now proceed to examine these numerals. And here I may be permitted to say that I alone am responsible for the arguments drawn from the evidence produced in this inquiry. So far as I know, these arguments have never been advanced previously; indeed, I am convinced that no one has ever discussed these numerals before, for it is commonly alleged that it is impossible to give any account of them.

1. *The Numeral 'One.'*

(*a*.) Of the words for 'one,' I take up first that which is least common, pir, 'one.' It is used in the Walarai country (see map). It must be an old and genuine word, for I know that, in another dialect, the word piriwal means 'chief,' and pir seems to me to bear the same relation to piriwal that the Latin primus, 'first,' bears to princeps, 'chief,' 'first,' or the Latin preposition pro, 'before,' to proceres, 'chiefs,' or our English word 'first' to the German fürst, 'a prince.' In fact, I regard pro and pir as the same word originally.

Now, do not mistake me here; for I do not assert that the languages spoken by our Australians are uterine brothers to the Latin and the Greek; but I do assert that all languages have one common, although ancient, origin, and that, in the essential words of these languages, there are proofs of that common origin. Pir, then, as allied to pro, means the number which comes 'before' all others in the row, the one that comes 'first.' The Latin primus is for pri-imus (*cf.* Sk. pra-thamas, 'first'), in which the root pri, not unlike pir, is the same as the Latin pro and prae. In the Aryan family, the nearest approach to the Australian pir is the Lithuanian pir-mas, 'first,' and pir-m (a preposition), 'before'; other remote kinsmen are the Greek pro-tos, 'first,' pru-tanis, 'a prince,' 'a president' (*cf.* piriwal), prin, 'before'; the Gothic fru-ma, 'first'; the Aryan prefixes pra, fra, pro, pru, prae, pre, and fore as in our English 'fore-ordain.' The Keltic languages drop the initial p or f, and say ro, ru, air, ari, to mean 'before.' In the Malay region ar-ung is a 'chief,' and in Polynesia ari-ki is 'a chief,' which the Samoans change into ali'i; these words, I would say, come from eastern forms corresponding to the Keltic ro, air, 'before.' In Samoan i lu-ma means 'in front,' and in Malay de-alu-wan; these are like ru; in Aneityum, a Papuan island of the New Hebrides, a 'chief' is called natimi arid, where natimi means 'man,' and arid is 'high,' 'exalted,' doubtless from the same root as ariki; and arid is to ariki as the Latin procērus, 'tall,' to procĕres, 'chiefs.' From the abraded from ru I take the New Britain* word lūa (Samoan lua'i), 'first.'

In the Dravidian languages of India, from which quarter, as I suppose, our Australian languages have come, there is a close parallel to our word pir, for pira means 'before,' and piran is 'a lord.' Dravidian scholars themselves acknowledge that piran comes from the Sanskrit preposition pra, 'before'; this corroborates my derivation of the Australian word piriwal and the Maori ariki. The Aroma dialect of New Guinea says pirana, 'face'; and in my opinion this pirana bears the same relation to the Dravidian pira that the Latin frons has to the preposition pro, the Samoan mua-ulu to mua, 'first,' and the English fore-head, to be-fore. The Motu dialect says vaira for 'face, front'; I take this to be a metathesis of pira, for the Motu also says vaira-nai, 'before'; another dialect says vari; with this compare pro, para, and frons. The negroes, to the west of Khartoum, also say ber, bera, for 'one.'

The Australian postposition bir-ung, 'away from,' seems to be connected with this root in the same way as the Greek para. The dictionary meanings of the Sanskrit preposition pra are 'before,' 'away,' 'beginning'; now, if these three meanings were

---

* New Britain and New Ireland are two tolerably large islands lying to the east of New Guinea, and Duke of York Island—a name corrupted by the natives into Tukiok—is a small island in the straits between these two. The natives of all these are Papuans.

carried to Australia through the Dravidian form pira, they abundantly justify my arguments as to the origin of the Australian word pir, 'one,' and birung, 'away from.' In New Britain pirai means 'odd,' 'not a "round" number' (*cf.* the game of 'odds and evens'), and this sense must be from a numeral meaning 'one.' In the Ebudan* language of Efate, 'a voice came from heaven' is nafisan sikei i milu elagi mai, in which milu elagi signifies 'away from (direction from) the sky.' Here milu is identical in form and meaning with the Awabakal birung. Further, in New Britain and in the Duke of York Is. (Melanesian), ka, kan mean 'from,' kapi, with verbs of motion, implies 'motion from,' and kabira means 'on account of.' These correspond very well with the forms and uses of the Awabakal postpositions kai, ka-birung, kin-birung. The simple form biru is therefore cognate to the Sanskrit para, *Gr.*, para, 'from.'

Some further light on this point may be got from another quarter. The Hebrew preposition corresponding to birung is min, or, without the *n*, mi, mä; in form this is not far removed from the bi of birung. Min, originally, is a noun meaning a 'part,' and, in its use as a preposition, it answers first to the partitive genitive or the preposition ex in the classic languages; then, from this primary notion, it is used to signify a 'departing from' any place, 'distance from,' 'proceeding *or* 'receding from'; in these respects it corresponds exactly with the Australian birung. Now, män, (min), 'a part,' comes from the *Heb.* root mânâh, 'to divide.' But, in Dravidian, the verb 'to divide' is per, piri, and that also is a close approximation to our Australian birung. In the chief Dravidian dialects, 'a part', 'a portion' is pâl; this again brings us to the Shemitic pâlâ, pârash, and many other forms of that verb, meaning 'to share,' 'to separate,' &c., and to the Sanskrit phâl, 'to divide,' *Gr.* meiromai, 'I share,' meros, 'a part,' *Lat.* pars, and a host of words from these. Now, if birung be the Dravidian piri, per, and if piri, per be the same word as the Sanskrit pâl and the *Heb.* pâlâ, and if these are all original root-words belonging to a common stock, I cannot see how it is possible for anyone to avoid the force of the argument from this that our Australian indigenes have a share in a common ancestry, and that, in language, their immediate ancestors are the Dravidians of India.

Results in this Section are:—Preposition forms to mean 'before' are, in the primitive languages, *pro, pri, pro, prae, pru*; other forms are *par-a, par-os, pur-as*; modes of all these are, *fra, fru, vor, fore*, and, without the initial letter, *ro, ru, air*; the Lithu-

---

* I have made the word 'Ebudan' (*Lat.* Ebudes *insulae*), and use it as more convenient to handle than 'New Hebridean.' The languages spoken on New Britain, New Ireland, Duke of York Island, Solomon Islands, Santa Cruz, and Banks Islands I call 'Albannic' (*cf. Lat.* Albion), and any root-words which are found in the Malay, Melanesian, and Polynesian languages I call 'Sporadic.'

anian has *pir*, and with this correspond the Dravidian *pir-a*, 'before,' the Australian *pir*, ' one,' and the Turkic, *bir*, ' one.' In Sanskrit, the old ablative form *purá* means ' formerly,' ' first '; cognates are the Gr. *paros*, ' before,' and the Zend *para*, 'before.'

(*b*). But the most common word for 'one' in New South Wales is wākul. In fact, it is our Sydney word for 'one,' and there can be no doubt of its genuineness, for it is noted by Lieut.-Colonel Collins as a Port Jackson word in his book on the Colony, published 1802; he spells it wogul. At Newcastle it was wākōl; in the Williams River district, wakul-bo, and on the Manning, waknl. From my manuscript notes I write down the various forms which this word assumes, beginning with Tasmania and passing northwards to the Timor Sea:— Tasmania, mara-i, mara-wa; in Victoria, bur; on the Murray River near Wentworth and Euston, mo, mata, máda, meta-ta; on the middle course of the Darling, waichola; on the Upper Murray, mala; on Monero Plains, yalla; at Moruya, medendal; in the Murrumbidgee district, mit-ong; at Jervis Bay, met-ann; on Goulburn Plains, met-ong; in the Illawarra district, mit-ung; at Appin, wógul; at Sydney and northwards to the Manning River and the Hastings, wakul; on Liverpool Plains, mal; at Wellington, mal-anda; in southern Queensland, byáda, muray, baja, byáya; in the Northern Territory of South Australia, mo-tu, wa-rat, wa-dat.

Besides these, some other words for the number 'one' are used in various parts of Australia, but those that I have given all proceed from the original root, which it will be our duty now to discover. And I notice, first of all, that one word in the list stretches along the whole extent of seaboard from the Illawarra district to the Hastings—the word wakul—and this fact affords the presumption that all that coast line was occupied by the same tribe, or by tribes closely akin; for the tribes a little inland say mal and mal-anda for 'one.' Wakul, then, was the word used by the Sydney blacks, as Collins testifies. If a chemist has a compound substance handed to him for analysis, he experiments on it, and tests it in order to discover its elements. Let us do so with wakul; it is a compound, for simple roots are usually monosyllables; but are its parts wa+kul or wak+ul? Here I remember that, in the same region where wakul exists, there is a word kará-kal, ' a wizard,' 'a doctor *or* medicine-man,' but inland he is called kará-ji. This satisfies me as proof that the -kul is merely a formative syllable, and that the root is wa. And this conviction is strengthened when I cast my eye over the above list of words; for they all begin with the syllable ma or some modification of it, the rest of each word consisting of various formative syllables. As I have now got hold of a clue to a solution, I reflect that the initial labial of a root-word may assume various forms; thus, *p*, *b*, *m* may interchange, and may easily become *f*, *wh*, *v*, *w*. There can be no doubt, for instance, that the Latin pater, the German vater, and the English father are the same word; there $p=f=v$; and in one district in Scotland the people always say fat for what and far for where; so also the Maori whatu is the Samoan fatu; that is $f=wh$; *b* and *m* also are interchangeable, in Oriental languages especially, for *m* is only the sound of the letter *b* modified by the omission of a breathing through the nose; *m* is therefore regarded as a *b* nasalized. I note also that the words under consideration all begin with the cognate sound of *m*, *b*, or *w*, except yalla; and this example 1 think must have been at one time walla, that is, u ala, of which the *u* has obtained the sound of *i* (y); or wa-la may come from the same root as wa-kul, the difference lying only in the termination. The other vowels of root word are *o*, *u*, *e*, *i*, *ai*, all of which in Australian are modifications of the original sound *a*.

Having now discovered the root-germ from which our Sydney friend wakul proceeded, and having noted the various guises which he has assumed in these colonies, we must next ask where he came from, and see if he has any kinsmen in other lands; for, when by searching we find that out, we may perhaps be justified in saying that the Australians brought the root-word with them from those lands. Before setting out on this quest, I observe that when a number of men are arranged in a row, he who is number one is (1) 'before' all the others, and 'in front' of them; he is thereby (2) 'first or foremost'; he has (3) the 'pre-eminence' in honour or authority, and (4) he may be regarded as the 'beginning or origin' of all the others.* We may therefore reasonably expect that words for 'one' will be akin to other words, bearing some one or other of these four meanings. I have already shown that the Kamalarai numeral pir, 'one,' is related to Aryan prepositions meaning 'before,' and to the Maori word ariki (Samoan ali'i), 'a chief,' as one having authority and eminence†; 1 shall now show that the kindred of wakul have the other meanings as well. And, first, I note that the word bokol is used for 'one' in the island of Santo, one of the New Hebrides. Bokol is so like wogul, the Port Jackson word, that I cannot doubt their identity; and yet it is impossible to suppose that the one word can be borrowed from the other. The islanders of Santo can never have had any intercourse with the blacks of Sydney; nor, if they had in any past time, can we believe that either language was so

---

* Cf. the *Heb.* âhâdh, kedam, rôsh, aûl or yaâl, for these meanings.
† The Insular-Keltic words for 'chief,' 'principal,' are priomh, ard, araid; and roimh is 'before.' It is evident that these are only corruptions of the root pri, pro, prae, pra, 'before.' In Ku, a Dravidian dialect, 'one' or 'first' is ra (cf. Sk. pra) and in Duke of York Island (New Britain Group), 'one' is ra, re.

miserably poor as to be without a word of its own for 'one.' The blacks of Santo are a frizzly-haired negroid race; I therefore argue, from the evidence of this word, that these blacks and our blacks have, in some way, one common origin.

I next take you to another Papuan region having a negroid population—a group of islands off the east end of New Guinea and consisting of New Britain, New Ireland, and some others. In the Duke of York Island there, I find the following words, all akin to wakul, viz., makala, 'for the 'first' time' mara, mara-kam, 'for the 'first' time,' marua, 'to bear fruit for the 'first' time, to enter on a new course, to begin,' mara, 100 (= the 'beginning' of a new reckoning), muka, 'first,' muka-na, 'first-' born son,' muka-tai, 'first,' mun, 'to go first.'* In all these, the root is ma, mu, as in Australia, and the abundance of these derived forms in this Tukiok language proves that the root is indigenous, not borrowed. Among them I observe mara, 'for the 'first' time,' and mara, 100, and this is exactly the Tasmanian word (marawa) for 'one'; another of them is muka, 'first,' and this word, by dropping the k, which is never† sounded in Samoan, becomes the Samoan mua, 'first,' and mua-ulu, 'the fore-head.'‡ Mua also is very common in Samoan (as in foe-mua, 'the 'first' or stroke oar,' a-fua, 'to begin'), and thus proves itself to be native to the language. Further, you may have observed that some of the Australian words for 'one' are mo, mata. With mo compare the Santo word mo-ig, 'to begin,'—another proof that the Santoans and the Australians are kinsmen; with mata compare the Motu word mata-ma, 'a beginning,' and mata-mata, 'new,' 'fresh'; the Fijian matai, 'first,' and tau-mada 'before-hand'; the Maori ti-mata, 'to begin'; the Samoan a-mata, 'to begin'; the New Britain a-ma-na, 'before, in front,' mata-na, 'the front,' biti-na 'the commencement'; the Motu badi-na, 'origin,' and the Aneityumese ni-mti-din, 'the front'; with mu compare the Fijian vuna, 'to begin,' and the New Britain wa-vuna, 'to begin,' and the Santo mul, 'a chief,' as being the 'first' man. All these I

---

* Compare with this the Tamil postposition mun, 'before.'
† The one solitary exception is puke, 'catch you'!—a child's play-word.
‡ An uncommon form of the root ba is va; and from it the Mangaians (Hervey Islands) say va-ri, 'a beginning'; but in the Koiari dialect of New Guinea this same word means 'the forehead,' 'the face.' This word thus illustrates the procession of meanings from the root pra (para), pro, 'before'; for vari is equivalent to 'that which is before,' hence 'a beginning,' 'the forehead' as the 'front' part of the human body, 'the face'; it also throws some light on the derivation of frons, which has so puzzled Latin etymologists that some of them derive it from the Greek ophrus, 'the eyebrow'! The Motumotu dialect of New Guinea says hali, instead of vari, for 'forehead'; several other dialects there say i-piri-ti, paru, para-na, pira-na, for 'face'; these are all connected with the Dravidian pira, 'before.' The Brahui of Afghanistan says mun, 'the face,' which is the same word as the Tamil, mun, 'before.'

have noticed in the course of my reading, but I believe there are many other words in these islands which are of the same origin as our Australian word wakul.* I pray you to remember that, with the exception of Samoa and New Zealand, these words all come from Papuan regions and afford indirect evidence that our Australians are allied to the Papuans.

As to the Maori and Samoan congeners that I have quoted, it is commonly alleged that these races are Malayo-Polynesians, on the theory that their languages are of Malay origin †; but let us look at this theory in the light of our present inquiry. It is said that the Polynesians are Malays. Well, let us see. If the Samoans are Malays, then the Duke of York Islanders are Malays; for the word mua, which is essential to the Samoan language, is the same word as the Tukiok muka; therefore the Papuans of that island also are Malays! But the corresponding Malay word is mūla, 'in front,' 'foremost,' 'at first,' and it is certain that muka can never be formed from mula; for, while k may become l, the letter l, when once established in a word, cannot revert to k. Thus the Malay language might be said to have come from the Duke of York Island, as least so far as the evidence of this word goes! But I acknowledge that they may both be taken from one common source, and this, I believe, is the true solution of the question. Where shall we find that common source? The root-form of mula, muka, mua, and of all the others, is ma, mu, and if we can find that root, it will be easy to understand how all these words have been formed independently from that original root; and it will then be unnecessary to say that the Samoan language is of Malay origin, or that the Papuans of the New Britain isles are using a Malay language. I now take you to Southern India, to a group of languages called the Dravidian, occupying the mountains of the Dekkan, and the coasts both to the east and the west of that. Some of these Dravidian tribes are considered by the best authorities to be certainly negroid, and, in England, Prof. Flower, from an examination of their crania, has classed them as kinsmen of the Australians. One of the most cultivated languages of the group is the Tamil, and the Tamilians are known to have class-marriage laws similar to those in Fiji and Australia. Now for 'first' the Tamil says mudal, and this mudal is a verbal noun meaning 'a beginning,' 'priority' in time or place. The root is mu, and dal is a formative syllable. The mu is, without doubt, our Australian

---

* These and all other words from the New Britain and Duke of York Islands I quote from manuscript dictionaries of these languages, prepared by the missionaries there.

† The name and authority of K. Wilhelm von Humboldt first gave this theory a standing; but we have now much fuller materials on which to form an independent judgment.

root ma, mo, mu. The late Bishop Caldwell says*—"Mudal is connected with the Tamil postposition mun, 'before'; mudal is used as the root of a new verb 'to begin.' Mu evidently signifies 'priority,' and may be the same as the Tamil mu, 'to be old,' mudu, 'antiquity.'" I think there is a better derivation than that. The Sanskrit mûla means 'origin, cause, commencement,' and is the same word as the Malay mula already referred to, and both of these I take from the Sanskrit root-word bhû, 'to begin to be, to become, to be,' with which is connected the Latin fore (fuere), 'to be about to be,' fui, &c. From bhû come such Sanskrit words as bhava, 'birth, origin,' bhâvana, 'causing to be,' bhuvanyu, 'a master or lord' (cf. piran, &c.), and many other words in the Aryan languages. At all events, wakul and these other Australian words for ' one ' are assuredly from the same root as the Dravidian mu-dal, 'first,' 'a beginnig.' I, for one, cannot believe that words so much alike both in root and meaning should have sprung up by accident over so vast an area as India, Malaya, New Guinea, Fiji, Samoa, and back again to the New Hebrides and Australia. The only rational explanation seems to me to be that these races were all at one time part of a common stock, that in their dispersion they carried with them the root-words of the parent languages, and that in their new habitations they dressed out these root-words with prefixes and affixes by a process of development, just as circumstances required.

Results.—The root in its simplest form is ba, 'to begin to be,' 'to begin'; other forms are bo, bu, bi; ma, mo, mu; ja, fu, vu; wa. The nearest approach to the Australian wakul, 'one,' is the Ebudan bokol, 'one,' and the Tukiok makal-a, 'for the first time,' but many other cognate words are found all over the South Seas in the sense of 'first,' 'begin.' The Tasmanian mara-wa, 'one,' is the same as the Tukiok mara, 'for the first time,' and mara, 100; and in New South Wales, mara-gai means 'first' in the Mudgee dialect.

2. *The Numeral Two.*

Almost the only other Australian numeral is bula, 'two.' It is true that several tribes have a distinct word for 'three,' and a few have a word for 'five' taken from the word 'hand,' but in most parts of Australia the number 'three' is expressed by 'two-one,' 'four' by 'two-two,' 'five' by 'two-two-one' and so on. But the wore bula is universal; with various changes of termination, it exists from Tasmania in the extreme south, right on to the Gulf

---

*All my knowledge of the Dravidian race and language comes from Dr. Caldwell's "Comparative Dictionary of the Dravidian or South Indian Family of Languages; second edition; London : Trübner and Co., 1875." In this Introduction, I quote from the notes which I made when I read the book some years ago, and now I cannot always tell whether I am quoting his words or only my own statement of them.

of Carpentaria. If you ask me why there is only one word for 'two,' while the words for 'one' are so numerous and different, I reply that, in other languages, and especially in those of the Turanian family, there is a similar diversity in the words for 'one'; and the reason is this, that, wherever there is a considerable number of words for 'origin,' 'commencement,' 'before,' &c., there will be a similar variety in the words for 'one,' which are formed from them. But the range of ideas for 'two' is somewhat limited; the only ideas possible are 'repetition,' or 'following,' or something similar. Let me show you this by a few examples. The Hebrew shenāim, 'two,' is a dual form, and is connected with the verb shânâh, 'to repeat;' the Latins also say 'vigesimo altero anno' to mean in the 'twenty second year;' but alter is 'the other of two,' and in French and English it means to 'change;' and secundus in Latin comes from sequor, 'I follow.' Thus we shall find that words for 'two' are the same as words for 'follow,' 'repeat,' 'another,' 'again,' 'also,' 'and,' and the like; and most of these ideas are usually expressed by forms of the same root-word.

As to the form of the word bula*, we have here no friendly karáji to tell us whether the -la is radical or not. I think that the -la is formative. The Tasmanian bu-ali (Milligan writes it pooalih) is probably the nearest approach to the original form, the bu being the root and the -ali the affix. In the Tasmanian pia-wa, the pia seems to me to be only a dialect form of bula, for the liquid *l* easily drops out, and in the Aryan languages a modified *u* approaches very nearly to the sound of *i* (*cf.* Eng., sir); in the Polynesian, *i* often takes the place of *u*. Thus bula would become bu-a, bi-a, pia. The syllable *wa* in pia-wa, as in marawa, 'one,' is only a suffix, the same as ba in our colony. All the other words for 'two' are only lengthened forms of bula.

As to the kindred of bula, I find that, in the Papuan island of Aneityum (New Hebrides), the word in-mul is 'twins'; there, *in* is the common prefix used to form nouns; the mul that

---

* In my manuscript notes I have the following forms :—From Tasmania, bura, pooali, piawah; Victoria, bûlum, pollit; South Australia, bulait, purlaitye; New South Wales, blula, buloara, bul̩oara-bo; Southern Queensland, bular, pūbul, bularro, bulao; Northern Queensland, bularoo. It is evident that some of these words have been written down by men who were not acquainted with the phonology of languages, and that the spelling does not adequately represent the real sounds. This is generally the case in vocabularies of Australian words, and is a source of much perplexity to linguists. One of the commonest mistakes is bular for bula. In pronouncing that word, our blackfellows let the voice dwell on the final *a*, and an observer is apt to think that this is the sound of *ar*; just as a Cockney will say 'idear' for 'idea,' 'mar' for 'ma,' or 'pianer' for 'piano.' In one vocabulary that I have seen almost every word terminates with *r* on this principle!

remains is bul, 'two'; there also u'm, for mu, is 'and'; in the other islands it is ma, mo. In New Britain, bal-et is 'again,' bul-ug, 'again,' 'also,' 'another,' mule, 'again,' bula, 'another,' 'an additional one' (*cf.* ma, 'and'), bula, ka-bila, 'also' (with -bila *cf.* Tasm. pia), muru, 'to follow.' In Samoan, muli is 'to follow,' fo'i is 'also,' ulu-ga (for fulu-) is a 'couple.' The Fijian has tau-muri, 'behind' in the sense of 'following,' just as tau-mada in Fijian means 'first' or 'before.' The Malay has ulang, 'to repeat,' and pula, 'again, too, likewise.' In some of the Himalayan regions, to which a portion of the aboriginal inhabitants of India was driven by the Aryan invasion, buli, pli, bli means 'four,' that is, as I suppose, 'two-twos,'—a dual form of 'two.'

It seems to me that the Dravidian words maru, 'to change,' muru, 'to turn,' muri, 'to break in two,' are from the same root as bula, and that root is to be found in Aryan words also, such as Lat. mu-to, mu-tu-us; for there is a Sk. root ma, 'to change.' It is known that the Sanskrit dvi, dva, 'two,' gives the Greek dis (for dvis), 'twice,' and the adjective dissos, 'double,' and that dvis gives the Latin bis; but the Sk. dva also gives the Gothic twa, 'other,' 'different,' and the Eng. twain, 'two,' as well as words for 'two' in many languages. Hence I think that our root bu, ba, gives the Samoan vae-ga 'a division,' vaega-lemu, 'the half,' and other words; because when people are 'at one' on any subject they are agreed, but when they are at 'twos and threes' they are divided in opinion; and in the same sense sense I would connect the Lat. divido with the Sk. root dvi. Probably the Latin varius and the English variance are connected with the root ba in that same sense.

I would only add a line to say that our blackfellows use the word bula also to mean 'many.' I do not believe that this is the same word as bula, 'two.' I consider it to come from the same root as the Sanskrit pulu, puru, 'many,' and that root, under the form of par, pla, ple, plu, has ramifications all through the Aryan languages in the sense of 'fill, full, much, more,' &c. The eastern form of this root gives, in New Britain, bula, 'more,' mag, 'many,' buka, 'full'; in Motu, badais 'much,' and hutu-ma, 'many,' 'multitude'; in Aneityum, a-lup-as (lup=plu), 'much'; in Fiji, vu-ga, 'many'; in Duke of York Island, bu-nui, 'to increase.' In Dravidian, pal is 'many,' pal-gu, 'to become many, to multiply, to increase.' It thus appears that the Australian bula, 'many,' has kindred, not only in Melanesia and the Dekkan, but also all through the Aryan region.

Results.—The root is *bu*, which denotes 'repetition,' 'change,' and this is the idea which resides in the Hebrew numeral 'two,' and in the Latin *alter*, 'second'; another, but cognate, idea for 'two' or 'second' is 'that which *follows*'; of the root *bu* other forms are *bu, bi, pi, ma, mo, mu, fu, fo,* and *u*; from *ma, mu,* come Dravidian words meaning 'to turn,' 'to change'; and from the same root-forms there are, in the New Hebrides, New Britain, and Polynesia, numerous words in the sense of 'follow,' 'again,' 'another,' "a couple,' 'also.' The Melanesian word *mu-le*, 'again,' and the Malay *pu-la*, 'again,' connect themselves, not only with the Dravidian *ma-ru, mu-ru*, but also with the Sanskrit word *pu-nar*, 'back,' 'again,' and also with the Greek *pa-lin*, 'again.'

VI. OTHER TEST-WORDS.
Words for 'Water,' 'Blind,' 'Eye.'

(*a*). In dealing with the Australian words for 'water,' 'fire,' 'sun,' 'eye,' &c., I must use brevity. All these can be proved to have their roots in India, and to have stems and branches from these roots in Aryan Europe, in Malay lands, and in the islands of the South Seas. First, let us take up the word for 'water.' Collins quotes b a d o as the Port Jackson word for 'water'; others write it b a d u; it is found in various parts of our colony and in Western Australia. The root is b a, m a, and the d u is a suffix; d u is also in Dravidian a formative to neuter nouns. The root m a means 'to be liquid,' 'to flow.' It is a very old word; for the Assyrian cuneiform inscriptions have m a m i, 'waters,' and this is a plural by reduplication; the Hebrew has m o, m a(i), 'water,' m o a, 'to flow'; the ancient Egyptian has m o, 'water,' whence, according to some, the name Moses; the Sanskrit has a m b u (a m *for* m a, by metathesis), 'water;' the Keltic has a m h a i n n, a b h u i n n, 'a river,' whence comes the river-name, 'Avon.' From m a come the words w a i and v a i which are so common for 'water' in the New Hebrides and in the Polynesian islands, and from the same root, in a sense known to the Arabs, by an appropriate euphemism, as 'the water of the feet,' come the Melanesian and Polynesian words m i, m i m, m i m i, m i a g a, &c., the Sanskrit m i h and the Keltic m ù n. From a m (=a b=a p) comes the Sanskrit plural form â p a s, 'water,' while from m a may come the Latin m a d-i d u s, 'wet.' We found that w a-k u l, 'one,' comes from root b a, m a; so, from the root of b a-d u, comes the Australian word w a-l a, which means 'rain,' and in some places, 'water.'

As to the kindred of our Sydney b a d u, I would remind you that 'water,' 'rain,' 'sea,' and 'wave,' are cognate ideas; hence the Samangs, who are the Negritos of the peninsula of Malacca, say b a t-c a o for 'water'; the Motu of New Guinea say m e d u, 'rain,' b a t u-g u, 'shower'; the Aneityumese i n-c a u-p d a,[*] 'rain';

---

[*] Can is the Fijian tau, 'to fall as rain,' and -pda is the same as the New Britain word b a t a, 'rain'; a u in Samoan is 'a current.'

New Britain says bata, 'to rain,' ta-va, 'sea,' and the Maori say awa, 'water.' As a coincidence, it is remarkable that the old high German word awa (*cf.* the Ger. wasser, Eng. water) means 'water,' and bedu is quoted as an old Phrygio-Macedonian word meaning 'water.'

Some observers have remarked that our blacks soon master the dialects spoken by other tribes, and have ascribed this to a natural readiness in learning languages. But the present inquiry shows that there is another cause for this. A man or woman of the Sydney tribe, which said ba-du for 'water,' would easily recognize ba-na in an adjacent tribe as the same word, the termination only being different, just as it is not hard for Englishmen to remember that the German wasser is water, and that brennen means burn. So also, a Kamalarai black, who says mu-ga, would soon know the Wiradhari mu-pai; and elsewhere mata, 'one,' is not much different from meta and matata for 'one,' or even from the Tasmanian mara.

Results.—*Ba, ma, mo, am, ap* are forms of an original root meaning 'water,' 'that which is liquid and flows'; derived forms are *mi, me, wa;* from *ba* comes the Sydney word *ba-du,* 'water'; the *du* here is a suffix in Dravidian also, and exists in the New Guinea word *ba-tu,* elsewhere *ba-ta;* the Samang Negritos say *bat-eao;* the old language of Java has *banu,* 'water,' where the *n* has the liquid sound of *gn,* and takes the place of *d* in the suffix *du.* From all this it is clear that our Australian *badu* is of good and ancient lineage.

(*b.*) In the Maitland district of New South Wales a 'blind' man is called boko; in Polynesia poko is 'blind,' or, more fully, mata-poko, mata-po, 'eyes-blind.' As there can be no suspicion of borrowing here, how is so striking a resemblance to be accounted for? Do you say that it is a mere coincidence? Well, if so, let us examine the matter. In the Kamalarai region, (see map) mu-ga means 'blind.' and in the Mudgee district, mu-pai is 'dumb'; in Santo (New Hebrides), mog-moga is 'deaf'; in Erromanga, another island of that group, busa is 'dumb'; in Fiji, bo-bo is 'blind'; in Duke of York Island, ba-ba is 'deaf'; in Sanskrit, mu-ka is 'dumb'; in Greek, mu-dos, mu-tis is 'dumb,' Lat. mut-us. In Keltic, bann is 'to bind, tie,' balbh is 'dumb,' and bodhar is 'deaf.' Now, there can be little doubt that in all these words the root is the same (mu, mo; ba, bo, bu; po), and yet these words extend over a very wide area indeed, from Tahiti right across through India to Greece, Italy, and even to John o' Groat's. The meanings are 'blind,' 'deaf,' 'dumb,' and yet the root is the same. The general root-meaning which suits them all is 'to close,' 'to bind'; this meaning shows itself in the Greek verb mu-ō—from which mudos comes—'to close the eyes or mouth,' and in the Sanskrit mu, 'to bind';

similarly the Hebrew (a) illām, 'dumb,' comes from the verb ālām, 'to bind,' 'to be silent'; in the Gospels, the blind man's eyes were 'opened,' and Zacharias, who had been for a time dumb, had 'his mouth opened and his tongue loosed.' The root of our Australian words boko, muga, is therefore the same as the Sanskrit mu, 'to bind.' From the same source come the Samoan pu-puni, 'to shut,' po, 'night'; the Aneityumese at-apn-es (apn=pan), 'to shut,' nā-poi, 'dark clouds'; the New Britain bog, 'clouded,' and the Tukiok bog, 'to cover up'; cf. the Sanskrit bhuka, 'darkness.' In Aneityum, a-pat is 'dark,' 'deaf,' and po-p is 'dumb.' In Malay, puk-kah (cf. mu-ga) is 'deaf,' and bu-ta is 'blind'; ba-bat (cf. ba-ba, bo-bo) is to 'bind'; Fiji has bu-ki-a, 'to tie,' 'to fasten'; New Zealand has pu-pu, 'to tie in bundles,' pu, 'a tribe,' 'bunch,' 'bundle.' It is even possible that our English words bind, bunch, bundle, come, through the Anglo-Saxon, from this same root, ba, bu, mu.

I suppose that these examples will suffice to prove that the similarity between the Australian boko and the Polynesian poko is not a mere coincidence. Where have we room now for the theory that the natives of the South Sea Islands are of Malay origin? I might, with equal justice, say that they came from the Hunter River district in Australia, if I were to look only at the words boko and poko!

Results.—The ideas 'blind,' 'deaf,' 'dumb,' may be reduced to the simple idea 'bound'—the eyes, ears, mouth, or tongue 'closed, bound, tied.' This idea is, in the Aryan languages, expressed mostly by *mu*, but, in our Eastern languages, by *ba, bo; mu, mo; pu, po;* all these root-forms are identical, and are the basis of cognate words spreading from the region of '*ultima Thule*' across the world to Tahiti. Can this be the result of accident, or of the spontaneous creation of language in several different centres? Is it not rather proof of a common origin? Even in the development of the root, there is a singular correspondence; for the Sanskrit adds -ka, and so do the Malay, the Kamalarai, the Santoan, and the Polynesian; others use *t* for *k*.

(c.) The word for 'eye' also may be useful as a sample test-word, for it is not likely to be subject to the influences of change to which I have already referred. In Tasmania a word for 'eye' is mongtena, and the common word in all Australia is mi or mil, or some other simple derived form from the root mi. Mongtena is in Milligan's "Vocabulary of the Dialects of the Aboriginal Tribes of Tasmania," but I have never found that Vocabulary to be satisfactory either as to its phonetics or its critical sagacity. I therefore suppose that the real form is ma-aġ-ta-na; for mong-ta-linna is there the word for 'eyelash,' and mong-to-ne is 'to see'; at all events, I consider ma to be its original stem, while the

INTRODUCTION.

Australian stem is mi, although there are, in various parts of the continent, words with the ma stem. The Australian words for 'eye,' then, are mi, mia, mikal, miki, mir, mil, mial, mina, minúk, miko, mirang; maal, mail; meur, mobara. These words extend from Port Darwin right across to Bass's Straits. Several words formed from the same root mean the 'face,' and compound words are:—wirtin-mirnu, 'eyelid,' turna-mirnu, 'lower eyelid,' wićin-mir, 'eye-lash,' genin-mir, 'eye-brow,' kráji-mring, 'white of the eye,' daami-mir, 'the temples,' katen-mirnu, 'a tear.'

Now, it is evident that all these words for 'eye' come from the root ma, mi, me, mo, and that those formed from mi are the most common. This ma is quite sporadic; for, in Samoan, which I take to be original and typical Polynesian, ma means 'clean,' 'pure,' 'bright-red,' maina is 'to shine,' said of fire; mā-lama means either 'the moon' or 'a light'; va-ai is 'to see,' and so on; the Ebudan ma is 'to see'; in New Britain me-me is 'scarlet,' 'bright-red,' and with the meaning of 'red' the Ebudan has me-me-a, miel, miala; in Samoan, mu-mu is 'to burn brightly,' and mú-mú is 'red,' and the Aneityumese ama-mud is 'to burn' transitively; the Maori has ma-hana, 'warm'; Papuan for 'eye' is mata, mara, maka, mana; the Malay has mata, 'eye,' and this is the sporadic word used everywhere for 'eye.'

From all these words, it appears that 'see,' 'clear,' 'shine,' 'eye,' 'burn,' 'fire,' 'red,' are allied terms, and that the root-idea from which they all proceed is that of 'shining brightly.' Now, so far as the eye is concerned, that is an appropriate designation for it; and this appropriateness is elsewhere confirmed by language; for the Sanskrit akshi, 'eye,' Latin oculus, and the Latin acer, 'sharp,' are founded on the root ak, meaning 'keenly bright' or 'sharp,' and the English word 'sheen' is, in Lowland Scotch, applied to the 'bright' part of the eye. Now, I find that meaning in the Sanskrit bhâ, 'to shine,' which is just our root ma. Sanskrit derivatives from this bhâ are bha, 'a star' (with which compare the Australian mirri, 'the stars'), bhaga, 'the sun,' and bhâ, 'light,' bhânu, bhâma, 'light,' 'the sun,' 'passion.' The Greek phai-no is from the same root.

The Dravidian language, like the Australian, seems to prefer the form mi; it has min, 'to glitter,' and hence mina is 'a fish,' so called from its phosphorescent scales.

A Samoan word 'to glisten,' 'to shine,' is ila-ila, applied to the eyes, and in the Papuan of Tagula (south-east cost of New Guinea) ira is 'bright'; at Port Essington (north coast of Australia) ira is the 'eye,' and in some parts of New South Wales ire, yir-oka is the 'sun.' In the Wiradhari dialect, iradu is 'day,' and the Ebudan of Erromanga has ire, 'to-day.' Further, a common word for 'eye' in Queensland is dilli; and

[c]

I have no doubt that this is the same Dravidian termination -illi which we shall find in ta-killi-ko and in many other Awabakal words, but here added on to the same root which we find in the Sanskrit di(p), 'to shine.'

The Ebudan of Baki has sembi to mean 'fire'; now sembu in Dravidian means 'red.' In Australia, a very general word for 'fire' is wi, win; in the north-west of Tasmania it is win-alia; these I take to be from the same root as our mil, 'the eye,' and the Dravidian min. In Tasmania also, tintya means 'red'; to which cognates are the Sanskrit damh, dah, ' to burn,' dams, damç, 'to bite,' 'to see'; in Tamil tind-u, is 'to kindle,' tittu, 'to whet'; cf. Anglo-Saxon tendan, 'to kindle,' English tinder.

Besides mata, the Maoris have another word for 'eye,' kanohi, which much resembles the Dravidian kan, 'the eye,' kân, 'to see'; and the root of kan may be the same syllable as in Sanskrit ak-shi, 'eye,' the ak being by metathesis changed into ka. At all events, the root kan is abundantly prevalent in the sporadic languages; for the Maori itself has kana, 'to stare wildly,' that is, 'to look keenly'; ka, 'to burn'; ka-ka, 'red-hot'; kana-pa, 'bright,' 'shining'; kana-ku, 'fire'; and cognate Polynesian dialects have kano-i-mata, 'the pupil (i.e., 'the sheen') of the eye'; 'a'ano, certain 'red berries,' ' the flesh of animals,' from its redness; ka-napa-napa, 'to glitter'; ka-napa, 'lightning.' The simple root ka gives la, ra, 'the sun,' and all the Polynesian words connected with these forms.

Nor is this root-word ka, kan confined to Polynesian dialects; in Ebudan, 'fire' is in-cap, kapi, kapu, gapu, av, avi; and the Papuan dialects have for 'fire,' kova, kai-wa; for ' burn,' ogabu, igabi. And kai-o in Greek is 'I burn.'

It is interesting to know, also, that in the states which form the Himalayan boundary of India the words for 'eye' are mi, mik, mighi, mak, mo, mak, mo; and, farther east, in Cochin-China and Tonkin, mot, mok, mu. It thus appears that, on the whole our common word mil, 'the eye,' is more akin to the non-Aryan races of India—the representatives of its earlier population.

In closing this section of my subject, I presume I need scarcely say that the evidence before us drawn from the words for 'water,' 'blind,' and 'eye,' fully justifies the opinion that the Australian languages are not isolated, but that, in their essential root-words, they have a close relation to the languages of the Southern Seas and to similar root-words in the languages of the great peninsula of India. I cannot conceive it to be possible that our blackfellows should have, by chance, invented words which, when analysed, show the underlying ideas expressed by them to be the same as those root-words spread over so vast an area elsewhere.

VII. Miscellaneous Test Words.

(*a.*) There are just two or three other words which I would glance at very rapidly. The Malay kutu means 'louse'; in all Polynesia also that word means 'louse'; therefore, as some persons say, the South Sea Islanders must be Malay-Polynesians. But I find that in Aneityum also, a Papuan region, in-ket is 'louse,' and in South Australia kŭta, and in other parts of Australia, kŭ-lo, gullun. To complete the analogy, these persons should now say that the Papuans of the New Hebrides and the blacks of South Australia are Malay. This looks like a *reductio ad absurdum*.

(*b.*) The word kutu reminds me that there are some very unsavoury words, which are a strong proof of identity of origin among races; for, if these words have not come from one common source, it is scarcely possible to imagine how they are so much alike. For instance, gū-nung here means *stercus hominis aut bestiae*; in Sanskrit the root-verb is gu. In Samoan, (k)i-no is 'excrement,' the same word as gū-nung. Among our Port Stephens blacks, the worst of the evil spirits is called gūnung-dhakia='*stercus edens*.' In Hebrew, a variant for the name Beelzebub is Beelzebūl, which means *dominus stercoris*. Again, kak is an Aryan root-verb; in New Guinea it becomes tage (*t* for *k*, as is common); in New Britain, tak; in Samoa, ta'e; in Aneityum, no-hok and na-heh. The Sanskrit bhaga, which I need not translate, is in Fiji maga; and in Tasmania maga; and pi, mi, as I have already shown, is as old as the Assyrians.

(*c.*) The Tasmanian word for 'sun' is pugganubrana or pukkanebrena *or* pallanubrana *or* panubrana, according to Milligan's list. Of these, the first is clearly the original form, for the last is merely a contraction of it, and the third substitutes *l* for *g*. The last syllable -na is formative, and is exceedingly common in Tasmanian words; it is, I may observe in passing, exactly the same syllable which is used as a common suffix to form nouns in New Guinea and in the Albannic group, and in a slightly different way also in Aneityum. The remainder of the Tasmanian word is pugga and nubra. Now, nubra or nubré in Tasmanian is 'the eye,' but the vocabularies of that language do not enlighten me as to the meaning of pugga. I would write it bŭg-a, and connect it with the New Britain word bŭg (pronounced bŭng), which means 'day'; thus bŭganubra would mean 'the eye of day,' that is, 'the sun'; and that is exactly the meaning of mata-ari, the Malay word for the 'sun.' The Ebudan of Santo has bog, 'day,' and the Fijian for 'sun' is mata-ni-senga. Bug is allied to the Dravidian pag-al, 'day.' Bŭg I take from the Sk. bhâ, 'to shine'; with this compare the derivation of the English word 'day.'

(*d*.) In the Kamalarai dialect (N.S.W.), kagal means 'bad,' 'no good'; the -gal here, as elsewhere, is formative, and ka is the root. Now kâ is a Sk. prefix meaning 'bad'; in Fiji, 'bad' is ca, and in the New Hebrides, sa; in New Britain it is a-ka-ina.

(*e*.) The Awabakal word for 'good' is murráraġ; in Wiradhari, it is marang; in Kamalarai, it is murraba; the Port Jackson tribe at Sydney called it bujári. The root is ma, mu, bu; Mr. Threlkeld's spelling should thus have been ma-ra-raġ, that is, ma-ra with the last syllable reduplicated and -aġ added; and murraba should be ma-ra-ba; in bu-jari, the -jari is a very common formative. Analogues to these are:—Albannic, bo-ina, 'good'; Ebudan (Aneityum), up-ene (up *for* bu); Malay, bā-ik; Papuan, māgē, bo-ēna, na-mo, na-ma. The Sanskrit bha-dra means 'best,' 'happy,' 'well'; and the insular Keltic ma-th is 'good,' 'wholesome,' 'happy.' I believe that the Latin bonus (of which Latin etymologists cannot trace the origin) is connected with these ancient roots; for the Keltic ma-th, *i.e.*, mad, would easily give bon-us.

(*f*.) The Wiradhari balun, 'dead,' seems to be the same word as the Dravidian mâ-l, 'to die,' and of the same origin as the Polynesian ma-te, 'dead,' and the Malay ma-ti, mang-kat, 'dead.' The old Assyrian has maatu, 'to die,' and the Sanskrit mri (mar), the Malay mi-ta, the Hebrew múth, mäth, are all cognate verbs. The Keltic has bath, bas, 'death.'

(*g*.) Korien is an Awabakal negative. If it were an Ebudan word, its form in -en would make it a verbal noun equivalent to 'the denying.' Now, it happens that, in the Motu dialect of New Guinea, gorea means 'to deny,' and the Maori ha-hore *or* hore means 'no' (*h* for *k*), and whaka-kore-kore, 'to deny.' The Ebudan of Efate has koro, 'to deny.' Another Awabakal negative is kya-wai, where the kya is for ka. The Maori ka-ua (imperative or optative) also means 'not.'

(*h*.) Wiyalli is to 'speak.' The Sanskrit vad, vaç, 'to speak,' would give the wiya, and the -alli is the usual verbal form. The Albannic has veti, 'speak.' Fiji has va-ka, 'to say,' and vei wali, 'to joke,' where vei is a reciprocal. The Awabakal wi-ya means 'say,' 'tell'; New Britain has wi, 'to tell, to inform.'

(*k*.) The Awabakal bún means 'to strike,' 'to beat,' 'to kill.' With this compare the Malay bunoh, 'to kill'; the Albannic bua-tari, 'to destroy,' and we-umi, 'to fight,' 'to kill,' of which the we is reciprocal.

(*l*.) For an adult 'woman,' the Wiradhari says inar; the Port Jackson (Sydney) sub-tribe said din or dhin*; other localities say yinan, ina; thus the *d* is radical. Several districts, far apart, in

---

*Hence comes the word jin—so commonly used in Australia to mean the 'wife' of a black man (kuri).

British New Guinea say ina-gu, 'my mother,' ia ina-na, 'his mother,' ine, 'mother,' where the ina is our Australian word; and, in Samoa, tinā is 'mother.' Are these languages not akin? Is it possible that the Papuans, the Polynesians, and the Australians could have borrowed from one another so essential a word as 'woman,' 'mother'? Moreover, in Tamil, inu means 'to bring forth young' (cf. Eng. yean), and in Malay indū is a word for 'mother.' Are these, too, not akin to our Australian word?

VIII. THE PRONOUNS AS TEST WORDS.

There are few languages in which the pronouns of the first and the second persons are declined throughout by the inflexion of the same base-stem. In the Aryan family, there are at least two bases for each of them, and these are often so disguised by the inflexions that it is difficult to detect them. In English, for instance, there does not seem to be any etymological connection between *I* and *me* and *we*, and a similar diversity exists in the Latin *ego*, *mihi* and *nos*, *tu* and *vos*; in the Greek *ego*, *mou*, *nōi*, *hēmeis*; in the Sanskrit *aham*, *mam*, *vayam*, or *tvad* and *yushmad*. In Melanesian regions, the corresponding Papuan, Albannic and Ebudan pronouns are apparently considered so volatile and evanescent that a strong demonstrative is added as a backbone for their support, and thus the pronoun itself almost disappears from view. But many of these Melanesian pronouns usually have two forms—a longer and a shorter; the longer and stronger is used for emphasis and can stand alone ; the shorter is suffixed to verbs and nouns, and it commonly shows the stem of the pronoun in its primary state. In Latin and Greek, we are already familiar with the strengthening use of demonstratives as regards these two personal pronouns, for we know that *ego-ipse*, *ego-met*, *vos-met-ipsi*, *ego-ge*, and the like, are used. As examples of the shorter Melanesian forms, I cite the Aneityumese etma-k, 'my father,' etma-m, 'thy father,' etma-n, 'his father,' where the *k*, *m*, and *n* represent the three pronouns of which the longer possessives are unyak, unyum, o un; corresponding suffixes are seen in the Papuan (Murua Is.) nima-gu 'my hand,' nima-mu, 'thy hand,' nima-na, 'his hand.' In Melanesian languages generally, either the separable possessive or its suffix form is used with nouns, although the one and the other use convey a slightly different shade of meaning ; thus, the Tukiok dialect says either a nug ruma or a ruma-ig, 'my house,' and the Fijian something similar ; but the Papuans say ia nima-na, 'his hand,' ina-gu, 'my mother.'

Each dialect in this volume has some peculiarity ; for the Wiradhari has something which looks like suffixed pronouns,*

---

* See girugal-*du* on page 111 of this Appendix, gaddal-*di* on page 112, and other instances in the same section.

and the Awabakal has a 'conjoined dual'; yet they all have long forms of the first and the second pronouns to be used alone or for the sake of emphasis, while other short forms always go with a verb as its subject. I add a list of the pronouns found in the whole of the Australian, Papuan, and Melanesian regions, so far as they are as yet known to linguists; for, although I shall make only a limited use of this list at present, yet it may be useful to students of language in Britain and elsewhere, especially as the sources from which I have compiled it are not generally accessible.

AUSTRALIAN PRONOUNS.

The *Awabakal* pronouns are :—

	Singular.	*Dual.*	*Plural.*
1st.—	Gatoa, baġ, emmo-uġ, tia	Bali, ġali	Geen, ġear-un
2nd.—	Ginto, bi, ġiro-ug	Bula	Nura
3rd. Masc.—	Niuwoa, noa, ġi-ko-uġ, bón	Buloara	Bara
3rd. Fem.—	Boun-toa, boun-noun		

For the purpose of comparison, I give the forms of these two pronouns as found in other parts of Australia :—

New South Wales.

1st Pronoun.

Sing.—Gaiya, ġa, ġaan, ġai, iya, ġata, ġaiagnġ; ġadthu, nathu, nathuna, athu, addu, thu, athol; mi, mina, mitua, motto; imiġdu, ġanna, nanna; ġera; maiyai; iaka; ġiamba; ġulaġi.

2nd Pronoun.

Sing.—Gind-a, (-u), yind-a, (-u), ind-a, (-e, -o, -u), nind-a, (-u); idno; numba; wonda; nindrua, natrua; yindigi, indiga; youra; beai, búbla; wiya, walbo; ġin; imiba; ġindiguġ; nagdu; gulaġa.
3rd Pro.; *Sing.*—Genna, noa, niuoa; *Plu.*—Garma, bara.

Victoria.

1st Pronoun.

Sing.—Gaddo, nadtha, gio, ġaiu, ġatúk; waan, aan, winnak; yatti, yanga, yandoġ, nitte; naik, naić, niak, ġe, ġen; wokok, yerrowik, wolúnyek, tiarmek; búrdop.

2nd Pronoun.

Sing.—Gind-a, (-e, -i,- o, -u), ġindúk; nind-i, (-e); ġinna, ġinya; nin, nindo, ninan, niam, winnin; yerrowin; tiarmin; waar, waanyen; wolaniġ; nutúk, utúk; mirambina; gulum; yerally.
3rd Pro.; *Sing.*—Nunthi, munniger, kiġa; *Plu.* Murra-milla,kinyet.

INTRODUCTION.

Tasmania.
1st Pro.; *Sing.*—Mina, mana, mena.   2nd Pro.; *Sing.*—Nina.
Central and South Australia.

1st Pronoun.

Sing.—Gai, ġann-a, (-i), ġinyi, onye, yiġa, yinna, ini, unnyi; ġapp-a, (-u), ġaap, appa, aupa; ġatto, attho, attu, autu, althu; ġúéa; ti; iyie.

2nd Pronoun.

Sing.—Gina, nia, nini, nina, yina; ġimba, imba, umpu, unga, unni, yinyi; nindo, yundo; tidni, yidni, yundru, andru, gundru; wuru, nuru, nuni; ġanna.
3rd Pro.; *Sing.*—Nulia, kitye, pa, panna, ninni; *Plu.*—Kinna(r), ka(r), pa(r)na, nana, ya(r)dna.

Western Australia.

1st Pronoun.

Sing.—Gatha, ġatuko, natto, ġadjo, ajjo, ġanya, ġuanga, ġanga, ġana, ġonya, nanya, nunna; ġarnii, ġeit; gi, ġida, ġika, ġiġ.

2nd Pronoun.

Sing.—Ginda, ġinna, yinda, yinna, nini, ninya, niya; ġinduk, yinnuk, nonduk, nundu, núnda, nunak; janna.   *Plural*—Nural.
3rd Pro.; *Sing.*—Bal; *Plu.*—Balgun, bullalel.

Queensland.

1st Pronoun.

Sing.—Gaia, ġia, ġio, nigo; ġanga, ongya, unéa; nutta, utthu, uda; yundu, ġiba, ipa; nia, ia, niu, iu, iuwa, yo; búrko; kuronya; ġúnġúl.

2nd Pronoun.

Sing.—Ninda, inda, imba; yinda, (-i), ind-a, (-i); yindua, yúndu, indu; innu, iu; inknu, ingowa, enowa, nowa; nino; nayon; nomún; yunúr; tini; wologa.
3rd Pro.; *Sing.*—Uġda, unda; *Plu.*—Ganna.

With these Australian Pronouns, compare the

DRAVIDIAN PRONOUNS.

1st Pronoun.

Sing.—Tamil—Nàn, yân, ên, en; Canarese—ân, yân, nâ, nânu, en, êne; Tulu—yân, yen, e; Malayâlam—âlam, ñân, ên, en, ena, eni, ini; Telugu—nênu, nê, ēnu, é, nâ, nu, ni; Tuda—ân, en, eni, ini; Kóta—âne, en, eni, ini; Gônd—annâ, nâ, ân, na; Ku—ânu, na, in, e; Râjmahâl—en; Orâon—enan.
Plu.—Mêmu, amât, yâm, âm, âmu, nâm, nângal, nâvu, âvu.

2nd Pronoun.

Sing.—Tamil—Ni, nin, nun, ei, i, ay, oy; Canarese—nin, ni, ninu, nin, ay, e, iye, i, i; Tulu, i, nin, ni; Malayâlam—ni, nin; Telugu—nivu, ivu, ni, nin, vu, vi; Tuda—ni, nin, i; Kóta—ni, nin, i; Gônd—imma, ni, i; Ku—inu, ni, i; Orâon—nien; Râjmahâl—nin. The Scythic of the Behistun tables has ni; the Brahui of Affghanistan has ni, na. *Plu.*—Miru, imat, nir, nivu, iru.

With these compare corresponding pronouns from several places in British New Guinea, thus :—

PAPUAN PRONOUNS.

1st.

Sing.—Gai, môu, da, yau, ye-gu, nau, nana, ara; *Dual*—Gabagaba, ni-mo-to, noni, kaditei, vagewu; *Plu.*—Ga-l-pa-ga-l-pa, 'we three,' ni-mo, 'we,' no-kaki, kita, ya-kaimi, ita.

2nd.

Sing.—Gido, gi, rôu, koa, ya-kom, oa, goi, oi; *Dual*—Gipel, nigo-to, ka-mitei; *Plu.*—Gita, nigo, yana, komiu, ya-kamiyi, umui, omi.

3rd.

Sing.—Ia, goi, nôu, añ-kaki, tenem; *Plu.*—Iamo, tana, nei, yabuia, sia, idia, ila, ira, isi.

Possessive forms are :—

1st.

Sing.—Lau-apu, gau, moro, dai-ero, yo-gu, ge-gu, egu; *Plu.*—Lai emai-apumai, ga-l-pan, yo-da, la-nambo.

2nd.

Sing.—Ia-apuga, eke-ero, apui-ero, li-nambo, gninu, oi-amu; *Plu.*—Komiai, gita-munu, yai-ero, amui, ami, gami.

EBUDAN PRONOUNS.

Corresponding Ebudan pronouns are :—

1st.

Sing.—E-nau, iau, na-gku, avau, ain-yak; *short forms*, na, a, ku, ne, iya, k; *Plu.*—Endra, hida, riti, kito, a-kity, a-kaija,

2nd.

Sing.—Eg-ko, e-nico, jau, aiko, yik, aiek; *Plu.*—Kamim, hamdi, ituma, akaua, aijaua.

Possessive forms are—

1st.

Sing.—No-ku, his-ug, kana-ku, kona-gku, rabak, tio-ku, unyak; *Plu.*—No-ra, isa-riti, kana-dro, kona-ra, otea, uja.

2nd.

Sing.—No-m, hisa-m, kana-mo, kona-mi, raba-m, o un; *Plu.*—No-nim, isa-hamdi, kana-miu, kona-munu, aua, un-yimia.

Fijian Pronouns.

Fijian pronouns are :—

Singular.		Binal.	Ternal.	Plural.
		First.		
Nom.—Koi-a-u†	inclu.	Koi-k-e-daru	Koi-k-e-datou	Koi-ke-da
	exclu.	Koi-keirau	Koi-keitou	Koi-keimami
Poss.— -nku	inclu.	I-ke-daru	I-ke-datou	I-ke-da
	exclu.	I-keirau	I-keitou	I-keimami
Obj. —Au	inclu.	Kedaru	Kedatou	Keda
	exclu.	Keirau	Keitou	Keimami
		Second.		
Nom.—Ko-i-ko		Koi-ke-mu-drau	Koi-ke-mu-dou	Koi-kemuni
Poss. — -mu		I-ke-mudran	I-ke-mudou	I-ke-muni
Obj. —Iko		Kemudrau	Kemudou	Kemuni
		Third.		
Nom. —Ko-koya		Koi-rau	Ko-iratou	Ko-i-ra
Poss. —I-keya; -na		I-rau ; drau	I-raton; dratou	I-ra ; dra
Obj. —Koya.		Rau	I-ratou	I-ra.

† Those syllables which are printed in italics may be dropped off in succession for various uses of the pronouns.

Demonstratives are :—

O ġuo, 'this, these'; o koya o ġuo, (*sing.*) 'this'; o ira o ġuo, 'these.' O ġori, 'that, those'; o koya o ġori (*sing.*), 'that'; o ira o ġori (*plu.*), 'those.'

Albannic Pronouns.

In the Albannic (Tukiok) dialect, the pronouns are :—

Singular.		Binal.*	Ternal.	Plural.
1st —Iau, io, yo	inclu.	da-ra	da-tul	dat
	exclu.	mi-ra	mi-tul	me-at
2nd—U *or* ui		mu-ru	mu-tul	mu-at
3rd—Ia *or* i		dia-ra	di-tul	di-at

This is a long list, and yet it may be useful, as showing how great a variety there is in the pronominal forms of the Australian and Melanesian languages. But these forms, if subjected to analysis and comparison, will be found to resolve themselves into a few simple elements. In examining the Australian pronouns now given, we must bear in mind that they are subject to some

* I prefer *Binal* and *Ternal*, because they signify 'two (three) each time.'

degree of error, which affects also many other lists of Australian words. Australian vocabularies are made often by Englishmen, who, in writing the words, follow the sounds of the vowels as used in English, and sometimes even their own vices of pronunciation; for instance, kinner is written down for kinna, and i-ya for ai-ya. Again, a blackfellow, when asked to give the equivalents for English words, sometimes fails to understand, and so puts one word for another; thus, in some lists that I have seen, the word for 'I' is set down as meaning 'thou'; and even in printing mistakes occur; for, in Mr. Taplin's list of South Australian dialects 'we' is ġun, and 'you' is ġun also; the former should probably be ġen; and kambiyanna is made to mean both 'your father' and 'his father.'

The First Pronoun.—Making all due allowance for such defects, I proceed to examine the Australian pronouns, and I find that, notwithstanding the multitude of their dialect-forms, they have only a very few bases. These are, for the first pronoun—Ga-ad, ġá-ta, ġa-ad-du, ba, mi, mo; and, for the second pronoun—Ġin, ġin-da, ġin-du, bi, bu, gula. I leave the demonstrative or third pronoun out of account, as it is not of so much importance to our inquiry. Now, the existence of the base ġa-ad is proved by the forms (given above), ġa-an, ġá-na; the base ġa-ta recurs in ġatha, ġa-ya, ni-te; ġa-ad-du, in ġád-thu, na-thu, a-thu, ġa-tu-ko, &c.; ba gives wa-an, a-an, and, in South Australia, ġa-pa, ġa-ap, a-pa; mo and mi are merely softened forms of ba, and are found in mo-to, wo-kok, mi-na, wi-nak, ġa-mi. Even so unpromising a form as ún-ća (Queensland) connects itself with the base ġa-ta through ġú-ća (South Australia); for some Melanesian dialects prefer to begin words with a vowel, and so transpose the letters of an initial dissyllable; thus, ún-ća is for úġ-ća= ġú-ća=ġá-ta.* Most of the dialect forms of this pronoun given above arise from the interchange of ng, n, and y; the Wiradhari dialect, for example, has ġaddu, naddu, yaddu, 'I,' and these become more liquid still in yallu, -ladu.† Let us observe here, also, that the Tasmanian forms ma-na, mi-na, 'I,' come from the base ma, mi. I have above given six bases for the first pronoun in Australian, and yet there are only two—ad *or* ta and ba; for mi and mo are only ba differently vocalised, and, in the other three, ġa- is a prefix, as will be shown further on, while the -du of ġa-ad-du is an emphatic suffix.

---

* The Aneityumese (Ebudan) language is so fond of an initial vowel that it constantly dislocates a consonant in favour of a vowel. Our Australian Vocabularies in this volume have very few words beginning with vowels.

† See Appendix, page 60. Dr. Caldwell was led into error by the form gadlu, which an authority told him meant 'we' in South Australia. Used alone, it is only 'I,' for gaddu.

Here comes in a most important question. Are these bases ta and ba exclusively Australian? Emphatically I say, No; for I know that, in Samoan, ta is the pronoun 'I,' and tā (for t ā-ua) is 'we two,' 'ita is 'me,' and ta-tou is 'we'; la'u (*i.e.*, ta-ku, *l* for *d*) is 'my.' I quote the Samoan as the representative of the Polynesian dialects. And yet the Maori pronouns of the first and second pronouns present some interesting features. They are:—

'I,' 'me'—Ahau, au, awau.
'We two'—Taua, maua.
'We'—Tatou, matou, matau.
'My'—Taku, toku, aku, oku, ahaku.
'Thou'—Koe; *dual*, korua, *plu.*, koutou.
'Your'—Tau, tou, au, ou, takorua, takoutou.

Here in 'we two,' 'we,' and 'my,' I see both of our Australian base-forms ta and ma; in 'my' I find the Australian possessive genitive suffix ku, gu*; and in 'we' I take the -tou to be for tolu the Polynesian for 'three,' three being used in an indefinite way to mean any number beyond two.† Then, in Fiji, I find that 'I,' 'me' is au, which may be for ta-u, for the binal form of it is -da-ru (*i.e.*, da+rua, 'two'), the ternal is -da-tou (*i.e.*, da+tolu, 'three'), and the plural is da. In the Motu dialect of New Guinea, 'I' is la-u, of which the plural is (*inclusive*) ai (for ta-i?) and (*exclusive*) i-ta. In other parts of New Guinea, 'I' is da, ya-u, nā-u, na-na, la-u, and, for the plural, ki-ta, i-ta (*cf.* Samoan). Ebudan parallels are—'I,' e-nau, iau, ain-ya-k; for the plural, hi-da, ki-to, a-kity; possessive forms are tio-ku, otea, u-ja. The Tukiok forms iau, io, yo; da-ra, da-tul, dat, correspond mainly with the Fijian, and are all from the root da, ta.

I think that I have thus proved that our Australian base ta is not local, but sporadic, and that, so far as this evidence has any weight, the brown Polynesians have something in common with the Melanesian race.

My next inquiry is this—Has this base, ta, da, ad, any connection with the other race-languages? And at once I remember that the old Persian for 'I' is ad-am, and this corresponds with the Sanskrit ah-am, of which the stem is agh-, as seen in the Græco-Latin ego and the Germanic ich. I assume an earlier form of this base to have been ak-, but, whether this Indian ak- or the Iranian ad- is the older, I cannot say. At all events, the change of ak into at and then into ad, and conversely, is a common phonetic change, and is at this moment going on copiously in Polynesia. The ak is now in present use in the Malay aku, 'I.'

*The possessive termination for persons in Awabakal is -umba; this I take to be for gu-mba, the gu being the possessive formative in Wiradhari; it corresponds to the Ebudan ki, which is used in the same way.

†*Cf.* Singular, Dual, and (all else) Plural.

The other Australian base-form of the first pronoun is ba, and this, in the forms of ma, me, mi, mo, is so common in all languages that I need scarcely quote more than Sanskrit mad (the base), 'I'; the Græco-Latin emou, mou; mihi, me; and the English, 'we.' This base, ba, gives us the Awabakal simple nominative báġ (for ba-aġ), -aġ being one of the most common of Australian formatives. Then, of the possessive form, emmo-ṅġ, which I would write emo-uġ, I take the e to be merely enunciative, the -ṅġ being a possessive formation; the mo that remains is the same as in the Australian mo-to, wo-kok, 'I,' the Papuan, mōu, 'I.' The Awabakal ba-li, 'we two' (both being present), is ba + li, where the -li is probably a dual form.

The Awabakal accusative of the first pronoun is tia, or, as I would write it, tya or ća; cf. ġuéa and únćá. This tia appears again in the vocative ka-tio-u, and is, I think, only a phonetic form of the ta which I have already examined.

I think, also, that the Hebrew pronoun an-oki, 'I,' is connected with our root ak, at, ta; for it seems to be pretty well assured that the an- there is merely a demonstrative particle placed before the real root-form -ok-i; for the Egyptian pronouns of the first and second persons have it (-an, -ant, -ent) also. And this quite corresponds with our Awabakal pronouns of the first and second persons, ġa-toa and ġin-toa; for, in my view, they both begin with a demonstrative ġa, which exists also in Polynesian as a prothetic nga, nge.* In Awabakal, I see it in ġa-li, 'this,' ġa-la, 'that,' and in the interrogative ġan, 'who'? for interrogatives come from a demonstrative or indefinite base (cf. the word minyuġ on page 3 of the Appendix). Here again, in the Awabakal word ġan, 'who'? we are brought into contact with Aryan equivalents; for, if ġán is for ká-an, as seems likely, then it leads us to the Sanskrit ka-s, 'who'? Zend, evañt = Latin quan-tus? Latin, quod, ubi, &c., Gothic, hvan = English, 'when'? Lithuanian, kà-s, 'who'? Irish, can, 'whence'? Kymric, pa, 'who'? Greek, pōs, 'how'? po-then, 'whence'?

In the Australian plural forms ġéanni, ġéen, we have again the prefix demonstrative ġa, but now softened into ge (cf. the Maori prefix nge) because of the short vowel that follows. The next syllable, an, is a liquid form of ad, ta, 'I,' and the ni may be a pluralising addition—the same as in the Papuan ni-mo. It should here be remembered, however, that the Australian languages seldom have special forms for the plural; for ta may mean either 'I' or 'we'; to indicate the plural number some pluralising word must be added to ta; thus in Western Australia 'we' is ġala-ta, literally 'all-I.' Some pronouns, however, seem to have absorbed these suffix

---

*In Maori, this nge is used as a prefix to the pronouns au and ona; thus, nge-au is exactly equivalent to the Australian ugatoa.

pluralising words, whatever they were, and thus to have acquired plural terminations; of this our ġeanni is an instance; in western Victoria, 'we' is expressed by ġa-ta-en, that is, ġata, 'I,' with the suffix -en—the same as the -ni of ġeanni. The Awabakal 'we' is ġeen. Such plurals are very old, for they are found in the Babylonian syllabaries; there the second pronoun is zu; its plural is zu enan, that is, 'thou-they' = ye; there also, 'I' is mu; with which compare ba, ma.

The Second Pronoun.—There are only two base-forms for the second pronoun, bi *or* bu and ġin. The latter is strengthened by the addition of -da, which may also be -de, -di, -do, -du, and these vocalic changes support my contention, that this syllable proceeds from the demonstrative ta, for if the original is da *or* ta, all the others may proceed from that, but it is not likely that, conversely, any one of them would change into -da. The -toa in the Awabakal ġin-toa is the same as in ġát-toa, and the initial ġ is the same as ġa, ġe. But what is the body of the word—the -in? I can only say with certainty that it is the base-form of the second pronoun, for I can give no further account of it. Possibly, it is for bin with the *b* (*v*) abraded; for the other base-form, although it now appears as bi, may have been originally bin—the same as the accusative; and yet, in the accusative dual, we have ġali-n and bulu-n, and in the singular bón for bo-un, where the *n* seems to be a case-sign. If the -in of ġintoa is for bin, then we get back to bi as the only base-form of the second Australian pronoun, and bi gives the forms wi-ye, wé, i-mi-ba, win-in, *q.v.* The other base-form of bi is bu, and this is attested in Australian by búbla, wuru, nuro, nuni, *q.v.*; the n'yuraġ in South Australia shows how the initial *n* has come in, for that plural is equivalent to ġvurag, from bu; it also shows the origin of the Awabakal plural nu-ra. The -ra there is certainly a plural form; for we have it in ta-ra, 'those,' from the singular demonstrative ta, and in ba-ra, 'they,' from ba. In the genitive ġear-unba, 'of us,' the -ar may be this -ra, but it may also be simply the -an of the nominative. This same -ra is a pluralising suffix in Melanesia. In many parts of Melanesia, likewise, this mu—often when used as a verbal suffix—is the pronoun 'thou.'

I may here venture the conjecture, without adding any weight to it, that, as the Sanskrit dva, 'two,' gives the Latin bis, bi, so, on the same principle, the Sanskrit tva, 'thou,' may be the old form to which our bi, bu is allied.

As to the prefix ġa, I know that, in New Britain, ngo is 'this,' in Aneityum, nai, naico, i-naico is 'that.' This nga, also, as a prefix, occurs in a considerable number of words in Samoan; for instance, tasi is 'one,' and tusa is 'alike,' solo is 'swift'; an intensive meaning of each is expressed by ġa-tasi, ġa-tusa, ġa-solo;

the numeral 'ten' is ga-fulu which I take to mean 'the whole' (sc. fingers). In Teutonic, it seems to have sometimes a collective force, as in ge-birge, 'mountains,' and sometimes an intensive, as in Gothic, ga-bigs, from Sanskrit bhaga, the 'sun.' In Latin the suffix c in sic is supposed to be the remains of a demonstrative.

Gátoa, then, is to me made up of ga+ad+do, the -do being the same suffix particle of emphasis which is elsewhere in Australia written -du, and the -do is extended into -toa, also for emphasis, as in the Wiradhari yama, yamoa, and other Australian words. It is quite possible that this -do also is only the demonstrative ta —so often used in composition in Awabakal—changed into -to, -do, according to the rules on pages 10 and 11 of this volume.

From the lists of pronouns given above, it will be seen that Fijian also prefixes a demonstrative ko, ko-i to its first and second pronouns. This same particle, ko, o is also prefixed to nouns, and especially to proper names. In Samoan, 'o, that is, ko, is placed before nouns and pronouns when they are used as the subject of a proposition—this, also, for emphasis, to direct attention to the agent, like the agent-nominative case in Awabakal.

In the Ebudan and Papuan pronouns, a similar prothetic demonstrative is found; there it has the forms of na, ain, en, a, ka, ha, ya, ye; in many of the Ebudan dialects,—the Aneityumese, for instance—the demonstrative in, ni, elsewhere na, is prefixed to almost every word that is used as a noun. In other parts of Melanesia, the na is a suffix.

Finally, I placed the Dravidian pronouns in my list in order to compare them with the Australian. And the comparison is instructive. They are, chiefly, nân, yân, for the first person, and nin, ni for the second. Dr. Caldwell himself considers the initial n in each case to be not radical, and the base forms to be ân and în. This is a close approximation to our Australian bases; for we have the three forms, gád-du, nád-du, yád-du, in which the n and the y proceed from the original nasal-guttural g̈, and that g̈, as I have shown, is only a demonstrative prefix. The d of nád and yád may easily pass into its liquid n, thereby giving the Dravidian nân and yân; and the Australian forms are older, for while d will give n, n, when established in a word, will not revert to d. So also, the Dravidian nin will come from the earlier g̈in, which we find in the Australian g̈inda.

IX. THE FORMATION OF WORDS.

Any one who examines the Vocabularies of the Awabakal and the Wiradhari dialects will see how readily the Australian language can form derivative words from simple roots, and how expressive those words may become. The language is specially rich in verb-forms. As an illustration of this, let us take from the Wiradhari dialect the root verb baṅga, of which the original meaning is that of 'breaking,' 'dividing,' 'separating.' From that root are formed—baṅg-ána, 'to break' (*intrans.*), baṅg-ára, 'to break' (*trans.*), baṅga-mára, 'to (make to) break,' and, with various other adaptations of the root-meaning, baṅga-bira, baṅga-dira, baṅga-nira, baṅga-naringa, baṅga-dara, baṅga-gambira, baṅga-dambira, baṅga-durmanbira, baṅg-al-gára. It is true that these varying formatives resolve themselves into a few simple elements, but they certainly convey different shades of meaning; else, why should they exist in the language? Nor is the root baṅga the only one on which such changes are made; for the Wiradhari vocabulary contains numerous instances of similar formations.

Then the modes of a verb are also usually abundant and precise. In the Indicative mood, the Awabakal dialect has *nine* different tenses, and the Wiradhari has one more, the future perfect. Our Australian verb thus rivals and excels the Greek and the Sanskrit, for it thus has four futures, and, for time past, it has three forms, marking the past time as instant, proximate, and remote. Corresponding to these tenses, there are nine participles, each of which may be used as a finite verb. Besides an Imperative mood and a Subjunctive mood, there are reflexive and reciprocal forms, forms of negation, forms to express continuance, iteration, imminence, and contemporary circumstances. Now, as the Australian language is agglutinative, not inflexional, the verb acquires all these modifications by adding on to its root-form various independent particles, which, if we could trace them to their source, would be found to be nouns or verbs originally, and to contain the various shades of meaning expressed by these modes of the verb. The Fijian verb—in a Melanesian region—is also rich in forms; for it has verbs intransitive, transitive, passive, and, with prefixes, intensive, causative, reciprocal, and reciprocal-causative. And among the mountains of the Dekkan of India—also a black region —the verb, as used by the Tudas and Gonds, is much richer than that of the Tamil, the most cultivated dialect of the same race.

And, in Australian, this copiousness of diction is not confined to the verbs; it shows itself also in the building up of other words. On page 102 of this volume, a sample is given of the manner in which common nouns may be formed by the adding on of particles. Mr. Hale, whom I have already named, gives other instances, doubtless derived from his converse with Mr. Threlkeld at Lake Macquarie, and, although some of the words he quotes are used for ideas quite unknown to a blackfellow in his native state, yet they are a proof of the facility of expression which is inherent in the language. I quote Mr. Hale's examples:—

EXAMPLES of the FORMATION of VERBAL NOUNS in *AWABAKAL*.

1. The agent.	2. The actor.	3. The instrument.	4. The action as subject.	5. The action.	6. The place.
Bún-ki-lli-kan	Bún-ki-ye	Bun-ki-lli-kanné	Bun-ki-lli-to	Bun-ki-lli-ta	Bunki-lli-ġeil
Gakuya-lli-kan	Gakuya-i-ye	Gakuya-lli-kanne	Gakuya-lli-to	Gakuya-lli-ta	Gakuya-lli-ġeil
Goloma-lli-kan	Goloma-i-ye	Goloma-lli-kanne	Goloma-lli-to	Goloma-lli-ta	Goloma-lli-ġeil
Gu-ki-lli-kan	Gu-ki-ye	Gu-ki-lli-kanne	Gu-ki-lli-to	Gu-ki-lli-ta	Gu-ki-lli-ġeil
Gurra-lli-kan	Gura-i-ye	Gura-lli-kanne	Gurra-lli-to	Gurra-lli-ta	Gurra-lli-ġeil
Kor-ri-lli-kan	Kor-ri-ye	Kor-ri-lli-kanne	Kor-ri-lli-to	Kor-ri-lli-ta	Kor-ri-lli-ġeil
Man-ki-lli-kan	Man-ki-ye	Man-ki-ili-kanne	Man-ki-lli-to	Man-ki-lli-ta	Man-ki-lli-ġeil
Pirri-ki-lli-kan	Pirri-ki-ye	Pirri-ki-lli-kanne	Pirri-ki-lli-to	Pirri-ki-lli-ta	Pirri-ki-lli-ġeil
Tiwa-lli-kan	Tiwa-i-ye	Tiwa-lli-kanne	Tiwa-lli-to.	Tiwa-lli-ta	Tiwa-lli-ġeil
Una-lli-kan	Una-i-ye	Una-lli-kanne	Una-lli-to	Una-lli-ta	Una-lli-ġeil
Upa-lli-kan	Upa-i-ye	Upa-lli-kanne	Upa-lli-to	Upa-lli-ta	Upa-lli-ġeil
Uwa-lli-kan	Uwa-i-ye	Uwa-lli-kanne	Uwa-lli-to	Uwa-lli-ta	Uwa-lli-ġeil
Wiroba-lli-kan	Wiroba-i-ye	Wiroba-lli-kanne	Wiroba-lli-to	Wiroba-lli-ta	Wiroba-lli-ġeil
Wiya-lli-kan	Wiya-i-yo	Wiya-lli-kanne	Wiya-lli-to	Wiya-lli-ta	Wiya-lli-ġeil
Wún-ki-lli-kan	Wún-ki-yo	Wún-ki-lli-kanne	Wún-ki-lli-to	Wún-ki-lli-ta	Wún-ki-lli-ġeil
Yallawa-lli-kan	Yallawa-i-yo	Yallawa-lli-kanne	Yallawa-lli-to	Yallawa-lli-ta	Yallawa-lli-ġeil

INTRODUCTION. xlix

If we follow the numbers on the columns, and remember that the word in column No. 1 always denotes the person who does the action of the verb, the meanings which these words bear—all springing from the verbal root-form and meaning—may be shown thus:—

From

Bún-ki-lli —2. a boxer; 3. a cudgel; 4. a blow; 5. the smiting; 6. a pugilistic ring; *root-meaning,* 'smite.'

Gakuya-lli —2. a liar; 3. a pretence; 4. deceit; 5. the deceiving; 6. a gambling-house; *rt.m.,* 'deceive.'

Goloma-lli —2. a saviour; 3. a safeguard; 4. protection; 5. the protecting; 6. a fortress; *rt.m.,* 'protect.'

Gu-ki-lli —2. an almoner; 3. a shop; 4. liberality; 5. the giving of a thing; 6. a market; *rt.m.,* 'give.'

Gura-lli —2. a listener; 3. an ear-trumpet; 4. attention; 5. the act of hearing; 6. a news-room; *rt.m.,* 'hear.'

Ko-ri-lli —2. a porter; 3. a yoke; 4. a carriage; 5. the carrying; 6. a wharf; *rt.m.,* 'carry.'

Man-ki-lli —2. a thief; 3. a trap; 4. a grasp; 5. the taking; 6. a bank; *rt.m.,* 'take.'

Pirri-ki-lli —2. a sluggard; 3. a couch; 4. rest; 5. the reclining; 6. a bedroom; *rt.m.,* 'recline.'

Tiwa-lli —2. a searcher; 3. a drag; 4. search; 5. the seeking; 6. the woods; *rt.m.,* 'seek.'

Uma-lli —2. an artisan; 3. a tool; 4. work; 5. the doing; 6. a manufactory; *rt.m.,* 'do.'

Upa-lli —2. a writer; 3. a pen; 4. performance; 5. the performing; 6. a desk; *rt.m.,* 'perform.'

Uwa-lli —2. a wanderer; 3. a coach; 4. a journey; 5. the walking; 6. a parade ground; *rt.m.,* 'walk.'

Wiroba-lli —2. a disciple; 3. a portmanteau; 4. pursuit; 5. the act of following; 6. the barracks; *rt.m.,* 'follow.'

Wiya-lli —2. a commander; 3. a book; 4. speech; 5. the speaking; 6. a pulpit; *rt.m.,* 'speak.'

Wún-ki-lli —2. a magistrate; 3. a watch-house; 4. resignation; 5. the leaving; 6. the jail; *rt.m.,* 'leave.'

Yallawa-lli —2. an idler; 3. a seat; 4. a session; 5. the act of sitting; 6. a pew; *rt.m.,* 'sit.'

As to the origin of these formatives, I think that kan equals k + an, the -an being a personal suffix from the same source as the demonstrative un-ni, 'this'; in Wiradhari it is -dain, that is d + ain, the -ain being the same as -an. We shall find further on that *k, d, t, g* and other consonants are used in this language merely to tack on the suffix. Similarly, in Fijian and Samoan, there is a great variety of consonants in use for this purpose. The -kanne seems to be a softer form of -kannai or -kanmai, the -mai being a common formative. The -ta of number 5 is a demonstrative which is used abundantly in the language as a strengthening particle; and the -to is the agent-nominative form (see pp. 10, 11) of -ta. The -ġeil of number 6, or, as I write it, -ġél, seems to me to be of the same origin as the suffix -kál (see page 18); a corresponding word in Dravidian is kál, 'a place.' The -yé of number 2 denotes a continued action, and may be the same as the imperative form -ia, that is -iya.

In the list given above, 'a magistrate' is called wúnkiye because he 'commits' the culprit to jail, and 'the watch-house' or jail is therefore wúnkilliġél. The wirroballikan are the 'light-horse,' who act as an escort to the Governor of the colony, and the place where they are housed is therefore wirroballiġél. In the Gospel, the disciples of Christ are called wirroballikan, and their following of Him for instruction—their discipleship—is wirro-balli-kanne-ta. Búnkillikanne may be a 'musket,' because it 'strikes' with a ball, or it may be a 'hammer,' a 'mallet,' which gives 'blows.'

The reader has observed that all the verbals in the first column above contain the syllable -illi, and, as that table has given us examples of synthesis, it may be profitable now to examine the formation of Australian words by employing etymological analysis. With this view, I take up the Awabakal verb takilliko, 'to eat,' and I take this word, because the idea expressed by it is so essential to a language, that it is impossible that the word should be a loan-word. Now, the verb 'to eat' has, in Australian, many forms, such as thalli, dalli, thaldinna, thilala, dira, chakol, taka, tala, and, in Tasmania, tuggara, tughli, te-ganna. Of all these, the simplest is taka, which is used by the northern portion of the Kuriġġai tribe (see map) in N. S. Wales. On comparing taka and tala, it is evident that the simple root is ta, and all the others come from this; chakol, for instance, is ta palatalized into ća, with -kál added; di-ra has the suffix -ra added on to the root ta, vocalized into di; and dira gives the universal Australian word for the 'teeth,'just as the Sanskrit dant, 'a tooth' (cf. Lat. dens), is a participial form of the verb ad, 'to eat.' The Tasmanian words, which I have here restored to something like a rational mode of spelling, are clearly the same as the Australian. Nor is the root ta contined to Australia; it is spread all over the East as ta or ka. In Samoa (Polynesian), it is tau-te, tau-mafa, and 'ai, that is (k)ai; in Aneityum (Melanesian), it is caig; in Efate, kani; in Duke of York Island, ani, wa-gan; in Motu (New Guinea), ania; in New Britain, an, yan. The Dravidian is un, and the Sanskrit is ad and khád. Our English word eat, Gothic ita, Latin edo, are from the same root. The Malay is ma-kan, of which the ma is also pa, ba, and with this corresponds the Melanesian (Efate) ba-mi, 'to eat.' Now, it seems to me likely that in primitive speech there were, alongside of each other, three root-forms, ba, ad, and kad, of which ba and ad passed to the West and produced the Greek pha-go, and e(s)thio, the Latin edo, the English eat, while kad spread to the East and is the source of all the other words; ba in a less degree accompanied it, and gives bami (Efate), -ma-fa (Samoa), and the Malay ma-kan. This root ba seems also to exist in Australia, for one dialect has has a-balli, 'to eat.'

In the Samoan tau-te (a chief's word), the tau is an intensive and therefore, in this case, honorific, prefix, and the tū is our root ta; it thus corresponds with the Tasmanian tū-ganna.

In various parts of British New Guinea, words for 'eat' are bai, uai, mo-ana, kani-kani, an-an, ye-kai; and for 'food,' kai, kān, ani-ani, ai-ai, mala-m, ala, wa-la. All these come from the roots ba and ka, kan; with an-an (an for kan) compare the Dravidian un, 'to eat.'

Thus I dispose of the Awabakal root ta, 'to eat'; and, if the analogies given above are well founded, then I am sure that our Australian blacks have a share with the rest of the world in a common heritage of language.

When the radical syllable, ta, is removed, the remainder of our sample word is -killi-ko, and both of these are formative. On comparing ta-killi-ko with other Awabakal verbs, such as um-ulli-ko, wi-yelli-ko, um-olli-ko, and with the Wiradhari verbs and verbals da-alli, d-illi-ġa, b-illi-ġa, it is obvious that the essential portion of the affix is -illi *or* -älli, the consonants before it being merely euphonic. In the Dravidian languages, similar consonants, *r, y, m, n, d, t, g*, are inserted to prevent hiatus, and in Fiji and Samoa there is also a great variety of consonants used to introduce suffixes. Then, as to the -illi *or* -álli, I find exactly the same formative in Gond—an uncultured dialect of the Dravidian; there the infinitive of a verb has -âlê *or* -îlê; and in Tamil, the verbal noun in -al, with the dative sign -ku added, is used as an infinitive; in Canarese the -al is an infinitive without the -ku. In all this we have a close parallel to the Awabakal infinitive in -álli-ko, -illi-ko, for some of our dialects have the dative in -ol, -ál.* Our formative, when attached to a verb-root, makes it a verbal noun, as bún-killi, 'the act of smiting'; hence the appropriateness of the suffix -ku, 'to,' a post-position.

The -ko in ta-killi-ko is equivalent to the English 'to' with verbs, except that it is used as a post-position in Awabakal, where it is the common dative sign. It also resembles, both in form and

---

*See page 49 of Appendix.

use, the Latin supine in -tum. This Sanskrit -tum is the accusative of the suffix -tu to express agency, and may thus correspond with our Australian suffix -to, -du, which is used in a similar manner. In the Diyeri dialect*, the infinitive ends in mi, which means 'to'; in Aneityumese imi means 'to.' Now, in all the Dravidian dialects, the sign of the dative case is ku, ki, ge; in Hindi it is ko, in Bengali kê; other forms in India are khê, -ghai, -gai; with this -gai compare the Minyung dative in -gai*. In the Kôta dialect of the Dravidian, the dative sign is ke, and the locative is -ol-ge; the infinitive ends in -alik, probably a compound of ali and ke; the Aneityumese infinitive in -aliek is very like that. A close parallel to our Awabakal infinitive in -ko is the Dravidian infinitive in -gu; as, kuru, 'short,' kuru-gu, 'to diminish.' In the Malay languages, transitive verbs are formed by prefixes and affixes; of the latter, the most common is kan, which may be the preposition ka, 'to.'

In the Ebudan languages, ki is a genitive and a dative sign, and in one of them, Malekúlan, bi, 'to,' makes an infinitive (cf. the South Australian mi), and this same bi is used like the Latin ut, 'in order that'; with this compare the Awabakal koa (page 75, et al.)—a lengthened form of -ko. In Fijian, some transitive verbs take ki, 'to,' after them, but a common termination for the infinitive is -ka, and the 'i (sometimes 'o) of many verbs in Samoan may be the same termination.

Our infinitive denotes the 'end' or 'purpose' for which anything is done; hence the dative sign; so also in Sanskrit, it would be correct to use the dative in -ana of the verbal noun. In the Wiradhari dialect, -ana is a very common termination for infinitives; but I do not know that it has any relation to the Sanskrit -ana.

I have taken this verb takilliko as an example of the formation of an infinitive in Awabakal; all other infinitives in that dialect are formed in the same way; the variations -ulli-ko, olli-ko, elli-ko proceed from -alli, which I would write -álli, so as to include the vowel changes all in one sign. In other dialects, there are many other forms for the infinitive, but this one in -illi is not confined to the Kuriġġai tribe, but is found also in Victoria.

Another similar and very important verb in the Awabakal is kakilliko, the verb 'to be.' On the same principles, as shown above, the -killiko here is terminational and the root is ka. Here again the Dravidian dialects assist us to trace the word; for the Tamil has á-gu, 'to become,' the Telugu has ká, the Canarese ágal, and the Gond ay-álê. Our Wiradhari dialect says ġinya (for ġi-ġa), 'to become.' It is possible that these forms have a parallel, but independent, relation to the Sanskrit roots gan and ga, 'to come into being,' Greek gigno-mai, gino-mai.

*See pp. 13 and 45 of Appendix.

X. Grammatical Forms and Syntax.

The consideration of the grammatical forms and the syntax of a language is a very important part of comparative grammar, and is a more potent proof of identity of origin than mere words can be; for, while words may be abundantly introduced from abroad, as the history of our English language testifies, yet the essential structure of allied languages is as little liable to change as the cranial character of a race. As none of the dialects spoken in Australia has had the chance of becoming fixed by being reduced to writing, the materials available for comparing them with themselves and with other languages are in a state of flux and decay, and any effort to determine their grammar will be only provisional at present, and subject to errors arising from the imperfect state of our information about them. Nevertheless, allowance being made for this source of imperfection and error, several of their features may be regarded as well-determined; and it will here be convenient to arrange these in numbered paragraphs.

1. The Australian languages are in the agglutinative stage; the relations which words and ideas bear to each other in a sentence are shown by independent words, often monosyllables, which do not lose their identity when attached to the word which they thus qualify. For example, 'he is the son of a good (native) man,' in Awabakal, is noa yinál mararáġ ko ba kúri ko ba, where the monosyllables ko and ba express the relation of yinál to kúri, and are otherwise in common use as distinct words; they can be combined and fastened on to kúri so that the whole may be pronounced as one word, kúrikoba, but they do not thus become lost as case-endings. These particles ko-ba, when thus united, may be also treated as an independent word, even as a verb, for koba-toara is a verbal form, meaning 'a thing that is in possession, gotten, acquired.'

Similarly, the tenses of the verb are indicated by particles added on to the stem; as, búm-mara-bún-bill-ai-koa baġ, 'that I may permit the one to be struck by the other'; here bún is the root-form, 'strike,' which may be almost any part of speech; ma-ra is an independent stem meaning 'make' (ma); bún is another verb conveying the idea of 'permission'; it is not used as a separate word, but it appears to be only a derived form of the verb ba, (ma), 'to make,' 'to let'; the rest of our sample word is bill-ai-koa; of these, koa is a lengthened form of the preposition ko, 'to,' and is equivalent to the Latin conjunction ut; the -ai has a reciprocal force, and b-illi is the same formative which we found in ta-killi-ko, q.v. Thus our sample-word is made up of three verbs, a formative (illi), which, perhaps, is of the nature of a demonstrative, a particle, and the infinitive post-position, which, as to its origin, may have been a verb.

2. Nevertheless, several dialects have forms which show the agglutinative words on the way to become inflexional. In the dialect of Western Australia, 'the woman's staff' is yago-äk wanna, in which the -äk has lost its independence, and is as much a case-ending as the æ, i, or *is* of the Latin genitive. So also in Awabakal; the -úmba of kokara emoúmba, 'my house,' may be regarded as inflexional; for, although the -ba can be detached and used as a separate word, not so the -úm. I believe the -úmba to be a weathering for gu-mba, the gu being a dialect form of the post-position ko, as in Wiradhari; yet the -ú cannot stand alone; the *m* belongs to the ba.

3. As to the *Cases* of nouns and pronouns, they are shown by separable post-positions which are themselves nouns, adjectives, or verbs. The post-position birung, for example, meaning 'away from,' is an adjective in the Wiradhari dialect, and means 'far distant,' while birandi, another form from the same root, is the post-position, 'from.' The other post-positions in the paradigm on page 16 are all taken from the monosyllables ka and ko. Of these, I take ko to be a root-verb, implying 'motion to,' and ka another, meaning 'to be' in a certain state or place; but of their origin I can give no account, unless ka be related to the Dravidian verb âgu, already noticed, and ko be a modified form of ka. These two roots, variously combined, become the post-positions kai, kin-ko, ka-ko, kin-ba, ka-ba, ka-birung, kin-birung on page 16; by the influence of the final consonant of the words to which they are joined, the initial *k* of these becomes *t*, *l*, or *r*.

A similar account of the post-positions in the Narrinyéri, the Diyéri, and other distant dialects could, no doubt, be given, but from the scantiness of our knowledge, that is at present impossible.

4. As to the *Gender* of nouns, that is either implied in the meaning of the word or to be guessed from the context. In Fijian, a word is added to mark the gender; for example, gone is 'child,' and, from it, a gone taganc is 'a boy,' but a gone alewa is 'a girl.' The Samoans say ulī po'a and ulī fafine to mean a 'male dog' and a 'female dog,' and the Ebudans something similar. Our Australians have no such devices, but they have some words in which the gender is clearly distinguished by an ending added on, or by a change of the vowel sound of the final syllable of the word. The most common feminine suffix is -gun; as, mobi, 'a blind man,' mobi-gun, 'a blind woman'; yinál, 'a son,' yinal-kun, 'a daughter'; another suffix is -in; as, Awabakal, 'a man of Awaba,' Awaba-kal-in, 'a woman of Awaba'; makoro-ban, makoro-bin, 'a fisher-man,' 'a fisher-woman,' show a change in the vowel sound. I think that, in proportion to the extent of the language, instances of this kind—the expression of

gender by change of termination—are quite as common in Australian as they are in English. To this extent, therefore, the Australian dialects are sex-denoting.

The -ban in makoro-ban seems to be a masculine suffix; in the Minyung dialect, yerrubil is 'a song,' yerrubil-gin, 'a singer,' and yerrubil-gin-gun is a 'songstress.' The Wiradhari -dain in birbal-dain, 'a baker,' from birbára, 'to bake,' and in many other words, is also a masculine termination.

5. As to *Number* of nouns and pronouns, the same word, and the same form of it, does duty both as singular and plural; the context shows which is meant; *e.g.*, kùri is 'a (native) man,' but kùri is also 'men'; if the speaker wishes to say, '*a* man came home,' that would be wakal kùri, 'one man'—the numeral being used just in the same way as our Saxon ' an,' ' ane '—but '*the* men ' would be bara kùri, 'they-man,' not kùri bara, as the Aryan arrangement of the words would be. Hence the pronoun ngaddu, ngadlu may mean either '1' or ' we'; to mark the number some pluralising word must be added to nouns and pronouns, such as in the gala-ta, ' we,' of Western Australia, where the gala is equivalent to 'they,' or perhaps ' all.' In Wiradhari, galang is added on to form plurals. Nevertheless, there are, among the pronouns, terminations which appear to be plural forms, as, nge-an-ni, ' we,' nu-ra, 'you,' which I have already considered in the section on the Australian pronouns.

The declension of yago, 'a woman' (page 49 of Appendix), is an example of a termination *added on* to form the plural of a noun, and shows how much akin our Australian language is to the Dravidian and other branches of the Turanian family. Yago takes -man as a plural ending, and to that affixes the signs of case which are used for the singular number. As a parallel, I cite the Turanian of Hungary; there, ur is 'master,' ur-am is 'my master,' ur-aim, 'my masters,' ur-am-nak, ' to my master,' ur-aim-nak, ' to my masters.' The Dravidian has not, in general, post-fixed possessives, but our Narrinyeri dialect has them, and they are quite common in the Papuan and Ebudan languages. In Fijian, the possessives, with nouns of relationship or members of the body or parts of a thing, are always post-fixed. And in Dravidian, when a noun denotes a rational being, the pronominal termination is suffixed.

6. The Minyung dialect (page 4, Appendix) makes a distinction between life-nouns and non-life nouns, and varies the endings of its adjectives accordingly. Something similar exists in Dravidian; for it has special forms for epicene plurals and for rational plurals and for neuter plurals; and, of course, in the classic languages the *a* of the neuter plural is distinctive. But in Fijian, the Minyung principle is carried out more fully, for possessives vary their radical form according as the nouns to

which they are joined denote things to be held merely in possession, or to be eaten, or to be drunk. In Samoan there is a somewhat similar use of lona and lana, 'his.'

7. In the Awabakal dialect (see the Gospel *passim*), a main feature is the use of the demonstrative ta as a suffix; it is added to nouns, adjectives, pronouns, and adverbs, and always has the effect of strengthening the word to which it is joined; as, unni ta kuri, 'this man,' wakäl-la purreäng, 'one day'; its plural is ta-ra; another form, apparently a plural, is tai, as in mararäng-tai, 'the good'; the singular form tarai means 'some one,' 'another.' Ta is simply a demonstrative particle, and may be related to the Sanskrit tad, 'this,' 'that.' Ta is always a suffix, and I consider it the same word as the demonstrative -na, which is so common as a suffix to nouns in all Melanesia, and sometimes in Polynesia. Some Ebudan dialects use it as a prefix, na, ni, in. In Telugu, ni and na are attached to certain classes of nouns before adding the case signs, as da-ni-ki, 'to that.' This ta is probably the same as the Dravidian da of inda, 'this,' anda, 'that.'

8. In Awabakal, a noun or adjective, when used as the subject of a proposition, takes ko (to, lo) as a suffix; so also in Fijian and Samoan, ko, 'o as a prefix. In Awabakal, this ko must be attached to all the words that are leading parts of the subject; as, tarai-to bulun kinbirug-ko, 'some one from among them.'

In Awabakal, there seems to be no definite arrangement of words in a simple sentence except that required by expression and emphasis; but an adjective precedes its noun and a pronoun in the possessive may either follow its noun or go before it. In Dravidian also, the adjective precedes its substantive; but the possessive pronouns are prefixed to the nouns.

These comparisons are general; those that now follow compare the Australian with the Dravidian.

9. In Gond and Tamil, the instrumental case-ending is -al. With this compare the Narrinyeri ablative in -il, and the -al of Western Australia (pp. 29, 32, 49 of Appendix).

10. The Tuda dialect alone in the Dekkan has the sound of *f* and the hard *th* of the English 'thin'; in Australia the Narrinyeri has the *th* of 'thin,' but there is no *f* anywhere.

11. The Tamil inserts a euphonic *m* before *b*; this is also exceedingly common in Australia. The Canarese dialect hardens mûru, 'three,' into mundru. Some of the dialects of Australia have a similar practice, and the Fijians do the same.

12. In Tamil, the conjunctive-ablative case has ôdu, dialect tôda, 'together with,' supposed to come from the verb to-dar, 'to join on.' The corresponding Awabakal word is katoa for kata (page 16).

INTRODUCTION.

13. In Dravidian, the 2nd singular of the Imperative is the crude form of the verb; so also in Australian.

14. In Tamil, the accusative case is the same as the nominative; so also with common nouns in Australian.

15. In Dravidian, there is no case ending for the vocative; some sign of emphasis is used to call attention; in Tamil, this is ê. In Awabakal, ela is used for the same purpose, and in Wiradhari ya. In Samoan e is used, but it usually comes after its noun.

16. In Dravidian, there are compound case-signs. So also in Australian (see pages 16, 17, and of Appendix, pages 30, 33, 58).

17. In Dravidian, comparison is expressed by using some adverb with the adjective; as, 'this indeed is good,' for 'this is very good.' There are no adjective terminations there to show comparison, but some Australian dialects seem to have them (see pages 45 and 51 of Appendix). Usually the Australian and the Melanesian languages are like the Dravidian in this matter.

18. In Turanian, the ma of the first pronoun often adds an obscure nasal making it something like máng. With this compare the Awabakal báng.

19. For the second pronoun, the Tamil has áy, óy, er. With these compare the Papuan second pronoun on page xl. of this Introduction.

20. In the Dravidian pronoun nin, 'thou,' the initial n is merely a nasalisation, for it disappears in the verbal forms. With this compare my analysis of the Awabakal pronoun gintoa.

21. In Dravidian generally, the pluralising particles are added on to the pronouns; but in Telugu these signs are prefixed, as in mi-ru. With this compare the Papuan ni-mo (page xl. of this Introduction), and the Awabakal ba-ra, nu-ra, and the like.

22. In almost all the Dravidian dialects, the first pronoun plural has both an inclusive and an exclusive form. This is so also in the Melanesian languages, especially those of the New Hebrides and Fiji.

23. The Canarese formative of adverbs is l, as in illi, alli, elli, 'here,' 'there,' 'where'; in Gond, âlê, îlê are the verb-endings. In Awabakal, these are the formatives of verbal nouns, as I have shown in another section. Now, it is an easy thing in language for a noun to be used adverbially, and hence the Canarese and Gond formatives may really be nouns. This would bring them closer to the Awabakal.

24. In the chief Dravidian dialects, the infinitive ends in -ku, a post-preposition, 'to.' So also in Awabakal, as has been already shown. I may add here that the Zulu infinitive ends -ku.

25. The Dravidian verb may be compounded with a noun, but never with a preposition. So also the Australian verb.

26. The Dravidian verb is agglutinative; particles are added on to the stem in order to express mood, tense, causation, negation, &c., no change being made on the stem. Tulu and Gond—both uncultured dialects—are exceptionally rich in moods and tenses. All this applies to the Australian, the Ebudan, and the Fijian verbs.

27. In Dravidian, there are no relative pronouns. So in Australian; for 'this is the book which you gave me,' a native would say 'this is the book; you gave it me.'

28. In Canarese, kodu, 'to give,' is used as a permissive. In Awabakal, bûn is the permissive, and appears to be formed from ba, a root-form meaning 'to make.' In English, the conditional conjunction 'if' is for 'gif,' 'give.'

29. The Dravidian verb has no passive, nor has the Australian. For 'it was broken,' our natives would say 'broken by me (you, &c.)'; a Dravida would say, 'it became broken through me.'

30. In Dravidian there are two futures—(1) a conditional future, and (2) a sort of indeterminate aorist future. For the latter, the Malayâlam adds -um to the verbal noun which is the base of the future. In Awabakal there are three futures; the third is an aorist future and adds -nûn to the verbal stem in -illi (see pages 25, 28 *ad finem*). This -nûn is probably equivalent to a formative -ûn with *n* interposed between the vowels to prevent hiatus. In Tamil also *n* (for *d*) is similarly inserted in verbs; as, padi(*n*)an, 'I sang.'

XI. The Origin of the Australian Race.

From these analogies and from the general scope of my argument in this Introduction, the reader perceives that I wish to prove a kinship between the Dravidian race and the Australian. This opinion I expressed in print more than ten years ago when it was not so generally held as it is now. Some of the very highest authorities have formed the same opinion from evidence other than that of language. But a theory and arguments thereon must be shown to be antecedently possible or even probable before it can be accepted; and to furnish such a basis of acceptance, one must go to the domain of history. This I now do.

In my opinion the ultimate home of origin of the negroid population of Australia is Babylonia. There, as history tells us, mankind first began to congregate in great numbers, and among them the Hamites, the progenitors of the negro races. It seems to have been those Hamites who were the first to try to break down the love-law of universal brotherhood and equality; for Nimrod was of their race, and wished to establish dominion over his fellows, and to raise an everlasting memorial of his power, like those which his kindred afterwards reared in Egypt. This attempt was frustrated by the 'Confusion of tongues,' at

Babel; and here begins, as I think, the first movement of the negro race towards India and consequently towards Australia. Here comes in also the 'Tôldoth Benê Noah' of Genesis x.

Accordingly, the position of the Hamite or black races at the opening of history is, in Genesis x. 6, indicated ethnically by the names Kush and Mizraim and Phut and Canaan, which geographically are the countries we call Ethiopia and Egypt and Nubia and Palestine. The Kushites, however, were not confined to Africa, but were spread in force along the whole northern shores of the Arabian sea; they were specially numerous on the lower courses of the Euphrates and Tigris, their original seats, and there formed the first germ whence came the great empire of Babylonia. The Akkadians were Turanian in speech, and, it may be, black in 'colour.' In this sense, the later Greek tradition (Odyssey I-23-24) speaks of both an eastern and a western nation of Ethiopians. And Herodotus tells us (VII-70) that in the army of Xerxes, when he invaded Greece, "the Ethiopians from the sun-rise (for two kinds served in the expedition) were marshalled with the Indians, and did not at all differ from the others in appearance, but only in their language and their hair. For the eastern Ethopians are straight-haired, but those of Libya have hair more curly than that of any other people."

It is clear, therefore, that the black races, many centuries before the Trojan war, had spread themselves from the banks of the Indus on the east right across to the shores of the Mediterranean, while towards the south-west they occupied the whole of Egypt and the Abyssinian highlands. Thus they held two noble coigns of vantage, likely to give them a commanding influence in the making of the history of mankind—the valley of the Nile, which, through all these ages to the present hour, has never lost its importance—and the luxuriant flat lands of Mesopotamia. A mighty destiny seemed to await them, and already it had begun to show itself; for the Kushites not only made the earliest advances towards civilisation, but under Nimrod, 'that mighty hunter,' smitten with the love of dominion, they threatened at one time to establish a universal empire with Babel as its chief seat. And not without reason; for the Kushite tribes were stalwart in stature and physique, in disposition vigorous and energetic, eager for war and conquest, and with a capacity and lust for great things both in peace and war. But a time of disaster came which carried them into the remotest parts of the earth— into Central Africa, into the mountains of Southern India, whence, after a while, another impulse sent them onwards towards our own island-continent; hither they came, as I think, many centuries before the Christian era, pressed on and on from their original seats by the waves of tribal migration which were so common in those early days. Similar was the experience of the Kelts, a very ancient tribe; soon after their first arrival in Europe, we find them occupying Thrace and the countries about the mouth of the Danube; but fresh immigration from the Caucasus plateau pushed them up the Danube, then into Belgium and France, thence into Britain, and last of all the invading Saxons drove them westwards into Ireland, and into the mountains of Wales and Scotland. So the successive steps of the Kushite displacement, in my opinion, were these:—first into the valley of the Ganges, where they were the original inhabitants, then into the Dekkan and into Further India, then into Ceylon, the Andaman Islands, and the Sunda Islands, and thence into Australia. These stages I will examine presently more in detail.

But, meanwhile, let us look at the old Babylonian kingdom. Its ethnic basis was Kushite; its ruling dynasty continued to be Kushite probably down to the time of the birth of Abraham, about 2000 B.C. But before that date, the Babylonian population had been materially changed. Nimrod had conquered Erech and Accad and Calneh in the land of Shinar; an Akkadian or Turanian element was thus incorporated with his empire; he had built Nineveh and Rehoboth and Calah and Resen (Genesis x. 11); a Shemite element was thus or in some other way superadded; other Turanians and Shemites and Japhetian Aryans too, perhaps attracted by the easy luxuriance of life on these fertile plains, had all assembled in Chaldæa and Babylonia. In consequence, we find that, about twenty centuries B.C., the Kushite kingdom had become a mixed conglomerate of four essentially different races—Hamite, Turanian, Shemite, and Japhetian—which on the inscriptions are called *Kiprat-arbat*, 'the four quarters.' Then, as the Babylonian worship of Mulitta demanded free intercourse as a religious duty, a strange mixture of physical types must have been developed among the children of these races, the Ethiopian, Scythic, Shemitic, and Iranian all blending—a rare study to the eye of a physiologist, who would have seen sometimes the one type sometimes the other predominating in the child. This Chaldæan monarchy—the first of the five great monarchies of ancient history—was overthrown by an irruption of Arab (Shemitic) tribes about the year 1500 B.C. And now, as I think, another wave of population began to move towards our shores; for these Arabs were pure monotheists, and in their religious zeal must have dashed to pieces the polytheistic and sensual fabric which the Babylonian conquests had extended from the confines of India westwards to the Mediterranean (*cf.* Chedorlaomer's expedition, Genesis xiv. 9). Those portions of the Chaldæo-Babylonian people that were unable to escape from the dominion of the Arabs were absorbed in the new empire, just as many of the Keltic Britons were in the sixth and seventh centuries merged in the newly-formed Saxon kingdoms. But the rupture of the Babylonian State and the proscription of its worship must have been so complete as to drive forth from their native seats thousands of the people of the four tongues and force them westwards into Africa, or eastwards through the mountain passes into the tableland of Pánjâb, and thence into the Gangetic Plain. Here, I imagine, were already located the pure Hamites of the Dispersion; but finding these to be guilty of a skin not exactly coloured like their own, and not understanding their language, these latter Kushites of mixed extraction regarded them as enemies and drove them before them into the mountains of the Dekkan, where, to this hour, the Dravidians and Kolarians are black-skinned and savage races. Ere long, these Babylonian Kushites were themselves displaced and ejected from the Ganges valley by a fair-skinned race, the Aryans, another and the last ethnic stream of invaders from the north-west. These Aryans, in religion and habits irreconcilably opposed to the earlier races of India, waged on them a relentless war. Hemmed up in the triangle of southern India, the earlier Hamites could escape only by sea; the Babylonian Kushites, on the other hand, could not seek safety in the mountains of the Dekkan, as these were already occupied; they must therefore have been pushed down the Ganges into Further India and the Malayan peninsula; thence they passed at a later time into Borneo, and the Sunda Islands, and Papua, and afterwards across the sea of Timor into Australia, or eastwards into Melanesia, driven onwards now by the Turanian tribes, which had come down from Central Asia into China and the Peninsula and islands of the East Indies.

Many arguments could be advanced in favour of this view of the origin of the Australian race, but the discussion would be a lengthy one, and this is scarcely the place for it. I may, however, be permitted to add here a simple incident in my own experience. A few months ago, I was staying for a while with a friend in the bush, far from the main roads of the colony and from towns and villages. One day, when out of doors and alone, I saw a black man approaching; his curly hair, his features, his colour, and his general physique, all said that he was an Australian, but his gait did not correspond. I was on the point of addressing him as he drew near, but he anticipated me and spoke first; the tones of his voice showed me that I was mistaken. I at once suspected him to be a Kalinga from the Presidency of Madras. And he was a Kalinga. This incident tells its own tale. In short, it appears to me that the Dravidians and some tribes among the Himalayas are the representatives of the ancient Dasyus, who resisted the Aryan invasion of India, and whom the Puranas describe as akin to beasts. The existence, also, of cyclopean remains in Ponape of the Caroline Islands, and elsewhere onward through the Pacific Ocean, even as far as Easter

Island in the extreme east—all these acknowledged by Polynesians to be the work of a previous race, which tradition, in various parts, declares to have been black—points out one of the routes by which the black race spread itself abroad into the eastern isles; while the presence of Negrillo tribes in detached portions nearer to India—like islands left uncovered by the floods of stronger races pouring in—the Mincopies in the Andaman Islands, the Samangs in the Malay Peninsula, and the Aëtas in the interior of Borneo, with the wild remnants of a black race in the heart of many of the larger islands of the Malay Archipelago—all this seems to me to show that the primitive Dasyus, driven from India, passed into Further India and thence—being still impelled by race movements—into our own continent and into the islands to the north and east of it. But this question must be left for separate investigation.

Thus, in my view, our island first received its native population, in two different streams, the one from the north, and the other from the north-west. Many known facts favour this view:—

(1.) Ethnologists recognise *two* pre-Aryan races in India. The earlier had not attained to the use of metals and used only polished flint axes and implements of stone; the later had no written records, and made grave mounds over their dead. The Vedas call them 'noseless,' 'gross feeders on flesh,' 'raw eaters,' 'not sacrificing,' 'without gods,' 'without rites'; they adorned the bodies of the dead with gifts and raiment and ornaments. All this suits our aboriginals; they are noseless, for they have very flat and depressed noses, as contrasted with the straight and prominent noses of the Vedic Aryans; they have no gods and no religious rites such as the Vedas demand.

(2.) The Kolarian and Dravidian languages have inclusive and exclusive forms for the plural of the first person. So also have many of the languages of Melanesia and Polynesia.

(3.) The native boomerang of Australia is used on the south-east of India, and can be traced to Egypt—both of them Hamite regions.

(4.) In the Kamalarai dialect, the four class-names form their feminines in -*tha*; as, Kubbi (*masc.*), Kubbi-tha (*fem.*); and that is a Shemitic formative. So also in the Hamitic Babylonian, Mul (*masc.*) gives Muli-tta (*fem.*), and Enu (*masc.*), Enu-ta (*fem.*). Although this formative is not common in the Australian languages, yet its unmistakable presence in Kamalarai may mean that our native population has in it the same mixed elements as existed in the old Babylonian empire. To the same effect is the fact that some tribes practise circumcision, while contiguous tribes do not; in many places the natives, in considerable numbers, have distinctly Shemite features; some have as regular Caucasian features as any of us; others, again, are purely negroid.

(5.) In Chaldæa, the dead were not interred; they were laid on mats in a brick vault or on a platform of sun-dried bricks, and over this a huge earthenware dish-cover, or in a long earthen jar in two pieces fitting into each other. Our blackfellows also, even when they do inter, are careful not to let the body touch the earth; in some places, they erect stages for the dead—the Parsee "towers of silence"; elsewhere, they place the dead body in a hollow tree; in South Australia, the corpse is desiccated by fire and smoke, then carried about for a while, and finally exposed on a stage. All this corresponds with the Persian religious belief in the sacredness of the earth, which must not be contaminated by so foul a thing as a putrifying human body. And it shows also how diverse are our tribal customs in important matters.

(6.) The Dravidian tribes, though homogeneous, have twelve varying dialects. The Australian dialects are a parallel to that.

(7.) There is nothing improbable in the supposition that the first inhabitants of Australia came from the north-west, that is, from Hindostan or from Further India. For the native traditions of the Polynesians all point to the west or north-west as the quarter from which their ancestors first came. So also the Indias are to the north-west of our island.

(8.) I now quote Dr. Caldwell; in diverse places, he says:—

"The Puranas speak of the Nishadas as 'beings of the complexion of a charred stick, with flattened features, and of dwarfish tature'; 'as black as a crow'; 'having projecting chin, broad ands flat nose, red eyes, and tawny hair, wide mouth, large ears, and a protuberant belly.' These Nishadas are the Kolarian tribes, such as the Kols and the Santals. But the Dravidians of the South have always been called Kalingas and Pandyas, not Nishadas."

"The Tudas of the Dekkan are a fine, manly, athletic race, with European features, Roman noses, hazel eyes, and great physical strength; they have wavy or curly hair, while the people of the plains are straight haired, have black eyes, and aquiline noses. The skin of the Tudas, although they are mountaineers, is darker than that of the natives of the Malabar coast. The physical type of the Gonds is Mongolian, that of the other Dravidians is Aryan."

"In Shamanism, there is no regular priesthood. The father of the family is the priest and magician; but the office can be taken by any one who pleases, and laid aside; so also in Southern India. The Shamanites acknowledge a Supreme God, but offer him no worship, for he is too good to do them harm. So also the Dravidian demonolators. Neither the Shamanites nor the Dravidians believe in metempsychosis. The Shamanites worship only cruel demons, with bloody sacrifices and wild dances. The Tudas exclude women from worship, even from the temples; they perform their rites in the deep gloom of groves. They have a supreme god, *Usuru Swâmi*; his manifestation is 'light,' not 'fire.' They have no circumcision. They have no forms of prayer. They believe in witchcraft and the work of demons. After the death of the body, the soul still likes and requires food."

"Dr. Logan thought that the Dravidians have a strong Melanesian or Indo-Afric element, and says that a negro race overspread India before both the Scythians and the Aryans. De Quatrefages agrees with him, and says that, long before the historical period, India was inhabited by a black race resembling the Australians, and also, before history began, a yellow race came from the northeast. Of the Tamilians Dr. Logan says:—'Some are exceedingly Iranian, more are Semitico-Iranian; some are Semitic, others Australian; some remind us of Egyptians, while others again have Malayo-Polynesian and even Semang and Papuan features.' Professor Max Müller found in the Gonds and other non-Aryan Dravidians traces of a race closely resembling the negro. Sir George Campbell thinks that the race in occupation of India before the Aryans was Negrito. Even in the seventh century of our era, a Brahman grammarian calls the Tamil and Telugu people Mlêchchas, that is, aboriginals. Dr. Muir thinks that the Aryan wave of conquest must have been broken on the Vindhya mountains, the northern barrier of the Dekkan."

CONCLUSION.

In this discussion, I have endeavoured to show the origin of our Australian numerals, the composition and derivation of the chief personal pronouns, and of a number of typical words for common things, and of these many more could be cited and examined in the same way. I have shown, so far as I can, that these pronouns, and numerals, and test-words, and, incidentally, one of the postpositions, are connected with root-words, which must be as old as the origin of the language; for such ideas as 'before,' 'begin,' 'first,' 'another,' 'follow,' 'change,' 'many,' seem to be essential to the existence of any language. I think I may safely say the same thing about the root-words for 'water,' 'dumb,' and 'eye.' It thus appears, from the present investigation, that our Australians have a common heritage, along with the rest of the world, in these root-words; for, if these blacks are a separate creation and so have no kindred elsewhere, or were never in contact with the other races of mankind, I cannot conceive how they have come to possess primitive words so like those in use over a very wide area of the globe. I therefore argue that they are an integral portion of the human race. If so, what is their origin? On this point, our present discussion may have thrown some light.

J.F.

PART I.

THE GRAMMAR AND THE KEY.

(A.)
THE GRAMMAR.

[THE ORIGINAL TITLE-PAGE.]

AN

AUSTRALIAN GRAMMAR,

COMPREHENDING

THE PRINCIPLES AND NATURAL RULES

OF THE

LANGUAGE,

AS

SPOKEN BY THE ABORIGINES,

IN THE VICINITY OF

HUNTER'S RIVER, LAKE MACQUARIE, &c.

NEW SOUTH WALES.

BY L. E. THRELKELD.

SYDNEY:
PRINTED BY STEPHENS AND STOKES, "HERALD OFFICE,"
LOWER GEORGE-STREET.

THE AUTHOR'S PREFACE.

In the year 1826, the writer printed a few copies entitled "Specimens of a dialect of the Aborigines of New South Wales," in which the English sounds of the vowels were adopted. Subsequently it was found that many inconveniences arose in the orthography, which could only be overcome by adopting another system. Many plans were proposed and attempted, but none appeared so well adapted to meet the numerous difficulties which arose, as the one in use for many years in the Islands of the South Seas,* wherein the elementary sounds of the vowels do not accord with the English pronunciation. This, however, does not meet all the difficulties, because there is a material difference in the idioms of the languages. For instance, in the Tahitian dialect, the vowels always retain their elementary sound, because a consonant never ends a syllable or word; in the Australian language, a consonant often ends a syllable or a word, and therefore its coalition with the sound of the vowels affects that sound and consequently shortens it; while, in many instances, the elementary sound of the vowel is retained *when closed by a consonant*, as well as when the syllable or word is ended by the vowel. To meet this, an accent will be placed over the vowel when the elementary sound is retained, but without such accent the sound is to be shortened. For example, the Australian words *bun, bún, tin, tín,* will be sounded as the English *bun, boon, tin, teen.*

A set of characters cast expressly for the various sounds of the vowels would be the most complete in forming speech into a written language, but in the present instance that could not be accomplished. The present orthography is therefore adopted, not because it is considered perfect, but from the following reasons, viz.:—

1. It appears, upon consideration, impossible so to express the sounds of any language to the eye, as to enable a stranger to pronounce it without oral instruction. The principal object, therefore, is to aim at simplicity, so far as may be consistent with clearness.

2. There appears to be a certain propriety in adopting universally, if possible, the same character to express the same sounds used in countries which are adjacent, as Polynesia and Australia, even though the languages be not akin; especially when those characters have been adopted upon mature consideration, and confirmed by actual experience in the Islands of the South Seas.

---

* Mr. Threlkeld was, for a time, a missionary at Raiatea, in the Society Islands.—Ed.

THE AUTHOR'S PREFACE.

Having resided for many years in the island of Raiatea, and having been in the constant habit of conversing with and preaching to the natives in their own tongue, I am enabled to trace the similarity of languages used in the South Seas, one with another, proving they are but different dialects, although the natives themselves, and we also, at the first interview, could not understand the people of neighbouring islands, who speak radically the same tongue!

In the Australian tongues there appears to exist a very great similarity of idiom, as respects the dual number and the use of the form expressive of negation; and yet it is observed by a writer in the article on 'Greek language,' *Rees's Cyclopædia*, that, "*The dual number is by no means necessary in language*, though it may enable the Greek to express the number 'two' or 'pair' with more emphasis and precision." But this assertion is not at all borne out by facts; because, in this part of the hemisphere, all the languages of the South Seas, in common with New South Wales, possess a dual number, and so essential is it to the languages that conversation could not be carried on, if they had it not. There is, however, a peculiarity in the dual of the Australian tongue which does not exist in the islands, namely, a conjoined case in the dual pronouns, by which the nominative and accusative are blended, as shown in the pronouns*, whilst the verb sustains no change, excepting when reflexive, or reciprocal, or continuative. But in the Islands there are dual verbs. The modes of interrogation and replication are very much alike in the idiom of both languages, and so peculiar as hardly possible to be illustrated in the English language; for they scarcely ever give a direct answer, but in such a manner as leaves much to be implied. The aborigines of this colony are far more definite in the use of the tenses than the Islanders, who have nothing peculiar in the use of the tenses. The subject of tenses caused me much perplexity and diligent examination. Nor did the observations of eminent writers on the theory of language tend to elucidate the matter; because the facts existing in the language of the aborigines of New Holland are in direct contradiction to a note to the article 'Grammar' in the *Encyclopædia Britannica*†, where certain tenses are represented as "peculiar to the Greek, and have nothing *corresponding to them in other tongues*, we need not scruple *to overlook them as superfluous*." Now, our aborigines use the tenses of the verb and the participle variously, to denote time past in general; or time past in particular, as, 'this morning only;' or time past remote, that is, at some former period, as, 'when I was in England,' or, 'when I was a boy.' The future time of the verb and of the participle is also modified in a similar manner, specifically, either now, or to-morrow

---

* See page 17.—ED. † Of that day.—ED.

morning, or generally as in futurity; and besides this, there is another curious fact opposed to the conclusion of the writer's note, which reads thus: "Of the paulo-post-futurum of the Greeks, we have taken no notice, because it is found only in the passive voice; to which if it were necessary, it is obvious that it would be necessary in all voices, *as a man may be about to act, as well as to suffer, immediately.*" Now, such is the very idiom of this language, as will be seen in the conjugation of the participle; for the pronoun, being used either objectively or nominatively, will place the phrase either in the one sense or the other, such change in the pronoun constituting the equivalent to the passive voice or the active voice. The most particular attention is necessary to the tense of the participle as well as that of the verb, each tense being confined to its own particular period, as shown in the conjugation of the verbs. The various dialects of the blacks may yet prove, as is already ascertained in the Islands, to be a difficulty more apparent than real; but when one dialect becomes known, it will assist materially in obtaining a speedier knowledge of any other that may be attempted, than if no such assistance had been rendered.

Although tribes within 100 miles do not, at the first interview, understand each other, yet I have observed that after a very short space of time they are able to converse freely, which could not be the case were the language, as many suppose it to be, radically distinct. The number of different names for one substantive may occasion this idea. For instance, 'water' has at least five names, and 'fire' has more; the 'moon' has four names, according to her phases, and the kangaroo has distinct names for either sex, or according to size, or different places of haunt; so that two persons would seldom obtain the same name for a kangaroo, if met wild in the woods, unless every circumstantial was precisely alike to both inquirers.* The quality of a thing is another source from which a name is given, as well as its habit or manner of operation. Thus, one man would call a musket 'a thing that strikes fire;' another would describe it as 'a thing that strikes,' because it hits an object; whilst a third would name it 'a thing that makes a loud noise;' and a fourth would designate it 'a piercer,' if the bayonet was fixed. Hence arises the difficulty to persons unacquainted with the language in obtaining the correct name of that which is desired. For instance, a visitor one day requested the name of a native cat from M'Gill, my aboriginal, who replied m i n n a r i n g; the person was about to write down the word m i n n a r i n g, 'a native cat,' when I prevented the naturalist, observing that the word was not the name of the native cat, but a question, namely,

---

* There are other reasons for this diversity of language.—ED.

'What' (is it you say? being understood), the blackman not understanding what was asked. Thus arise many of the mistakes in vocabularies published by transient visitors from foreign parts.*

In a "Description of the Natives of King George's Sound (Swan River Colony)," which was written by Mr. Scott Nind, communicated by R. Brown, Esq., F.R.S., and read before the Royal Geographical Society, &c., 14th February, 1831, there is an interesting account of the natives, and also a vocabulary, not one word of which appears to be used or understood by the natives in this district; and yet, from a passage at page 24, the following circumstance leads to the supposition that the language is formed on the same principles, and is perhaps radically the same tongue; the writer observes: "It once occurred to me to be out shooting, accompanied by Mawcurrie, the native spoken of, and five or six of his tribe, when we heard the cry, coowhie, coowhiecácá, upon which my companion stopped short, and said that strange blackmen were coming." Now in this part of the colony, under the same circumstances, a party of blacks would halloo, kaai, kaai, kai, kai; which, allowing for the difference in orthography, would convey nearly, if not precisely, the same sound; the meaning is 'halloo, halloo, approach, approach.' Also, at page 20, the same word, used by the natives here in hunting and dancing, is mentioned as spoken by those aborigines in the same sort of sports, viz., wow, which in this work is spelt wun; it means 'move.' Also, at page 28, the phrase 'absent, at a distance' is rendered búcun, and 'let us go away' by búcun oola, *or* wat oola; here the natives would say waita wolla; see the locomotive verb, in the conjugation of which a similarity of use will be perceived. At Wellington Valley, the names of the things are the same in many instances with those of this part, although 300 miles distant; and, in a small vocabulary with which I was favoured, the very barbarisms are marked as such, whilst mistaken names are written, the natural result of partial knowledge; for instance, kiwung is put down as the 'moon,' whereas it means the 'new moon,' yellenua being the 'moon.' In the higher districts of Hunter's River, my son was lately conversing with a tribe, but only one man could reply; and he, it appears, had a few years back been in this part, and thus acquired the dialect. Time and intercourse will hereafter ascertain the facts of the case.

---

* Many mistakes of this kind have been made by collectors of vocabularies; even the word 'kangaroo,' which has now established itself in Australasia, does not seem to be native; it is not found in any of the early lists of words. The settlers in Western Australia, when they first came into contact with the blacks there, tried to conciliate them by offering them bread, saying it was 'very good.' So, for a long time there, ' very good ' was the blackman's name for bread!—ED.

The arrangement of the grammar now adopted is formed on the natural principles of the language, and not constrained to accord with any known grammar of the dead or living languages, the peculiarities of its structure being such as totally to prevent the adoption of any one of these as a model. There is much of the Hebrew form in the conjugation; it has also the dual of the Greek and the deponent of the Latin. However, these terms are not introduced, excepting the dual, the various modifications of the verb and participle exemplifying the sense in which they are used.

The peculiarity of the reciprocal dual may be illustrated by reference to a custom of the aborigines; when a company meet to dance, each lady and gentleman sit down opposite to one another, and reciprocally paint each other's cheek with a red pigment; or, if there is not a sufficiency of females, the males perform the reciprocal operation. Also, in duelling, a practice they have in common with other barbarous nations, the challenge is expressed in the reciprocal form. The terms I have adopted to characterise the various modifications of the verb may not ultimately prove the best adapted to convey the various ideas contained in the respective forms, but at present it is presumed they are sufficiently explicit. Many are the difficulties which have been encountered, arising, principally, from the want of association with the blacks, whose wandering habits, in search of game, prevent the advantages enjoyed in the Islands of being surrounded by the natives in daily conversation. It would be the highest presumption to offer the present work as perfect, but, so far as opportunity and pains could conduce to render it complete, exertion has not been spared.

BARBARISMS.

It is necessary to notice certain barbarisms which have crept into use, introduced by sailors, stockmen, and others, who have paid no attention to the aboriginal tongue, in the use of which both blacks and whites labour under the mistaken idea that each one is conversing in the other's language. The following list contains the most common in use in these parts:—

Barbarism.	Meaning.	Aboriginal proper word.
Boojery,*	good,	murrorong.
Bail,	no,	keawai.
Bogy,	to bathe,	nurongkilliko.
Bimble,	earth,	purrai.
Boomiring,	a weapon,	turrama [the 'boomerang'.]
Budgel,	sickness,	munni.

* Captain John Hunter (1793) gives *budgeree*, "good," and Lieut.-Col. Collins (1802) gives *boodjerre* "good," both at Port Jackson. Some of the other words condemned here as barbarisms are used in local dialects.—ED.

Cudgel,	*tobacco,*	kuttul, *lit.,** smoke.
Gammon,	*falsehood,*	nakoiyaye.
Gibber,	*a stone,*	tunung.
Gummy,	*a spear,*	warre.
Goonyer,	*a hut,*	kokere.
Hillimung,	*a shield,*	koreil.
Jin,	*a wife,*	porikunbai.
Jerrund,	*fear,*	kinta.
Kangaroo,†	*an animal,*	karai, and various names.
Carbon,	*large,*	kauwul.
Mije,	*little,*	mitti; warea.
Mogo,	*axe,*	baibai.
Murry,	*many,*	muraiai; also, kauwul-kauwul.
Pickaniuney,	*child,*	wounai.
Piyaller,	*to speak,*	wiyelliko.
Tuggerrer,	*cold,*	takara.
Wikky,	*bread,*	kunto, vegetable provisions.
Waddy,	*a cudgel,*	kotirra.
Wommerrer,	*a weapon,*	yakirri; used to throw the spear.

* Used for *literally,* throughout.
† See note, page viii.—ED.

CHAPTER I.

PRONUNCIATION AND ORTHOGRAPHY.

PRONUNCIATION is the right expression of the sounds of the words of a language.

Words are composed of syllables, and syllables of letters. The letters of the language of the aborigines of New South Wales are these:—*

A B D E G I K L M N Ng O P R T U W Y.

Note.—It is very doubtful if *d* belongs to their alphabet; the natives generally use the *t*.

VOWELS.

A is pronounced as in the English words 'are,' 'far,' 'tart.' E is pronounced as slender *a* in 'fate,' or *e* in 'where.' I is pronounced as the short *i* in 'thin,' 'tin,' 'virgin,' or *e* in 'England.' O is pronounced as in the English 'no.' U is pronounced as *oo* in the words 'cool,' 'cuckoo.'

When two vowels meet together they must be pronounced distinctly; as, noa, niuwoa, the pronoun 'he'; bounton, 'she;' so also when double vowels are used in the word; as, wiyéen, 'have spoken.'

A diphthong is the union of two vowels to form one sound: as,
1. *ai*, as in kúl-ai, 'wood'; wai-tawán, 'the large mullet.'
2. *au*, as in nau-wai, 'a canoe'; tau-wil, 'that...may eat.'
3. *iu*, as in niu-woa, the pronoun 'he'; paipiu-wil, 'that it may appear.'

Note.—*ai* is sounded as in the English word 'eye'; *au* as in 'cow'; *iu* as in 'pew.'

CONSONANTS.

G is sounded hard, but it often has also a soft guttural sound; *g* and *k* are interchangeable, as also *k* and *t*.

Ng is peculiar to the language, and sounds as in 'ring,' 'bung,' whether at the beginning, middle, or end of a word.

R, as heard in 'rogue,' 'rough'; whenever used, it cannot be pronounced too roughly; when double, each letter must be heard distinctly.

---

* See PHONOLOGY, page 3.—ED.

The other consonants are sounded as in English.

Europeans often confound *d* with *t*, because of a middle sound which the natives use in speaking quickly; so also they confound *t* with *j*, from the same cause.

ACCENTS.

The language requires but one marked accent, which serves for the prolongation of the syllable; as, b ó n, 'him'; b ú n, the root of 'to smite.' The primitive sound is thus retained of the vowel, which otherwise would be affected by the closing consonant; as, b u n, the root of the verb 'to be' accidental, rhymes with the English word 'bun,' but b ú n, 'to smite,' rhymes with 'boon.'

ORTHOGRAPHY.

In forming syllables, every consonant may be taken separately and be joined to each vowel. A consonant between two vowels must go to the latter; and two consonants coming together must be divided. The only exception is Ng, which is adopted for want of another character to express the peculiar nasal sound, as heard in h a n g e r, and, consequently, is never divided. The following are general rules :—

1. A single consonant between two vowels must be joined to the latter; as, k ŭ - r i, 'man'; y u - r i ġ, 'away'; w a i - ta, 'depart.'
2. Two consonants coming together must always be divided; as, t e t - t i, 'to be dead,' 'death'; b u ġ - g a i, 'new.'
3. Two or more vowels are divided, excepting the dipthongs; as, ġ a t o - a, 'it is I'; y u - a i p a, 'thrust out.' A hyphen is the mark when the dipthong is divided; as, k á - u w a, 'may it be' (a wish); k a - a m a, 'to collect together, to assemble.'
4. A vowel in a root-syllable must have its elementary sound; as, b ú n k i l l i, 'the action of smiting'; t a, the root-form of the verb, 'to eat.'

ACCENTUATION.

In general, dissyllables and trisyllables accent the first syllable; as, p u n t i m a i, 'a messenger'; p i r i w à l, 'a chief *or* king.'

Compound derivative words, being descriptive nouns, have the accent universally on the last syllable; as, w i y e l l i k á n, 'one who speaks,' from w i y e l l i, 'the action of speaking'; so also, from the same root, w i y e l l i - ġ é l, 'a place of speaking,' such as, 'a pulpit, the stage, a reading desk.'

Verbs in the present and the past tenses have their accent on those parts of the verb which are significant of these tenses; as, t a t á n, 'eats'; w i y á n, 'speaks'; w i y á, 'hath told.' This must be particularly attended to; else a mere affirmation will become an imperative, and so on; as, k á - u w a, 'be it so, (a wish); k a - u w á, 'so it is' (an affirmation).

In the future tenses, the accent is always on the last syllable but one, whether the word consists of two syllables or of more; as, tánún, 'shall or will eat'; wiyánún, 'shall or will speak'; búnkillínún, 'shall or will be in the action of smiting'; búnnún, 'shall or will smite.' Present participles have the accent on the last syllable; as, búnkillín, 'now in the action of smiting'; wiyellín, 'now in the action of talking, speaking.' Past participles have their accent on the last syllable but one; as, búnkilliála, 'smote and continued to smite,' which, with a pronoun added, means 'they fought.' But the participial particle, denoting the state or condition of a person or thing, has the accent on the antepenultimate; as, búntóara, 'that which is struck, smitten, beaten.' Thus, there are two accents—one the radical accent, the other the shifting one which belongs to the particles.

Emphasis.

The aborigines always lay particular stress upon the particles in all their various combinations, whether added to substantives to denote the cases, or to verbs to denote the moods or tenses. But, when attention is particularly commanded, the emphasis is thrown on the last syllable, often changing the termination into -o ú; as, wálla-wálla, the imperative, 'move,' or 'be quick'; but to urgently command would be wálla-wáll-o ú, dwelling double the time on the -o ú. To emphatically charge a person with anything, the emphasis is placed on the particle of agency; as, ġatóa, 'it is I;' ġintóa, 'it is thou.'

[The Phonology of the Australian Languages.

Of late years increasing attention has been given to the consideration of the Australian languages, and numerous vocabularies have been collected. But it is somewhat unfortunate that these collections of words have been made, in most instances, by those who did not appreciate the principles of phonology; often the spelling of the words does not adequately represent the sounds to be conveyed. Enough, however, is now known to permit a general estimate to be made of the sounds in the languages or rather dialects, for—notwithstanding many tribal variations in vocables and grammar—the Australian language is essentially one.

General Features.

Looking at the language as a whole, and examining its features, we at once observe the prominence of the long vowels, á and ú, and the frequency of the guttural and nasal sounds; the letter r with a deeper trill than in English, is also a common sound.

Vowels.

The essential vowels are á, í, ú, all pronounced with a full and open voice; *a* as in the English word 'father'; *i* as in 'seen'; and *u* as oo in 'moon.' The Australian *a* long is, in fact, a guttural sound, and is so deceptive to the ear that in many vocabularies the syllable *ba* is written *bah*, or even *bar*; this *a* has a strong sympathy for the letter *r*, which is nearly a guttural in Australia, and when the two come together, as in *mar*, the sound of both is deepened, and so *mar* is pronounced something like *mah-rr*. This guttural combination of *a* and *r* has hitherto been represented by *arr*, as in the word bundarra; but, as both the sounds are normal, I prefer to write bundara, especially as the accent in such a word always falls on the penult. Our blacks also are Orientals in this respect, that, while in English there is a tendency to hurry over the open vowels in a word, they dwell on them, and say *bá-bá*, where we say pă-pă, or even pă-pă.

The Australian *i* is *ee* long; sometimes the sound of it is prolonged, and then resembles the sound of *e* in 'scene'; this sound of *i* is represented by í in this volume.

In Australian names and words, the sound of *u* long is commonly indicated by *oo*. This is quite unnecessary; for the sound of *u*, as it is in 'pull,' is its natural sound. I will, therefore, make it a rule that *u*, before a single consonant, stands for that sound.

There are two more long vowels, ē and ō; these come from a combination and modification of the sounds of á, í, and ú ; ē comes from the union of a and i, as in the English 'sail'; ō from a and u, as in the French 'faute,' or perhaps from â direct. Wherever necessary, an accent has been placed on *e* and *o* (thus, é, ó), to show that they are the long vowels.

Besides these, there are the short vowels, ă, ĕ, ĭ, ŏ, ŭ. As a matter of convenience, it has been usual to indicate the short sound of these vowels, wherever they occur in Australian words, by doubling the consonant which follows them; thus also, in English, we have 'manner,' and, in French, 'bonne,' 'mienne.' This plan seems unobjectionable, and has been followed here; such a word, then, as bukka will have the short sound of *u*; and such words as bundara, where the *u* is followed by a hardened consonant, or by two different consonants, will have the *u* short, unless marked otherwise. If any one of those vowels which are usually short be followed by a *single* consonant, the vowel may then be pronounced long; as ĕlla, ēla; but the short sound of *u*, in such a position, will be marked by û in this volume. In the declension of the verbs, our author writes -mulla, -kulli, and the like; this spelling I have allowed to stand, although I think that it should have been -mûlla, -kâlli.

Besides these ten, there is in Australian a peculiar vowel sound which appears only in a closed syllable, and chiefly before the nasal *ng*; it takes the short sound of either *a, e, i, o,* or *u*. For instance, we have the word for 'tongue' set down as t a l l a n g, t a l l e n g, t u l l i n g, t a l l u n, and the word for 'hand' as m a t a, m e t a, m i t a; and so also with other examples. I regard these variations as proceeding from an obscure utterance of ă, the same dulled *a* which appears in English in the word 'vocal,' and is represented by other vowels in the English 'her,' 'sir,' 'son.' I have introduced ȧ as the sign for this sound; ȧ, therefore, as in the syllables of t ȧ l ȧ ġ, &c., will mean a dull, volatile sound of ă, which, in the various dialects, may have any one of the other short vowels substituted for it. In the Malay language similarly, the *a*—that is, the letter *ain*, not *ghain*—takes the sound of any one of the short vowels.

These six paragraphs seem to contain all that is noticeable in the long and short sounds of the vowels a, e, i, o, u.

Then, we have the diphthongs; *ai*, as in 'eye'; *oi*, as in 'coin'; *au*, as in 'cow'; *iu*, as in 'new'; but *ai* is apt to become *oi*, and sometimes, though rarely, *ei*.

The summary of the vowel sounds will thus be:—

Vowels—â, î, û; i; ē, ō; ă, ĕ, ĭ, ŭ; ủ; ȧ (volatile).
Semi-vowels—w, y.
Diphthongs—ai, oi, au, iu.

I have admitted *w* and *y*, because they are already established in Australian words. I consider *w*, as a vowel, to be entirely redundant in our alphabet; *y* may be useful at the end of an open syllable to represent the softened sound of *i*. Even when *w* or *y* stands as an initial letter in such words as w a t a, y u r i n g, they are both superfluous, for w a t a might as well be written u a t a, and y u r i n g as i u r i n g. But in words such as w a-k ȧ l, 'one,' the *w* stands for an original *b*, and is therefore a consonant; and, similarly, in y a r r o, 'an egg,' the *y* probably represents a primitive *k*. In such cases, *w* and *y* are consonants.

CONSONANTS.

The *gutturals* are *k, g, h, ng*. The *k* is a much more frequent sound in Australian than its softer brother *g*; indeed, I am inclined to think that we could safely regard *k* as the native sound of this guttural, and set down *g* as merely a dialect variety of it. For the reasons given above, I discard the use of *h* at the end of an open syllable; as an initial, *h* occurs in only a few words, such as h i l ȧ m ȧ n, 'a shield'; but the guttural-nasal *ng* is one of the distinctive sounds of the Australian alphabet, and is the same sound as the *ng* in the English word, 'sing.' It appears both as an initial and as a final; its use at the beginning of a syllable severs the Australian language from the Aryan family, and gives it kinship with the African.

B

In Samoan and in other Polynesian dialects, *ng* is very common as an initial, and as a final too in the whole of Melanesia. In this respect the Polynesian and the Melanesian languages are akin to the Australian. The Malay also uses *ng* both as an initial and as a final. Some Australian dialects nasalise the *k*, as in the English word 'ink'; to this there are parallels in the Melanesian languages, and there the sound is represented by *k* or *q*.

In Tamil, one of the Dravidian languages of India, with which our Australian language is supposed to be connected, one formative suffix is *gu*, nasalised into *ngu*; it is used as the initial sound of a syllable, as in *ni-ngu*, 'to quit'; to this extent it corresponds with our *ng*.

Our author, in his edition of 1834, has in some words a doubled *guttural-nasal*, as in bu n gn ga i. As the second of these is only a *g* attracted by the nasal that precedes it, I have written such words with ġ-g. In fact, the double sound proceeds from the one nasal, as in our English word 'finger.' Some of the Melanesian languages have this double sound both with *g* and with *k*.

But in both of its uses, initial and final, the Australian *ng* arises from the nasalisation of the guttural *g*; it is a simple sound, and should therefore be represented by only one letter, not by the digraph *ng*. In Sanskrit, the symbol for it as a final, for there it is never used as an initial and seldom as a final, is n·; but, as the Australian *ng* comes from *g*, 1 prefer to use ġ as its symbol. If we compare the Dravidian pag-al, 'a day,' with the Melanesian bung, 'a day,' it is clear that the *ng* proceeds from a *g*, for the original root of both words is the verb bha, 'to sine.' Further examination may, perhaps, show that our *ng* is, in some cases, a modification of the sound of *n*, as in the French 'bon,' 'bien,' or even of a final vowel, but at present that does not seem to me at all likely.

Besides *ng*, there are the two subdued *nasal* sounds of *n* and *m*—that is, *n* before *d*, and *m* before *b*; these harden the consonant that follows, and produce such sounds as *nda*, *mba*. The same sounds are common in Fiji—a Melanesian region—but not in Polynesia.

Of the *palatals*, the language has *ch*, as in the English word 'church,' and *j*, as in 'jam'; to these may be added the consonant *y*. The *ch* and the *j* sounds are, in some vocabularies, printed as *tch* and *dj*; that is quite unnecessary. I have adopted ċ as the symbol for *ch*, because it is a simple sound.

The only *cerebral* that we have is *r*, although the sound of it is often so asperated as to resemble the Dravidian rough and hard *r*. Our *r* is neither the Arabic vibrating *ghr*, nor the Northumbrian *burr*, but is more like the rolled *r* of the Parisians.

The *dentals* are *t, d, n, l*. As in the case of the gutturals *k* and *q*, so with the dentals *t* and *d*; it is often difficult to decide whether a native, in pronouncing a word, is using the one or the other; so also with *p* and *b* in the next paragraph. The liquids *n* and *l* are really dentals, their sound being produced by the movement of the tongue on the teeth. In connection with the dentals *t* and *d*, it would be interesting to know if our natives ever cerebralise them in pronunciation; for, if they do, that would be another link to connect them with the Dravidians; but the difference of sound is too minute to be detected by an ordinary observer.

A variant of *t* is *th*, for our blacks say both Ippatha and Ippata; the *th* has the same sound as in the English words, 'thin,' 'breath.' It is possible that, in Australian, this *th* sometimes takes the place of the absent *s*. In the Melanesian region also this sound of *th* is common, and is represented often by *d*. Some Australian tribes have also *th* sonant, as in the English words 'this,' 'that'; the Melanesians have a corresponding sound which is represented in Fijian by *c*. If we could revive the Anglo-Saxon characters for these simple sounds, such anomalies would cease.

The *labials* are *p, b*, and *m*; the *m*, as in other languages, is only a *b* sound with the breathing allowed to escape through the nose. Some collectors of words have set down the sounds of *f* and *v* as existing in Queensland, but I cannot admit them without further evidence; they are not found in New South Wales; the natives here say Uëbiny for Waverley.

In addition to these elementary sounds, there are the conjunct sounds obtained by adding the aspirate *h* to some of the consonants. These are *ph, bh, th, dh, kh, gh*, and in each of them the aspirate is separated, in pronouncing it, from the consonant to which it is attached, as in Sanskrit, or as in the English words, u*p*-*h*ill, do*g*-*h*ouse, &c. Some of these combined sounds I have heard distinctly from the lips of a native, and I have no doubt that the others also exist.

The *sibilants* have no place in Australia. One vocabulary gives *stha* as an initial syllable, but that must be a mistake; another gives *dtha*; that also must be a mistake.

It ought to be noted here that in many Australian tribes, when a young man passes through the Bora ceremonies of initiation, one or two of his upper front teeth are knocked out, and this is a portion of the accustomed rites. The loss of these teeth must have had an important influence on the utterance of the dentals and sibilants in past time, and so on the language itself.

PECULIARITIES.

In some dialects, there is a tendency to insert the sound of *y* after *t* and *k*; as, t y a l a, 'to eat,' instead of t a l a. So also in English we sometimes hear *gyarden* for *garden* and *kyind* for *kind*.

Some dialects say k e d l u, for which the usual form would be k e l l u. But it is possible that the *d* here is radical, and so maintains its place.

In the Dieyerie tribe, near Cooper's Creek, South Australia, many words have in them the peculiar sound *ndr*, as m u *n d r* u, 'two,' which is also the Tamil word for 'three.' The Tamil is fond of this sound, and so is the language of Madagascar; the Fijian prefixes the sound of *n* to *d*, so that d u a is pronounced n d u a. The sound of *ndr* comes by accretions from a single *r*, and so the simpler forms of the Tamil m u n d r u are m u r u, m u d u.

The dialect of King George's Sound, Western Australia, has this peculiarity, that it delights in closed syllables; for there the t w o n g a of the inland tribes is pronounced t w o n k, and k a t t a is k a t.

SUMMARY.

The consonants, then, may be thus arranged :—

Gutturals—	k	kh	g	gh	ġ	h.
Palatals—	ć	...	j̣	...	...	y.
Cerebrals—	?	...	...	...	...	r.
Dentals—	t	th	d	dh	n	l.
Labials—	p	ph	b	bh	m	...
Liquids—	...	...	...	...	n	l.

The vowels are *five* in number. If we reckon the guttural-nasal *g* as a separate sound (which, considering its place in the language, we may justly do), but omit the nasalised *k* as uncommon, and count *n* and *l* as dentals only, the simple consonant sounds are *fifteen* in number. To these add the two sounds of *th*, and *w* and *y* as consonants; but omit the six aspirated consonants, for they are not simple sounds. The Australian alphabet thus consists of *twenty-four* simple elementary sounds.—ED.]

CHAPTER II.

THE PARTS OF SPEECH.

Of the Substitute for the Article.

The general meaning of a noun is expressed by using its simple form; as, m a k o r o, 'a fish' or 'fishes'; t i b b i n, a 'bird' or 'birds,' in a general sense ; k ù l a i, ' wood,' or 'a stick.' To make these plural, the plural pronoun would be attached; as, u n n i m a k o r o, t a r a m a k o r o, 'this fish,' 'these fishes,' meaning that they are here present; to express 'the fish' as an active agent we must say ġali m a k o r o, 'this fish,' sc., did some action. And so also with respect to all nouns, as will be explained under the head of pronouns.

Of Substantives.

Nouns are the 'names of persons, things, actions, and places.' They are Proper, when used as the name of any individual person or thing; Common and Collective, when denoting the names of things singly or together; as, k ù r i, 'man' or 'mankind'; k a r a i, 'kangaroo'; m a k o r o, 'fish.' A pronoun attached shows the number, whether singular or plural. Nouns which describe particular applications of the meaning of the verb are formed from the roots of their verbs ; e.g., w i, the root of the verb 'speak,' gives w i y e l l i k á n. ' one who speaks,' ' a speaker'; w i y a i y ó, ' one who always talks,' 'a talker,' 'chatterer.' When names of things are appropriated to a person so as to be the person's name, that name must be declined in the first declension of nouns, to show it is the name of a person and not of the thing ; e.g., t i n t i ġ ' a crab,' belongs to the third declension, and the genitive would be t i n t i ġ - k o b a, ' belonging to a crab'; but when it is the name of a person, its genitive would be t i n t i ġ - ú m b a, 'belonging to Crab,'—Mr. or Mrs., according to the context. There are a few terminations of gender in certain nouns, but not generally; as, p o r i - b a i, 'a husband'; p o r i k ù n - b a i, 'a wife'; y i n á l, ' a son'; y i n á l k ù n, 'a daughter'; but p i r i w á l, means a 'king' or 'queen,' according to the gender of the pronoun attached. To animals, in most instances, there are different words used for the male and for the female; as, warikál, 'a he-dog'; tinko, 'a she-dog.' Names of places are generally descriptive, as, puntéi, the 'narrow' place; búlwára, the 'high' place; tirabínba, the 'toothed' place; búnkilli-ġél, 'the place for fighting,' the field of battle. Names of countries have a declension peculiar to place, and in the genitive have a feminine and a masculine termination; *e.g.*, Englandkál, means 'Englishman,' the termination being masculine; but Englandkálin, means 'Englishwoman,' the termination being feminine; so also, untikál, 'of this place,' masculine; untikálin, 'of this place,' feminine. A noun is an adjective, a verb, or an adverb, according to the particle used with it, or the position of the word in the sentence; as, pitál, 'joy'; pitálmálli, 'to cause joy'; pitállikán, 'a joyful being'; pitálkátán, 'to exist joyfully'; murráráġ, 'good'; murráráġtai, 'the good,' *sc.*, person; murráráġ umá, 'good done,' 'well done,' 'properly done.'

Of the Declension of Nouns, etc.

There are seven declensions of nouns, according to which all adjectives and participles, as well as nouns, are declined.

Nouns are declined according to their use and termination. When used for the name of an individual person, they are declined in the first declension, whatever may be the termination of the word; but when used as the names of places, they follow the declension of place-names. Common nouns are declined in the second, third, fourth, fifth, and sixth declensions, according to their respective terminations.

Of the two nominative cases, the one is simply declarative, and in it the subject is inactive; as, 'this is a bird,' unni ta tibbin; the second nominative is used when the subject is represented as doing something; as, tibbin to tatán, 'the bird eats'; in which case the particles ending in *o* are affixed, to denote the agent, according to the terminations of the respective nouns*; hence the following general rules for the use of the particles of agency:—

1. Nouns or participles ending in *i* or *n* affix -*to*; as,
    Kikoi, 'a native cat,' kikoi-to, 'the cat   '†;
    Gurrulli, the active participle, or the infinitive, ' to hear, believe, obey,' gurrulli-to, 'faith, belief   .'
2. Nouns ending in *ng, a, e, o, u*, require -*ko*; as,
    Maiyá, 'a snake,' maiya-ko, 'the snake   ';
    Kúri, 'a man,' kúri-ko, 'the man   ';
    Woiyo, 'grass,' woiyo-ko, 'the grass   .'
    But when *r* precedes *o*, the noun belongs to the fifth declension.

---

* See '*Agent-nominative case*,' page 11.
† Supply here, and wherever the space occurs, some transitive predicate, as 'did, does, or will do, something.'

3. Nouns ending in *l* require -*lo* to be annexed; as, Punnàl, 'the sun,' punnàl-lo, 'the sun '; Yinàl, 'a son,' yinàl-lo, 'the son .'
4. Nouns of three syllables ending in *r o* require the accent to be shifted to the *o*; as, Makoro, 'fish,' makor-ó, 'the fish .'
5. Nouns of three syllables ending in *r a* change the *a* into *ó*; as, Kokera, 'a hut, house,' koker-ó, 'the house .' Màttàra, 'the hand,' màttàr-ó, 'the hand .'
6. Nouns of four syllables ending in *r* require *r ó* to be added; as, Kulmotiur, 'a woman's name,' Kulmotiur-ró .

NOTE.—The participle form of the verb in the passive voice, when used as an agent, changes the last syllable into *r ó*; as,

Búntoara, 'that which is struck,'
búntoar-ó, 'that which is struck ';
Yellawaitoara, 'that which sits, squats,'
yellawaitoar-ó, 'that which sits .'

OF THE CASES OF NOUNS AND PRONOUNS.

It is by the particles that the whole progress of the mind of the speaker is shown, and only by the right use of them may we expect to render ourselves correctly intelligible to the aborigines. The following are used in the declension of nouns and pronouns, according to the terminations and cases of these:—

1. *The Simple-nominative case* merely declares the person or thing, or the quality, and has no particle added; as, gatoa, 'I'; kùri, 'man'; kùlai, 'wood'; kekàl, 'sweet'; murràràg, 'good.' But particles are used to form nouns; as, búnkiyé, 'a smiter,' from the root bún, 'to smite'; kekàlke, 'sweetness'; or, are used to transform the noun into a verb, which merely declares the abstract action; as, búnkilli, 'the action of smiting.'

2. *The Agent-nominative case* denotes the person who operates, and is always known by the addition of the particle *o*; but this particle of agency is preceded by a servile consonant, or is accented according to the last syllable of the noun. The personal and instrumental interrogatives, to? 'who?' ko? 'what thing?' are unchangeable; the particles of agency thus attached to the noun are -to,-ko,-lo,-o,-ro.

3. *The Genitive case* shows the relation of one thing considered as belonging, in some manner, to another; in the interrogative 'who,' and in the names of persons, it requires -úmba; as, gan-umba? 'whose?' Threlkeld-umba, 'Threlkeld's'; piriwàl-umba, 'the king's'; but things and persons require -koba; as, minarig-koba? 'belonging to what thing?' kùri-koba, 'belonging to man.' The dual, the plural, and the singular feminine pronouns form the genitive by affixing -ba

to the accusative; as, ġalín-ba, 'belonging to us two'; ġearun-ba, 'belonging to us,' 'ours'; bounnoun-ba, 'belonging to her,' 'hers.' The other singular pronouns add the particles to a variant form of the root-word; as, emmo-umba, 'belonging to me,' 'mine'; ġiro-umba, 'belonging to thee,' 'thine.' But time and place require -kál, and -kálin; as, buġgai-kál, 'belonging to the present' period of time now becoming; England-kál, 'a man belonging to England,' 'an Englishman'; England-kálin, 'a woman belonging to England,' 'an Englishwoman'; untikál, 'hereof,' 'belonging to this place.'

4. *The Dative case* shows the ultimate object to which an action tends; as, for a person to possess and use a thing in any way; it is expressed by adding -nuġ to the interrogative pronoun and to names of persons only, but -ko to all other nouns, and to the abstract action, which is thereby formed into a supine or a construct infinitive; as, búnkilliko, 'for-to smite.'* But motion towards a person or thing, as opposed to motion from the place where the person or thing is, requires the following particles according to the various terminations of the nouns; viz., -tako, -kako, -lako, -ako, -rako; that is, the particle -ko, preceded by a syllable, the consonant of which varies according to the termination of the noun to which it is affixed; the personal pronoun requires -kinko, and place takes -kako; see table of declensions.

5. *The Accusative case*, which marks direct action on the person, not merely towards the person, is the object of a transitive verb. The personal pronouns have distinct particles; see their declension. But names of persons have the terminating particle -nuġ added; so also the interrogatives of person, place, and thing; as, ġan-nuġ? 'whom?' *or* 'who is the direct object?' won-nuġ? 'where?' *or* 'where at?' min-nuġ? 'what?' *or* 'what object?' so also, Threlkeld-nuġ is the objective or accusative case. All other common substantives, not derivatives, are placed before the active verb without any change from the simple nominative; nor can error arise therefrom; because when they are used as agents, the sign of that case will be attached; as, karai búwa, 'smite the kangaroo; but karaito tia búnkulla, 'the kangaroo struck me,' equivalent to, 'I was struck by the kangaroo.'

6. In *the Vocative case*, the particle a-la *or* e-la, calling for attention, is prefixed to the form of the nominative, not the agent-nominative, case; as, ala piriwál! 'O king!' equivalent to 'May it please your majesty.'

7. *Ablative case.* Certain postpositions are used to indicate this case; as, (1) kai, meaning 'from,' 'concerning,' 'about,' 'on account of,' used only to proper names and pronouns; but for

---

* See footnote, page 24.

common nouns, -tin, -lin, -in, -rin, 'from,' 'on account of,' the consonant varying according to the termination of the word to which it is attached; (2) kin-biruġ, meaning 'from,' used only to pronouns, is opposed to the dative of 'motion towards'; proper names, whether of persons or places, require ka-biruġ; but common nouns require, according to their terminations, -ta-biruġ, -ka-biruġ, -la-biruġ, -a-biruġ, -ra-biruġ, to mark 'motion from,' as opposed to the dative; (3) katoa, meaning to be 'with' as an agent, is affixed to personal pronouns and proper names of persons only; but persons, things, and places annex, according to their respective terminations, -toa, -koa, -loa, -oa, -roa, meaning 'by,' 'through,' 'with,' 'near'; no causative effects are implied in any of these particles; (4) ka-ba, meaning 'at' or 'on,' and kin-ba, present 'with' a person at his place, are locative.

For nouns, these postpositions are annexed mostly to the form of the simple nominative; for pronouns, commonly to the first dative form.

Of Adjectives and Participles.

Adjectives have no distinctive endings; it depends entirely on their situation, or on the particles used, whether words are nouns, adjectives, verbs, or adverbs. For instance, if murràràġ, 'good,' yarakai, 'bad,' and konéin, 'pretty,' be declined according to their terminations, with the particles of agency affixed, they would then become agents, and consequently nouns; as, murràràġko, 'the good,' yarakaito, 'the bad *or* evil,' konéinto, 'the pretty' *or* 'the beauty,' respectively, ... ;* but participles in the passive voice terminate always in the compound particle -tóara; the root of the verb is prefixed either with or without the causative particles, according to the sense required; as, from kiyu, the verb 'to roast with fire, to scorch, to broil,' comes kiyuba-tóara, 'that which is roasted'; kiyuba-tóara baġ, 'I am roasted'; kiyuba-toaró, 'that which is roasted '*.

Adjectives denoting abundance are often formed by a reduplication; as, murràràġ, 'good'; murràràġ-murràràġ, 'excellent, abundance of good'; kauwàl, 'great, large, big'; kauwàl-kauwàl, 'many, abundant.'

Adjectives denoting want are expressed by affixing a negative word; as, murràràġ-korien, 'worthless,' *lit.*, 'good-not.'

Adjectives denoting resemblance require the particle -kiloa, 'like,' to be affixed; as, wonnai-kiloa, 'child-like,' 'like a child'; but, if they denote habit, the particle -koi is affixed; as, wonnai-kei, 'childish.'

---

* See footnote, page 10.

Adjectives denoting character, manner, or habit, are formed from the roots of verbs, and have the particles y e *or* k o i added; *e.g.*, b ú n, the root of the verb 'to smite,' gives b ú n k i y é, 'a smiter'; whereas b ú n k i l l i-k á n would be 'one who smites'; w o ġ k á l 'to be a fool'; w o ġ k á l-k o i, 'foolish'; so also ġ u r a-k o i 'wise, skilful'; b u k k a-k o i, 'ferocious, savage'; k e k á l-k o i, 'sweet, nice, pleasant.' Derived forms of the verb also give nouns in - y é; as w i y - a i - y é, 'a talker.'

Of Comparatives and Superlatives.

The following are the methods used in comparison, there being no particles to express degrees of quality:—
1. The comparative of equality is formed thus:—
K e k á l-k e i u n n i y a n t i u n n o a-k i l o a, 'sweet this as that-like,' *i.e.*, 'this is as sweet as that.'
2. The comparative of inferiority is formed by putting the negative particle k o r i e n after the adjective; thus:—
K e k á l-k o r i e n u n n i y a n t i u n n o a-k i l o a, 'sweet-not this as that-like,' *i.e*, 'this is not so sweet as that.'
3. The comparative of superiority is formed by the use of the word k a u w á l-k a u w á l, a reduplication of 'great,' and the particle of negation added to that which is inferior; as:—
K e k á l-k e i u n n i k a u w á l-k a u w á l k e a w a i u n n o a, 'sweet this great-great, not that,' *i.e.*, 'this is most sweet.'

Of Words denoting Number.

Numerals are only cardinal; they are declined as nouns, so far as they extend; namely, w a k á l, 'one'; b u l a, b u l ó a r a, 'two'; ġ o r o, 'three'; w a r á n, 'four'; beyond this there are no further numbers, but the general term k a u w á l-k a u w á l, 'much *or* many' is used. The interrogative of quantity or number, m i n n á n? 'which present?', means 'how many?'; the answer would be given by any of the above numbers; or by k a u w á l-k a u w á l k ú r i, 'many men'; or by w a r e a k ú r i, 'few men.' Ordinal numbers can be expressed only by declining the noun to which they may be attached, the ordinal adjective being also subject to declension, according its own termination, independently of the termination of the noun; as:—
P u r r e á ġ-k a ġ o r o-k a, 'the third day'; k ú l a i-t o a ġ o r o-k o a, 'by, beside the third tree.' B u l ó a r a is used in the dual, and is of the sixth declension.

There are also two other expressions which may be noticed here; namely, w i n t a, equivalent to 'a part *or* portion of, some of'; also, y a n t i n, equivalent to 'the whole *or* all'; as, u n t i-b o w i n t a k ú r i, 'here be part of the men,' 'some of the men are here'; u n t i-b o y a n t i n k ú r i, 'here be all the men,' 'all the men are here.'

Of Pronouns.

The personal pronouns of the first, second, and third persons singular, have two forms, the one used with the verb as a subject to it, the other used absolutely in answer to an interrogative, or with the verb for the sake of emphasis. The latter form, when used as a subject, precedes the predicate, and always calls attention to the person and not to the verb. These forms will therefore be designated Personal-nominative pronouns, and marked as such; thus, Nom. 1 means Personal-nominative; but the personal pronouns used as the nominative to verbs and never by themselves, nor in answer to interrogatives, will be marked Nom. 2, to denote Verbal-nominative, as the verb is then the prominent feature to which attention is called, and not the person; these always follow the verb. The strictest attention must be given to the use of the pronouns in all their persons, numbers, and cases; for by them the singular, dual, and plural numbers are known; by them the active, the passive, the reciprocal, and reflexive states of the verb; as will be exemplified in the conjugation of the verbs, as well as in the declension of the pronouns. The plural personal pronouns have only one nominative form to each person; so also, the singular feminine pronoun, which is only of one description. The dual number also has but one pronoun in the nominative case; but it has a case peculiar to this language —a nominative and an accusative case conjoined in one word; just as if such English pronouns as I and thee, thou and him, could become I-thee, thou-him. This will be called the Conjoined-dual form.

DECLENSION OF THE NOUNS AND PRONOUNS.

[The declension of the nouns and pronouns is effected by means of postpositions, as has been already explained in this chapter. The forms of the ablative case may be indefinitely multiplied in number by using other postpositions than those shown in the following paradigms.*—ED.]

[* In the paradigms of the pronouns and the nouns, *Nom.* 1 is the nominative case in its simple form, used absolutely; *Nom.* 2 is the form used as the nominative of the agent or instrument; the *Gen.* means, as usual, ' of,' or 'belonging to'; *Dat.* 1 is the dative of ' possession' or 'use,'=' for' (him, her, it), to have and to use; *Dat.* 2 is a sort of locative case 'towards' (him, &c.); the *Acc.* is the ' object' form of the word; the *Voc.* is used in ' calling'; *Abl.* 1 denotes 'from,' 'on account of,' as a cause; *Abl.* 2, 'from,' 'away from,' 'procession from'; *Abl.* 3, 'with,' 'in company with'; *Abl.* 4, 'being with,' 'remaining with,' 'at'; occasionally there is an *Abl.* 5, which means merely place where, ' at.'—ED.]

PARADIGM OF THE DECLENSION OF NOUNS.

Declensions.

	(1st.) Bi-ra-ban. 'A man's name.'	(2nd.) Bi-ra-ban. 'An englehawk.'	(3rd.) Kú-ri. 'Man.'	(4th.) Pi-ri-wal. 'A chief.'	(5th.) Ma-ko-ro. 'A fish.'	(6th.) Ko-ke-ir-ur. 'A kangaroo (fem).'
Nom. 1.	Biraban	Biraban	Kuri	Piriwal	Makoro	Kokeirur
2.	Biraban-to	Biraban-to	Kuri-ko	Piriwal-lo	Makor-ó	Kokeir-ro
Gen.	Biraban-úmba	Biraban-ko-ba	Kuri-ko-ba	Piriwal-ko-ba	Makoro-ko-ba	Kokeirur-ko-ba
Dat. 1.	Biraban-nũng	Biraban-ko	Kuri-ko	Piriwal-ko	Makoro-ko	Kokeirur-ko
2.	Biraban-kin-ko	Biraban-ta-ko	Kuri-ka-ko	Piriwal-la-ko	Makor-rí-ko	Kokeir-rí-ko
Acc.	Biraban-nũng	Biraban	Kuri	Piriwal	Makoro	Kokeirur
Voc.	Ala Biraban	....	Ala kuri	Ala piriwal	....	....
Abl. 1.	Biraban-kai	Biraban-tin	Kuri-tin	Piriwal-lin	Makor-rin	Kokeir-rin
2.	Biraban-ka-birung	Biraban-ka-ta-birung	Kuri-ka-birung	Piriwal-la-birung	Makor-rá-birung	Kokeir-rá-birung
3.	Biraban-ka-to-a	Biraban-to-a	Kuri-ko-a	Piriwal-lo-a	Makor-ró-a	Kokeir-ró-a
4.	Biraban-kin-ba	Biraban-ta-ba	Kuri-ka-ba	Piriwal-la-ba	Makor-rá-la	Kokeir-rá-ba

THE GRAMMAR. 17

PARADIGM OF THE DECLENSION OF THE PERSONAL PRONOUNS.

Singular.

	1st.	2nd.	3rd (Mas.)	3rd (Fem.)
Nom.	1. Nga-toa 2. Bang	Ngin-toa Bi	Niu-woa Noa	} Boun-toa
Gen.	Emmo-umba	Ngiro-umba	Ngiko-umba	Boun-no-umba
Dat.	1. Emmo-ung 2. Emmo-ung-kin ko	Ngiro-ung Ngiro-ung-kin-ko	Ngiko-ung Ngiko-ung-kin-ko	Boun-no-un-ko Boun-no-un-kin-ko
Acc.	Tia	Bin	Bón	Boun-no-un
Voc.	Ka-tioá	Ala bi	......	......
Abl.	1. Emmo-ung-kai 2. Emmo-ung-kin-birung 3. Emmo-ung-ka-toa 4. Emmo-ung-kin-la	Ngiro-ung-kai Ngiro-ung-kin-birung Ngiro-ung-ka-toa Ngiro-ung-kin-la	Ngiko-ung-kai Ngiko-ung-kin-birung Ngiko-ung-ka-toa Ngiko-ung-kin-la	Boun-no-un-kai Bounoun-kin-birung Boun-no-un-ka-toa Boun-no-un-kin-la

Dual.

	We two (thou and I).	We two (he and I).	We two (she and I).	Ye two.	They two.
Nom.	Bali	Bali-noa	Bali-boun-toa	Bula	Bul-o-ara
Gen.	Ngali-n-ba	Ngali-n-ba-bón	Ngoli-n-ba-no-un	Bul-un-la	Bul-o-ara-koba, bul-un-la
Dat.	1. Ngali-n-ko. 2. Ngali-n-kin-ko.				
Acc.	Ngali-n	Ngali-n-bón	Ngali-n-no-un	Bul-un	Bul-o-ara ; bul-un (fifth declension).
Abl.	1. Ngali-n-kai. 2. Ngali-n-kin-birung. 3. Ngali-n-kin-toa. 4. Ngali-n-kin-la.				

Plural.

	1st.	2nd.	3rd.
	Ngé-en	Nú-ra	Ba-ra.
	Ngear-umba	Nur-umba	Bar-umba.
	Ngear-un-ko Ngear-un-kin-ko		
	Ngear-un	Núr-un	Bar-un.
	Ngear-un-kai Ngear-un-ka-birung. Ngear-un-ka-toa. Ngear-un-kin-la.		

The two.
Nom. { 1. Bul-o-ara.
2. Bul-o-aṟa (the two as agents).

Conjoined Dual.

Ba-búng, I-thee   Ba-noun, I-her   Bi-tia, thou-me   Bi-núng, thou-him   Bi-noun, thou-her   Bi-loa, he-thee   Bin-toa, she-thee.

DECLENSION OF PLACE-NAMES.

All Nouns, whatever may be their original signification, when used as proper names of places, are of this declension, if they end in *a*.

Mulubinba, the site of 'Newcastle.'

Nom. Mulubinba, the name of the place, *M* . . . . .
Gen. 1 Mulubinba-koba, any thing belonging to *M*. . .
     2 Mulubinba-kàl, a male belonging to *M* . . . .
     3 Mulubinba-kàlin, a female belonging to *M*. . .
Dat. 1 Mulubinba-kako, for *M* . . , — to remain there.
     2 Mulubinba-kolaġ, to *M* . . , to proceed to *M*. .
Acc. 1 Barun Mulubinba-kàl, them (*masc.*) of *M* . . .
     2 Barun Mulubinba-kàlin, them (*fem.*) of *M* . .
     3 Barun yantín Mulubinba-kàl, them all of *M*. .
Voc. Yapállun Mulubinba-kàl, alas! people of *M*.   .
Abl. 1 Mulubinba-tin, from, on account of *M*. . . . . .
     2 Mulubinba-kabiruġ, from, away from *M* . . .
     3 Mulubinba-koa, by, by way of, through *M* . . .
     4 Mulubinba-kaba, at, on, in *M*. . . . .

NOTE 1.—To form the *Acc.* singular or dual here, put their pronouns in the place of barun.

2.—The interrogative pronoun signifying place is wonta? 'where is it?' and this may be substituted for Mulubinba; the example would then become interrogative; as, wontakàl? 'belonging to what place?' wontakaba? 'where is it at?' 'at what place is it?' &c.

DECLENSION OF THE FIRST PERSONAL PRONOUN.

The cases of the three personal pronouns and the manner of using them are similar to those of the nouns. Thus, for the first pronoun:—

Nom. 1. Gatoa, *I.*—This form is used in answer to an interrogative of personal agency; as, Gánto wiyán? 'Who speaks?' The answer would be ġatoa, 'it is I who,' the verb being understood. The next form, baġ, would simply declare what I do.

    2. Baġ, *I,*—is used in answer to an interrogative of the act; as, Minnuġ ballin bi? 'What art thou doing now?' tatán baġ, 'I eat;' baġ must be used, and not the personal-nominative, ġatoa.

THE GRAMMAR.

Gen. E m mo - ú m b a, *My* or *mine*,—is used with a noun, or with a substantive verb; the noun always precedes; as, k o k e r a e m m o u m b a, 'my house'; but e m m o u m b a t a, 'it is mine.'

Dat. 1. E m m o - u ġ, *For me*,—personally to receive or use.
2. E m m o - u ġ - k i n - k o, *To me*,—to the place where I am.

Acc. Ti-a, *Me*,—governed by transitive verbs. This pronoun is used to form the equivalent for the passive voice; as, b ú n t á n b a ġ, 'I strike;' but b ú n t á n t i a, 'I am struck,' *lit.*, 'strikes me.'

Voc. K a - t i - o ú,—merely an exclamation; as, *Oh me! Ah me!*

Abl. 1. E m m o - u ġ - k a i, *From me*,—through me, about me.
2. E m m o - u ġ - k i n - b i r u ġ, *From me*,—away from me.
3. E m m o - u ġ - k a - t o a, *With me*,—in company with me.
4. E m m o - u ġ - k i n - b a, *With me*,—at my place.

These case-endings have the same force for the second and the third pronouns also.

DEMONSTRATIVE PRONOUNS.

These are so compound in their signification as to include the demonstrative and the relative; *e.g.*—1. ġ a l i is equivalent to 'this is that who *or* which,'—the person *or* thing spoken of being here present; 2. ġ a l a, 'that is that who *or* which,'—being at hand; 3. ġ a l o a, 'that is that who *or* which,'—being beside the person addressed, or not far off. They are thus declined: —

		Instant.	*Proximate.*	*Remote.*
Nom.	1.	Ga-li	Ga-la	Ga-loa.
	2.	Un-ni	Un-noa	Un-toa.
Gen.		Gali-ko-ba	Gala-ko-ba	Galoa-ko-ba.
Dat.	1.	Gali-ko	Gala-ko	Galoa-ko.
	2.	Un-ti-ko	Un-ta-ko	Un-toa-ko.
Acc.		Un-ni	Un-noa	Un-toa.
Abl.	1.	Gali-tin	Un-ta-tin	Galoa-tin.
	2.	Un-ti-biruġ	Un-ta-biruġ	Un-toa-biruġ.

The pronouns attached to these demonstratives determine their number, whether they are to be singular or plural; as, ġ a l i - n o a, 'this is he who'; ġ a l i - b a r a, 'these are they who'; ġ a l i - t a, 'it is this that'; ġ a l i - t a r a, 'these are they that.' Other combinations are ġ a l i - n o a, 'this is he who,' as an agent; u n n i - n o a, 'this is he,' the subject. Gali-koba bón, 'this belongs to him,' an idiom; ġ a l o a - k o b a bón, 'this is that which belongs to him'; these and the other similar genitives, are always followed by the accusative case.

Reciprocal Pronouns.

Gatoa-bo, 'I myself'; ġintoa-bo, 'thou thyself'; niu-woa-bo, 'he himself'; bali-bo, ' our two selves,' and so on. The *bo* here attached is merely an intensive particle.

Possessive Pronouns.

These are the genitive cases of the personal pronouns, and are used thus:—emmoumba ta, 'mine it is'; unni ta emmoumba kokera, 'this is my house'; unnoa ta ġiroumba, 'that is thine'; tararán ġiroumba korien, 'it is not thine,' *lit.*, 'not thine not,' for the idiom of the language requires two negatives here.

Indefinite Pronouns.

Yiturrabúl, 'some one,' 'some person or persons', is declined like the fourth declension of nouns; tarai, 'other,' like the second declension.

Absolute Pronouns.

Ta, 'it is,' from the substantive verb; tara, 'they are,' is of the fifth declension; unni tara, 'these are they which,' as a subject; ġali taro, 'these are they which,' as agents; yantin, 'all,' 'the whole,' is of the second declension; yantin-to, 'all who,' as agents; wakállo, 'one only,' as an agent.

Interrogative Pronouns.

The interrogative pronouns are,—ġan, 'who?'; min (*neut.*), 'which? what?'; won, 'where?'; ya-koai, 'how? in what manner?'; ya-kounta, 'when? at what time?'

EXAMPLES OF THE PARTICLES USED AS AFFIXES TO THE INTERROGATIVES.

The Interrogative, Gán-? who?

Nom. 1 Gan-ke? who is?
      2 Gan-to? who is the agent?
Gen.   Gan-úmba? whose?
Dat. 1 Gan-núġ? for whom?—to possess or use.
      2 Gan-kin-ko? to whom?—towards whom?
Acc.   Gan-núġ? whom? *or* who is the object?
Voc.   ....
Abl. 1 Gan-kai? from whom? on account of whom?
      2 Gan-kin-biruġ? from, away from whom?
      3 Gan-katoa? in company with whom?
      4 Gan-kin-ba? with whom? remaining with whom?

The Interrogative, Min-? what? which?,
applied to things only.

Min-a ri ġ? what? as, min a ri ġ ke unni? what is this?
Min-n á n? what are? *i.e.*, how many?
Min-a ri ġ-ko? what?—as the agent or instrument.
Min-a ri ġ-ko ba? belonging to what?
Min-a ri ġ-ko la ġ? towards what?
Min-n u ġ? what?—the object of the verb.
Min-a ri ġ-tin? from what cause? why? wherefore?
Min-a ri ġ-bi ru ġ? from what? of what? out of what?
Min-a ri ġ-ki lo a? like what?
Min-a ri ġ-ko a? with what? together with what?
Min-a ri ġ-ka ba? on what?

The Interrogative of place,
Won-? what place? where?

Won-ta? where is the place? what place?—definite.
Won-u ein? where? which place?—indefinite.
Won-ta-kál? *masc.*, belonging to what country or place?
Won-ta-kálin? *fem.*, belonging to what country?
Won-ta-ko la ġ? towards what place?
Won-ta riġ? to what place? whither?
Won-n u ġ? what place? where?—the object of a verb.
Won-ta-tin to? from what place? (causative); where at?
Won-ta-bi ru ġ? from what place? out of what place?
Won-ta-ko a? through what place? by what place?

Interrogative adverbs. { Yako ai? how? in what manner?
{ Ya ko un ta? when? at what time?

All these particles are used strictly according to the meanings shown above, and cannot be used loosely like some interrogatives in English; for example, y a k o a i? 'how?' cannot be used to to ask the question 'how many?' for it is an adverb of manner; 'how many' must be min n á n.

c

CHAPTER III.

OF THE VERB.

The verbs undergo no change to indicate either number or person, but the stem-forms vary in respect to the sort of agency employed, whether personal or instrumental, and also according to the manner of doing or being; as, (*a*) when I do anything to myself, or (*b*) to another; or (*c*) I do anything to another and he reciprocally does it to me; or (*d*) when I continue to be or to do; or (*e*) when the action is doing again, or (*f*) when permitted to be done by this or that agent; or (*g*) by another agent; or (*h*) when a thing acts as an agent, or (*i*) is used as an instrument. Verbs are reduplicated to denote an increase of the state or action. All verbs are declined by particles, each of which particles contains in its root the accident attributed to the verb in its various modifications; as, assertion, affirmation, negation, privation, tendency, existence, cause, permission, desire, purpose; thus are formed moods, tenses, and participles. The participles are formed after the manner of their respective tenses, and are declined either as verbal nouns or as verbal adjectives.

Of the Kinds of Verbs.

Verbs are either *Transitive* or *Intransitive*, both of which are subject to the following accidents, viz. :—

1. *Active-transitive*, or those which denote an action that passes from the agent to some external object; as, 'I strike him,' búntán bón bag. This constitutes *the active voice*, which states what an agent does to another, or, what another agent does to him, in which latter case it is equivalent to the English passive voice; *e.g.*, búntán bón (literally, 'strikes him,') implies that some agent now strikes him, and means 'he is now struck,' the nominative pronoun being omitted in order to call attention to the object. But when this accusative or object is omitted, the attention is then called to the act which the agent performs; as, búntán bag, 'I strike,' expressed often by 'I do strike.'

2. *Active-intransitive*, or those which express an action which has no effect upon any external object except the agent or agents themselves; that is, the agent is also the object of his own act; consequently the verb is necessarily reflexive; as, búnkilléún bag, 'I struck myself.' This constitutes the 'reflexive' modification of the verb.

3. *Active-transitive-reciprocal*, or those verbs that denote an action that passes from the agent to some external object, which object returns the action to the agent who then becomes the object, and thus they act reciprocally one towards the other. Consequently the dual and plural numbers are always the subject to this form of the verb; as, búnkillán bali, 'thou and I strike' each other reciprocally; búnkillán bara, 'they strike' each one the other reciprocally, or they fight with blows. This constitutes the 'reciprocal' modification of the verb.

4. *Continuative*; as when the state continues, or the action is, was, or will be, continued without interruption; as, búnkillilín baġ, 'I am now continuing in the action of making blows', such as thrashing or beating. This is called the 'continuative' modification of the verb.

5. *Causative* (1) by permission, or, with a negative, *prohibitive*; as, when we do or do not permit a person to do the act, or another to do the act to him; as, búmmunbilla bón, 'let him strike,' búmmarabunbilla bón, 'cause some one to strike him,' equivalent to, 'let him be struck'; búmmarabunbi yikora bón, 'let no one strike him.'

6. *Causative* (2) by personal agency, denoting the exertion of personal energy to produce the effect upon the object; as tiir ta unni, 'this is broken'; tiir buġ-ga unni also means 'this is broken,' but then personal agency is understood, for the phrase is equivalent to 'some person has broken this,' *or* 'this is broken by some one.'

7. *Causative* (3) by instrumental agency, denoting an effect produced by means of some instrument; as, tiir burréa unni, 'this is broken,' *sc.*, by means of something.

8. *Effective*, or those which denote an immediate effect produced by the agent on the object; as, umá baġ unni, 'I made this'; pitál baġ, 'I am glad'; pitálmá bón baġ, 'I made him glad.'

9. *Neuter* verbs, or those which describe the quality, state, or existence of a thing; as, kekál láġ unni, 'this is sweet'; tetti láġ unni, 'this is dead'; wonnuġ ke noa? 'where is he?' unni ta, 'this is it'; móron noa kátán, 'he is alive'; unnuġ noa ye, 'there he is.' In these the particles, láġ, ke, ta, kátán, ye, are rendered into English by the neuter verb *is*.

10. *Reduplicate*, or those which denote an increase of the state, quality, or energy; as, pitál noa, 'he is glad'; pitál-pitál noa, 'he is very glad'; tetti bara, 'they are dead'; tetti-tettéi bara, 'they are dead-dead,' *or* 'a great death is among them'; kauwál, 'great'; kauwál-kauwál, 'very great'; tauwa, 'eat'; tauwa-tauwa, 'eat heartily.'

11. *Privative*, or those which denote the absence of some property. Affirmatively, u m á n b a ġ u n n i, 'I make this,' *or* 'I do this'; u p á n b a ġ u n n i, 'I do this,' not directly, but with something or by means of something else; *e.g.*, 'I write on this paper with a quill' would be u p á n b a ġ u n n i y i r i ġ k o w i y e l l i k o, *lit.*, 'I make this quill for-to speak *or* communicate'; whereas u m á n b a ġ u n n i y i r i ġ p o n k a k i l l i k o would mean 'I make this quill for-to* be a pen.' Negatively, when it is implied that the act itself has not taken place, the expression would be u m a p a b a ġ b a, 'had I made'; again, if the act existed, but no effect produced by the action were implied, it would be expressed thus, u m a i-ġ a b a ġ u n n i, 'I had almost done this.'

12. *Imminent*, or those which denote a readiness to be or to do; as p i r i w á l k a t é a k u n k o a b a ġ, 'lest I should be king'; b ú n t é a k u n k o a b ó n b a ġ, 'lest I should strike him.'

13. *Inceptive*, or those which describe the state as actually about to exist, or the action as going to put forth its energy at the time spoken of; as, k a k i l l i k o l a ġ b a l i, 'we two are now going to live reciprocally together'; b ú n k i l l i k o l a ġ b a ġ, 'I am now going to strike.'

14. *Iterative*, or those which denote a repetition of the state or action; as, m ó r o n k a t é a k á n ú n, 'shall live again'; b ú n t é a k á n ú n, 'will strike again.'

15. *Spontaneous*, or those which denote an act done of the agent's own accord; as, t i i r k u l l i n u n n i, 'this is breaking of its own accord'—not by external violence (*cf.* No. 6); p ó r k u l l é ú n n o a, 'he has just been born,' *lit.*, 'he has dropped himself.'

Of the Moods.

There are three moods, the *Indicative*, the *Subjunctive*, and the *Imperative*.

1. *The Indicative*, which simply declares a thing; as, b ú n t á n b a ġ, 'I strike'; u n n i t a, 'this is it', the subject; ġ a l i n o a 'this is he,' the agent.

2. *The Subjunctive*, which subjoins something to the meaning of the verb, such as a wish, a desire, a purpose; as, b ú w i l b a ġ, 'I wish to strike,' b ú u w a b a ġ, 'I desire to strike,' *or* 'I want now to strike'; t a n á n b a u w á b ú n k i l l i k o, 'had I come hither for-to strike.'

---

* This form of the verb, as will afterwards be shown, denotes *purpose;* our author expresses that everywhere by *for-to*. I have allowed that prepositional form to stand.—Ed.

3. *The Imperative*, which expresses command; as, b ú w a b i, 'do thou strike'; but in b ú m m u n b i l l a, 'let strike,' the person or persons addressed are desired to permit the person named to strike; in b ú m m a r a b u n b i l l a, 'let strike,' the person addressed is desired to permit any one to strike the person named; in b ú n t é a - k a, 'strike again,' the person or persons addressed are desired to repeat the action. The imperative form is often used with the first and the third personal pronouns; in this sense it denotes the desire of the agent to do the act at the time spoken of; as, b ú w a b a n u ġ, 'I want to strike thee'; b ú w a b i l o a, 'he wants to strike thee.'

NOTE.—The equivalent, in many instances, to the English infinitive mood is the construct form of the verb which denotes the purpose of the subject; as, M i n a r i ġ k o u n n i? What is this for? b ú n k i l l i k o, is the answer, 'for-to strike.'

OF THE TENSES.

1. *The Present*, which asserts the present existence of the action or being of the verb, at the time in which the assertion is made. The signs of this tense are the following affixed particles, of which the first consonant is varied by the terminations of the respective conjugations of the verbs, viz., -á n to the simple verb, -l á n to the reciprocal verb, and -l í n to the participle; as, b ú n t á n, 'strikes' now; b ú n k i l l á n, now 'reciprocally strike one another'; b ú n k i l l í n, now 'striking'; b ú n k i l l i l í n, now 'continuing in the act of striking.'

2. *The Perfect-definite*, which asserts the act as having been completed in a past period of the present day; as, b ú n k é ú n, 'has struck,' sc., this morning; b ú n k i l l é ú n b a ġ, 'I have struck myself,' sc., this day.

3. *The Perfect-past-aorist*, which asserts the act as completed, without reference to any particular period in past time; as, b ú n k u l l a, 'struck.' This is not the participle.

4. *The Pluperfect*, which asserts the act as completed prior to some other past circumstance. It is formed by the affirmative particle, t a, affixed to the past aorist, and is equivalent only to the English pluperfect; as, b ú n k u l l a t a, 'had struck.'

5. *The Future-definite*, which asserts the act as taking place at a certain definite period, future to the time at which the act is spoken of; as, b ú n k í n, 'shall *or* will strike,' sc., to-morrow morning.

6. *The Future-aorist*, which asserts the mere future existence of the act, without reference to any other circumstance, in some indefinite time to come; as, b ú n n ú n b a ġ, 'I shall strike'; b ú n n ú n n o a, 'he will strike.'

Of the Participles.

1. *The Present.* This has already been described; but it may be necessary to mention, that the present participle can be used only with reference to present time, not to the past and future, as is the case in English; as, búnkillín, 'striking' now.

2. *The Imperfect-definite,* which represents the action as being in progress at some definite past period; as, búnkillikéún, 'striking,' sc., this morning.

3. *The Imperfect-past-aorist,* which represents the action as being in progress at any recent time; as, búnkilliela noa, , he was striking.'

4. *The Past-present-aorist,* which asserts the action as having been engaged in and completed at some former period; as, búntálla baġ, wounnai baġ ba, 'I struck when I was a child'; wiyálla baġ wonnai-kiloa, wonnai baġ ba, 'I spoke as a child when I was a child.'

5. *The Pluperfect,* which indicates the action as having been completed prior to some other past event mentioned; as, búnkilliela ta, 'had struck,' sc., prior to something.

6. *The Inceptive-future,* which asserts that the action is now about to be pursued; as, búnkilli kolaġ baġ, 'I am going to strike,' *or* 'I am going a-striking'; makoro kolaġ baġ, 'I am going a-fishing.'

7. *Future-definite,* which asserts the action as about to be engaged in at some future definite period; as, bunkillikín baġ, 'I am going to strike,' sc., to-morrow morning.

8. *The Future-aorist,* which asserts that the action will exist at some future undefined period; as, búnkillinún baġ, 'I am going to strike,' sc., at some time or other, hereafter.

[*PARADIGM OF THE TENSES AND THEIR MEANINGS.*

The Tenses of the verb and their meanings, as given above, may be concisely expressed thus:—

Indicative Mood and Participles.

Tense.	Meaning.
1. *Present tense,*	I am or do—now.
2. *Imperfect-definite,*	I was or was doing—this morning.
3. *First-aorist,*	I was or was doing—recently.
4. *Second-aorist,*	I was or did—at some former period.
5. *Perfect-definite,*	I have been or done—this morning.
6. *Pluperfect,*	I had been or done—before some event.
7. *Inceptive-future,*	I am going to or shall, be or do—now.
8. *Future-definite,*	I am going to or shall, be or do—to-morrow morning.
9. *Future-aorist,*	I am going to or shall, be or do—at some time hereafter.

Subjunctive Mood.

Our author has four *Aorists* in this Mood, namely:—

10a. *Past aorist*,		I had almost been *or* done.
b. *Aorist of the past*,		Had I been *or* done.
c. „ „		I wish I had been *or* done.
d. „ „	*negatively*,	I have not been *or* done.

The Moods have various mode-forms, thus:—

In the Indicative.

Reciprocal mode,	We [*e.g.*, strike] one another.
Reflexive mode,	I [strike] myself.

In the Subjunctive.

Iteration mode,	I [strike] again.
Imminence,	Lest I should [strike].
Contemporary circumstance,	While I *or* when I [strike].
Implied negation of actual becoming or of actual effect,	See 10 a
Implied negation of being or action,	See 10 b., c., d.

In the Participles.

Continuative mode,	Continuing to be *or* to do.
Reflexive mode,	Doing to one's self.
Reciprocal mode,	Doing to one another.

It is clear that the native language recognises three varieties of time and place. The pronouns ġa l i, ġa l a, ġa l o a (*q.v.*) show these variations as to *place*; and so the principal tenses of the indicative mood, as above, mark *time* (1) *present*, (2) *recent*, (3) *remote*. English and other languages show the same distinctions in such words as *here, there, yonder*.—Ed.]

DECLENSION of the VERBS.

[☞ The reader will remember that the tense-form of the verb is always constant, and is therefore not affected by its subject. The subject shown in the declension of the verb is the pronoun ba ġ, 'I,' and the direct object with a transitive verb is bón, 'him'; but any other suitable pronouns may be substituted for these; for the pronouns that are thus used as subjects, see note on next page; their objective cases are shown in the paradigm of the pronouns. Each tense may thus be declined in full, as in English, by using in succession the pronouns of the first, second, and third persons as the subject of the verb. The shades of meaning conveyed by the tenses are given in the paradigm above, and are applicable to all verbs. The numbers, affixed to the various tenses in the declension of the verbs, correspond with the numbers on that paradigm of tenses, and the *T*. stands for Tense.—Ed.]

DECLENSION OF THE SUBSTANTIVE VERB.

Kakilliko, 'to be,' 'to exist,' 'to remain.'

Example of the Declension of a Verb in the Present Tense of the Indicative Mood.

Any Tense may be declined in full in a similar manner.

T. 1. *Sing.* Unnibo† baġ* ka-tán,   I am here.
                „   bi   „   Thou art here.
                „   noa „   He is here.
Dual.   „   bali* „   We two (*inclusive*) are here.
           „   balinoa „   We two (*exclusive*) are here.
           „   bula   „   You two are here.
           „   buloara „   They two are here.
Plu.   „   ġeen, „   We are here.
           „   nura   „   You are here.
           „   bara   „   They are here.

Reciprocal.

Dual. Unnibo bali* ka-kill-án, We two are, *or* live, here together.
Plu.   „   ġeen* „   We are, *or* live, here together.

* Or, such other nominative cases of pronouns of the singular, dual, and plural, as the sense may require; *e.g.*, for the *sing.*, b a u ġ, *I*; b i, *thou*; n o a, *he*; b o u n t o a, *she*; t a, *it*; n g a l i, *this* (here); n g a l a, *that* (near me); n g a l o a, *that* (near you); for the *dual*, b a l i, *thou and I*; b a l i n o a, *he and I*; b a l i b o u n t o a, *she and I*; b u l a, *ye two*; b u l o-a r a, *they two*; for the *plu.*, n ġ é e n, *we*; n u r a, *you*; b a r a, *they.*

† *Lit.,* this-self-same-place I am

INDICATIVE MOOD.

T. 1. *Baġ ka-tán   *T.* 6. *Baġ ka-kulla-ta
   4. „   ka-kulla   8. „   ka-kín
   5. „   ka-kéùn   9. „   ka-nùn.

Aorist participle—kán; as, kinta kán baġ, 'afraid being I.'

[*Throughout the verb 'to be,' both in this Declarative form and in the Permissive, a predicative adverb, 'unnibo,' or any other suitable word, may be inserted here in all the tenses.—ED.]

PARTICIPLES.

T. 1. Baġ ka-killín   *T.* 6. Baġ ka-killi-ela-ta
   2. „   ka-killi-kéùn   7. „   ka-killi-kolaġ
   4. „   ka-tala   8. „   ka-killi-kín
               T. 9. Baġ ka-killi-nùn.

Continuative.

T. 1. Baġ ka-killi-lín *T.* 3. Baġ ka-killi-li-ela.

Reflexive.

T. 1. Kán baġ bo.

Reciprocal.

T. 1. Bali ka-kill-án* *T.* 6. Bali ka-kill-ala-ta
4. „ ka-kill-ala   7. „ ka-kill-ai-kolaġ
5. „ ka-kill-ai-kéún   8. „ ka-kill-ai-kín
  T. 9. Bali ka-killá-nún.

* = 'We two are living together, the one with the other, now.'

SUBJUNCTIVE MOOD.

1. *The construct verb, denoting purpose.*

T. 10.

Ka-killi-ko, 'to be, exist, remain.'
Ka-killi-koa, ' to continue to be *or* live.'
Ka-kill-ai-koa, ' to live one with another.'

2. *The construct verb, denoting the immediate purpose of the action in the preceding clause; when no clause precedes, the form of the verb denotes a wish.*

T. 10. Ka-uwil-koa baġ, 'that I may *or* might be,' ' I wish to be.'

Iteration.

T. 1. Ka-téa-kún baġ T. 9. Ka-téa-ka-nún baġ

Imminence.

T. 9. Ka-téa-kún-koa baġ.

Contemporary circumstance.

T. 1. Ka-tán baġ ba* *T.* 3. Ka-killi-ela baġ ba
  T. 9. Ka-nún baġ ba.

* The whole of the indicative mood may be thus declined with *ba.*

Implied negation of actual becoming.

T. 10a. Ka-mai ġa baġ

Implied negation of entity or being.

T. 10b. Ka-pa baġ ba *T.* 10c. Ka-pa-ta baġ ba
 T. 10d. Keawarán* baġ ka-pa
   *Keawarán is a negative.

IMPERATIVE MOOD.

Ká-uwa bi, 'be thou.'
Ka-kill-ía bi, 'continue thou to be, live, remain.'
Ká-uwa bi ġintoa bo, ' be thou thyself.'
Ká-killá bula (dual and plural only), ' be ye two.'
Ka-téa-ka bi, ' be thou again.'

PERMISSIVE FORM OF THE VERB 'KAKILLIKO.'

Ka-mun-billiko 'to permit to be, exist, remain.'

Indicative Mood.

T. 1. Ká-mún-bin   bón baġ*   T. 6. Ká-mún-bin-bia-ta bón baġ
4.   „   -bin-bia   „   „   8.   „   -bi-kín   „   „
5.   „   -bi-kéún „   „   9.   „   -bi-nún   „   „
* = 'I permit him to be.'

Participles.

T. 1. Ká-mún-bill-ín   T. 6. Ká-mún-billi-ola-ta
3.   „   -billi-ola   7.   „   -kolaġ
4.   „   -bi-ala   8.   „   -kín
5.   „   -billi-kéún   9.   „   -nún.

Reciprocal.

T. 1. Ká-mún-bill-án   †   T. 6. Ká-mún-bill-ala-ta   †
4.   „   -bill-ala   „   7.   „   -bill-ai-kolaġ „
5.   „   -bill-ai-kéún „   8.   „   -bill-ai-kín   „
T. 9. Ká-mún-billá-nún bulun baġ.

† Here insert in each tense 'bulun bang,' or any other suitable words, as subject and personal object. T. 1. is equivalent to 'I permit them to live together.'

Subjunctive Mood.

1. *To express purpose.*

T. 10. Ká-mún-billá-ko, 'to permit to be'.
   „   -billá-koa, 'to permit to be together, the one with the other'.

2. *To express immediate purpose.*

T. 10. Ká-mún-bin-uwil-koa, 'that ... may or might permit to be together.'

Iteration.

T. 1. Ká-mún-béa-kán bón baġ   T. 9. Ká-mún-béa-ká-nún bón baġ*
* = 'I shall again permit him to be.'

Imminence.

T. 9. Ká-mún-béa-kún-koa biloa,† 'lest he permit thee to be.'

Contemporary circumstance.

T. 1. Ká-mún-bin bón baġ ba   T. 3. Ká-mún-billi-ola binuġ† ba
     T. 9. Ká-mún-bi-nún bitia† ba

† For banung, biloa, bitia, binung, see paradigm of Pronouns.

Implied negation of actual becoming.
T. 10 a. Kà-mai-gɩ bón bag
Implied negation of entity or being.
T. 10 b. Kà-mùn-bi-pa bag ba   *T.* 10 c. Kà-mùn-bi-pa-ta bag ba
     T. 10 d. Keawarán* bag mùn-bi-pa
       * Keawarán is a negative.

IMPERATIVE MOOD.

Kà-mùn-billa   *   'permit * to' . . . .
Kà-mùn-bill-a   ,,   'permit ,, self to continue to' . . .
Kà-mùn-béa-ka   ,,   'permit ,, again to' . . . .
      * Insert here the pronoun in the *Acc.*

DECLENSION OF TRANSITIVE VERBS.

DECLENSION OF THE VERB 'TO STRIKE.'

Bun-killi-ko, 'to strike'.

EXAMPLES OF THE DECLENSION OF THE TENSES OF THE INDICATIVE MOOD.

T. 1. *Sing.*, Búntán bag.†   *Dual*, Búntán bali.†
     Plu., Búntán géen.†
     Conjoined Dual, Búntán banug.†

† Or any other suitable pronoun as a subject. The personal object must be placed after the verb, but the neuter object after the subject.

INDICATIVE MOOD.

T. 1. Búntán   bón bag*   *T.* 6. Bún-kulla-ta bón bag
4. Bún-killa ,, ,,   8. ,, -kín bón bag
5. ,, -kéún ,, ,,   9. ,, -nún ,, ,,

PARTICIPLES.

T. 1. Bún-killín   bón bag   *T.* 6. Bún-killi-ela-ta bón bag
2. ,, -killi-kéún ,, ,,   7. ,, ,, -kolag ,, ,,
3. ,, -killi-ela ,, ,,   8. ,, ,, -kín ,, ,,
4. ,, -tala ,, ,,   9. ,, ,, -nún ,, ,,

        Continuative.
T. 1. Bún-killi-lín bón bag*   *T.* 3. Bún-killi-li-ela bón bag
    * = 'I am striking with many blows, now.'
        Reflexive.
T. 5. Bún-kill-éún bag, 'I have struck myself.'

Reciprocal.

T. 1. Bún-killán   bali   T. 6. Bún-kill-ala-ta   bali
4.   „ -kill-ala   „   7.   „ -kill-ai-kolaġ   „
5.   „ -kill-ai-kéún „   8.   „ -kill-ai-kín   „
            T. 9. Bún-killá-nún bali

Subjunctive Mood.
1. *To express purpose.*
T. 10.

Bún-killi-ko, 'to strike,' 'for the purpose of striking.'
Bún-killi-koa, 'to strike continually,' 'to beat,' 'to thrash.'
Bún-kill-ai-koa, 'to strike each one the other,' 'to fight.'

2. *To express immediate purpose.*
T. 10. Bún-wil *or* bú-wil-koa bón baġ, 'that I might strike him.'

3. *Iteration.*
T. 1. Bún-téa-kán bón baġ   T. 9. Bún-téa-ká-nún baġ

4. *Imminence.*
T. 9. Bún-téa-kún-koa bón baġ

5. *Contemporary circumstance.*
T. 1. Bún-tán bón baġ ba   T. 3. Bún-killi-ela bón noa ba
     T. 9. Bún-nún bón baġ ba

6. *Implied negation of actual effect.*
T. 10a. Búm-mai ġa bón baġ

7. *Implied negation of action or entity.*
T. 10b. Búm-pa bón baġ ba   T. 10c. Búm-pa-ta bón baġ ba
     T. 10d. Keawarán bón baġ búm-pa

Imperative Mood.
Bú-wa bi, 'strike thou'; búwa-búwa bi, 'continue thou to strike.'
Bún-killá bula, 'strike on, ye two, the one with the other.'
Bún-kill-ía, 'strike on,' 'be striking self.'
Bún-téa-ka bi, 'strike again'; bún-kéa, 'strike instantly.'

NOTE.—This imperative, if written in full, with a subject and an object, would be:—

Bú-wa bi (*or* bula, *or* nura) tia; instead of tia, any other object may be used; such as, unni, 'this,' unnoa, 'that,' and the accusative cases of all the pronouns.

Continuative.
Bún-killi-lía bi (bula, nura) tia, &c., as above.

Reflexive.   *Emphatic.*   *Reciprocal.*
Bún-kill-ía bi kotti, Bu-wa bi ġintoa,   Bún-killá bula
'strike thou thine own 'strike thou thyself.' 'strike ye two, the one the
     self.'   other.'

PERMISSIVE FORM of the VERB 'TO STRIKE.'

Búm-mara-bun-billiko 'to permit (some other) to strike.'

EXAMPLE OF THE DECLENSION OF THE TENSES.

1. *Form to be used for the Active Voice.*

INDICATIVE MOOD.

T. 1. *Sing.* Búm-mún-bín bi† tia,† 'thou permittest me to strike,' *or* 'I am permitted to strike.'

IMPERATIVE MOOD.

1. *Present;* 2. *Continuative;* 3. *Reflexive;* 4. *Emphatic;* 5. *Reciprocal.*

1.	Búm-mún-billa bi† tia,†	'permit thou me to strike,' *or* 'let me strike.'
2.	„ -billi-lía bi tia	'permit me to continue in striking.'
3.	„ -bill-ía bi kotti,	'permit thyself to strike thine own self.'
4.	„ -billa bi ġintoa bón,	'do thou thyself permit him to strike.'
5.	„ -billa bula,	'permit ye two, the one the other, to strike one another.'

2. *Form to be used for the Passive Voice.*

INDICATIVE MOOD.

1. *Present;* 2. *Continuative;* 3. *Reflexive;* 4. *Reciprocal.*

1.	Búm-mara-bún-bin bi† tia,†	'thou permittest (any one) to strike me,' *or* 'I am permitted to be struck.'
2.	„ bún-billi-lía,	'continue thou to permit (any one) to be struck.'
3.	„ bún-bill-ía tia ġatoa bo,	'I myself permit myself to be struck.'
4.	„ bún-billa bulun,	'permit, the one the other, to be struck.'

† Any other suitable pronouns may be placed here.

Declension of this Verb,

when it is used so as to have the meaning of a passive voice.

Indicative Mood.

T. 1. Búm-mara-bún-bin bón baġ   4. Búm-mara-bún-bía bón baġ
T. 9. Búm-mara-bún-bi-nún bón baġ

Participles.

T. 1. Búm-mara-bún-bill-in   T. 4. Búm-mara-bún-bi-ala
T. 9. Búm-mara-bún-billi-nún

Reciprocal.

T. 1. Búm-mara-bún-billán   T. 4. Búm-mara-bún-bill-ala
T. 9. Búm-mara-bún-billa-nún

Subjunctive Mood.
T. 10.

Búm-mara-bún-billi-ko,	'to permit (somebody) to be struck.'
„ -bún-bill-ai-koa,	'to permit the one to be struck by the other.'
„ -bún-bi-uwil-koa,	'that...might permit...to be struck.'
„ -bún-bia-kún-koa,	'lest (somebody) should be permitted to be struck.'
„ -bún-bi-nún bón baġ ba,	'when I permit (any person) to be struck.'
„ -bún-bai-ġı bón baġ,	'I had almost permitted him to be struck.'
„ -bún-bi-pa bón baġ ba,	'had I permitted him to be struck.'

Imperative Mood.
Búm-mara-bún-billa bi tia.

DECLENSION OF THE VERB 'TO MAKE.'

Umulliko, 'to do,' personally, 'to make,' 'to create.'

Indicative Mood.

T. 1. Umán   baġ unni   T. 6. Umá-ta   baġ unni
   4. Umá   „   8. Uma-kín   „
   5. Uma-keún   „   9. Umä-nún   „

THE GRAMMAR. 35

Participles.

T. 1. Umull-ín   baġ unni   T. 4. Umala   baġ unni
2. Umulli-kéûn   „   6. Umulli-ela-ta   „
3. Umulli-ela   „   7. Umulli-kolaġ   „
T. 9. Umulli-nùn baġ unni

Continuative.

T. 1. Umulli-lín baġ unni   T. 3. Umulli-li-ela baġ unni

Reflexive.

T. 5. Umull-éûn baġ unni

Reciprocal.

T. 1. Umull-án   bali unni   T. 6. Umull-ala-ta   bali unni
4. Umull-ala   „   „   7. Umull-ai-kolaġ   „ „
5. Umull-ai-kéûn   „   „   8. Umull-ai-kín   „ „
T. 9. Umullá-nùn bali unni

Subjunctive Mood.

1. *To express purpose.*
T. 10.
Umulli-ko, 'to do, make, create.'
Umulli-koa, 'to continue to do.'
Umull-ai-koa, 'to do reciprocally.'

2. *To express immediate purpose.*
T. 10. Uma-uwil-koa baġ unni, 'that I may *or* might make this.'

Iteration.

T. 1. Uméa kán baġ unni   T. 9. Uméa ká-nùn baġ unni

Imminence.

T. 9. Uméa kùn koa baġ unni

Contemporary circumstance.

T. 1. Umán baġ ba unni   T. 3. Umulli-ela baġ ba unni
T. 9. Umú-nùn noa baġ unni

Implied negation of actual effect.

T. 10a. Umai-ġi baġ unni

Implied negation of action or entity.

T. 10b. Uma-pa baġ unni   T. 10c. Uma-pa-ta baġ unni
T. 10d. Keawarán baġ uma-pa unni

Imperative Mood.

Umulla bi, 'make thou.'
Umáu-umulla bi, (reduplication) 'make thou diligently.'
Umullá bula, 'make ye two' (reciprocally).
Umull-ía bi, 'make thou thyself' (reflexive).
Uméa-ka, 'make again'; uma-kéa, 'make instantly.'
Uma-bún-billa bón unni, 'permit him to make this.'
Umara-bún-billa unni, 'permit this to be made.'

DECLENSION OF THE VERB 'TO DO,' 'TO PERFORM.'

Upulliko 'to do,' 'to perform,' 'to use in action.'

Indicative Mood.

T. 1. Upán baġ ġali ko   T. 4. Upá baġ ġali ko
         T. 9. Upá-nún baġ ġali ko.

Participles.

T. 1. Upullín baġ ġali ko   T. 4. Upala baġ ġali ko
3. Upulli-ela „ „ „   7. Upulli-kolaġ „ „ „
       T. 9. Upulli-nún baġ ġali ko

Continuative.

T. 1. Upulli-lín baġ ġali ko   T. 3. Upulli-li-ela baġ ġali ko

Reflexive.

T. 5. Upull-éún baġ ġali ko

Reciprocal.

T. 1. Upull-án bali ġali ko

Subjunctive Mood.

T. 10.

Upulli-ko, 'to do, to use in action.'
Upulli-koa, 'to continue to do,' as, 'to work with.'
Upan-uwil-koa baġ, 'that I might do.'
Upéa-kún-koa baġ, 'lest I should do.'
Upá-nún bi ba, 'when thou doest,' *or* 'if thou do.'
Upai-ġa baġ, 'I had almost done.'
Upa-pa baġ ba, 'had I done,' *or* 'if I had done.'

Imperative Mood.

Upulla, 'do,' 'use' in action.

DECLENSION of the VERB 'TO BREAK'
by personal agency.

Tiir-bung-gulliko, 'to break' by personal agency, not by instrumental means.

Indicative Mood.

T. 1. Tiir-buġ-gán baġ unni   T. 4. Tiir-buġ-ga baġ unni
T. 9. Tiir-buġ-gá-nún baġ unni

Participles.

T. 1. Tiir-buġ-gullín   baġ †   T. 4. Tiir-buġ-galla   baġ †
3. Tiir-buġ-gulli-ela ,, ,,   7. Tiir-buġ-gulli-kolaġ ,, ,,
T. 9. Tiir-buġ-gulli-nún baġ unni

† Here insert 'unni' or any other neuter object.

Continuative.

T. 1. Tiir-buġ-gulli-lín bag   T. 3. Tiir-buġ-gulli-li-ela bag †

Reflexive.

T. 5. Tiir-buġ-gull-éún bag unni

Reciprocal.

T. 1. Tiir-buġ-gull-án bali unni

Subjunctive Mood.

T. 10.

Tiir-buġ-gulli-ko, 'to break' (something).
Tiir-buġ-ga-uwil-koa, 'that ... may *or* might break.'
Tiir-buġ-géa-kún-koa, 'lest ... should break.'
Tiir-buġ-ga-nún baġ ba, 'when I break,' *or* 'if I break.'
Tiir-buġ-gai-ġa baġ, 'I had almost broken.'
Tiir-buġ-ga-pa bag ba, 'had I broken,' *or* 'if I had broken.'

DECLENSION of the VERB 'TO BREAK'
by instrumental agency.

Tiirburrilliko, 'to break,' by instrumental, not by personal, agency.

Indicative Mood.

T. 1. Tiir-bur-rín baġ unni   T. 4. Tiir-bur-réa baġ unni
T. 9. Tiir-bur-ri-nún baġ unni

Participles.

T. 1. Tiir-bur-rill-ín baġ †   *T*. 4. Tiir-bur-rala baġ †
3. „ -bur-rilli-ela „ „   7. Tiir-bur-rilli-kolaġ „ „
       T. 9. Tiir-bur-rilli-nùn baġ unni

Continuative.

T. 1. Tiir-bur-rilli-lín baġ †   *T*. 3. Tiir-bur-rilli-li-ela baġ †
    † Here insert 'unni' or any other neuter object.

Reflexive.

T. 2. Tiir-bur-rill-éùn baġ unni

Reciprocal.

T. 1. Tiir-bur-rill-án bali unni

Subjunctive Mood.

T. 10.

Tiir-bur-rilli-ko, 'to break' by means of some instrument.
Tiir-burr-uwil-koa, 'that... may *or* might break.'
Tiir-bur-réa-kùn-koa, 'lest ... should break.'
Tiir-bur-ri-nùn baġ ba, 'when I break', *or* 'if I break.'
Tiir-bur-ri-pa baġ ba, 'had I broken', *or* 'if I had broken.'

DECLENSION of the VERB '*TO SPEAK*,' '*TO TELL*.'

Wiyelliko, 'to speak, say, talk, converse, communicate.'

Indicative Mood.

T. 1. Wiyán bón baġ*   *T*. 6. Wiya-ta bón baġ
4. Wiyá „ „   8. Wiya-kín „ „
5. Wiya-kéùn „ „   9. Wiyá-nùn „ „
     * = 'I tell him.'

Participles.

T. 1. Wiyellín bón baġ   *T*. 6. Wiyelli-ela-ta bón baġ
2. Wiyelli-kéùn „ „   7. Wiyelli-kolaġ „ „
3. Wiyelli-ela „ - „   8. Wiyelli-kín „ „
4. Wiyala „ „   9. Wiyelli-nùn „ „

Continuative.

T. 1. Wiyelli-lín   *T*. 3. Wiyelli-li-ela

Reflexive.

T. 5. Wiyel-léùn baġ = 'I talked to myself.'

Reciprocal.

T. 1. Wiyell-án bara*   T. 6. Wiyell-ala-ta bara
4. Wiyell-ala   ,,   7. Wiyell-ai-kolaġ ,,
5. Wiyell-ai-kéûn ,,   8. Wiyell-ai-kín ,,
   T. 9. Wiyellá-nûn bara
* = 'They say to one another.'

Subjunctive Mood.

1. *To express purpose.*

T. 10.
Wiyelli-ko, 'to tell, say.'
Wiyelli-koa, 'to continue to tell *or* preach.'
Wiyell-ai-koa (reciprocal), 'to talk,
 the one with the other.'

2. *To express immediate purpose.*

  T. 10. Wiyán-uwil-koa baġ

Iteration.

T. 1. Wiyéa kán baġ   T. 9. Wiyéa ká-nún baġ

Imminence.

  T. 10. Wiyéa kún-koa baġ

Contemporary circumstance.

T. 1. Wiyán noa ba   T. 3. Wiyelli-ela noa ba
  T. 9. Wiyá-nûa noa ba

Implied negation of actual effect.

  T. 10a. Wiyai-ġa bón baġ

Implied negation of action or entity.

T. 10b. Wiya-pa bón baġ ba   T. 10c. Wiya-pa-ta bón baġ
  T. 10d. Keawarán† bón baġ wiya-pa
  † Keawaran is the negative.

Imperative Mood.

Wiya, 'say, will you?' (interrogative).
Wiyella, 'speak, tell.'
Wiya-wiyella (reduplication), 'speak! be quick!'
Wiyella, 'speak' reciprocally.
Wiyell-ía, 'continue to ask.'
Wiya-wiyall-ía, 'ask urgently.'
Wiyéa-ka, 'tell again,' 'repeat.'
Wiya-kéa, 'speak presently.'
Wiya-bún-billa bón, 'permit him to speak.'

DECLENSION OF INTRANSITIVE VERBS.

DECLENSION OF THE VERB 'TO GO.'

Uwolliko, 'to go, come, walk, tend, move.'

Indicative Mood.

T. 1. Uwán baġ   *T*. 4. Uwá baġ
T. 9. Uwá-nùn baġ

Participle.
T. 1. Uwoll-in baġ   *T*. 4. Uwala baġ
3. Uwolli-ela baġ   9. Uwolli-nùn baġ

Continuative.
T. 1. Uwolli-lin baġ   *T*. 3. Uwolli-li-ela baġ

Reflexive.
T. 5. Uwoll-éùn baġ

Reciprocal.
T. 1. Uwoll-án bara   *T*. 4. Uwoll-ala bara
T. 9. Uwolli-nùn bara

Subjunctive Mood.
T. 10.
Uwolli-ko, 'to come,' 'to go away' (according to the meaning of the adverb with it).
Uwa-uwil-koa, 'that I may *or* might come *or* go.'
Uwéa-kùn-koa, 'lest . . should come *or* go.'
Uwá-nùn baġ ba, 'when I go *or* come.'
Uwai-ġa baġ ba, 'I had almost come *or* gone.'
Uwa-pa baġ ba, 'had I come *or* gone.'

Imperative Mood.
Tanan uwolla, 'come hither.'
Waita uwolla, 'go away.'
Wolla-wolla, 'come *or* go quickly.'
Uwollá, 'depart each.'
Uwoll-ía, 'come *or* go' (of self).
Uwéa-ka, 'come *or* go.'
Uwa-bùn-billa, 'permit to come *or* go.'
Uwa-kéa, 'come *or* go,' *sc.*, in the morning.

DECLENSION OF THE VERB 'TO BREAK.'

Türkulliko, 'to break' spontaneously.

PARTICIPLES.

Tiir rán unni, 'this is broken' spontaneously.

- T. 1. Tiir-kull-ín unni
- 2. „ -kulli-kéùn unni
- 3. „ -kulli-ela unni
- 4. „ -kull-ala unni
- T. 5. Tiir-kull-éùn unni
- 6. „ -kulli-ela-ta unni.
- 7. „ -kulli-kolaġ unni
- 8. „ -kulli-kín unni
- T. 9. Tiir-kulli-nùn unni

Continuative.

- T. 1. Tiir-kulli-lín unni
- T. 3. Tiir-kulli-li-ela unni

SUBJUNCTIVE MOOD.

T. 10.

Tiir-kulli-ko, 'to break of its own accord.'
Tiir-kulli-koa unni, 'that this may *or* might break.'
Tiir-kull-éa-kùn-koa, 'lest . . . should break.'
Tiir-kulli-nùn unnibo, 'when *or* if this breaks.'
Tiir-ka-ġa-léùn unni, 'this had almost broken.'
Tiir-kulli-ba-pa unni, 'had this broken.'

IMPERATIVE MOOD.

Tiir-kull-ía unni, 'I wish this to break of itself.'
Tiir-kull-éa-ka unni, 'I wish this to break of itself again.'
Kamùnbilla unni tiir-kulli-koa, 'let this break spontaneously.'

DECLENSION OF THE VERB, 'TO DIE.'

Tetti bulliko, 'to be in the act of dying,' 'to die'.

INDICATIVE MOOD.

- T. 1. Tetti bán noa
- 4. „ ba noa
- 5. „ ba-kéùn noa
- T. 6. Tetti ba-ta noa
- 8. „ ba-kín noa
- 9. „ ba-nùn noa

PARTICIPLES.

- T. 1. Tetti bullín noa
- 2. „ bulli-kéùn noa
- 3. „ bulli-ela noa
- T. 4. Tetti bala noa
- 7. „ bulli-kín noa
- 9. „ bulli-nùn noa

Continuative.

- T. 1. Tetti bulli-lín noa
- T. 3. Tetti bulli-li-ela noa

Subjunctive Mood.
T. 10.

Tetti bulli-ko, 'to die.'
Tetti ba-uwil-koa noa, 'in order that he might die.'
Tetti béa-kûn-koa noa, 'lest he should die.'
Tetti lä-nûn noa ba, 'when he dies,' 'if he should die.'
Tetti bai-ġa noa, 'he had almost died.'
Tetti ba-pa noa, 'had he died,' 'if he had died.'

Imperative Mood.

Tetti ba-uwa, 'proceed to die' (optatively).
Tetti bûn-billa bón, 'permit him to die.'
Tetti béa-ka, 'die again.'

PARTICLES used instead of the VERB 'TO BE.'

1. *The verb, with a substantive attribute:* ta, 'it is'; tararán, 'it is not.'
2. *The verb, with an adjective attribute:* láġ, 'it is'; kora láġ, 'it is not.'
3. *The verb, with a personal attribute:* (1) bo, is 'self'; (2) ġali, 'this' is the agent who.

Examples of 1, 2, *and* 3 :—

Unni bo baġ, 'this is I' (the subject of the verb); ġatoa bo unni, 'this is I myself (the personal agent), who' . . ; unni ta, 'this is' (the subject); unni bo ta, 'this is itself' (the subject); ġali noa wiya, 'this is he who spoke.'

Pulli, 'salt' (a *subst.*); pulli ta, 'it is salt' (a *subst.*); pulli láġ, 'it is salt' (an *adj.*); pulli kora láġ, 'it is not salt' (an *adj.*); tararán* pulli korien, 'it is not salt' (a *subst.*)

* There are two negatives here, as usual, but the former of them may be omitted.

4. *The verb, with an attribute of manner:* yanti, 'it is so'; yanti bo ta, 'it is so itself'; *imperative:* yanóa, 'let be as it is'; ya-ai (used negatively), 'let it not be so.'

Example:—

Yaai, búnki yikora, 'let it not be so, strike not.'

5. *The verb, expressing tendency:* wal, 'is,' 'shall,' 'will' (denoting tendency of the mind or thing); *imperative:* wiya, 'say,' 'declare what you wish.'

Examples:—

Tiir wal unni, 'this is broken'; wiya, unni murráráġ, 'say, is this good?'

6. *The verb, expressing being or existence:* ke, 'be,' 'is.'

Example:—
   Minarig ke unni? 'what (thing) is this?'

[NOTE.—I am not sure that all these particles are used as substitutes for the verb 'to be.'—ED.]

THE VERB used NEGATIVELY.

INDICATIVE MOOD.

Affirmatively.   *Negatively.*

T. 1. Kaáwá, bún-tan bón bag.   Keawarán, bón bag bún korien.
    'Yes, I strike him.'   'No, I strike him not.'
5. Bún-keún bón bag.   Keawai, bón bag bún-ki-pa.
    'I have struck him.'   'No, I have not struck him.'
6. Bún-kulla bón bag.   Keawarán, bón bag búm-pa.
    'I had struck him.'   'No, I had not struck him.'
8. Bún-kin bón bag.   Keawai, bón bag bún-kin.
    'I shall strike him.'   'No, I shall not strike him.'
9. Bán-nún wal bón bag.   Keawai, wal bón bag bún korien.
    'I shall strike him.'   'No, I shall not strike him.'

PARTICIPLES.

T.
1. Bún-kill-ín bón bag.   Keawaran, bón bag bún-killi korien.
    'I am striking him.'   'No, I am not striking him.'
3. Bún-killi-ela bón bag.   Keawaran, bón bag bún-killi kora kal.
    'I was striking him.'   'No, I was not going to strike him.'
9. Bún-killi-nún bón bag.   Keawai, bón bag bún-killi kora ke.
    'I am going to strike him.'   'No, I am not going to strike him.'

IMPERATIVE MOOD.

Mandatory—
Búwa bón, 'strike him.'   Ma, búwa bón, 'do, strike him.'
Yanoa, bún-ki yikora bón, 'let be, strike him not.'
Bún-killá, 'strike on,' 'continue to strike.'
Yanoa, bún-killa-ban kora, 'let be, cease striking.'
Búm-mara-bún-billa bón, 'permit him to be struck.'
Yari, bón bi búm-mara-bún-bi yikora, 'hold! let him not be struck.'

Entreaty—
Búm-mún-billa-bón. 'permit him to strike.'
Yanoa, búm-mún-bi yikora bón, 'let be, permit him not to strike.'

Interrogative—
Minarig-tin binug bún-kulla? 'why did'st thou strike him?'
Kora koa binug búm-pa? 'why hast thou not struck him?'

Idioms—
Wiwi, 'be quiet,' 'do not what you tend to do.'
Yaai, 'refrain,' 'do not,' 'cease acting,' 'hold'! 'let not.'
Yari, yanoa, 'let be,' 'let alone,' 'do not.'

ADVERBS.

The use of the word determines whether it should be called a noun, an adjective, or an adverb. A word used with the particle of agency would be considered a noun; but the same word, if attached to a noun, would be an adjective; used with a verb, it would be an adverb; as, pórról, 'heavy'; pórról ta unni, 'this is heavy'; pórról noa wiyán, 'he speaks heavily.' Adverbs are classed in the following manner:—

1. *Of Number.*

Wakál bo ta, 'once only.' Bulóara bo ta, 'twice only.'
Ngóro bo ta, 'thrice only.'

2. *Of Order.*

Bonén, 'the first to be done.' Kurri-kurri, 'the beginning, the
Gánka, 'the first,' *or* 'before.' first.'
Willuġ, 'the last,' *or* 'behind.'

3. *Of Place.*

Unti, 'here.' Bará-kolaġ, 'downwards.'
Unnuġ, 'there.' Muriṅg-kolaġ, 'forwards.'
Wonnuġ? 'where?' Willuġ-kolaġ, 'backwards.'
Wonta-kolaġ, 'whither'? Wonta-biruġ? 'whence? from
Unti-kolaġ, 'hither.' what place?'
Untoa-kolaġ, 'thither.' Unta-biruġ, 'thence.' [time.
Wokka-kolaġ, 'upwards.' Unti-biruġ, 'hence'; place or

4. *Of Time.*

Ba, 'when; at the time that'; Keawai-wál, 'never, not at any
ġai-ya, 'then,' must always time'; 'no, never.'
be after it. Kún-ba, 'yesterday' (when the
Buġ-gai, 'this present period, verb is in a past tense); 'to-
now, to-day'; 'the time now morrow' (when used with a
passing.' verb in the future tense).
Buġ-gai-kál, 'of the present Kún-ba kén ta, 'the day after
period; fresh, new, recently.' to-morrow.'
Gai-ya, 'then, at that time'; Murá-ai, 'sometimes.'
it is governed by the par- Murrín-murrín, 'often, repeat-
ticle ba. edly, frequently.'
Kabo, 'presently.' Tága, 'before, prior to.'
Kabo ka ta, 'presently it is,' Tanoa-nuġ bo, 'soon.'
for 'not yet.' Toan-ta, 'afterwards.'

Unnuġ bo, 'hitherto.'
Wakàl-wakàl, 'once-once,'—an idiom *for* ' seldom.'
Yaki-ta, 'now'; at the time spoken of.
Yaki-ta bo, 'instantly'; at the selfsame moment spoken of.

Yakoun-ta? ' at what time? when?'
Yanti-kat-ai, 'hence forward,' 'for ever'; *lit.*, 'thus always.'
Yuki-ta, 'afterwards.'
Yuraki, 'long since, formerly, long ago.'

NOTE.—Iteration is expressed by a particular form of the verb; as, Búntéa-kanun, ' will strike again.'

5. *Of Quantity.*

Butti, 'more'; meaning, 'continue the action.'
Kauwàl-láġ, 'largely, much, abundantly.'
Kirun, ' all.'

Minnán? 'what quantity? how much? how many?'
Tantoa, 'enough, sufficiently.'
Waréa-láġ, 'little, sparingly.'
Winta, ' a part, a portion.'

6. *Of Quality or Manner.*

Kára, 'slowly, deliberately.'
Kurra-kai, 'quickly'; also equivalent to the phrase 'make haste.'

Pór-ról, ' heavily'; *cf.* pór-ról.
Wir-wir, 'cheerfully, lightly'; *cf.* wir, as a verb, 'to fly like the down of a bird.'

Woġkàl-láġ, 'foolishly '; *cf.* woġkàl, 'deaf, stupid, foolish.'

7. *Of Doubt.*

Mirka, 'perhaps.'   Mirka-ta, 'perhaps so, possibly.'

8. *Of Affirmation.*

E-é, 'yes.'
Kau-wá, 'yea.'
Tokól bo ta, 'truly, in truth itself'; *cf.* tokól, 'straight.'

Yanti bo ta, 'yes, just as it is.'
Yuna bo ta, 'verily, certainly, really '; *lit.*, 'there it is itself.'

9. *Of Negation.*

Kea-wai, ' nay.'
Kea-wa-rán, 'no.'

Ta-rarán, 'it is not,' *sc.*, the thing affirmed.

Yikora, kora, korien, ' no, not.'

10. *Of Interrogation.*

Kora-koa? 'why not?'
Minariġ-tin? ' why? wherefore?'
Wonnén? 'how? which way?'

Yako-ai? 'how?' meaning 'in what manner?' answer, yanti, 'thus.'
answer, ġia-kai, 'this way.'

NOTE.—Other modifications will be better understood from the Illustrative sentences.

PREPOSITIONS.

Ba, 'of'—denoting possession, when used with the personal pronouns.

Birug̣, 'of, out of, from'; opposed to ko-lag̣.

Ka, 'in,' or 'at' such a period; as, tarai-ta yellánna-ka, 'in another moon.'

Ka-ba, 'in, on, at'—a place; as, Sydney-ka-ba, 'at Sydney.'

Kai,—the same meaning as tin; only this is used to personal pronouns, but 'tin' goes with nouns.

Kál, 'part of'; as, unti-kál, 'of this, part of this, hereof.'

Katoa, 'with, in company with,'—not instrumental.

Ko, -lo, -o, -ro, -to,—particles denoting agency or instrumentality.*

Ko-ba, 'of'—the same as 'ba,' but used only with nouns.

Ko-lag̣, 'to, towards, tendency towards,'—opposed to birug̣.

Murrarig̣, 'into.'

Murrug̣, 'within.'

Tin, 'from, on account of, for, because of, in consequence of.'

Warrai, 'outside, without,'—opposed to 'within.'

* Expressed by *with*, *by*, *for*, but only when instrumental.

CONJUNCTIONS.

THE idiom of the language is such, that sentences connect with sentences without the aid of conjunctions, the subjunctive mood answering all these purposes. The dual number also does away with the necessity of using connectives to unite two expressions. The following are the principal conjunctions, viz., g̣atun, 'and'; kulla, 'because, for'; g̣ali-tin, 'therefore, on account of this.' But the particles 'lest,' 'unless,' 'that,' and the disjunctives, are expressed by modifications of the verb in the subjunctive mood, as will be shown in the Illustrative sentences.

INTERJECTIONS.

NOTE.—The following are used under the circumstances mentioned.

A, 'hearken! lo! behold!'

Ela-beára, of wonder, surprise, astonishment.

Ginoa, of salutation at parting; as, 'farewell.'

Katio-katia, of pain, anguish.

Wau, 'attention!' a call to attend.

Wi-wi, of aversion.

Yapallun, of sorrow; 'alas!'

CHAPTER IV.

VOCABULARY.

(1) MYTHOLOGY.

G a k ó n ; k ú r i m a ; *m.*,* bones put through the septum of the nose for ornament.

G ó r r o ; p u m m e r i ; y o n e i , *m.*, varieties of grass-tree. To form the native spears, pieces of the flower-stalks of this are cemented together at the ends by a resinous substance which exudes from the root; they are made from eight to twelve feet long; a piece of hard wood forms the last joint, on which is cemented a splinter of pointed bone, as a barb. A deadly weapon this is; thrown by means of a lever nearly four feet long, *cf.* 'w o m m à r a', which is held in the hand, and on it the poisoned spear.

K o i n, T i p p a k á l, P ó r r á g̀ are names of an imaginary male being, who has now, and has always had, the appearance of a black; he resides in thick brushes or jungles; he is seen occasionally by day, but mostly at night. In general, he precedes the coming of the natives from distant parts, when they assemble to celebrate certain of their ceremonies, as the knocking out of tooth in the mystic ring, or when they are performing some dance. He appears painted with pipe-clay, and carries a fire-stick in his hand; but generally it is the doctors, a kind of magicians, who alone perceive him, and to whom he says, 'Fear not; come and talk.' At other times he comes when the blacks are asleep, and takes them up, as an eagle his prey, and carries them away for a time. The shout of the surrounding party often makes him drop his burden; otherwise, he conveys them to his fire-place in the bush, where, close to the fire, he deposits his load. The person carried off tries to cry out, but cannot, feeling almost choked; at daylight K o i n disappears, and the black finds himself conveyed safely to his own fire-side.

K o y o r ó w é n, the name of another imaginary being, whose trill in the bush frequently alarms the blacks in the night. When he overtakes a native, he commands him to exchange cudgels, giving his own which is extremely large, and desiring the black to take a first blow at his head, which he holds down for that purpose†; after this he smites and kills the person with one blow, skewers him with the cudgel, carries him off, roasts, and then eats him.

---

* The *m*, throughout, stands for *meaning*.
† This is a common mode of duelling among the blacks.—ED.

Kurriwilbán, the name of his wife; she has a long horn on each shoulder, growing upwards, with which she pierces the aborigines, and then shakes herself until they are impaled on her shoulders, when she carries them to a deep valley, roasts, and eats her victims. She does not kill the women, for they are always taken by her husband for himself. Yaho has, by some means, come to be used by the blacks as a name for this being.

Múrramai, *m.*, the name of a round ball, about the size of a cricket-ball, which the aborigines carry in a small net suspended from their girdles of opossum yarn. The women are not allowed to see the internal part of the ball. It is used as a talisman against sickness, and it is sent from tribe to tribe for hundreds of miles, on the sea-coast and in the interior. One is now here from Moreton Bay, the interior of which a black showed me privately in my study, betraying considerable anxiety lest any female should see the contents. After he had unrolled many yards of woollen cord, made from the fur of the opossum, the contents proved to be a quartz-like substance of the size of a pigeon's egg. He allowed me to break it and retain a part. It is transparent, like white sugar-candy. The natives swallow any small crystalline particles that crumble off, as a preventive of sickness. It scratches glass, and does not effervesce with acids. From another specimen, the stone appears to be agate, of a milky hue, semi-pellucid, and it strikes fire. The vein from which it appears to have been broken off is one and a quarter inch thick. A third specimen contained a portion of carnelian partially crystallised, a fragment of chalcedony, and a fragment of a crystal of white quartz.

Murrokun, *m.*, the name of a mysterious magical bone, which is obtained by the karákáls, *q.v.* Three of these sleep on the grave of a recently interred corpse; in the night, during their sleep, the dead person inserts a mysterious bone into each thigh of the three 'doctors,' who feel the puncture not more severe than that of the sting of an ant. The bones remain in the flesh of the doctors, without any inconvenience to them, until they wish to kill any person, when by magical power, it is said and believed, they destroy their ill-fated victim, causing the mysterious bone to enter into his body, and so occasion death.

Nauwai, *m.*, a canoe; pupa, *m.*, bark, a canoe. The canoes are made of one sheet of bark, taken whole from the tree and softened with fire, and then tied up in a folded point at each end. A quantity of earth forms a hearth, on which the natives roast their bait and fish, when fishing.

N u ġ - g ú n, *m.*, a song. There are poets among the tribes, who compose songs ; these are sung and danced to by their own tribe in the first place, after which other tribes learn the song and dance; and so the thing itinerates from tribe to tribe throughout the country, until, from change of dialect, the very words are not understood correctly by distant blacks.

P ó r o b u ġ, the name of a mystic ring, in which certain ceremonies of initiation are performed ; from p ó r, ' to drop down, to be born.'

P u n t i m a i, *m.*, a messenger, an ambassador. These men are generally decorated with the down of the swan or of the hawk on their heads, when on an embassy. They arrange the time, place, and manner of preparations for a battle or for the punishing of a supposed offender or real aggressor. They bring intelligence of the movements of hostile tribes, or the last new song and dance (*cf.* n u ġ - g u n). When they travel at night, a fire-stick is always carried by them as a protection against the powers of darkness, the evil spirits, of which they are in continual dread.

P u t t i k a n, another imaginary being, like a horse, having a large mane and a tail sharp like a cutlass ; whenever he meets the blacks, they go towards him and draw up their lips to show that the tooth is knocked out *; then he will not injure them ; but should the tooth be still there, he runs after them, and kills and eats them. He does not walk, but bounds like a kangaroo, and the noise of his leaps on the ground is as the report of a gun; he calls out as he advances, 'P i r r o l ó ġ, P i r r o l ó ġ.'

T i l m ú n, *m.*, a small bird of the size of a thrush. It is supposed by the women to be the first maker of women ; or to be a woman transformed after death into the bird ; it runs up trees like a woodpecker. These birds are held in veneration by the women only. The bat, k o l u ġ - k o l u ġ, is held in veneration on the same ground by the men, who suppose the animal a mere transformation.

T i p p a k a l i n, M a i l k u n, and B i m p ó i n, are names of the wife of K o i n, *q.v.* She is a much more terrific being than her husband ; him the blacks do not dread, because he does not kill them ; but this female being not only carries off the natives in a large bag-net and drags them beneath the earth, but she spears the children through the temples ; she thus kill them, and no one ever sees again those whom she obtains.

T u r r a m a, *m.*, an instrument of war, called by Europeans a 'b o o m e r a n g.' It is of a half-moon shape ; when thrown in the air it revolves on its own centre and returns, forming

---

* This is a proof that the black man has been duly initiated at the ceremonies of the Bora. See *s.v.* Yarro.—ED.

a curve in its orbit from and to the thrower; to effect this, it is thrown against the wind; but in war it is thrown against the ground; it then rebounds apparently with double violence, and strikes some distant object, and wounds severely with its sharpened extremities.

Yárro, *m.*, an egg. But, used in a mystic sense, to the initiated ones it means 'fire *or* water.' And by the use of this term in asking for either element, the fraternity can discover themselves to each other. The men, after the tooth is knocked out in the Bora rites, call women k u n n a i k a r á, and themselves v i r a b a i; previous to which the men are styled, k o ro m u n. The ceremony of initiation takes place every three or four years as young lads arrive at the age of puberty; mystic rings are made in the woods, and numerous ceremonies are gone through before the operation of displacing a tooth from the upper jaw; this is effected by three steady blows with a stout piece of hard wood, in shape like a punch, from the hand of the k a r á k á l; after that, the youth may seize a woman; he becomes a member of the tribe and engages in their fights.

Yulug̈, the name of the ring in which the tooth is knocked out. The trees are marked near the ring with rude representation of locusts, serpents, and other things, on the bark; these are chopped with an axe; and copies of the nests of various quadrupeds are formed on the ground near the spot. The celebrants dance for several days every morning and evening, continuing the whole of the night; no women are allowed to join in the ceremony.

(2) GEOGRAPHICAL NAMES.

A w a b a, Lake Macquarie; the word means 'a plain surface.'
B i w o g̈ k u l a, the place of red ti-trees; from b i w o g̈, 'red ti-tree.'
B o i k ó n ú m b a, a place of ferns; from b o i k ó n, 'fern.'
B o u n, the site of Wallis's Plains; from a bird of that name.
B ú l b a, an island; any place surrounded with water.
B u l k á r a, any mountain; from b u l k a, 'the back' of a man or a beast.
B u t t a b a, the name of a hill on the margin of the Lake.
G a r a w a n t á r a, any plain, a flat.
G o l o y á u w é, a point of land on the south side of the Lake.
G ó r r ó i n b a, the female-emu place; from g ó r r o i n, 'the female emu'; 'the male emu' is k ó g̈ k o r ó g̈, from his cry.
G u r r á n b a, a place of brambles; from g u r r á n, an inferior sort of 'bramble.'
K a i á r a b a, a place of 'sea-weeds.'
K á r a k u n b a, a place of 'swamp-oaks,' which is a species of pine.
K é e l - k é e l b a, a place of 'grass-tree.'

THE VOCABULARY.   51

Kintíirrabín, the name of a small extinct volcano on the sea-coast, near Red Head, north-east of Lake Macquarie.

Koikaliġba, a place of brambles; from koikaliġ, a sort of 'bramble,' bearing a berry like a raspberry.

Koiyóġ, the site of any native camp.

Kona-konaba, the name of the place where the stone called kona-kona is found. There are veins in the stone, which contain a yellow substance used for paint in warlike expeditions. It is the name of a large mountain, at the northern extremity of Lake Macquarie.

Kopurraba, the name of the place from which the blacks obtain the kopurra, a yellowish earth, which they wet, mould up into balls, and then burn in a strong fire; the fire makes it change into a brilliant red, something like red ochre; the men and women paint themselves with it, after mixing it with the kidney fat of the kangaroo; this paint they use always at their dances.

Kurrà-kurrán, the name of a place in which there is almost a forest of petrifactions of wood, of various sizes, extremely well defined. It is in a bay at the north-western extremity of Lake Macquarie. The tradition of the aborigines is, that formerly it was one large rock which fell from the heavens and killed a number of blacks who were assembled there; they had gathered themselves together in that spot by command of an immense iguana, which came down from heaven for that purpose; the iguana was angry at their having killed lice by roasting them in the fire; those who had killed the vermin by cracking them, had been previously speared to death by him with a long reed from heaven! At that remote period, the moon was a man named Póntobuġ; and hence the moon is called *he* to the present day; but the sun, being formerly a woman, retains the feminine pronoun *she*. When the iguana saw all the men were killed by the fall of the stone, he ascended up into heaven, where he is supposed to be now.

Kuttai, the site of Sydney Light-house; any peninsula.

Mulubinba, the name of the site of Newcastle, from an indigenous 'fern' named mulubin.

Mulluġ-bula, the name of two upright rocks about nine feet high, springing up from the side of a bluff head on the margin of the Lake. The blacks affirm, from tradition, that they are two women who were transformed into rocks, in consequence of their being beaten to death by a black man. Beneath the mountain on which the two pillars stand, a seam of common coal is seen, many feet thick, from which Reid obtained a cargo of coals when he mistook the entrance of this lake for Newcastle. A portion of a wharf built by him still exists at this place, which is still called Reid's Mistake; [*i.e.*, in 1834].

Munuġ-gurraba, the place to which 'sea-snipe' resort.
Múnukáu is the name of a point, under which is a seam of cannel coal, and beneath that is a thick seam of superior common coal, and both jut into the sea betwixt three and four fathoms of water. The government mineral surveyor found, on examination, that the two veins were nearly nine feet in thickness, and the coal of excellent quality; [*i.e.*, in 1834].
Nikkinba, a place of coals, from nikkin, 'coal.' The whole Lake, twenty-one miles long by eight broad, abounds with coal.
Niritiba, the name of the island at the entrance of the lake; from niriti, the 'mutton bird,' which abounds there.
Pitoba, a place of pipe clay; from pito, 'pipe clay,' which is used at a death by the deceased's relatives to paint their whole body, in token of mourning.
Puntei, a 'narrow' place; the name of any narrow point of land.
Purribáġba, the 'ant's-nest place'; from within these nests a yellow dusty substance is collected, and used by the blacks as a paint for their bodies, called purribáġ. The ants gather the substance for some unknown purpose.
Tirabéenba, a tooth-like point of land; from tira, 'a tooth.'
Tulkaba, the soft ti-tree place; from tulka, 'ti-tree.'
Tulkiriba, a place of brambles; from tulkiri, 'a bramble.'
Tumpoaba, a clayey place; from tumpoa, 'clay.'
Wárawállnġ, the name of a high mountain to the west of Lake Macquarie. This has been partly cleared of timber, by order of the Surveyor-General; as a land-mark it is seen from a considerable distance. The name is derived from wálluġ, the 'human head,' from its appearance.
Wauwarán, the name of a hole of fresh water in the vicinity of Lake Macquarie, betwixt it and the mountains westerly; said by the blacks to be bottomless, and inhabited by a monster of a fish much larger than a shark, called wauwai; it frequents the contiguous swamp and kills the aborigines! There is another resort for these fish near an island in Lake Macquarie named boroyiróġ, from the cliffs of which if stones be thrown down into the sea beneath, the ti-tree bark floats up, and then the monster is seen gradually arising from the deep; if any natives are at hand, he overturns their canoe, swallows the crew alive, and then the entire canoe, after which he descends to his resort in the depths below!
Yiránnálai, the name of a place near Newcastle on the sea beach, beneath a high cliff; it is said that if any persons speak there, the stones fall down from the high arched rocks above; for the crumbling state of these is such that the concussions of air from the voice cause the pieces of the loose rock to come down; this once occurred to myself when I was in company with some blacks here.

(3) COMMON NOUNS.

B.

Baibai, m.,* an axe.
Baiyaġ-baiyaġ, m., a butterfly.
Bato, m., water; cf. ġapoi
Berabukkán, m., sperm whale; the natives do not eat this; cf. toroġ-gun.
Biġgai, m., an elder brother.
Bintunkin, m., a father.
Birraba, m., a small shell fish.
Biruġ, m., 'father,' addressive.
Biṛuġbai, m., a father.
Boalúġ, m., mangrove seed.
Boarriġ, m., misty rain.
Boata, m., the cat-fish.
Boawál, m., the curlew.
Buġkin, m., vermin, as fleas.
Bukkai, m., the bark of a tree; the skin of animals.
Bulbuġ, m., a small species of kangaroo.
Búnkun, m., a red sea-slug which adheres to the rocks, and is known to Europeans as 'kunjewai.'
Búruġ, m., hair on the head.
Wúrun, m., hair on the body.
Kituġ, m., the short hair of animals.
Yirriġ, m., the fur of the opossum tribe.
Buttikáġ, m., any beast.

G.

Gapál, m., a concubine.
Gapoi, ġaiyuwa, ġatóġ, kulliġ, m., names for fresh water; cf. kokoin, bato, and yarro.
Garawan, m., a plain flat place.
Garóġ-ġaróġ, m., a rough place.
Garo-ġéen, m., an old woman.
Garo-mbai, m, an old man.
Gauwo, m., a sea-gull.
Girrinbai, m., first-born female.
Wúġ-gunbai, youngest "
Golokonuġ, m., a large kind of schnapper.
Gorokán, m., the morning dawn
Guraki, m., one initiated; hence, a wise person.

K.

Kán; kurriwirára; m., a brown diamond snake.
Maiyá, m., the general name for snakes.
Kanin, m., a fresh-water eel.
Karai, m., flesh of any sort, but chiefly of the kangaroo.
Karákál, m., a wizard, doctor, sorcerer.
Karoburra, m., a large whiting.
Karóġ-karóġ, m., a pelican.
Kéarapai, m., the white cockatoo.
Waiila, m., the black cockatoo; its breeding place is unknown to the blacks.
Keilai, m., urine.
Kikoi, m., a native cat; is very destructive to poultry.
Kinnun, m., the women's nets; used as bags.
Kipai, m., fat, grease, &c.
Kira-kira; kúneta; m., the male and the female king-parrot.
Kirika and korunnáġ, m., two kinds of native honey.
Mipparai, m., the honey-comb.
Nukkuġ, m., the small stingless bee of this country.
Mikál, m., the honey in the blossoms of the honeysuckle tree.
Káraka, m., the honey in the blossom of the grass-tree.

---
* The m, throughout, stands for meaning; it is inserted merely to divide the native word from its signification.—Ed.

E

Kirrin, *m.*, pain.
Kógka, *m.*, a reed.
Kógkoróg, *m.*, an emu; from the noise it makes.
Koiwon, *m.*, rain.
Koiyóg, *m.*, a native camp.
Koiyug, *m.*, fire.
Kokabai, *m.*, a wild yam.
Kokoi; wimbi; winnug; *m.*, native vessels made of the bark of trees, and used as baskets or bowls.
Kokera, *m.*, a native hut.
Kokoin, *m.*, water; *cf.*, gapoi
Kókug, *m.*, frogs; are so called from the noise they make.
Kómirrá, *m.*, a shadow.
Konug; kintárig; *m.*, dung.
Kónug-gai, *m.*, a fool.
Koreil, *m.*, a shield.
Koropun, *m.*, fog, mist, haze.
Korowa-tálág, *m.*, a cuttle fish; *lit.*, 'wave-tongue.'
Korro, *m.*, the wind-pipe.
Kotara, *m.*, a club, a waddy.
Kotumág, *m.*, the land tortoise.
Kúlai, *m.*, trees, wood, timber.
Kullára, *m.*, a fish-spear.
Kullearig, *m.*, the throat.
Kullig, *m.*, a shell.
Kulligtiella, *m.*, a knife.
Kullo, *m.*, the cheeks.
Kúmara, *m.*, blood.
Kúmba, *m.*, to-morrow.
Kumbàl, *m.*, a younger brother.
Kunbul, *m.*, the black swan.
Kúri, *m.*, man, mankind.
Kurratág; murrin; *m.*, the body.
Kurrábun, *m.*, a murderer.
Kurraka, *m.*, the mouth.
Kurrakóg, *m.*, the oldest male.
Taiyól, *m.*, the youngest male.
Kurra-koiyóg, *m.*, a shark.
Kurrugkun; muttaura; *m.*, the schnapper.
Kuttàl, *m.*, the smoke of a fire; tobacco; *cf.* poito.
Koun, *m.*, the mangrove bush.

M.

Makoro, *m.*, the general name for fish.
Malama, pirig-gun, pinkun, *and* wóttól, *m.*, lightning.
Marai, *m.*, the soul, the spirit; 'the same as the wind, we cannot see him,' was the definition given by a black.
Meini, *m.*, sand-flies.
Minmai, *m.*, the gigantic lily.
Miroma, *m.*, a saviour.
Moani, *m.*, the kangaroo.
Mokoi, *m.*, mud oysters.
Molakán, *m.*, the season of the wane of the moon.
Móto, *m.*, a black-snake.
Múla, *m.*, a boil.
Mulo, *m.*, thunder.
Múmuya, *m.*, a corpse, a ghost.
Múnbónkán, *m.*, the rock oyster.
Munni, *m.*, sickness.
Murabán, *m.*, blossom, flowers.
Murrakin, *m.*, young maidens.
Murrin, *m.*, the body.
Murri-nauwai, *m.*, a ship, boat.

N.

Nukug, *m.*, a woman, women.
Nulka; anulka; *m.*, iron; this is a kind of iron-stone, which abounds on the sea-coast. There is a vein of iron ore running over coal at the sea entrance of Lake Macquarie.

P.

Paiyabúra, *m.*, the large ti-tree.
Pillapai, *m.*, a valley *or* hollow.

Pimpi, *m.*, ashes.
Pippita, *m.*, a small hawk; so called from its cry.
Pirama *and* wommarakán, *m.*, a wild duck and drake.
Piriwál, *m.*, a chief *or* king.
Pirrita, *m.*, an oyster which grows on the mangrove tree.
Pittóġ; talowai; *m.*, two kinds of roots of the arum species; the taro of Tahiti.
Poito, *m.*, the smoke of a fire.
Póno, *m.*, dust.
Poribai, *m.*, a husband.
Porikunbai, *m.*, a wife.
Porowi, *m.*, an eagle.
Porun, *m.*, a dream *or* vision.
Porun-witilliko, *m.*, to dream.
Pukko, *m.*, a stone axe.
Pulli, *m.*, salt.
Pullí, *m.*, voice, language.
Puna, *m.*, sea sand.
Punbuġ, *m.*, sea-slug, blubber.
Punnál, *m.*, the sun.
Púrai, *m.*, earth, land, the world.
Purreáġ, *m.*, day.
Purramai, *m.*, a cockle.
Purramaibán, *m.*, an animal like a ferret, but amphibious; it lives on cockles.
Purrimunkán, *m.*, a sea-salmon.

T.

Taiyol, *m.*, the youngest male.
Tembiribéen, *m.*, a death adder. The aborigines, when bitten, usually suck the wound, as a remedy.
Tibbin, *m.*, a bird.
Tibún, *m*, a bone.
Tiġko, *m.*, a bitch.
Tirál, *m.*, a bough of a tree.
Tirriki, *m.*, the flame of fire; the colour red.

Tirril, *m.*, the tick, a venomous insect in this country that enters the skin of young dogs, pigs, lambs, cats, and is fatal, but not to man; it is exactly similar in size and shape to the English tick, but its effects are soon discovered; for the animal becomes paralyzed in its hind quarters, sickness comes on, and death follows in two or three days after the paralysis has taken place.
Tokoi, *m.*, night.
Topiġ, *m.*, a mosquito.
Toróġ-gun, *m.*, the black whale; this the blacks eat, whilst the sperm whale is not eaten.
Tukkára, *m.*, winter.
Tullokán, *m.*, property, riches.
Tulmun, *m.*, a grave.
Tulun, *m.*, a mouse.
Tunkán, *m.*, a mother, a dam.
Tunuġ, *m.*, a rock, a stone.
Tupea-tarawoġ *and* nináġ, *m.*, names of the flat-head fish.
Turea, *m.*, a bream-fish.

W.

Wairai, *m.*, the spear for battle, or for hunting.
Motiġ, *m.*, the spear for fish.
Waiyóġ, *m.*, a sort of yam.
Wákun, *m.*, a crow; from its cry, wak-wak-wak.
Wárikál, *m.*, a dog; the species.
Wárikál *and* waiyi, *m.*, the male and female tame dog.
Yuki *and* mirri, *m.*, the male and female native dog.
Murroġkai, *m.*, the wild dog species,
Waroi, *m.*, the hornet.
Waropára, *m.*, the honeysuckle.

Willai, *m.*, an opossum.
Wimbi, *m.*, a bowl; generally made from the knot of a tree.
Wippi *or* wibbi, *m.*, the wind.
Wirripág, *m.*, the large eagle-hawk, which devours young kangaroos, lambs, &c.
Woiyo, *m.*, grass.
Wombál, *m.*, the sea-beach.
Wommára, *m.*, the instrument used as a lever for throwing the spear; *cf.* ġorro.
Wonnai, *m.*, a child, children.
Woropil, *m.*, a blanket, clothes.
Worowai, *m.*, a battle, a fight.
Worowán, *m.*, a kangaroo-skin cloak.
Wattawán, *m.*, a large mullet.
Wúġgurrapin, *m.*, young lads.

Wúġgurrabula, *m.*, yo two lads.
Wunál, *m.*, summer.
Wurunkán, *m.*, flies.

Y.

Yapuġ, *m.*, a path, a broad way.
Yarea, *m.*, the evening.
Yareil *and* yurá, *m.*, the clouds.
Yilén, *m.*, bait.
Yinál, *m.*, a son.
Yinálkun, *m.*, a daughter.
Yirra, *m.*, a wooden sword.
Yirriġ, *m.*, a quill, a pen.
Yulo, *m.*, a footstep, a track.
Yunuġ, *m.*, a turtle.
Yuroin, *m.*, a bream-fish.

(4) PARTS OF THE BODY.

The Head.

Kittuġ, *m.*, the hair of the head.
Wálluġ, *m.*, the head.
Káppára, *m.*, the skull.
Kúmborokán, *m.*, the brain.
Yintirri; ġolo; *m.*, the forehead.
Tukkál, *m.*, the temples.
Gúréuġ; turrákurri; *m.*, the ear.
Yulkára, *m.*, the eye-brows.
Woipín, *m.*, the eye-lashes.
Gaikuġ; porowuġ; *m.*, the eye.
Tarkin; ġoara; *m.*, the face.
Nukoro, *m.*, the nose.

Kullo, *m.*, the cheeks.
Tumbiri; williġ; *m.*, the lips.
Kurráka, *m* , the mouth.
Gunturra; tirra; *m.*, the teeth.
Tálláġ, *m.*, the tongue.
Wattán, *m.*, the chin.
Yarrei, *m.*, the beard.
Untáġ, *m.*, the lower jaw.
Kulleuġ, *m.*, the neck; it is also called 'wuroka.'
Kulleariġ, *m.*, the throat.
Koro, *m.*, the windpipe.

The Trunk.

Kurrabáġ, *m.*, the body.
Murrin, *m.*, the body.
Múmurrákun ⎫ *m.*, the collar-
Milka-milka, ⎭ bone.

Mirruġ, *m.*, the shoulder.
Kopa, *m.*, the upper arm.
Turruġ, *m.*, the lower arm.
Guna, *m.*, the elbow.

The Hands and Feet.

Máttára, *m.*, the hand.
Tunkánbéen, *m.*, the thumb; *lit.*, the mother *or* dam.

Númba, *m.*, the first finger.
Purrokulkun, *m.*, the second „
Kotán, *m.*, the third „

Garákonbi, m., the little finger.
Tirri; tirreil; m., the nails of the fingers and toes.
Wará, m., the palm of the hand; cf. warapal, m., level, plain.
Túġ kaġ keri, m., the right hand.
Wúntokeri, m., the left hand.
Bulka, m., the back; either of the hand or of the body.
Paiyil, m., the breasts.
Gapug. m., the nipple.
Wajára, m., the chest, breasts.
Nara. m., the ribs.
Kurrälaġ, m., the side or body.
Turoun, m., the right side.
Goraón, m., the left side.
Parrá or warra, m., the belly.
Parra, m , the bosom.
Winnal, m., the loins.
Gakáġ, m. the hips.

The Limbs.

Búloinkoro, m., the thighs.
Wóloma or tára, m., the calf of the leg.
Gári, m., the shins.
Warombuġ, m., the knees.
Tinna, m., the toes; the foot.
Papinán, koróg-gai, and mokul-mokul. m., the knee-pan.
Wiruġkáġ, m., the ankles.
Mukko; monuġ; m., the heels.
Yúllo, m., the sole of the foot.

The Intestines.

Búlbúl, m., the heart.
Purrānai, m., the kidney; also a cockle, from its shape.
Munuġ, m., the liver.
Yokól, m., the lungs.
Konariġ; konuġ; m., the bowels.
Purriuġ; puttara; m., the flesh.
Meya, m., the sinews.
Turrakil, m., the reins.
Tóġ-tóġ, m., the marrow.
Tibún, m., the bone.
Moika, m., the fatty substance betwixt the joints.
Bukkai, m., the skin.
Wurun, m., the downy hair on the skin.

Goróġ, m., the blood.

(5) VERBS.

B.

Béelmulliko, m., to mock, to deride, to make sport.
Birrikilliko, m., to lie along, to lie down so as to sleep.
Boibulliko, m., to know carnally.
Boinkulliko, m., to kiss.
Bómbilliko, m., to blow with the mouth.
Bouġ-buġ-gulliko, m., to cause another to arise, to compel to arise.
Bouġ-gulliko, m., to raise one's self up, to arise.
Búġ-búġ. m., to salute.
Bukka, m., to be wrathful, to be furious.
Bulpór-buġ-gulliko, m., to cause to be lost property, to lose.
Bum-buġ-gulliko, m., to cause to be loose, to open a door.
Búmmarabunbilliko, m., to permit another to be struck.
Bummilliko, m., to find.
Búmmunbilliko, m., to permit another to strike.
Búnkilliko, m., to strike, smite; to aim a blow with a weapon.
Bunbilliko, m., to permit, to let; this is an auxiliary verb.

Búnmulliko, *m.*, to rob, to take by violence, to snatch.
Bur-buġ-gulliko, *m.*, to cause to be light *or* well, to cure.
Burkulliko, *m.*, to be light as a bird, to fly; to be convalescent.
Buruġ-buġ-gulliko, *m.*, to cause to be loose, to set at liberty.

G

Gakilliko, *m.*, to see, to look, to observe with the eye.
Gakómbilliko, *m.*, to deceive, to cheat.
Gakóntibunbilliko, *m.*, to disregard, not to mind.
Gakoyelliko, *m.*, to lie, to tell a falsehood.
Gamaiġulliko, *m.*, to see, to look, but not to notice.
Garabo, *m.*, to sleep.
Garawatilliko, *m.*, to lose one's self.
Garbuġ-gulliko, *m.*, to convert into, to cause to become.
Gári-ġári, *m.*, to pant.
Garo-ġaro, *m.*, to fall down.
Garokilliko, *m.*, to stand upon the feet.
Garokínbilliko, *m.*, to stand up.
Gimilliko, *m.*, to know by the eye, as a person or place.
Giratimulliko, *m.*, to feed, to give food.
Girulliko, *m.*, to tie.
Goitiġ, *m.*, to be short.
Goloin, *m.*, to be complete or finished.
Gukilliko, *m.*, to give, to present.
Gumaiġulliko, *m.*, to offer.
Gupaiyiko, *m.*, to give back, to pay, to return in exchange.
Guraki, *m.*, to be wise, skilful.
Gurrà-korien, *m.*, not to hear.

Gurramaġ, *m.*, to be initiated.
Gurramaiġulliko, *m.*, to hear, but not to obey.
Gurrara, *m.*, to pity.
Gurrawatilliko, *m.*, for remembrance to pass away, to forget any place, or road; *cf.* woġúntilliko.
Gurravelliko, *m.*, to hearken, to be obedient, to believe.
Gurrulliko, *m.*, to hear, to obey, to understand with the ear.
Gurrunbórburrilliko, *m.*, to let fall tears, to weep, to shed tears.

K.

Ka-amulliko, *m.*, to cause to be assembled together, to assemble.
Kaipulliko, *m.*, to call out, to cry aloud.
Kaiyu, *m.*, to be able, powerful, mighty.
Kakilli-bán-kora, *m.*, do not be.
Kakilliko, *m.*, to be, to exist in any state.
Kaki-yíkora, *m.*, be not.
Kapirri, *m.*, to be hungry.
Kapulliko, *m.*, to do; without the idea of effect upon any object.
Karabulliko, *m.*, to spill.
Karakai, *m.*, to be active, to be quick, to hasten.
Karákál-umulliko, *m.*, to cure, to make well; a compound of 'karákál,' a doctor, and 'umulliko,' to do, to make.
Karól, *m.*, to be hot, to perspire from the heat of the sun.
Kauwál, *m.*, to be large, great.
Kekál, *m.*, to be sweet, pleasant, nice, delightful.
Kia-kia, *m.*, to be courageous, strong, powerful; to conquer.

Kilbuġ-gulliko, *m.*, to compel to snap.
Kilburrilliko, *m.*, to snap at by means of something, as a hook is snapped at by a fish.
Kilkulliko, *m.*, to snap asunder, as a cord of itself.
Killibinbin, *m.*, to shine, to be bright, to be glorious.
Kimulliko, *m.*, to wring, to squeeze as a sponge, to milk.
Kimmulliko, *m.*, to broil meat on coals of fire.
Kinta, *m.*, to be afraid.
Kintai; kintelliko; *m.*, to laugh.
Kinúkinári, *m.*, to be wet.
Kirabarawirrilliko, *m.*, to twirl the stem of grass-tree until it ignites.
Kirilliko, *m.*, to lade out water, to bail a canoe or boat.
Kiroapulliko, *m.*, to pour out water, to empty water.
Kirrai-kirrai, *m.*, to revolve, to go round.
Kirrawi, *m.*, to be lengthy, to be long; *cf.* 'goitiġ,' *m.*, to be short in length.
Kirrin, *m.*, to pain.
Kitelliko, *m.*, to chew.
Kiunuriġ, *m.*, to be wet.
Ko, *m.*, to be, to come into existence.
Koakilliko, *m.*, to rebuke, to scold, to quarrel.
Koinomulliko, *m.*, to cough.
Koipulliko, *m.*, to smell.
Koitta, *m.*, to stink.
Koiyubulliko, *m.*, to burn with fire.
Koiyun, *m.*, to be ashamed.
Kolayelliko, *m.*, to keep secret, not to tell, not to disclose.
Kólbi, *m.*, to sound, as the wind or sea in a storm.
Kólbuntilliko, *m.*, to chop with an axe or scythe, to mow.

Kóllabilliko, *m.*, to fish with a line. The line is held in the hand.
Kóllamulliko, *m.*, to make secret, to conceal anything told.
Konéin, *m.*, to be handsome, pretty.
Kóntimulliko, *m.*, to wear as a dress.
Korawalliko, *m.*, to watch, to stay by a thing.
Korien, *m.*, not to be; the negative form of 'ko.'
Korokál, *m.*, to be worn out, threadbare.
Korokón, *m.*, to roar. as the wind or sea; *cf.* kólbi.
Korun, *m.*, to be silent, to be quiet.
Korunpaiyelliko, *m.*, to remain silent.
Kotabunbinla, *m.*, to permit to think, to remember.
Kotelliko, *m.*, to think.
Kóttán, *m.*, to be wet and chilly, from rain.
Kugun, *m.*, to be muddy.
Kulbilliko, *m.*, to lean, to recline.
Kulbun-kulbun, *m.*, to be very handsome, elegant.
Kulwun, *m.*, to be stiff, claycold, as a corpse.
Kum-bárá-paiyelliko, *m.*, to be troublesome, to give one a headache by noise.
Kumbáro, *m.*, to be giddy, to have a headache from dizziness.
Kunbúu, *m.*, to be rotten, as a skin or cloth.
Kunbuntilliko, *m.*, to cut with a knife.
Kunuá, *m.*, to be burned.
Kurkulliko, *m.*, to spring up, to jump, to leap.
Kur-kur, *m.*, to be cold.

Kurmúr, *m.*, to be rotten, as wood; *cf.*, kuubún.
Kurrá, *m.*, to be slow.
Kurrágkopilliko, *m.*, to spit.
Kurrál, *m.*, to be disabled, to be wounded.
Kurrilliko, *m.*, to carry.
Kuttawaiko, *m.*, to be satisfied with food, satiated, drunk.

M.

Ma, *m.*, to challenge, to dare; to command to do.
Mánkilliko, *m.*, to take, to accept, to take hold of.
Mánmunbilliko, *m.*, to cause to take, to let take, to let have.
Marógkoiyelliko, *m.*, to proclaim, to make known.
Matelliko, *m.*, to be gluttonous.
Meapulliko, *m.*, to plant.
Mimulliko, *m.*, to detain, to compel to wait.
Minki, *m.*, to sorrow, to sympathize.
Minkilliko, *m.*, to remain, to dwell.
Miromulliko, *m.*, to keep.
Mirral, *m.*, to be without, to be poor, miserable; a desert place.
Mirrilliko, *m.*, to sharpen into a point, as a spear.
Mirrínupulliko, *m.*, to cause to be sharp.
Mitti, *m.*, to be small.
Mittilliko, *m.*, to wait, to stay, to remain.
Mituġ, *m.*, to be cut, wounded, sore.
Morilliko, *m.*, to wind up as a string.
Morón, *m.*, to be alive.
Moroun, *m.*, to be tame, quiet, docile, patient.
Móttilliko, *m.*, to pound with a stone, like pestle and mortar.

Mulamulliko, *m.*, to vomit.
Múmbilliko, *m.*, to borrow, to lend.
Munni, *m.*, to be sick, ill, *or* to be diseased.
Muntilliko, *m.*, to be benighted, to be overtaken with darkness.
Mupai, *m.*, to fast; to keep the mouth closed; to be silent, dumb.
Mupaikaiyelliko, *m.*, to remain silent, to continue dumb.
Murralliko, *m.*, to run.
Murráraġ, *m.*, to be good, excellent, valuable.

N.

Neilpaiyelliko, *m.*, to shout; the noise of war *or* play.
Niġulliko, *m.*, to play, to sport.
Nillán-nillán, *m.*, to be smashed into pieces.
Nimulliko, *m.*, to pinch.
Ninmilliko, *m.*, to seize, to snatch.
Niuwara, *m.*, to be angry, displeased.
Nuġ-gurrawolliko, *m.*, to meet.
Núġkilliko, *m.*, to be successful, fortunate; to obtain.
Nummulliko, *m.*, to press, to force down.
Numulliko, *m.*, to touch with the hand.
Nupulliko, *m.*, to try, to learn, to attempt.
Nurilliko, *m.*, to throw the 'boomerang.'

P.

Paikulliko, *m.*, to act of its own power, to act of itself.
Paikulliko, *m.*, to show one's self spontaneously.
Paipilliko, *m.*, to appear, to become visible.

Paipilliko, *m.*, to act; excluding the idea of cause.
Tálŋál, *m.*, to vibrate, to swing, as in a swing.
Papai, *m.*, to be close at hand.
Peakulliko, *m.*, to fetch water.
Pillatoro, *m.*, to set; as the sun, moon, and stars.
Pillobuntilliko, *m.*, to be sunk, wrecked.
Pillokulliko, *m.*, to sink.
Pinkurkulliko, *m.*, to burst as a bladder, of itself.
Pinnilliko, *m*, to dig.
Pintakilliko, *m*, to float.
Watpulliko, *m.*, to swim.
Pintilliko, *m.*, to knock down, as with an axe; to shock, as with electricity.
Pipabunbilliko, *m.*, to permit to stride, to let stride.
Pipelliko, *m.*, to stride, straddle.
Pirra, *m.*, to be tired.
Pirral-mulliko, *m.*, to urge.
Pirriko, *m.*, to be deep.
Pirrírál, *m.*, to be hard, strong; *cf.* kunbón, *m.*, to be soft.
Pirun-kakilliko, *m.*, to be glad, to be pleased.
Pitál-kakilliko, *m.*, to be glad, to be pleased, to be happy.
Pitál-mulliko, *m.*, to cause joy, to make happy.
Pittabunbilliko, *m.*, to permit to drink, to let drink.
Pittalliko, *m.*, to drink.
Pittamulliko, *m.*, to make to drink, to cause to drink.
Poaibug-gulliko, *m.*, to compel to grow.
Poai-buntilliko, *m.*, to cause to grow.
Poai-kulliko, *m.*, to grow up of itself.
Poiyeakulliko, *m.*, to be suspended, to hang on; to infect.
Poiyelliko, *m.*, to beg, to entreat.

Pónkég, *m.*, to be short.
Pór-bug-gulliko, *m.*, to compel to drop.
Pórburrilltko, *m.*, to cause to drop by means of something.
Porei, *m.*, to be tall.
Pór-kakilliko, *m.*, to be dropped, to be born.
Porobulliko, *m.*, to smooth.
Porógkúl, *m.*, to be globular, to be round.
Porról, *m.*, to be heavy; to be slow.
Pórunwitilliko, *m.*, to dream a dream.
Potobuntilliko, *m.*, to cause a hole, to bleed a person.
Potoburrilliko, *m.*, to burst a hole with something.
Potopaiyaùún-wal *m*, will burst.
Pulluntara, *m.*, to shine, as with ointment.
Pulóg-kulliko, *m.*, to enter, to go *or* come into.
Púlúl-púlúl, *m.*, to shake with cold, to tremble.
Punta, *m.*, to be mistaken in anything.
Puntimulliko, *m.*, to cause to fall, to throw down.
Purkulliko, *m.*, to fly.
Puromulliko, *m.*, to lift up.
Puto, *m.*, to be black.
Puttilliko, *m.*, to bite.

T.

Ta-killiko, *m.*, to eat.
Taleamulliko, *m.*, to catch any thing thrown.
Talig-kakilliko, *m.*, to be across.
Ta-munbilliko, *m.*, to permit to eat, to let eat.
Tanán, *m.*, to approach.
Tarógkamulliko, *m.*, to cause to mix, to mingle.
Tetti, *m.* to be dead.

Tetti-ba-bunbilliko, *m.*, to permit to die, to let die.
Tetti-ba-bun-burrilliko, *m.*, to permit to be put to death by some means.
Tetti-buġ-gulliko, *m.*, to compel to be dead, to kill, to murder.
Tetti-bulliko, *m.*, to die, to be in the act of dying.
Tetti-búnkulliko, *m.*, to smite dead, to strike dead.
Tetti-burrilliko, *m.*, to cause to die by some means, as poison.
Tetti-kakilliko, *m.*, to be dead, to be in that state.
Tiir-buġ-ga-bunbilliko, *m.*, to let break.
Tiir-buġ-gulliko, *m.*, to compel to break.
Tiirburribunbilliko, *m.*, to permit to break by means of ... .
Tiirburrilliko, *m.*, to break by means of something.
Tiirkullibunbilliko, *m.*, to allow to break of itself.
Tiirkulliko, *m.*, to break of its own itself, as wood.
Tiraġ-kakilliko, *m.*, to be awake.
Tirriki, *m.*, to be red hot; the colour red.
Tittilliko, *m.*, to pluck.
Tiwolliko, *m.*, to seek, to search.
Tiyumbilliko, *m.*, to send any kind of property, *cf.*, yukulliko.
Tokól, *m.*, to be true; the truth; this takes 'bo ta' with it.
Tolóġ-tolóġ, *m.*, to separate.
Tolomulliko, *m.*, to shake any thing.
Torololäl, *m.*, to be slippery, slimy.
Tóttóġ *and* tóttoriġ; *m.*, to be naked. This word must be carefully distinguished from 'tótóġ,' news, intelligence.

Túġ-gunbilliko, *m.*, to show.
Túġkamulliko, *m.*, to find; *lit.*, to make to appear.
Túġkilliko, *m.*, to cry, to bewail.
Tuirkulliko, *m.*, to drag along, to draw.
Tukín-umulliko, *m.*, to preserve, to keep, to take care of.
Tukkára, *m.*, to be cold.
Tulbulliko, *m.*, to run fast, to escape.
Tullamulliko, *m.*, to hold by the hands.
Tulla-tullai, *m.*, to be in a rage.
Tuloin, *m.*, to be narrow.
Tulutilliko, *m.*, to kick.
Túnbilliko, *m.*, to exchange.
Túnbamabunbilliko, *m.*, to permit to string together.
Túnbamulliko, *m.*, to string together.
Turabunbilliko, *m.*, to permit to pierce.
Turakaiyelliko, *m.*, to convince.
Turinwiyelliko, *m.*, to swear the truth, to adjure to speak the truth.
Turól, *m.*, to be in a state of healing, to be well; as a cut or wound.
Turónpiri, *m.*, to suffer hunger.
Turrál, *m.*, to split.
Turrál-buġ-gulliko, *m.*, to cause to split, to make to split.
Turrámulliko, *m.*, to throw a stone.
Turruġ, *m.*, to be close together.
Turukónbilliko, *m.*, to punish.
Turukilliko, *m.*, to grow up, to shoot up.
Túrulliko, *m.*, to pierce, prick, stab, sting, lance, spear.
Tútóġ, *m.*, to be stunned, insensible, apparently dead.

U.

Umulliko, *m.*, to do, to make, to create.
Unmulliko, *m.*, to make afraid, to affright, to startle.
Úntelliko, *m.*, to dance.
Upulliko, *m.*, to do with, to use, to work with.
Uwolliko, *m.*, to come *or* go; to walk, to pass, &c.

W.

Waipilliko, *m.*, to wrestle.
Waipulliko, *m.*, to hunt.
Waita, *m.*, to depart, to be away.
Wamulliko, *m.*, to bark a tree, to skin.
Wamunbilliko, *m.*, to permit to go, to let go away.
Warakarig̈, *m.*, to be full, to be satiated.
Warekulliko, *m.*, to put away, to cast away; to forgive.
Warin-warin, *m.*, to be crooked.
Wari-wari-kulliko, *m.*, to strew, to scatter about, to sow seed.
Waran, *m.*, to be flat *or* level, to be plain.
Waruwai, *m.*, to battle, to engage in fighting.
Watpulliko, *m.*, to swim, to stretch the hands to swim.
Wattawalliko, *m.*, to tread, to stamp with the foot or feet.
Wauwibunbilliko, *m.*, to permit to float, to let float.
Wauwilliko, *m.*, to float; as a cork or feather.
Weilkorilliko, *m.*, to flog, whip, scourge.
Weir-weir, *m.*, to be lame.
Willug̈, willuntin, *m.*, to be behind, to come after, to be last.
Willug̈bo, willug̈, *m.*, to return.
Winelliko, *m.*, to burn with fire, to scorch.
Wirabakilliko, *m.*, to heat, to be becoming hot.
Wirakakilliko, *m.*, to be hot.
Wirrig̈bakilliko, *m.*, to close up, to shut a door.
Wirrilliko, *m.*, to wind up, as a ball of string.
Wirrobulliko, *m.*, to follow after.
Witelliko, *m.*, to smoke a pipe.
Wittilliko, *m.*, to sing.
Wittimulliko, *m.*, to fall, to be thrown down.
Wiyelliko, *m.*, to speak, to say, to tell, to command, to ask.
Wiyabunbilliko, *m.*, to permit to speak, to let speak.
Wiya-lei-illiko,* *m.*, to talk and walk.
Wiyavelliko, *m.*, to speak in reply, to answer.
Wiyayimulliko, *m.*, to accuse.
Wiyéa, *m.*, to say again, to repeat.
Woatelliko, *m.*, to lick.
Wog̈kàl, *m.*, to be foolish, not clever, stupid.
Wog̈úntilliko, *m.*, to forget any thing told; *cf.*, g̈urrawatilliko.
Woro-woro, *m.*, to swell.
Wotùra, *m.*, to be shallow.
Wúnkilliko, *m.*, to leave.
Wúnmarabunbilliko, *m.*, to permit to be left, to let be left.
Wuno, *m.*, to stoop or bend in walking.
Wupilliko, *m.*, to put, to place.
Wurunbarig̈, *m.*, to be hairy; as an animal.
Wntilliko, *m.*, to cover, to put on clothes.

* NOTE.—Other verbs also take this form whenever the act is conjoined with walking; as, ta-tei-illiko, 'to eat and walk.'

Y.

Yarakai, *m.*, to be bad, evil.
Yaöälkulliko, *m.*, to move away, as the clouds.
Yariġkulliko, *m.*, to laugh.
Yellawa-buġ-gulliko, *m.*, to compel to sit, to force to sit.
Yellawa-bunbilliko, *m.*, to permit to sit down.
Yellawolliko, *m.*, to cross legs down on the ground; to sit, to remain, to rest.
Yemmamulliko, *m.*, to lead; as by the hand, or as a horse by a rope.
Yiirkulliko, *m.*, to tear of itself, as cloth; to break.
    Yiirkabunbilliko, *m.*, to permit to tear, to let tear.
    Yiirburririlliko, *m.*, to tear, by means of something.
    Yiirburri-bun-billiko, *m.*, to permit to tear, by means of something.
    Yiirbuġ-gulliko, *m.*, to compel to tear.
    Yiirbuġ-ga-bunbilliko, *m.*, to permit compulsively to tear.
Yimulliko, *m.*, to make light, as fur is caused to lie lightly before the blacks twist it into cord; to encourage, to cheer up.
Yinbilliko, *m.*, to kindle a fire.
Yiremba, *m.*, to bark; as a dog.
Yitelliko, *m.*, to nibble *or* bite; as a fish the bait.
Yunaipilliko, *m.*, to push away, to thrust out.
Yukulliko, *m.*, to send, as a messenger, to send property; *cf.*, tiyumbilliko.
Yuntilliko, *m.*, to cause pain, to hurt.
Yuriġ. *m.*, to go away.
Yuróġkilliko, *m.*, to dive.
Yuropulliko, *m.*, to conceal from view, to hide
Yurruġ-gun, *m.*, to be faint with hunger.
Yutilliko, *m.*, to guide, to show the way by guiding.
Yútpilliko, *m.*, to pulsate, to beat, to throb.

CHAPTER V.

ILLUSTRATIVE SENTENCES.

Aboriginal sentences literally rendered into English.*

1. ON THE SIMPLE-NOMINATIVE CASE.

Gán ke bi? ġatoa, Bonni; *m.*, who are you? it is I, Bonni.
Who be thou?   I,
Gán ke unni, unnoa, unnuġ? *m.*, who is this, that,
Who be this?   that?   there?   there?
Kúri unni, nukuġ unnoa, wonnai unnuġ;
Man this,   woman that, child   there.
   m., this is a man; that is a woman; there is a child.
Minariġ ke unni? warai ta unni; *m.*, what is this? it is
What   be this? spear it is this.   a spear.
Minariġ-ko ke unnoa? turulliko; *m.*, what is that for?
What   -for be that?   for-to-spear.   to spear with.

2. ON THE AGENT-NOMINATIVE CASE.

Gán-to bín wiyá? niuwoa tia wiyá; *m.*, who told you?
Who thee told?   he   me told.   he told me.
Gali-noa, ġali-bountoa, tia wiyá; *m.*, this man, this
This-he   this-she,   me told;   woman, told me.
Gali-noa unni umá; *m.*, this is the man who made this.
This-he this made.
Minariġ-ko bón búnkulla tetti?; *m.*, what smote him
What   him   struck   dead?   dead?
Nukuġ-ko, piriwàllo, puntimaito;
The woman —, the king —,   the messenger —.
m., the woman —, the king —, the messenger —, *sc*, smote him.
Wakun-to minariġ tatán?; *m.*, what does the crow eat?
Crow   what   eats?
Minariġ-ko wakun tatán?; *m.*, what eats the crow?
What   crow   eats?
Naġún-to tia pitàl-mán; *m.*, the song rejoices me.
Song   me joy-does.
Kúlai-to tia búnkulla wokka-tin-to;
Stick   me struck   up-from.
   m., the stick fell from above and struck me.

---

*NOTE.—The line under the native words is a literal translation of them; that which follows the *m* is the equivalent English.—ED.

3. ON THE GENITIVE CASE.

Gán-úmba noa unni yinál? *m.*, whose son is this?
Whom-belonging-to he this son?

Emmoumba ta; gali-ko-ba bón; *m.*, it is mine; this belongs to him.
Mine it is; this-belongs him.

Birabán-umba, gikoumba wonnai; *m.*, Birában's, his child.
Birabán-belonging-to, his child.

Minarig-ko-ba unni? gali-ko-ba bón; *m.*, what does this belong to?
What-belongs this? this-belongs him.

Wonta-kàl bara? England-kal bara?
What-place-of *(mas.)* they? England - of they.
m., what country are they of? they are Englishmen.

Wonta-kálin bara? England-kalin bara?
What-place-of *(fem.)* they? England - of they.
m., what countrywomen are they? they are Englishwomen.

Bug-gai-kàl; *m.*, to-day; *lit.*, belonging to the present period.
To-day-of.

Makoro-ko-ba ta unni górróg; *m.*, this is the blood of a fish.
Fish-belonging-to it is this blood.

Governor- kai-kàl bag; *m.*, I belong to the Governor's place.
Governor - place-belonging-to I.

Governor-úmba bag; *m.*, I am the Governor's, *sc.*, man.
Governor-belonging-to I.

Murrárág-ko-ba kùri-ko-ba; *m.*, a good man's.
Good-belonging-to man-belonging-to

4. ON THE DATIVE.

Makoro bi guwa; gán-nug? give the fish; to whom?
Fish thou give; whom-for?

Piriwàl-ko? Keawai; giroug bo; *m.*, to the chief? no; for yourself.
Chief-for? no, for-thee self.

Karai tia guwa emmoug takilliko; *m.*, give me flesh to eat.
Flesh me give for-me for-to-eat.

Yurig bi wolla; gikoug-kin-ko; *m.*, be off; go to him.
Away thou go him-to.

Gán-kin-ko? piriwàl-la-ko; kokerá-ko;
Whom-to? chief-to; house-to.
m., to whom? to the chief; to the house.

Wontarig? untarig; untarig;
To-what-place? that-place; that-place-there.
m., to what place? to that place; to that place there.

Mulubinba-ka-ko; England-ka-ko; *m.*, to Newcastle; to England.
To Newcastle; England to.

5. ON THE ACCUSATIVE.

Gán-to bón búnkulla tetti kulwun? *m.*, who smote him dead?
Who him smote dead stiff.

Gánnug? Birabannug; *m.*, whom? Biraban.
Whom? Biraban.

Gatoa bón turá; turá bón baġ; *m.*, it is I who speared
 I   him speared; speared him I.   him; I speared him.
Kaibulla bounnoun; ġánnuġ? *m.*, call her; which?
 Call   her;   which?
Unnuġ-yóġ unnoanuġ nukuġ; *m.*, that woman there.
 There-there   that   woman.
Mánki yikora unnoanuġ; *m.*, do not take that.
 Take   not   that.
Mára bi unnoanuġ; *m.*, take that; take it.
 Take thou   that.
Mára bi unti-kál, untoa-kál, *m.*, take some of this, of that.
 Take thou hereof,   there-of.
Makoro tia ġuwa; ġúnùn banuġ; *m.*, give me a fish; I
 Fish   me give. give-will I-thee   will give thee.
Puntimán tia barán; *m.*, I am thrown down.
 Throws   me down.
Makoro bi turulla warai-to; *m.*, spear the fish with the
 Fish   thou pierce spear-with.   spear.
Tibbin bi buwa musketto; *m.*, shoot the bird with the
 Bird thou smite musket-with.   musket.
Wiyella bón; wiyella binuġ; *m.*, tell him; you tell him.
 Tell   him; tell   thou-him.
Búnkulla tia; wonné?; *m.*, I am struck; where?
 Smote   me; where?
Wálluġ tia noa wiréa; *m.*, he hit me on the head.
 Head me he struck.
Minariġ bo bali wiyellá? *m.*, what shall you and I say?
 What self thou-I say.
Gán-to bounnoun turánùn? *m.*, who will spear her?
 Who   her   pierce-will?
Gánto unnoanuġ umá-nùn? *m.*, who will make it?
 Who that-there make-will?

6. ON THE VOCATIVE.

Ela! kaai, tanán unti-ko; *m.*, I say, come hither.
Hallo! come, approach this-place-for.
Wau! kaai, kaai, karakai; *m.*, I say, come, make haste.
Hallo! come, come, be quick.
Bouġkalinùn-wal baġ waita biyuġbai-tako
 Arise-self-will   I   depart Father-to
 emmouġ-ka-ta-ko, ġatun wiyá-nùn-wal, Biyuġ,
   my-to   and   say-will,   Father,
 yarakai baġ umá mikán ta morokoka ġatun
  evil   I   made, presence-at heaven-at and
 ġirouġ-kin;
  thee.
m., I will arise and go to my father, and will say unto him, Father
 I have sinned against heaven, and before thee.

7. ON THE ABLATIVE.

Koakillán bara; gán-kai? gán-kai-kán;
Quarrelling-now they; whom-from? whom-from-being?
  m., they are now quarrelling; about whom?
Bounnoun-kai; Taipamearin; *m.*, about her; about T—.
Her-from, Taipamear-from.
Minarig-tin? minarig-tin-kán; *m.*, about what? don't
What-from? what-from-being. know.
Makorrin gatun kúri-tin; *m.*, about the fish and the men.
Fish-from and men-from.
Gán-kin-birug unni puntimai? *m.*, from whom came
Whom-from this messenger? this messenger?
Jehova-ka-birug Piriwäl-la-birug, *m.*, from Jehovah the
Jehovah-from King-from. King.
Wonta-ka-birug noa? *m.*, from what place did he come?
What-place-from he?
Wokka-ka-birug moroko-ka-birug; *m.*, from heaven above.
Up-from heaven-from.
Sydney-ka-birug; Mulu-binba-ka-birug; *m.*, from Sydney;
Sydney-from; Newcastle-from. from Newcastle.
Minarig-birug unnoa umá? *m.*, what is that made of?
What-from that made?
Kùlai-birug; brass-birug; *m.*, of wood; of brass.
Wood-from; brass-from.
Copper-birug gárabug-ga brass; *m.*, brass is made
Copper-from converted brass. of copper.
Yurig bi wolla emmoug-kin-birug; *m.*, go away from me.
Away thou move me-from.
Yellawolla bi emmoug-katoa; *m.*, sit with me.
Sit thou me-with.
Gán-katoa bountoa? Tibbin-katoa ba;
Whom-with she? Tibbin-with.
  m., with whom is she? with Tibbin.
Minarig-koa noa uwá? *m.*, how did he go?
What-by he go?
Murrinowai-toa; purrai-koa; *m.*, on board a ship; by land.
Large-canoe-by; land-by.
Wonta-kál-loa? korug-koa; *m.*, which way? through the
What-place-by? bush-by. bush.
Kokeróa bag uwa; *m.*, I came by the house.
House-by I came.
Wonnug ke wurnbil? Biraban-kin-ba;
Where-at be skin-cloak? Biraban-at
  m., where is the blanket? at Biraban's.
Wonnong ke noa? Sydney-ka-ba noa;
Where-at be he? Sydney-at he.
  m., where is he? he is at Sydney.
Wonta-wontá-ka-ba kokera? *m.*, whereabouts is the house?
Where-where-at house?

Papai-ta-ba Mulubinba-ka-ba; *m.*, close to Newcastle.
Close-at   Newcastle-at
Broken-bay-tin-to* natán Sydney-heads;
Broken-Bay-from   see   Sydney-heads.
   m., at Broken Bay is seen Sydney Heads.
Wonta-tin-to? unti-tin-to; unta-tin-to;
What-place-from? this-place-from; that-place-from.
   m., at what place? at this place; at that place.

8. ON THE ARTICLE.

Minnán kûri tanán-ba? *m.*, how many men are now coming?
What   men   approach?
Wakál-bo ta noa tanán-ba; *m.*, one man only is coming.
One-self   it is he   approaches.
Buloara-bo ta bula tanán uwá; *m.*, only the two came.
Two-self   it is two approach came.
Kólbirán-bo ta bara nukuġ; *m.*, only a few women.
Few-self   it is they women.
Tibbin-to noa tatán; *m.*, the bird eats.
Bird   he   eats.
Gali-noa tibbin-to pittán; *m.*, this is the bird which drinks.
This-he   bird   drinks.
Tibbin-to noa unnuġ; *m.*, that is a bird.
Bird   he there.
Unni-tara tibbin bi búnkulla tetti; *m.*, these are the birds
These   birds thou smotest   dead.   you killed.
Gintoa-bo ta unnoa kûri; *m.*, thou art the man.
Thou-self it is that man.
Maiya-ko putti-nùn tetti koa kauwil kûri;
Snake   bite-will   dead   ut†   may-be   man.
   m., the snake will bite in order to kill the man.
Tira-ko ġikoumba-ko; *m.*, with his teeth.
Teeth   his-with.
Tetti bón horse-ko witti-má; *m.*, the horse threw him,
Dead him   horse   violence-made.   and killed him.

9. CONJUGATION OF THE NEUTER VERB.

Wibbi unni kauwál kátán; *m.*, this is a high wind.
Wind   this   great   it exists.
Kauwau, kauwál láġ unni; *m.*, yes, very powerful.
So it is, great acts   this.
Kapirra baġ kakilliela, kátán; *m.*, I was, I am, hungry.
Hungry   I   was-being,   am.
Gán unti kátán? *m.*, who lives here?
Who this-place exists?
Bara-bo unti kátán; *m.*, they themselves dwell here.
They-self this-place exist.

---

* NOTE—Here Broken Bay is spoken of both as the cause and the agent, so that the meaning is—on account of Broken Bay being the agent, you see Sydney Heads. The particle *tin*, 'from,' 'on account of,' denotes the cause, and *to (ko)* marks the agency.
  † The English expression 'in order that' is too long to stand under and correspond with 'koa' in the above. I have, therefore, substituted for it, throughout, the Latin 'ut.'

F

Kiakia baġ kakéún unni ġorokán; *m.*, I was conqueror
Conqueror I   was this morning   this morning.
Bukka baġ kakulla; *m.*, I was very angry.
Rage I   was.
Búntoara noa tetti kakulla; *m.*, he is the man who
That-which-is-smote he dead was.   was killed.
Kakulla-ta baġ Sydney-ka táġa bi ba kakulla unta;
Was I Sydney-at before thou wast at-that-place
m., I was at Sydney before ever you were there.
Kúmba baġ kakéún Sydney-ka; *m,*, to-morrow I shall be
To-morrow I shall-be Sydney-in.   in Sydney.
Kánún-ta unni murráráġ; *m.*, it will be good, this.
Be-will this   good.
Mirka noa tetti kánún; *m.*, perhaps he will be dead.
Perhaps he dead be-will.
Gán-ke kiakia kánún? *m.*, who will be the victor?
Who conqueror be-will?
Piriwal kánún-wal bi; *m.*, you will certainly be king.
Chief be-wilt thou.
Kabo baġ kánún Sydney-ka; *m.*, by and by I shall be
By and by I be-will Sydney-at.   at Sydney.
Kánún baġ tarai ta yellenna-ka; *m.*, in another
Be-will I another it is moon-at.   month I shall.
Kaiyu kán baġ; kaiyu korien baġ;
Able being I; able not I.
m., I am powerful; I am not powerful.
Wirrobulli-kán bara ġikoumba; *m*, they are his fol-
Followers   they   his.   lowers.
Tulbulléun baġ kinta kán; *m.*, I escaped, being afraid.
Escaped I fear being.
Pirra-pirrá bara kakillín úntelli-tin; *m.*, the dancing
Fatigued they becoming dance-from. is tiring them.
Wunál unni kakillín; *m.*, the summer is coming on.
Hot-season this becoming.
Store-ba kakillín bountoa; *m.*, she is now living near
Store existing she.   the store.
Store-ka-ba kakillín bountoa; *m.*, she is now living at
Store at   existing   she.   the store.
Musket tia katala Awaba-ka; *m.*, I had a musket at
Musket me existed Awaba-at.   Lake Macquarie.
Kinta baġ katala, yakita keawai; *m.*, I used to be afraid,
Afraid I existed, now not.   but now I am not.
Katala baġ Raiatea-ka; *m,*, I used to live at Raiatea.
Existed I Raiatea-at.
Unta baġ katala yuraki M—ka; *m.*, I lived formerly
There I existed formerly M— at.   at M—.
Piriwál baġ kakilli-kolaġ; *m.*, I am now going to be
Chief I   to-be-towards   king.
Korien kakilli-nún yanti kata¡; *m.*, I will not be so for
Not be-will so for ever.   ever.

ILLUSTRATIVE SENTENCES.

Morón noa kakilli-nún tetti korien;
  Live   he   be-will   dead   not.
    m., he is going to live for ever and never die.

Wibbi kakillilín waréa; *m.*, the wind is lessening.
  Wind now-continuing-to-be less.

Gatoa-bo, yaki-ta-bo, unti-bo;
  I myself,   instantly,   this self same place.
    m., I myself, at this very place and instant.

Kakillán bali-bountoa; *m.*, she and I live together.
  Live-together we two-she.

Gintoa-bo ka-pa piriwál kakilliko; *m.*, you ought to
  Thou-thyself oughtest chief to be. be chief.

Yakoai bag tetti kámúnbin-nún bón?;
  In-what-manner I dead let-be-will him?
    m., how shall I cause his death?

Kakillai koa bali muroi; *m.*, I wish you and me to
  To-continue-to-be ut we two quiet;   continue at peace.

Kauwil-koa-poré goro yards; *m.*, I want it three yards long.
  That-may-be   long three „ ;

Munni noa katéa kan; *m.*, he is sick again.
  Sick he is-become again.

Yanoa; munni koa noa katéa-kún; *m.*, do not; lest he be
  Do-not; sick lest he should-be.   sick.

Munni kánún bag ba; *m.*, if I should be sick.
  Sick be-will I if.

Gán-ke tetti kámai-ga? *m.*, who had almost been dead?
  Who dead like-to-have-become?

Tetti bag kámai-ga; *m.*, I was almost dead.
  Dead I   had-like-to-have-been.

Piriwál bi ba-ka-pa pitál gaiya bag ka-pa;
  Chief thou if-hadst-been joy then I had-had.
    m., if you had been king, I should have been glad.

Ka-pa bi ba unta gorokán-ta, na pa gaiya banug;
  Hadst-been thou if there this-morning, seen had then I-thee.
    m., if you had been there this morning, I should have seen you.

Korun kauwa, túnki yikora; *m.*, be still, do not cry.
  Quiet be wail not.

Kauwa, bi tetti kakilliko; *m.*, yes, you are to die.
  Yes, thou dead for-to-be.

Kakillá nura pitál kakilliko; *m.*, be at peace one with
  Be ye peace for-to-be.   the other.

Morón bón ká-múnbilla; *m.*, let him live.
  Alive him permit-to-be.

Ká-múnbi-nún banug piriwál kakilliko;
  Permit-will I-thee chief for-to-be.
    m., I will let you be king.

Piriwál bi katéa-ka; *m.*, be king again.
  Chief thou be-again.

Piriwál bón ká-mún bi yikora; *m.*, prevent his being
  Chief him permit-to-be thou not.   chief.

10. THE CONJUGATION OF THE ACTIVE VERB.

Gánnuġ búnkulla? unni bón ye; *m.*, who was beaten?
Whom   struck?   this him   be.   this is he.

Minariġ-tin biloa ġala búnkulla?; *m.*, why did that
What-from   he-thee that struck?   person beat you?

Unni bulun búnkulla noa; *m.*, these are the two he struck.
These them-two struck   he.

Tanán tia, wolla-wolla; búntán tia butti kirrín-kirrín!
Approach me, move-move, beats me more pain pain.
  m., come to me, make haste; I am beaten more and in pain.

Gan-to bin búnkulla? wiyella bi tia; mupai yikora;
Who   thee struck? tell thou me; secret   not.
  m., who beat you? tell me; do not conceal it.

Gali-noa tia búnkulla; *m.*, this is he who struck me.
This-he   me   struck.

Minariġ-ko biloa búnkulla? *m.*, with what did he strike
What-with he-thee struck?   you?

Máttárró ġikoumba-ko; *m.*, with his hand.
Hand-with   his-with.

Kotárró noa tia búnkulla; *m.*, he struck me with a cudgel.
Cudgel-with he me struck.

Kora koa binuġ búm-ba? *m.*, you ought to have beaten him.
Not *ut* thou-him struck had.

Búwil   koa bón, kaiyu korien baġ;
That-might-strike *ut* him, able   not   I.
  m., I wish to beat him, but am unable.

Kotára bi tia ġuwa buwil koa bón baġ;
Cudgel thou me give to-strike *ut* him I.
  m., give me a cudgel that I may beat him.

Búm-ba bo ta bón baġ, wonto baġ-ba kinta kán kakulla;
Struck-had surely him I, but   I   fear being was.
  m., I should certainly have struck him, but I was afraid.

Búnkéún bón baġ; *m.*, I have beaten him, *sc.*, this morning.
Struck-have him I.

Búnnún bón baġ ka-bo; *m.*, I will beat him by-and-by.
Strike-will him I   by-and-by.

Búnkillaibán kora nura; *m.*, do not be striking one
Striking-be not   ye.   another.

Búnkillín bón bara yakita; *m.*, they are striking him now.
Are-striking him they now.

Búnkilliela bón baġ, tanán bi ba uwá;
Was-striking him I, approach thou came.
  m., I was striking him when you came.

Búntala tia bara wonnai baġ ba;
Struck me they   child   I
  m., they beat me when I was a child.

Waita-kolaġ noa búnkilli-kolaġ; *m.*, he is gone a-
Depart-towards he to-strike-towards.   fighting.

Búnkillilín   noa wheat; *m.*, he is thrashing wheat.
Is-continuing-to-strike he wheat.

Búnkillilía binuġ; *m.*, beat him; thrash it.
Continue-to-strike thou-him.
Gán-bo nura búnkillán? *m.*, who are fighting with you?
Who-self ye strike-reciprocally?
Búnkillala bara-bo bara-bo; *m.*, they fought amongst
Fought they-self they-self. themselves.
Búnkillala bali-noa Bulai wonnai bali-noa ba;
Struck-reciprocally we-two-he Bulai children we-two-he when.
m., when Bulai and I were children, we fought with one another.
Búnkillá-nún bula; *m.*, the two are going to fight.
Strike-reciprocally-will the-two.
Yanoa; búnkillai bán kora; cease fighting.
Let be; striking-reciprocally be not.
Yanoa; búnki yikora; *m.*, do not strike.
Let be; strike not.
Búnkillai-kín bali-noa kúmba; *m.*, to-morrow he and I
Strike-each-will we-two-he to-morrow will fight a duel.
Yakounta-ke bara búnkillá-nún? *m.*, when will they fight?
At-what-time they fight-will?
kúmba-kén-ta; *m.*, the day after to-morrow.
Waita-kolaġ baġ búnkilliko musket-to;
Depart-towards I for-to-strike musket-with.
 m., I am now going to shoot with a musket.
Yakoai tia buwil koa bón baġ; *m.*, take care that I
How me may-strike *ut* him I. may beat him.
Wiyella bón buwil koa bón; *m.*, command him to beat
Tell him strike *ut* him. him.
Buwil baġ Pattynuġ; *m.*, I wish to beat Patty.
May-beat I Patty.
Yari bi núti-nún, búntéa-kún koa bin;
Do-not thou wait-will, should-strike lest thee.
 m., do not wait lest you be struck.
Bún-nún noa tia ba turulla ġaiya binuġ;
Strike-will he me if pierce then thou-him.
 m., when he strikes me, then spear him; *or*, if he, &c.
Búmmai-ġa tia, wonto baġ ba murra;
Struck-has-nigh me, but I ran.
 m., I should have been struck, but I ran away.
Keawarán tia búm-ba-ka-pa baġ-ba unti bo;
Not me struck-had-been I-if at this self same place.
 m., I should not have been struck, had I remained here.
Gali-ta tia tetti búm-ba; *m.*, this might have killed me.
This me dead struck-had.
Yuriġ, binuġ búnkéa yakita; *m.*, go, strike him again now.
Away thou-him strike-again now.
Wiya, bón baġ búm-ba, búm-ba ġaiya bi-tia;
Say him I struck-had, struck-had then thou-me;
 m., if I had struck him, then you would have struck me.
Yari bón búntéa kánún, *m.*, prevent his being beaten again.
Prevent him strike-again be-will.

Búmmúnbia bi-tia; *m.*, you permitted me to be beaten.
Permitted-to-strike thou-me.
Búmmúnbillín bón baġ; *m.*, I am permitting him to strike.
To-strike-permitting him I.
Búmmúnbi yikora bón; *m.*, do not permit him to strike.
To-strike-permit not him.
Búmmúnbilla bi-tia bón; *m.*, let me strike him.
To-strike-permit thou-me him.
Kamulla bi-tia búmmarabúnbia-kún koa tia;
To-be-cause thou-me some-one-should-strike lest me;
m., protect me, lest anyone should beat me.
Búnkillá nura; *m.*, fight on.
Continue-to-strike ye.
Wakállo binuġ buwa, ma búntéa-ka tia;
Once thou-him strike, do strike-again me.
m., smite him once, smite me again.
Búmmúnbilla binuġ, buwil koa noa tia,
Permit-to-strike thou-him, may-strike *ut* he me.
m., permit him to strike, that I may be beaten by him.
Yakoai, búwil koa barun baġ; *m.*, take care that I beat
Mind, may-strike *ut* them I. them.
Kinta kora bi; keawarán bin bún-nún;
Fear not thou; not thee strike-will.
m., fear not; thou shalt not be beaten.
Kora koa bi-tia búntán? *m.*, why do not you beat me?
Not *ut* thou-me strike?
Ma, búwa bi-tia, binuġ (a challenge); *m.*, do strike me, him.
Do, strike thou-me, thou-him.
Búnkia binuġ; *m.*, strike him, *sc.*, to-morrow morning.
Strike thou-him.
Búnkilli-tin noa murrá; *m.*, he ran away because of the
Striking-from he ran. fighting.
Búnkillai bara yanti katai; *m.*, they are always fighting
Striking they then for ever. amongst themselves.
Kauwál unnoa búnkilli-kan-né; *m.*, that is a great thing
Great that striking-thing. to strike with.
Unnoa-ta noa búnkilli-kán; *m.*, that is the striker.
That he striking-being.
Gali-noa búnkilli-kán-to tia búnkulla;
This - he striking-being me struck.
m., this is the striker who struck me.
Búnki-ye bara unnoa kúri; *m.*, they are the fighters.
Fighter they those men.
Waita-kolaġ baġ búnkillai-ġél-kolaġ;
Depart about I striking-place-towards.
m., I am going to the field of battle.
Búntoara baġ gali-biruġ bón; *m.*, I was struck by
That-which-is-struck I this-from him. him.
Búnkilli-tin baġ katán unti; *m.*, I remain here because
Striking-from I remain here. of the fight.

Munni géen kapaiyin búnkilli-birug;
Sick   we   suffering   striking-from.
   m., we are ill through fighting.
Gali tia noa búntoaró búnkulla; *m.*, this is the wounded
This me he the-wounded struck.   man who struck me.
Wonnug-ke bara búntoara? *m.*, where are those who
Where   they that-be-struck.   were struck?
Búntoarin bara tetti kakulla; *m.*, they died of their
Wounded-from they dead were.   wounds.

11. CONJUGATION OF SOME OTHER VERBS.

Minarig bi umán? warai? *m.*, what thing do you make?
What thou makest? spear.   a spear?
Gán-to unni umá? gali; *m.*, who made this? this person
Who this made? this.   did
Gán-to tia morón umá-nún? *m.*, who will save me alive?
Who me alive make-will?
Gán-to unnoa punnál umá? Jehova-ko;
Who   that sun made?   Jehovah.
   m., who made the sun? Jehovah did.
Mumin winta kakulla, uma noa barun nakilli-kán;
Blind some were,   made he them   seers;
   m., some were blind, he made them to see.
Umabúnbi yikora, tetti koa noa katéa-kún;
Permit-to-do not, dead lest he become;
   m., do not let him do it, lest he die.
Umai-ga-ta bag unni yarakai; *m.*, I had almost spoiled
Like-to-have-done I this bad.   this.
Wiyella bón uma-uwil koa unnoa; *m.*, tell him to make it.
Tell   him may-do   ut that.
Wiyella bón upa-uwil koa unnoa;
Tell   him to-do   ut that;
   m., tell him to use it; or, to make it act.
Soap umatoara kipai-birug; *m.*, soap is made of fat.
Soap   made   fat-from.
Upulli-gél kúlai-ta-birug; *m.*, the acting place of wood;
Doing-place wood-from.   a wooden table.
Warai bag umullin; *m.*, I am making a spear.
Spear I am-now-making.
Mirrin bag upullin; *m.*, I am sharpening *or* putting a
Point I am-now-doing.   point.
Wonnug-ke mirrin wirritoara? *m.*, where is that which
Where   be point that-which-is-done?   is pointed.
Umatoara   kúmba-birug; *m.*, that which was made
That-which-is-done yesterday-from.   yesterday.

12. CONJUGATION OF THE VERB 'TO GO.'

Wonta-kolaġ bi uwán? Syḋney-kolaġ.
Whither-towards thou movest? Sydney-towards.
   m., where are you going? to Sydney.

Wontariġ bi uwán? untariġ; Sydney-ka-ko.
To-what-place thou movest? to that place; Sydney-for
   m., to what place do you go? to that place; to Sydney.

Wonta biruġ bi uwá? *m.*, from what place did you come?
What-place from thou movedst?

Koiyóġ-tin baġ uwá; *m.*, I started from the camp.
Camp-from I moved.

Kaiyóġ-biruġ baġ uwá, *m.*, I came out from the camp.
Camp-from I moved.

Wiya, baġ uwá-nún? *m.*, may I go?
Say, I move-will?

Keawarán wal bi uwá-nún; *m.*, you shall not go.
Not shalt thou move-wilt.

Yanoa, uwa yikora; *m.*, do not go.
Let be, move not.

Wiya, bi tanán uwá-nún? *m.*, will you come?
Say, thou approach move-will?

Wiya, bi waita uwá-nún? *m.*, will you go?
Say, thou depart move-will?

Wiya, bi waita uwolla? *m.*, do you wish to go?
Say, thou depart move?

Wiya, bi tanán uwolla? *m.*, do you wish to come?
Say, thou approach move?

Wiya, bali uwolla; *m.*, let us, you and me, go.
Say, thou-I move?

Waita ġeen uwolla wittim ulli-kolaġ; *m.*, let us go a
Depart we move to-hunt-about.   hunting.

Wonnén ġeen uwolla? ġiakai; *m.*, which way shall we
Which-way we move? this way.   go? this way.

Wonnén kán? *m.*, don't know; *or*, which way can it be?
Which-way being?

Wa-uwil bali Pakai kabo; *m.*, I want you to go with
Move-may I-thou Pakai by-and-by.   me to Pakai by-and-by.

Yanoa; uwá-nún bo-ta baġ; *m.*, no; I will go by myself.
Let be; move-will self I

Wiya, bali-baġ wa-uwil; *m.*, I wish you to go with me.
Say, we-two-I move-may.

E-e, waita bali; waitá-láġ bara;
Yes, depart we-two-I; departed they.
   m., yes, I will go with you; they are gone.

Yuriġ bula uwollá, ġarabo ka-ko baġ waita;
Away ye-two move, sleep for-to-be I depart;
   m., go away you two; I am going to sleep.

Waitá ka-ba bountoa parkai; *m.*, she is gone to the
Departed is she southward.   southward.

ILLUSTRATIVE SENTENCES. 77

Waita-wal baġ uwà-nùn; *m.*, I am determined I will go.
Depart-shall   I   move-will.

Waita koa baġ; mimai yikora; *m.*, I must go; do not
Depart   *ut* I;   detain   not.   detain me.

Winta bara waita uwà-nùn; *m.*, some of them will go.
Part   they depart move-will.

Waita *wà-nùn noa ba, waita ġaiya ġéen;
Depart move-will he if, depart then we.
m., when he goes, we will go.

Wonta punnàl kakulla, uwà ġaiya nura ba?
Where sun   was   come then ye?
m., what time was it when you came?

Uwolliela noa ba, nuġurrurwà ġaiya bòn noa;
Moving-was he   met   then him he.
m., while he was walking, he met him.

Wiya, bi uwa-kéùn koiyóġ-kolag? *m.*, have you been
Say, thou moved-hast camp-towards? to the camp?

Keawai, kùmba baġ waita wokkìn; *m.*, I have not, but
No, to-morrow I depart move. to-morrow I shall.

Kabo, waita wà-nùn baġ; *m.*, by-and-by I shall go.
By-and-by, depart move-will I.

Kurrikai-kurrikai-ta kàtàn uwolliko gaol-
Quick   it is for-to-move gaol-
kolaġ, keawaràn willuġ-ko;
towards   not for-to-return.
m., it is very easy to go to goal, but not so easy to get out again.

Waita baġ uwà-nùn tóttóġ ġurrulliko.
To-depart I   move-will news for-to-hear.
m., I will go and bear the news.

Pitàl mà-pa bi-tia ba, keawai ġaiya baġ wa-pa;
Joy done-had thou-me, not then I moved-had.
m., if you had loved me, I would not have gone.

Wà-mùnbilla tia Sydney-kolaġ; *m*, permit me to go to
Permit-to-move me Sydney-towards. Sydney.

Wà-mùnbi-nùn banuġ; *m.*, I will let you go.
Permit-to-move-will I-thee.

Yari bi wà-nùn, turea-kùn-koa bin kùri-ko bara;
Do-not thou move-wilt, pierce-should-lest thee men they.
m., do not go, lest you should be speared by the men.

Keawai banuġ wà-mùnbi-nùn; *m.*, I will not permit
Not I-thee permit-to-move-will. you to go.

Uwa-ta noa yanti-ta punnàl ba polóġ-kàlléùn;
Came he at-the-time sun sinking-was.
m., he came just as the sun was setting.

---

* NOTE.—The *u* is often omitted when another verb takes the government, forming it into an auxiliary; but as a principal verb the *u* is generally retained.

Kcawáran noa wa-pa yanti-ta punnàl-ba pólog-
　Not　　　he moved-had at-the-time　sun　　sinking-
kàlléùn;
　was.
　　m., he had not come, when the sun was setting.
Tanàn bi wolla yanti-ta punnàl-ba pológ-kàllinún;
　Approach thou move　at-the-time　sun　　sinking　will-be.
　　m., come at sunset.

13. CONJUGATION OF OTHER VERBS.

Kurrawán unni　　yiirkullin;　*m.*, the weather is
　Clear　this　breaking (as the clouds).　clearing up.
Pór-kàlléùn tia wonnai emmoumba; *m.*, unto me my
　Dropped-has　me　child　　mine.　　child is born.
Tiirrán unni; minnug?　*m.*, that is broken; what is?
　Broken　this;　what.
Tiir-bug-ga unni; ganto unni tiir-bug-gá?
　Broken　　this;　who　this　　broken?
　　m., this is broken by some person; who broke it?
Tiirburréa unni; yakoai?　wibbi-ko;
　Broken　　this;　how?　　wind-for.
　　m., this is broken; how? by the wind.
Wibbi-ko tia pórburréa hat emmoumba;
　Wind　me　dropped　hat　my.
　　m., the wind has blown off my hat.
Wiwi, tiirkulléa-kùn-koa　spade; *m.*, mind, lest the
　Mind,　break-should-lest　spade.　　spade break.
Wiwi, tiir-bug-géa-kùn-koa bi unnoa spade;
　Mind,　break-shouldst-lest　thou　that　spade.
　　m., mind, lest you break that spade.
Wiwi, tiirburréa-kùn-koa bi unnoa spade gali
　Mind,　break-shouldst-lest　　thou　that　spade that
kùlai-to; *m.*, mind, lest you break the spade with that stick.
　stick-with.
Tiir-bug-ga-pa bag ba, minnug bànún gaiya bara-tia?
　Broken-had　I,　what　act-will　then　they-me?
　　m., had I broken it, what would they have done to me?
Minnug bàllin bi? wiyellin bag;
　What　about-doing thou?　talking　I.
　　m., what are you doing? I am talking.
Minnug ba bin? *m.*, what is the matter with you?
　What　do-to thee?
Minnug bànún gaiya biloa? *m.*, what will he do to you?
　What　do-will　then　he-thee?
Minnug bànún bi bug-gai? *m.*, what will you do to-day?
　What　do-will thou to-day?
Minnug bànún? gatóg; *m.*, I don't know; nothing (an idiom).
　What　do-will?　nothing.
Pitàl bali kakillán; *m.*, we two rejoice together.
　Joy　we-two are-being.

Minnuġ bàlli-ka-ke? *m.*, of what use is it? of what profit?
What   do-for-to-be?
Minnuġ bàlli-kolaġ noa uwà-nùn? *m.*, what is he
What   to-be-about-to-do she move-will?   going about?
Na-nùn bountoa biyuġbai bounnounba; *m.*, to see
See-will   she father   her.   her father.
Kàti! kàtià! tetti-ba-bunbéa tia; *m.*, alas! alas! I am
Alas! alas! to-die-permitted me.   left to die.
Tetti ba bùnbilla bón; *m.*, let him die; (*trans. verb*).
Dead   permit him.
Tetti bùġ-gulla bón; ġán-to? *m.*, kill him; who shall?
Dead force him ; who?
Tetti ba bunbi-nùn banuġ; *m.* I will let you die.
Dead   permit-will I-thee.
Tetti burri-nùn banuġ *m.*, I will cause you to die, as by
Dead   cause-will I-thee.   poison, &c.
Tetti buġ-gànùn banuġ; *m.*, I will compel you to die;
Dead force-will I-thee.   murder you.
Minnuġ ba-uwil koa bali bón? *m.*, what shall you
What   may-do   *ut* thou-I him?   and I do to him?
Yanoa, tetti-béa-kùn-koa noa, *m.*, let alone, lest he die.
Let be,   die-should lest he.
Birrikillía noa untoa tetti bauwil koa noa;
Lie   he at-that-place dead may-be *ut* he.
m., he may (I wish him to) lie there until he dies.
Tetti burrilléùn baġ; *m.*, I have destroyed myself; I have
Dead cause-self I.   killed myself.

14. CONJUGATION OF THE VERB 'TO SPEAK.'

Gànto wiyán? ġaliko, ġali-taró; *m.*, who speaks? this
Who speaks? this,   these.   man does; these.
Wiyán ġali clock-ko; *m.*, the clock strikes.
Speaks this clock.
Wiyán kùri-ko; wiyán tibbin-to; *m.*, the man speaks;
Speaks man; speaks bird.   the bird sings.
Wiyán bullock-ko; *m.*, the bullock roars.
Speaks bullock.
Wiya-uwil bitia yakoai bara-ba wiyá bin;
Tell-may thou-me how they told thee.
m., I wish you to tell me how they spoke to you.
Wiyá ġaiya ġearun bara yanti; ma; *m.*, they spoke to
Told then them they so; do. us in bravado.
Ga binuġ wiyá? wiyá bón baġ; *m.*, did you tell him?
Is it thou-him told? told him I.   I told him.
Ganto bin wiyá? yitàrabùllo tia wiya;
Who thee told? such-a-one me told.
m., who told you? that man did.

Gán unnuġ wiyellín yóġ? *m.*, who is talking out there?
Who there talking there?
Gánnuġ bi wiyán? *m.*, whom do you tell? to whom do you
Whom thou speakest? speak?
Emmouġ? ġalín? barun? *m.*, me? us two? them?
Me? us-two? them?
Kúri-ko-ba wiyella bitia; *m.*, speak to me in the black's
Man-belonging-to speak thou-me. language.
Wiyéa-ka bitia; kárá tia wiyella; *m.*, tell me again;
Speak-again thou-me; slowly me tell. speak distinctly.
Wonnuġ borin bali wiyella? *m.*, what shall we two
Where first thou-I speak? first talk about?
Kabo-kabo, wiya-wiyelli koa baġ; *m.*, stay. stay, that I
Presently, talk-talk-may ut I. may have some talk.
Wonnén baġ wiyánùn unni yitára? *m.*, how am I to
Which-way I speak-will this name? call this?
Yakounta biloa wiya? *m.*, when did he tell you?
At-what-time he-thee told?
Wiyán banuġ ġarokilli-ko; *m.*, I command thee to arise.
Tell I-thee for-to-arise.
Unta bali-bi wiyellala yuraki; *m.*, this is where we
There thou-I conversed formerly. conversed together.
Kaiyalléùn ġaliclock wiyelli-biruġ; *m.*, the clock has
Ceased-has this clock talking-from. done striking.
Yakoun-ta ke binuġ wiyá-nùn; when will you tell
At-what-time be thou-him tell-will? him?
Wiyá-nùn binuġ ba, wiyá-nùn ġaiya tia;
Tell-will thou-him when, tell-will then me.
m., when you tell him, let me know.

15. PROMISCUOUS SELECTIONS.

Patin ġali koiwon-to; *m.*, it is raining.
Drop this rain.
Kabo-ka-ta turá-nùn ġaiya bin; *m.*, by-and-by you will
By-and-by pierce-will then thee be speared.
Bulka-ka ba noa buttikán-ka-ba; *m.*, he is on horseback.
Back he beast - at.
Keawai kolaġ baġ ġután; *m.*, I am not going to give.
Not towards I give.
Gukillá bali unnoa; *m.*, let you and me give one
Give-reciprocally thou-I that another, *i.e.*, exchange.
Kora koa napál uwán kúri-katoa? *m.*, why do not women
Not ut women move men - with? go with the men?
Yanoa, yirriyirri ka-ke; *m.*, because it is a sacred concern.
Let-be, sacred is.
Pitál korien baġ shoe-tin; *m.*, I am displeased with the
Joy not I shoe-from. shoe.
Pulli ġowi-ko-ba; *m.*, a strange language; a foreign tongue.
Voice strange-belonging-to.

ILLUSTRATIVE SENTENCES.

Minarig̈-tin bi kóttán untoa-tin? *m.*, what think you
What-from   thou thinkest   that-from?   of that?
Kóttalliela bag̈ tokoi-ta tetti bag̈ ba ka-pa;
Thinking-was   I   last-night   dead   I should-have-been.
    m., I thought I should have died last night.
Tirág̈ bag̈ kátán; *m.*, I am awake.
Awake   I   remain.
Tirág̈ bug̈-gulla bón boug̈kulli koa noa;
Awake   compel   him   to-arise   *ut*   he.
    m., make him awake and get up.
Konéin-ta unni nakilli-ko, *m.*, this is pretty to look at.
Pretty   this   for-to-see.
Turi wiyelli-ko; *m.*, to swear the truth; to speak convincingly.
Truth   for-to-speak.
Yuna bo ta bag̈ wiyánùn tuloa; *m.*, I will certainly speak
Certain   I   speak-will   straight.   the truth.
Minarig̈-tin nura tia bukka bug̈gán? *m.*, why do ye
What-from   ye   me   to-rage   compel?   enrage me?
Minarig̈-tin nura tia bukka kátán? *m.*, why are ye en-
What-from   ye   me   to-rage   remain?   raged at me?
Kamullala noa yantin-birug̈ umulli-birug̈;
Ceased   he   all-from   doing-from
    m., he rested from all his work.
Kauwa, wiyalléùn bag̈ g̈atoa-bo; *m.*, yes, I was talking
Yes,   talked-reflexively I   I-self.   to myself.
Gintoa-bo ba; *m.*, do as you like; (an idiom).
Thou-thyself   act.
Nauwa wirrobán bountoa-tia ba; *m.*, look while she fol
Look   follows   she-me.   lows me.
Nakillán bali; *m.*, we two are looking one at the other.
Look-reciprocally thou-I.
Nakilléùn bag̈ g̈atoa-bo nakalli-g̈él-la;
Saw-reciprocally   I   my-self   looking-place-at.'
    m., I saw myself in the looking-glass.
Minarig̈-tin bón búnkulla? kulla noa bukka barig̈;
What-from   him   struck?   because he   angry   always.
    m., why was he beaten? because he is always angry.
Yanti, bán kora; *m.*, do not do so.
Just so,   act   not.
Múmbilla tia g̈aloa; múmbitoara unni;
Lend   me   that;   that-which-is-lent   this.
    m., lend me that; it is lent.
Múmbéa bag̈ tarai-kán; *m.*, I have lent it to another.
Lent-have   I   another-being.
Gumai-g̈a bin unni wonto bi ba keawai mán-ba*;
Given-had   thee   this   where   thou   not   taken-hadst.
m., it would have been given you, but you would not have it.

---

* NOTE.—It is extremely difficult to ascertain whether this particle should be spelt Pa or Ba; in the conjugations of the verb it is spelled Pa. But many natives say it should be Ba, whilst others affirm that it ought to be Pa.

Tunuġ unni Turkey-ko-ba; *m.*, this is a Turkey stone.
Stone this Turkey-belonging-to.

Kùri unni Turkey-kàl; *m.*, this is a Turkish man, a Turk.
Man this Turkey-of.

Tirriki-ko tia winnà; *m.*, the flame burns me.
Red me burns.

Makoro ġuwa, ġatun karai, ġatun tibbin, ġatun
Fish give and flesh, and fowl, and

kokoin, ta-uwil koa baġ pitta-uwil koa baġ;
water eat-may *ut* I drink-may *ut* I.

m., give fish, flesh, fowl, and water, that I may eat and drink.

(B.)

THE KEY.

[THE ORIGINAL TITLE-PAGE.]

A KEY

TO THE STRUCTURE OF THE

ABORIGINAL LANGUAGE;

BEING AN ANALYSIS OF THE

PARTICLES USED AS AFFIXES, TO FORM

THE VARIOUS MODIFICATIONS OF THE VERBS;

SHEWING THE

ESSENTIAL POWERS, ABSTRACT ROOTS, AND OTHER PECULIARITIES
OF THE LANGUAGE

SPOKEN BY THE ABORIGINES

IN THE VICINITY OF HUNTER RIVER, LAKE MACQUARIE, ETC.,

NEW SOUTH WALES:

TOGETHER WITH COMPARISONS OF POLYNESIAN AND OTHER DIALECTS.

By L. E. THRELKELD.

SYDNEY:

THE BOOK FOR PRESENTATION AT THE ROYAL NATIONAL EXHIBITION, LONDON, 1851,
UNDER THE AUSPICES OF HIS ROYAL HIGHNESS PRINCE ALBERT.

PRINTED WITH COLONIAL TYPE CAST BY A. THOMPSON, AND BOUND WITH
COLONIAL MATERIAL.

PRINTED BY KEMP AND FAIRFAX,
LOWER GEORGE-STREET.

1850.

THE AUTHOR'S PREFACE.

This work was intended to be a paper for the Ethnological Society of London, to accompany some very interesting researches and observations made by a friend, relative to the customs and language of the aborigines of this colony. Through his making an inquiry respecting the meaning and difference of the words *ba* and *ka*, either of which can only be rendered into our language by the verb *to be* in some one or other of its modifications, I was led to the tracing out of the various meanings of many particles of a similar description, so that the work swelled to a size much larger than was anticipated. It was, therefore, thought advisable to print the work in its present form, especially as a public announcement asks for "A book, printed with colonial type, filled with colonial matter, and bound and ornamented with colonial materials," for presentation at the Royal National Exhibition, London, 1851.

The subject is purely colonial matter, namely, the language of the aborigines, now all but extinct; and the other conditions have been strictly attended to, as far as the circumstances of the colony would allow, the paper alone being of English manufacture. The author was the first to trace out the language of the aborigines, and to ascertain its natural rules; his "Australian Grammar" was published here in the year 1834, under the auspices of his late Majesty's Government, by the Society for Promoting Christian Knowledge, which generously carried the work through the press free of expense. His late Majesty King William IV. was graciously pleased to accept a copy of the book, and direct it to be placed in his library. Copies were likewise forwarded to several public institutions in England and elsewhere, where, it is presumed, they may still be found,—a testimony against the contemptible notion entertained by too many, who flatter themselves that they are of a higher order of created beings than the aborigines of this land, whom they represent as "mere baboons, having no language but that in common with the brutes!"; and who say, further, that the blacks have "an innate deficiency of intellect, and consequently are incapable of instruction." But if the glorious light of the blessed Gospel of God our Saviour had never shed its divine lustre around the British Crown, or never penetrated the hearts of the people with its vivifying power, the aborigines of Albion's shores might still have remained in the state described by the eloquent Cicero, in one of his epistles to his friend Atticus, the Roman orator; for he says, "Do not obtain your *slaves* from *Britain*, because they are *so stupid* and *utterly incapable of being taught* that they are *not fit* to form a part of the household of Atticus!"

Reminiscences of Biraban.

An aboriginal of this part of the colony was my almost daily companion for many years, and to his intelligence I am principally indebted for much of my knowledge respecting the structure of the language. Biraban was his native name, meaning 'an eagle-hawk,' but the English called him M'Gill. His likeness was taken at my residence, Lake Macquarie, in 1839, by Mr. Agate, and will be found in the "Narrative of the United States' Exploring Expedition," commanded by Charles Wilkes, U.S.N. The "Narrative," vol. II, page 253, says :—" At Mr. Threlkeld's, Mr. Hale saw M'Gill, who was reputed to be one of the most intelligent natives ; and his portrait was taken by Mr. Agate. His physiognomy was more agreeable than that of the other blacks, being less strongly marked with the peculiarities of his race ; he was about the middle size, of a dark-chocolate colour, with fine glossy black hair and whiskers, a good forehead, eyes not deeply set, a nose that might be described as aquiline, although depressed and broad at the base. It was very evident that M'Gill was accustomed to teach his native language, for when he was asked the name of anything he pronounced the word very distinctly, syllable by syllable, so that it was impossible to mistake it. Though he is acquainted with the doctrines of Christianity and all the comforts and advantages of civilization, it was impossible for him to overcome his attachment to the customs of his people, and he is always a leader in the corrobborees and other assemblies."

Both himself and Patty, his wife, were living evidences that there was no "innate deficiency of intellect" in either of them. He had been brought up from his childhood in the Military Barracks, Sydney, and he understood and spoke the English language well. He was much attached to us, and faithful to a chivalrous extreme. We never were under apprehensions of hostile attacks when M'Gill and his tribe encamped nigh our dwelling. A murderous black, named 'Bumble-foot,' from his infirmity, and 'Devil-devil,' from his propensities, had attempted to murder a European by chopping off the man's head with a tomahawk, and had nearly effected this; but the man recovered, and I had to appear at a Court of Justice as a witness; this displeased 'Bumble-foot,' and he avowed openly, in the usual manner, that he would slay me in the bush at the first opportunity ; this came to the ears of M'Gill, who immediately applied to me for the loan of a fowling-piece ' to go and shoot that fellow for his threat'; this was, of course, refused. M'Gill was once present with me at the Criminal Court, Sydney, assisting as interpreter, when he was closely examined by Judges Burton and Willis, in open Court, on the trial of an aboriginal for murder, 1834, in order that M'Gill might be sworn as interpreter in the case; but, though his answers were satisfactory to the general questions proposed to him by the Judges, yet, not understanding the nature of our oath in a Court of Justice, he could not be sworn. Patty, his wife, was pleasing in her person, "black but comely," kind and affectionate in her disposition, and evidenced as strong a faculty of shrewdness in the exercise of her intellectual powers over M'Gill as many of the fairer daughters of Eve, who, without appearing to trespass on the high prerogative of their acknowledged lords, manage their husbands according to their own sovereign will ; this might perhaps have arisen from the circumstance that M'Gill, once, when intoxicated, had shot at his wife, although he deeply deplored this when he became sober; the injury sustained was not much, but ever afterwards he treated her with much affection, which appeared to be reciprocal. It was a romantic scene to behold the happy pair, together

BIRABAN
(McGILL).

This Portrait of McGill was taken in Pencil by Mr Agate of the U. S. Exploring Expedition in 1839.

Reproduced by Heliotype.

with many others, on a moonlight night, under the blue canopy of heaven, preparing for the midnight ball to be held on the green sward, with no other covert than a growing bush, with none other blaze than that from the numerous fires kindled around the mystic ring in which to trip the light fantastic toe. Then they might be seen reciprocally rouging each other's cheek with pigment of their own preparing, and imparting fairness to their sable skin on the neck and forehead with the purest pipeclay, until their countenances beamed with rapturous delight at each other's charms. The cumbrous garments of the day were laid aside, and in all the majesty of nature they danced as Britons did in days of old.

On points of aboriginal honor M'Gill was exceedingly sensitive. "I must go," said he one day, "to stand my punishment as a man of honor, though I have done no wrong." The hostile message had been duly sent, and faithfully delivered by the seconds; one of these was an elderly female, who made her verbal communication with all the accustomed vituperation of daring challenge to the offended party; it was duly accepted; the weapons named, the cudgel, shield, and spear; the time was appointed, a certain day when the sun was one quarter high; the place, a plain in a certain well-known vicinity attached to our dwelling. Messengers were despatched to gather in the distant tribes, and on the mountain-tops were seen the signal-fires announcing their approach to witness the affair of honor. When the tribes had assembled, a mutual explanation ensued betwixt the parties, and the evening dance and supper of game peacefully terminated the business of the day. The course usually pursued when matters take a hostile form is this: the offending party is the first to stoop and offer his head for his antagonist to strike with his weapon; and, if not disabled or killed by the blow, he rises from his bending posture, shaking the streaming blood from his bushy hair, and then his opponent fairly and honorably bends forward his head, and presents it in return to receive his blow; and so this reciprocally continues until the assembled parties and the combatants themselves are satisfied. But should either strike dishonorably on the temple, thus showing an intention to kill, or in any other way than on the fairly offered cranium of his antagonist, a shower of well-directed spears would instantly be sent against the cowardly assailant, who should dare to be guilty of such a breach of the laws of honor. M'Gill informed me that formerly it was a custom amongst certain of the northern tribes that, when the first blow actually killed the person, the spectators would roast and eat the body of him who so nobly fell in the cause of honor, if he were a young man in good condition of body; as a matter of taste, M'Gill expressed himself dissatisfied with the custom, and stated that he thought it had fallen into desuetude, as it tended to no good purpose but to check the spirit of duelling.

Picturesque or alarming as in many instances these scenes were, all have for ever passed away, and the once numerous actors, who used to cause the woods to echo with their din, now lie mingled with the dust, save some few solitary beings who here and there still stalk abroad, soon, like their ancestors. to become as "a tale that is told."

THE KEY:

BEING

AN ANALYSIS OF THE PARTICLES USED AS AFFIXES.

AT the time when my "Australian Grammar" was published in Sydney, in the year 1834, circumstances did not allow me a sufficient opportunity to test the accuracy of the supposition that *every sound forms a root*, and, consequently, that every character which represents those sounds becomes, likewise, a *visible root*, so that every letter of the alphabet of the language is in reality *a root*, conveying an abstract idea of certain prominent powers which are essential to it.*

My present object is, therefore, to demonstrate the correctness of this supposition by explanation and illustration, and to place on record, along with the first attempt to form the aboriginal tongue into a written language, my last remarks on the speech of tribes, which, in this portion of Australia, will soon become extinct! Death has triumphed over these aborigines; for no rising generation remains to succeed them in their place, save that generation of whom it is written, "God shall enlarge Japheth, and he shall dwell in the tents of Shem."

In attempting to show the natural structure and peculiarities of the language, I hope that the philologist may here find some assistance in his researches, as well as any others who may be endeavouring to acquire a knowledge of barbarous languages, in which there are difficulties unsuspected, because they are not commonly found in the languages of Europe.

I cannot too strongly recommend to those who are endeavouring to attain a knowledge of the language of savage nations, the necessity of dismissing from the mind the trammels of European schools, and simply to follow out the natural rules of languages which have not been sophisticated by art. The almost sovereign contempt with which the aboriginal language of New South Wales has been treated in this colony, and the indifference shown toward the attempts to gain information on the subject, are not highly indicative of the love of science in this part of the globe; for this it is difficult to account, except on the ground of that universal engagement in so many various employments incidental to a new colony, where every individual must be dependent on his own exertions for the necessaries and the comforts of life.

---

* I hope that, in reprinting "The Key," I shall not be held as supporting this theory.—ED.

In tracing analogies with this aboriginal language, I find that the Indians of North America have a 'transitive conjugation,' which expresses the conjoined idea both of the persons acting and acted upon; 'the form has excited much astonishment and attracted the attention of the learned in different parts of the world.' The aborigines of this colony have a similar form of expression, as is explained fully in my "Australian Grammar";* this I have denominated therein 'active-transitive-reciprocal'; with the dual and the plural number, it constitutes 'the reciprocal modification'; as, bún-kil-lán bali, 'thou and I strike one another' reciprocally, or 'we-two fight'; which phrase would be thus analysed:—bún, the root, 'to strike'; -kil, the sign of the infinitive, 'to be, to exist'; -lán denotes the present time and that the action is reciprocal; bali is the dual pronoun 'we-two.' 'I fight with him' would be expressed by bún-kil-lán bali-noa, in which the noa means 'he'; v. page 17; but to say 'he and I fight another' would be bún-tan bali-noa.

The Cherokees use no distinct word for the articles *a* and *the*; but, when required, they use a word equivalent to the numeral *one*, and the demonstrative pronouns *this* and *that*, agreeably to the original use and nature of the words which we call articles; so likewise the aborigines of this colony; they too use wakäl for *a*, and for *the* the pronoun demonstrative both of thing and of place; as, unni, 'this here'; unnuġ, 'that there.' The Delaware dialect, according to Mr. Du Ponceau's notes in Elliot's Grammar, possesses an article wo *or* m', which is used for *a* and *the*, but not frequently, because these words are sufficiently understood without it. The Tahitians possess a definite article te, used for our *the*; but they express *a* by tehoe, 'one.' The American Indians have, in common with the Tahitians, an extra plural denoting *we*, including the party addressed. But this peculiarity the aborigines of New South Wales have not in their language, though they have, in common with the American Indians and the Tahitians, a dual of that kind; beside which, they have an extra dual denoting the object and the agent conjoined.

The Use of the Personal Pronouns.

The following are examples of the way in which these pronouns are used in our aboriginal dialect:—

Examples:—1. Pitál balinoa kakillán, 'we-two love one another'; *lit.*, 'he and I are joyful (*i.e.*, live peaceably) with one another.' 2. Búnnún binuġ, 'thou wilt beat him'; búnnún binoun, 'thou wilt beat her'; búnnún banuġ, 'I shall beat thee.'

---

* See pages 23 and 32 of this volume.—ED.

Analysis.—1. Pitúl* is 'joy, peace, delight'; bali is the dual pronoun, 'we two'; kakillán, which is the verb 'to be' in state of continuation, consists of three parts—ka, the root of the verb 'to be, to exist'; -ki, the sign of the infinitive, -lán, the sign of continuation at the present time.

The negative form of this example would be keawaran bal- pitál korien, 'we do not love one another,' *or* 'we do not agree the one with the other.' Here keawaran is the denial in the present tense, from keawai, the negative infinitive; the imperative negative is kora; as, pitál bán kora, 'do not be peaceable', where bán is the present tense of the verb 'to be doing'; the last word, korien, in the aboriginal sentence, is the negative adverb 'not'; thus, in this sentence there are *two* negatives, both of which are essential to express the negation.

2. The aboriginal phrase búnnúnbanuġ, 'I shall smite thee,' shows at once the similarity of construction of this Australian language with that of the Indians of America; for, though I may write it separately, as búnnún banuġ, because I know the words to be the verb and the conjoined dual pronoun, yet it is pronounced as one word, and would be so considered by a stranger. If 'determination' is to be expressed, the particle wal must be inserted; as, búnnún wal banuġ, 'I shall and will smite thee'; this would be thus analysed:—bún, the root of the verb 'to smite'; -nún, the particle denoting futurity; wal denotes determination; ba, is part of the *verbal* pronoun baġ, 'I', while the *personal* pronoun is ġatoa, 'I'; bi is the *verbal* pronoun 'thou'; -nuġ is the pronoun 'him' in the objective case; and the termination -noun in the next example is part of bounnoun, the feminine pronoun 'her,' in the objective case. Thus, our blacks carry out the dual beyond any known language in the world, whether ancient or modern; and they also complete their dual by carrying it out to the feminine in the conjoined dual case, which the American Indians do not in the " second personal form."

Nuġ is pronounced núġ when applied to a person, but nuġ when applied to a thing. So likewise, bún, 'to smite,' is accented, and is pronounced like the English word boon, 'a gift'; but bún, 'to permit to be,' is unaccented, and rhymes with the English word bun, 'a little cake.'

Our blacks say waita bali for 'I go with thee,' *or* 'we two go now together'; but waita baġ would mean 'I go by myself'; waita bali noa, 'he and I go together'; waita bali bountoa, 'she and I go together'; to say 'I go,' emphatically, meaning no other but myself, would be ġatoa waita uwánún; which would be construed thus:—ġatoa is the personal pronoun 'I'; waita

---

* *Pitul* in this language is the nearest word to express *love*.

is 'to go *or* depart'; uwánún is the future tense of the verb of motion, 'to come' *or* 'to go,' according as the word waita, 'to go,' *or* tanan, 'to come,' is attached to it. The Tahitians have a similarity of form in the expression haere, 'to come' *or* 'to go,' according as the particle mai *or* atu is attached; thus, haere mai, 'come,' haere atu, 'go.'

Mr. Elliot, in his Grammar, shows that the Massachusetts dialect has numerous conjugations of its verbs; and Mr. Reisberger has divided the Delaware language into eight conjugations of verbs. In my Grammar, also, I have traced out eight modifications of the Australian verb as spoken at Lake Macquarie; and its tenses are not confined simply to the past, present, and future, but have various modifications of each time; for instance, they have a present with the termination -án for the verb, and -lin for the participle; as, wiy-án bag, 'I speak' now; wiyel-lin, 'speaking' now; a definite past tense has the particle -kéún; as, wiya-kéún, 'have spoken' this morning; wiy-elli-kéún, 'have been speaking' this morning; and an indefinite past is wiya, 'told *or* spoke', and wiyelli-ela, 'spake,' both terminating in *a*. There are three varieties of the future; as, wiyelli kolag, 'to be about to speak'; where wiyelli is the bare form of the infinitive wiyelliko, 'to speak,' and kolag is 'towards'; then there is also a definite future; as, wiya-kin, 'shall *or* will speak' to-morrow morning; and besides, an indefinite future, wiyánún, 'shall *or* will speak' some time or other. These peculiar tenses are not noticed in the Indian Grammars, and, therefore, it is presumed that they are peculiar to the languages of the aborigines of this land.

The South Sea Islanders make no change in the endings of the verb; neither do the aborigines of Australia; for each tense-form of the verb may be made available to any person, according to the pronoun substituted. The change of person is seen only in the English translation, and not in the Australian word; thus, from wiyelliko, 'to speak,' 'to communicate by speech or sound'—applied to the speech of man, the crowing of a cock, or the striking of a clock—come wiyán bag, 'I speak'; wiyán bi, 'thou speakest'; wiyán noa, 'he speaks'; wiyán bountoa, 'she speaks'; wiyán gali, 'this speaks'; wiyán géen, 'we speak'; wiyán banug, 'I speak to thee'; wiyán bali bulun, 'we two speak to you two'; wiyellin bag, 'I am speaking'; wiyellin banug, 'I am speaking to thee'; wiyellán banug, 'I speak and continue to speak,' 'I tell'; wiyellán banug, 'I tell thee'; wiyellán bali, 'we two tell one another,' 'we converse'; wiyellilin bag, 'I am speaking and continue to speak,' 'I am talking'; wiyán gali-ko clock-ko, 'the clock strikes.' Muk-kă-ká tibbin-to wiyán, 'the cock crows'; here mukkăká is the nearest sound to express the cackling of fowls; literally the sentence is, 'the bird says mukkăká.'

The affixes used in the language of the aborigines of this colony show the nature of the verb, whether causative, declarative, or active; whether personal, instrumental, self-active, or locomotive ; and whether negative, affirmative, privative, apparent, or actual. It is only by a strict attention to the root-meaning of the affixes, that they can be properly applied to express the modified uses of the principal word to which they are joined, whether that principal be a verb, a proper name of a person or place, or a common substantive.

Illustrative Sentences,*
to show the force of the variations of the consonants in the suffix-forms of the verb.

Suffixes.

1. **-b-**-*illi-ko ;* m., *for the purpose of—the root-meaning of the verb.*

Examples :—1. Gatun tunbilliela· noa barun talokan, and he divided unto them the property.' 2. Túgun-billia nura, 'show yourselves.' 3. Kapirró wirri ban-billin, 'I am perishing with hunger.'

Analysis :—1. Gatun, 'and'; tun, the root of the verb 'to apportion, divide, separate, count '; -billiela, the past participle of billiko ; noa, 'he,' the verbal-nominative form of the pronoun ; barun, 'them'; talokan, ' property, goods.'

2. Túgun, as a verb, 'to show'; as a noun, 'a mark for a sign,' 'a chop on a tree to show the road.' .

3. Kapirri, 'hunger'; the *o* makes the word an instrumental case ; wirri is the root of the verb wirrilliko, 'for motion to act,' as an instrument ; ban, 'doing, acting '; -billin is the form of the present participle of that verb.

2. **-b-**-*ulli-ko ;* m., *to be doing effectively what the verb implies.*

Ex.:—Minnug ballin bi ? 'what object art thou effecting ? what are you doing ? what are you about ' ? Tetti ballin bag, 'I am dying.'

---
* I have here omitted twelve pages of "The Key"; in them our author sets forth his theory that the vowels and consonants of the suffix-forms of verbs and pronouns have each of them a determinate and essential meaning ; a portion of this theory appears in the headings of the twenty sections of "Illustrative Sentences" which now follow. These Illustrative Sentences I print for the sake of the examples of analysis which they contain ; and yet I do not think that that analysis is in every instance correct.—Ed.

-p-*ulli-ko;* m., *to be doing what the verb implies, without the idea of effect.*

Ex.:—Up-ullin baġ yirriġko wiyelliko, 'I am writing'; *lit.*, 'I am using the quill for-to * communicate, speak, say.'
Anal.:—Yirriġ, 'a quill'; yirriġko, 'the quill as an agent'; um-ullin baġ yirriġko pen kakilliko, 'I am making a pen'; *lit.*, ' I am causing the quill to become a pen.'

3. -k-*illi-ko;* m., *to become, to come to be in some state.*

Ex.:—1. Tetti kakulla noa, wonto ba yakita moron noa katéa kan, 'he was dead, whereas now he is alive again.' 2. Wunàl unni kakillin, 'this is summer season,' *or* ' this is-becoming (now) warm.'
Anal.:—1. Tetti, 'dead, *or* death'; kakulla, 'was' in that state; noa, the inseparable verbal pronoun 'he'; wontoba, 'whereas it is'; yakita, 'at this time'; moron, 'alive'; katéa-kan, 'one who exists again'; tetti kaba noa, 'he is actually dead'; *lit.*, ' he (died and so he) is in a state of death.'
2. Wunàl means 'warm'; the aborigines have no word for time in the abstract; unni, 'this'; kakillin, 'a state of being,' the present participle form of the verb kakilliko, *q.v.* Wunàl unni kakullin, 'the summer is now coming'; *lit.*, 'the warmth is of its own power becoming to be in the present state'; a reduplicate form of the participle kakullin, 'becoming,' is kakullilin, 'becoming and continuing to become'; *cf.* next paragraph for the difference in meaning between kakillan and kakullin.

4. -k-*ulli-ko;* m., *to bring into being any act done by one's own power.*

Ex.:—1. Bouġ-kulléùn yuna bo ta Piriwàl to, ġatun pai-kulléùn Thimon-kin, 'the Lord hath risen indeed, and hath appeared unto Simon.' Each of these acts is of the Lord's own power. 2. Punnàl ba poloġ-kulli-ġél, is 'the west'. 3. Por-kullitoara means 'that which is born'; *lit.*, 'that which has dropped itself of its own power,' 'that which has fallen of itself.' 4. Poai-kulléùn ba, ' as soon as it sprung up.' 5. Pai-kul-linùn bara ba, ' when they will shoot forth.'
Anal.:—2. Punnàl, 'the sun'; ba, 'is being', a verbal particle; poloġ, 'to sink'; -kulli, 'of his own power'; -ġél, 'the place of the action.' This phrase then means ' the place of the sun's sinking of his own power.'
4. Poai, 'to shoot up, to grow up, to spring up as grass'; -kulléùn, 'has... of its own power'; ba, equivalent to ' when.'
5. Pai, 'appear'; -kullinùn, 'will of their own power'; bara, 'they'; ba, equivalent to ' when.'

---

* Occasionally I still allow this phrase to stand.—See note, page 24.—Ed.

5. **-l-iko;** m., *for the purpose of initiating the action of the verb.*

Ex :—Tetti kolaġ baġ, 'I am about to die'; waita kolaġ baġ, 'I am about to depart'; piriwȧl kolaġ noa, 'he is about to be king'; worowai kolaġ bara, 'they are about to fight'; tanan baġ wiyelliko, 'I come to speak,' 'I am come for the purpose of speaking'; tanan baġ wiya-uwil koa banuġ, 'I am come in order to speak to thee,' 'I am come that I may speak to thee'; wiya-uwil koa banuġ, 'I wish to speak to thee'; ġurrulli ta, 'it is the act of hearing'; ġurrulliko, 'for the purpose of the act of hearing'; 'to hear, to hearken.'

6. **-m-**illi-ko; m., *for the purpose of the initiation of the act of causation.*

Ex.:—Kai, umillia tia, 'come and help me'; *lit.*, 'come exercise causative power on me'; umillia bi tia, 'help thou me, assist me'; *i.e.*, 'cause the exercise of power to me.'

7. **-m-**ulli-ko; m., *for causation and effective power.*

Ex.:—Tariġ ka-mulliko, 'to mix'; *lit.*, 'for-to cause to be across and across'; ġurra-mulla bon, 'cause him to hear *or* know'; ka-mullala noa yantin-biruġ umulli-biruġ, 'he rested from all the work'; *lit.*, 'he caused himself to be from all, from the act of causation and effective power.' Uma noa yantin tara, 'he made all things'; umȧn baġ unni, 'I make this'; nu-mulliko, 'to make a personal effort, to try, to attempt'; pirral-mulla bon, 'urge him, constrain him'; *lit.*, 'be hard at him'; pirral umulla bon, 'make him hard, cause him to be hard'; pirriral-mullin bon, 'strengthening him'; na-mȯnbilliko tia umulla, 'cause me to be permitted to see'; kȧmȯnbilla bin nakilliko, 'let it be permitted to cause thee to see'; equivalent to, 'receive thy sight.'

8. **-n;** m., *present time.*

Ex.—Unni, 'this' present; unnoa, 'that' present; untoa, 'that other' present; unnuġ, 'that,' as an object, present there; unti, 'this present place' here; unta, 'that place' spoken of; pitȧl kȧnȯn bi, 'thou wilt be joyful'; pitȧl banȯn bi, 'thou wilt rejoice.'

9. **-g-**ulli-ko; m., *for one to act with effective power.*

Ex.—Buġ-buġ-gulla, 'kiss,' that is, 'effect a kiss'; buġ-buġ-kȧmȯnbilla bon, 'let him kiss'; buġ-buġ gatoa,' it is I who kiss'; buġ-buġ-gan baġ, 'I kiss'; buġ-buġ-gatoara, 'that which is kissed'; tetti buġ-gulliko, 'to effect death by personal power'; 'to kill'; tetti buġ-ga bon, 'he is killed'; *lit.*, 'some person hath killed him'; tetti buġ-ga bon baġ, 'I have killed him.'

10. **-p-*illi-ko*;** m., *to act, excluding the idea of causation.*

Ex.—Up-illiko, 'to exercise personal power,' without causation; up-ai-ġa, 'to exercise personal power,' without completion; pai-pilliko, 'to seem,' 'to appear'; pai-pilliko maraito, 'for the spirit to appear'; pai-péa uoa Eliath, 'Elias he appeared'; pai-péa bon aġelo, 'an angel appeared to him.'

11. **-p-*ulli-ko*;** m., *to exercise power, but excluding the idea of effect.*

Ex.—1. Up-ulliko, 'to exercise personal power,' exclusive of effect; upán baġ unni, 'I do this'; upán baġ ġali-ko, 'I use this'; upullin baġ ġali-ko broom-ko, 'I am sweeping with the broom'; *lit.*, 'I am exercising personal power with the broom,' exclusive of effect; in ġali-ko broom-ko upullin murráráġ, 'the broom is sweeping well,' the broom is the instrumental agent; upullin baġ ġatoa-bo kipai-to, 'I am anointing myself with ointment'; *lit.*, 'I am doing myself with grease,' *or* 'I am greasing myself.' 2. Upulla binoun kopurró konéin kakilliko, 'paint her with red to be pretty.' 3. Konéin ta upatoara bountoa, 'she is prettily done'; *lit.*, 'she is pretty that which is done.' 4. Kabo-kabo ġalitin upatoarin kopurrin, 'stay, stay, on account of the painting red.'

Anal.:—2. Upulla, the imperative, 'do'; binoun, the conjoined dual pronoun, 'thou-her'; kopurró, 'red,' with the instrumental sign *o* affixed; konéin, 'pretty'; kakilliko, the verb 'to be,' 'for the purpose of being.' The sentence then means, 'do thou her with red, that she may be pretty.'

3. Konéin ta, 'it is pretty'; upatoara is a compound of the verb, and means 'that which is done'; bountoa, the emphatic personal pronoun, 'she it is who,' 'she who' is emphatically so.

4. Kabo-kabo, equivalent to 'stay'; ġali-tin and the two words following it are all in the ablative case and mean, 'on account of this, on account of the doing, on account of the red.'

12. **-r;** m., *negation.*

Ex.—Murráráġ ta unni, 'this is good'; keawai, murráráġ korien, 'no, it is not good'; kipai ta unni, 'this is actually fat'; tararan, 'it is not'; this is used as the negation of a thing, but not of a quality. Keawaran baġ murráráġ korien, 'I am not comfortable.'

Anal.:—Keawaran, the present tense of the verb 'to be,' in the state of negation; baġ, the verbal pronoun 'I'; murráráġ 'good'; korien, the aorist of negation of the verb 'to be not.' The sentence thus means, 'I am not in a state of being good.' The two negatives here are essential and govern one another; they do not destroy each other, as in English; this arises from the very nature of the language, which can express actuality, negation of actuality, and negation absolutely;

hence the variety of the forms of verbs 'to be'; for instance, natán baġ means 'I see'; na korien baġ, 'I see not'; nakulla baġ, 'I saw'; na pa korien baġ, 'I saw not.' This last cannot be written nakulla korien baġ, 'I saw not,' because the -kulla would affirm that the agent actually of his own power did whatsoever the root affirms; and the root-form na implies that the thing is actually seen, while the -kulla added makes the meaning to be that it presents itself before you, and you must see it, unless you are blind or do not exercise the faculty of sight; hence the privative affix, pa, must be used instead, to show that, although the object spoken of was there, I could not see it, because it was not presented to my sight.

Ex.—Yanoa, na-mai-ġa yikora. This is a peculiar but common phraseology throughout all verbs, and is hardly translateable into English; the nearest phrase would be ' do not be seeing and yet perceive not,' *or* ' do not in your manner be looking without causing yourself to exercise your faculty of sight.' In this there is an affirmation of the abstract action performed by the agent, but a suspension of effect; the whole is something similar to the phrase ' you look but you will not see', that is, 'you are determined not to see.' But, on the other hand, yanoa, naki yikora means 'do not look'; yanoa, nakilli-ban yikora, 'do not thou be looking'; and yari bi nanún, 'thou must not look'; -nùn is the sign of the future tense, for prohibition requires the future.

Gan ke unnoa kùri? 'who is that man'? to this, ġannug? is the answer, if you do not know the person; *lit.*, 'whom'? a question in reply. To express 'I do not know,' would be ġurra korien baġ; but this would really mean 'I do not know what is said,' *or* 'I do not perceive by the ear what is spoken.' To know personally anyone is ġimilli; thus, ġimilli bon baġ, 'I know him personally'; keawaran baġ nurun ġimilli korien, 'I personally know you not.' To deny that you have the knowledge of a person whom you really do know is expressed by the peculiar form ġan? 'who'? thus ġan-bulliko means 'to be who-ing' interrogatively, that is, asking who the person is when he is already known, with the intention of denying a knowledge of the person. Wonto ba niuwoa ġan-bullinùn tia emmouġ mikan-ta kùri-ka, ġan-bullinùn wal bon mikan-ta aġelo-ka Eloi-koba-ka; 'whereas he who will be 'who-ing' of me in the presence of men, certainly I will be 'who-ing' of him in the presence of angels belonging to Eloi,' *i.e.*, God; this is an aboriginal translation of the words "But he that denieth me before men, shall be denied before the angels of God." Emmouġ means 'concerning me,' whilst tia means 'me,' the object; the passive form of the English verb is always expressed by the active form of the Australian.

13. -r-*illi-ko;* m., *for instrumentality to be in some act.*

Ex.—Gatun wélkorinùn wal bara bon, ġatun tetti wal bon wirrinùn, 'and they shall scourge him and put him to death.'

Anal.—Gatun, 'and'; wélkorinùn, 'will instrumentally wale' him. The wél is from the English word wale, 'a mark in the flesh'; -ko is the usual affix of agency; -ri-nùn is the future tense of instrumental action; wal is the certainty thereof; bara, 'they'; bon, 'him'; tetti, 'death'; wirrinùn, the future tense of instrumental violence; *cf.* wirrin wibbi-ko, the 'wind moves,' *sc.*, it.

14. -r-*ulli-ko;* m., *for instrumentality to act of itself.*

Ex.—1. Turuliin tia topiġ-ko, 'the mosquito is stinging, piercing me'; tura bon warai-to, 'the spear speared, pierced, him'; turànùn banuġ lancet-o, 'I will pierce thee with the lancet'; turànùn, 'will pierce'; banuġ, conjoined dual case, 'I-thee'; lancet-o, the English word 'lancet' with *o* the affix of agency. 2. Niuwoa ba ġurréuġ-kan ġurrulliko, ġurrabùnbilla bon, 'he who hath ears to hear, let him hear.' Here the ear is the instrument that perceives of its own power.

Anal.—2. Niuwoa, the emphatic personal pronoun, 'he'; ba, a particle; ġurréuġ, 'the ear'; -kan, a personal particle; ġurréuġkan therefore means 'a person who is eared, who has ears'; ġurrabùnbilla, the imperative, 'permit to hear'; bon, 'him'; ġurrulliko, 'to hear'.

15. -t-*illi-ko;* m., *for the thing to act, as a verbal noun.*

Ex.—Poai-bùntinùn koiwon to, 'the rain will cause it to grow'.

Anal.—Poai, the bare form of the verb 'to grow'; bùn, is the active permissive form of the verb ' to suffer *or* permit the act,' 'to let actively'; -tinùn, the future-tense form of the verb; koiwon, 'rain'; -to, an affix, to show that the word to which it is affixed is the agent that purposes to act. In the sentence koiwon-to ba tin, 'it rains,' the ba is the aorist of the verb 'to be doing' some act; tin, is the present tense of tilliko, and when used as a preposition means 'from, on account of it'; *e.g.*, tetti-tin, 'on account of death'; ġali-tin, 'on account of this'; but 'from, *i.e.*, out of,' is biruġ; as, Thydney-biruġ, 'from Sydney'; London-biruġ, ' from London '.

16. -t-*elli-ko*; m., *to indicate itself, as a verbal noun.*

Ex.:—1. Yantin bara piriwàl bùntelliko, 'for all who exalt themselves.' 2. Moron ta katéa-kànùn tetti kabiruġ, ' the resurrection from the dead.'

Anal.:—1. Yantin, 'all'; bara, 'they'; piriwàl, 'chief'; bùn, 'topermit' actively; telliko, 'for it to be' as indicated. Moron, 'life'; ta, 'it is'; ka, 'is'; -téa, the past tense of tolliko, 'it actually was' as indicated; ká-nún, 'will be' in the state mentioned; tetti, 'death'; ka, 'is'; biruġ, 'from, out of.' The sentence thus means 'the future becoming alive again from the dead'; *cf.* yanoa, tetti katéa kûn, 'let be, lest it become dead'; yanoa, tetti burréa kûn, 'let be, lest it die.' Yanoa is prohibitory of the manner of being.

17. -w-*illi-ko*; m., *to be in motion to; to tend towards; to incline towards.*

Ex.:—U wil koa baġ, 'I wish to move, I tend towards, I incline towards'; ta-uwil koa baġ, 'I wish to eat'; ta is from ta-killiko, 'for-to eat'; waita wa-uwil koa baġ, 'I now wish to depart'; 'I intend to depart'; tanan bi wolla waita, koa baġ uwa-uwil, 'I wish to go'; *lit.*, 'approach thou *or* come, in order that I may depart'; wiya-uwil koa bon baġ, 'I wish to tell him'; wiya is from wiyelliko, 'to speak, to utter a sound,' &c.

18. -wir-*rilli-ko*; m., *to act with instrumental motion; as, to knock with anything; to whip or flog with anything; to smite with the fist; to stir with a stick; to do any act of motion by any instrumental means.*

Ex.:—Wirrilléûn bara wapara, 'they smote their breasts'; wirrilliâuûn wirrillikanné-to, 'will sweep with the sweeper', 'will swab with a swab'; *lit.*, 'will knock away with that which knocks away'; because, when the blacks sweep, they knock the ground with boughs, and so remove the rubbish.

19. -w-*olli-ko*; m., *to act and move of purpose.*

Ex.:—Uwolliko, 'to come, to go, to move away'; *lit.*, 'to be in a state of motion and action,' with power of purpose to effect change of place; waita wâ-nûn baġ England kolaġ, 'I will depart and will go to England'; tanan noa uwollin England kabiruġ, 'he approaches coming from England'; 'he is coming from England'; uwéa kânûn baġ, 'I will come again' (tanan, understood); uwéa kânûn baġ, 'I will go again' (waita, understood); yanoa, uwa yikora, 'do not go'; uwolli ban kora, 'do not be moving away,' *sc.*, hither or thither.

20. -y-*elli-ko*; m., *to be in a certain manner of action.*

Ex.:—1. Gakoiyelliko, 'to act in a certain manner of personification'; 'to feign to be another person'; ġakoiyellikan, 'one who feigns to be another'; 'a spy, a deceiver'; wonta noa ba ġurra ġakoiya barunba, 'but he perceived their craftiness'; *lit.*, 'whereas he knew their deception,' their feigning to be just men; yanti bi wiyella, 'thou shalt say thus', in this manner; yanti baġ wiya, 'I said so'; yakoai bin wiyan, 'how, *i.e.*, in what manner, is it told to thee'? ġiakai baġ wiya bon yanti, 'this is that which I actually told him'; *lit.*, 'thus I told him thus'; mupai kaiyelliko, 'to be silent'; *lit.*, 'for-to be in manner dumb'; 'to be really dumb' would be mupai-kan, 'one who is dumb.'

Ex.:—2. Kaiyelléûn clock-ko wiyelli-biruġ, 'the clock has ceased to strike'; *lit.*, 'the clock has' been and continues in the state and manner of being now 'ceased' from a certain manner of motion, *i.e.*, 'from talking'; wiyelli-kan, 'one who speaks'; wiyai-yé, 'a talker,' one in the habit of talking, one whose manner is to continue to speak; wiyelliko, 'to utter a sound'; 'to speak'; wiya-bûnbilliko, 'to permit to speak'; wiyai-yelliko, 'to say on, to reply, to answer'; wiya-yimulliko, 'to make accusation, to accuse'; wiya-pai-yelliko, 'to demand'; wiyella bon, 'speak to him'; wiyellin noa, 'he is talking'; wiyellán bali, 'we two are conversing'; wiyán baġ, 'I speak'; wiyán clock-ko, 'the clock strikes'; wiya, 'say'; this is used to ask a person if he will be or do; *e.g.*, wiya, bali wiyellinûn? 'say, shall we two converse?'

The Formation of Words.

Yarr is a word which the aborigines now use in imitation of the sound made by a saw in sawing; with the verbal formative-affix -bulliko, it becomes yarr-bulliko, 'to be in the act of causing by its own act the sound of yarr'; or, in English, 'to saw.' Yaġ is another introduced word, formed from the imitation of the sound of the sharpening of a saw.

From these roots come the following derivatives:—Yarr-bulliko, 'to saw'; yarr-bulli kolaġ, 'to be about to saw'; yarr-bulli korien, 'not to saw'; yarr-bulli yikora, 'saw not'; yarr-bulli ban kora, 'be not sawing'; yarr-bulli-kan, 'one who does sawing'; 'a sawyer'; yarr-bulli-kanné, 'that which saws'; 'a saw'; yarr-bulli-ġél, 'the sawing-place'; 'a saw-pit'; yarr-ba-toara, 'that which is sawn'; 'a plank'; yarr-ba-uwa, 'saw' (optative), 'do saw'; yarr-bulla, 'saw (mandatory), 'do saw'; yarr-bulli-buġ-gulla, 'compel to saw'; yarr-bulli-buġ-gulliko, 'to compel to saw'; this last form may undergo all the changes given above for yarr-bulliko; and so of every verb in the infinitive form.

Yaġ-ko-bulliko, 'to sharpen a saw'; yaġ-ko-bulli-ta, 'the sharpening of the saw'; yaġ-ko-bulli-kan, 'one who sharpens the saw'; yaġ-ko-bulli-kanné, 'that which sharpens the saw'; 'a file'; and so on.

[The common root-words of the language also give forth verbal derivatives in a similar way. If we take the verb 'to strike' as an example, the formatives and their meanings may be arranged thus, a verbal suffix always intervening between the root and the formative :—

	Root + Suff. + Formative.			Meaning.
1.	,,	,,	yé	a continual striker.
2.	,,	,,	to-ara	the person or thing that is struck.
3.	,,	,,	kán	the person who strikes.
4.	,,	,,	kan-né	the thing which strikes.
5.	,,	,,	to	the action, as an agent.
6.	,,	,,	ta	the action, as a subject.
7.	,,	,,	ġél	the place where the action is done.

EXAMPLES.

Root.—Bún, 'strike.'

1. Bún-ki-yé, 'a fighting man.'
2. Bún-to-ara, 'a wounded man.'
3. Bún-killi-kán, 'a striker.'
4. Bún-killi-kan-né, 'a cudgel.'
5. Bún-killi-to, 'the stroke.'
6. Bún-killi-ta, 'the striking.'
7. Bún-killi-ġél, 'a pugilistic ring.'

Root.—Um-a, 'make.'

1. Um-ai-yé, 'a tradesman.'
2. Um-ulli-to-ara, 'anything made.'
3. Um-ulli-kán, 'a worker.'
4. Um-ulli-kan-né, 'a tool.'
5. Um-ulli-to, 'the work.'
6. Um-ulli-ta, 'the working.'
7. Um-ulli-ġél, 'a workshop.'

Root—Up-a, 'do, use in action.'

1. Up-ai-yé, 'a cobbler, a mason,' &c.
2. Up-ulli-to-ara, 'a piece of work.'
3. Up-ulli-kán, 'a worker.'
4. Up-ulli-kan-né, 'a spade, an awl.'
5. Up-ulli-to, 'the operation.'
6. Up-ulli-ta, 'the operating.'
7. Up-ulli-ġél, 'a operating-room.'

The difference in the use of the fifth and sixth forms may be illustrated by such sentences in English, as,—The *stroke* killed him; the *striking* of the iron heats it; the *work* was done, but the *working* of the machine went on; the *operation* did no harm, for the *operating* was in skilful hands.]

Analysis of the name Biraban.

1. Declension of 'Biraban,' as a common noun.

The word is formed from bira, the cry of the bird which we call the 'eagle-hawk.' The -ban postfixed denotes the one who does the action. As applied to M'Gill, the name may have been given to him from some circumstance in his infancy, perhaps his infantile cry.*

Nom. 1. Konéin ta biraban ta, 'the hawk is pretty.'
    2. Biraban to wiyan, 'the hawk cries,' *lit.*, speaks.
Gen. Yarro unni biraban koba, 'this egg is the hawk's.'
Dat. 1. Unni ta biraban ko takilliko, 'this is for the hawk to eat.'
    2. Waita baġ biraban tako, 'I depart to the hawk,' *i.e.*, to where the hawk is.
Acc. Tura bon biraban unnuġ, 'spear him, the hawk there.'
Voc. Ala *or* ola biraban! 'O hawk'!
Abl. 1. Minariġ tin tetti noa? biraban tin; 'from what cause is he dead'? 'from the hawk,' as a cause.
    2. Tul-bulléùn noa tibbin biraban ka tabiruġ, 'he, the bird, hath escaped from the hawk.'
    3. Buloara bula biraban toa, 'the two are in company with the hawk.'
    4. Tibbin ta biraban taba, 'the bird is with the hawk.'
    5. Wonnuġ ke noa kàtan? biraban kinba, 'where does he exist'? 'at the hawk's place.'

Minariġ unnoa tibbin? 'what is that bird'? tibbin ta unnoa bukka-kan, 'it is a savage bird that.'
Yakoai unnoa ta yitàra wiyá? 'how is that such-a-one spoken'? equivalent to 'what is its name'? ġiakai unnoa yitàra biraban wiyá, 'this way, that such-a-one is spoken *or* called biraban.'
Minariġ tin yitàra biraban wiyá? 'from-what-cause is such-a-one spoken *or* called biraban'? ġali tin wiyelli tin bira-bira tin, 'from this, from speaking, from bira-bira'; *i.e.*, because he says 'bira.'

2. Declension of 'Biraban,' as a proper name.

Nom. 1. Gan ke bi? ġatoa Biraban, 'who art thou'? 'it is I, Biraban'; yakoai bi yitàra wiyá? ġiakai baġ yitàra Biraban, 'in what manner art thou such-a-one spoken'? 'thus am I such-a-one, Biraban,' *sc.*, called.

---

* 'Eagle-hawk' may have been his *totem* or family name; or, as our blackfellows name their children from some trivial incident at the time of birth, he may have been called Biraban, because an 'eagle-hawk' was seen or heard then.—Ed.

2. Ganto bon tura? Biraban to bon tura, 'who did spear him'? 'Biraban speared him.'
Gen. Gan-úmba unni wonnai? Biraban-úmba unni wonnai, 'whose child is this'? 'Biraban's, this child.'
Dat. 1. Gannuġ unni? Birabannuġ, 'for whom this'? (*i.e.*, who is to have this?) 'for Biraban' to have personally or to use.
2. Kurrilla unni Biraban kinko, ' carry this to Biraban,' locally.
Acc. Gannuġ tura? Birabannuġ, 'whom speared'? (meaning, who is speared?) 'Biraban.'
Voc. Ala Biraban ġurrulla! 'O Biraban, hearken.'
Abl. 1. Gan kai kaokillai bara? Biraban kai, 'concerning whom are they quarrelling'? 'about Biraban.'
2. Wonta biruġ bi? Biraban kabiruġ, 'whence dost thou come'? 'from Biraban.'
3. Gan katoa bountoa? Biraban katoa, 'with whom is she'? ' with Biraban'; that is, in company with him.
4. Gan kinba? Biraban kinba, ' with whom is she'? ' with Biraban '; that is, living with him.
Wontakál noa Biraban? Mulubinbakál, ' of what place is he, Biraban'? ' Of Newcastle.'*
Wontakàlin bountoa Patty? Mulubinbakálin, 'of what place is she, Patty'? 'Of Newcastle.'

Selections from the Scriptures.†

WINTA 1.

1. Yantin kokera wittima tarai to kuri ko; wonto ba noa yantin wittima, Eloi ta noa.—Heb., iii. 4.
2. Wakál noa Eloi ta.—Gal., iii. 20.
3. Eloi ta pitál noa.—1 John, iv. 8. Eloi ta marai noa.—John, iv. 24.
4. Gearunba Eloi ta winullikan koiyuġkan.—Heb., xii. 29.
5. Unnuġ ta noa wakál bo ta Eloi ta.—Mark, xii. 32.

---

* See page 18 of this volume.
† As the suffix-forms of the nouns, verbs, and other parts of speech have been fully shown in the previous part of this volume by the use of hyphens, I do not think it so necessary now to continue that aid. All postpositions will now be detached from their nouns and pronouns, and every compound postposition will be printed as one word. Those suffix particles which are used as enclitics, and the inseparable case-endings, will be attached to their words. The tense-forms of the verbs will be printed as shown on pages 28 to 41, but without the use of the hyphens. In the Analysis of the selections which now follow, the hyphens are sometimes retained to show the composition of the words.—ED.

SELECTIONS FROM THE SCRIPTURES.

6. Keawai wal wakál tarai ta, murrárag ta wakál bo ta Eloi ta.—Luke, xviii. 19.

7. Gatun gearunba wakál bo ta Eloi ta, Biyugbai ta, gikoug kai yantin ta, gatun géen gikoug kinba; gatun wakál bo ta Piriwál, Iéthu Kritht, gikoug kinbirug yantin ta, gatun géen gikoug kinbirug.—1 Cor., viii. 6.

WINTA 2.

8. Eloi ta kaibug noa; gatun keawai wal gikoug kinba tokoi korien.—1 John, i. 5.
9. Yuna bo ta, keawai wal taraito kúriko na pa korien bon, Eloinug.—1 John, iv. 12.
10. Túgumbilléun noa Eloi puttárakan.—1 Tim., iii. 16.
11. Niuwara noa Eloi ta kátan yantin ta purreág ka yarakai ko.—Psalm, vii. 11.
12. Kauwálkan noa Eloi ta, waréa ta gearunba búlbúl, gatun gurrán noa yantin minnugbo minnugbo.—1 John, iii. 20.
13. Kaiyukan noa Eloito yantin ko minnugbo minnugbo ko.—Matt., xix. 26.

WINTA 3.

1. Eloi ta Piriwál ta noa.—Psalm, cxviii. 27.
2. Iéthu Kritht Piriwál ta noa yantin koba.—Acts, x. 36.
3. Piriwálto Eloi ta gearunba wakál bo ta Piriwál ta.—Mark, xii. 29.
4. Gurrulla nura yanti Piriwál ta noa Eloi ta noa; niuwoa ta gearun uma, keawai wal géenbo umulli pa; géen ta gikoumba kúri, gatun ćipu takilligél koba gikoumba.—Psalm, c. 3.
5. Piriwál gintoa ta Eloi ta, gintoa ta moroko umá, gatun purrai, gatun wombul, gatun yantin gali koba.—Acts, iv. 24.
6. Piriwál ta noa Eloi kauwálkan ta.—Psalm, xcv. 3.
7. Piriwál ta noa murrárag ta.—Psalm, c. 5.
8. Guraki noa Eloi ta Piriwál ta, upin noa umulli tin gearunba tin.—1 Sam. ii., 3.

WINTA 4.

9. Piriwál ta noa Eloi tuloakan ta, niuwoa ta Eloi moron kakillikan ta, gatun Piriwál kauwál yanti katai kakilliko; pululpulul wal purrai kánún bukka tin gikoumba tin, gatun yantin bara konara kaiyu korien wal bara kátan niuwarin gikoumba tin.—Jerem. x. 10.
10. Bapai ta ba noa Piriwál kátan barun yantin ko wiyan bon ba.—Psalm, cxlv. 18.
11. Kalog ka ba noa Piriwál kakillin barun kai yarakai tin.—Prov., xv. 29.
12. Piriwál ta noa wirrillikan ta emmoumba; keawai wal bag mirrál kánún.—Psalm, xxiii. 1.
13. Gurrárakan noa Piriwál kauwál kátan, gatun gurráramulli kan noa.—James, v. 11.

WINTA 5.

1. Unnuġ ġoro ta kakilli wokka kaba moroko kaba, Biyuġbai ta, Wiyellikan ta, ġatun Marai ta yirriyirri laġ; ġatun unni ta ġoro ta wakál bo ta.—1 John, v. 7.
2. Biyuġbaito yuka bon yinal miromullikan noa kakilliko, yantin purrai ko.—1 John, iv. 14.
3. Eloito noa pitál ma kauwál yantiu kúri, ġukulla ta noa wakál bo ta yinal ġikoumba, ġali ko yantinto ba ġurran ġikouġ kin, keawai wal bara tetti kánún, kulla wal yanti katai barunba kakillinún moron.—John, iii. 16.
4. Pulli ta noa Eloito upéa barun Ithárachúmba, wiyelliliko pitálmulliko Iéthu ko Kritht to; niuwoa bo Piriwál kátan yautin ko.—Acts, x. 36.
5. Iéthu Kritht yinal noa Biyuġbai koba.—2 John, 3.
6. Guarunba kátan Wiyellikan, Iéthu Kritht, Biyuġbai toa ba kátan.—1 John, ii. 1.

WINTA 6.

7. Eloi ta Marai noa.—John, iv. 24.
8. Piriwál ta unnoa ta Marai.—2 Cor., iii. 17.
9. Maraito yirriyirri laġ ko wiyánún wal nurun.—Luke, xii. 12.
10. Murrin nurunba kokera yirriyirri ta Marai yirriyirri laġ koba.—1 Cor., vi. 19.
11. Wakálla murrin, ġatun wakálla Marai, yanti nurun wiya wakálla kotulli ta nurunba wiyatoara; wakálla Piriwál, wakálla ġurrulli ko, wakálla kurrimulli ko; wakálla Eloi ta Biyuġbai ta yantiu koba; wokka kaba noa yantiu ko, ġatun noa yantiu koa, ġatun murruġ kaba nurun kinba.—Ephes., iv. 4, 5, 6.
12. Yantiu barun yemmamáu Marai to Eloi koba ko, wonnai ta bara Eloi koba.—Rom., viii. 14.
13. Niuwara buġ-ga kora bon Marai yirriyirri laġ Eloi koba.—Ephes., iv. 30.
14. Ganto ba yarakai wiyánún ġikouġ yinal kúri koba, kámúnbinún wal bon; wonto noa ba yarakai wiyánún ġikouġ Marai yirriyirri laġ, keawai wal bon kámúnbinún.—Luke, xii. 10.

WINTA 7.

Luke, ii. 9–14.

9. Gatun noa aġelo Yehóa-úmba tanan uwa barun kin, ġatun killaburra Yehóa-úmba kakulla barun katoa; kinta ġaiya bara takulla.
10. Gatun noa aġeloko wiya barun, Kinta kora; kulla nurun baġ wiyan totóġ murráraġkakillıko pitál ko, kakilliko yantiu ko kúri ko.

SELECTIONS FROM THE SCRIPTURES. 107

11. Kulla nurunba porkulléŭn unni purreáġ kokerá Dabidúmba ka, Golomullikan ta, noa Kritht ta Piriwál ta.
12. Gatun unni túga kánùn nurunba; nanùn nura boboġuuġ ġımatoara kirrikin taba, kakillin ba takilliġél laba.
13. Gatun tanoa-kal-bo paipéa konara morokokúl ġikouġ katoa aġelo katoa, murráráġ wiyellin bon Eloinuġ, ġiakai,
14. Wiyabúnbilla bon murráráġ Eloinuġ wokka kaba moroko kaba, ġatun kámúnbilla pitál purrai tako, murráráġ umatoara.

WINTA 8.

1. Eloito noa ġurrára ma korien barun aġelo yarakai umullikan, wonto ba wareka noa barun barau koiyuġ kako, tartaro kako.—2 Peter, ii. 4.
2. Wiyatoara ta yantin kùri ko waká:la tetti bulliko, ġatun yukita ġaiya ġurrulli ko.—Heb., ix. 27.
3. Yakoaikan baġ moron kánùn ? Gurrulla bou Piriwálnuġ Iéthunuġ Krithtnuġ, moron ġaiya bi kánùn.—Acts, xvi. 30, 31.
4. Gatun kirrikin ta temple kako, yiir-kulléùn bulwa koa wakka kabiruġ unta ko barau tako.—Mark, xv. 38.

The preceding eight Wintas or 'Portions,' are taken from an "Australian Spelling Book, in the Language spoken by the Aborigines," published by the author in 1826. In the following translation, the Section figures are those of the paragraphs in the Wintas, and the words, as they become translated and explained, are not again referred to.

Analysis of the foregoing Wintas.

WINTA 1.—PART 1.

Section 1.

Winta, 'a part, a portion.'
Eloi, 'God,' a word taken from Elohim, is introduced into the language of the aborigines, because Koin, the name of the being whom they dread, is a word of an equivocal character.*
Yantin, 'all, every,' is singular or plural, according to the number of the noun or pronoun used with it.
Kokera, 'a covert, shelter, habitation, hut, house, palace, temple.'
Wittima, 'built'; hence wittimulliko, 'to build' in any way; to prepare a place for habitation by removing obstacles; to put up a shelter of bushes or bark.

---
* See page 47.—Ed.

Tarai, 'some one, another, other', is singular; but tara, 'others,' is plural.

Taraito is tarai, with the particle of agency postfixed.

Kùri, 'man, men,' according to the singular or plural idea expressed or understood in the context.

Kùriko is kùri, with the particle of agency postfixed.

Wonto ba, 'whereas,' a compound phrase; from won, 'where'? the interrogative adverb of place.

Wonto ba-ba, 'is as'; the ba is a particle which verbalizes the word to which it is affixed.

Noa, the inseparable verbal pronoun, 'he'; the separable emphatic pronoun 'he' is niuwoa.

Eloi ta; for Eloi, see above; ta is the substantive verb, 'it is actually'; this phrase affirms that it is God who is the agent.

Section 2.

Wakàl, 'one'; buloara, 'two'; goro, 'three'; wara, 'four'; beyond which the aborigines have no word to express higher numbers. For 'five' they hold up one hand and say yantin, 'all,' i.e., all the five fingers; or both hands with a part of the fingers up to describe the numbers 6, 7, 8, 9; for 10 they hold all the fingers up and say yantin; or they double both hands and say kauwàl-kauwàl, a 'great many,' and repeat the same as often as required, to give some idea of the greatness of the number.

Section 3.

Pitàl, 'joy, peace, gladness, happiness, love.'

Marai, 'spirit'; not the 'ghost' of a departed person, which is mamuya.

Section 4.

Gearun, 'us'; géen, 'we'; gearunba, 'our,' 'belonging to us'; see pronouns.

Winulli, 'to burn,' to consume by fire only, and not in any other way; hence winulliko, 'to consume,' 'to burn.'

Winullikan means 'one who consumes or burns.' The particle -kan means 'the person who,' and is equivalent to the English particle -er, affixed to verbs to form the substantive person, as lover, consumer. To express the thing, the particle -né is postfixed; as, winullikanné, 'the burning thing which consumes.'

Koiyug, 'fire'; the particle -kan, in the text, is affixed to show that the 'fire' is to be construed with the preceding word, by which it is thus connected and governed.

Section 5.

Unnug, 'there.' Bo ta, 'only,' a compound of bo, 'self,' and ta, 'it is'; meaning it is 'that self same thing only' to which it is affixed; as, wakol bo ta, 'one only, one by itself, one alone.'

Section 6.

Keawai is the verb 'to be' in the negative form, with **korien**, understood; it is equivalent to 'there be not,' a universal denial; **wal** positively affirms the assertion whether negative or affirmative; **keawai wal wakál**, 'there be certainly not one.'

Murrárág, 'good, well.'

Section 7.

Gatun, 'and.'

Biyuġ-bai, 'father.' The address to a father or elderly person is **biyuġ**; to a brother or equal, **biġ-gai**.

Gikouġ, 'him,' the separable emphatic pronoun; the objective pronoun is **bon,** 'him.'

Gikouġ kai, 'on account of him, for him.'

Géen, 'we,' *v.* page 17. There is only this one form in the nominative case plural; **ġearun,** 'us,' is the objective case, from which all the oblique cases are formed by the addition of particles; as, **ġearun-ba,** 'ours'; **ġearun kai,** 'on account of us'; **ġéen-bo** is 'we ourselves.'

Gikouġ-kinba, 'with him'; 'remaining with him.'

Piriwál, 'chief, lord, king.'

Biruġ, 'from, out of'; **tin,** 'from, on account of.'

WINTA 2.—PART 2.

Section 8.

Kaibuġ, 'light,' as opposed to darkness.

Tokoi, 'darkness, night,' as opposed to day.

Section 9.

Na, 'see'; hence **na-killiko,** 'to see,' 'to perceive by the eye.' The negative of this is formed by affixing the negative particle, **korien,** to the principal verb, divested of the verbal affix **-killiko**; as, **na-korien,** 'see not.'

Bon, 'him,' is the verbal pronoun in the objective case; **gikouġ** is the emphatic form, 'him,' when governed by particles; **-nuġ** is the suffixed particle that denotes the object, as, **Eloi-nuġ.** Eloi is here the object spoken of, and so is in the objective case along with the pronoun, to show that both are under the same government of the verb **na-korien.**

Section 10.

Túġun-billéún, 'was manifested, shown'; from **túġun-billi-ko,** 'to show as a mark shows'; 'to manifest of itself *or* of oneself.'

Puttára-kan, 'a flesh-being,' one who is flesh; from **puttára,** 'flesh.'

Section 11.

Niuwara, 'anger'; *cf.* bukka, 'wrath, rage, fury.'
Kátan, 'is,' the present tense of kakilliko, 'to be' in a state.
Purreáġ, 'day.'
Yarakai, 'evil, bad'; opposed to murráráġ, 'good.'
Yarakai kinko, 'on account of the wicked.'

Section 12.

Kauwál, 'great'; kauwál-kauwál, 'very great.' The comparison is drawn always by what the one is and the other is not; hence, kauwál kan noa, 'he is great'; Eloi ta, 'God is'; waréa ta ġearunba bulbul, 'little it is our hearts.'
Waréa, 'little,' in size.
Bulbul, 'heart' of animals and man; not 'heart' of oak or the like.
Gurran, 'knows'; the present tense of ġurrulliko, 'to know, to perceive by the ear, to understand,' but not in any other sense; to know a person by sight is ġi-milliko; to know a thing by sight, na-killiko; to know carnally, boi-bulliko; and to know by the touch, nu-mulliko.
Minnuġ, as a question, means 'what thing' is the object? The reduplication, with the particle bo affixed, means 'everything itself' as an object.

Section 13.

Kaiyu, 'able, powerful, mighty'; kaiyu-kan, 'one who is able'; noa, 'he'; Eloi ta, 'God is'; yanti-ko, 'for all'; minnuġ-bo minnuġ-bo-ko, 'for every thing.'

WINTA 3.—Part 3.

Section 2.

Yantin koba, 'of all'; koba is the genitive particle used with things, while -úmba is used with person; as, ġan-úmba? 'whose'? 'belonging to what person'? minariġ koba? 'belonging to what thing'? makoro koba, 'belonging to the fish'; emmo-úmba, 'mine', 'belonging to me'; Threlkeld-úmba; 'belonging to Threlkeld.'

Section 4.

Gurrulla, imperative, 'know, hearken, listen.'
Nura, the personal plural nominative pronoun, 'ye'; the objective case is nurun, 'you'; nurunba, 'belonging to you.'
Yanti, 'thus, in this manner.'
Niuwoa, the emphatic separable personal pronoun, 'he,' 'it is he'; the inseparable verbal pronoun is noa, 'he'; the inseparable verbal pronoun in the objective is bon, 'him', and the separable oblique case is ġikouġ. 'him'; ġikouġ ko means 'for him'; ġikouġ kai, 'on account of him.'

Gearun, 'us,' the objective case of ġeen, 'we.'
Uma, 'made,' the aorist of the verb 'to make'; hence umulliko, 'to make, create, do'; 'to cause power, to effect.' In this sentence the use of the two forms of the pronoun, 'he,' is seen; niuwoa ta, 'it is he,' emphatically; noa, he,' verbally; ġearun, 'us'; uma, 'made'; the whole means, 'it is he, he us made.'
Keawai-wal, a universal, absolute denial.
Ġeen-bo, 'we ourselves.'
Umulli-pa, 'made,' excluding reality of effect; this is expressed by the particle, pa, postfixed, along with the negative keawai-wal.
Giko-umba, 'his,' 'belonging to him.'
Kùri, 'man,' individually or collectively, or 'people,' according as the pronoun with it is singular, dual, or plural; ġali kùri, 'this man,' as an agent; unni kùri, 'this man,' as a subject; bara kùri, 'they the men,' 'they the people'; buloara kùri, 'the two men.'
Cipu, an adopted word, from the English, 'sheep.'
Takilli, the act of 'eating'; hence takilliko, 'to be in the act of eating'; 'to eat.'
Ġél, the inseparable verbal particle denoting place, 'the place of'; takilliġél, 'the pasture, the eating-place, the feeding-place'; ġikoumba, 'belonging to him,' 'his.'

Section 5.

Gintoa, the emphatic separable personal nominative pronoun, 'thou.' 'it is thou who'; ta, 'it is.'
Gintoa ta, 'it is thou who dost, didst, wilt do,' according to the tense of the verb, which in this case is uma, and that, being a past aorist, renders it 'didst make,' without reference to any particular past time.
Moroko, 'heaven,' the visible Heavens, the sky, the space above our heads.
Purrai, 'the earth, the land, the ground.'
Wombul, 'the sea.'
Yantin ġali koba, 'all belonging to these'; yantin, 'all,' pluralizes the emphatic demonstrative pronoun ġali, 'this'; yantin gali, 'all these'; yantin gala, 'all those.'

Section 8.

Guraki, 'skilful, wise.'
Upin, the present tense of upilliko, 'to exert power,' exclusive of the idea of effect upon the object; as, to put a thing anywhere.
Tin, 'from, on account of'; 'therefore' as a cause, 'because of'; umulli tin, 'on account of doing'; ġearunba tin, 'on account of our.'

WINTA 4.—PART 4.
Section 9.

Tuloa, 'straight,' opposed to crooked'; 'upright' as to character; 'truth' as to expression, opposed to falsehood; tuloa kan ta, 'one who is straight, upright, true.'
Moron, 'life,' opposed to death; animal, not vegetable, life.
Kakilli-kan ta, 'it is one who remains, who is, who exists'; kakilli from kakilliko, 'to be' in some state.
Kauwăl, 'great'; piriwăl kauwăl, 'lord or king,' *lit.*, 'great chief'; kauwăl-kauwăl, 'great-great,' 'very great.'
Yanti katai kakilliko, 'thus to be always,' 'to be for ever.'
Pulul-pulul, 'trembling, shaking.' Kănŭn, 'will be.'
Bukka, 'wrath, rage, fury'; bukka tin, 'on account of wrath'; ġikoumba tin, 'on account of his.'
Konara, 'a flock, herd, an assembly, a mob, a nation'; yantin bara konara, 'all they, the assemblies *or* nations.'
Niuwarin, the causative case of niuwara, 'anger'; niuwarin, 'because of anger'; 'from *or* on account of anger,' as a cause.

Section 10.

Bapai, 'nigh at hand, close to'; bapai ta ba, 'it is nigh to.'

Section 11.

Wiyan, the present tense of wiyelliko, 'to communicate by sound, to speak, tell, say, call out'; yantinko wiyan bon ba, 'all when they call on him.' The verbalizing particle, ba, is equivalent to 'when,' *or* 'at the time when' the verbal act or state shall be or was, according to the tense of the verb.
Kaloġ, 'afar off, distant.'
Kakillin, 'continues to be,' 'is now being'; the present participle of the verb kakilliko, 'to be' in some state.
Barun kai, 'from, on account of them,' *sc.*, persons.
Yarakai tin, 'from, on account of the evil,' *sc.*, thing.

Section 12.

Wirrilli; hence wirrilliko, 'to wind up as a ball of string.' The blacks do this to their long fishing-lines, and opossum-fur cords, to take care of them, to preserve them; hence the verb means 'to take care of, to preserve, to keep together, to guide,' as a flock of sheep; wirrilli-kan, 'one who takes care of' by some act of locomotion, as a watchman going his round.
Mirrăl, 'desert, desolate, miserable'; 'a state of want'; mirrăl ta unni, 'this is a desert place'; mirrăl-laġ unni, 'this is desolate *or* miserable,' because in a desert there is nothing to eat or drink; mirrăl kătan, 'is now at present in a miserable *or* desolate state, in a state of want'; keawai, 'not to be.'
Keawai wal, 'certainly shall not be'; equivalent therefore to 'shall not'; mirrăl kănŭn, 'shall be in want.'

Section 13.

Gurrára-kan, 'one who personally attends to'; ġurrárakan kauwál, 'one who is very pitiful.'
Gurrára-mulli-kan, 'one who causes or exercises attention,' 'one who does attend to'; the phrase means 'he is a merciful Being.'

WINTA 5.—PART 5.
Section 1.

Goro, 'three'; see page 108.

Kakilli, 'state of being'; hence kakilliko, 'to be, to exist' in some state; we cannot express 'is dead' by tetti kátan, because kátan implies existence, though we may say moron kátan, 'is alive,' because existence is implied; 'is dead' must be tetti ka ba, which means 'is in the state of the dead'; generally the blacks say kulwon, 'stiff, rigid' for 'dead'; thus tetti ka ba kulwon is equivalent to 'dead and stiff,' in opposition to 'a swoon,' which might be the meaning, unless circumstances led to another conclusion.

Wokka, an adverb, 'up,' opposed to bara, 'down'; wokka kaba moroko ka ba, 'are up in heaven.'

Biyuġbai ta, 'the father it is.'

Wiyelli-kan ta, 'the one who speaks it is'; this is the form of the word when applied to a person; to a thing, it would be wiyellikanné.

Marai ta, 'the spirit it is,' in opposition to corporeal substance; but kurrábáġ is 'the body,' and mamuya is 'a ghost' murrin is another word for 'the body.'

Yirriyirri, 'sacred, reverend, holy'; not to be regarded but with awe, as is the place marked out for mystic rites; a separate place not to be profaned by common use, hence holy; a person reverend, to be held in reverence, sacred. Native heralds and messengers pass as sacred persons; they are held in reverence, and are unmolested by hostile parties, when on embassies of war or peace; yirriyirri-laġ means 'one who acts sacredly,' one who is holy, separate by privilege of being held sacred or in reverence. In the South Sea Islands, a pig devoted to the god Oro, in former times, was made sacred by having a red feather thrust through and fastened to its ear, and thus the reverend pig was privileged to feed anywhere unmolested, as being sacred; nor was he confined to a tithe of the produce if he broke through into any plantation, but was permitted to eat his fill, not, however, without a murmur at the sacred intrusion.

Unni, 'this,' as subject or object; ġali, 'this,' as agent; unni ta ġoro ta, 'this it is, the three it is'; wakál bo ta, 'one it is, one-self only it is.'

Section 2.

Yuka, 'sent'; hence yukulliko, 'to send' a person; but to send property is tiyumbilliko. Yinal, 'son.'

Kakilliko, 'for-to be'; here the infinitive form, as usual, denotes the purpose.

Miromulli-kan means 'one who keeps or takes care of'; from miromulliko, 'to keep with care'; miromullikan noa kakilliko means 'he is for-to-be one who keeps with care,' hence a 'Saviour.' From the same root, miroma also is a 'Saviour.' 'A deliverer' would be mankilli-kan, 'one who takes hold of'; but then the evil must be expressed out of which the person is taken or to be taken.

Yantin purrai ko, 'for all lands'; 'for all the earth'; 'for the whole world.'

Section 3.

Eloi-to noa, 'God he,' as a personal agent; pitál ma kauwál, 'causes great joy,' sc., towards.

Yantin kúri, 'all men.'

Gukulla ta noa, 'it is he gave'; from ġukilliko, 'to give'; the ta, 'it is,' affirms the act.

Wakál bo ta, 'only one'; lit., 'one-self only.'

Gali ko, 'for this purpose'; ġali, the emphatic pronoun, 'this'; ġala, 'that'; ġaloa, 'the other'; the demonstrative pronouns are unni, 'this'; unnoa, 'that'; untoa, 'the other.'

Yantin-to ba, 'that all who'; the particle, to, denotes agency, and ba verbalizes.

Gurran, 'believe,' the present tense of ġurrilliko, 'to hear, to believe.'

Gikouġ kin, 'on account of him,' as a cause; for, if he speaks, you hear; he is therefore the cause of your hearing, and if you assent to that which he says, you continue to hear; if not, you do not hearken to him, or else you only pretend to hear him; the verbal objective pronoun 'him' is bon; ġurran bon is the present tense, 'hear him,' but has no reference to the effect of that hearing, whereas the use of the other pronoun ġikouġ kin implies that they hear him so as to attend to what he says and believe.

Keawai wal bara tetti kánún, 'they certainly shall not be in a state of death.'

Kulla wal, 'but certainly' shall, or 'because certainly' they shall.

Yanti katai, 'in this manner always.'

Barunba, 'belonging to them,' 'theirs.'

Kakillinún, 'will be and continue to be'; from kakilliko, 'to be, to exist' in some state.

Moron, 'life'; kakillinún moron means 'a future state of being, and continuing to be, alive.'

Section 4.

Pulli, 'voice.'
Upéa, 'put forth'; from upilliko, 'to exert power.'
Itháracl-úmba; Israel is the proper name, introduced; -úmba, the particle denoting 'belonging to' a person only; 'belonging to' a thing is koba; 'belonging to a place' is -kál (*masc.*), -kálin (*fem.*).
Wiyelliko, 'to speak.'
Pitál-mullikó, 'to cause peace, joy, gladness.'
Iéthu-ko Kritht-ko, 'Jesus Christ,' as the agent; the particle ko, denoting agency, must be added to each word, to show that both are in the same relation to the verb.
Niuwoa-bo, 'himself it is who is,' emphatic.

Section 6.

Gearunba kàtan, 'is belonging to us' and remains so; equivalent to, 'for we have.'
Wiyelli-kan, 'one who speaks'; 'an advocate.'
Biyugbai toa ba kátan, 'it remains with the Father.'

WINTA 6.—PART 6.

Section 10.

Murrin, 'body' of a person; murrin nurunba, 'your body.'
Kokera yirriyirri ta, 'it is a sacred house,' 'a temple.'
Marai yirriyirri koba, 'belonging to the sacred Spirit.'
Wakálla murrin, 'one body is.'

Section 11.

Yanti nurun wiya, 'in the manner as called you'; equivalent to, 'you are called'; nurun is in the objective case.
Kotelli ta, 'in the thinking.'
Nurunba, 'belonging to you,' 'your'; 'of you.'
Wiyatoara, 'that which is said.'
Wakálla Piriwál, 'one Lord is'; wakálla Marai, 'one Spirit is.'
Wakálla gurrulliko, 'one is for-to hear *or* obey.'
Wakálla kurrimulliko, 'one is for-to cleanse' with water.
Wakálla Eloi ta, 'one is God it is.'
Biyugbai ta yantin koba, 'father it is of all.'
Wokka-kaba noa yantin ko, 'up above he is for all.'
Gatun noa yantin koa, 'and he all with.'
Gatun murrug kaba nurun kinba, 'and within you,' *sc.*, all; murrug, 'within, inside.'

Section 12.

Yantin barun yemmaman marai-to Eloi koba ko, 'all them lead the spirit does, belonging-to-God does,' equivalent to the passive; the to and ko are only signs of agency and not the verb 'to do'; in the translation the verb 'does' is only used to show the effect of the particles; no reason can be assigned why the particles may not be used indiscriminately the one for the other, excepting euphony, because the agency is in the *o*, which denotes purpose.

Yemmamulliko, 'to lead as by the hand'; the to in the text is added to Marai, because that is the subject of the verb, and the ko (=to) is added to Eloi koba, because that, too, is an essential portion of the subject.

Wonnai ta bara Eloi koba, 'children it is they of God.'

Section 13.

Niuwara buġ-ga kora bon, ' angry purposely cause not him.'
Marai yirriyirri-laġ Eloi koba, 'Spirit sacred of God.'

Section 14.

Gan-to ba yarakai wiyanùn ġikouġ, 'whosoever-there-be evil will-speak concerning him.'
Yinal kùri koba, 'the son belonging-to man'; 'the son of man.'
Kàmùnbinùn wal bon, 'suffered-to-be shall-certainly-be he.'*
Wonta noa ba yarakai wiyanùn ġikouġ marai yirriyirri-laġ, 'whereas he evil will-speak concerning-him, the spirit sacred.'
Keawai wal bon kàmùnbinùn, 'not certainly he shall-be-suffered-to-be,' or remain, or exist; according to the idea of punishment which the speaker wishes to convey.*

WINTA 7.—Part 7.
Luke, ii. 9–14.
Verse 9.

Gatun noa aġelo Yehóa-ùmba, 'and he the angel belonging-to-Jehovah.'
Tanan uwa noa barun-kin, 'approached them'; 'came to them.'
Gatun killiburra Yehóa-ùmba, 'and shining belonging-to-Jehovah'; from killibinbin, ' to be bright; for the verbal form burra, see page 37.
Kakulla barun katoa, ' was them with.'
Kinta ġaiya bara kakulla, 'fear then they were-in-a-state-of.'

Verse 10.

Gatun aġeloko noa wiya barun, 'and he the angel told them.'
Kinta kora, 'fear not.'
Kulla nurun baġ wiyan, 'because you I tell.'
Totoġ murràràġ kakilliko pitàlko, ' news good, for-to-be joy-for.'
Kakilliko yantin ko kùri ko, 'to-be all-for men-for.'

---
*Bon is here in the objective ; for the reason why, see pages 22 and 30.

Verse 11.

Kulla nuruuba porkulléún unni purreåġ, 'because belonging-to-you born-of-itself-is this day.'
Kokerá Dabid-úmba ka, 'house-at belonging-to-David-at '; the -rá of kokerá is an ablative form; see page 16.
Golomullikan ta noa, Kritht ta Piriwàl ta, 'one-who-saves (by personal causation) it-is he, Christ it-is, the Chief *or* Lord it-is.'

Verse 12.

Gatun unni túġa kánún nuruuba, 'and this mark will-be yours.'
Nanún nura b'oboġnuġ, 'see-will ye the-babe.'
Gamatoara kirrikin taba, 'that-which-is-wrapped in-the garment,' *i.e.*, 'soft raiment.'
Kakillin ba takilliġél laba, 'remaining-at the-eating-place-at.'

Verse 13.

Gatun tanoa-kal-bo, 'and at-that-self-same-instant.'
Paipéa konara moroko-kal ġikouġ katoa aġelo katoa, 'appeared host Heaven-of him-with angel-with.'
Murráráġ wiyellin bon Eloinuġ ġiakai, 'good, telling him, God (the object), thus'; equivalent to, 'praising God, and saying.'

Verse 14.

Wiyabúnbilla bon murráráġ Eloinuġ, 'let him speak well God' (the object); *i.e.*, 'let persons speak good *or* well of God.' This is the native way of expressing our passive voice, 'let God be praised'.
Wokka kaba moroko kaba, 'up-in Heaven-in.
Gatun kámúnbilla pitàl purrai tako, 'and let-there-be-caused-to-be peace earth for.'
Murráráġ umatoara kúri ko, 'good what-is-done men-for.'

WINTA 8.—Part 8.

Section 1.

Eloi-to noa ġurrára-ma korien barun aġelo yarakai umullikan, 'God he regarded not them angels evil who-do.'
Wonto ba wareka noa barun bara koiyuġ kako tartaro kako, 'whereas cast-away he them down fire for tartarus for'; 'tartarus' is a word introduced.

Section 2.

Wiyatoara ta yantin kúri-ko wakálla tetti bulliko, 'that-which-is-said it-is all men-for once dead to become.'
Gatun yukita ġaiya ġurrulliko, 'and afterwards then to-perceive-by the car,' *sc.*, the sentence.

I

Section 3.

Yakoai-kan baġ moron kánùn? 'in-what-maunner-of-being 'l life will-be-in-a-state-of'? *i.e.*, 'how can I be alive.'
Gurrulla bon Piriwálnuġ, Iethunuġ Krithtnug, 'hear him, the Lord Jesus Christ.'
Moron ġaiya bi kánùn, 'life then thou wilt-be-in-a-state-of.'
Gatun kirrikin ta tempel kako, 'and the-veil it-is the temple-at.'
Yiir-kulléùn bulwa koa, 'rent-of-its-own-power in-the-midst, in-order-to-be.'
Wokka-kabiruġ unta-ko baran-tako, 'from the top thence to the bottom'; *lit.*, 'up-from there-to down-to.'

☞ The peculiarity of the verbal form of yiir, 'a rent,'—so called from the noise of a piece of cloth when tearing,—is shewn in the following specimen:—

Yiir-kulléùn, 'rent,' 'has rent' of itself, of its own power.
Yiir-buġ-ga, 'rent,' some person has.
Yiir-burréa, 'rent,' some instrument has.
Yiir-laġ, 'rent,' is declaratively.
Yiir-wirréa, 'rent,' some motion has rent; as when a flag, or a sail of a ship flapping in the wind, is rent.

Thus, without a clear idea of the nature of the roots of the affixes, no one could understand the difference of the five kinds of 'rending.'

Compound Words.

Like the North American Indians, although to a less extent, our aborigines have long composite words in their language. For instance, to express the abstract idea contained in the English word 'lust,' they would say kotilliyarakaigearúnba, 'our evil thinking'; and for the contrary idea, kotillimurráráġ-gearúnba, 'our good thinking.' Now, either of these words, when pronounced, appears to be but one word, whereas each contains three words combined, namely:—

(1.) Kotilli (from simple root kot), 'the act of thinking'; (2.) ġearúnba, 'belonging to us'; (3.) yarakai, 'evil'; murráráġ, 'good.' From the root kot come the forms, kotilliko, *infin.*, 'to think,' kotan, *pres. indic.*, kotinùn, *fut. indic.*, kotta, *past indic.*, kotillin, *pres. part.*, kotilliela, *past participle.*

Again, such a word as tiirburréabúnbilliko, 'to permit to be torn,' is made up of tiir, a root which expresses the idea of tearing, -burréa, the verbal particle of instrumental agency, -bún, 'permit,' -illi, the formative of a verbal noun, and -ko, for the purpose of.' And so also with other examples.

THREE AUSTRALIAN ABORIGINAL DIALECTS,
SHOWING THEIR AFFINITY WITH EACH OTHER.

1. *Eastern Australia* (Threlkeld) ; 2. *South Western Australia* (Captain Grey's Vocabulary); 3. *South Australia* (Teichelmann).

I (emphatic)—1. Gatoa; 2. Ganya; Nadjo; Gaii.
Thou—1. Gintoa; 2. Ginnei; 3. Ninna.
We—1. Géen; 2. Ganéel; 3. Gadlu.
Ye—1. Nura; 2. Nurag; 3. Na.
They—1. Bara; 2. Balgúu; 3. Barna.
We two (dual)—1. Bali; 2.   ; 3. Gadlukurla.
Ye two—1. Bula; 2. Bulala; 3. Niwadlukurla.
This (emphatic)—1. Gali; 2. Gali; 3. Gadlu.
That (emphatic)—1. Gala; 2. Gala; 3. Parla.
Who?—1. Gan?; 2. Gan?; 3. Ganna?
Who (is the agent)—1. Ganto?; 2. Gando?; 3. Ganto?
Whose?—1. Gannug?; 2. Gannog?; 3. Gaityurlo?
To strike (imperative)—1. Buwa; 2. Buma; 3. Bumandi.
To be wroth—1. Bukka; 2. Bukkan; 3. Tagkarro.
Yes (assent)—1. E-e; 2. E-ee; 3. Ne.
On account of?—1. -tin ke?; 2. -gin ge?; 3. birra.
Cold—1. Kurkur; 2. Gurgal; 3. Manyapaianna.
Heat—1. Karrol; 2. Kallarruk; 3. Wottita.
Where?—1. Wonti?; 2. Winji?; 3. Wanti?
To tear (*pres.*)—1. Yiiran; 2. Jiran; 3. Yarurendi.
Presently—1. Kabo; 2. Kaabo; 3. Gaiinni; Yagadti.
To take (imperative)—1. Mara; 2. Mara; 3. Marrar.
More—1. Bati; 2. Mate; 3. Muinmo.
Go quickly—1. Wollawollag; 2. Welawellag; 3. Warruanna.
To see—1. Nakilli; 2. Nago; 3. Nakkondi.
To blow (*i.e.*, puff)—1. Bombilli; 2. Bobon; 3. Búntondi.
To fly—1. Burkilli; 2. Burdag; 3.   .
To speak—1. Wiyelli; 2. Wagon; 3. Wagondi.
Water (fresh)—1. Kokoin; Bato; 2. Kowin; Badto; 3. Kowi.
Dung (excrement)—1. Konug; 2. Konug; 3. Kudna.
The tongue—1. Tulluu; 2. Tallug; 3. Tadlaga.
The throwing stick—1. Wommára; 2. Meera; 3. Meedla.
Smoke—1. Poito; 2. Buyu; 3. Poiyu.
Wood—1. Kúlai; 2. Kalla; 3. Karla.
The hand—1. Máttára; 2. Mara; 3. Murra.
The ribs—1. Narra; 2. Narra; 3. Tinninya.
The toes—1. Tinna; 2. Tjenna; 3. Tidna.
A crow (from its cry)—1. Wakun, 2. Quaggun; 3. Kui.
The wind—1. Wibbi; Wippi; 2.   3. Waitpi.

The Lord's Prayer,
In the language of the Aborigines of Lake Macquarie.

Biyuġbai ġearunba wokka kaba moroko kaba kàtan;
Father   our   up   in   heaven   in   art;
kámúnbilla yitirra ġiroumba yirriyirri kakilliko;
let-caused-to-be name thy sacred for-to-be;
paipibúnbilla Piriwál koba ġiroumba; ġurrabúnbilla
let-to-appear King-belonging-to thy; let-to-obey
wiyellikaune ġiroumba; yanti purrai taba, yanti ta
word thy; as earth in as
moroko kaba, ġuwa ġearun purrcáġ ka yanti katai
heaven in; give to-us day at as always
takilliko; ġatun warekulla ġearunba yarakai
for-to-eat; and cast-way our evil
umatoara yanti ta ġćen wareka yantin ta wiyapaiyéeu
that-is-done as we cast-away all spoken-but-not-done
ġearunba; ġatun yuti yikora ġearun yarakai
belonging-to-us; and guide not us evil
umulli-kan kolaġ; miromulla ġearun yarakai
one-who-causes-to-do towards; cause-to-deliver us evil
tabiruġ; kulla ta ġiroumba ta Piriwál koba ġatun
from; because thine King-belonging-to and
killibiubin yanti katai. —— Amen.
bright-shining thus always. —— Amen.

The Author trusts that he has now placed on permanent record the language of the aborigines of this part of the colony, before the speakers themselves become totally extinct; and if, in his endeavour to aid the purpose of scientific enquiry, his work may seem to fall short, and so disappoint the expectations of those who take an interest in ethnological pursuits, he can only state that, in the midst of attention to manifold engagements in other paramount duties, no pains have been spared on the subject, and therefore his only apology is, that with slender means he has done his best.

L. E. THRELKELD.

Sydney, New South Wales,
    November 26, 1850.

PART II.

THE GOSPEL BY ST. LUKE.

THE

GOSPEL BY ST. LUKE

TRANSLATED INTO

THE LANGUAGE

OF THE

AWABAKAL

BY

L. E. THRELKELD.

NOW FOR THE FIRST TIME PRINTED.

FROM THE ORIGINAL MANUSCRIPT,
IN THE 'SIR GEORGE GREY COLLECTION' OF THE PUBLIC LIBRARY,
AUCKLAND, N.Z.

Sydney:
CHARLES POTTER, GOVERNMENT PRINTER.
1891.

THE AUTHOR'S PREFACE.

It is a matter of fact that the aborigines of these colonies and of the numerous islands of the Pacific Ocean are rapidly becoming extinct. The cause of their extinction is mysterious. Does it arise from the iniquity of this portion of the human race having become full ?—or, that the times of these Gentiles are fulfilled ?—or, is it but the natural effects of iniquity producing its consequent ruin to the workers thereof in accordance with the natural order of God's government of the universe ? Whatever may be the result of speculative theories in answer to these queries, there remains one grand question incontrovertible, " Shall not the Judge of all the Earth do right ?"

The providence of God has permitted ancient nations, together with their languages, and numerous tribes, with their various tongues, to pass away and others to take possession of and dwell in their tents, just as we in New South Wales and the neighbouring colonies now do, in the place of the original inhabitants of the land.

The numbers of the aborigines, both in Australia and the South Sea Islands, have always been overrated, and the efforts that have been made, on Christian principles, to ameliorate their condition, have been more abundant in proportion to the number of these aborigines, than have ever been any similar efforts towards the hundreds of millions of heathens in other parts of the world.

My own attempt in favour of the aborigines of New South Wales was commenced in the year 1824, under the auspices of the London Missionary Society, at the request of the deputation from that Institution sent out for the purpose of establishing Missions in the East, and urged likewise by the solicitations of the local Government of this colony. The British Government sanctioned the project by authorizing a grant of 10,000 acres of land, at Lake Macquarie, in trust for the said purpose, at the recommendation of Sir Thomas Brisbane, the then Governor of the Australian Colonies.

In 1839, the London Missionary Society abandoned the mission, broke faith with me, and left me to seek such resources as the providence of God might provide, after fifteen years' service in their employ. The Colonial Government, being perfectly acquainted with all the circumstances of the case, stepped in and enabled me to continue in my attempt to obtain a knowledge of the aboriginal language, and the British Government subsequently confirmed the new arrangement.

Circumstances, which no human power could control, brought the mission to a final termination on December 31, 1841, when the mission ceased, not from any want of support from the Government, nor from any inclination on my own part to retire from the work, but solely from the sad fact that the aborigines themselves had then become almost extinct, for I had actually outlived a very large majority of the blacks, more especially of those with whom I had been associated for seventeen years. The extinction of the aborigines is still progressing throughout these colonies. The last man of the tribe which formerly occupied the site of Sydney may now be seen sitting by the way side, a paralytic, soliciting alms from passers by, and this he does from choice, rather than enter the Benevolent Asylum. Those who drive by in their carriages along the South Head Road often throw him a sixpence or so, and thus he is bountifully provided for in his native and beloved state of freedom.

Under such circumstances, the translation of the Gospel by St. Luke can only be now a work of curiosity,*—a record of the language of a tribe that once existed, and would have, otherwise, been numbered with those nations and their forgotten languages, and peoples with their unknown tongues, who have passed away from this globe and are buried in oblivion.

Elliot, the missionary to the North American Indians, made a translation of the Scriptures into their language, which has recently been published; but only one Indian now remains who knows that dialect.

This translation of the Gospel of Luke into the language of the aborigines, was made by me with the assistance of the intelligent aboriginal, M'Gill, whose history is attached.† Thrice I wrote it, and he and I went through it sentence by sentence, and word for word, while I explained to him carefully the meaning as we proceeded. M'Gill spoke the English language fluently. The third revisal was completed in 1831. I then proceeded with the Gospel of Mark, a selection of prayers from the Book of Common Prayer, with which to commence public worship with the few surviving blacks; I prepared a Spelling book; I had also commenced the Gospel of Matthew, when the mission was brought to its final close.

Not long ago, I accidentally found at a book-stall a copy of the first specimens of an Australian language, which I published some

---

* Our author did not know that his Awabakal blacks were only a sub-tribe, and that their brethren, for some hundreds of miles along the coast to the north and south of Lake Macquarie, spoke a language which is essentially the same. Northwards from the Hunter River to the Macleay, this language is still spoken.—ED.

† See page 88.—ED.

time in 1826; this was done to satisfy my friends of the impropriety of introducing the English sound of the vowels instead of those of the Continent, which are also in use in the South Sea Islands.

This present copy of the Gospel by Luke is the fourth re-written revisal of the work, and yet it is not offered as a perfect translation; it can only be regarded by posterity as a specimen of the language of the aborigines of New Holland, or, as a simple monumental tablet, on which might be truthfully inscribed, as regards the unprofitable servant who attempted to ameliorate the pitiable condition of the aborigines and attain a knowledge of their language:—" He has done what he could."

L. E. THRELKELD,
Minister.

Sydney, New South Wales,
15th August, 1857.

[NOTE.—The original manuscript was illuminated for Sir George Grey by Annie Layard, daughter of Sir A. H. Layard, the explorer of Nineveh.

The original title page is this:—

EVANGELION

UNNI TA

JESU-ŪM-BA CHRIST-KO-BA.

UPATŌARA

LOŪKA-UMBA.

Translated into the language of the aborigines, located in the vicinity of Hunter's River, Lake Macquarie, &c., New South Wales, in the year 1831, and further revised by the translator, L. E. Threlkeld, Minister, 1857.—ED.]

EUANGELION upatúara LUKA-ÚMBA.

WINTA I.

Wonto ba kauwállo mankulla unnoa tara túġunbilliko ġurránto ġéen kinba,

2. Yanti bo ġearun kin bara ġukulla, unnoa tara nakillikan kurri-kurri kabiruġ ġatun mankillikan wiyellikanne koba.

3. Murráráġ tia kátan yantibo, koito haġ ba tuiġ ko ġirouġ, Teopolo muriáiáġ ta,

4. Gurra-uwil koa bi tulon, unnoa tara wiyatoara banuġ ba.

5. Yanti-kalai ta Herod noa kakulla, Piriwál noa kakulla Iudaia ka, kakulla noa tarai †hiereu Dhakaria yitirra, Abia-úmba konara : ġatun nukuġ ġikoúmba yinálkun koba Aaron-úmba, ġiakai bounton yitirra Elidhabet.

6. Buloara bula kakulla muriáráġ Eloi kin, mikan ta ġurraiyelléún bula Yehóa-ko noa ba wiyellikanne yarakai ma korien.

7. Keawaran bula wonnai korien kulla, bountoa Elidhabet ġurrauwai ; ġatun bula ba ġurróġbai kakulla.

8. Gatun yakita kakulla, umulliela noa ba Eloi kin makan ta, yirruġ ka ġikouġ kin †hiereu koba,

9. Yanti kiloa †hiereu koba uman, yirruġ ka ġikoúmba ta upulliko bon porapora koiyuġ ko uwa noa ba †nao koba Yehóa kai koba.

10. Gatun yanti bo yantinto konara kùri wiyelliela warai ta yakita winelliela ba porapora.

11. Gatun paipéa noa †aġelo Yehóa-úmba ġikouġ kin, ġarokilliela noa túġkaġkirri ka koiyuġ kún ta porapora ka.

12. Gatun nakulla bon noa ba Dhakaria ko, unma bon noa ba, kinta ġaiya noa ba kakulla.

13. Wonto ba aġelo wiya noa, Kinta kora bi kauwa, Dhakaria; kulla ġurra ta wiyellikanne ġiroúmba, ġatun nukuġ ko ġiroúmba ko wonnai kánún ġiroúmba, ġatun wiyánún bi ġiakai yitirra Ioanne.

14. Gatun pitál bi kánún, pitál kauwálkan kánún pórkullin'in ġikouġ kinbiruġ.

15. Kauwál wal noa kánún, mikan ta Yehóa kin, ġatun keawai wal noa †wain pitánún, keawai tarere, ġatun warakaġ wal noa witellinún Marai yirriyirri kan biruġ ko, waraka biruġ tunkán ta biruġ.

16. Gatun noa wiyánún wal barun kauwál-kauwál wonnai Itháraeĺ-úmba Yehóa-kin ko Eloi ta barúnba.

† This mark is placed before all common nouns which are adapted from Greek, Latin, or English ; whichever equivalent word in these languages suits the aboriginal tongue best, that word I have introduced into the text. In the original text, many of the borrowed words, and especially the proper names, could not be pronounced by a native black.—Ed.

17. Gatun wal noa uwánún ġikouġ kin mikan ta kaiyu ka Marai ta Elía-úmba, warbuġgulliko búlbúl biyuġbai tara koba wonnai kolaġ, ġatun barun kinko tuloa kako; uma-uwil koa barun kúri kurrikurri Ychóa kinko.

18. Gatun noa Dhakariako wiya bon aġelonuġ, Yakoai kan baġ ġurránún unni? kulla baġ ġurroġbai, ġatun nukuġ emmoúmba ġurróġ ġéen.

19. Gatun noa aġeloto wiya bon, Gatoa Gabriel, ġakillin Eloi kin mikan ta; ġatun yuka tia wiyelliko ġiroug, ġatun túġun billiko ġali tara ko pitálmullikanne ko.

20. A! ġurrulla bi, ¿óġ ko wal bi kánún, ġatun kaiyu korien wal bi kánún wiyelli ta, yaki-kalai tako purreáġ kako unni tara kánún ba, kulla bi ba ġurra korien wiyellikanne emmoúmba, kabo kánún wal unni tara.

21. Gatun bara kúri ko mittia Dhakarianuġ, ġatun kotelliela minnuġ-bulliela noa tunkéa noa †nao ka.

22. Gatun noa ba paikulléún warrai ta, kaiyu korien noa wiyelli ko barun; ġatun bara ġurra Marai noa nakulla †nao ba; kulla noa wanwál-wauwál uma barun ġatun, ġarokilliela noa ġóġ ko.

23. Gatun kirun kabulla purreáġ ġikoúmba umullikanne, waita ġaiya noa uwá kokera ko ġikouġ ka tako.

24. Gatun yukita purreáġ ka Elidhabet ġikoúmba nukuġ warakáġ bountoa, ġatun yuropulléún bountoa warán yellenna ka, wiyelliela bountoa,

25. Yanti noa tia Yehóako umá nakulla noa tia ba purreáġ ka, mankilliko barun ba béelmulli tin kúri tin.

26. Tarai ta yellenna ka †hek ka, Gabriel ta aġelo ta puntimai ta wiyabunbia bon Eloi kinbiruġ uwolliko, purrai kolaġ Galilaia koba, ġiakai Nadharet,

27. Mirrál lako wiyatoara ko, kúri kako Yothep kinko yitirra ko, wonnai taro noa Dabidúmba; ġatun mirrál ġiakai yitirra Mari.

28. Gatun noa aġelo uwa bounnoun kin, ġatun wiyelliela, A! murráráġ umatoara bi Ychóa kátan ġiroug katoa ba; murráráġ umatoara bi nukuġ ka.

29. Gatun bountoa ba nakulla bon, kinta bountoa kakulla wiyellita ġikouġ kin, ġatun kotelliela bountoa minariġ unni totóġ kátan.

30. Gatun aġeloko wiya bounnoun, Kinta kora bi, Mari : kulla bin pitálmatoara Eloito noa.

31. A, ġurralia bi, warakáġ bi kánún, wonnai kan ġiroug kin pika ka, ġatun yinal pórkullinún, ġatun bi ġiakai yitirra IETHU.

32. Gatun wal noa kauwál kánún, ġatun wal bon wiyánún ġia kai Yinal ta wokka ka ko ; ġatun noa Yehóako Eloito gúnún wa. bon yellawollikanne biyuġbai koba Dabidúmba ġikoúmba :

33. Gatun noa wiyánún wal yanti-katai barun Yakobúmba; ġatun ġikoúmba piriwálkanne keawai wal kánún wirán.

34. Wiya ġaiya bountoa bon aġelonuġ Mariko, Yakoai ke unni kánún, kulla baġ kúri korien ?

35. Gatun noa aġeloko wiya bounnoun, Tanan wal noa uwánún Maraikan murráráġkan ġirouġ kinko, ġatun kaiyuko wokka tinto wutinún wal ġirouġ, koito ba unnoa ta murráráġ pórkullinún ġirouġ kin ; wiyánún ġinkai yinal ta Eloi koba.

36. A, ġurralía, ġiroúmba wuġgunbai Elidhabet, warakaġ bountoa yinal ġurroġéen koba bounnoun ba ; ġatun unni ta yellenna †hek ta bounnoun-kai-kan wiyatoara ġurra-uwai.

37. Kulla ġurakito ke noa Eloito kaiyukanto ke.

38. Gatun bountoa Mariko wiya, Kauwá yanti kámunbilla tia wiya bi ba ; ġatoa mankillikan Ychóa-úmba. Gatun noa aġelo púntirkulléún bounnoun kinbiruġ.

39. Gatun bountoa Mari buġkulléún unti-tara purreáġ ka, ġatun uwa bountoa karakai bulkára kolaġ, kokerá kó Yuda kako ;

40. Gatun bountoa uwa kokera ko Dhakaria-úmba kako, ġatun búġbúġ ka bounnoun Elidhabetnuġ.

41. Gatun yakita ġaiya ġurrá bountoa ba Elidhabetto pullí Mariúmba, tulutilléún ġaiya wonnai bounnoun kin pika ka ; ġatun warapál bounnoun ba Elidhabet kin Maraikanto murráráġko :

42. Gatun bountoa wiyelléún pullí wokka wiyellicla, murráráġ umatoara bi nukuġ ba ; ġatun murráráġ umatoara peil ġiroúmba pika koba.

43. Gatun minariġ tin tia unni, tanan uwa tunkan piriwál koba emmoúmba ?

44. Kullá baġ ba ġurrá pulli ġiroúmba ġurréuġ ka emmouġ kin, wonnai ġaiya tia tulutilléún emmouġ kin pika ka pitál ko.

45. Gatun murráráġ umatoara bountoa ġurrá ; kulla unnoa tara kánún umatoara, wiyatoara bounnoun kin Yehóa kinbiruġ.

46. Gatun Mariko bountoa wiya, " Maraito emmoúmba ko wiyan murrai bon Yehóanuġ,

47. Gatun maraito emmoúmba ko pitál umulléún Eloi kin Miroma emmoúmba.

48. Kulla noa nakulla mirrál bountoa ba umullikan ġikoúmba; A, unti biruġ yantinto tia wiyánún murráráġ upatoara.

49. Kulla noa tia kaiyukanto unnoa tara kauwál uma; ġatun yitirroa ġikoúmba murráráġ upatoara kátan.

50. Gatun murrai ġikoúmba barun kinba kintakan bon kátan willuġġél kúri kabiruġ tarai kúri kabiruġ.

51. Túġunbilléún noa kaiyukan turruġ ġikoúmba ; wupéa noa barun ġaruġ ġara yaroyaro búlbúl ban kotellikanne.

52. Upéa noa baran parrán kaiyukan yellawolliġél labiruġ barúnba, ġatun wupéa noa barun mirrál wokka laġ.

53. Gukulla noa kapirrikan ko múrráráġ ta ; ġatun noa barun parólkan yuka mirrál ko.

54. Umulléún noa gikoúmba umullikan Itháraelnuġ, ġurrulli Liruġ ġikouġ kinbiruġ murrai ta ġikoúmba;

55. Yanti wiya noa ba barun biyuġbai to ġearúnba, Abáramnuġ, ġatun barun wonnai tara ġikoúmba yanti katai."

56. Gatun Mari bountoa kakulla bounnoun katoa ġoro ka yellenna ka, ġatun willuġ ba ġaiya bountoa bounnoun ka tako kokera ko.

57. Yakita ġaiya Elidhabetúnba kakulla wonnai pórkullinún; ġatun yinal bounnoun ba pórkulléún.

58. Gatun ġurra bara kótita ko bounnoun bako, yanti Yehóako noa ba murráráġ uma bounnoun kin; ġatun bara pitál kakulla ġatun bountoa.

59. Gatun yakita ġaiya purreáġ ka, uwa ġaiya bara kullabulliko wonnai ko; ġatun bara wiya bon ġiakai Dhakaria, biyuġbai tin yitirra tin.

60. Gatun tunkanto wiya bountoa, Yanoa; kulla bon wiyánún ġiakai Ioanne.

61. Gatun bara bounnoun wiya, Keawaran ġiroúmba kótita wiya ba ġiakai unni yitirra.

62. Gatun bara túġa umulléún bon biyuġbai ko ġikoúmba ko, wonnén noa bon yitirra wiyánún ?

63. Gatun noa wiya upulliġél ko, ġatun noa upa wiyelliela, Yitirra noa ġiakai Ioanne. Gatun bara yantinto kota.

64. Gatun tanoa-kal-bo kurraka buġkulléún ġikoúmba, ġatun bon ġikoúmba tállaġ balbal kakulla, ġatun noa wiya, ġatun noa wiya murrai Eloinuġ.

65. Gatun bara kinta kakulla yantin ta untakál; ġatun unni tara wiyellikanne totóġ kakulla yantin ta kaloġ koa bulkaroa Yuda ka.

66. Gatun bara yantinto umnoa tara ġurra wúnkulla barun kin búlbúl la, wiyelliela, Yakoai unni ta wonnai kánún! Gatun máttára Yehóa-úmba ġikouġ kin kátan.

67. Gatun noa Dhakaria ko biyuġbai ġikoúmba, warapal bon wupéa Marai to yirriyirri to, ġatun noa wiyelliela ġiakai,

68. "Kámunbilla bon Yehóanuġ Eloinuġ Itháracl koba pitálliko; kulla noa uwa barun nakilliko, ġatun wirrilliko kúri ko ġikouġ kaiko.

69. Gatun bouġbuġga noa nulka-nulka ġolomullikan ġearun, kokerá Dabid-úmba ka ġikoúmba mankillikan;

70. Yanti noa ba wiya kurraka ko †propet koba ko yirriyirrikan to yantin to, purrai yantin kurrikurri kabiruġ:

71. Goloma-uwil koa ġearun ġearúnba bukka tukulla birúġ, ġatun máttára biruġ barun kinbiruġ yantin tabiruġ yarakai willuġ kabiruġ,

72. Umulliko murrai ko wiyatoara barun kin biyuġbai ko ġearúnba, ġatun ġurrulliko ġikoúmba wiyatoara yirriyirri ta;

73. Pirral-man noa ġali wiyelliela bon Abáramnuġ biyuġbai ġearúnba,

74. Gúwil koa ġearun noa, mankilliko ġearun máttára biruġ bukkakan tabiruġ ġearúnba, ġurra-uwil koa ġeen bon kinta kerien ko,

75. Yirriyirrikan ġatun murráráġkan mikan ta ġikouġ kin, yantin ta purreáġ ka moron ġearúnba.

76. Gatun ġintoa, wonnai ta, wiyánún bin yitirra †propet ta wokka kako ; kulla bi uwánún ġanka mikan ta Yehóa kin, upulliko yapuġ ko ġikoúmba ;

77. Gukilliko ġurrulliko moron ko ġikouġ kaiko kúri ko, warewarekan yarakai barúnba,

78. Murrai tin kauwollin Eloi koba tin ġearúnba, ġurrakan wokka kabiruġ tanan uwa ġearun kinko,

79. Gukilliko purreáġ barun ko yellawolli ta ba ko ġoroġorá ba ko, ġatun komirra kaba tetti koba, yutilliko tinna ko ġearúnba ko yapuġ koa pitál koba koa.

80. Gatun wonnai poaikulléún, ġatun ġuraki noa maraikan ko, kulla noa koruġ koa yakita ko purreáġ kako paipéa noa ba Itharael kinko.

WINTA II.

YAKITA purreáġ ka, wiya noa Kaitharíko Augútoko, upa-uwil koa bara yantin kuri murrapulliko.

2. Gatun unni murrapullikanne una yakita Kurinio noa ba †kobána kakulla Thuria ka.

3. Gatun yantin bara uwa murrapulliko barun ka tako.

4. Gatun noa Yothep uwa wokka-laġ Galilaia kabiruġ, kokerá birug Nadharet tabiruġ, Iudaia kolaġ, kokerá kolaġ Dabidúmba kolaġ, ġiakai yitirra Bethlehem ; (kulla noa kokera koba ġatun kotita koba Dabidúmba ;)

5. Murrapulliko bon ġatun Mari bounnoun katoa, wiyatoara nukuġ ġikoúmba, wonnai kan bountoa warakaġ.

6. Gatun yakita kakulla, kakulla bara ba unta, purreáġ ka kátan pórkulli'koa bountoa ba wonnai.

7. Gatun bountoa pórbuġġulléún kurri-kurri yinal, ġatun bountoa muġġama bon kirikin to, ġatun bon wúnkulla takilliġélla buttikaġ koba ka ; kulla wal tantullan kokera takilliġél.

8. Gatun bara †éipu-kál untoa kakulléún, tumimillin wirrál barun ba tokoi ta.

9. Gatun noa aġelo Yehóa-úmba tanan uwa barun kin, ġatun kullaburra Yehóa-úmba kakulla barun katoa ; kinta ġaiya bara kakulla.

10. Gatun noa aġeloko wiya barun, Kinta kora ; kulla nurun baġ wiyan murráráġ totóġ kakilliko pitál ko, kakilliko yantin ko kúri ko.

11. Kulla nurúnba pórkulléún unni purreáġ, kokerá Dabidúmba ka, Golomullikan ta, noa Kritht ta Piriwál ta.

12. Gatun unni túġa kánún nurúnba; nanun nura boboġnuġ ġamatoara kirikin taba, kakillin ba takilliġél laba.

13. Gatun tanoa kal bo paipéa konara morokokál ġikouġ katoa aġelo katoa, muriáráġ wiyellin bon Eloinuġ, ġiakai,

THE GOSPEL BY LUKE, c. 2. 133

14. Wiyabúnbilla bon murrárág Eloinuġ wokka kaba moroko kaba, ġatun kámúnbilla pitál purrai tako, murrárág umatoara barun kúri ko.

15. Gatun kakulla ba, waita uwa bara ba, aġelo barun kinbiruġ moroko kolaġ, wiyellan bara †ćipu-kál taraikan-taraikan, Waita ġéen yakita Bethlehem kolaġ, na-uwil koa unnuġ tara kakulla ba, ġala Yehóako noa wiya ġéarun.

16. Gatun bara uwa kurrakai, ġatun nakulla Marinuġ, ġatun boboġ pirikilliela takilliġél laba.

17. Gatun nakulla bara ba, wiyabúnbéa bara yantin ta purrai ta unnoa wiyellikanne wiyatoara barun wonnai tin.

18. Gatun bara yantinto ġurra, kotelliela unnuġ tara, wiya barun bara †ćipu-kál-lo.

19. Wonto ba bountoa Mariko miromá unni tara, ġatun kota bountoa minki ka búlbúl-la bounnoun kin.

20. Gatun bara †ćipu-kál willuġ ba kakulla, murrárág wiyellin ġatun pitálmullin bon Eloinuġ ġala biruġ natoara biruġ ġurratoara biruġ bara yantita wiyatoara ba barun kai.

21. Gatun purreáġ †ét ta kakulla ba, kullintiela ko túġa-witia wonnai, ġiakai bon wiya Iéthu, ġala ba wiya noa aġeloko kurrikurri noa ba pika ka kakulla kunto ka.

22. Gatun purreáġ ka ġoloin ta killibínbín bounnoun ba, yanti Mothé-ko noa ba wiya, mankulla bara bon †Hierothalem kolaġ, ġukilliko bon Yehóa kin ;

23. (Yanti wupa ba wiyellikanne ta Yehóa-úmba ġiakai, Yantin kúri tara ġanka-ġanka pika kabiruġ yirri-yirri wal kánún yitirroa Yehóa koba ;)

24. Gatun ġukilliko ġutoara, ġala wupa ba wiyellikanne taba Yehóa-úmba, ġiakai, Buloara purrouġkan ġa keawai wuroġ buloara poppolameri.

25. A ! ġatun kakulla noa tarai kúri †Hierothalem kaba, ġiakai noa yitirra Thimeon ; ġatun unnoa kúri wiyellikan tuloakan, ġatun ġurrullikan, mittillin pitál ko Itháraeí-úmba ko ; ġatun Marai yirri-yirri-kan kakulla ġikouġ kin.

26. Gatun bon wiyatoara Maraito yirri-yirri-kan-to, keawai noa nanún tettibullikanne, na-uwil koa noa Krithtnuġ Yehóa-úmba.

27. Gatun noa uwa Marai toa †hieron kako : ġatun bula ba porikullaito puruma wonnai Iéthu kin, unulliko bon yanti ko upatoara ko wiyellikanne tako,

28. Mankulla ġaiya bon noa ġikouġ kin turruġ ka, ġatun pitálma noa bon Eloinuġ, ġatun wiyelliela,

29. "Wamúnbilla bi tia Yehóa yakita pitálkan, yanti wiya bi ba :

30. Kulla baġ nakulla ġaikuġ ko ġolomullikan ġiroúmba,

31. Gali ko kakilliko ġintoa yantin ko kúri ko mikan tako ;

32. Kaibuġ kakilliko barun †ethánékál ko, ġatun pitál kakilliko kúri ko Ithárael ġiroúmba ko."

K

33. Gatun bula Yothep gatun Mari kotelliela unnoa wiyatoara gikoug kai.

34. Gatun Thimeon ta noa pitálma barun, gatun wiyelliela Mariuug tunkan gikoúmba, "A ! kátan noa unni wonnai kakilliko puntimulliko, gatun bougkulliko kauwál-kauwál barúnba Itl árael koba; gatun túga ko wiyéa kánún;

35. (Kauwa, yirrako bin turánún wal marai giroúmba kóti,) paipi-uwil koa kotatoara búlbúl labirug kauwál-kauwál labirug."

36. Gatun kakulla wakál Anna, †propetkun, yinálkun Panuel koba, konara koba Ather koba; bountoa ta gurrogéen gagkakalín, gatun kakulla bountoa poribai ta wunál la †hepta ta, murrakin tabirug bountoa katalla;

37. Gatun bountoa mabogun kukulla wunál la †éty-wara yantikalai tabirug, waita uwa korien bountoa †hieron kabirug, wonto ba gurrulliela Eloinug bon purreág ka gatun tokoi ta ta-korien.

38. Gatun bountoa uwolliela tanoa-kal-bo, wiyapaiyéin bon Yehóanug, gatun wiyelliela yantin barun gikoug kin barun, nakillikan gupaiyiko †Hierothalem kako.

39. Gatun upá bara ba unni tara yanti wiyatoara Yehóa koba, willugbo gaiya bara kakulla Galilaia kako, barun ka tako kóti kako Nadharet tako.

40. Gatun wonnai poaikulléún guraki noa maraikan kátan; gatun pitálmatoara bon Eloi koba.

41. Waita uwa bula gikoúmba tunkan gatun biyugbai Hierothalem kolag yanti-katai wurál la takilligél lako kaiwitoara wokka koa.

42. Gatun noa ba wurál la †dodeka ka, waita gaiya uwa bara †Hierothalem kolag wirikai ko takilli ko.

43. Gatun kirun kakulla purreág, willugbo bara ba, wonnai Iéthu noa minka willug ka †Hierothalem ka; gatun noa Yothepko gatun tunkanto gurra korien bula.

44. Wonto bara ba punta bon barun kin konara, uwa purreág ka wakál la; gatun bara bon tiwa kóti ta ka.

45. Gatun bara na korien bon ba, willugbo gaiya bara katéakún †Hierothalem kolag tiwolliko bon.

46. Gatun purreág ka goro kulla, nakulla gaiya bara bon murrug ka †hieron ka, yellawolliela willi ka barun kin †didathkaloi ka, gurrulliela barun, gatun wiyelliela barun wiyellikanne pullí.

47. Gatun yantinto bara bon gurra, kotellela bara bon guraki gatun wiyatoara gikoúmba.

48. Gatun nakulla bara bon ba, unma gaiya barun; gatun tunkanto gikoúmba-ko wiya bon, Nai, minarig tin bi kakulla gearun kai ? a ! biyug ta uwa bali, tiwolliela bali bin, miuki-kan-to.

49. Gatun noa wiya barun, Minarig tin nura tia tiwolliela ? keawai nura ba gurran-upa-uwil koa bag píutunúmba-kan wiya noa tia ba?

50. Gatun bara gurra korien unnoa wiyelli ta wiya noa ba barun.

51. Gatun noa uwa barun katoa barán Nadharet tako, gatun gurrullikan noa kakulla barun kin : wonto bountoa ba tunkan to gikoúmba miromá unni tara wiyellikanne murrug ka búlbúl la bounnoun kin.

52. Gatun noa Iéthuko poaikulléún guraki kakilliko, gatun kauwàl kakilliko, gatun pitálmulliko bon Eloito gatun kúriko.

WINTA III.

YAKITA kakulla wunál la †pipátín ta piriwàl koba Tiberio Kaithar koba, †kobàna noa Pontio Pilato Iudaia ka, gatun tetrák noa Herod Galilaia ka, gatun gikoúmba kóti Pilip tetrák noa Ituréa ka, gatun yantin tako Trakoniti ka, gatun Luthanio tetrák noa Abiléné ka,

2. Annath gatun Kaiapath †thiereu piriwàl bula kakulla, wiyellikanne Eloi koba uwa Ioanne kinko bon, yinal Dhakaría koba, korug kaba.

3. Gatun noa uwa yantin toa purrai toa Ioiádan toa, wiyelliela korimulliko kanumaiko, warekulliko yarakai ;

4. Yanti wupaitoara †biblion ka wiyellikanne Ethaia koba †propet koba, giakai, Pullí wakál koba wiyelléún korug kaba, Yapug Yehóa koba murràràg umulla nura, tuloa kakilliko yapug gikoúmba.

5. Yantin ta pilabai warapal upinún, gatun yantin ta bulkára umánún puntig ; gatun warín-warín ta umánún tuloa, gatun yapug yarakai wollugbiara umánún poitog ;

6. Gatun yantinto nanún wal golomullikanne Eloi koba.

7. Wiya gaiya noa barun konara uwa bara korimulliko gikoug kinko, Ela béara ! konara maiya kiloa nura ! ganto nurun wiya murralliko bukka tin tanan ba uwánún ?

8. Koito nura ba umullia murràràg minki kabirug; gatun kota yikora nura kóti ka minki ka nurun kin wiyelliko, Abáram gearun noa gcarúnba biyugbai ; kulla bag wiyan nurun, Eloi noa kaiyukan kàtan umulliko unti tara birug tunúg kabirug wonnai kakilliko Abáram kinko.

9. Gatun yakita baibai wúnkulla kúlai ta wirrá ka ; koito ba yantin kúlai keawai kàtan murràràg kólbúntil!ánún wal barán, warekulliko koiyug kako.

10. Gatun kúriko bon wiya, wiyelliela, Minnug banún gaiya géen?

11. Wiya noa barun, wiyelliela, Niuwoa †kót-kan buloarakan gikoúmba, gumunbilla bon keawai ko; gatun niuwoa kuntokan gumúnbilla bon yanti kiloa.

12. Uwa gaiya bara †telóné korimulliko, gatun wiya bon, Piriwàl, minnug banún géen ?

13. Gatun noa wiya barun, Manki yikora untoa-kál unnoabo mara wiyatoara nurúnba.

14. Gatun bara †army-kanko wiya bon wiyelliela, Minnug banún géen? gatun noa wiya barun, Bukkamai yikora yantin kúri, gatun wiyéa-yemmai yikora gakoyellaikan yantin kúri ; gatun murrai kauwa nura galoakan gutoarakan nurúnba.

15. Gatun bara ba kúri kotelliela, ġatun yantinto kúriko kotelliela murruġ ka ba ko, búlbúl la ba ko barun kin ba ko ġikóuġ Ioannenuġ, minariġ noa Kritht ta, mirka keawaran.
16. Ioanneto noa wiya barun yantin ta, wiyelliela, Korimulliko baġ katan nurun bato ko ; wonto ba wakál kaiyukan kauwál-kauwálkan ġatoa kiloa uwánún, murráráġ korien baġ poruġbuġgulliko túġġanúġ ko ġikoúmba ko; niuwoa ta korimanún nurun Marai to yirri-yirri ko ġatun koiyuġ ko :
17. †Pituon ġikoúmba mankillin máttára ba, ġatun murkun noa umánún búnkilliġél laba ġikoúmba, ġatun noa ka-umánún †wíet ġikoúmba tako kokerá ko ; wonto ba tirri koiyuġ-banún wal noa koiyuġ ka talokulli korien ta.
18. Tarai ta yantin kauwál-kauwál wiya noa : ġatun wiyelli ta ba ko barun kúri.
19. Wonto noa ba Herodnuġ †tetráknuġ piralma bon, noa boun noun kin Herodia kin nukuġ ka Pilip-úmba ġikoúmba kóti koba, ġatun yantin yarakai noa ba uma Herodto,
20. Yanti unni uma, wirriġbakulla bon noa Ioannenuġ †jail ka.
21. Yakita barunbo karima yantin kúri, kakulla ġaiya korimullicla bon Iéthunuġ, ġatun wiyelliela, moroko ġaiya waruġkalléún,
22. Gatun uwa barán Maraikan yirri-yirrikan murrin kiloa purrouġkan kiloa, ġikouġ kin; ġatun wakál pullí kakulla moroko tin, wiyelliela, Gintoa ta emmoúmba yinal pitálmullikanne ; pitálman baġ ġirouġ.
23. Gatun niuwoa bo Iéthu kakillilicla wunál la †triakontaka ġiko-úmba, puntelliela bon yinal Yothepúmba, wonto yinal Eli-úmba;
&c., &c.,
38. Wonto yinal Enoth-úmba, wonto yinal Thet-úmba, wonto yinal Adam-úmba, wonto yinal Eloi-úmba.

WINTA IV.

GATUN noa Iéthu warapálkan Maraikan yirri-yirri-kan, willuġbo kakulla Iorádan tabiruġ, ġatun bon yutéa Maraito koruġ kolaġ,
2. Nupitoara bon purreáġ ka †tettarakonta ka †diabollo. Gatun unta tara purreáġ ka keawai noa ta ba : ġatun ġoloin ba unta tara kakulla, kapirri ġaiya noa kakulla.
3. Gatun noa †diabollo wiya bon, Wiya, bi ba yinal Eloi koba, wiyellía unni tunuġ ka-uwil koa kunto.
4. Gatun noa Iéthuko bon wiya, wiyelliela, Wupatoara ta, Keawai kúri kánún moron kunto kabiruġ, wonto ba Eloi koba pullí tabiruġ.
5. Gatun noa †diabollo yutéa bon waita bulkárá ko, nanunbéa bon yantin piriwál koba purrai ta ba tanoa-kal-bo kurrakai.
6. Gatun noa †diabollo wiya bon, yantin kaiyu kako ġunún baġ ġirouġ, ġatun pitálmulliko ġali tara ko ; koito ba ġukulla tia emmouġ ; ġatun baġ ġutan ġanúmbo pitál baġ ba kátan.

7. Gintoa ba wiyánún tia, kánún bin yantin giroúmba.

8. Gatun noa Iéthuko wiya bon, Kauwa bi, Thátan, willug ka emmougkin ; koito ba wupatoara, Wiyánún wal bi Ychóanug giroúmba Eloinug, gatun gikoug bo gurránún wal bi.

9. Gatun noa bon yutéa †Hierothalem kolag, gatun wúnkulla bon búlwarra ka †hieron ka, gatun wiya bon, Yinalla bi ba unni Eloikoba, warekulla bi unti birug barán :

10. Kulla ba wupatoara ta, Wiyánún noa barun agelo ko nakilliko giroug, golomulliko giroug;

11. Gatun bara bin manún máttárró wokka lag, tinna koa giroug pultéa-kún tunug ko yantin ta.

12. Gatun Iéthuko, wiyelliela, wiya bon, Wiyatoara ta, Yanoa wal bi numa yikora bon Ychóanug Eloinug giroúmba.

13. Gatun noa †diabollo goloin kakulla unni tara nupatoara, waita gaiya noa uwa gikoug kinbirug yakita ko.

14. Gatun noa Iéthuko willug ko kakulla, kaiyukan Maraikan, Galilaia kako: gatun totóg bon kakulla yantin ta purrai karig ka.

15. Gatun noa wiyelliela †thunagóg ka barun ka ta, pitál wiyatoara bon yantinto.

16. Gatun noa uwa Nadharet tako, kakulla noa poaikulléún unta; gatun, yanti katai noa ba, uwa noa †thunagóg kako purreág ka thabbat, gatun garokéa wokka lag wiyelliko.

17. Gatun gukulla bon †biblion ta †propet koba Ethaia koba : gatun bugbugga noa ba †biblion, nakulla gaiya noa giakai upatoara,

18. Marai ta unni Yehóa koba emmoug kinba, kulla noa tia putía wiyelliko Euagelion barun kin mirrál la; yuka noa tia turon umulliko minkikan ko, wiyelliko barun wúntoara ko wamunbilliko, gatun na-uwil koa bara munmin to, burug buggulliko barun búntoara,

19. Wiyelliko * * * gurrabunbilliko wunál la pitálmullikanne Yehóa koba.

20. Gatun noa wirrig-bugga †biblion, gatun noa gutéa kan bon umullikan ko, gatun yellawa barán. Gatun bara bon pimilliela gaikug ko, yantin †thunagóg ka ba ko.

21. Gatun noa barun tanoa bo wiya, Turin-pai-béa unni wiya upatoara nurun kin gurréug ka unti purreág ka.

22. Gatun yantinto bara gurrulliela bon, gatun kota bara pulli murrai kurraka kabirug gikoug kinbirug. Gatun bara wiya, Wiya, unni ta Yothepúmba yinal ?

23. Gatun noa barun wiya, Nura ta wiyánun tia unni wiyellikanne, Karákal, turon bi umulla ginton bo; gurra géen ba umatoara Kapernaum ka, umulla bi unti yantin ta purrai ta giroúmba ka.

24. Gatun noa wiya, Tuloa nurun bag wiyan, keawai †propet gurrá korien gikoug ka ta purrai ta kóti ka.

25. Wonto bag ba nurun wiyan tuloa, kauwál-kauwál ta mabogun Ithárael kulléún purreág ka Elía-úmba ka, yakita wirrigbakulla moroko ta wunál ta goro gatun yellenna †hek ta, tara-wará kakulla yantin ta purrai karig ka ;

26. Keawai Elíanuġ yuka ba barun kinko, wonto ba Tbarepta kako Thidoni kako nukuġ kako mabogun tako.

27. Gatun kauwá'-kauwá!kan †leprokan Itháracl ka, yaki-kalai Elíću koba †propet koba; keawaran wakál barun kinbiruġ turon umatoara, wonto ba noa Naaman Thuriakúl.

28. Gatun yantin bara kakulla †tthunagóg ka, ġurra bara unni tara, bukka kauwál kakulla,

29. Gatun bouġkullċún, ġatun yipa bon kokerá biruġ, ġatun bon yutéa pita kako bulkará ko kokerá ko wittitoara ko, wareka uwil koa bara bon walluġġón barán.

30. Wonto noa ba uwolliela willi koa barun katća, waita uwa.

31. Gatun noa uwa barán Kapernaum kako, kokerá ko Galilaia kako, ġatun wiyelliela barun purrċáġ ka thabbat ka.

32. Gitun bara kota wiyellikanne tin ġikoúmba tin; kulla ġikoumba pulli kaiyukan.

33. Gatun kakulla wakál kúri †tthunagóg ka, ġikouġ kin minki ka marai kakulla †diabol koba yarakai koba, ġatun noa kaipulléun wokka,

34. Wiyelliela, Ká nunbilla ġearun; minnuġ banún ġéen bin ġinton Iéthu Nadharetkál? uwa bi ġearun tetti-umulli kolaġ? ġimillin bannġ ġintoa ta; wakál bo ta yirri-yirri-kan Eloi koba.

35. Gatun bon Iéthuko koakulla, wiyelliela, Kaiyellía bi, ġatun paikulléa ġikouġ kinbiruġ. Gatun bon ba wareka willi ka †diabollo, paikulléan noa ġikouġ kinbiruġ. ġatun keawai bon tetti búntima ba.

36. Gatun bara yantinto kota, ġatun wiyelliela barabo-barabo, Minariġ unni wiyellikanne! kulla noa wiya kaiyu-kan-to barun †diabolnuġ yarakaikan, ġatun barun paikulléan warrai tako.

37. Gatun totóġ ġikoumba kakulla yantin toa purrai kariġ koa.

38. Gatun noa uwa †tthunagóg kabiruġ, ġatun pológkulléun Thimon kinko kokera ko. Gatun tunkan Thimonúmba nukuġ koba munni kakulla karinkan; ġatun bon bara wiya bounnoun kai kolaġ.

39. Gatun noa ġarokéa bounnoun kin turruġ ka, ġatun noa koakulla karin; ġatun wareka ġaiya bounnoun karinto; ġatun bountoa bouġkullé in tanoa-kal-bo, ġatun umulliela barun kaiko.

40. Gatun punnál ba pulóġ-kulliléan, yantin bara mankulla munni-munni-kan ġikouġ kinko; ġatun noa wupilléan barun kin mátára yantin ta, ġatun turon unia barun.

41. Gatun †diabol kauwál-kauwál paikulléun kauwá'-kauwál labiruġ, kaibulliela, Gintoa ta Kritht ta, yinal ta Eloi-koba. Gatun noa barun koakulla wiya korien; kulla wal bara ġimilléun bon Kritht ta noa unnoa.

42. Gatun purrċáġ ba kakulla, waita noa uwa korariġ; ġatun bara kúriko tiwa bon, ġatun uwa ġikouġ kin, ġatun niima bara bon, keawai noa waita wapa barun kinbiruġ.

43. Gatun noa wiya barun, Wiyánun bo ta wal baġ piriwá'ġél la Eloi koba taraikan ta kokera; kullá wal tia ġaliko yuka.

WINTA V.

Gatun yakita kakulla, warapa bon ba bara kuriko, ġurrulliko wiyellikanne Eloi koba, ġarokéa noa pitta ka waraka Gennetharet ta,

2. Gatun nakulla buloara murrinauwai kakilliela wara ka; wonto ba bara makoroban waita uwa murrinauwai tabiruġ, ġatun bara umulliela pika mirkun.

3. Gatun noa uwa wakál la murrinauwai ta Thimon koba ka, ġatun wiya bon yóġyóġ umullia purrai tabiruġ. Gatun noa yellawa barán, ġatun wiyelliella barun kúri murrinauwai kabiruġ.

4. Gatun ġoloin noa ba wiya, wiya noa Thimónnuġ bon, Tuirkullia pirriko kako, ġatun wura pika nurúnba mankilliko.

5. Gatun Thimónto, wiyelliela, wiya bon, Piriwàl, uma ġéen tokoi ta yanti-katai, ġatun mán korien; kulla bi wiyán wupinún wal baġ barán pika.

6. Gatun uma bara ba unni, kokoi-kokoi bara uma makoro katai kal; ġatun pika kilpaiya.

7. Gatun bara wokkaimullé in barúnba tarai taba murrinauwai taba; wa-uwil koa barun wintamulliko. Gatun bara uwa, ġatun warapál bara wupéa buloara murrinauwai, pillukulliela ġaiya bara.

8. Nakulla noa ba Thimónto Peterko, puntimullé in noa Iéthu kin warómbuġ ka, wiyelliela, Ela Piriwál! yuriġ bi wolla emmouġ kinbiruġ; kulla baġ yarakairán kúri kátan.

9. Kulla noa kota, ġatun yantin bara ġikouġ katoa ba, kauwá!-lin makorrin mankulla bara ba.

10. Gatun yantibo bara Yakobo ġatun Ioanne, yinal ta Lebedaio koba, mankillai bula ba Thimon katoa. Gatun Iéthuko noa wiya bon Thimónnuġ, Kinta kora bi; yakita biruġ man in wal bi barun kúri.

11. Gatun mankulla bara ba murrinauwai barán purrai tako, wánkulla bara yantin, wirroba bon bara.

12. Gatun yakita kakulla, kakulla noa ba tarai ta kokerá, a! wakál kúri kauwál †leprokan; nakilliela noa Iéthunuġ puntimulléin ġoarrá ko, ġatun wiya bon, wiyelliela, Piriwál, wiya, bi ba kaiyukan kánún, umánún bi tia turon.

13. Gatun noa bon wupilléin máttára ġikouġ kin, wiyelliela, Kauwá; turon bi kauwa. Gatun tanoa-kal-bo †leprota wareka ġikouġ kinbiruġ ko.

14. Gatun noa bon wiya, wiyéakún koa noa barun k'iri; wonto ba yiruġ uwa túġunbilliko ġintoa bo †thiereu kinko, ġatun ġúwa kulla bi turon umatoara, yanti to Mothé ka noa ba wiya, ġurrulliko kakilliko barun.

15. Wonta ba yantin kakulla totóġ ġikouġ yantin toa purrai toa: ġatun kauwálko naro uwa ġurrulliko, ġatun turon kakilliko barun munni-munni ġikouġ kinbiruġ ko.

16. Gatun noa uwa koruġ kako, ġatun wiyelliela.

17. Yakita kakulla tarai ta purrcáġ ka, wiyelliela noa ba, yellawa ba Parithaioi ġatun †didathkaloi wiyellikanne koba, yantin

tabiruġ kokerá biruġ Galilaia kabiruġ, ġatun ludaia kabiruġ, ġatun †Hierothalem kabiruġ; ġatun kaiyuto Yehóa-úmba kakulla turon umulliko barun.

18. A! ġatun bara kúri wakál kúri kurréa pirrikilliġél la munnikan karál; ġatun numa bara bon kurrilliko kokerá kolaġ, ġatun wúnkilliko bon ġikouġ kinko mikan tako.

19. Gatun keawai bara napa wonnén kurrilliko murruġ kolaġ konara tin, uwa bara wokka laġ kokera búlwarra ka, ġatun wupéa bon barán kulla koa willi-willi kako pirrikilliġélkan léthu kin mikan ta.

20. Gatun nakulla noa ba kotellikanne barúnba, wiya noa bon, Ela kúri, yarakai ġiroúmba wareka ġirouġ kinbiruġ.

21. Gatun bara †gárammateu ġatun Parithaioi kota, wiyelliela, Gan-ke unni wiyan ba yarakai? Ganto kaiyu-kan-to warekulliko yarakai, wonto ba wakállo Eloito?

22. Wonto noa ba Iéthuko ġurra kotatoara barúnba, niuwoa wiya wiyelliela barun, Minariġ tin nura kotelliela búlbúl lako nurun kin ba ko.

23. Wonnén murráraġ wiyelliko, Giroúmba ko yarakaito wareka ġirouġ kinbiruġ; ġa wiyelliko, Bouġkullia ġatun uwolliko?

24. Wonto ba ġurra-uwil koa nura kaiyukan noa yinal kúri koba purrai taba yarakai warekulliko (wiya noa munni karál), Wiyan banuġ, bouġkullia ġatun mara ġiroúmba pirrikilliġél, ġatun waita unwolla ġirouġ ka tako kokerá ko.

25. Gatun tanoa-kal-bo bouġulléún noa barun kin mikan ta, ġatun mánkulla unnuġ ġikoúmba pirrikéa noa ba, ġatun waita uwa ġikouġ ka tako kokerá ko koti kako, pitálmulliela bon Eloinuġ.

26. Gatun yantin bara kotelliela, ġatun bara ġaiya pitálma bon Eloinuġ, ġatun kinta laġ bara kauwál, kátan wiyelliela, Nakulla ġéen minariġ konéin buġgai.

27. Gatun yakita yukita waita uwa noa, ġatun nakulla wakál †telónénuġ, ġiakai yitirra Lebi, yellawollin wúnkilliġél la; ġatun noa wiya bon, Yettiwolla tia.

28. Gatun noa wúnkulla yanti bo bouġkulléún, ġatun noa bon yettiwa.

29. Gatun Lebiko bon noa upéa kauwál takillikanne ġikouġ ka ta kóti ka kokera: ġatun kauwál kakulla konara telónai ko ġatun tarai to yellawa barun katoa.

30. Wonto ba barúnba †gárammateu ġatun Parithaioi koakillan bara barun wirrobullikan ġikoúmba, wiyelliela, Minariġ tin nura tatan ġatun pittan barun katoa †telónai koa ġatun yarakai toa?

31. Gatun noa Iéthuko wiya barun, wiyelliela, Bara ba moron tai kátan keawai bara wiyan karákál; wonto ba bara munni kátan.

32. Uwa baġ wiya korien ko murroġ taiko, wonto ba yarakai willuġ ko minki kakilliko.

33. Gatun wiya bon bara, Minariġ tin bara mupai kátan mur-

rínmurrín wirrobullikan Ioannc-úmba, gatun wiyan wiyellikanne, gatun yantibo bara Parithaioi koba; wonto ba giroúmba ko tatan gatun pittan?

34. Gatun noa wiya barun, Wiya, nura kaiyukan mupai umulliko barun wonnai kakillaikanne, yakita-kalai poribai ba katan barun katoa ba?

35. Wonto ba purreág kánún wal, mánún wal bon ba poribai barun kinbirug, gatun yakita gaiya bara mupai-kakillinún purreág ka unta tara.

36. Gatun wiya noa barun wakál †parabol giakai : Keawai kúri ko wupillinún buggaikál korokál la ; ga ba, yanti buggaikál yiirbugganún gaiya wal, gatun pontol buggaikál labirug keawai korokál kiloa kátan.

37. Gatun keawai kúri ko wupinún buggaikál †wain pika ka korokál la; kulla buggaikállo potopai-yánún wal pika ka, gatun kiroabullinún, gatun pika kánún yarakai.

38. Wonto ba buggaikál †wain wunún wal buggaikál la pika ka; gatun buloara murrárág kátan.

39. Gatun keawai kúri koba pittánún korokál †wain keawai noa manún buggaikál †wain, kulla noa wiyan korokál ta murrárag.

WINTA VI.

Gatun yakita thabbat ka buloara, yukita thabbat ka kurri-kurri, uwa gaiya noa murrug koa yeaigél loa ; gatun bara wirrobulli-kanto gikoug ka to tittia wollug yeai, gatun takulla mirro-mirromá máttára barun kin.

2. Gatun taraikanto Parithaioi koba wiya barun, Minarig tin nura uman unnoa keawaran murrárág umulliko unti tara purreág ka thabbat ka?

3. Gatun noa Iéthuko wiya, wiyelliela, Wiya nura, wiya nura, wiya ba unni, Dabid-to noa ba upa, niuwoabo ba kapirri kakilla gatun bara gikoug katoa ;

4. Uwa noa ba kokera kai Eloi koba, gatun mankulla takulla nulai nakillikanne, gatun gukulla barun gikoug katoa ba ko, keawaran murrárág takilliko, wonto ba barúnba ko †hiereu koba?

5. Gatun noa barun wiya, Yinal ta kúri koba, piriwál noa kátan yantin ko thabbat ko.

6. Gatun yakita kakulla tarai ta thabbat ta, uwa gaiya noa †thunagóg ka gatun wiyelliela : gatun wakál kúri unta kakulla, máttára gikoúmba túgkagkeri tirrai kakulla.

7. Gatun bara †gárammateuko gatun Parithaioiko tumiméa bon, wiya bon noa ba turon umulla purreág ka thabbat ta ; wiyayemma-uwil koa bara bon.

8. Wonto noa ba kota barúnba gurrulliela, wiya bon noa máttárakan tirraikan, Bougkullia, gatun garokilla willi ka. Gatun noa bougkulléún, gatun garokéa.

9. Wiya gaiya noa Iéthuko barun, Wiyánún wal bag nurun

unni ; wiya tuloa ta umulliko, murrárág ḡa yarakai umulliko purreáġ ka thabbat ta ? moron umulliko, ḡa warekulliko?

10. Gatun nakilliela kari-kari yantin barun, wiya bon noa, Tutullia bi máttára ġiroúmba. Gatun upulléún ġaiya noa, ḡatun máttara ḡaiya bon turon uma yanti tarai ba.

11. Gatun bara warapalkan bukkakan kakulla; ġatun murrárág wiyellan barabo-barabo, minnuġ banún bara bon ba léthunuġ.

12. Yakita unta purreáġ ka, uwa noa bulkára kolaġ wiyelliko, yanti-katai noa tokoi ta wiyelliela bon Eloi-nuġ.

13. Gatun yakita purreáġ ta, kaai ba noa barun wirrobullikan ġikoúmba; ġirimulléún noa barun kinbiruġ †dodeka niuwoa, barun wiya ḡiakai yitirra †apothol ;

14. Thimóunuġ (wiya noa ġiakai yitirra Peternuḡ), ġatun ġikoúmba kurrakóġ Andrea, ḡatun Yakobo ġatun Ioanne, ġatun Pilip ġatun Bátolomai,

15. Mattaio ḡatun Thoma, ġatun Yakobo Alpai-úmba, ḡatun Thimon ġiakai wiya yitirra Dheloté,

16. Gatun Iudath kurrakóġ ta Yakobo-úmba, ġatun Iudath Ithákariot, niuwoa ġakoiyayé noa.

17. Gatun noa uwa barán barun katoa, ġatun ġarawan tako ḡarokéa noa, ġatun konaró wirrobullikan ġikoúmba, ḡatun kauwál konara kúri Iudaiakál, ġatun †Hierothalemkál, ġatun korowátari Turokúl ġatun Thidonikál, uwa bara ġurrulliko bon, ġatun turon umulliko barun ba munni ;

18. Gatun bara wonkálman yarakai to marai to : gatun barun uma turon.

19. Gatun yantinto konaró numulla bon bara ; kulla murrárág paibéa ġikouġ kinbiruġ, ġatun noa turon uma yantin barun.

20. Gatun noa wokkalan nakulla ġaikuġ ko ġikoúmba wirrobullikan, ġatun wiya, Murrárág umatoara mirrálko ; kulla nurun ba piriwálġél la Eloi koba.

21. Murrárág umatoara nura kapirrikan yakita : kulla nura warapan wal kakilliko. Murrárág umatoara nura túnkillin yakita, kulla nura kintellinún wal.

22. Murrárág umatoara nura, yarakai umánún ġaiya nurun kúri ko, ġatun warekanún nurun, ġatun yarakai wiyánún nurun, ġatun warekanún yitirra nurúnba yanti yarakai ba, ġikouġ kin biruġ yinal kári koba kabiruġ.

23. Pitál nura kauwa ġatun úntellia unta purreáġ ka ; kulla nurúnba ġukillikanne kauwál kátan moroko kaba; yanti uma bara biyuġbai tako barun ka to barun †propetnuġ.

24. Yapal nura porólkan kátan ! kulla nura mankulla ta pitál nurúnba.

25. Yapál nura warakan! kulla nura kapirrikánún. Yapal nura kintellan yakita ! kulla nura ġirellinun ġatun túnkillinún.

26. Yapal nura, murrárág wiyánán ba yantinto kuriko nurun ! yantibo barúnba biyuġbai ta ko barun ġakoyaye †propetnuġ.

THE GOSPEL BY LUKE, c. 6. 143

27. Giakai bag wiyan nurun gurrullikan, Pitálumulla barun yarakai willug nurúnba; murrárág umulla barun yarakai nurúnba uman,

28. Murrárág barun wiyella koatan nurúnba; gatun wiyella bon Eloinug wiyella barun yarakai nurúnba uman.

29. Gatun búnnún ba wakál gan kulló tarai to, tarai gukillia; gatun niuwoa manún wurabil giroúmba, wiya yikora wiwi manki yikora unni doan.

30. Guwa barun yantin ko wiyellinún ba giroug kin; gatun niuwoa ba mankulla tullokán giroúmba wiya yikora kari bon.

31. Gatun unnoa la kotan nura la murrárág umulliko barun kúri nurun, umulla nura yantibo ta barun.

32. Kulla nura pitálman barun pitálman nurun, minarigko-ke unnoa? kulla bara yarakai-kan-to yantibo uman.

33 Gatun murrárág nura umánún ba barun gali murrárág nurun uman, minarigko-ke unnoa? kulla bara yarakai-kan-to yantibo uman.

34. Gatun mumbinún nura ba barun kotan nura willugbo upilliko barun, minarigko-ke unnoa? kulla bara yarakai willug mumbillan barun willugbo upilliko yantibo.

35. Wonto ba nura pitálumulla barun yarakai willug nurúnba; gatun murrárág umulla, gatun mumbilla kotan keawai willugbo upulliko; gatun gutoara kauwál kánún nurúnba, gatun nura wonnai kánún wokka koba; kulla noa murrárag uman barun wiyapaiyo korien gatun barun yarakai.

36. Kauwa nura minkikan, yantibo Biyugbai nurúnba minki kátan.

37. Kota yikora yarakai, gatun keawai nurun kotánún yarakai: pirriralmai yikora nura, gatun keawai nurun pirriralmanún: warekilla nura, gatun nurúnba warekánún.

38. Guwa, gatun gunún wal nurun; warapal, upulla barán, gatun tolomulla kaumulliko, gatun kiroabullin barán, gunún wal kúri nurun gielkag ka nurun kin. Kulla yantibo upitoara nura upullin, upéa kánún nurun.

39. Gatun noa wiya barun wakál †parabol; wiya, munminto yutinún tarai mummin? wiya, wal bula-buloarabo warakullinún barán kirun tako?

40. Wirrobullikan ta keawaran noa kauwál korien gikoug kin piriwál la; wonto ba tuloa kátan, kánun noa yanti piriwal ba gikoug ba.

41. Gatun minarig tin bi natan morig giroug ka ta ba gaikug kaba kurrikóg kaba, wonto ba na korien bi tulkirri gaikug kaba giroug kinba kóti kaba?

42. Ga, yakoai bi wiyan bon kurrikóg giroug ba, Biggai, yakoai tia porugbuggabunbilla morig giroug kinba gaikug kaba, keawai bi ba nakillin tulkirri giroug kaba? Gintoa gakoiyaye! burugbug gala kurri-kurri tulkirri gaikug kaba giroug kinba kóti

kaba, ġatun nanún ġaiya bi murra-murráráġ umulliko moriġ ġaikuġ kaba kurrikóġ kaba ġirouġ ka ta ba.

43. Kulla ba kúlai murráráġ ta kátan, keawai yeai yarakai upin ; ġa keawai kúlai yarakai ta kátan, yeai murráráġ upin.

44. Wonto ba yantin kúlai ġimilliko kóti tin yeai tin ; kulla bara kúri mán korien kokuġ tulkirri-tulkirri tin, ġa titi korien bara †botru maro tin.

45. Murráráġko noa kúriko wupillin noa murráráġ wunkilliġél labiruġ minki kabiruġ búlbúl labiruġ ġikouġ kinbiruġ ; ġatun noa yarakai wupullin noa yarakai wunkilliġel labiruġ yarakai ta biruġ minki kabiruġ búlbúl labiruġ ġikouġ kinbiruġ ; kulla ġikoúmba ko kurraka ko wiyan kauwál labiruġ ko búlbúl labiruġ ko.

46. Gatun minariġ tin nura tia wiyan, Piriwál, Piriwál, ġatun uwa korien nura unnoa tara wiyan nurun baġ ba.

47. Gan tia ba uwánún emmouġ kin, ġatun ġurran wiyellita emmoúmba, ġatun ġaloa uman, túġunbinún baġ nurun ġan kiloa noa :

48. Niuwoa ba wakál yanti kúri kiloa, wittia noa kokera ġatun pinnia pirriko, ġatun wupéa tuġga tunuġ ka ; ġatun poaikulléún ba tunta-tunta, waiumbul murrá koribibi kokeroa, ġatun ġeawai tolomá pa ; kulla wal wittia tunug ka.

49. Wonto ba ġurran ġatun uma korien, kúri kiloa noa wittia kokera tuġga korien purrai ta : waiumbul murrá koribibi ġali, ġatun warakulléún tanoa-kal-bo ; kauwálla unnoa warakullin kokera koba.

WINTA VII.

WIYA noa ba ġoloin ġikoúmba wiyellikanne, mikan ta yantin ta kúri ka, uwá noa Kapernaun kako.

2. Gatun tarai koba †kapátin koba umullikan munni kakilliela, muluġkilliliela tetti, pitál umatoara noa ġikoúmba.

3. Gatun, ġurrá noa ba Iéthunuġ, wiyabunbéa noa barun ġarokál Hebáraioi koba, wiyelliela bon uwa-uwil koa noa pirbuġgulliko ġikoúmba ko umullikan ko.

4. Gatun uwá bara ba Iéthu kin, wiya ġaiya bon bara tanoa-kal-bo, wiyelliela, Murráráġ noa uma-uwil koa noa bon yanti :

5. Kulla noa pitálman ġearúnba kúri, ġatun uoa wittia ġearun †thunagóg.

6. Uwa ġaiya noa Iéthu barun katoa. Gatun kaloġ korien ta noa ba kakulla kokerá kolaġ, yuka noa barun †kapátinto kóti ta ġikouġ kin, wiyelliela bon, Piriwál, yanoa bi ; kulla baġ keawaran murráráġ korien uwa-uwil koa bi emmouġ kin kokerá :

7. Yaki tin baġ kota murráráġ korien baġ uwolliko ġirouġ kinko ; wonto ba wiyella wakál wiyellikanne, ġatun emmoúmba umullikan pirkullinún wal.

8. Kulla baġ ba kaiyukan wiyelliko, emmouġ kinba bara kakillin †army-kan ; ġatun baġ wiya wakál, Yuriġ, ġatun waita ġaiya noa uwa ; ġatun tarai, Kaai, ġatun noa uwa tanan ; ġatun emmoúmba umullikan, Umulla unni, ġatun uma ġaiya noa.

9. Iéthuko noa ba ġurrá unni tara, kotelliela noa ġikouġ, ġatun warrakulléún noa, wiya ġaiya noa barun wirroba bon ba, Wiyan baġ nurun, keawaran baġ na pa yanti ġurrullikanne kauwál, keawai yanti Ithárael la kátan.
10. Gatun bara yukatoara, willuġbo uwolliela kokerá kolaġ, nakulla bon umullikan munni biruġ pirbuġgatoara.
11. Gatun yakita purrcáġ ka yukita, uwa noa kokeroa, ġiakai yitirra Nain ; ġatun kauwál uwa ġikoúmba wirrobullikan ġatun taraikan kúri ġikouġ katoa.
12. Gatun uwa noa ba papai puloġkulliġél la kokerá kolaġ, ġa, tetti kulwon kurrilliela kúri warai kolaġ, wakál bo ta yinal tunkan koba bounnoun ba, ġatuu maboġun bountoa, ġatun kauwál-kauwál kúri kokerá biruġ uwa bounnoun katoa.
13. Gatun nakulla bounnoun noa ba Piriwállo, ġurrirra bounnoun noa kakulla, ġatun wiya ġaiya noa bounnoun, Túġki yikora.
14. Gatun uwa ġaiya noa, numa kurrilliġél ; ġatun bara kurriá bon ba ġakéa korun. Gatun noa wiya, Wuġgurra, wiyau banug, Bouġkullia.
15. Gatun niuwoa tetti kabiruġ yellawa, ġatun tanoa-kal-bo wiya. Gatun willuġbo bon noa ġukulla bounnoun kin ġikoúmba ka tunkan ta.
16. Gatun bara kakulla kinta yantin ; ġatun bara bon pitálman Eloinuġ, wiyelliela, Kauwál †propet ta paipéa ġearun kin, ġatun noa Eloito nakulla ġikoúmba kúri.
17. Gatun unni totóġ ġikoúmba kakulla yantin to Iudaia koa, ġatun yantin toa purrai kariġ koa.
18. Gatun Ioanne-úmba-ko wirrobullikanto wiya bon unni tara.
19. Gatun noa Ioanneto wiya bulun wirrobullikan ġikoúmba, yuka bulun Iéthu kinko, wiyelliko, Gintoa ta uwánún ? ġa, na-téa kánún ġéen taraikan ?
20. Uwa bara ba kúri ġikouġ kinko wiya bara, Ioanneto korimullikanto ġearun yuká ġironġ kinko, wiyelliko, Gintoa ta uwánun ? ġa, na-téa kánún taraikan ?
21. Gatun tanoa-kal-bo †hora ka pirbuġga noa kauwál-kauwál munni-munni, ġatun marai yarakaikan ; ġatun kauwál-kauwál munmin uma noa barun nakilliko.
22. Wiya ġaiya noa barun Iéthu, wiyelliela, Waita laġ nura, ġatun wiyella bon Ioanuenuġ unni tara nakulla nura ba ġatun ġurra ; munmin-tabiruġ-ko natan, wiirwiir-biruġ-ko uwan, wamunwamun-tabiruġ turon kakulla, woġkál-labiruġ ġurran, tetti-kabiruġ bouġkulléún, barun mirrál ko wiyan ta Euaġelion.
23. Gatun pitál-umatoara yantinto niuwara korien kánún emmouġ kin.
24. Gatun waita ka ba bara ba puntimai Ioanne-úmba, wiya ġaiya noa barun kúri Ioannenuġ bon, Minariġ tin nura koruġ kolaġ nakilliko ? koġka toloman wibbi ko ?

25. Minarig ko nura uwa korug kolag nakilliko? wakal upulléún kúri poitog korikin to? A! bara upulléán konéin to ġatun bara murrárág kátan takilliko, yellawa bara piriwálġél la.

26. Minarig ko nura uwa korug kolag nakilliko? wakal †propet? Kauwa, wiyan nurun bag kauwállan noa ba †propet kiloa.

27. Gali noa wiyatoara upa unni, A! yukan bag puntimai emmoúmba giroug kin mikan ta, umánun wal noa yapug giroug.

28. Kulla bag wiyan nurun, Keawai †propet kauwäl kátan yanti Ioanne noa ba korimullikan porkullitoara nukug labirug: niuwoa waréa ta kátan piriwálġél la Eloi koba ka, kauwál noa kátan niuwoa kiloa.

29. Gatun yantinto kúriko ġurra bon, ġatun bara †telónai, pitálma bon Eloi-nug, korimatoara kátan bara Ioanne kaibirug karimulli birug.

30. Wonto ba bara Parithaioi ġatun bara †nomikoi ġurramaiġa wiyellikanne Eloi kola barun kin, keawai korimatoara korien Ioanne kai.

31. Gatun noa Piriwállo wiya, Yakoai kiloa bara kúri untikál willuġġél? ġatun minarig kiloa bara?

32. Bara yanti wonnai kiloa yellawollin ġukilliġél la, ġatun kaipullin taraikan, ġatun wiyellin, Tirkima ġéen nurun, ġatun keawai nura úntelli korien; minki ġéen kakulla nurun, ġatun keawai nura tugkilli korien.

33. Kulla noa Ioanne korimullikan uwa, keawai kunto ta pa ġa †wain keawai pitta pa; ġatun nura wiyan, †diabol noa ġikoug katoa ba.

34. Yinal ta kíri koba uwa takilliko ġatun pittelliko, ġatun nura wiyan, A! mataye kúri unni, ġatun †wain pittaye, kóti ta †telónai koba ġatun yarakai willug koba!

35. Wonto ba yantinto wonnaito ġuraki koba ko piralman bon ġuraki.

36. Gatun wakállo Parithaioi koba ko wiya bon ta-uwil koa noa ġikoug katoa. Gatun uwa noa kokera Parithaio koba, ġatun yellawa noa barán takilliko.

37. Gatun, a! ġapal wakál yarakaikun bountoa ġurrá bountoa ba Iéthunug bon yellawai takilli taba kokera Parithaio koba ka, mankulla bountoa wúnkilliġél alabathro putillikanne,

38. Gatun ġarokéa bountoa tinna ka bulka ka ġikoung kin, túġkillin, ġatun bountoa puntia bounnoun ka to ġurrun to tinna ġikoúmba, ġatun pirripa bounnoun ka to kittug ko wollug koba ko bounnoun ka to, ġatun búġbúġka bon tinna ġikoúmba, ġatun putia bon putilliġél lo.

39. Yakita nakulla noa ba unni ġali Parithaio, wiya bon ba, wiyelléún ġaiya noa niuwoabo minki ka, wiyelliela, Unni kúri †propet ba noa ġurra pa noa wonta-kan-to ka ġapallo numa bon; kulla bountoa yaraikan.

40. Gatun Iéthuko noa wiyayelléún, wiyelliela bon, Thimón, wiya-uwil koa banuġ. Gatun noa wiya, Piriwál, wiyellia.
41. Tarai ta kakulla ġukillikan wakál buloara mumbitoara ġikoúmba ; wakállo noa mumbillé in †pentakothioi †denari, ġatun tarai ta †pentékonta mumbilléún.
42. Gatun keawai bula ġupaiye pa ba yaruġ ka bon, wareká ġaiya noa bulun ba. Wonta kin bulun kinbiruġ pitálman in kauwál bon!
43. Thimónto noa wiya, wiyelliella, Mirka ġikouġ wareka noa ba kauwál. Gatun noa wiya bon, Kota bi tuloa.
44. Gatun noa warrakulléún ġapal ko, ġatun wiya Thimónnuġ Natan bi unni ġapal ? uwa baġ kokera ko ġirouġ ka ta ko, keawai bi tia ġupa bato tinna ko ; wonto bountoa ba puntia tia tinna bounnoun ka to ġurrun to, ġatun watia bounnoun ka to wolluġ kabiruġ ko kittuġ ko.
45. Keawai bi tia búġbúġ ka pa : wonto ba unni ġapal, búġbúġ-kulliela tia tinna yakita biruġ uwa baġ ba.
46. Keawai bi puti pa emmoúmba wolluġ kipai to, wonto ba unni ġapal putia emmoúmba tinna kipai to.
47. Giakai tin banuġ wiyan, Yarakai umatoara bounnoun ba kauwál ta warekatoara bounnoun ba ; kulla bounnoun pitál-ma kauwál: kulla barúnba warekatoara waréa, pitál-ma bara waréa.
48. Gatun noa bounnoun wiya, Wareká umatoara ġiroúmba yarakai.
49. Gatun bara yellawan ġikouġ kinba takilli taba, bara bo wiyatan minki ka, Gan-ke unni warekan noa yarakai.
50. Gatun noa bounnoun wiya, Gurrulli ta biruġ ġiroúml-a moron bi kátan ; yuruġ bi pitál kakilliko.

WINTA VIII.

Gatun yakita yukita uwa noa yantin toa purrai toa kokera, wiyelliela ġatun túġunbilliela totóġ pitálmullikanne †bathileia koba Eloi koba : ġatun bara †dodeka ta ġikouġ katoa ba.
2. Gatun bara nukuġ taraikan, turon umatoara marai yarakai tabiruġ ġatun munni kabiruġ, Mari yitirra ġiakai Magdalakálin, bounnoun kinbiruġ paipéa †diabol †hepta ta,
3. Gatun Ioanna porikunbai Kutha-úmba, Herod-úmba umullikan, ġatun Thuhanna, ġatun taraikan kauwál, ġala bara ġukulla bon untakál tullokan ba biruġ barun kai.
4. Gatun uwittillin bara ba kúri kauwál-kauwál, ġatun uwa ġikouġ kinko, yantin tabiruġ kokerá biruġ, wiya noa unni †parabol :
5. Upillikan noa uwa yeai ko upulliko ġikoúmba ko ; ġatun upulliela noa ba, winta porkulléún kaiyinkon ta yapuġ ka ; ġatun waita-wa barán, ġatun tibbinto takulla moroko tinto.
6. Gatun winta porkullé in tunuġ ka ; ġatun poaikullé in ba wokka laġ tetti ġaiya kakulla, koito ba bato korien ta.
7. Gatun winta porkulléún tulkirri-tulkirrá ; ġatun poaikullé in tulkirri-tulkirri matti, ġatun murruġkama.

8. Gatun tarai ta porkulléún purrai murráráġ purrai ta, ġatun poaikulléún wokka laġ, ġatun yeai kurria †hekaton ta. Gatun noa ba wiya unni tara, kaaipulléún ġaiya noa, Niuwoa ba ġurréuġ kan katan ġurrulliko ġurrunbunbilla bon.

9. Gatun wirrobulli-kan-to ġikoúmba ko wiya bon, wiyelliela, Minariġ ke unni †parabol?

10. Gatun noa wiya, Gutan ġurrulliko nurun pirriral †bathileia koba Eloi-úmba; wonto barun tarai ta †parabol la; natan bara keawai bara na pa, ġatun ġurran bara keawai bara ġimilli pa.

11. Giakai ta unni †parabol: Yeai ta wiyellikanne ta Eloi koba.

12. Bara kaiyinkon taba yapuġ kaba ġurrullikan bara; uwa ġaiya noa †diabol, ġatun mankulla wiyellikanne barun ba minki kabiruġ búlbúl labiruġ, ġurréa-kún koa bara ġatun moron koa bara katéa-kún.

13. Bara tunuġ kaba ġurra bara ba wiyellikanne pitálkan to; ġatun unni tara wirra korien kátan, kota bara waréa ba, ġatun yakita numullikanne ta waraka ġaiya bara.

14. Gatun unnoa tara porkulléún tulkirri-tulkirrá, bara ba ġurra, waita uwa ġaiya, ġatun murruġkana umullikannéto ġatun porollo ġatun pirunto moron koba, ġatun yeai kurri korien murrárag kakilliko.

15. Wonto ba unnoa murráraġ kaba purrai taba, bara ba ġurra wiyellikanne, tuloakan ġatun murráruġkan búlbúlkan, tuman bara, ġatun yeai kurrin murroi to.

16. Keawai kúriko wirroġbanún kaibuġ, wutinún ġaiya tenti ko, ġa wutinún bara ka pinkilliġélla; wonto ba wupinún kaibuġ-ġél la, na-uwil koa bara uwollita ba ko kaibuġ.

17. Kulla yantin ta ġetti biruġ ġurranún wal kakilliko; ġatun yantin ta yuropatoara biruġ ġurranún wal kakilliko, ġatun paipi-nún wal.

18. Yakoai nura ġurrulla; kulla ġikouġ kinba ġunún wal ġiko-uġ kin; ġatun keawai noa ka korien, mantillinún wal bon ġikouġ kinbiruġ unnoa ta paipitoara ġikouġ kinba.

19. Gatun tunkan ġikouġ kinko ġatun bara kóti ta ġikoúmba uwa, ġatun keawai bara wa pa ġikouġ kinko konarrin, kulla kauwál waitawollan.

20. Wintako bon wiya ġiakai, Garokillin bara warrai taba ġiko-úmba tunkan ġatun kóti ta, na-uwil koa bara ġirouġ.

21. Gatun noa wiyayelléún barun, wiyelliela, Unni tara tia kátan emmoúmba tunkan ġatun kóti ta, ġurrullikan wiyellikanne Eloi koba ġatun umullikan.

22. Gatun yakita tarai ta purreáġ ka, uwa noa murrinauwai ta ko ġikouġ katoa wirrobullikan toa ġikoúmba; ġatun noa barun wiya, Waita ġéen waiġa-uwil kaiyin kolaġ wara kolaġ. Gatun bara tolka murcuġ kolaġ.

23. Wonto ba bara uwolliela, pirrikéa noa kóġóġ; ġatun wibbi ka-uwál kakulla wara ka; ġatun bara warapal, ġatun kinta kakilliela.

24. Gatun bara uwa ġikouġ kin, bouġbuġga ġaiya bon, wiyellielia, Piriwál, piriwál, tetti kolaġ ġéen! Bouġkulléun ġaiya noa, ġatun wiya noa wibbi, ġatun tulkun wombul koba; ġatun korun kakulla, ġatun yuraġ ġaiya kakulla.

25. Gatun noa wiya barun, Wonnuġ-ke nurun kotellita? Gatun bara kinta kakulla, kotelliela, wiyalan taraikan-taraikan, Wontakan unni kúri! kulla noa wiyan wibbi ġatun bato, ġatun ġurra ġaiya bon.

26. Gatun bara uwa purrai tako Gadarén tako, kaiyin taba Galilaia kaba.

27. Gatuu noa ba yankulléún purrai tako, nuġgurrawa bon wakállo kúriko kokera biruġ ko, †diabolkan noa katalla yuraki, ġatun keawai noa upillipa kirrikin to, keawai noa kátan kokera, nikki ka noa kakulla.

28. Nakulla noa ba Iéthunuġ, kaaibulléun ġaiya noa, ġatun puntimulléún ġikouġ kin mikan ta, ġatun wokka wiyelléún wiyelliela, Minnuġ banún ke bi tia, Iéthu, Yinal ta Eloi koba wokka kaba koba? Yanoa bi tia piralmai yikora.

29. (Kulla noa wiya marai yarakaikan paikulliko kúri kabiruġ. Kulla bon mankulla murrin-murrin; ġatun wirria bon tibon ko; ġatun noa tiirbuġga tibon, ġatun yuaipéa bon †diabollo korug kolaġ).

30. Gatun Iéthuko noa wiya bon, wiyelliela, Wonnén bi yitirra? Gatun noa wiya, †Léjun baġ; kulla kauwál-kauwál †diabol uwa murrariġ ġikouġ kinko minki kako.

31. Gatun bara bon wiya, Yanoa, wiya yikora ġearun bi pirriko kolaġ kakilliko.

32. Gatun kakulla untakál wirrul takilliela bulkára ba ko; ġatun bara wiya bon pulóġkulliko barun minki kako †porák kako. Gatun noa wamunbéa barun.

33. Uwa ġaiya bara waita †diabol minki tabiruġ kúri kabiruġ, ġatun pulóġkulléún †porák ka koiro ka; ġatun wirrul murra barán karakai pirriko koba wara kako, kurrin to ġaiya bara.

34. Nakulla bara ba tamunbéa unnoa tara umatoara, murra ġaiya bara, ġatun waita uwa kokerá kolaġ, ġatun ġoruġ kolaġ; wiya ġaiya ġaloa.

35. Uwa ġaiya bara nakilliko umatoara ko; ġatun uwa Iéthu kin, ġatun nakulla bara bon unnoa kúri, paipitoara biruġ bara waita uwa, yellawolliela Iéthu ka ta tinna ka, kirrikinkan ġatun tuloa ġurrullikan; ġatun kinta bara kakulla.

36. Yantinto nakulla unnoa wiya barun, yanti bon ba turon uma †diabolkan kauwálkan.

37. Gatun yantinto konaró purrai tako Gadarén tako wiya ġaiya bon waita uwolliko barun kinbiruġ; kulla bara kintakan kauwál kakulla. Gatun noa uwa murrinauwai tako, ġatun wulluġbo kakulla.

L

38. Gatun unnoa kúri kabiruġ †diabol bara waita uwa, wiya bon ka-uwil koa noa ġikouġ katoa: wonto noa Iéthuko yuka bon waita, wiyelliela,

39. Willuġbo bi wolla ġirouġ ka tako kokerá ko, ġatun gurra-bunbilliko unnoa tara uma noa ba Eloito ġirouġ. Gatun noa waita uwa, ġatun wiya yantin toa kokeroa, yanti Iéthuko noa uma bon.

40. Gatun yakita kakulla, willuġbo noa ba Iéthu kakulla, pitál tara kakilliela kûri, kulla bara bon mittilliela yantinto.

41. Gatun yakita uwa wakál kûri tanan, ġiakai yitirra Yaeiro, wiyellikan noa †tḣunagóg kako; ġatun noa puntimulléún Iéthu kin tinna ka, ġatun wiya uwolliko ġikouġ kinko kokera ko;

42. Kulla bon wakál yinálkun kakulla, †dodeka wunál ta boun-noun ba, ġatun bountoa pirrikilliela tetti kakilliela. Gatun uwa ġaiya noa, kûriko bon murruġkama.

43. Gatun wakál nukuġ, kumarakan †dodeka wunál ta boun-noun ba, ġukilléún bountoa kirun tullokan bounnoúnba karákál ko, keawai bara bounnoun turon uma pa,

44. Uwa bountoa bulka kako, ġatun numa pita ġikoúmba kir-rikin: ġatun tanoa-kal-bo kumara ġaiya kakulla korun.

45. Gatun noa Iéthuko wiya ġaiya, Ganto tia numa? Yantin-to wiya keawai, wiya ġaiya noa Peterko ġatun bara ġikouġ katoa, Piriwál, konaro bin murruġkama ġatun waita wa, ġatun bi wi-yan, Ganto tia numa?

46. Gatun noa Iéthuko wiya, Wakállo ta tia numa: kulla baġ ġurran waita ka ba kaiyu emmouġ kinbiruġ.

47. Gatun bountoa ba nukuġko nakulla yuropa korien boun-toa, uwa bountoa pulul-pulul, ġatun puntimulléún ġikouġ kin mikan ta, wiya bon bountoa mikan ta yantin ta kûri ka, minariġ tin bountoa numa bon, ġatun tanoa-kal-bo bountoa kakulla turon.

48. Gatun noa bounnoun wiya, Yinálkun, kauwa bi pitál; ġurrullito ġiroúmba-ko turon bin uma; yuriġ waita pitál kakilliko.

49. Gatun wiyelliela noa ba, tanan uwa wakállo wiyellikan ta biruġ kokera biruġ, wiyelliela bon, Giroúmba yinálkun tetti kakul-la; yanoa, Piriwál pirriralmai yikora bon.

50. Wonto noa ba Iéthuko ġurra, wiyayelléún noa bon wiyel-liela, Kinta kora bi; ġurrulla wal bi, ġatun turon ġaiya wal boun-toa kánún.

51. Gatun noa ba uwa kokera ko ba murrariġ, keawai noa tarai kan wommumbi pa ġikouġ kin, wonto ba Peternuġ ġatun Yako-bonuġ, ġatun Ioannenuġ, ġatun biyuġbai ġatun tunkan murrakín koba.

52. Gatun yantin tuġkilléún ġatun minki kakulla bounnoun kai: wonto noa ba wiya, Tuġki yikora; keawaran bountoa tetti korien, wonto ba ġarabo kakillin.

53. Gatun bara bon béelma, nakilliela tetti bountoa kakulla.

THE GOSPEL BY LUKE, c. 8. 151

54. Gatun noa kirun barun yipa warai tako, gatun noa mankulla bounnoun muttárrin, gatun wiya, Murrakín, bougkullia.
55. Gatun bounnoun ba marai katéakan, gatun bountoa bougkulléún tanoa-kal-bo : gatun noa wiya bounnoun takilliko.
56. Gatun kintakan biyugbai gatun tunkan bounnoun ba : wonto noa ba wiya barun, yanoa wiya yikora taraikan kúri unni umatoara.

WINTA IX.

Wiya gaiya noa barun †dodeka ta gikoúmba kaumulliko, gatun gukulla barun kaiyu kakilliko gatun wiyellikan kakilliko yantin ko †diabol ko, gatun turon umulliko yantin munnikan ko.
2. Gatun noa barun yuka wiyelliko †bathileia Eloi koba, gatun turon umulliko munni ko.
3. Gatun noa wiya barun, Manki yikora waita kolag, keawai tupa-tupa manún, keawai yinug, keawai kunto, keawai †money, keawai buloara manún kirrikin taraiko-taraiko.
4. Gatun uwánún nura ba tarai ta kokera, tanoa kauwa, gatun waita uwolla untoa birug.
5. Gatun bara keawai nurun wommunbi korien, waita nura ba uwánún untoa birug kokera birug, tirri-tirrillia yullo kabirug morig tinna kabirug nurun kinbirug, túga kakilliko barun kinko.
6. Gatun waita bara uwa, gatun uwa kokeroa willi koa, wiyelliela Euagelion, gatun turon umulliela yantin ta purrai ta.
7. Gatun noa Herodto tetrákko gurra unni tara uma noa ba ; gatun kotelliela niuwoa bo, kulla wiyatoara tarai-kan-to Ioanne noa bougkulléa tetti kabirug ;
8. Gatun winta ka, paipéa noa Elía ; gatun tarai-kan-to, wakúl gagka-kúl †propet tabirug bougkalléún.
9. Gatun noa Herod wiya, Kolbúntia bag bon Iaonuenug wollug ; gan-ke unni gurran bag unni tara ? gatun noa na-uwil koa bon.
10. Gatun bara †apothollo willugbo bara ba kakulla, wiya gaiya bon yantin unni tara uma bara ba. Gatun noa barun yutéa, gatun kara uwa mirrulla ko, kokera ko yitirra Betáthaida kako.
11. Gatun bara kúri gurra bara ba, wirropa bara bon ; garokéa noa wiyelliko barun †bathileia Eloi koba, gatun uma barun turon kakilliko munnikan.
12. Gatun purreág kakilliela yaréakúl, uwa gaiya bara †dodeka ta, gatun wiya bon, Yukulla barun konara waita lag, uwa-uwil koa bara yantin toa purrai karig koa, yellawolliko, gatun takilliko ; kulla géen kátan unti mirrul la.
13. Wonto noa ba barun wiya, Guwa barun galoa ko takilliko. Gatun bara wiya, Keawai gearúnba kulla unni †pente kunto gatun buloara makoro ; wiya géen wirrilla barun gali ko takilliko yantin ko kúri ko.

14. Kulla wal kúri kauwäl †pentakikilioi ta. Gatun noa wiya barun wirrobullikan, Yellawabunbilla barun konara kakilliko †pentékonta tarai taba kakilliko.

15. Gatun unia gaiya bara yanti, gatun yellawabunbéa barun yantin barán.

16. Mankulla gaiya noa unnoa tara kunto †pente gatun makoro buloara; gatun nakilliela wokka lag moroko koba, murroi wiyelliela unni tara, gatun yiirbugga, gatun gukulla barun wirrobullikan ko wunkilliko barun kin mikan ta konara.

17. Gatun takulla bara, gatun warakan gaiya bara kuttawan yantin; gatun mankulla bara wanan †dodeka ka wimbi ka wuntawai birug barun kai.

18. Gatun yakita wiyellicla noa ba niuwoa-bo púnbai, gikoúmba wirrobullikan gikoug katoa; gatun noa wiya barun, wiyelliela, Gannug wiyan kúri ko gan bag ba.

19. Wiyayelléún bara, wiyelliela, Ioanne ta bi korimullikan; wonto ba taraito wiyan Elía ta ba; gatun taraito wiyan wakál gagka-kál †propet koba, bougkulliakan katéa-kán.

20. Wiya noa barun, Ganto tia nura wiyan gan bag ba? Peterko noa wiyayelléún, wiyelliela, Kritht ta bi Eloi-úmba.

21. Gatun noa barun piralma, wiyéa-kán koa bara unnoa tara tarai ko kúri ko;

22. Wiyelliela, Yinal ta kúri koba yarakai kauwál wal bon umán'ín, gatun warekánún wal bon bara gagkakal gatun bara †hiereukan piriwal, gatun bara †gárammateukan, gatun búnnún wal tetti, gatun boug̈gánún gaiya bon tarai ta purreág goro ka.

23. Gatun wiya noa barun yantin, Wanún tia ba taraikan kúri uwánún, gurrullia noa niuwoa-bo, gatun mara-uwil koa noa taligkabillikanne gikoúmba yantin ta purreág ka, gatun wirrobulla tia.

24. Ganto ba miromán in moron gikoúmba, warekánún wal noa? kulla noa warekánún moron gikoúmba emmoug kin, galoa noa moron umánún.

25. Wonnug̈-ke murrárág kúri ko, mankilliko purrai karig ko, gatun noa tetti wal gaiya kánún niuwoa-bo, ga warekánún wal?

26. Gan tia ba koiyun kánún emmoug kai, gatun wiyellikanne emmoúmba, Yinal kúri koba koiyun gikoug kai, uwánún noa ba killibinbinkan kóti gikoug kinba, gatun Biyug̈bai koba, gatun agelo yirri-yirri-kan koba barúnba.

27. Kulla bag wiyan nurun tuloa, unni winta garokéún ba, keawai bara tetti kánún, kabo na-uwil koa bara †bathileia-nug Eloi koba.

28. Gatun yakita kakulla purreág ka †ét ta yurika-ta unni tara wiyellikanne, yutéa noa barun Peternug, gatun Ioannenug, gatun Yakobonug, gatun uwa wokka lag bulkára kolag wiyelliko.

29. Gatun noa ba wiyelliela, takin bon tarai warrakulléún, gatun gikoúmba kirrikin purrul kakulla, gatun killibinbin kakulla.

30. Gatún wiyelliela bon kúriko Mothéko gatun Elíako:
31. Paipéa bula killibinbin, gatun wiya bula gikoúmba teun tin ka-uwil koa †Hierothalem ko.
32. Wonto ba Peter noa gatun bara gikoug katoa porrólkan bara birikéa kógóg; gatun bara kakulla tirag, nakulla bara gikoúmba killibinbin, gatun buloara bula k:iri garokéa gikoug katoa.
33. Gatun kakulla yakita bula ba waita uwolliela gikoug kinbirug, Peterko noa wiya bon Iéthunug, A! Piriwàl, murrárag géarun unti ko kakilliko; gatun umabunbilla goro kokera; wakal bin, gatun wakal Mothénug, gatun wakal Elíanug, gurra korien minarig noa wiya.
34. Wiyelliela noa ba, yareil kakulla, gatun wutéa barun; gatun bara kinta kakulla, waita bara ba wolliela murrarig yareil la.
35. Gatun pullí kakulla yareil labirug, wiyelliela, Unni ta emmoúmba kóti yinal pitàlmullikan; gurrulla bon.
36. Gatun pullí ba kakulla korun, Iéthu noa kakilliela púnbai. Keawai bara unni tara wiya pa untatoara, natoara purreag ka taraikan ta.
37. Gatun yakita kakulla purreag ka tarai ta unta, uwa bara ba barán buikára birug, kauwàllo kúriko nuggurra wa bon.
38. A! gatun wakal kúri konara koba kaaibulléun, wiyelliela, Piriwàl, kai bi, na-uwillia yinal emmoúmba; kulla noa emmoúmba wakal wonnai.
39. A! gatun maraito bon mankulla, gatun gaiya noa kaaibulléin wokka; gatun yiirbugga bon, gatun kurragtoanbugga; gatun búntoara noa, waita gaiya gikoug kinbirug uwa.
40. Gatun bag wiya barun wirrobullikan giroúmba warekulliko bon; keawai bara kaiyu korien.
41. Gatun noa Iéthuko wiya, wiyelliela, A! gurra korien gatun pirriral unni willug-géel! Yakounta-lag bag kánún nurun kin, gatun wal bag kámunbinún nurun? Mara bon tanan giroúmba yinal unti ko.
42. Gatun uwolliela noa ba tanan †diabollo bon puntima barán gatun yiiryiir uma. Gatun noa Iéthuko koakulla bon marai yarakai ka, gatun bon wonnai turon uma, gatun gutéakan gaiya bon biyugbai ta gikoúmba tin.
43. Gatun yantin bara kinta kakulla kaiyu tin kauwàl lin Eloi koba tin; gatun kotelliela bara ba yantin unni tara Iéthuko noa ba uma, wiya gaiya noa barun wirrobullikan gikoúmba,
44. Kámunbilla unni tara wiyellikanne murrarig gurréug kako nurun kin; kulla noa Yinal kúri koba wupinún wal bon mattára kúri ka.
45. Keawai bara gurra pa unni wiyellikanne, gatun yuropa gali barun kinbirug, keawai bara gimilli korien; gatun bara kinta kakulla wiyelliko bon gali tin wiyellikanne tin.
46. Yakita gaiya bara wiyellan barabo-barabo, gan-ke kàn in kauwàl piriwàl barun kinbirug.

47. Gatun Iéthuko noa gimilléûn kotatoara búlbúl labirug barun kinbirug mankulla noa wonnai, gatun yellawabunbéa bon gikoug kin tarug ka,

48. Gatun noa barun wiya, Ganto ba unni wonnai pitálmanún kinba, pitál manún gaiya tia; gatun ganto ba tia pitálmanún, pitálmanún bon gala yuka tia ba; gatun niuwoa katan waréa nurun kinba yantin taba, yantibo ta wal noa kauwál kánún.

49. Gatun noa Ioanneto wiya, wiyelliela, Piriwál, nakulla géen wakállo paibuggulliela barun †diabol giroug katoa birug yitirra birug; wiya géen bon yanoa, koito ba keawai noa wa pa gearun katoa.

50. Gatun noa Iéthuko bon wiya, Wiwi yikora; koito noa ba keawai bukka korien gearun, niuwoa gearun katoa ba.

51. Gatun yakita kakulla purreág manún bon ba wokka kolag, pirral noa kakilliela waita †Hierothalem kolag,

52. Gatun noa yuka barun puntimai gikoúmba ganka; gatun bara uwa kokerá kolag Thamaria kako, umulliko gikoug.

53. Gatun bara bon keawai pitálma pa, kulla noa pirral kakulla wa pa †Hierothalem kolag.

54. Gatun bula wirrobullikan gikoúmba, Yakobo gatun Ioanne, nakulla bula unni, wiya bula, Piriwál, wiya bi, wiya-uwil koa géen koiyug koa kauwál barán moroko kabirug wina-uwil koa barun, yanti Elia noa ba unnoa?

55. Wonto noa ba wakulléûn, koakulla gaiya barun noa, gatun wiya, Keawaran nura gimilli korien nurúnba kóti búlbúl.

56. Koito ba noa yinal kúri koba keawaran noa tanan wa pa, búnkilliko kúri ko barun, wonto ba murrin umulliko. Gatun bara uwa tarai tako kokera ko.

57. Gatun yakita kakulla, uwolliela bara ba yurig yapug koa, taraito bon wiya, Piriwál, wirrobugbinún banug, wontarig bi ba uwánún.

58. Gatun noa Iéthuko bon wiya, Murrog-kai-ko kumiri barúnba, gatun tibbin moroko ka koba kunta barúnba, wonto ba yinal kúri koba keawaran bon gikoúmba birrikilli-gél wallug ko gikoúmba ko.

59. Gatun noa tarai wiya, Wirrobulla tia. Wonta noa ba wiya, Piriwál, wamunbilla tia ganka bapa-uwil koa bag emmoúmba biyugbai.

60. Wiya bon noa Iéthuko, Bapabunbilla barun tetti-tetti barúnba; gintoa yurig bi wolla wiyelliko piriwál koba Eloi koba.

61. Gatun taraito wiya, Piriwal, wirrobanún banug; wamunbilla tia ganka wiyellikoa barun bag unni emmoug kinba kokera ba.

62. Gatun noa Iéthuko bon wiya, Keawai tarai-kan-to upillinún máttara purrai-gél lo, gatun willug-wuminún, keawaran noa murrárag korien kakilliko piriwál ko Eloi koba ko.

WINTA X.

Yakita ġaiya kakulla unni tara, Piriwàllo noa ġearimulléún †the benty taraikan ta, ġatun yuka barun buloara-buloara ġikouġ kiɥ mikan ta, yantin tako kokera ko uwànun noa ba niuwoa-bo.

2. Gatun noa barun wiya, Kauwàl-lan unni nulai kàtan, keawai bo katillikan kúri kauwàlkàl; ġali tin wiyella nura bon, Piriwàl nulai-ġél koba yuka-uwil koa noa barun katillikan nulai ko katilliko ġikouġ kaiko.

3. Waita nura yuriġ wolla: A! yukan nurun baġ waita kolaġ yanti kiloa waréa ta ćipu barun kin murroġ ka ta.

4. Kurri yikora yanoa munniġél, ġatun yinuġ, keawai tuġganuġ; ġatun yanoa wiya yikora yapuġ koa taraikan kúri.

5. Gatun uwànún nura ba kokera ko taraikan tako, wiyella kurri ġiakai, Pitàl kauwa unni kokera ba.

6. Gatun ba yinal koba pitàl koba kànun unta, nurúnba pitàl kànún ġaiya unta; keawai ba nurun kin katéa kànún willuġbo.

7. Gatun yellawànún nura unta kokera, takilliko ġatun pittelliko, ġunún bara ba nurun; kulla noa umulli-kan-to man ba ġutoara ġikoúmba. Uwai yikora kokera kolaġ kokera kolaġ.

8. Gatun uwànún nura ba yantin ta kokeroa, ġatun bara nurun pitàlmanún, ta-uwa untoa tara wunún ba mikan ta nurun kin.

9. Gatun turon barun umulla unta tara; ġatun wiyella barun, Piriwàl koba Eloi koba papai uwa nurun kinba.

10. Uwànún nura ba tarai ta kokeroa, ġatun bara keawai pitàlma korien nurun, uwéa ka nura warai tako yapuġ kako, ġatun wiyella,

11. Umulléún ġeen punul untikàl ġearun kinba nurun kin; A! kotellia nura unni ta uwan ta papai kàtan nurun kin piriwàl koba Eloi koba.

12. Wiyan nurun baġ, murràraġ kànún unta ta tarai ta purreàġ, ka Thodom kako, keawaran ġala ko kokera ko.

13. Yapallun bi Koradhin! yapallun bi Betàthaida! kulla umatoara ba kauwàl-kauwàl kaiyu biruġ ka pa Turo ka ġatun Thidoni ka uma ġirouġ kin, minki bara ka pa yuraki, yellawa pa bara pirral la kirrikin ta ġatun bonoġ ka.

14. Murràraġ buloara kànún Turo ġatun Thidoni unta purreàġ wiyellaikanne ta keawaran bi.

15. Gatun ġintoa, Kapernaum, wunkulla wokka laġ moroko ka, yuaipinún wal barán pirri kako.

16. Niuwoa ġurran nurun ba, ġurran ta noa tia; ġatun niuwoa waitiman nurun ba, waitiman noa tia; ġatun niuwoa tia waitiman, waitiman noa bon yuka noa tia ba.

17. Gatun bara †thebenty ta willuġbo kakulla pitàlkan, wiyelliela, A Piriwal! ġurrullikan bara †diabollo ġearun ġirouġ katoa yitirroa.

18. Gatun noa barun wiya, Nakulla bon baġ Thatannuġ puntimulléùn barán moroko tin yanti málma kiloa.
19. A! ġutan baġ nurun kaiyu waitawolliko maiya ko ġatun wuarai ko, ġatun yantin ko kaiyu bukkakan ko; ġatun keawai wal nurun yarakai umulliko.
20. Pitál-mai yikora nura-nura, ġali tin ġurullikan tin bara marai nurun ba; unti biruġ pitálma nura, kulla yitirra nurúnba upatoara moroko ka ba.
21. Yakita ta noa pitál-lan kakulla marai ta, ġatun wiyelliela, Kauwa tia yanti, Biyuġ, Piriwál ta moroko koba ġatun purrai koba, kulla bi ba unnoa tara yuropa ġali unti biruġ ġuraki ta biruġ, ġatun bi túġkaiya unnoa tara barun boboġ ko; kauwa yanti, Biyuġ, koito ba murráráġ ta ġirouġ kin kátan mikan ta.
22. Yantin ta tia wupéa emmouġ kinko Biyuġbaito; ġatun keawai kúriko bon yinal ġimilli pa, wonto ba Biyuġbaito; ġatun Biyuġbai yinallo ġimilléùn, ġatun niuwoa yinallo túġunbinùn bon Biyuġbai.
23. Gatun noa willariġ kakulla ġikouġ kai koba wirrobullikan koba, ġatun wiyelliela kara, Kauwa yanti murráráġ ta natan ġaikuġ ko unni tara natan nura ba:
24. Kulla baġ nurun wiyan, kauwállo †propetto ġatun piriwállo na pa unni tara natan nura ba, ġatun bara keawai na korien; ġatun ġurra pa unni tara ġurran nura ba, ġatun keawai ġurra korien.
25. A! tarai wakál †nomiko ġarokéa wokka laġ, ġatun wiya bon, wiyelliela, Piriwál, minnuġ banún baġ moron kakilliko yantikatai?
26. Wiya bon noa, Minariġ upa wiyellikanne? yakoai bi wiyan?
27. Gatun noa wiyayelléùn, wiyelliela, Pitál kakilliko bi Piriwál ko Eloi ko ġiroúmba ko yantin to búlbúl lo ġiroúmba ko, ġatun yantin to marai to ġiroúmba ko, ġatun yantin to kaiyu ko ġiroúmba ko, ġatun yantin to kotellitó ġiroúmba ko; ġatun kóti ta ġiroúmba yanti ġintoa bo ba.
28. Gatun noa wiya bon, Gintoa wiyayelléùn tuloa; unni ta umulla ġatun moron koa bi kauwál
29. Wonto noa ba kotelliela tuloa ko niuwoa bo, wiya bon noa Iéthunuġ, Gan-ke tia kóti ta emmoúmba?
30. Gatun noa Iéthuko wiya, Taraikan waita uwa barán †Hicrothalem kabiruġ Jeriko kako, ġatun nuġgurrawa mankiye, mantillé in bon kirrikin, ġatun búnkulla, ġatun bara waita uwa wareka ġaiya bon búntoara.
31. Yakita ġati uwa wakál †thiereu barán yapuġ koa; ġatun nakulla bon noa ba, uwa noa taruġ koa kaiyin ta koa.
32. Ganti yanti kiloa wakál Lebikan kakulla noa ba unta, uwa nakulla ġaiya bon, ġatun noa uwa taruġ koa kaiyin ta koa.
33. Wonto ba wakál kúri Thamariakál uwolliela ba, uwa yapariġ kakilliela noa ba; ġatun nakulla bon noa ba, minki bon noa kakulla ġikouġ kai,

THE GOSPEL BY LUKE, c. 10. 157

34. Gatun uwa ġikouġ kai koba, ġatun ġira bon búntoara ġikoúmba, kiroabulliela kipai ġatun †wain, ġatun yellawabunbéa bon ġikouġ ka ta kóti ka buttikaġ, ġatun yutéa bon tákilliġél lako, ġatun miroma bon.

35. Gatun tarai ta purreaġ ka wakál la waita noa ba uwa, mankulla ġaiya noa buloara †denari, ġatun ġukulla kokeratín ko, ġatun bon wiya, Golomulla bon ; kirun bi ba upinún, uwéa kánún baġ ba willuġbo, ġutéa kánún ġaiya banuġ.

36. Wounuġ-ke kóti ta ġikoúmba nuġgurrawa mankiye unti biruġ ġoro kabiruġ kuri kabiruġ, kotella bi ?

37. Gatun noa wiya, Niuwoa ġoloma bon. Wiya noa bon Iéthu ko, Yuriġ, yanti kiloa umulla bi.

38. Gatun yakita kakulla, uwa bara ba, uwa noa murruġ koa kokeroa ; ġatun taraito nukuġko, Maráthako yitirra, wamunbéa bon bounnoun kin kokera.

39. Wúġgunbai bounnoun ba ġaiya kai, yitirra Mari, yellawa bountoa Iéthu kin yullo ka, ġatun ġurra bon wiyellita

40. Wonto ba Marátha kámullan buntoa marai-marai umullita, ġatun uwa bountoa ġikouġ kin, ġatun wiya, Piriwál, kora bi natau tia wareka tia wúġgunbai cmmoúmba umulliko wakállo ? wiyella bounnoun umulli koa bountoa tia.

41. Gatun noa Iéthuko wiyelléún, ġatun wiya bounnoun, Ela ! Marátha, Marátha, ġintoa kámullan marai-marai minnambo-minnambo ka ;

42. Wonto ba wakál murráraġ kátan : ġatun Mariko bountoa ġeremulléin unnoa murráraġbo, keawai wal mantillinún bounnoun kinbiruġ.

WINTA XI.

Gatun yakita kakulla, wiyelliela noa ba tarai ta purrai ta, kaiulléún noa ba wiyelli ta, wakállo bon wiya ġikouġ-ka-to wirrobullikanto, Piriwál, wiyella ġearun bi wiyelliko, yanti kiloa Ioanneto noa wiya barun ġikoúmba wirrobullikan.

2. Gatun noa wiya barun, wiyánún nura ba, ġiakai nura wiyanún nura, Biyuġbai ġearúmba wokka ka ba moroko ka ba kátan, Kámunbilla yitirra ġiroúmba yirri-yirri kakilliko. Paipibunbilla Piriwál koba ġiroúmba. Gurrabunbilla wiyellikanne ġiroúmba, yanti moroko ka ba, yanti ta purrai ta ba.

3. Guwoa ġearun purreaġ ka takilliko.

4. Gatun warekilla ġearúnba yarakai umatoara, kulla ġéen yanti ta wareka yanti ta wiyapaiyeún ġearúnba. Gatun yuti yikora ġearun yarakai umullikan kolaġ ; miromulla ġearun yarakai tabiruġ.

5. Gatun noa barun wiya, Gan nurun kinbiruġ kóti ġikoúmba, ġatun uwánún ġikouġ kin tokoi ta, ġatun bon wiyánún, Ela ! kóti, mumbilla tia wokkai to ġoro ko ;

6. Kulla noa emmoúmba kóti uwa kaloġ tin emmouġ kinko, ġatun keawai baġ wún korien ġikouġ kin mikan ta takilliko?
7. Niuwoa murruġ ka ba ko wiyanún, Wai tia wiyellan; kulla unni kurraka wirriġbakulla, kulla wonnai tara emmoúmba emmouġ katoa ba birrikilliġél laba; keawaran baġ bouġkulli korien ġukilliko ġirouġ.
8. Wiyan nurun baġ, Keawai noa bouġkulli korien ġulliko bon, kulla noa ba ġikoúmba kóti; kulla wal noa bon pirriral-mulli tin bouġkullinún ġaiya noa ġulliko bon wiyellinún noa ba.
9. Gatun nurun baġ wiyan, Wiyella, ġatun ġunún ġaiya nurun; ġatun tiwolla, ġatun karawollinun ġaiya nura; wirrillia, ġatun umánún ġaiya nurun.
10. Yantin ba wiyellinún, manún wal; gatun noa tiwollinún, karawollinún ġaiya noa; ġatun ġikouġ wirrillinún noa ba, umánún ġaiya wal.
11. Yinallo ba wiyúnún nulai yantin ta nurun kin, biyuġbai ta ba, wiya, noa ġunún tunuġ? ġa makoro, wiya, noa maiya ġunún makoró?
12. Ga ba wiyellan noa ba yarro, wiya, noa bon ġupaiyinún wuarai?
13. Nura ba yarakaikan kátan, ġukilliko ġutoara murráraġ wonnai ko nurúnba ko; kauwa yanti ġunún noa Biyuġbaito moroko ka ba ko Marai murráraġ barun wiya bon ba?
14. Gatun noa ba paibuġġulliela wakál †diabol, ġatun noa ġoġo. Gatun yakita ġaiya kakulla, waita ba uwa †diabol, wiya ġaiya noa ġoġo kabiruġ ko; ġatun bara kúri kotelliela.
15. Wonto ba tarai-kan-to wiya, Paibuġġa noa barun †diabol Béeldhebul kátan biruġ, piriwálloa biruġ †diabol koba ko.
16. Gatun tarai-kan-to wiyelliela, wiya bon túġa moroko tin.
17. Wonto noa ba ġimilléún barúnba kotellikanne, wiya barun, Yantin piriwál koba ġaruġgara umulla barabo tetti bara kanún; ġatun kokera koba barabo warakullia bara.
18. Thatan noa ba ġaruġġara kánún niuwoa-bo, yakoai ġikoúmba piriwál koba kánún? kulla nura wiyan paibuġġa baġ ba barun †diabol Béeldhebul katoa biruġ.
19. Gatun ġatoaba paibuġġánún barun †diabol Béeldhebul biruġ, ġan katoa biruġ nurúnba-ko yinal-lo paibuġġa?
20. Gatoa paibuġġánun máttárroa biruġ Eloi koba ko barun †diabol, kauwa tuloa uwa ġaiya piriwál koba Eloi koba nurun kin ba.
21. Golománún noa ba tarai kúri mokál porrol ġikouġ kin kokera, ġikoúmba tullokan murroi kátan.
22. Wonto ba tanan uwánun tarai mokál porrolkan kauwál kan ġikouġ kin, ġatun kéakéa-ma noa bon, mantillinún ġaiya wal bon kirun mokál ġikoúmba pirriral-matoara; ġatun ġutillinún noa mokúl ġikoúmba.

23. Niuwoa keawai emmouġ katoa, niuwoa katan kóti korien ; ġatun noa keawai boa-ma korien emmouġ katoa, ware-ware-kan.
24. Paikullinùn ba marai yarakai kùri kabiruġ, uwan noa yu-riġ purroi toa tarawaroa, nakilliko korilliko ; ġatun noa keawai na korien, wiyan noa, Willuġbanùn wal baġ willuġbo kokera ko emmouġ ka ta ko, unta biruġ uwa baġ ba.
25. Ġatun uwànùn noa ba, nakulla ġaiya noa ba wiréa kiriiri ġatun konéin.
26. Uwan ġaiya noa ġatun yutéa taraikan †theben ta marai ya-rakai kauwàl yanti niuwoa ba ; ġatun bara uwa murrariġ ġatun kakulla ġaiya bara unta ; ġatun yarakai kauwàl noa unnoa katan yakita, kakulla noa ba kurri-kurri.
27. Ġatun yakita kakulla, wiyellicla noa ba, kaaibulléùn tarai nukuġ ġali koba konara koba, ġatun wiya bon bountoa, Murràràġ kauwa yanti pika kurréa bon ba, ġatun paiyil pitta bi ba.
28. Wonto noa bo wiya, Kauwa yanti, murràràġ kauwàl katan bara ġurrullikan wiyellikanne Eloi koba, ġatun mirromulli-ko.
29. Ġatun yakita kakulla, wittillan bara ba kùri, wiya noa kurri-kurri, Unni ta yarakai katan willuġġél ; nakillin bara túġa ; keawai wal barun ġunùn, unni bo ta wal túġa Iona-ùmba †propet koba.
30. Yanti kiloa Iona túġa kakulla noa barun kùri Ninebi ka, yanti bo ta wal kànùn noa yinal kùri koba barun ġali ko willuġġél ko.
31. Bouġkullinùn wal piriwal kirín pakai biruġ purreàġ ka wiyelliġél la kùri koa untikàl loa willuġġél loa, ġatun pirralmanùn barun ; kulla bountoa uwa kaloġ kabiruġ purrai tabiruġ wiran tabiruġ ġurrulli bon ġuraki ko Tholomón ko ; A! kauwàl katan Tholomón kiloa unnibo.
32. Bouġkullinùn wal bara kùri Ninebikàl purreàġ ka wiyelli-ġél la kùri koa untikàl loa willuġġél loa, ġatun pirral-manùn barun ; kulla bara minki kakulla wiyelli ta Iona-ùmba ka ; A! kauwàl katan Iona kiloa unnibo.
33. Keawai kùriko tarai-kan-to wirrouġ buġġanùn kaibuġ wu-nùn ġaiya ġati ta, keawai bará ka wimbi ka, wonto ba kaibuġġél la, bara ba uwànùn na-uwil koa bara kaibuġ.
34. Kaibuġ ta murrin koba ġaikuġ ; wonto ba giroúmba ġaikuġ tuloa katan, yantin bin katan murrin kaibuġkan ; wonto bin ba ġaikuġ yarakai, kànùn murrin bin warapa tokoi to.
35. Yakoai bi, mirka unnoanuġ kaibuġ ġirouġ kinba tokoi ta ba katan.
36. Kulla ba yantin ta ġiroúmba murrin ta ba warapan kaibuġ ko, keawai taraikan tokoi, kànùn yantinbo ta wal warapan kaibuġ ko, yanti kaibuġ koba wupin ġatun binkirréùn.
37. Ġatun wiyellicla noa ba, taraito Parithaioko wiya bon ta-uwil koa noa ġikouġ katoa ; ġatun noa uwa murrariġ ġatun yel-lawa takilliko.

38. Gatun noa ba Parithaioko nakulla, umulli korien noa bato ka kurri-kurri takilli kolaġ, kotellicla noa.
39. Gatun bon noa Piriwállo wiya, Yakita nura Parithaioiko umullia mirkun karai-ġon tunti ġatun pikirri ; wonto ba nurúnba murrin warapan williró ġatun yarakai to.
40. Woġkál nura! yan ta noa uma unnoa yanti unnoa ba warrai ta ba, yantibo uma noa murruġ ka ba ?
41. Guwa nura untoakál nurun kinbiruġ, ġatun yantin nurun ba tuloa ka kátan.
42. Yapal nura Parithaioi ! kulla nura ġukillan wintakál †mentha tabiruġ, ġatun †ruta tabiruġ, ġatun yaki tara, ġatun ġurramaiġan tuloa ġatun pitálumullikanne Eloi koba : unni tara nura uma pa, ġatun keawai taraikan wareka pa uma korien.
43. Yapal nura Parithaioi ! kulla nura pitálman yellawollikanne wokka kaba †thunagóg kaba, ġatun umullikanne ġukilliġél lako.
44. Yapal nura †ġarammateu ġatun Parithaioi, ġakoiyaye ! kulla nura yanti tulmun kiloa paipi korien, ġatun bara kúri uwan wokka laġ tulmun toa, keawaran bara na korien.
45. Wiyayelléan ġaiya wakállo †nomiko-ko wiyelliela bon, Piriwál, ġiakai bi wiyan, pirralman bi ġearun.
46. Gatun noa wiya, Yapal nura †nomikoi yantinbo ! kulla nura wuntan kúri ka porrol ta lo kauwai porrol kurrilliko, ġatun keawai nura unnoa porrol numa korien nurun ka to máttárró.
47. Yapal nura ! kulla nura ba wittiman tulmun barúnba †propet koba, ġatun biyugbaito nurúnba-ko bunkulla barun tetti kulwon.
48. Kauwa tuloa ta pirralman nura umatoara biyuġbai koba nurúnba ; kulla bara yuna bo ta barun búnkulla tetti, gatun nura wittillin tulmun barúnba.
49. Yaki tin wiya ġurakita Eloi koba ko, Yukán in wal baġ barun †propet ġatun †apothol barun kin, ġatun winta barun kinbiruġ búnn.in wal bara ġatun yarakai umánún ;
50. Wiya-uwil koa ġoroġ yantin koba †propet koba kiroabatoara yaki tabiruġ kurri-kurri tabiruġ purrai tabiruġ, unni barun willuġġél ;
51. Goroġ kabiruġ Abelúmba kabirug, ġoroġ kako Dhakaríaúmba kako búntoara willi ka †bómo ta ġatun †hieron ; kauwa tuloa to wiyan nurun baġ, wiya-uwil koa unni barun willuġġél.
52. Yapal nura †nomikoi ! kulla nura mankulla wirriġbakilliġél ġurakita koba ; keawai nura wa pa, ġatun nura miya barun uwa bara ba.
53. Gatun wiya noa ba unni tara barun, pirriralma bon bara gárammateuto ġatun Parithaioiko, wiya-uwil koa noa minnambo wiyelliko ;
54. Mittillin bara bon, ġatun nakillin ġurrulliko ġikouġ kin ba ko kurraka ba ko, wiyayeán koa bara bon.

WINTA XII.

YAKITA kakulla, wittillan bara ba yantibo konara kùri, wata-wata-
wollan barabo, wiya noa kurri-kurri barun wirrobullikan ġikoúmba,
Yakoai nura †lebben barúnba Parithaioi koba, ġakoiyaye ta unnoa.
2. Yantin ba wutéa ta túġunbinún ġaiya wal; ġatun yantin
yuropa ta namunbinún ġaiya wal.
3. Yaki tin, wiyellan nura tokoi ta ġurrabunbinún wal kaibuġ
ka; ġatun unni ta wiya nura ba ġurréuġ ka waiyakan ta, wiyellinún wal wokka ka kokera.
4. Gatun baġ nurun wiyan kóti ta emmoúmba, Kinta kora nura
barun kin búnkillikan tin murrin tin, ġatun yukita tantoa bo ta
wal bara kaiyukanto banún.
5. Túġunbinún wal baġ nurun ġan-kai nura kinta wal kánún:
Kinta bon kauwa ġikouġ kai, yukita noa ba búnkulla kaiyukan
noa warekulliko koiyuġ kako pirriko kako; kauwa wiyan baġ
nurun, Kinta bon kauwa ġikouġ kai.
6. Wiya, †pente tibbin waréa ta ġupaiye ko buloara †assari, ġatun keawai wakál unti biruġ woġgunti korien ġikouġ kin Eloi kin?
7. Kulla yantin wolluġ kaba kittuġ murrapatoara kátan. Kinta
kora nura ġali tin; kulla nura murráráġ kauwálkan kátan, keawaran ġali tarako tibbinko waréa-ta-ko kauwál-kauwál-ko.
8. Unni ta nurun baġ wiyan, Yantinto emmouġ wiyánún mikan
ta kúri ka, ġikouġ wiyánún noa Yinal kúri koba mikan ta aġelo
ka Eloi koba ko.
9. Wonto ba niuwoa ġanbullinún tia emmouġ mikan ta kúri
ka, ġanbullinún wal bon mikan ta aġelo ka Eloi koba ka.
10. Gatun ġanto ba yarakai wiyánún ġikouġ Yinal kúri koba,
kámunbinún wal bon; wonto bon ba yarakai wiyellikan Maraikan
yirri-yirri-kan, keawai bon kámunbinún.
11. Gatun manún nurun bara †thunagóg kako ġatun wiyellikan tako, ġatun kaiyukan tako, kota yikora nura wonnuġ nura ba
wiyayellinún, ġa minnuġ nura wiyánún.
12. Kulla nurun Marai-kan-to yirri-yirri-kan-to wiyánún wal
yakita bo ġaiya minnuġ wal nura wiyánún.
13. Gatun wiya bon wakállo konara biruġ ko, Piriwal, wiyella
emmoúmba biġgainuġ, ġukulli koa noa purrai emmouġ kai.
14. Gatun noa bon wiya, Kùri, ġanto tia uma wiyellikan, ġa
ġukillikan ġirouġ kin?
15. Gatun noa barun wiya, Yakoai ġatun murroi kauwa williri
koba; kulla moron kùri koba ka korien ta kauwál-kauwál la tul
lokan ka ġikouġ ka ta.
16. Gatun noa wiya barun unni †parabol, wiyelliela, Purrai ta
porrólkan koba poaikulléún kauwál:
17. Gatun noa kotelléún niuwoabo, wiyelliela, Minnuġ banún
baġ, kulla wal unni tuntan uwa, wiya wal baġ wonta wura-uwil
unni tara emmoúmba?

18. Gatun noa wiya, Unni bag umánún ; umánún wal bag barán wunkilligél commoúmba, gatun wittia kánún kauwál ; gatun unta bag wunún yantin emmoúmba nulai gatun tullokan.
19. Gatun bag wiyánún emmoúmba marai, A marai! kauwál tullokan giroúmba wúnkulla kauwál lako wunál lako; yellawolla murroi bi, tauwa, pittella, gatun pitál kauwa.
20. Wonto ba Eloito bon wiya, Wogkál-lan bi ! unti tokoi ta giroúmba marai mantillinún wal giroug kinbirug; ganto gaiya unnoa tara tullokan manún tuigko bi ba uma ?
21. Yanti niuwoa ba wupéakan tullokan gikoúmba ko, gatun keawai porrol korien Eloi kai koba.
22. Gatun noa wiya barun wirrobullikan, Yaki tin wiyan bag nurun, Yanoa, kota yikora nurúnba moron takilliko ; ga keawai murrin ko wupulliko.
23. Moron ta kauwál kátan murrárag takillikanne keawaran, gatun murrin ta kauwál kátan murrárag kirrikin keawaran.
24. Kotella wákun barun ; koito bara ba keawai wupa korien, gatun keawai kol bunti korien ; keawai barúnba tuigko wupilligál, keawai barúnba kokera ; gatun noa Eloito giratiman barun ; kauwál-kauwál nura kátan murrárag tibbin bara keawaran.
25. Gatun gan nurun kinbirug kotellita kánún, uméa kánún moron gikoúmba waréa ka kakilliko †kubit kako ?
26. Wiya nura ba kaiyu korien to umulliko unni waréa, minarig tin nura kotellin unnoa tara ?
27. Kotella nura kenukún turukin bara ba ; keawai bara uma korien, wupi korien bara ; gatun bag wiyan nurun, Tholomón noa ba, konéinkan, keawai bon wupa korien yanti kiloa wakál unti tara birug.
28. Upánún noa ba Eloito woiyo yanti, yakita purreág ka unta ba purrai ta kátan, gatun kumba warekakin murrug ka wollo ka ; wiya, nurun noa upánún, A! nura gurrullikan waréakan ?
29. Gatun na-ki yikora nura minarig nurúnba takilliko gatun pittelliko, ga kota yikora nura minki ko.
30. Koito ba bara yantinto purrai ta ba ko natan yantin unni tara ; gatun nurúnba-to Biyugbai-to gurran unni tara gukillikanne nurun ba murrárag kakilliko.
31. Wonto ba nura nauwa piriwál koba Eloi koba, gatun yantin unni rara gunun nurun kin.
32. Kinta kora, wirrul waréa ; kulla pitálman bon Biyugbai nurúnba gukilliko piriwál-gél ta nurun kin.
33. Gukilléa nurúnba, gatun guwa gukillikanne : umulla nura yinug nurúnba, keawai koa korokál katéa-kún, porrólkan ta moroko ka ba kakilliko ka korien kakilliko, keawai ba unta ko uwa korien mankiye, gatun keawai ba yarakai puntaye.
34. Wonnun ta nurúnba tullokan, untabo kánún nurúnba búl-búl yantibo.

35. Girullia nura winnal nurúmba, ġatun nurúnba kaibuġ winabunbilla;
36. Gatun nurabo yanti kiloa kúri ba mittillin barúnba ko Piriwál ko, willuġ-banún noa ba mankilliġél labiruġ; uwánún noa ba ba tanan ġatun wirrillinún, umánún ġaiya bon tanoa-kal-bo.
37. Pitálmatoara kánún bara unnoa tara mankillikan, yakita Piriwál noa ba uwánún, noa ba barun kin nanún noa ba barun nakilli ta; wiyan baġ tuloa nurun, ġirullinún noa kótibo, ġatun yellawabumbéa barun takilli kolaġ, ġatun uwánún noa ġukilliko barun.
38. Gatun tanan uwánún noa ba, yakita buloara nakillikan ta, yakita ġoro ka nakillikan ta, ġatun nanún barun yantibo nakilli ta, pitálmatoara bara unnoa tara mankillikan.
39. Gatun ġurrulla unni, wiya noa ba kokera-tín-to ġurra pa, yakounta ba uwa pa mankiye na pa noa, keawai ġaiya kokera ġikoúmba potobunti pa.
40. Yanti tin kauwa nura nakilliko; kulla noa Yinal kúri koba uwánún yakita kota korien nura ba.
41. Wiya ġaiya noa bon Peterko, Piriwál, wiyan bi unni †parabol ġearunbo, ġa ġearun yantin?
42. Gatun noa Piriwállo wiya, Gan-ke noa mankillikan murráraġ ġatun ġuraki, piriwállo noa umánún bon wiyellikan kakilliko kokera ko ġikouġ ka ta ko, ġu-uwil koa noa takilliko yakita ġukilliġél la?
43. Pitálmatoara kátan unnoa mankillikan, umánún noa ba ġikoúmba piriwál nanún ġaiya noa bon umulli ta yanti.
44. Wiyan baġ tuloa, umánún bon noa wiyellikan kakilliko yantin tako.
45. Wonto noa ba wiyánún ġala mankilli-kan-to, búlbúl la, Emmoúmba piriwál minkin uwa korien; ġatun ġaiya noa búnkilli kolaġ barun kúri mankillikan ġatun ġapal, ġatun takilli kolaġ, ġatun pittelli kolaġ, ġatun kuttawai kolaġ;
46. Piriwál ġala koba mankillikan koba uwánún wal noa purreaġ ka na korien ta, ġatun yakita ġaiya kota korien ta bon, ġatun búnnún bon buloarakan, ġatun ġunún bon winta ġikouġ kai barun kin ġurra korien ta.
47. Gatun unnoa mankillikan ġurran noa kotelli ta piriwál koba ġikoúmba, ġatun keawai uma korien, keawai noa uma pa yanti kotelli ta ġikoúmba, búnnún wal ġaiya bon kauwál-kauwál.
48. Wonto noa ba niuwoa ġurra korien, ġatun yarakai umatoara yaki tin bún ba bon, búnnún wal waréa. Kulla bon ġupa kauwál, wiyapaiyánún wal kauwál ġikouġ kinbiruġ; ġatun kúriko ġukulla kauwál, wiyellia kánún bara ġaiya kauwál-kauwál ġikouġ kinbiruġ.
49. Uwan ta baġ unni yukulliko koiyuġ ko purrai ta ko; minnuġ-bullinún baġ kauwa ba tanoa-kal-bo wirroġ-kulléa?

50. Kulla tia korimullikanne emmoug kinba korimulliko; gatun yakoai bag katan goloin koa ka-uwil kakilliko !

51. Kotan nura, uwa bag ba pital gukilliko purrai ta ko? wiyan bag ba, keawai ; wonto ba gurruggurra kakilliko ;

52. Kulla wal unti birug kanún kakilliko †pente kokera wakal la, gurruggurra birug, goro bulun kinbirug, gatun buloara goro kabirug.

53. Biyugbai gurruggurra kanún yinal labirug, gatun yinal biyugbai tabirug ; gatun tunkan yinalkun tabirug, gatun yinalkun tunkan tabirug, túngaikun bounnoun ba kurrinanbai tabirug, gatun kurrinanbai bounnoun ba túngaikun tabirug.

54. Gatun noa barun kúri wiya, Nanún nura ba yareil wokka lag punnál ba pulógkulligél lin, wiyanún gaiya nura koiwon tanan ba ; gatun kauwa yanti.

55. Gatun kareawug ba kanún, wiyellinún gaiya nura, karol kanún ; gatun yanti gaiya kanún.

56. A nura nakoiyaye ! natan nura tarkin moroko koba gatun purrai koba ; minarig tin koa nura na korien unti yakita?

57. Kauwa, kora koa nura kota ba nurun kinbirug tuloa?

58. Uwanún bi ba gikoug katoa bukkakan toa gikoug kinko wiyellikan tako, yapug koa nuiyellia bi bon, wamunbi-uwil koa biloa murroi kakilliko gikoug kinbirug; yutéa-kún koa biloa wiyellikan kauwal lako, gatun wiyellikanto kauwallo wamunbinún biloa yarakan tako, gatun yarakanto wupinún biloa †jail kako.

59. Wiyan banug, keawai bi waita uwa korien unta birug, gukillinun bi ba †lepton ta kirun waréa ta.

WINTA XIII.

KAKULLA bara unta yakita taraikan, wiya bon barun Galilaiakal, gorog barúnba tarogkama Pilato-to †thuhia barun barúnba.

2. Gatun noa Iéthuko wiyayelléún, wiyelliela noa barun, Wiya, nura kotellin unnoa tara Galilaiakál yarakai bara kakulla kauwal barun kinbirng Galilaiakál labirug, kulla barun ba mankulla unnoa tara?

3. Wiyan nurun bag, Keawai ; kulla nura keawai minki katan, yantin gaiya nura tetti-tetti kanún.

4. Ga barun †tetín ta wunkulléún kokera barán, gatun tetti-tetti barun wirria, wiya, nura kotellin barun yarakai bara ba kakulla kauwal barun kúri kabirug kakillin †Hierothalem ka?

5. Wiyan nurun bag, Keawai ; kulla nura keawai minki katan, yantin gaiya nura tetti-tetti kanún.

6. Wiya noa unni yanti †parabol : Taraikan ta kúriko wupéa yirriwilbin purrai ta gikoug ka ta ; gatun noa uwa yeai ko nakilliko, gatun noa keawai gaiya na pa.

7. Wiya gaiya noa bon upullikan, Ela! goro ka wunal la unti, uwa bag nakilliko yeai ko unti birug ko yirriwiltabin tako, gatun

keawai gaiya bag na pa ; kólbúntilla unnoa barán ; minarig tin unnoa kátan purrai ta ?

8. Gatun noa wiyayelléún, wiyelliela bon, Piriwal, kámunbilla unnoa unti wunál la, pinni-uwil koa bag untoakál ko, gatun konug koa bag wupi-uwil ;

9. Gatun yeai ba kúnún, murrárág gaiya kánún ; gatun ka korien ba, gatun yukita gaiya kólbúntinún wal bi unni barán.

10. Gatun noa wiyelliela wakál la †tkunagog ka purreág ka thabbat ka.

11. Gatun, a! kakulla unta wakál nukug munni-lan bountoa ba kauwál-kauwál wunál †étín ta, gatun woinu bountoa, gatun keawai bountoa kaiyu korien wokka-lan kakilliko.

12. Gatun nakulla noa ba Iéthuko bounnoun, kaaipa bounnoun noa, gatun wiyelliela bounnoun, Nukug, gintoa burug-kulléún woinu kabirug giroug kinbirug.

13. Gatun noa upilléún máttára bounnoun kin ; gatun tanoakal-bo bounnoun tuloa uma, gatun bountoa pitálma bon Eloinug.

14. Gatun piriwállo †thunagóg kako wiyayelléún bukka-kan-to, kulla noa Iéthuko turon uma purreág ka thabbat ka, gatun wiya barun kúri, †Hek ta purreág ka umilliko kúri ko ; unti tara purreág ka tanan uwolla turon umulliko, gatun keawai thabbat ta purreág ka.

15. Piriwállo noa bon wiyayelléún gatun wiyelliela, Gintoa gakoiyaye ! wiya, yantinto nura burugbuggan gikoúmba †boo gatun †athino, purreág ka thabbat ka, unta birug kokera birug, yemmama-uwil koa kokoin kolag pittelliko?

16. Gatun keawai wal unni gapal, yinálkun ta Abáramúmba, giratoara bounnoun Thatánto noa unni tara †étín ta wunál la, burugbuggulliko yanti birug, unti thabbat ta purreág ka ?

17. Gatun wiya noa ba unni tara, koiyun bara gaiya kátan yantin bukkamaiye gikoug kai ; gatun yantin kúri pitál kakulla yantin tin umatoarrin kauwál lin gikoug birug.

18. Wiya gaiya noa, Minarig kiloa Piriwál koba Eloi koba ? gatun yakoai kiloa paggunbinún ?

19. Yanti kiloa ta yeai ba †mutard koba, mankulla kúriko, gatun meapa purrai ta gikoug kai ta ; gatun boaikulléún wokka lag, gatun kakulla kauwál kúlai ; gatun tibbin moroko tin yellawa wiran ta.

20. Gatun noa wiyéa-kún, Yakoai kiloa bag túgunbinún piriwál koba Eloi koba ?

21. Yanti †lebben kiloa, mankulla gapallo gatun yuropa goro ka gukilligél la nulai ta, kakulla wal yantibo †lebben kiloa.

22. Gatun noa uwa kokeroa gatun kauwál loa kokeroa, wiyatin, gatun uwollin †Hierothalem kolag.

23. Wiya gaiya bon wakállo, Piriwál, wiya, warai moron kakilliko ? Gatun noa wiya barun,

M

24. Nuwolla pulógkulli kolag tuloa tin yapug tin : kulla bag nurun wiyan, kauwál-kauwállo nuwanún murrárig pulógkulli kolag gatun keawai wal kaiyu korien.

25. Bongkullinún noa ba kokeratín wokka lag, gatun wirrigbakulla pulógkulligél, gatun nura garokéa warrai ta, gatun wirrilléún toto pulógkulligél, wiyellin, Piriwál, Piriwál, umulla gearun ; gatun noa wiyayellinún gatun wiyánún, Keawaran bag nurun gimilli korien wonta birug wal nura :

26. Wiyánún gaiya wal nura, Takéún géen gatun pittakéún giroug kin mikan ta, gatun gintoa wiyakéún gearun kin yapug ka.

27. Wonto wal noa ba wiyánún, Wiyan bag nurun, keawaran bag nurun gimilli korien, wonta birug wal nura ; yurig tia uwolla emmoug kinbirug, yantin nura yarakai umullikan.

28. Unta ta wal tugkillinún gatun tirra-gatpuntullinún, nanún gaiya nura ba barun, Abáramnug, gatun Itháknug, gatun Yacóbnug, gatun yantin †propetnug, kakillin bara ba piriwál koba ka Eloi koba, gatun nurunbo yuaipéa warrai tako.

29. Gatun bara uwánún muring tin, gatun krai tin, gatun kummari tin, gatun pakai tin, gatun yellawánún wal piriwál koba ka Eloi koba ka.

30. Gatun, a ! bara willug kátan, kabo wal bara ganka kánún gatun bara ganka kátan, kabo wal bara willug kánún.

31. Unta purreág ka winta uwa Parithaioi kabirug wiyellin bon, Yurig ba waita wolla unta birug, kulla noa Herodto biloa búnnún tetti.

32. Gatun noa barun wiyá, Yurig nura wolla, wiya-uwil koa bon unnoa †alópék, A ! paibuggan bag barun †diabol, gatun turon bag uman buggai gatun kúmba, gatun kúmba-ken-ta wal goloin tia kánún.

33. Yantin tin uwánún wal bag buggai gatun kúmba, gatun kúmba-ken-ta ; kulla wal keawaran wal wakál †propet ka korien tetti †Hierothalem kabirug.

34. Yapallun †Hierothalem, Hierothalem ! búnkiye tetti wirriye barun †propet, gatun pintia barun tunug ko yupitoara giroug kinko; murrin-murrin bag kauma pa bag barun wonnai tara giroúmba, yanti kiloa tibbinto ba kauma-uwil yirrig ka bara ka bounnoun ba waréa tara, gatun keawaran nura kauma korien.

35. A ! nurúnba kokera kakillin mirrál kakilliko : gatun bag wiyan tuloa nurun, Keawai nura tia nanún, yakita ko kánún ba wiyánún wal nura ba, Pitálkámunbilla bon uwan noa ba yitirroa Piriwál koba koa.

WINTA XIV.

Gatun yakita kakulla, uwa noa ba murrarig kokera piriwál koba ka Parithaioi koba takilliko nulai ko purreág ka thabbat ka, tumiméa gaiya bon bara.

2. Gatun, a ! garoka ba kakulla wakál kúri kokoin-kan warakag.

3. Gatun Iéthuko noa wiyayelléún wiya barun †nomikoinuġ ġatun Parithaioinuġ, wiyelliela, Wiya, murráráġ turon umulliko purreàġ ka thabbat ka?
4. Gatun bara tullama pullí. Gatun noa bon turon uma, ġatun wamunbéa bon;
5. Gatun wiyayelléún noa barun, wiyelliela, Ganto nurun kinbiruġ-ko puntimanún buttikaġ ba †athino ba ġa †boo ba nurúmba kirai ta, ġatun keawai ġaiya bon manún wokka laġ purreáġ ka thabbat ka?
6. Gatun keawai bara bon wiyayelli pa unni tara.
7. Gatun noa wiya wakál †parabol barun ġala ko wiyatora ko, nakulla noa ba ġiriméa bara murráráġ waiyakan; wiyelliela barun,
8. Wiyánún bin ba taraito kúriko uwa-uwil koa bi mankilli kolaġ nukuġ kolaġ, yellawa yikora wokka waiyakanto, mirka ta tarai kúri piriwál wiyatoara ta;
9. Gatun noa niuwoa wiya biloa ġatun ġikouġ tanan uwolliko ġatun wiyelliko bin, Guwa bon ġali ko; ġatun ġintoa koiyun bi ba kánún waita uwánún waiyakan kolaġ bará ka bo.
10. Wonto ba bin wiyánún ba, yuriġ bi yellawolli ta ka bará kako waiyakan kako; ġatun uwánún noa ba wiya biloa ba wiyánún biloa, Kóti, yuriġ wokka laġ uwolla: yakita ġaiya pitálmánún bin mikan ta barun kin tanún ba kunto ġirouġ katoa.
11. Gan umullinún niuwoa bo wokka kako, umánún wal bon bará kako; ġatun niuwoa umullinún niuwoa ba bará kako, umullinún wal wokka kako.
12. Wiya ġaiya noa ġala wiya bon noa ba, Gunún bi ba takilliko búlwára ka ġa yaréa ka, wiya yikora bi ġiroúmba kóti, ġa kótita, ġa porrólkan; wiyéa kánún bin ba bara, ġatun ġupaiyéa kánún bin yaruġ ka.
13. Wonto bi ba umánún takilliko, wiyella barun mirrál-mirrálkan, ġatun munni-munni-kan, ġatun wiir-wiirkan, ġatun munminkan :
14. Gatun bin pitálmanún; kulla bara keawai ġupaiye korien yaruġ ka; kulla bin ġupaiyéa kánún yaruġ ka, yakita ba moron kánún murráráġ-tai tetti-tetti kabiruġ.
15. Gatun wakál barun kinbiruġ yellawa ġikouġ kin takilliela, ġurra noa ba unni tara, wiya bon noa, Pitálmatoara noa tanún wal kunto piriwál lako Eloi koba ka.
16. Wiya ġaiya noa bon, Taraito kúriko wupéa kauwál takilliko yaréa ka, ġatun wiya barun kauwál-kauwál kúri:
17. Gatun yaréa ka yuka noa bon ġikoúmba mankillikan, wiyelliko barun wiyatoara ko, Tanan ; kulla yantin umnuġ tara wupéa yakita.
18. Gatun bara yantin wiyellan wakál-wakál ġakoiyellan. Kurri-kurrito wakállo wiya ġikouġ, Gukilléún baġ winta purrai, ġatun waita wal baġ uwánún nakilliko ġala ko ; wiyan biloa wamunbilliko tia.

19. Gatun taraito wiyá, Gukilléun bag †pente tumba †boo butti-kag, gatun bag waita uwan numulliko barun ; wiyan biloa wamun-billiko tia.
20. Gatun taraito wiyá, Mankulla bag nukug emmoúmba, yaki tin keawai bag uwa korien.
21. Uwa gaiya noa unni mankillikan, gatun wiya bon piriwál gikoúmba unni tara. Wiya bon gaiya noa kokeratinto bukka-kan-to gikoúmba mankillikan, Yurig wolla kurrakai yapug koa koke-roa, gatun yutilla barun tanan untiko mirrál-mirrál-kai, gatun munni-munni-kai, gatun wiir-wiir-kai, gatun munmin-kai.
22. Gatun noa mankillikanto wiyá, Piriwál, upatoara ta yanti bi ba wiya, gatun kauwál-kauwál lako ka untiko.
23. Gatun noa bon piriwállo wiya mankillikan, Yurig uwolla yapug koa gatun korug koa, gatun pirriralmulla barun tanan uwolliko, emmoúmba koa kokera warapa-uwil.
24. Kulla bag wiyan nurun, Keawai wal bara untoakállo wiya-toara nutmuún emmoúmba kunto.
25. Gatun kúri kauwál-kauwál uwa gikoug katoa : gatun noa willarig warkulléun, gatun wiya gaiya barun,
26. Uwánún tia ba taraikan kúri emmoug kin, gatun wareka korien gikoúmba biyugbai gatun tunkan, gatun nukug, gatun wonnai tara, gatun kóti tara, gatun wuggunbai, kauwa, gikoúmba kata moron, keawai noa kánún emmoúmba wirrobullikan.
27. Ganto-bo ba kurri korien gikoúmba talig-kabillikanne, gatun uwolla emmoug katoa, keawai noa kánún emmoúmba wirrobulli-kan.
28. Ganto nurun kinbirug-ko, kotellin wittimulliko kokera, wi-ya, noa yellawánún kurri-kurri, gatun tuigko umulliko, mirka kea-wai goloin witti korien?
29. Mirroma, yukita wupéa noa ba tugga, gatun keawai noa kaiyu korien goloin wittilliko, yantinto ba namún béelmanún gaiya bon,
30. Wiyellinún, Gali kúriko nutéa wittimulliko, gatun kaiyu korien noa goloin wittimulliko.
31. Ga, gan piriwál uwánún noa ba wuruwai kolag tarai ko piriwál ko, yellawa noa kurri-kurri, gatun kotelliela, wiya, noa ba kaiyukan uwa-uwil koa †dekem-millia to nuggurrawa-uwil koa bon taimin to ke †bith-dekem-millia to ?
32. Ga ba, kalog ka ba noa piriwál taraito, yuka noa wakál puntimai wiyelliko pitál koa kakillai.
33. Yanti kiloa, yantinto nurun kinbirug-ko wareka korien noa yantin gikoúmba, keawai noa kánún emmoúmba wirrobullikan.
34. Pulli ta unni murrárág ; wonto ba pulli ka korien, yakoai kánún upilliko !
35. Keawai murrárág korien ta purrai ko, ga ba konuggél ko ; wareka gaiya kúriko. Niuwoabo gurréugkan gurrulliko, gurrabilla bon.

WINTA XV.

Papai gaiya bara uwa gikoug kin yantin †telónai gatun yarakai-willug gurrulliko bon.

2. Gatun koiya bara Parithaioiko gatun †garammatcuko, wiyelliela, Unni kúri murrárag koríen, noa uman barun yarakai-willug gatun tatan noa barun katoa.

3. Gatun noa wiya barun unni †parabol, wiyelliela,

4. Gan kúri nurun kinbirug, †hekaton ta †ćipu gikoúmba, wakál noa ba yuréa umánún barun kinbirug, wiya, noa wunún barun †nainty-nain ta korug ka, gatun waita noa uwánún na-uwil koa noa yuréa-matoara, kara-uwilli koa noa ?

5. Gatun karawolléún noa ba, wúnkilléún gaiya noa ba mirrug ka gikoug kin, pitállo ba.

6. Gatun uwa noa ba gura kako, wiya noa barun kótita gatun taraikan, wiyellin barun, Pitállía kauwa emmoug katoa ; kulla bag karawolléún †ćipu ta emmoúmba unni, yuréa ba kakulla.

7. Wiyan bag nurun, yanti kiloa pitál kánún kauwállan moroko ka ba minki noa ba wakál yarakaikan, keawai barun kai murrárágtai tin †nainty-nain ta tin, minki korien.

8. Ga wonnug-ke nukug púndol †targuro †ten ta bounnoun kinba, yuréa bountoa ba umánún wakál púndol, wiya, bountoa wirrogbanún kaipug, gatun wirrillinún wirrillikanneto kirra-kirra-uwilli koa bountoa ?

9. Gatun karawolléún bountoa ba, wiya gaiya bountoa ba kótita gatun taraikan tuigko, wiyellin, Pitállía kauwa emmoug katoa ; kulla bag karawolléún yuréa bag ba uma.

10. Yanti kiloa, wiyan bag nurun, unnug ta pitál kátan mikan ta agelo ka Eloi koba wakál lin ba yarakai-willug minki kánún.

11. Gatun noa wiya, Taraito kúriko yinal bula-buloara gikoúmba :

12. Gatun mittiko bulun kinbirug-ko wiya bon biyugbai gikoúmba, Biyug, gnwa tia winta tullokan ka-uwil koa emmoúmba. Gatun túnbilliela noa bulun tullokan.

13. Gatun keawai kauwál-kauwál korien ta purreág ka yukita, kau-ma noa mittiko yinallo, gatun waita noa uwa kalog koba, gatun unta noa wari-wareka tullokan gikoúmba pittelligél la.

14. Gatun wari-wareka noa ba kirun, kauwál kakulla unta kunto korien ; gatun tanoa-kal-bo kakulla gaiya noa kapirrikan.

15. Gatun uwa gaiya noa umulliko kúri kako unta ko purrai ta ko ; gatun noa bon yuka gikoug ka tako purrai tako giratimulliko buttikag ko †porák ko.

16. Pitál gaiya noa kakulla takilliko, ta-uwil ba buttikagko: gatun keawai kúriko bon gupa.

17. Gatun noa kakilliela ba niuwoabo, wiyelliela gaiya noa, Kauwál-kauwálla umullikan biyugbai koba emmoúmba koba kun-

to kauwál barúnba takilliko gatun gukilliko, gatun gatoa kapirró wirribanbillin !

18. Bougkullinún wal bag, waita biyugbai tako, gatun wiyánún wal bon, Biyug, yarakai bag nna mikan ta moroko ka, gatun giroug kin,

19. Gatun keawai bag murráräg korien wiya-uwil koa tia giroúmba yinal yitirra; umulla tia wakál yanti umullikan giroúmba.

20. Gatun noa bougkulléún, uwa gaiya noa biyugbai tako. Wonto noa ba kalog ka kauwál kakulla, nakulla noa bon biyugbaito gikoúmba-ko, minki gaiya noa kakulla, murrá gaiya noa, puntimulléún gaiya noa gikoug kin wuroka, gatun búnbúmbéa-kan gaiya bon.

21. Gatun noa bon yinallo wiyá, Biyug, yarakai bag umulléún mikan ta moroko ka gatun giroug kin, keawai bag murráräg korien wiya-uwil koa tia giroúmba yinal yitirra.

22. Wonto noa ba biyugbaito wiya barun mankillikan giroúmba, Mara unnoa-unnug upilligél, gatun upilla bon konéin kako, gatun upilla †rig gikoug kin máttára, gatun upilla bon tugganog yulo ka gikoug kin :

23. Gatun mara tanan untiko buttikag †italo giratimatoara kipai, gatun turnlla; tamunbilla gearun, gatun pitál koa géen kauwál :

24. Koito ba unni emmoúmba yinal tetti kakulla, yakita gaiya noa moron kátan; garawatilléún noa, gatun yakita bummilléún gaiya bon. Gatun pitál bara kakilli kolag.

25. Unta ta garro gikoúmba kakilliela upulligél la purrai ta ; gatun uwolliela noa ba papai kokera koba, gurra noa tekki gatun untelli ta.

26. Gatun noa kaaipa wakál mankillikan, gatun wiya minnugban gali tara minarig tin.

27. Gatun wiya bon noa, Unni ta uwan giroúmba biggai ; gatun giroúmba-ko biyugbaito tura giratimatoara buttikag †italo kipai ta, kulla wal pitál noa gikoug kai moron tin kátan.

28. Gatun noa minwara kakulla, keawai noa murrug kolag uwa pa; yaki tin noa biyugbai gikoúmba uwa gatun pirriralma bon.

29. Gatun noa bon wiyayelliela gikoúmba biyugbai, Ela ! kauwál-kauwálla wunálla unala bag giroug; keawai bag giroúmba wiyellikanne uma korien ; gatun keawai bi tia gupa waréa buttikag †kid, pitál koa tia ka-uwil bara emmoúmba kótita :

30. Wonto ba tanoa-bo giroúmba yinal uwa gali, wari-wareka giroúmba tullokan yarakai-willug koa ko gapal loa, tura gaiya bi gikoug buttikag †italo giratimatoara.

31. Gatun noa wiya bon, Yinal, yellawan bi emmoug kin yantikatai, gatun yantin unni tara emmoúmba giroug kin kánún.

32. Murräräg ta kakulla takilliko gatun pittelliko ; koito ba unni giroúmba umbeara-kóg tetti kakulla, gatun moron katéakan; gatun garawatilléún, gatun bummilléún bon yakita.

WINTA XVI.

Gatun noa wiya barun ġikoúmba wirrobullikan, Untoa ta tarai ta wakál kûri tullokan porrólkan, mankillan piriwál ġikoúmba; ġatun wiyayéma bon ġikouġ wareka noa ġikoúmba tullokan.

2. Gatun noa wiya bon, wiyelliela, Yakoa baġ ġurra ġirouġ kinba? wiyella bi tia minariġ bi ba umulliela; keawai bi kara kánún umullikan.

3. Wiyelléún ġaiya noa mankillikan niuwoabo, Minnuġ banún baġ? kulla wal lia piriwállo emmoúmba ko mantilléún keawai baġ mankillikan kánún; keawai baġ pinninún; koiyun baġ poiyelliko.

4. Gali wal baġ umulliko, yipánún tia ba emmoúmba mankilliġél labiruġ, wamunbi-uwil koa tia bara kóti ko kokera ko.

5. Yanti ba wiya noa barun wiyatoara piriwál koba ġikoúmba, ġatun noa wiya wakál kurri-kurri ka, Minnan ba wiyapaiyéún emmoúmba piriwál koba?

6. Gatun noa wiyá, †Hekaton ta wimbi ka karauwa. Gatun noa wiya bon, Mara bi unni, yellawa kurrakai, upulla †pentékonta koa ka-uwil.

7. Wiya ġaiya noa tarai, Minnan bi wiyapaiyéún piriwál koba? Gatun noa wiyá, †Hekaton ta wimbi †wiet. Gatun bon noa wiyá, Mara bi unni, upulla †éty koa ka-uwil.

8. Gatun noa piriwallo murráráġ bon wiya unnoa mankillikan yarakai ka, kulla noa una ġurakito; kulla bara wonnai tara unti ko purrai tako barúnba willuġġél koba ġuraki bara, keawai bara wonnai kaibuġ koba.

9. Gatun ġatoa nurun wiyan, Umulla nura bo kótita kakilliko tullo-yarakai tabiruġ; tetti nura ba kánún, wamunbilla ġaiya nurun kokera yuraki ba kátan yanti-katai.

10. Niuwoa miroman ġali waréa ta, yanti miroman noa kauwál ġali ta; ġatun niuwoa yarakai-maye ġali waréa ta, yanti yarakaimaye ġali kauwál ta.

11. Yaki tin keawai nura ba miroma pa tullo yarakai ta, ġanto wal nurun ġunún tullo tuloa ta miromulliko?

12. Gatun keawai nura ba miroma pa tarai koba, ġanto wal ġunún nurúnba kóti tako?

13. Keawai wal mankillikanto umánún buloara-bulun piriwál bula; kulla noa yarakai umánún wakál bon, ġatun murráráġ umánún tarai; ġa ba kánún noa wakálla, ġatun béelmánún bon tarai. Keawai nura kaiyu korien umulliko Eloi ko ġatun tullokan ko yarakai ko.

14. Gatun unni tara bara ġurra Parithaioiko, willirrikan bara kátan, ġatun bon bara béelma.

15. Gatun noa barun wiyá, Kauwa murráráġ koa nura ka-uwil mikan ta barun kin kûri ka; wonto noa ba Eloito ġurran nurúnba búlbúl la ba; kulla unni tara murráráġ ta kátan barun kinba kûri ko, yakaran ta kátan mikan ta Eloi kin.

16. Wiyellikanne-ta gatun bara †propet kakulla Ioanne noa ba paipéa ; yaki tabirug piriwál koba Eloi koba wiyabunbéa, gatun yantin kúri waita-waitawolléún murrug kolag.
17. Gatun moroko ta gatun purrai ta kaiyukan kanún waita kolag, keawai waréa ta wiyellikanne koba ka korien kakilliko.
18. Ganto ba warekullinún porikunbai gikoúmba gatun tarai búmbéa ka, yarakai búmbéa noa: gatun ganto ba búmbinún warekatoara poribai tabirug, yarakai búmbéa noa.
19. Kakulla ta noa wakál porrólkan, upulléún noa gorog-gorog ko gatun murrárag ko karigkareug ko, gatun bon kakulla minnugbo-minnugbo kauwál takilliko gatun pittelliko yantin ta puréag ka:
20. Gatun kakulla ta wakál poiyaye giakai yitirra Ladharo, wúnkulla bon ba yapuggél gikoug ka ta, warapal mita-mitag,
21. Gatun wiya bon ba mutug ko takilliko gikoug kai porrólbin tin takilligél labirug ; gatun warikál uwa bara, woatá gaiya bon mita-mitag.
22. Yakita-kalai tetti kakulla poiyaye, gatun kurriá bara bon agelo-ko Abáram kinko parrag kako : tetti gaiya noa porrólkan kakulla, gatun bon núlká.
23. Gatun noa unta koiyug ka †bell ka bougkulléún gikoúmba gaikug, kakilliela tirriki ka, gatun nakilliela bon Abáramnug kalog ka, gatun noa Ladharo parrag ka kakilliela Abáram kin.
24. Gatun noa kaaibulléún, wiyelliela, Biyug Abáram, gurrara tia kauwa, gatun yukulla bon Ladharonug, kurrimulli· koa noa kokoin to, gatun moiya koa tia tállag wupi-uwil ; kulla wal bag kirrin kátan unti tirriki ka koiyug ka.
25. Wonto noa ba Abáramko wiyá, Yinal, gurrulla gintoa yakita moron ta mantala murrárag-tai giroúmba, wonto noa ba Ladharo yakaran mantala ; gatun noa yakita pitál kátan, wonto bi ba kirrin kátan.
26. Gatun yanti unni ba, gearun kinba willika ba pirriko wúnkulla ; keawai uwánún untikál untoa kolag : keawai bara unta birug uwánún untiko gearun kinko.
27. Wiya gaiya noa, Wiyan banug, Biyug, yuka-uwil koa bon bintun kinko kokera kolag :
28. Kulla wal lia emmoúmba kótita †pente; wiya-uwil koa noa barun, yanoa bara ba tanan uwánún unti kolag tirriki-tirriki kako.
29. Abáramko noa wiya bon, Mothé noa gatun bara †propet barun katoa ba ; gurrabunbilla barun.
30. Gatun noa wiyá, Keawaran, biyug Abáram ; wakál ba uwolla barun kin unta birug tetti kabirug, gurránún gaiya wal bara.
31. Gatun noa bon wiyá, Keawai bara ba gurránún bon Mothénug gatun barun †propetnug, keawai wal bara gurránún wakál ba paikullinún moron tetti kabirug.

WINTA XVII

Wiya gaiya noa barun wirrobullikan gikoúmba, Kauwa yanti kanún bo ta wal yarakai ; yapalla noa gikoug kinbirug yarakai tabirug !

2. Murrai ka ba noa gira-uwil koa kulleug koa bon tunug, gatun wareka-uwil koa bon korowa ka, unni noa yanoa yarakai umabunbi yikora unti tara birug wakál wonnai tara birug.

3. Yakoai nura kauwa : Kótiko ba giroug yarakai umánún giroug ka to, wiyella bon ; gatun minki noa ba kánún, kámunbilla bon.

4. Gatun kauwál-kauwál-la biloa ba yarakai umánún wakál la purreág ka, gatun kauwál-kauwál-la biloa willarig noa kánún wakál la purreág ka, wiyellinún biloa, Minki bag kátan ; kámunbinún wal binug.

5. Gatun bon bara †apothol wiyá, Piriwál, kauwál koa gearúnba gurrulli-ta ka-uwil kakilliko.

6. Gatun noa Piriwállo wiyá, Ka ba nurúnba gurrulli-ta yanti kiloa mitti yeai †mutard koba, wiyella wal nura ba unni kúlai †thukamín, Wokka lag bi kauwa wirrakan-bo, gatun meapullía bi korowa ka ; gatun gala nurun gurránún gaiya wal.

7. Gan nurun kinbirug-ko upullin purrai nurun ka to mankillikan-to. ga tamunbin buttikag, wiyánún bon kabo, uwánún noa ba upulliggél labirug, Yurig bi wolla, yellawolliko ta-uwil koa ?

8. Gatun wiya bon noa wiyánún, Kurrakai umulla ta-uwil koa bag, gatun girullia bi gintoabo, gatun mara-uwil koa bi tia ta-uwil koa bag gatun pitta-uwil ; gatun willug gaiya bi tanún gatun pittánún ?

9. Wiya noa, wiyapaiyéún bon mankillikan, koito noa ba uma unni tara·wiya bon ba ? Kotan bag kearan.

10. Yanti nura wiyella, umánún nura ba yantin unni tara wiyatoara nurun, Umullikan géen murrárág korien kátan ; umá ta géen unni wiyatoara umulliko gearun.

11. Gatun yakita kakulla, uwolliela noa ba †Hierothalem kolag, uwa willi koa noa Thamaria koa gatun Galilaia koa.

12. Gatun noa uwolliela ba tarai toa kokeróa, nuggarawa bon bara kúri †ten ta purrul-wommun-wommun, garokéa kalog ka ;

13. Gatun bara paibugga pullí, gatun wiya Iéthu, Piriwal, gurráramulla gearun.

14. Gatun nakulla noa barun, wiya barun noa, Yurig nura wolla, túgunbillía nura barun kin †hiereu ko. Gatun yakita kakulla, uwolliela bara ba, turon bara kakulla tanoa-kal-bo.

15. Gatun wakállo barun kinbirug-ko, nakilléún noa ba turon noa kakulla, willugbo noa uwa, gatun kaaipulléún noa wokka, pitálmulliela bon Eloinug,

16. Gatun puntimulléún noa barán goara ko gikoug kin tinna ka, murrárág noa bon wiyelléún ; gatun noa Thamaria-kál.

17. Gatun noa Iéthuko wiyayelléůn, wiyelliela, Wiya, †ten ta turon kakulla? ga wonnuġ-ke bara taraikan †nain ta?
18. Keawai bara willuġ pa ba pitálmulliko bon Eloinuġ, wakál ba noa unni ġowikan ko.
19. Gatun noa wiya bon, Bouġkullía, yuriġ bi wolla; ġirouġ ka ba ko ġurrulli biruġ ko turon bi kátan.
20. Gatun wiya bon ba Parithaioiko, yakounta-ke paipinůn piriwál koba Eloi koba, wiyayelléůn noa barun, wiyelliela, Tanan uwan piriwál koba Eloi koba keawai na korien.
21. Keawai bara wiyánůn wal, A unni ta! ġa unta ta! kulla, a! piriwál koba Eloi koba murruġ kaba kátan nurun kinba.
22. Gatun noa wiya barun wirrobullikan, A! purreáġ ta wal kánůn, na-uwil koa nura wakál purreáġ Yinal koba kúri koba, ġatun keawai wal nura nanůn.
23. Gatun bara nurun wiyánůn wal, Na-uwa unni; ġa, na-uwa unnuġ: yanoa barun uwa yikora, wirroba yikora.
24. Yanti kiloa pirruġgun-to uwan tarai tabiruġ ko moroko biruġ ko, tarai ta kako moroko kako; kauwa yanti kiloa wal kánůn Yinal kúri koba purreáġ ka ġikouġ ka ta.
25. Gatun kurri-kurri ta bon umánůn minnuġbo-minnuġbo, ġatun warekatéa wal bon ġali koba willuġġél koba.
26. Gatun yakita ba kakulla purreáġ ka Noe-úmba ka, yanti bo ta wal kánůn purreáġ ka Yinal koba kúri koba.
27. Takillala bara, pittellala bara, búmbillala bara nukuġ, ġukillala búmbilli ka, yakita purreáġ ka kakulla noa ba Noe uwa murrariġ murrinauwai ka, ġatun tunta-tunta kakulla, ġatun kirun ġaipa barun nuropa.
28. Gatun yanti yakita ba kakulla purreáġ ka Lot-úmba, takillala bara, pittellala bara, wirrilliala bara, ġukillala bara, meapala bara, wittiala bara;
29. Wonto ba yakita unta purreáġ ka Lot noa uwa Thodóm kabiruġ, patéa ġaiya koiyuġ-ko ġatun †brimtón-ko wokka tin moroko tin, ġatun kiyupa barun yantin kirun tetti-tetti.
30. Yanti kiloa kánůn yakita purreáġ ka paipinůn noa ba Yinal kúri koba.
31. Unta yakita purreáġ ka kátan noa ba wokka kokerá, ġatun ġikoúmba tullokan murruġ kaba kokera ba, keawai bon uwabunbi yikora barán mankilliko tullokan ko; ġatun kátan noa ba upulliġél laba, keawai bon uwabunbi yikora willuġ kolaġ.
32. Kotella bounnoun kai nukuġ Lot-úmba tin.
33. Ganto ba ġikoúmba moron mirománůn moron kakilliko, woġúntinůn wal noa; ġatun ġanto ba woġúntinůn ġikoúmba moron, kánůn wal moron kakilliko.
34. Wiya nurun baġ, yakita unta-unta tokoi ta buloara ta kánůn birrikilliġél la wakál la; manůn wal wakál, ġatun tarai ġaiya wunůn.

35. Buloara umullinûn bula; manûn wal wakál, gatun tarai gaiya wunûn.

36. Buloara katéa-kánûn upulligél la; manûn wal wakál, gatun tarai gaiya wunûn.

37. Gatun wiyelléûn bon bara, wiyellicla, Piriwál, wonnug-ke? Gatun noa wiya barun, Unta wonto ba katéa-kánûn murrin ta, unta kolag ba kautillinûn bara porowi.

WINTA XVIII.

Gatun noa wiya barun wakál †parabol, wiya-uwil koa bon bara kûriko Eloinug, gatun yari koa bara kaiyaléa-kún;

2. Wiyelliela, Unta ta kokerá tarai ta wakál wiyellikan piriwál kakulla, kinta korien kakulla noa bon Eloi kai, gatun keawai noa tuma korien barun kûri:

3. Gatun kakulla wakál mabogun unta kokerá; gatun bountoa uwa gikoug kin, wiyellicla, Timbai kakillía tia emmoúmba bukkakaye.

4. Gatun keawai wal noa gurra pa kabo kakullai tako; wonto noa ba yukita wiya gikoug kinko minki ka, Keawai bag kinta korien bon Eloi kai kátan, ga keawai kûri tuman korien;

5. Kulla bountoa tia unni mabogunto pirralman, gatoa timbai kánûn bounnoun kin, murrin-murrin koa bountoa tia uwa-uwil kumburrobawan bounton tia.

6. Gatun noa Piriwállo wiyá, Gurrulla bon unni yarakai wiyellikan piriwál wiyan ba.

7. Gatun wiya noa Eloito timbai katillinûn barun gikoúmba girimatoara, bara wiyan bon purreag ka gatun tokoi ta, gurralin noa barun wiyelli ta kalog tinto?

8. Wiyan nurun bag, timbai wal noa katillinûn barun kurrakai. Wonto noa ba uwánûn wal Yinal kûri koba tanan, wiya, noa nanûn gurrullikanne purrai taba?

9. Gatun noa wiya barun unni †parabol tarai tako kotelléûn bara ba murrárag-tai barabo, gatun yarakai bara kotellin taraikan :

10. Buloara-bula kûri uwa †hieron kolag wiyelliko : wakál la noa Parithaio gatun tarai ta †telóné;

11. Garokéa noa Parithaio gatun noa yanti wiyelliela niuwoabo giakai : A Eloi! pitálman bag giroug, kulla bag ka korien yanti tarai ba kátan, bara kau-maye, tuloa uma korien mankiye nukug ka, ga ka korien bag yanti unni noa ba †telóné:

12. Ta korien bag buloarakál kátan wakál la thabbat birug ka, gutan bag winta untikál emmoug kai yantin tabirug.

13. Gatun noa †telóné garokilliela ba kalog ka, keawai noa gaikug ka wokka lag na pa moroko koba, wonto noa ba minki motilliela wiyelliela ba, A Eloi! miromulla bi tia, yarakai bag ba kátan.

14. Wiyan nurun bag, unni noa kûri uwa barán kokera koba gikoug ka tako gurrámatoara, keawai tarai ta : kulla yantin bara

piriwäl-buntelliko, känún wal bara koiyun-barátoaro : gatun niuwoa bo koai-koai korien bon, umánún kauwäl bon kakilliko.

15. Gatun mankulla bara gikoug kinko wonnai tara numa-uwil koa barun noa : wonto ba nakulla bara ba wirrobullikanto, yipa bara barun.

16. Wonto ba noa Iéthuko wiya barun, wiyelliela, Wamunbilla barun wonnai tara emmoug kinko, gatun yanoa barun yipai yikora : kulla barun-kai-käl katéa-känún piriwäl koba Eloi koba.

17. Wiyan bag tuloa nurun, Ganto ba gurra korien piriwäl koba Eloi koba yanti wonnai waréa ba, keawai wal noa pulógkullinún unta kolag.

18. Gatun taraito umullikanto piriwällo wiya bon, wiyelliela, Piriwäl murrárág-tai, minnug-bullinún bag moron kakilliko yantikatai ?

19. Gatun noa Iéthuko wiya bon, Minarig tin bi tia wiyan murrárág-tai emmoug ? keawai wal wakäl murrárág-tai, wonto noa ba wakälbo, Eloi ta.

20. Gurran bi yantin wiyellikanne, Yanoa manki yikora nukug taraikan koba, Yanoa búnki yikora tetti, Yanoa manki yikora, Yanoa nakoiya yikora, Gurulla bon biyugbai gatun tunkan giroúmba.

21. Gatun noa wiyá, Gurra bag unni tara wiyellikanne yakikalai tabirug, wonnai bag ba kakulla.

22. Gatun yakita gurra noa ba Iéthuko unnoa tara, wiya bon noa, Wakäl unnoa-unnug uma korien bi ba; gukillía yantin tullokan giroúmba, gu-uwil koa barun mirräl ko, gatun tullokan giroúmba känún wal wokka ka moroko ka ; gatun kaai, wirroba-uwil koa bi tia.

23. Gatun gurra noa ba unni, minki noa kakulla kauwäl ; kulla noa porrol kakulla kauwälkan.

24. Gatun noa ba Iéthuko nakulla bon minki noa ba kakulla kauwäl-lan, wiya gaiya noa, Pirral ta pulógkulliko bara tullokan ta ba piriwäl koba kako Eloi koba kako !

25. †Kamel noa kaiyukan kátan pulógkakilliko tigkugkoa ko taku lako, keawai porrólkan pulógkakilliko piriwäl koba kako Eloi koba kako.

26. Gatun bara ba gurrá, wiya bara, Gan-ke wal moron känún kakilliko ?

27. Gatun noa wiyá, Unni tara kaiyu korien kúri ko umulliko, kaiyu-kan-to Eloito noa umulliko.

28. Gatun Peterko noa wiyá, Ela ! wúnkulla géen yantin ta, gatun wirroba géen bin.

29. Gatun noa wiya barun, Wiyänún bag tuloa, Niuwoa wareka kokera gikoúmba, ga biyugbai, ga tunkan, ga gapal, ga wonnai, gikoug kinko piriwäl koba tin Eloi koba tin,

30. Manún wal noa kauwäl unti yakita, gatun untoa tarai ta purrai ta tanan kakilliko, moron noa känún yanti-katai.

31. Mankulla ġaiya noa barun †dodeka ta wirrobullikan, ġatun wiya barun, A! waita ġeen wokka kolag †Hierothalem kolag, ġatun yantin tara wiyatoara †propet to ġikouġ kai Yinal lin kûri koba tin kânûn wal umatoara kakilliko.

32. Gatun bon ġunûn wal barun kin †ethânékâl kinko, ġatun bon bukka-manûn wal, ġatun karaġkobinûn :

33. Gatun wélkorinûn wal bara bon, ġatun wal bon wirrinûn : ġatun kûmba-ken-ta bouġkullinûn ġaiya noa willuġbo.

34. Gatun keawai bara ġurrapa unni tara wiyatoara : ġatun unni wiyellikanne yuropa barun kai, keawai bara ġurrápa unni tara wiyatoara.

35. Gatun yakita kakulla, uwolliela noa ba papai Yeriko ka, wakâl munmin kûri yellawolliela yapuġ ka bitta ka, poiyelliela :

36. Gatun ġurrulliela noa barun konara yapuġ koa, wiya noa minariġ unni ?

37. Gatun bara bon wiyá, Uwan noa Iéthu Nadharet-kâl.

38. Gatun noa kaaipulléûn, wiyelliela, Ela Iéthu! yinal Dabidûmba, ġurrára-mulla bi tia.

39. Gatun bara uwa ġanka, wiya bon koiyelli koa noa : wonto noa ba butti paiyelléûn, Yinal Dabidûmba ġintoa, ġurrára-mulla bi tia.

40. Gatun ġarokéa noa Iéthu, ġatun wiya bon yutilliko bon ġikouġ kinko ; ġatun uwa noa ba papai, wiya bon noa,

41. Wiyelliela, Minnuġ-bulliko bi tia wiyan ? Gatun noa wiyan, Piriwâl, namunbilliko tia umulla.

42. Gatun noa Iéthuko wiya bon, Kâmunbilla bin nakilliko ; ġiroûmba tin ġurrulli tin moron uma.

43. Gatun noa tanoa-kal-bo nakulla, ġatun bon noa wirropa, pitâlmulliela bon Eloinuġ ; ġatun yantin unni kûri nakulla bara ba, pitâlma bon Eloinuġ.

WINTA XIX.

1. GATUN noa Iéthu uwa willi koa Yeriko koa.

2. Gatun kakulla untakâl wakâl kûri ġiakai Dhakké yitirra, piriwâl †telónékâl noa kakulla, ġatun noa porrólkan.

3. Gatun noa numéa nakilliko Iéthunuġ, ġan noa ba ; ġatun noa keawai, kulla konaró núntima, kulla noa waréa ġoiyoġ.

4. Gatun noa murra ġanka, ġatun noa kulliwa wokka-laġ kûlai tin nakilliko bon, kulla noa unta kolaġ uwolli kolaġ.

5. Gatun Iéthu noa ba uwa untako, nakulla noa wokka-laġ, ġatun bon nakulla, ġatun bon wiyá, Ela Dhakké! tanan kurrakai tirabulla, kulla buġgai koa baġ yellawánûn ġirouġ ka ta kokerá.

6. Gatun tiraba noa kurrakai barán, ġatun pitál ma-uwa bon.

7. Gatun nakulla bara ba, wiyellan niuwarakan bara yantinto, wiyelliela, Waita noa uwa yarakai toa kóti kakilliko.

8. Gatun noa Dhakké ġarokéa, ġatun wiya bon Piriwálnuġ, Ela Piriwál! winta baġ ġutan emmoûmba tullokan kabiruġ mirrál

kai ko ; gatun mankulla baġ ba tullokan taraikan tabiruġ yaki tin gakoiyayc tin, wupinún gaiya bon baġ willuġbo waran tako.

9. Gatun noa Iéthuko bon wiyá, Tanan uwa moron unti buġgai purreáġ ka unti ko kokera ko, kulla noa kátan yinal ta Abáramúmba.

10. Kulla Yinal kúri koba uwa tiwolliko gatun tumulliko wogúntitoara ko.

11. Gatun gurra bara ba unni tara, wiyéakan butti noa gatun wiva wakál †parabol, kulla noa papai ta ba †Hierothalem ka, gatun kulla bara kota paipillinún piriwäl koba Eloi koba tanoa-kal-bo.

12. Yaki tin noa wiyá, Tarai ta piriwäl uwa tarai tako purrai tako kaloġ kako, mankilliko gikouġbo piriwálkanne-ta, gatun willuġbulliko.

13. Gatun wiya noa barun gikoúmba mankillikan †ten ta, gatun gukulla noa barun kin †mina ta †ten ta, gatun wiya barun. Miromulla uwánún baġ ba willuġbo.

14. Wonto ba gikoúmba-ko konara niuwama bon, gatun yuka bon puntimai gikouġ, wiyelliela, Keawai wal noa unni piriwäl katillinún gearun.

15. Gatun kakulla yakita, willuġ ba noa ba, mantoara piriwälkoba, wiya gaiya noa barun unnoa mankillikan gan kin noa ba gukulla †money, tanan gikouġ kin, gurra-uwil koa noa minnan barun kinba gutoara gukilli tabiruġ.

16. Tanan gaiya uwa kurri-kurri wakál, wiyelliela, Ela Piriwäl! giroúmba ta †mina unni wittia kauwäl †ten †mina ta.

17. Gatun bon noa wiyá, Kauwa yanti, gintoa mankillikan murráráġ; kulla bi miroma unnoa waréa ta, kaiyukan bi kauwa †ten ta kokera.

18. Gatun tarai uwa, wiyelliela, Ela Piriwäl! giroúmba ta †mina unni wittia kauwäl †pente †mina ta.

19. Gatun noa wiya gaiya bon, Kauwa bi kaiyukan †pente ta kokera.

20. Gatun tarai uwa, wiyelliela, Ela Piriwäl! na-uwa unni ta †mina giroúmba, wúnkulla baġ ba koroka wurobilla :

21. Kulla baġ kinta kakulla girouġ kai, kulla bi bukka kauwäl : mantan bi wokka-laġ keawai bi ba wunpa barán, gatun kólbúntia bi unnoa keawai bi ba meapa ba.

22. Gatun noa bon wiyá, Girouġ kinbiruġ kóti ko kurraka ko wiyan pirriral-manún banuġ, gintoa ta mankillikan yarakai. Gurra bi tia bukka kauwäl baġ; mantillin wokka-laġ keawai baġ wunpa barán, gatun kólbúntillin unnoa keawai bag ba meapa ba:

23. Kora koa bi gupa emmoúmba †money gukilliġél lako, maraúwil koa baġ emmoúmba kóti gatun kopatoara ta, emmouġ ka ta uwolli ta ?

24. Gatun noa wiya barun garokilliela bara ba taruġ ka, Mantillía unnoa †mina unti biruġ bon, gatun guwa bon gala ko †tenkan ko gikouġ.

25. (Gatun bara wiya bon, Piriwäl, †ten ta †mina mantan noa).
26. Wiyan nurun baġ, Yantinko barun mantan bara ba ġunún wal butti; ġatun keawaran noa ba, unnoa ta mantan noa ba mantillinún wal bon ġikonġ kinbiruġ.
27. Kulla bara unnoa emmoúmba niuwa-maye, keawai bara emmouġ känún bi ba piriwäl barun, mara barun, bú-uwil koa barun emmouġ kin mikan ta.
28. Gatun wiya noa ba unnoa, waita ġaiya noa ġanka uwa wokka-laġ †Hierothalem kolaġ.
29. Gatun kakulla yakita, uwa noa ba papai Bethäbage tako ġatun Bethany tako, bulkära ta ġiakai yitirra †Elaión ka la, yakunbéa noa buloara-bulun ġikoúmba wirrobullikan,
30. Wiyelliela, Yuriġ nura wolla kokerä ko kaiyin tako; uwollinún nura ba untariġ, nanún ġaiya nura wirritoara waréa buttikaġ, keawai yellawa pa kúri bulka ka: buruġbuġgulla unnoa, ġatun yemmamulla untiko.
31. Gatun tarai-kan-to ba wiyanún, Minariġ tin nura unnoa ta buruġbuġgan? ġiakai nura wiyella bon, Kulla noa Piriwällo wiyä.
32. Gatun bara ba yukatoara, waita uwa, ġatun nakulla ġaiya bara yanti noa ba wiya barun ba.
33. Gatun buruġbuġgulliela bara ba unnoa waréa buttikaġ, ġikoúmba-ko wiya barun, Minariġ tin nura buruġbuġgan unni waréa buttikaġ?
34. Gatun bara wiyä, Piriwällo noa wiya ġala.
35. Gatun bara yemmama bon kinko: ġatun bara wupéa barun ba kirrikin bulka ka buttikaġ ka, ġatun wupéa bon bara Iéthunuġ wokka ka.
36. Gatun uwolliela noa ba, wupéa bara yapuġ ka kirrikinkan nurúnba.
37. Gatun uwa noa ba papai, barä ka †Elaión ka ba koba bulkära koba, yantin konara wirrobullikan pitäl ġaiya kakulla, ġatun pitälmulliela bon Eloinuġ kauwäl lo pullí to, yantin tin kauwäl lin uma ba nakulla bara ba;
38. Wiyelliela, Pitälmabunbilla bon Piriwäl ta uwan noa ba Yehóa-úmba koa yitirroa: pitäl-kämunbilla moroko ka, ġatun killibinbin kämunbilla wokka ka.
39. Gatun winta-ko Parithaioi kabiruġ konara biruġ wiya bon, Piriwäl, koawa bi barun ġiroúmba wirrobullikan.
40. Gatun noa wiyayelléún barun, wiyelliela, Wiyan nurun baġ, wiya, bara ba kaiyellinún mupai, kaibullinún wal ġaiya unni tara tunuġ tanoa-kal-bo.
41. Gatun uwa noa ba papai, nakulla noa kokera kariġ, ġatun noa tuġkillimilléún ġaloa rin,
42. Wiyelliela, Gurrapa bi ba, ġintoa ta, unti purreäġ ka ġirouġ ka ta unni tara pitäl-kakilliko ġiroúmba ko! wonto ba yakita yuropa ta ġirouġ kai nakilli tin ġaikuġ tin.
43. Kulla purreäġ ta känún ġiroug kin, bukka-kan-to ġirouġ

wirrinún wal bara kirrai karai-karai ģirouģ, ģatun karai-karai wirrinún ģirouģ, ģatun mirrámanún bin willi ka yantin ta kaiyinkaiyin ta,

44. Gatun pirikibunpinún bin purrai ta, ģatun ģiroúmba wonnai tara murruģ kaba ģirouģ kinba; ģatun keawai bara wupinún tunuģ tarai ta wokka ka; kulla keawai bi ba ģurra pa yakita natala ba ģiroúmba.

45. Gatun noa uwa murrariģ kolaģ, ģatun yipa ģaiya noa barun ģukillikan, ģatun barun mankillikan unta biruģ;

46. Wiyelliela barun, Upatoara unni, Emmoúmba kokera ta wiyelliģél kokera; wonto ba nura uma unni wollo kakilliko barun mankiye-ko.

47. Gatun wiyelliela noa purreáģ ka yantin ta murruģ ka †hieron ka. Wonto ba piriwál †hiereu, ģatun bara ģárammaten, ģatun bara piriwál kúri koba, numa bara bon búnkilli kolaģ;

48. Yakoai bara ba umulliko ģatun keawai bara, kulla yantin ta kúri pitál kakilliela ģurrulliko bon.

WINTA XX.

Gatun yakita kakulla, wakál la tarai ta purreáģ ka, wiyelliela noa ba barun kúri ka, ģatun wiyelliela euaģelion, uwa ģaiya bon bara piriwál ģatun bara †ģárammateu ģatun bara †párethbuteroi,

2. Gatun wiya bon, wiyelliela, Wiyella ģearun, minariģ tin kaiyu tin umullia bi unni tara? ģa ģanto-ke noa bin unni ta kaiyu ģukulla ģirouģ?

3. Gatun noa wiyayelléun, ģatun wiyelliela barun, Gatoa wiyánún nurun unni ta wakál; ģatun wiyayelléa tia;

4. Korimullikanne-ta Ioanne-úmba, wiya, ta morokó kabiruģ, ģa kúri koba?

5. Gatun bara wiyatan barabo, wiyelliela, Wiyánún ģéen ba, Morokó kabiruģ ta; wiyánún ģaiya noa, Kora koa nura ģurrapa bon?

6. Kulla ģéen wiyánún ba, Kúri koba ta; yantinto ģaiya ģearun kúriko pintinún tunuģ ko: kulla bara kotan bon Ioannenuģ †propet ta kakulla.

7. Gatun bara wiyá, keawai bara ģurrapa wonta biruģ ta.

8. Gatun noa barun Iéthuko wiya, Keawai baģ wiyánún nurun minariģ tin kaiyu tin umau baģ unni tara.

9. Gatun potopaiyá ģaiya noa barun kúri wiyelliko unni-ta †parabol: Taraito kúriko meapa †wain-ģél la, ģatun wúnkulla barun kin upullikan ta, ģatun uwa ģaiya noa kaloģ kolag, yuraki.

10. Gatun yakita poaikulléún ba, yuka noa bon wakál umullikan barun kin upullikan ta, ģu-uwil koa bara bon yeai †wainģél labiruģ; wonto bara ba búnkulla bon, ģatun yuka bara bon waita yeai korien.

11. Gatun noa toanta yukéa-kan tarai umullikan: ģatun bara bon búntéa-kan yantibo, ģatun yarakai uma bara bon, ģatun bon bara yuka waita yeai korien.

12. Gatun noa toanta yukéa-kan goro-ta, gatun bara bon mularéa-kan, gatun wareka bara bon warrai tako.
13. Wiya gaiya noa piriwállo †wain-gél koba, Minnug banúñ kan bag? Yukánún wal bag emmoúmba yinal pitálmatoara; mirka bara bon gurránún, nanún bon bara ba.
14. Wonto bara ba upulli-kan-to nakulla bon ba, barabo gaiya wiyellan, wiyelliela, Unni ta wúggurra piriwál: kaai géen baiwil bon, purrai koa ka-uwil gearúnba.
15. Yanti bon bara wareka †wain-gél labirug, gatun búnkulla gaiya bon tetti. Minnug banún noa barun piriwállo †wain-gél koba ko?
16. Uwánún wal noa tanan búnkilliko barun upillikan-ko, gatún gunún wal †wain-gél taraikan ko. Gatun gurra bara ba unni. wiya gaiya bara, Kámumbi yikora Eloito.
17. Gatun noa barun nakilliela, gatun wiyá, Minarig-ke unni upatoara yanti, Tunug ta wareka wittilli-kan-to, unnoa ta katéakánún wokka ka waiyakan ta wollug?
18. Gan-ba puntimullinún untoa tunug ka tiirpuntimullinún, wal; gan kinba puntimullinún, minbinún wal bon muta-mutan.
19. Gatun tanoa-kal-bo kota bara piriwállo †hiereuko gatun †gáranmmateuko mankilliko bon; gatun bara kinta kakulla konará tin; kulla bara gurrá, wiya noa ba unni †parabol barun kin.
20. Gatun bara bon tumiméa, gatun yuka barun gakoiyellikan, gakogkilliko barunbo kúri murrarág-tai, gurra-uwil koa bara gikoúmba wiyellikanne, yaki tin mara-uwil koa bara bon kaiyu kabo †kobána kinko.
21. Gatun wiya bon bara, wiyelliela, Piriwál, gurran géen wiyan bi ba tuloa, kinta kora bi kauwa taraikan tin kúri kurrig tin, wonto bi ba wiyan tuloa wiyellikanne Eloi koba:
22. Wiya tuloa ta gukilliko gearun tullokan gikoug kin †Kaithari kin, ga keawai?
23. Wonto noa ba gurra gakoiya barúnba, gatun wiya barun, Yakoai nura tia numan?
24. Túgunbilla tia wakál †denari. Gan kiloa unnoa goara gatun upatoara unni ta? Wiyayelléun bon bara gatun wiyelliela, †Kaitharúmba ta.
25. Gatun noa wiya barun, Koito †Kaithari kinko guwa †Kaitharúmba ta, gatun Eloi kinko unnoa tara Eloi-úmba ta.
26. Gatun keawai bara man pa gikoúmba wiyelli-ta mikan ta barun kin kúri ka: gatun mupai kakulla bara.
27. Uwa gaiya taraikan barun kinbirug Thadukaioi kabirug, bara gurramaigaye moron ta katéa-kánún tetti kabirug; gatun bara bon wiyá,
28. Wiyelliela, Ela Piriwál! Mothéto noa upa gearun, Taraikan koba ba kóti tetti kánún ba porikunbai gikoúmba ta, gatun tetti noa ba kánún, wonnai korien, mara-uwil koa gikoúmba kóti

N

bounnoun gikoúmba porikunbai ka-uwil koa wonnai gikoúmba kóti koba.

29. Yakita gaiya warán kakulla kótita †theben ta: gatun kurri birug ko búmbéa porikunbai kakilliko, gatun tetti kakulla, wonnai korien.

30. Gatun willi-kaba-ko †deutero-to búmbéa bounnoun porikunbai kakilliko, gatun tetti noa kakulla, wonnai korien.

31. Gatun willi-kaba-ko †trito-to bumbéa bounnoun porikunbai kakilliko; gatun yaki-bo †thebento; gatun bara keawai wimba wonnai, gatun tetti bara kakulla.

32. Willug ta tetti ba bountoa nukug.

33. Ganúmba barun kinba unnoa porikunbai kanún kakilliko moron ba katéa-kanún tetti kabirug? kulla bara †thebento bounnoun búmbéa porikunbai kakilliko.

34. Gatun noa Iéthuko wiyayelléún, wiyellicla barun, Wonnai ta untikál búmbillan porikunbai gatun gukillaiko búmbilliko:

35. Wonto ba bara murrárág-tai kanún uwolliko unta kolag tanai tako purrai tako, gatun moron kakilliko tetti kabirug, keawai bara búmbúmbillan, keawai gukitan búmbilliko:

36. Keawai wal bara tetti banún yukita; kulla bara yanti katan †agelo kiloa; gatun wonnai tara kátan Eloi-úmba, kátan bara wonnai tara gali koba moron kanún tetti kabirug.

37. Gatun Mothéko noa ba túgaiya wakál la kúlai ta, bougbugga barun tetti-tetti kabirug, wiya noa ba bon Yehóanug, Eloi ta Abáramúmba, gatun Eloi ta Ithákúmba, gatun Eloi ta Yacobúmba.

38. Keawai noa Eloi ta barúnba tetti-tetti koba, wonto ba barúnba moron koba; kulla yantin moron kátan gikoug kin.

39. Tarnito bara †gárammateukállo wiya gaiya, Piriwál, murrá rág bi wiyan.

40. Gatun yukita keawai bara bon wiya pa kinta-kan-to.

41. Gatun noa barun wiyá, Yakoai bara wiya Kritht ta yinal ta Dabidúmba?

42. Gatun Dabidto noa niuwoabo wiyá, †biblion kaba †tchillím koba, Yehóako noa wiya bon Piriwál emmoúmba, Yellawolla bi túgkagkeri ka emmoug kin,

43. Uma-uwil koa bag barun bukkakan gikoúmba yulogél ko kakilliko gikoug.

44. Dabidto noa ba wiya bon Piriwál yitirra, yakoai gaiya noa yinal ta gikoúmba?

45. Wiya gaiya noa barun gikoúmba wirrobullikan mikan ta yantin ta kúri ka,

46. Yakoai nura barun kai †gárammateu tin, pitál koa bara uwa-uwil kurrawitaikan, gatun umulliko gukilligél laba ko, gatun yellawolligél la wokka ka †thunagóg ka, gatun piriwál-gél takilligél laba;

47. Mantan bara kokera ba mabogun koba, gatun umanùn wiyellikanne-ta kurra-uwai túgunbilliko: yaki tin bara kànùn kauwàl tetti kakilliko.

WINTA XXI.

Gatun noa nakulla wokka-lag, gatun nakulla barun porrólkan wúnkilliela gutoara barúnba wúnkilligél la.

2. Gatun noa nakulla tarai mabogun mirrálkan wúnkilliela bountoa †lepto buloara unta ko tarog kako.

3. Gatun noa wiya barun, Wiyan bag nurun tuloa, gali mabogunto mirrállo wúnkulla kauwál ta bara yantin kearan.

4. Kulla yantin gali wúnkulla bara tullokan barúnba kauwàl labirug gutoara Eloi koba ko : wonto bountoa ba bounnoun kinbirug mirrál koba wúnkulla yantin tullokan bounnoúnba.

5. Gatun winta koba wiyelliela †hieron tin, umatoara unni korien tunug ko murrärág ko gatun gutoara, wiya noa,

6. Unni tara natan nura ba, uwanùn ta purreág karig ka, korien gaiya ba wakál tunug wokka-ka-wokka-ka, yantin wal warekullinùn barán.

7. Gatun bara bon wiyá, wiyelliela, Piriwál, yakounta-ke unni tara kànùn? gatun minarig túga kànùn unni tara ba gaiya kànùn?

8. Gatun noa wiyá, Yakoai nura, gakoiya kora koa nura ka-uwil; kulla kauwál-kauwállo tanan uwànùn emmoug kin yitirra, wiyellinùn, Gatoa ta (Kritht ta); gatun papai ta kakillin : yanoa uwa yikora nura barun.

9. Gurránùn gaiya nura ba wuruwai kauwál gatun koakillai ta ba, kinta kora nura : kulla unni tara kànùn wal kurri-kurri, kulla wiran keawai kànùn kabo.

10. Wiya gaiya noa barun, Bara kúriko wuruwai wal kànùn barun kúriko, gatun bara piriwál koba barun piriwál koba ko :

11. Gatun purrai tako pulululu kakilliko winta ka bo, gatun kunto korien ta ko, gatun munni kauwálkan ; gatun kinta nakilli tara gatun kauwál kánùn túga morokó kabirug.

12. Wonto ba kurri-kurri ka unni tara ba kànùn, manùn wal bara máttárro nurun, gatun yarakai nurun umánùn, gumuliinùn nurun †thunagóg kako, gatun †jail ko, mantoaro nurun mikan ta ko piriwál lako, gatun wiyellikan tako emmoug kinko yitirra ko.

13. Gatun unni ta kánùn nurun túga kakilliko.

14. Yanoa nura kota yikora minki ko, minarig nura wiyayellinùn.

15. Kulla bag gunùn nurun kurraka gatun guraki kakilliko, keawai wal yantin bara nurúnba bukka-kan-to kaiyu kànùn wiyayelliko ga pirriral umulliko.

16. Gatun nura gakoiyellinùn wal nurun biyugbaito gatun kóti tako karig ko, gatun winta nurun kinbirug búnnùn wal tetti barun kai.

17. Gatun nurun yarakai umánùn yantinto, emmoúnba tin yitirra tin.

18. Wonto ba keawai wal wakál kittuġ ġikouġ kinbiruġ wolluġ kabiruġ tetti kánún.
19. Murrái kakillikanne nurúnba ka, miromulla nura marai nurúnba ?
20. Gatun nanún nura ba †Hierothalem kirrai-kirrai ta ba konara ba, ġurrulla papai ta ba gaiya wari-warekulli ta ba unnuġ.
21. Murrabunbilla ġaiya barun Iudaia kaba waita bulkárá kolaġ; ġatun uwabunbilla barun willi kaba waita warai tako; ġatun uwabunbi yikora barun tanan koruġ kaba untako.
22. Kulla yakita unti tara purreáġ ka bukka kakillikanne, kauwil koa yantin upatoara kánún wal kakilliko.
23. Yapallun bara wonnaikun ġatun bara pittallikun, yakita ġaiya purreáġ ka ! kulla wal kánún kauwál yarakai purrai ta, ġatun bukka unti yantin ta kúri ka.
24. Gatun bara tetti kapaiyinún yirrá biruġ, ġatun barun yutinún wal mantoara kakilliko yantin tako purrai kariġ kako : ġatun †Hierothalem wattawánún barán bara †ethánékál-lo, yakita kalai tako barúnba koba ġoloin kánún †ethánékál.
25. Gatun ġaiya kánún wal túga punnál la, ġatun yellana ka, ġatun mirri ka ; ġatun purrai taba yarakai ta barun kin kúri ka, ġatun kinta kauwál ; korowa ta ġatun bókkaloġ kólbilaġbullín ;
26. Kúri koba búlbúllo kotan kinta-kan-to, ġatun nakilli tabiruġ ġaloa tara kotanan ba uwánún purrai kolaġ ; kulla wal barun tolománún wal kaiyukan ta moroko koba.
27. Gatun yakita ġaiya wal nanún Yinal ta kúri koba tanan uwollinún yareil loa kaiyu koa. ġatun killibinbin koa kauwál loa.
28. Gatun kánún ba unni tara paipinún, na-uwa wokka-laġ, ġatun wokka-laġ kauwa kia-kia nurúnba wolluġ ; kulla tanan uwánún paipai nurúnba wommunbillikanne-ta.
29. Gatun noa wiya barun wakál †parabol ; Na-uwa kokuġ ta, ġatun yantin kúlai ta ;
30. Paikullinún bara ba, nanún nura ġatun ġurránún nura nurun kinbiruġ wunál kátan paipai taba.
31. Yaki kiloa nura, nanún nura ba unni tara paikulliko, ġurrulla ġaiya nura piriwál koba Eloi koba kátan papai taba.
32. Wiyan tuloa nurun baġ, Keawai unni willuġġél tetti-tetti kánún, yakita-ko ġoloin ba kánún.
33. Moroko ta ġatun purrai ta kánún wal waita uwánún, wonto ba keawai wal emmoúmba wiyellikanne unni tara keawai wal waita uwánún.
34. Gatun yakoai nura nurabo, kauwa ba yantin ta nurúnba búlbúl matayei koa katéa-kún ġatun kuttawaiban koa katéa-kún, ġatun umillikéún koa katéa-kún ġali koba moron koba, ġatun yantita purreáġ ka paipinún ġati nurun kin.
35. Kulla pika kiloa yanti uwánún untoa purreáġ ka barun kin yellawan yantin ta yaki tin purrai ta.

36. Tumimilla nura, gatun wiyellía yanti-katai to, ka-uwil koa nura murrárág kakilliko moron ko unti tara birug paikullinún wal, gatun garokilliko mikan tako yinal lako kúri koba ko.

37. Gatun purreág ka wiyelliela noa murrug ka †hieron la; gatun noa uwa waita tokoi ta, gatun yellawa noa bulkara giakai yitirra †Elaión ka la.

38. Gatun yantin bara kúri uwa gorokan ta gikoug kinko †hieron lako, gurrulliko bon.

WINTA XXII.

YAKITA kakulla papai takillikanne nulai †lebben korien koba, giakai yittira †Pathak.

2. Gatun bara piriwäl †hiereuko gatun garammateuko nukilliela búnkilli kolag bon tetti wirrilliko ; kulla bara kinta kakulla kúri tin.

3. Pulógkulléún noa Thatánto murrug ka bon Iudathkin, tarai yitirra giakai Ithákariot, wakál noa †dodeka kabirug.

4. Gatun noa waita uwá, gatun wiyelliela barun piriwäl †hiereunug gatun barun †kapátin, yakoai noa ba gakoyánún bon barun kin.

5. Gatun pitál kakulla, gatun bara wiya gukilliko bon †arguro.

6. Gatun noa wiyai, gatun mittilliela noa gakomulliko bon barun kin, yakita bara ba konara waita gaiya uwa.

7. Kakulla gaiya purreág nulai †lebben korien ta, yakita †Pathak búnnún wal ba tetti.

8. Gatun noa yuka Peternug gatun Ioannenug, wiyelliela, Yurig uwolla umulliko †Pathak ta, ta-uwil koa géen.

9. Gatun bara bon wiyá, Wonta-ke géen umánún ?

10. Gatun noa barun wiyá, A! nauwa nura, yakita uwánún nura ba kokerá karig ka, unta gaiya nurun wakállo kúriko wimbi-kaba-kan-to kokoin-kan-to nuggurra uwánún nurun ; wirrobulla bula bon murrug kolag kokerá kolag unta-ko pulógkullinún noa ba.

11. Gatun wiyánún nura bon kokeratin, Piriwallo wiyan bin, Wonnug waiyakan takilligél, untoa bag ba tanún †Pathak ta emmoúmba katoa wirrobullikan toa ?

12. Gatun nurun túgkaiyánún wal noa kauwál ta waiyakan wokka kaba wupitoara: unnug umulla.

13. Gatan bara waita uwa, gatun nakulla bara unni tara yantin ba wiya barun : gatun bara upéa †Pathak ta.

14. Gatun yakita kakulla †hóra ba, yellawa noa barán, gatun †dodeka ta †apothol ta gikoug katoa.

15. Gatun noa barun wiyá, Kauwál ta emmoúmba kotatoara takilliko unni †Pathak ta nurun katoa, ta-uwil koa kurri-kurri tetti kolag ke bag :

16. Kulla bag wiyan nurun, Keawai wal bag tanún unta-kál kabo ba kánún piriwál koba ka Eloi koba.

17. Gatun noa mankulla wimbi, gatun pitalma gaiya noa, wiyelliela, Mara unni gukillai koa nurabo :

18. Kulla bag wiyan nurun, Keawai wal bag pittanùn yeai tabirug †ampelo tabirug, kabo koa uwa-uwil piriwal koba Eloi koba tanan.

19. Gatun noa mankulla †arto ta, gatun pitalma gaiya noa, gatun yiirbugga, gatun gukulla barun, wiyelliela, Unni ta emmoùmba murrin gutoara nurun kin : umulla unni yanti gurrulliko tia.

20. Yantibo wimbi takilli birug yaréa ka, wiyelliela, Unni wimbi ta wiyatoara ta buggaikal emmoug kinbirug gorog kiroapa nurun kai.

21. A! na-uwa, unni ta mattara gikoúmba gakoyelli-kan-to tia, emmoug katoa ba takilligél laba.

22. Yuna bo ta wal noa uwanùn Yinal kùri koba, yanti wiyatoara ; yapallun umnoa kùri gakoyelli-kan-to bon ba !

23. Gatun bara wiyellan barabo, gan-to barun kinbirug-ko umanùn ta unni.

24. Gatun koakillan bara barabo, gan-ke kanùn piriwal barun kinbirug.

25. Gatun noa wiya barun, Bara ta piriwàl ethanékal koba katilléùn bara ; gatun bara ta katillikan giakai yitirra murrog-tai.

26. Wonto nura ba keawai yanti kanùn ; wonto noa kurrikóg nurun kinba, kamunbilla bon yanti mitti ; gatun noa piriwàl katan, yanti umullikan ta.

27. Wonnug-ke kauwàl unnug, niuwoa yellawan noa ba takilli ta, niuwoa umanùn noa ba ? wiya, unni ta noa yellawollin ba takilli taba ? wonto bag ba kàtan nurun kinba yanti niuwoa ba umullikan ta.

28. Nura ta emmoug kin minkéa emmoug ka ta numatoara :

29. Gatun gutan nurun bag kakilliko piriwalgél lako, yanti tia emmoùmba Biyugbaito gukulla tia ;

30. Ta-uwil koa nura gatun pitta-uwil emmoug ka ta takilligél la emmoug ka ta piriwalgél la, gatun yellawa-uwil yellawolligél la piriwàl koba ka, wiyellin barun konara †dodeka ta Ithàrael koba.

31. Gatun noa piriwàllo wiyá, Ela Thimon, Thimon ! gurrulla, Thantànto noa wiyan bin mankilliko kirrai-kirrai koa biloa uma· uwil yanti †wiet kiloa :

32. Wonto bag ba wiyelléùn giroug kai gurra-uwil koa bi ; gatun minki bi ba kanùn, pirralmulla gaiya barun bi kòti ta giroùmba.

33. Gatun noa wiya bon, Piriwàl, katan bag unni mirigil uwolli kolag gikoug katoa ko †jail kolag gatun tetti kakilli kolag.

34. Gatun noa wiyá, Wiyan banug, Peter, keawai wal mukkaka ko tibbinto wiyànùn unti purreàg ka, kurri-kurri ka bi ba gakoyànùn tia goro-ka gimillin bi tia ba.

35. Gatun noa wiya barun, Yuka nurun bag ba yinug korien,

gatun pika korien, gatun tugganóg korien, wiya, nura minarig lo? gatun bara wiyá, Keawai.

36. Wiya gaiya noa barun, Wonto ba yakita unti, niuwoa ba yinugkan, mamunbilla bon unnoa, gatun yanti pika; gatun niuwoa yirra korien, gumunbilla kirrikin gikoúmba, wakál koa noa gukilli ko.

37. Wonto bag ba wiyan nurun, unni ta upatoara ka-uwil koa emmoug kin kakilliko giakai, Tumbitoara noa barun kin yarakai willug ka: kulla unni tara emmoug kin ba kakillinún goloin ko.

38. Gatun bara wiyá, Piriwál, na-uwa unni tuloa buloara yirra. Gatun noa wiya barun, Tantoa-bo-ta.

39. Gatun noa uwa warrai koba, gatun waita uwa uwolli kolag bulkára kolag †Elaión ko la kako; gatun gikoúmba wirrobullikan wirroba bon.

40. Gatun uwa noa ba unta, wiya gaiya noa barun, Wiyella, keawai koa nura pulógkulli korien yarakai kolag.

41. Gatun noa waita uwa barun kinbirug yanti kiloa tunug koba pintia, gatun warogbugko upullin barán, gatun wiyá,

42. Wiyelliela, Biyug, wiya bi unni wimbi manún emmoug kinbirug: yanoa emmoúmba kotellikanne giroúmba ta kámunbilla kakilliko.

43. Gatun paipéa wakál agelo moroko kabirug pirriralmallin bon.

44. Gatun kirrinkan noa kauwálkan, wiyelliela noa pirriral butti; gatun gikoúmba kurrol upulléún barán purrai kolag yanti kiloa komonba kauwál gorog koba.

45. Gatun bougkulléún noa ba wiyelli tabirug, gatun uwa gikoúmba tako wirrobullikan tako, nakulla gaiya noa barun birriki birriki minkikan,

46. Gatun noa wiya barun, Minarig tin nura birrikin? Bougkullía gatun wiyella, uwéa-kún koa nura yarakai kolag.

47. Gatun yakita wiyelliela noa ba, a! konara, gatun noa yitirra giakai Iudath, wakál ta †dodeka kabirug, uwa ganka barun kin, gatun uwa gaiya noa papai Iéthu kin, búmbúmkakilliko.

48. Wonto noa ba Iéthuko bon wiyá, Ela Iudath! gakoman binug Yinal kúri koba búmbuggullito?

49. Nakulla bara ba gikoug kinba minnug-bulli kolag, wiyabon bara, Ela piriwál! wiya, géen búntan yirra ko?

50. Gatun wakál barun kinbirug kunbuntéa wakál umullikan †thiereu koba piriwál koba, gatun kunbuntéa bon túgkag-keri gurréug.

51. Gatun Iéthuko noa wiyayelléún, gatun wiyelliela, Kámunbilla nura unni. Gatun bon noa numa gurréug gatun turon bon uméa-kan.

52. Wiya gaiya Iéthuko barun piriwál †thiereu koba, gatun barun †kapátin †thieron koba, gatun barun garrokál, uwa bara gi-

koug̣ Lin, Wiya, nura tia uwan yanti mankiye ko yarakaikan ta, yirrakan gatun kotarakan?

53. Kakulla bag̣ ba nurun kin yanti-katai purreäg̣ ka †hieron ka, keawai nura tia manpa máttárro: wouto ba unni yakita ta kátan nurúnba gatun kaiyukan tokoi tako.

54. Mankulla g̣aiya bara bon, gatun yutéa bon, mankulla g̣aiya bon kokera ko piriwäl koba kako †hiereu koba kako. Gatun Peterko noa wirroba kalog̣ kolag̣.

55. Gatun upilléün bara ba koiyug̣ ko willi ka kokera, gatun yellawa yantin, Peter g̣aiya noa yellawa barun kin.

56. Gatun taraito murrakinto nakulla bon, yellawa noa ba koiyug̣ ka, gatun pimmillicla bon pirrallo, gatun wiyá, Unni noa kúri kakulla g̣ikoug̣ katoa.

57. Gatun noa g̣akoiya bon, wiyellicla, Ela murrakin! keawai bon bag̣ g̣imilli korien.

58. Gatun toanta taraito bon nakulla, gatun wiyellicla, Giutoa ta yanti bo barúnba. Gatun noa Peterko wiyá, Kúri, keawaran bag̣.

59. Gatun, yakita toanta, wakäl †hora ta yukita, taraito wiya pirralma wiyelliela, Yuna bo ta unni kúri kakulla g̣ikoug̣ katoa; kulla noa Galilaiakäl.

60. Gatun noa Peterko wiyá, Ela kúri! keawai bag̣ g̣urran yakoai bi ba wiyan. Gatun wiyellicla noa ba, tanoa-kal-bo mukkaka-ko g̣aiya wiya tibbinto.

61. Gatun noa Piriwäl warkulléün, gatun nakilléün bon Peternug̣. Gatun Peterko noa g̣urra wiyellita Piriwäl koba, wiya bon noa ba giakai, Gikoyánún wal bi tia kurri-kurri tibbinto mukkaka ko wiyánún goro-ka.

62. Gatun Peter noa uwa warrai koba, gatun túg̣killéün g̣aiya noa kauwäl.

63. Gatun bara kúriko mankulla bon Iéthunug̣ béelma bon, gatun búnkulla bon.

64. Gatun munmin bara ba upéa bon, búnkulla g̣aiya bon bara goará, gatun wiya bon, wiyellicla, Wiyella bi, g̣anto-ke bin búnkulla?

65. Gatun kauwäl-kauwäl taraikan yarakai wiya bara g̣ikoug̣ kin.

66. Gatun purreäg̣ ba kakulla, kau-umullan g̣aiya bara g̣arrotai kúri koba, gatun bara piriwäl †hiereu koba, gatun bara g̣arammateu, gatun yutéa g̣aiya bon kau-umulligél lako barúnba tako,

67. Wiyelliela, Kritht ta bi unni? wiyella g̣earun. Gatun noa wiya barnu, Wiyánún nurun bag̣ ba, keawai g̣aiya wal nura g̣urránún:

68. Gatun wiyánún nurun bag̣ ba, keawai wal nura wiyaiyellinún tia, keawai wal nura tia wamunbinún.

69. Kabo noa Yinal kúri koba yellawánún túg̣kag̣ ka kaiyukan ta Eloi koba ka.

70. Wiya ġaiya bara yantinto, Yinal ta bi unni Eloi koba? Gatun noa wiya barun, Wiyan nura ġatoa ta unni.
71. Gatun bara wiya tantoa ta, Yanoa ġearun kin ġurrullikanto taraito? kulla ġeen ġurra ġeenbo kurraka kabiruġ ġikouġ kinbiruġ kóti kabiruġ.

WINTA XXIII.

GATUN bara yantin konara bouġkulléùn. ġatun yutéa bon Pilato kin.
2. Gatun bon bara pirralma, wiyelliela, Gurra ġeen bon unni ġakoyelliela noa ba barun kùri willuġġél, ġatun wiyelliela, yanoa ġuki yikora tullokan Kaitharinuġ, wiyelliela, niuwoa-bo-ta Kritht ta wakál ta Piriwál.
3. Gatun Pilato-to wiya bon, wiyellicla, Ga ġintoa ta Piriwál kátan barúnba Iudaioi koba? Gatun noa wiyayelléùn bon, ġatun wiyá, Gintoa ta wiyan.
4. Wiya ġaiya noa Pilato-to barun piriwál †hiereu ġatun barun kùri, Keawai baġ ġurra pa yarakai unti kùri ka.
5. Gatun bara bukka-buttibuġkéa, wiyellicla, Pirralman noa barun kùri, wiyellin, yantin ta Iudaia ka, Galilaia tinto unti kolaġ.
6. Gurra noa ba Pilato-to Galilaia ka, wiya noa, Unni kùri Galilaiakál?
7. Gatun ġurra noa ba Herodúmba-kan noa wottaikan, yuka bon noa Herod kinko, yakita ġaiya niuwoabo kakulla †Hierothalem ka.
8. Gatun nakulla bon noa ba Herodto Iéthunuġ, pitál ġaiya noa kátan kauwál, kulla noa natelli ba bon yuraki tabiruġ, kulla noa ġurra kauwállan ġikouġ kinba : ġatun nakilliko tarai umatoara ġikouġ kai.
9. Wiya ġaiya bon noa wiyellikanne kauwál-kauwál ; wonto noa ba keawai wiyelli pa bon.
10. Gatun bara piriwál †hiereu ġatun bara ġarammateu ġarokilliela, ġatun pirralmulliela bon kauwál.
11. Gatun Herod katoa ba bara wurunwai koba ġurramaiġa bon bara, ġatun béelma bon, ġatun wuda bon konéin to kirrikin to, ġatun yukéa-kan bon Pilato kinko.
12. Gatun unta purreáġ ka wakál la, Pilato ġatun Herod kóti bula umullan : yakita unta kakillan bula bukkakan bula-bo.
13. Gatun Pilato-to noa kau-wiya noa ba barun piriwál †hiereu, ġatun barun piriwál, ġatun barun kùri,
14. Wiya ġaiya barun, Mankulla nura bon unni kùri emmouġ kinko, yanti wakál noa ġakoya-uwil ba kùri ; ġatun, a! ġurulla, nuiya ta bon baġ unni mikan ta nurun kin keawai baġ ġurrapa yarakai ġikouġ kin, ġinoa-tara tin pirralma bon nura :
15. Keawaran, keawai Herodto : kulla baġ yuka nurun ġikouġ kin; ġatun, nauwa, keawai ġali tin tetti korien noa kánùn.
16. Wélkorinùn wal bon baġ, ġatun wamunbinùn ġaiya bon.
17. (Kulla noa burugbugġanùn wal wakál yakita ta takillikanne ta.)

18. Gatun bara kaaibulléún wakálla purawai, wiyelliela, Yurig unni kuri; gatun burugbuggulla bon Barabbanug gcarun kinko:
19. (Gali noa wakál wuruwai tin kokera gatun búnkilli tin tetti tin, wúnkulla bon †jail ka.)
20. Koito noa ba Pilato-to kotelliela burugbuggulliko bon Iéthunug, wiyéa ka barun.
21. Wonto bara ba wiyá, wiyelliela, Buwa bon tetti, buwa bon tetti.
22. Gatun noa barun wiya yukita goro-ka, Minarig tin? minarig noa yarakai uma? keawai bag gurrapa taraikan gikoug kin galoa kolag búnkilli kolag tetti wirrilliko; wélkorinún wal bon bag, gatun wamunbinún bon.
23. Gatun bara tanoa-kal-bo pullí kakulla kauwál, wiyelliela, búwil koa bon tetti. Gatun pullí barúnba gatun barúnba piriwál †hiereu pirral kakulla.
24. Gatun Pilato-to noa wiyá, ka-uwil koa yanti wiya bara ba.
25. Gatun noa bon burugbugga barun kin unni bon wuruwai tin gatun bunkilli tin tetti tin wunkulla bon †jail ka wiyatoara barúnba; gatun noa bon Iéthunug wamunbéa barun kin.
26. Gatun yutéa bon bara ba yurig, mankulla gaiya bara wakál Thimónnug Kureniakál ta, tanan uwolliela korug tin, gatun wupéa bara gikoug kin taligkabillikanne, kurri-uwil koa noa willug tin Iéthu katoa.
27. Gatun wirroba bon bara kauwállo konaro, gatun bara nukug-ko, túgkilliela gatun minki kakilliela gikoug kai.
28. Wonto noa ba Iéthu warkulléún barun kai koba, wiyá, Yinálkun †Hierothalemkálín, túgki yikora emmoug kai, wonto ba túgkillía nura nurunbo, gatun nurun kaiko wonnai tara ko.
29. A! na-uwa, purreág karig tanan uwollinún, yakita unta wiyanún bara ba, Murrárág bara wonnai korien, gatun unnug tara pika keawai pórkulli korien, gatun paiyil keawai pittelliko.
30. Yakita gaiya bara wiyellan bulkára karig, Puntimullía gearun kin, gatun yúnko ko, Wutilla gearun.
31. Gatun uwullinún bara ba unni tara kúlai ta kirug ka, minnug banún wal kúlai ta turrál la?
32. Gatun unnug bula taraikan yarakai willug, yutéa gikoug katoa wúnkilliko tetti wirrilliko.
33. Gatun uwa bara ba unta ko, giakai yitirra Kalábary, unta gaiya bara búnkulla bon gatun bulun yarakai bula, wakál ta túgkag-keri ka gatun tarai ta wunto-keri ka.
34. Wiya gaiya noa Iéthuko, Biyug, kámúnbilla barun, kulla bara keawai gurra korien umulli ta. Gatun toinbillan bara kirrikin gikoúmba, gatun wupillan woiyo.
35. Gatun bara nakilliela garokito. Gatun bara piriwál yantibo barun katoa béelmulliela, wiyelliela, Mironá noa taraikan; miromabunbillía bon gikoug kóti, wiya noa ba Kritht ta, girimatoara Eloi-úmba.

THE GOSPEL BY LUKE, c. 23. 191

36. Gatun bara †militiko béelma bon, uwolliela gikoug kin, gatun nupilliela bon †taket,

37. Gatun wiyelliela, Wiya bi ba piriwàl Iudaioi koba, miromullía bi gintoabo kóti.

38. Gatun upulléún wakál upatoara wokka ka gikoug kin pulli †Hellenik koba, gatun Latin koba, gatun Hebàraio koba, giakai, Unni ta Piriwàl Iudaioi koba.

39. Gatun wakállo yarakai bulun kinbirug-ko, kakilliela ba kúlai ta, béelmulliela bon, wiyelliela, Wiya bi ba Kritht ta, miromullía bi gintoabo gatun gearun.

40. Wonto ba taraito wiyayelléún, koakilliela bon, wiyelliela, Keawai bi kinta korien Eloi kai, gatun gintoa ta kàtan wakál la umatoara?

41. Gatun galin yakita murràrág uma; yaki tin galin kai umatoara tin: wonto noa ba gali kúriko, keawai noa yarakai uma pa.

42. Gatun noa wiya Iéthunug, Piriwàl, gurrulla bi tia, uwànún gaiya bi ba piriwàlgél lako giroug ka tako.

43. Gatun noa Iéthuko wiya bon, Yuna bo ta wal bag wiyan giroug, Unti buggai purreág ka kànún bi tia emmoug katoa Paràdeith ka tako.

44. Gatun yakita kakulla †hora ka †hekto ta, tokoi ta kakulla yantin ta purrai ta katéa ka †hóra kako †nain tako.

45. Gatun punnál ta tokoi kakulla, gatun kirrikin ta †hieron kako yiirkulléún búlwa koa.

46. Gatun noa ba Iéthuko kaaibulléún wokka wiya noa, Biyug, wunún bag emmoúmba marai giroug kin màttàra; gatun wiyelléún noa ba unni, wúnkulla gaiya noa marai.

47. Yakita gaiya noa ba kenturionko nakulla unni umatoara, pitàlma noa Eloinug, wiyelliela, Yuna bo ta wal murràrág unni kúri.

48. Gatun bara yantin kúri uwà nakilliko gala ko umatoara ko, wirrilléún bara wapara, gatun willugbo bara uwa.

49. Gatun yantin gikoúmba kóti ta, gatun bara nukug wirroba bon Galilaia kabirug, garokéa kalog ka, nakilliela unni tara.

50. Gatun kakulla wakál kúri, giakai yitirra Yothep, wiyellikan kàtan; murràrág kakillikan, gatun tuloa kakillikan:

51. Gali keawai noa pitàl korien barúnba ko wiyellikanne ko gatun barúnba umatoara ko; Arimathéakàl noa, wakál ta kokera Iudaioi koba; niuwoa ba mittilliela piriwàl lako Eloi koba kako.

52. Unni noa uwa Pilato kin, bon wiyelliko murrin ko Iéthu koba ko.

53. Gatun noa mankulla barán, gatun muggama kirrikin ta, gatun wúnkulla tulmun ta umatoara tunug ta; keawai ba unta kúri wúntelli ta.

54. Gatun unta purreág ka tupoi-tupoi-kanne-ta, gatun papai kakulla thabbat ta.

55. Gatun bara nukuġ uwa ġikouġ katoa Galilaia kabiruġ wirroba yukita, ġatun nakulla tulmun, yakoai ba wúnkulla murrin.
56. Gatun bara willuġbo, ġatun mankulla †aromata ġatun †mura; ġatun koréa purreáġ ka thabbat ta, yaki tin wiyatoara tin.

WINTA XXIV.

YAKITA kakulla purreáġ ka yukita thabbat biruġ ka, ġoiokan ta, uwa bara unti ko tulmun tako, mankillin †aromata uma bara ba, ġatun taraikan uwa barun katoa.
2. Gatun bara nakulla tunuġ umatoara kurrai-kurrai biruġ kurraka ko tulmun tabiruġ.
3. Gatun bara uwa murrariġ, ġatun keawai bara na korien murrin ta Piriwál koba Iéthu koba.
4. Gatun yakita kakulla, kotelliela bara ba ġe tin, a! buloara kúri bula ġarokéa barun kin killibinbin kaba kirrikin taba,
5. Gatun bara ba kinta kakilliela, ġatun wúnkulliela barúnba ġoara barán purrai tako, wiya bula barun, Minariġ tin nura nakillin moron-kan ta unti tetti-tetti ka ?
6. Keawai noa unti, kulla noa waita ka ba bonġkulléún: ġurrulla nura yanti wiya nurun noa ba, yakita noa ba kakulla Galilaia ka,
7. Wiyelliela, Yinal ta kúri koba wunún wal bon máttára yarakai-willuġ koba ka, ġatun búnnún wal tetti, ġatun purreáġ ka tarai ka kúmba-ken bonġkullía kánún noa.
8. Gatun ġaiya bara kotelliela ġikoúmba wiyelli tara,
9. Gatun willuġbo bara uwa tulmun tabiruġ, ġatun wiya unni tara barun kin †dódeka ta, ġatun barun yantin ta.
10. Gala bountoa Mari-ko Magdalakálín-to, ġatun bountoa Ioanna-ko, ġatun bountoa Mari-ko tunkan-to Yacóbo-úmba-ko, ġatun taraikan-to bara nukuġ-ko barun katoa, wiya unni tara barun †apotholnuġ.
11. Gatun bara ba wiyelli tara kakulla barun kin yanti kiloa ġakoyelli tara, ġatun bara keawai ġurraiyelli pa barun.
12. Peter ġaiya noa ġarokéa, ġatun murra tulmun tako ; ġatun woinkulliela barán, nakulla noa kirrikin wuntoara pitaka, ġatun waita noa uwa, kotelliela unni tara kátan ba.
13. Gatun yakita purreáġ ka yantibo, buloara-bula barun kinbiruġ uwa kokera kolaġ, ġiakai yitirra Emmaou, yakita kaloġ †Hierothalem kabiruġ purloġ †hekékonta ta.
14. Gatun bara wiyellan unni tara kakulla ba.
15. Gatun yakita kakulla, wiyelliela ba, ġatun kotelliela bara ba, Iéthu noa niuwoabo uwa papai barun kin, ġatun uwa barun katoa.
16. Wonto ba ġaikuġ barúnba tullamá, ġimilli korien koa bara bon.
17. Gatun noa wiya barun, Minariġ nura unni tara wiyellan, uwollin nura ba, ġatun minki kátan ?

18. Gatun wakál bulun kinbiruġ, ġiakai noa yitirra Kleopa, wiyayelléůn, wiyelliela bon, Gintoa bo ta wakál ġowikan †Hierothalemkál, ġatun keawai unni tara ġurrapa kakulla ba unti tara purreáġ ka?
19. Gatun noa wiya barun, Minariġ-ke unni wonnuġ? Gatun bon bara wiyá, Gikouġ kin Iéthu kin Nadharetkál unni kakulla †propet ta kaiyukan umulliko ġatun wiyelliko mikan ta Eloi koba kin, ġatun yantin ta barun kin kûri ka :
20. Gatun yakoai bara ba piriwál †hiereu, ġatun ġearúnba piriwál kariġ wúnkulla bon wiyayelliko tetti kolaġ, ġatun bara bon búnkulla tetti.
21. Wonto ġéen ba kota niuwoa miromulliko Itháraelnuġ : ġatun yantin unni tara ba, unni buġġai kúmba-ken-ta kátan unnoa tara umatoara biruġ.
22. Kauwa, tarai bara nukuġ ġearúnba konara biruġ kota bunbéa bara ġearun, bara ġoiokéen kátan tulmun ta :
23. Gatun keawai bara ba na pa ġikoúmba murrin, uwa ġaiya bara, wiyelliela, nakéún bara natoara †aġelo kariġ koba wiya moron noa kakulla.
24. Gatun taraikan barúnba ġearun kinba uwa tulmun kolaġ, ġatun nakulla yanti bara nukuġko wiya ; keawai bon bara na korien.
25. Wiya ġaiya noa barun, A! woġkál nura, ġatun pirriral búlbúl ġurrulliko yantin ta wiyatoara bara ba †propet to!
26. Keawai noa Kritht kámúnġinbia ta umatoara ba unni tara, ġatun uwolliko kirrikin kolaġ ġikouġ ka tako?
27. Gatun kurri-kurri Mothe ko noa ba wiya, ġatun yantin to †propet kariġ ko, ġurrabunbéa ġaiya noa barun unnoa tara upatoara biruġ ġikouġ kai.
28. Gatun bara papai uwa unta kolaġ kokerá kolaġ, unta kolaġ bara : ġatun noa puntelliela kaloġ kolaġ.
29. Wonto bara ba pirralma bon, wiyelliela, Kauwa ġearun katoa ; kulla wal yaréa kakillilin, ġatun purreáġ ta waita uwollilin. Gatun noa uwa murrariġ kakilliko barun katoa.
30. Gatun yakita kakulla, yellawa noa ba barun katoa takilliko, mankulla noa †arto, ġatun pitálma noa, ġatun yiirbuġġa, ġatun ġukulla ġaiya barun.
31. Gatun ġaikuġ barúnba buġkulléún, ġatun ġimilléún ġaiya bara bon ; noa ġati kakulla barun kinbiruġ.
32. Gatun bara wiyellan barabo, Wiya, ġearúnba búlbúl winna ba ġearun kinba ko murruġ kaba ko, wiyelliléún noa ba ġearun katoa, ġatun ġurrabunbéún noa ba ġearun upatoara ta?
33. Gatun bonġkulléún tanoa-kal-bo ġatun williġ ba kakulla †Hierothalem kolaġ, ġatun nakulla barun †hendeka ta, ġatun barun taraikan barun katoa,
34. Wiyelliela, Bonġkulléún bo ta yuna Piriwál ta, ġatun paikulléún Thimon kir.

35. Gatun bara wiya unni tara upatoara yapiġ koa, ġatun ġimilléún bara bon yiirbuġgullicla noa ba ✝arto.

36. Gatun bara ba wiyellicla, Iéthuko noa niuwoabo ġarokéa willi ka barun kin, ġatun wiya barun noa, Pitál nura kauwa.

37. Wonto bara ba pulul-pulul kakulla ġatun kinta-kan, ġatun kotellicla bara marai ta bara nakulla.

38. Gatun noa wiya barun, Minariġ tin nura kinta kátan? ġatun minariġ tin nurúnba búlbúllo kotun?

39. Nauwa tia máttára emmoúmba, ġatun yulo emmoúmba, Gatoa bo : numulla tia, ġatun nauwa ; kulla keawai marai koba purriúġ korien ġatun tibun korien, yanti nakulla nura tia ba emmoúmba.

40. Gatun wiya noa ba unni, túġumbéa barun noa ġikoúmba máttára ġatun yulo.

41. Gatun keawai bara ba ġurra pitál ko, ġatun kotelliko, wiya noa barun, Wiya, nurúnba kunto unti?

42. Gatun bara bon ġukulla pundol koiyubatoara makoro biruġ, ġatun pundol nuparai kabiruġ.

43. Gatun noa mankulla, ġatun takulla barun kin mikan ta.

44. Gatun noa wiya barun, Unni tara wiyellikanne-ta wiya nurun baġ ba, kakulla baġ ba nurun katoa, yantin koa ka-uwil kakilliko upatoara wiyellikanne-ta Mothé-únba, ġatun barun ba ✝propet koba, ġatun ✝tehillim kaba, emmouġ kai.

45. Gurrabunbéa ġaiya noa barun, ġurra-uwil koa bara upatoara ta ;

46. Gatun wiya noa barun, Yaki upatoara, ġatun yaki murráraġ ta Kritht ko ġikouġ kakilliko tetti ko, ġatun bouġkulliko kúmba-ken-ta purreáġ ka tetti kabiruġ :

47. Gatun wiyabunbi-uwil koa minkikanne-ta ġatun warekullikanne-ta yarakai umullikan ko ġikouġ katoa biruġ yitirra biruġ yantin ta konara, kurri-kurri kabiruġ ✝Hierothalem kabiruġ.

48. Gatun nura nakillikan kátan ġali tara ko.

49. Gatun, ġurrulla, wupin baġ nurun kin wiyatoara emmoúmba koba Biyuġbai koba : wonto nura ba minkéa kokerá ✝Hierothalem ka, kaiyu koa nurun kauwál búlwára tin.

50. Gatun yutéa noa barun kaloġ kolaġ Bethany ka bo, ġatun noa wupilléún máttára ġikoúmba wokka-laġ, ġatun pitálma noa barun.

51. Gatun yakita kakulla, yaki pitálmullicla noa ba barun, mantilléún ġaiya bon barun kinbiruġ, ġatun kurréa bon wokka-laġ moroko kako.

52. Gatun bara bon murráraġ koiyellicla, ġatun willuġ ba kakulla ✝Hierothalem kolaġ kauwál-kan pitál-kan :

53. Gatun kakillicla murruġ ✝hieron ka, murráraġ wiyellicla ġatun pitálmulliela bon Eloinuġ.

AMEN.

PART III.

THE LEXICON.

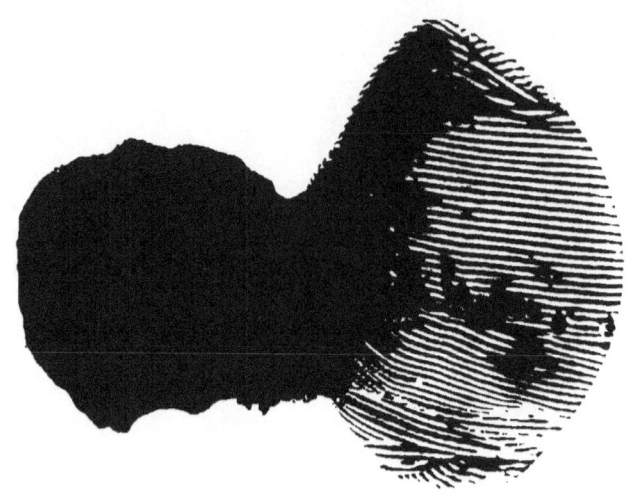

AWABAKALIN:
OR
'A WOMAN OF THE LAKE MACQUARIE TRIBE.'

ÆTAT. 65.

[FROM THE ORIGINAL MANUSCRIPT.]

AN

AWABAKAL-ENGLISH

LEXICON

TO THE

GOSPEL ACCORDING TO SAINT LUKE

BY

L. E. THRELKELD

NOW FOR THE FIRST TIME PRINTED.

Sydney:
CHARLES POTTER, GOVERNMENT PRINTER.
1892.

THE AUTHOR'S PREFACE.

It was during the year 1827, being the third year after the commencement of my mission to the aborigines, that the first work of this kind was produced—the result of my researches, assisted by M'Gill. The work was entitled "Specimens of the Language of the Aborigines of New South Wales," and was printed in Sydney, the only attempt that had then been made by anyone to obtain a thorough grammatical knowledge of the aboriginal language of Australia, in any of its various dialects, and to render it into a written form.

In 1834, on the recommendation of the Rev. W. G. Broughton, the then Arch-Deacon of New South Wales, the Colonial Government, and the Society for the Promotion of Christian Knowledge, London, conjointly advanced sufficient funds to enable me to to publish a small edition, now out of print, of "An Australian Grammar of the Language as spoken by the Aborigines in the Vicinity of Lake Macquarie, New South Wales." In 1850, I published, on my own account, "A Key to the Structure of the Aboriginal Language, being an Analysis of the Particles used as Affixes, to form the various modifications of the Verbs, showing the essential powers, abstract roots, and other peculiarities of the language." Both of these works were presented to, and exhibited at, the Royal National Exhibition, London, 1851.

This Lexicon will contain only those words which are used in the Gospel by Saint Luke. For the exemplification of such tenses and cases as may not be used therein, reference must be made to the "Australian Grammar," and to the "Key to the Structure of the Aboriginal Language."

A few illustrative sentences will be found at the end of the Lexicon, showing the mode in which certain forms of English phraseology are expressed in the aboriginal language.

As a tribute of respect to the departed worth of M'Gill, the intelligent aboriginal, whose valuable assistance enabled me to overcome very many difficulties in the language much sooner than otherwise could have been accomplished, his likeness is also attached to this work.

L. E. THRELKELD.

Sydney,
   New South Wales,
     1859.

ABBREVIATIONS.

abl.	for	*ablative*	*interr.*	for	*interrogative.*
acc.	,,	*accusative*	*Lat.*	,,	*Latin.*
adv.	,,	*adverb.*	*lit.*	,,	*literally.*
aor.	,,	*aorist.*	*mand.*	,,	*mandatory.*
cf.	,,	*refer to.*	*masc.*	,,	*masculine.*
conj.	,,	*conjoined.*	*neg.*	,,	*negative.*
dat.	,,	*dative.*	*opt.*	,,	*optative.*
def.	,,	*definite.*	*part.*	,,	*participle.*
emph.	,,	*emphatic.*	*perf.*	,,	*perfect.*
Eng.	,,	*English.*	*plu.*	,,	*plural.*
exclam.	,,	*exclamation.*	*prep.*	,,	*postposition.*
fem.	,,	*feminine.*	*pres.*	,,	*present.*
fut.	,,	*future.*	*priv.*	,,	*privative.*
Gr.	,,	*Greek.*	*pr.n.*	,,	*proper noun.*
Heb.	,,	*Hebrew.*	*proh.*	,,	*prohibitory.*
imper. or *imp.*	,,	*imperative.*	*pron.*	,,	*pronoun.*
indef.	,,	*indefinite.*	*sing.*	,,	*singular.*
i.q.	,,	*the same as.*	*subj.*	,,	*subjunctive.*
intens.	,,	*intensive.*	*subst.*	,,	*substantive.*

cf.* *This is a reference to the foot-note on page* 204.

AN
AWABAKAL-ENGLISH LEXICON
TO THE
GOSPEL ACCORDING TO SAINT LUKE.

The letters in the English alphabet, with some modifications, are here used to convey the sounds of letters and words in the aboriginal language. The meaning of the verb is given in the third person singular only, but it should be remembered that the verb, when rendered into English, must be made to agree with its subject, whether singular, plural, or dual—first, second, or third person, as the case may require; for example,—búntán, 'smites,' may have to be translated 'I smite,' 'thou smitest,' 'he, she, or it smites,' 'we, ye, or they (*dual* and *plural*) smite'; *cf.* Grammar, p. 31. So likewise with respect to nouns; for they are singular, dual, or plural, according to the particle attached to show the number; as, kúri, 'man'; kúri ta, 'the man'; kúri tara, 'the men'; yantin kúri, 'all manner of men'; 'all men'; 'all people'; 'all mankind.'

[Hyphens are used to show the composition of some of the words.—ED.]

A

A—the sound of this letter is the same as heard in *Eng.* ah!
A—retains the long sound, especially when accented as in bán; à sounds shorter than *a*. See 'Phonology,' page 5.
A!—a call of attention; hark!
Aaron—*pr.n.*, Aaron.
Aaronúmba—belonging to A.
Abáram—*pr.n.*, Abraham.
Abáramúmba—belonging to A.
Abáram kinko—to be with A.; *dat.* 2.
Abáramnug—for A. to have or possess; *dat.* 1.
Abáramnug—A. as the object.
Abel—*pr.n.*, Abel.
Abelúmba—belonging to A.
Abelnug—Abel; the *acc.* case.

Abia—*pr.n.*, Abia.
Abia-úmba—belonging to A.
Abiléné—*pr.n.*, Abilene.
Agelo—*Gr.*, an angel.
Ai—sounds as *i* in *Eng.* 'nigh.'
Akéto—*Lat.*, vinegar.
Aku—*Lat.*, a needle.
Alabathro—*Gr.*, alabaster.
Alpai—*Gr. pr.n.*, Alpheus.
Altar—*see* bomo.
Andrea—*pr.n.*, Andrew.
Apothol—*Gr.*, an apostle.
Arguro—*Gr.*, silver.
Army—*Eng.*, army.
Army-kan—*Eng.*, a soldier.
Arto—*Gr.*, bread, a loaf.
Atthari—*Gr.*, a farthing.
Ather—*pr.n.*, Asher.
Athino—*Lat.*, an ass.

B

B—is sounded as in *Eng.* 'be.' In many instances it is difficult to ascertain whether the sound be *b* or *p*, or a compound sound of both letters.

Ba—sounds as *Eng.* 'bah'!
Ba—when, as if; postfixed to pronouns, it forms the *poss.**
Baġ—the verbal *pron.*, I.
Bai—is sounded as *Eng.* 'by.'
Baibai—a stone-axe ; an axe.
Bal, ban—are sounded as *Eng.* 'marl, barn,' omitting the *r*.
Ban—a suffix to certain nouns ; as, makoro, 'fish'; makoroban, 'one who fishes,' 'a fisherman'; makorobin, 'a fisherwoman.'
Banuġ—the *conj. dual*, I-thee ; the first person *nom.*, and the second person *acc.*
Bapai—nigh, near, close at hand.
Bapabunbilliko—*inf.*, to let bury.
Bapabunbilla—*imp.*, permit to bury.
Bapa-uwil—*opt.*, (a wish) that ...may bury.
Bapa-uwil koa—*subj.*, (a purpose) in order to bury ; that may...bury.
Bapilliko—to bury, to inter.
Bará—down ; below.
Barabba—*pr.n.*, Barabbas.
Barabbanuġ—B.; in the *acc.*
Bará kako—actually down.
Bará kolaġ—tending down.
Bara—they.
Barabo—they themselves.
Barabo-barabo—*recip.*, they (do it) themselves, one to another.
Barán—down ; now is down.
Barun—them ; *acc.* case.

Barúnba—belonging to them ; their ; theirs ; *gen.* case.
Barun kai, barun kaiko—from them, as a cause ; on account of them ; *abl.* 1.
Barun kinbiruġ—*locally* away from them; out of them ; from amongs them.
Barun kako—with them *locally*.
Barun katoa—in company with them ; with them.
Bathileia—*Gr.*, kingdom.
Bathileu—*Gr.*, a king.
Bátolomai—*pr.n.*, Bartholomew.
Bato—fresh-water ; *cf.* kokoin.
Batoto—with water, as agent.
Bato kabiruġ—out of the water ; from the water, *locally*.
Bau—sounded as *Eng.* 'bough.'
Ba-uwil—*opt.*, a wish as to the action of the verb to which it is joined.
Ba-uwil koa—*sub.*, in order that ...may...
Be—is sounded as *Eng.* 'bay.'
Béelidhebul—*pr.n.*, Beelzebub.
Béelma—mocked ; did mock.
Béelmanún—will mock.
Béelmulliko—to mock, deride, despise ; to make game of.
Béelmulli tin—because of the mocking.
Béelmulliela—mocked and continued to mock ; was mocking.
Béelmullinún—will be mocking.
Bethany—*pr.n.*, Bethany.
Bethany kolaġ—towards B.
Bethlehem—*pr.n.*, Bethlehem.
Bethápagé—*pr.n.*, Bethphage.
Betháhaida—*pr.n.*, Bethsaida.
Bi—is sounded as *Eng.* 'bee.'
Bi—thou ; the verbal *nom.*
Biblion—*Gr.*, book, *cf.*, book.

---

*For all personal pronouns, and for the case-endings of nouns, see pp. 16, 17 of the Grammar.—Ed.

Biggai—the affectionate address to a brother; brother!
Biloa—he-thee; *conj. dual.*
Bin—thee; *acc.* case.
Bintun—a male parent; a father.
Binug—thou-him; *conj. dual.*
Bir—sounds as in *Eng.* 'bird.'
Birrikéa—slept; was asleep.
Birriki-birriki—sound asleep.
Birrikilligél—the lying (resting, sleeping) place; a bedroom, &c.
Birrikilliko—to lie along; to take rest, as by lying down to sleep.
Birrikin—*pres. part.*, sleeping; being asleep.
Birug—from; apart from; out of.
Bith-dekem-millia—*Lat.*, 20,000.
Bitta—the edge or sides.
Biu—rhymes with *Eng.* 'pew.'
Bi-uwil—auxiliary sign of the optative mood.
Bi-uwil koa—auxiliary sign of the subjunctive mood.
Biyug—the affectionate address to a male parent; father!
Biyugbai—a father; the male parent.
Biyugbai-nug—*acc.*, the father, as the object.
Biyugbai-ta—the father, as the subject; it is the father.
Biyug-ta-uwa bali—*dual*; both father and I have ....
Biyugbai-to—the father, acting as an agent *or* as the subject to an active verb.
Bo—the self-same; as, gatoa-bo, 'I myself'; unti-bo, 'this self-same place.'
Boaikulléun—grew, of itself.
Boaikulliko—to grow *or* shoot up, of itself.
Boa-má—gathered together, collected.
Boamá korien—did not gather together.
Boamulliko—to gather together, to collect.
Bobog—a babe; an infant.
Bokatog—the surf of the sea; a wave.
Bomo—*Gr.*, an altar.
Bon—*acc.*, the pronoun 'him.'
Bonig—ashes.
Boo—*Gr.*, an ox.
Book (†biblion, *Gr.*)—*Eng.*, book.
Book kaba—in (on) the book.
Bo-ta—itself; it itself.
Botru—*Gr.*, grapes.
Bougbuggá—has caused to arise; did cause to arise; arose.
Bougbuggánún—will cause to arise by personal agency; will be made to rise; shall be raised up.
Bougbuggulliko — to cause to arise by personal agency; to raise up.
Bougkatéa-kánún—will be raised again by command; will again stand up.
Bougkulléun—arose, got up.
Bougkullía—*imp.*, arise, get up.
Bougkullía kan—one who has arisen by command.
Bougkullía-kan-katéa-kan—one who has arisen again by command.
Bougkulliko—to arise, to get up, to stand up.
Bougkulli korien—not to arise.
Bougkullinún—will rise.
Bougkullinún-wal—shall arise; will certainly rise.
Bougkullía-kánún—will arise by command.
Bounnoun—*acc.*, her.
Bounnoúnba—belonging to her.
Bounnoun kai—because of her.
Bounnoun kinbirug—from her; away from (apart from) her.
Bountoa—she.
Bredd (†arto, *Gr.*)—*Eng.*, bread.

Bredd ta—the bread, as a subject; it is bread.
Bredd-to—the bread, as agent.
Brimtón—*Eng.*, brimstone.
Bu—sounds as *Eng.* 'bull'; *cf.**
-bug̀—sounds as *Eng.* 'bung.'
-bug̀—as an auxiliary particle, postfixed to the verb, denotes personal and causative agency.
-bug̀gulliko—to act effectually by personal agency; to cause to.
Bág̀—sounds as in *Eng.* 'boon,' but with the strong nasal *ng* instead of the *n*; *cf.**.
Búg̀búg̀—to salute.
Bug̀bug̀gá—unloosed; did open.
Bug̀bug̀gulliko—to act upon so as to unloose; to open a book.
Búg̀búg̀-ka—saluted, did salute with a kiss.
Búg̀búg̀kulliko—to salute with a kiss.
Bug̀gai—now; to-day; present time.
Bug̀gaikál—of to-day; belonging to the present period; of this time; new; fresh.
Bug̀kulléún—did become.
Bug̀kulliko—to cause to be, by its own power; to become.
Bukk—sounds as *Eng.* 'buck.'
Bukka—anger; ferociousness.
Bukka-butti-bug̀kéa—the more wrathful (angry, enraged).
Bukka-ka-ke—to be in an angry, wrathful, savage state; to be an avenger.
Bukka-kakilli-kanne—anything which is in a state of anger; wrath; enmity.

Bukka-kakilliko—to be in a state of anger (wrath, rage, enmity).
Bukka-kan—one who is angry; being angry; an enemy.
Bukka-kan-to—one who is angry (or an enemy) acting as agent.
Bukka-kan-toa—the angry one, as an agent; the adversary; the enemy.
Bukka kauwál—great anger.
Bukka-mai-ye—one who is habitually angry.
Bukka-mai yikora—*imp. neg.*, be not angry.
Bukka manún—will do angrily.
Bukka-ta-kál—in a state of rage.
Bula—*dual*, ye two.
Búl—for its sound *cf.**.
Bul—sounds as *Eng.* 'bull.'
Búlbúl—the heart.
Búlbúl la—in the heart.
Búlbúl-lo—the heart, as agent.
Búlbúl labirug̀—out of the heart
Bulka—the back of the hand *or* body; any hill *or* mountain; a protuberance.
Bulka kako—at *or* on the back.
Bulkárá—to (unto) the back, &c.
Bulkára karig̀—all the mountains *or* hills.
Bulkárá kolag̀—towards the hill.
Bulkára-ta—it is the mountain; the mountain.
Bulkároa—throughout the back (*or* hill, mountain).
Buloara—two.
Buloara-bula—*dual*, they two; the two; both.
Buloara-buloara—two and two.

---

*Note.—ú always, and u before a *single* consonant, are sounded like *u* in *Eng.* 'bull.'

ú always, and u before *two* consonants, are sounded as *u* in *Eng.* 'hull.' See page 4.

Throughout the Lexicon, reference to this Note is made by *cf.**
—Ed.

Bulun—*dual acc.*, them two.
Bulun kinbirug — from (apart from) them two.
Bulun-kinbirug-ko—from them two, as an agent.
Búlwára—high, lofty.
Búlwára ka—at the height ; on high ; noon ; high noon.
Búlwarai tin—on account of the height ; on high.
Bům—for its sound *cf.**.
Bum—is sounded as *Eng.* 'boom.'
Búmbéa—was and is married.
Búmbéa-ka—is in the married state.
Búmbillala—did marry at some definite time past.
Búmbillan—do *or* does marry.
Búmbilli-ka—was in the act of marrying at some indefinite time past.
Búmbilliko—to marry ; to take a wife ; to kiss reciprocally.
Búmbinún—*fut.*, will marry.
Búmbuggulliko—to take a kiss by force.
Bumbuggulliko—to cause to be loose ; to open a door.
Búmbuggulli-to—the kiss given, as agent ; with *or* by a kiss.
Búm-búm—kisses ; kissing.
Búmbúm-ka—was kissed.
Búmbúm kakilliko - to be in a state of kissing ; to kiss.
Búmbúm-ka-pa—did not kiss.
Búmbúm-kullicla—did continue to kiss.
Búmbúm-kullielliko — to continue to kiss.
Bummilléán—found ; did find.
Bummilliko—to find.
Bun—is sounded as *Eng.* 'boon.'
Bůn—for its sound *cf.**.
Bůn—*permissive*, let ; permit.
Búnbá—smitten ; smote.
Búnbéa—did permit ; did let.
Bůnbilla—*imp.*, permit ; let.

Bůnbilliko—to permit ; to let.
Bůnbin—*pres.*, permits.
Bůnbinún—*fut.*, will permit.
Bůn-bi-uwil—*opt.*, wish to let.
Bůn-bi-uwil koa—*subj.*, in order to permit ; that…might let.
Búnkilligél—the place of smiting ; the threshing floor ; the pugilistic ring ; the field of battle.
Búnkilli-kan—one who smites.
Búnkilli-kan tin—from (on account of) him who smites.
Búnkilliko—to smite *or* strike ; to make a blow ; *cf.**.
Búnkilli kolag—towards smiting ; about to smite.
Búnkilliko tetti—to smite dead ; to kill with a blow.
Búnkilli tin—from (on account of) the smiting.
Búnkiye tetti wirriye—one who habitually smites to death ; one who kills with blows ; a murderer.
Búnki yikora—*proh.*, smite not ; strike not ; must not strike.
Búnkulla—smote ; did beat.
Búnnún wal—shall smite ; will certainly smite.
Búnnún-wal-ba—when …should smite ; if…should smite.
Búntan—*pres.*, strikes.
Buntimai—a messenger ; an ambassador ; a herald ; *b=p*.
Búntoara—that which is smitten *or* struck.
Burrilliko—to do a thing spoken of by some violent instrumental means ; *cf.* tetti-burrilliko.
Burroug—a dove.
Burugbuggá—did set at liberty ; unloosed, released, unbound.
Burugbuggan—does set at liberty (release, unbind).
Burugbuggánún—will set loose.

Burugbuggulla—*mand.*, set at liberty; set loose.
Burugbuggulliela—was causing to be set at liberty; was unloosing *or* releasing.
Burugbuggulliela ba—while (as, when)...was setting at liberty.
Burugbuggulliko—to cause to be set at liberty; to unloose; to release; to unbind.
Burugkulléun—did set at liberty, unloosed (of itself).
Burugkulliko—to set itself at liberty of its own power; to unloose itself; to unbind itself; to go off spontaneously.
Butti—more; to do more; to continue the action.
Butti-butti—*mand.*, more more; go on, go on.
Buttikag—any animal; ass, ox.
Buttikag ba—when (if) an animal ..., as an ox.
Bu-uwil—*opt.*, wish to smite.
Bu-uwil koa—*subj.*, in order to smite; that...might smite; on purpose to strike.
Buwa—*mand.*, smite; strike.

C.

There is no sibilant sound in the language, consequently there is no *c* soft, or *s*, or *z* in the native alphabet. These letters, therefore, occur only in words of foreign origin introduced into the aboriginal tongue. The hard sound of *c*, as in *Eng.* 'cubit,' would be represented by the letter *k*. The letter ć (Ć) represents the sound of *ch.*, as in *Eng.* 'church.'

Ćipu—*Eng.*, sheep.
Káf(†italo, *Gr.*)—*Eng.*, calf.

Kalábary—*pr.n.*, Calvary.
Kenturion—a centurion.
Kenturion-ko—the centurion, as an agent.
Kubit—*Eng.*, a cubit.
Kurenia—*pr.n.*, Cyrenia.
Kurenia-kál—belonging to Cyrenia; a Cyrenian (*masc.*).
Kurenia-kálin—belonging to Cyrenia; a Cyrenian (*fem.*).

D.

D has a middle sound betwixt *t* and *d*; it often confounds the sounds of *d* and *t*. D is used in foreign words, while *t* belongs to the language. The aborigines do not pronounce the *Eng.* *v* or *f*, generally substituting *b* for *v*, and *p* for *f*.

Dabid—David.
Dabid-to—David, as the agent.
Dabidùmba—belonging to D.
Debbil (†diabol, *Gr.*)—devil.
Debbil-debbil—*intensive*; a term used for an evil being of whom the aborigines are much afraid.
Dekem-millia—*Lat.*, 10,000.
Denari—*Lat.*, a penny.
Deutero—*Gr.*, second.
Dhakaría—*pr.n.*, Zacharias.
Dhakké—*pr.n.*, Zacchaeus.
Dhélot—*Gr.*, a zealot.
Diabol-lo *or* diabol-to—the devil, as an agent.
Diabol-kan—one having a devil.
Didathkalo (-oi)—*Gr.*, teacher.
Dodeka—*Gr.*, twelve.

E.

E—sounds as *a* in *Eng.* 'may.'
Ela *or* ala!—*exclam.*, ho! hallo!

Ela-beara! — emphatic *exclam.* of astonishment or surprise; oh, dear! dear me! well!
Elaión—*Gr.*, Mount of Olives.
Elebben—*see* hendeka.
Elebben-ta—eleven it is; eleven.
Elía—*pr.n.*, Elias.
Elía-úmba—belonging to Elias.
Elidhabet—*pr.n.*, Elizabeth.
Elitheu—*pr.n*, Eliseus.
Eloi—*Hebrew Elohim*, God.
Eloi kai—on account of Eloi.
Eloi kai koba—on account of and belonging to God.
Eloi kin—in place before Eloi; before (in presence of) God.
Eloi kinko—for *or* to Eloi.
Eloi koba—belonging to Eloi; belonging to God, as property.
Eloi-ta—Eloi it is, as the subject.
Eloi-to—Eloi, as the agent; God.
Eloi-úmba—belonging to Eloi, personally; God's.
Eloi-úmba-ta—belonging to Eloi it is; it is of God; it is God's.
Emmaou—*pr.n.*, Emmaus.
Emmaou kolaġ—towards E.
Emmouġ—*acc.*, me.
Emmouġ kai—from me; on account of me; about me.
Emmouġ katoa—with (in company with, together with) me.
Emmouġ kin—at me; with me.
Emmouġ kinbiruġ—from me; away from me.
Emmouġ-ta—it is mine; mine.
Emmoúmba—my, mine, belonging to me. Also, Emmoemba.
Emmoúmba katoa — with (in company with) my.
Emmoúmba koba—belonging to my; of my.
Emmoúmba tin—from mine; on account of mine, as a cause.
Et (ét)—*Eng.*, eight.
Ethaia—*pr.n.*, Esaias.

Ethané—*Gr.*, nations.
Ethané-kál—*Gr. and aboriginal*, the Gentiles. *See* Gentail.
Etín (étín)—*Eng.*, eighteen.
Etín-ta—the eighteen it is, as a subject.
Ety-wara—*Eng. and aboriginal*, eighty-four.
Ety koa—in order to be eighty.
Euagelion—*Gr.*, the gospel.

F.

The sound of *f* is not found in the native language; when it is introduced by foreign words, the aborigines pronounce it *p*.

Parthiġ—*Eng.*, farthing.
Pente—*Gr.*, five.
Pente-ta—five it is; the five.
Pentaki-kilioi—*Gr.*, 5,000.
Pentakothioi—*Gr.*, 500.
Pentékonta—*Gr.*, fifty.
Pipátín—*Eng.*, fifteen.
Pipáty—*see* pentékonta.
Pipáty koa—in order that it may be fifty.
Pipáty koa ka-uwil—in order that there may be fifty.
Pok (†alópék, *Gr.*)—*Eng.*, fox.
Purloġ—*Eng.*, furlong.
Purloġ hikty—*Eng.*, sixty furlongs.
Purloġ hikty-ta—sixty furlongs it is; three-score furlongs.

G.

G is always the English *g* hard.
Gabriel—*pr.n.*, Gabriel.
Gabriel-ta—Gabriel it is.
Gabrielúmba—belonging to G.
Gadara—*pr.n.*, Gadara.
Gadara-kál—a woman of G.
Gadarén—*pr.n.*, Gadarene.

Galilaia—*pr.n.*, Galilee.
Galilaia kaba—at Galilee.
Galilaia kabirug—out of G.
Galilaia-kál—(*masc.*) belonging to Galilee; a Galilean.
Galilaia-kálín — (*fem.*) belonging to Galilee; a Galilean.
Galilaia tin—from (on account of) Galilee.
Galilaia tin-to—on account of Galilee, as an agent.
Gárammateu—*Gr.*, scribes.
Gárammateu-kál—belonging to the scribes.
Gárammateu-kál-lo — belonging to the scribes, acting as agents.
Gárammateu-kan—he who is a scribe.
Gárammateu ko—for the scribes.
Gárammateunug—the scribes, as the object.
Gárammateu tin—on account of the scribes; from the scribes, as a cause.
Gárammateu-to—the scribes, as agents.
Garép (†botru, *Gr.*)—*Eng.*, grape.
Gennetharet—*pr.n.*, Gennesaret.
Gentail (†ethané-kál)—Gentiles.
Gentail kinko—for (unto) the G.
Gentail koba—belonging to G.
Gentail-to—G., as the agents.

G.

G sounds as *ng* in *Eng.* 'bung'; it has the nasal sound of *ng* in the English alphabet. The sound is invariably the same whether at the beginning, the middle, or the end of a word, and cannot be too strongly nasalised.

Ga—or; or it is.
Ga ?—is it ?
Ga !—lo ! behold !
Ga ba—or as; it is as; while as.
Ga wiya ?—or say? or is it not ?
Gagga, gagka—*see* ganka.
Gai—rhymes with *Eng.* 'nigh.'
Gaikug—the eye; the eyes.
Gaikug birug—from (away from, out of) the eye.
Gaikug tin—because of the eye.
Gaiya—then; at that time or period spoken of. It is used as a correlative to yakounta? 'when'? in the reply, 'gaiya' follows the word that indicates the time when; as, kúmba gaiya, 'to-morrow then.'
Gakéa—stood; did stand.
Gakilliko—to stand upright.
Gakillilin — now standing and continuing to stand.
Gakillin—standing upright.
Gakogkilliko—to feign; to sham *or* pretend.
Gakoiman—deceives; betrays.
☞ This and the word-forms below may be written either gakoi- *or* gako-.
Gakoimulliko — to cause deception; to deceive; to betray.
Gakoiyá—deceived; denied; betrayed; perverted.
Gakoiya—deception; hypocrisy; deceit; betrayal.
Gakoiyanún—will make believe *or* sham; will deceive *or* deny.
Gakoiya-uwil—*opt.*, wish to deceive *or* betray.
Gakoiya-uwil ba—as...might deceive.
Gakoiya-uwil koa—*subj.*, that... might deceive *or* betray.
Gakoiya-uwilliko—to wish to deceive.
Gakoiyaye—habitual deception.
Gakoiyaye tin—on account of habitual deception; from hypocrisy *or* deceit.

Gakoiya yikora—*mand.*, beware of deception.
Gakoiyellan—does now deceive.
Gakoiyellela—was deceiving or perverting.
Gakoiyelli-kan—one who lies or deceives or acts the traitor.
Gakoiyelli-kan-to—one who deceives, acting as the agent.
Gakoiyelliko—to act in such a way as to deceive; to betray; to feign; to lie; to act the spy.
Gakoiyellilin—now deceiving.
Gakoiyellinún—will betray.
Gakoiyelli-ta—(*sing.*) the deception; the deceiving.
Gakoiyelli-tara—(*plu.*) the deceptions; the deceivings.
Gala—that (demonstrative).
Gala ko—for that; to that.
Gali—this (demonstrative).
Gali birug—from (out of) this.
Gali koba—belonging to this.
Gali noa—this is he who.
Gali-ta—this is it that; this is that which.
Gali-tara—these are they which.
Gali tin—from (on account of) this, as a cause.
Galoa—that (there at hand.)
Galoa-ko—that there, spoken of as an agent.
Galoa kolag—towards that.
Galoa-rin—from (on account of) that, as a cause.
Gan?—*interr.* who?
Gan-ba—who as; whoever.
Gan...ba?—who is (he)?
Ganbulliko—(a peculiar idiom, *lit.*, to be 'whoing' a person when you know who he is; hence,) to deny all knowledge of a person when at the same time you know him; to deny a person; to deny personal knowledge.

Ganbullin in—will be 'whoing'; will deny.
Ganbullin in wal—will certainly be 'whoing'; shall deny.
Ganka—first; before; foremost; prior; elder; *i.q.* gag-ga or -ka.
Ganka—before; in presence of.
Ganka-ganka—the very first.
Ganka kakilliko—to be before; to be the first.
Ganka-kal—relating to the first or the elder.
Ganka-kalléún—having been be-before or first.
Ganka kanún—will be first.
Ganke?—personal *interr.*, who is the person? who? who is?
Gan kiloa?—whom like?
Gan kiloa unnoa—like whom is that?
Gan kin?—upon whom? *locally.*
Gan kinba—upon whomsoever, *locally.*
Gannug?—*acc.*, who is the personal object? whom?
Gan-to?—who did or does? who is the personal agent?
Gan-to ba—whosoever shall act as a personal agent; whosoever does or will do.
Ganto-bo ba—whosoever may be the selfsame personal agent; whosoever will.
Ganto-ko?—who is the personal agent? who is he that does?
Ganúm?—to whom (to have or to possess)?
Ganúmba?—whose? to whom belongeth...?
Ganún-bo—whosoever hath.
Gapal—a woman, a concubine.
Gapal toa—with (in company with) a woman or women.
Gar—rhymes with the *Eng.* 'far,' pronouncing the *r* very rough.
Garabo—sleep; repose.

Garabo-kakilliko—to be in a state of repose; to sleep.
Garabo kakillin—*present part.*, sleeping; reposing.
Garaka—the entrance *or* mouth of anything; *i.q.* kurraka.
Garaka-ko—the entrance, as the subject.
Garawàlliko—to lose one self.
Garawàllilléún—lost; did lose.
Garawàn—a plain; a flat place; a level; *i.q.* gararawan.
Garo—the eldest son; the first born son; *cf.* kurri *and* koro.
Garogéeu—an elderly woman; an old woman.
Garokàl—aged; elder; old.
Garokéa—stood up; arose.
Garokéún—stood up, at some definite time past.
Garokilla—*mand.*, stand up.
Garokilléa—*mand.*, stand up and continue to stand.
Garokillicla — *past. part.*, continued to stand; stood.
Garokilliko—to stand upright on the feet; to be in a standing position.
Garokilli korien — *neg.*, not to be standing upright; not to stand.
Garokillin — *pres. part.*, standing; now standing upright.
Garombai—an elderly man; an old man.
Garkulléún—turned round.
Garkulliko—to revolve of itself; to turn one's self round.
Garug—rough; rugged.
Garuggara—rugged; proud.
Gati—happened of itself; accidental; perchance; unawares; without cause; secret; unrevealed.
Gati—nothing; nought; not.
Gati kakilliko—to be nothing.

Gati kakulla — was not; evanished; disappeared.
Gati-ta—the secret place.
Gaton—*emphatic*, I who; it is I.
Gatoa-ta—*emphatic*, it is I who.
Gatoa-bo—*emph.*, it was (is) I myself who.
Gatun—*conj.*, and.
Ge—rhymes with the *Eng.* 'nay,' sounding strongly the nasal *ng* at the beginning.
Gearimulléún—choose; elected.
Gearimulliko—to pick out; to choose; to cull; to elect.
Gearun—*pron.*, we.
[*Incomplete:* see note at the end of the Lexicon.—Ed.]

H.

The aborigines seldom sound *h* as an initial aspirate; consequently the letter *h* is not much used in the language, save in words of foreign extraction.

Hebáraio—*pr.n.*, a Hebrew.
Hebáraioi-úmba — belonging to the Hebrews.
Hek—*Gr.*, six.
Hekaton—*Gr.*, a hundred.
Hekékonta—*Gr.*, sixty.
Hellenik—*Gr.*, Greek.
Hendeka—*Gr.*, eleven.
Hepta—*Gr.*, seven.
Herod—*pr.n.*, Herod.
Herodiath—*pr.n.*, Herodias.
Herod katoa—with (in company with) Herod.
Herodnug—H., as the object.
Herod-to—Herod, as the agent.
Herodúmba—belonging to H.
Herodúmba-kan—being H's.
Hiereu—*Gr.*, a priest; priests.
Hiereu-kan—one who is a priest.
Hiereu-ko—the priest, as agent.

Hiereu-nug—the priest or priests,
as the object.
Hieron—*Gr.*, temple.
Hieron ka—at the temple.
Hieron tin—from (on account of)
the temple.
Hierothalem—*Gr.*, Jerusalem.
Hierothalem ka—at or in J.
Hierothalem kabirug—out of J.;
from (away from) J.
Hierothalem-kal—belonging to
Jerusalem (*masc.*); a man of
Jerusalem.
Hierothalem-kalín — belonging
to Jerusalem *(fem.)*; a woman
of Jerusalem.
Hour (†hora, *Gr.*)—*Eng.*, hour.
Hour ba—when (at) the hour.
Hour ka—was at the hour.
Hour-ka-ta—it was at the hour.
Hundared—*see* hekaton.
Hundared-ta—hundred it is; the
hundred.

I.

I (i)—sounds as *e* in *Eng.* 'cat.'
I (í)—sounds as *ee* in *Eng.* 'e'en.'
Iaeiro (Yaeiro)—*Gr.*, Jairus.
Iakob (Yakob)—*pr.n.*, Jacob.
Iakobnug—Jacob, as the object.
Iakobúmba—belonging to Jacob
Iakóbo (Yakóbo)—*Gr.*, James.
Iakóbo-úmba—of or belonging to
James ; James's.
Iakóbo-úmba-ko — belonging to
J., as the agent.
Yehóa—*Heb. pr.n.*, Jehovah.
Yehóanug—J., as the object.
Yehóa kin—to Jehovah.
Yehóa-ko—J., as the agent.
Yehóa-úmba—belonging to J.
Iéthu—*Gr. pr.n.*, Jesus.
Iéthu katoa—with (in company
with) Jesus.
Iéthu kin—to Jesus, *locally*. [is.

Iéthu kinko—to Jesus, where he
Iéthu-ko—Jesus, as the agent.
Iéthunug—Jesus, as the object.
Ioanna—*pr.n.*, Joanna.
Ioanna-ko—Joanna, as an agent.
Ioanne—*Gr. pr.n.*, John.
Ioannenug—J., as the object.
Ioanne-úmba—of or belonging to
John ; John's.
Iona—*Gr.*, Jonas.
Ioràdan—*pr.n.*, Jordan.
Iothep (Yothep)—*pr.n.*, Joseph.
Yothep kinko—to Joseph.
Yothepúmba—belonging to J.
Italo—*Gr.*, a calf.
Ithák—*pr.n.*, Isaac.
Itháknug—Isaac, as the object.
Ithákúmba—belonging to I.
Ithákariot—*pr.n.*, Iscariot.
Ithárael—*pr.n.*, Israel.
Itháraelnug—Is., as the object.
Ithárael koba—belonging to Is.
Ituréa—*pr.n.*, Iturea.
Iudaia—*Gr. pr.n.*, Judea.
Iudaio (-oi)—*Gr. pr.n.*, a Jew.
Iudaio koba—of or belonging to
a Jew or Jews.
Iudath—*pr.n.*, Judas.
Iudath kin—to Judas.
Iudath kinko—to Judas (for him
to have).

J.

[Other tribal dialects have the
palatals j and ć, but this Awabakal has not; in it j occurs only
in imported words.—ED.]

Jail—*Eng.*, jail.
Jeriko—*pr.n.*, Jericho.
Jerusalem—*see* Hierothalem.

K.

K is sounded as in *Eng.* 'Kate.'

Ka is sounded as in *Eng.* 'cart.'
Ka korien—*neg.*, not ; am not.
Kaai—*a call*, here! come hither!
Kaaibulliko—to cry out ; to call aloud ; to 'kaai'; because the blacks use that word as we do hallo! hoy!
Kaaibullinŭn—will cry out.
Ka ba—to be in such a state or condition (as mentioned).
Ka ba (at the beginning of a sentence)—if it is (as stated).
Kabirug—from ; out of ; away from; apart from.
Kabo—presently ; by-and-by.
Kabo koa—in company with by-and-by ; in order to be by-and-by ; until.
Kai—rhymes with *Eng.* 'eye.'
Kai—*imp.*, be (an entreaty).
Kaiapath—*pr.n.*, Caiaphas.
Kai-ba—cried out ; called. The word 'kai' is used, as well as 'kaai,' to call attention.
Kaibug—a light (of any kind) ; a lamp *or* candle.
Kaibug-gél—the place of a light, as the candlestick.
Kaibulla—*imp.*, call; cry aloud.
Kaibulléïn—cried out ; did cry out ; did shout aloud.
Kaibullía—*imp.*, call out and continue to call.
Kaibulliela—was lifting up the voice ; was shouting.
Kaibulliko—to cry out ; to lift up the voice; to call aloud; to shout. Also, Kaipulliko.
Kaibullinŭn—will call; will cry out ; will shout aloud.
Kaibullinŭn wal—certainly will call *or* shout ; shall call.
Kain—sounds as *Eng.* 'kine.'
Kain—in possession of ; having.
Kaithar—*Lat. pr.n.*, Cæsar.
Kaithar kinko—for (to) Cæsar.
Kaithari-ko— C., as the agent.

Kaitharnug—Cæsar, as the object, *acc.* ; to Cæsar, *dat.*
Kaitharúmba—Cæsar's.
Kaitharúmba-ta—it is what belongs to Cæsar ; that which is Cæsar's.
Kaiulléŭn—ceased; ended.
Kaiulliko—to cease ; to finish.
Kaiwitoara (†Pathak)—passed over ; the Passover.
Kaiyálléa—*imp.*, be silent ; be mute ; cease; leave off.
Kaiyálléakŭn—again to cease *or* leave off.
Kaiyellía—*imper.*, be silent *or* mute ; cease.
Kaiyelliko—to be silent *or* mute ; to cease.
Kaiyellinŭn—will cease.
Kaiyin—an edge; the other side.
Kaiyin-kaiyin—*(plu.)* all sides ; every side.
Kaiyin kolag—over towards the other side.
Kaiyinkon—the side *or* edge.
Kaiyinkon taba—at *or* on the other side *or* edge.
Kaiyin tako—to be over against on the other side.
Kaiyu—power, ability; powerful, able.
Kaiyu kako—unto the power.
Kaiyu-kan—being powerful; being able ; one having power; one having ability.
Kaiyu-kan kanŭn—will be able.
Kaiyu-kan-to—a person having power, as agent.
Kaiyu koa—with (in company with) power ; accompanied by power.
Kaiyu korien—not powerful *or* able ; unable.
Kaiyu-korien-to—unable to act, as an agent.
Kaiyu tin—from (on account of) the power.

BUNTIMAI—'A MESSENGER.'

THE LEXICON.   213

Ka-keún—*definite tense*, it was (early in the morning) this day *or* of the day spoken of.
Kakillai—being and continuing to be.
Kakillan—did remain in a state of (whatever is spoken of).
Kakillieliko—to be and to continue to be.
Kakilli-kan—one who is and continues to be.
Kakilliliela—was being and continuing to be (in such a state).
Kakilliko—to be.
Kakillin—being now actually (in such a state).
Ka korien kakilliko—not to be; to fail to be.
Kakulla—was (in such a state).
Kakullai—to be awhile; to be for a season.
Kakullai-ta—it is for awhile; it endures for a season.
-kál—(*masc.*) belonging to a time *or* place; in a state of; a man of such a place.
-kálín—(*fem.*) belonging to a place; a female of such a place.
Kalog—afar off; far; distant.
Kalog ka—at a distance.
Kalog kaba—being afar off *or* at a distance.
'Kalog-kolag—towards afar off; to a distance.
Kamel—*Eng.*, camel.
Kámunbilla—*imp.*, forgive; let be; permit to be.
Kámunbilla kakilliko—to permit to be in any state or condition.
Kámunbilliko—to cause to let be; to permit to be.
Kámunbin in—will cause to let be; will permit to be.
Kámunbin in wal — will certainly cause to permit to be; shall cause to let be.

Kámunbi yikora—*imp. prohib.*, let not be permitted to be; forbid permission to be; let not be; forbid to be.
Kan — is sounded as *Eng.* 'can.'
Kan-kan—*pres. tense* of the verb to be (in any state); *subst.*, one who is (whatever is stated).
Kanumaiko—to repent.
Kánún—*fut. indef.*, will be; *e.g.*, tetti kánún, 'will be dead,' will be in a state of death.
Kánún kakilliko—to be in such a state; will be; will become; will come to pass.
Kánún wal kakilliko—shall certainly come to pass.
Ka-pa—a particle which implies a denial; 'if it had been.'
Kapaiyinún—will become.
Kapátin—*Eng.*, a captain.
Kapátin-to—a captain, as agent.
Kapernaum—*pr. n.*, Capernaum.
Kapirri—hunger.
Kapirri-kan—one who hungers; being hungry.
Kárá—private; secret; *adv.*, privately; secretly.
Kárá—*the negat.* of being in such a state; equivalent to 'no longer to be.'
Karag—spittle.
Karag-kabilliko—to do spittle; to spit spittle; to spit.
Karai-karai—round about; all round.
Karaigon—*subst.*, the outside; *adv.*, outside.
Karaka—the mouth; an entrance gate *or* door; *i.q.* kurraka.
Karakai—quick; *imp.*, be quick; make haste; *i.q.* kurrakai.
Karákál—one who pretends to cure by charms; a medicine-man; a sorcerer; a doctor.
Karal—trembling; shaking; the palsy.

P

Karauwa—oil.
Kara-uwilliko—to seek carefully with a wish to find.
Kara-uwilli-koa—that ... might find ; in order to find.
Karawolléun — *aorist*, found ; shall have found.
Karawolliko—to find.
Karawollinún—*fut.*, will find.
Kareawuġ—the south wind.
Kári—the first ; *i.q.* kurri.
Kári-kári—a *reduplication* denoting intensity *or* plurality ; the very first.
Kariġ—all through ; throughout the whole.
Kariġ-kareuġ—fine raiment.
Kariġ-kareuġ-ko—fine dress, as the agent.
Karin—pain.
Karín-kan—one who is in pain.
Karol—heat of any kind ; hot.
Katai—always ; to be always ; for ever ; ever.
Kataikál—of every sort.
Ka tako—to be with.
Katalla—had been ; had lived ; had existed.
Kátán—(*present tense* of kakilliko, 'to be in any state') am ; art ; is ; are ; it is used with singular, dual, and plural pronouns.
Katéa—to be again.
Katéa ka—to be until.
Katéa-kan—one who is again ; being again.
Katéa-kanún—will be again.
Katéa-kanún wokka ka—will become again up ; will be again.
Katéa-kún—*subj.*, may be again.
Katilli-kan—one who is the thing spoken of and acts as such ; one who is...
Katilliko—to be (substantively) the thing spoken of ; to be in any state or condition.

Katillín—(substantively) existing as ; if preceded by piriwál, 'chief, lord, king,' it means —does exercise lordship.
Katillinún — will be (substantively), as above.
Kau—sounds as *Eng*, 'cow.'
Kau-ka-uwil—*opt.*, would wish to be.
Kau-ka-uwil koa—*sub.*, in order to be... ; that might be...
Kau-má—gathered together ; assembled.
Kau-ma korien—did not assemble together.
Kau-ma pa—*priv.*, would have gathered together, but
Kau-manún—will cause to come together ; will gather together.
Kau-ma-uwil—*opt.*, wished to gather together ; would gather together.
Kau-ma-ye—one who habitually causes to assemble *or* collect together ; a collector.
Kau-mullan—did assemble together ; did take council.
Kau-mulli-ġél—the place where the gathering together is made ; the place of assembly ; the council chamber ; the parliament house.
Kau-mulliġél lako—*dat.*, to the place of assembly ; to the council.
Kau-mulliko—to cause to gather together ; to collect ; to gather together, as quails their young or a hen her chickens.
Kau-tilliko—to assemble *or* collect together, of themselves.
Kau-tillinún—will of themselves assemble together.
Kauwa—*imp.*, be ; be in such a state. Also, Ka-wa.
Kauwa ba—be it so ; let it be in this manner.

Kauwäl—great; large; big.
Kauwäl kakilliko—to be great.
Kauwäl kakulla—was great.
Kauwäl-kan—one who is great; being great.
Kauwäl-kauwäl—a great many; intensely great; very great.
Kauwäl-kauwäl-la—the many, as the subjects.
Kauwäl-kauwäl-lo—very many, as the agents.
Kauwäl koa—with (in company with) the great...
Kauwäl-la—great, as the subject; much; abundance.
Kauwäl-laġ—is great, large, or abundant; a great deal.
Kauwällan—does greatly...
Kauwäl-lo—great, as an agent.
Kauwäl loa—through the many or great.
Kauwäl loa kokeroa—through the many houses; through the village, town, or city.
Kauwäl-lo konaró—a great multitude (as agents) did, does, or will...(according to the tense of the verb.)
Kauwa yanti—be it so; be it in this manner; be it thus.
Ka-uwil koa yanti—in order to be thus; that ... might be in this manner.
Kau-wiyelliko—to command by word of mouth to assemble together; to call a council; to summon a congregation.
Ke—sounds as *ca* in *Eng.* 'care.'
-ke?—an *interrogative* particle.
Kea-kea—courageous, victorious. Also, Kia-kia.
Kea-kea-má—did cause to conquer; has conquered.
Kearan—*pres. tense neg.*, no, not.
Keawai—*simple negation*, nay; no; not.
Keawai wun-ba—did not leave.

Keawai wal—*determinate negation*, shall not; certainly shall not.
Keawaran—*pres. tense of nega.*, no, it is not; no; not.
Keawaran baġ—*denial*, not I; I am not.
Keawaran-keawai—no; nor.
Kenukun—the large white rock lily; a lily.
Kerun—complete; *i.q.* kirun.
Ki—sounds as *Eng.* 'key.'
Kia-kia—upright; this denotes conquest, victory; because one left standing upright after a combat or battle is the victor.
Kid—*Eng.*, a kid.
-kil—a particle used in the infinitive form of the verb 'to be.'
-killi—particle used as the auxiliary sign of the verb 'to be.'
-killiko—'to be,' as an auxiliary, to indicate the initiation of the action implied by the verb to which it is joined; *e.g.*, búnkilliko — to proceed to smite; from the root bún, 'a blow.'
Kilbuġgulliko—to cause to snap by personal agency; to snap, as a piece of rope; to break, as a cable.
Kilburrilliko—to cause to snap by an instrument.
Kilkulliko—to snap of itself; to break.
Killibinbin—clear; unspotted; bright; shining; pure; glorious.
Killibinbin kaba—in a state of shining glory; in a pure, unspotted, glorious condition.
Killibinbin kakilliko—to be in a bright, glorious state.
Killibinbin kámunbilla—*imper.*, let there be brightness, splendour, glory; glory be.

Killibinbin koa—with (in company with) glory; accompanied with splendour or glory.
Kiloa—like; likeness; resemble; resemblance.
Kilpaiyá—did snap as a cord; broke as a rope breaks.
Kilpaiyelliko—to snap, as a cord snaps when it breaks.
Kin—*prep.*, to; to a *person*.
Kin-ba—with; at; is at; *locally*.
Kinta—fear.
Kinta kakillicla—was afraid; feared and did fear: feared.
Kinta kakilliko—to be in a state of fear; to fear; to be afraid.
Kinta kakulla—was in a state of fear; was afraid.
Kinta-kan—being afraid; one who is afraid; a coward.
Kinta-kan-to—one who fears, as an agent.
Kinta kora—*imp.*, fear not.
Kinta korien—not to fear; no fear.
Kinta-lag—does now fear; is now afraid.
Kinta nakilliko—fearful to see.
Kinta nakilli-ta—(*sing.*) it is fearful seeing; a frightful sight.
Kinta nakilli-tara—*(plu.)* fearful sights.
Kintelléun—did laugh.
Kintelliko—to laugh.
Kintellinún — *fut.*, will laugh.
Kintellinún wal—will certainly laugh; shall laugh.
Kipai—fat; ointment; unction.
Kirai—a ditch; canal.
Kirín—queen; *cf.*, piriwál.
Kiroabatoara—that which is poured out or spilled.
Kiroabullicla—did pour out.
Kiroabullielliko—to continue to pour out; to continue spilling.

Kiroabulliko— to pour out all; to spill. Also, Kiropulliko.
Kiroabullin—now spilling.
Kiroabullinún—will pour out.
Kiroa-pa—shed; is shed or spilt.
Kirrá—gently, carefully.
Kirrai— *see* krai.
Kirrai-kirrai—round about.
Kirrai-kirrai ta ba—surrounded.
Kirrai-kirrai-umulliko—to cause to go round about or revolve, as a windmill; to sift grain, as with a sieve; to bring the chaff to the top.
Kirra-uwolliko—to seek wishing to find; *i.q.* kara-uwilliko.
Kirra-uwolli koa—in order to seek diligently; that...might seek diligently.
Kirráwolliko—to move carefully; to seek diligently.
Kirrikin—clothing; a garment of any kind; cloak; veil; curtain; covering.
Kirrikin-ta—it is the garment.
Kirrikin taba—with the raiment
Kirrikin-to— clothing (raiment, robe), as an agent.
Kirrikin-wuntoara—the raiment or clothes which were left.
Kirrín—light; as, daylight.
Kirrín—pain; fever; agony.
Kirrin kakilliko—to be in a state of pain (fever, agony).
Kirrin-kan—one being in pain or suffering agony.
Kirrin-kan noa—he being in an agony.
Kirrin kátan—is in pain; is in a state of anguish or agony.
Kirul—green, as a young tree.
Kirun—all; the whole.
Kirunta—a creek; a ditch.
Kittug—hair (of the head only).
Kiyubanún—will do with fire.
Kiyubatoara—that which is done with fire (roasted, broiled).

Kiyubulliko—to do with fire; to roast or broil.
Kiyu-pa-ba—done or destroyed by fire; roasted; burned.
Kleopa—*pr.n.*, Cleopas.
Ko-—*particle*, for the purpose of.
Koa—in order to; that...might.
Koai-koai-kakilliko—to be strutting like a turkey-cock; to be lifted up or proud.
Koai-koai-kan — being proud; one who is proud.
Koai-koai korien—not proud.
Koai-koai-umulliko — to make proud.
Koakillai-ta—contention; any strife of words.
Koakillan—strives with words; does quarrel or rebuke.
Koakilléún—did rebuke, &c.
Koakillicla—did rebuke.
Koakilliko—to scold; to quarrel; to contend; to rebuke.
Koakulla—rebuked.
Koatan—swears at. [at.
Koatelliko—to curse; to swear
Koawa—*imp.*, chide; rebuke.
Koba—of or belonging to any *thing*; -ůmba—of or belonging to any *person*.
Kobana—*Eng.*, governor.
Kobana kinko—*dat.* 2, to the governor.
Koba-toara—that which is in possession; that which is obtained.
Koiro—an herb.
Koito—therefore; for; because; consequently.
Koito-ba—therefore as; because it is so.
Koito noa ba—for as he...; for when he...; because he....
Koiwon—rain.
Koiwon tanún ba—as the rain approaches.
Koiyá—murmured; repined.

Koiyelliko—to murmur; to repine; to rebuke.
Koiyelli koa—in order to rebuke; that...might rebuke.
Koiyuġ—fire.
Koiyuġ ka—in the fire; is in the fire.
Koiyuġ kako—in (into) the fire.
Koiyuġ-ko—fire, as an agent.
Koiyún—shyness; shame.
Koiyún-bará-toaró—down ashamed; to be abased.
Koiyún-batoara—that which is become ashamed.
Koiyún kakilliko—to be in a state of shame; to be ashamed.
Koiyún kanun—will be ashamed.
Kokera—habitation; hut; shelter; tent; tabernacle; house; palace; temple.
Kokerá—*dat.*, at or in the house, temple, &c.
Kokerá biruġ—away from out of) the house.
Kokerá ka—*dat.* 1, to the house.
Kokerá kolaġ—*dat.* 2, towards the house.
Kokera kariġ—all the houses; the whole of the houses; the village, town, city.
Kokerá kolaġ kokerá kolaġ—towards the houses; from house to house.
Kokeratín—the master (owner, landlord) of the house.
Kokeratín-to—the master of the house, as an agent.
Kokeroa—through the house.
Kokerrin—from (on account of) the house.
Kokoi-kokoi — surrounded; inclosed.
Kokoin—fresh water; *cf.* bato.
Kokoin-kan—one having water; possessing water; dropsical.
Kokoin-kan-to—a dropsical person, as an agent.

Kokoin-kan warakaġ—one filled with water ; one having the dropsy.
Kokoin kolaġ—to (towards) the water ; going to water.
Kokug—an indigenous fig; a fig.
Kolaġ—towards ; now about to.
Kólbi—sound ; noise ; roar.
Kólbi-laġ-bulliko—to make a sound or noise ; to roar.
Kólbi-laġ-bullin—now making a noise or sounding; roaring as the wind or sea.
Kólbúnti korien—not to chop.
Kólbúntia—chopped ; reaped.
Kólbúntilla—*imp.*, cut down.
Kólbúntilliko—to chop, as with an axe ; to hew ; to mow ; to reap with a hook or any other thing that cuts or chops ; to cut with a sword.
Kólbúntillin—*pres. part.*, chopping ; hewing ; reaping.
Kólbúntillinún—will chop, &c.
Kólbúntinún—will chop, &c.
Kólbúntinún-wal — shall cut ; will certainly chop.
Koli—water; *cf.* kori *and* bato.
Komarra — shade ; a shadow.
Komónba—a drop or clot.
Kóġ—sounds as the *Eng.* 'gong,' but with the o long.
Kóġka—a reed.
Kóġgóġ, kóġóġ—the noise made by any person sound asleep ; hence, to be overpowered with sleep.
Kóġóġ-kan—being sleepy ; one who sleeps.
Kóġóġ-kan-to—one who sleeps, being the agent.
Kón—sounds as the *Eng.* 'cone,' but rather longer, laying the accent on the o.
Konára—tribe ; host; company ; assemblage ; family ; army ; herd ; nation.

Konárrin—from the tribe, as a cause ; because of the tribe, company, assemblage, &c.
Konéin—good to look at; pretty ; handsome ; noble in appearance.
Konéin kakilliko—to be in a beautiful state ; to be pretty; to be handsome ; to be garnished.
Konéin kako—to being pretty.
Konéin-kan—one who is pretty ; being handsome.
Konéin-ta—it is pretty, &c.
Konéin-tara—the pretty things.
Konéin-taró—the pretty (persons or things), as agents.
Konéin-to—pretty, as an agent.
Koin — an unknown being of great power, of whom the aborigines are very much afraid.
Kón-ta—that person, as an agent.
Kón-to-ka—that person as an agent is…
Konuġ—dung ; excrement.
Konuġ-ġél—the place of dung ; a dunghill.
Konuġ-ġél ko—for the dunghill.
Kora—*a mandatory prohibition*; *e.g.*, kinta kora, 'fear not.'
Koradhin—*pr.n.*, Chorazin.
Korakál—*see* korokál.
Kora koa—*interrogative of negation*, why not ?
Korariġ—a lonely place.
Koréa—ceased action ; rested.
Koribibi—strong, rushing, violent ; as a stream of water or the tide of the sea.
Korien—*denial*, not.
Korilliko—to cease action ; to rest ; to be still.
Korimá—did cleanse ; baptised.
Korimanún—will use water to cleanse ; will baptise.
Korimulliela — being cleansed or baptised.

Korimulli-kan—one who cleanses with water ; a baptist.
Korimullikanne—baptism.
Korimullikan-ta—the baptism.
Korimulliko—to use water in any way ; cleanse with water ; *cf.* kori, koli. ' water '; mulliko means ' to do with ' ; hence korimulliko is used to mean ' to baptize,' in any form.
Korimulli koa — that ... might cleanse with water ; that ... might baptise.
Koro-ka—concealed ; was hidden.
Korokál—old, worn out ; said of clothes or property, not of persons.
Koro-kakilliko—to be in a state of concealment ; to hide one's self ; to be concealed.
Korokál la—*dat.*, to the old.
Korokál katéa-kanún—will be again old.
Korowa—the sea ; the waves of the sea.
Korowa tarig—the sea coast ; the seaside ; the coast.
Korug—the inland part of the country ; the interior ; the bush ; the wilderness.
Korug-ka—in the wilderness ; in the bush ; in the interior.
Korug kabirug—from (out of, away from) the bush ; from the country ; from the interior.
Korug tin—from (on account of) the wilderness, as a cause.
Korun—still ; silent ; calm.
Kót—*Eng.*, coat.
Kót-kan—one having a coat.
Kotá—thought ; did think.
Kota ba—when (if)...did think.
Kota-ban kora—*mand.* (participial form), cease thinking.
Kota-bumbilliko—to permit to cause to think ; to let think.

Kota-bunbéa—allowed to cause thought ; did astonish ; made astonished.
Kota korien—thought not.
Kotan—thinks ; does think.
Kotánún—*fut.*, will think.
Kotatoara—thought ; the thing which is thought.
Kota yikora—*mand.* (the verbal form) do not think ; think not ; take no thought.
Kotára—an aboriginal instrument of war called by the Europeans 'a waddy '; a cudgel, made of iron wood, stout in the middle but tapering to a point.
Kotára-kan—one having a cudgel.
Kotáró — the cudgel, as an agent ; with *or* by the cudgel.
Kotella—*mandatory* (the verbal form), do think ; remember ; reflect.
Kotellan—does think.
Kotelléún—*aor.*, did, does, will think ; thought ; thinks.
Kotellía—*mand.* (the participial form), think ; be thinking ; remember ; reflect ; meditate.
Kotelliela—thought ; did think ; was thinking.
Kotelliélliko—to think and continue to think ; to be thinking.
Kotellikanne—the thing which is thought ; imagination ; idea.
Kotelliko—to think ; to be in thought.
Kotellin—*part. pres.*, the action of thought ; thinking.
Kotelli-ta—the thought.
Kóti—a kinsman *or* a neighbour ; a friend ; a guest.
Kótí—personally belonging to self ; own-self ; *e.g.*, giroúmba kótí, ' thine own-self.'

Kóti bula umullan—the two became friends again ; *lit.*, the two were caused to be akin.

Kóti kabirug̃—from (out of) the the self-same.

Kóti kakilliko—to be near of kin; a kinsman, friend, neighbour.

Kóti-ta—(*sing.*) the kinsman or neighbour; friend; guest.

Kóti-tara—(*plu.*) the kinsfolk ; kinsmen ; neighbours ; friends.

Krai—the west ; westward ; inland ; *i.q.* kirrai. [west.

Krai tin—from (because of) the

Kritht—*pr.n.*, Christ.

Kritht-ta—it is the Christ ; the Christ, emphatic.

-kŭl—*particle masc.*, belonging to any locality ; *i.q.* -kál.

-kŭlín—*part. fem.*, belonging to any locality ; *i.q.* -kálín.

Kúlai—wood ; timber ; a tree of any kind.

Kulla—because, for.

-kulla—*postfix particle*, the sign of an aorist tense ; *e.g.*, ka, 'to be' ; ka-kulla, ' was.'

Kullabulliko—to cut round ; to circumcise.

Kullaburra—shining ; glorious ; bright ; resplendent ; glory.

Kulla wal—because certainly ; surely.

Kulla-wal-léa—because certainly ...has *or* did.

Kulleug̃, kulliug̃—the neck.

Kulligticla—cut ; did cut.

Kulligticlliko—to cut, as with a knife or some such cutting instrument.

Kullimulliko—to make use of the toe ; hence, to climb ; because the blacks cut notches in the bark, and, to ascend the trunk of a tree, place the toe therein.

Kulliwá—climbed ; did climb.

Kullo—cheek.

Kulwon—stiff, as a corpse.

Kŭm—sounds as *Eng.* 'come'; *cf.**

Kumara—blood.

Kumara-kan—a bloody person.

Kúmba—to-morrow.

Kúmba-ken-ta—the period of time after to-morrow; the day after to-morrow ; the third day.

Kumbarapaiyelliko—to be troublesome, clamorous, noisy.

Kumbarawan—does trouble, as by some movement or bustle.

Kumbarawilliko—to trouble *or* tease ; to worry.

Kumiri—a shady place ; a hole in a rock ; a cave.

Kummari—northward ; north.

Kummari tin—from the north.

Kummulliko—to cause trouble, anxiety ; to be anxious.

Kummullan—troubled; anxious.

Kŭn—for its sound *cf.**.

Kunbúntéa—did smite with a knife *or* a sword ; cut ; smote.

Kunbúntilliko—to cut with a knife ; to smite with a sword or any similar edged instrument. [be.

Kŭn koa—lest…should *or* might

Kunta—nest ; the nest of a bird.

Kunto—food ; vegetable food, as bread, but not animal food.

Kunto-kan—one having food ; one possessed of food.

Kúri—man ; mankind ; men.

Kúri koba—belonging to men ; of mankind ; of man (*sing.* or *plu.*).

Kúri koba ko—*dat.*, to man's.

Kurinio—*Gr. pr.n.*, Cyrenius.

Kúri tin—from man, as a cause ; on account of man.

Kúri willug̃-g̃él—the men of this place ; those of this generation.

Kurr—sounds as *Eng.* 'cur.'
Kurrag—froth; foam.
Kurrag-to—froth, as an agent.
Kurragtoanbuggulliko—to cause by personal agency to foam.
Kurragtoanbugga—was caused to foam; foamed.
Kurrai-kurrai—to turn round: to go round about; to roll.
Kurraka—the mouth; entrance; doorway; gateway.
Kurraka birug—from (out of) the mouth, &c.
Kurrarakai—be quick; haste ye; *i.q.* karakai.
Kurrauwai—long; length.
Kurrawitai-kan—being clothed with long raiment; robed.
Kurrea—carried; did carry.
Kurri—first; *cf.* kara.
Kurri birug ko—from (out of) the first; from the first.
Kurrig—any.
Kurrig tin—from (on account of) any.
Kurrikog—the first-born male; *cf.* karakog, the elder brother.
Kurri korien — not to carry: carries not; bears not.
Kurri-kurri—*intensive*, the very first; the beginning.
Kurri-kurri ka—is the first.
Kurri-kurri kabirug—from the first; from the beginning.
Kurri-kurri-to—the first, as an agent.
Kirrilliela—bore; was carrying.
Kurrilli-gel—the place of carrying; the carrying places, as the railway.
Kurrilliko—to carry; to bear.
Kurrin — choked; suffocated; stifled; drowned.
Kurrin—carries, bears, brings forth; *cf.* karin.
Kurrinanbai—daughter-in-law.

Kurri-uwil koa—in order that... might carry.
Kurriwulliko—to carry away; to bear away.
Kurri yikora—*mand.*, carry not.
Kurrol—perspiration; sweat.
Kutha—*pr.n.*, Chusa.
Kuttawai — satiety; intoxication; drunkenness; gluttony; giddiness.
Kuttawai-ban—one who satiates; a glutton; a drunkard.
Kuttawai-kan—one who is in a state of satiety.
Kuttawaiko—to be satiated with food or drink; drunkenness; gluttony.
Kuttawai kolag—to be about to satiate with food or drink.
Kuttawaiye—one whose manner is habitually that of being satiated; one habitually a drunkard or a glutton.
Kuttawan—satiated.

L

L—pronounced as *Eng*, 'ell.'
La—is sounded as in *Eng.* 'large.'
Ladharo—*pr.n.*, Lazarus.
Latin—*pr.n.*, Latin.
Latinumba — belonging to the Latin people *or* language.
Le—rhymes with *Eng.* 'lay.'
Lebben—*Eng.*, leaven.
Lebben kiloa—like leaven.
Lebben korien koba—not having leaven; unleavened.
Lebi—*pr.n.*, Levi.
Lebi-kal—a Levite.
Lebi-ko—Levi, as the agent.
Léjun—*Eng.*, legion.
Lepro—*Eng.*, leprosy.
Lepro-kan—one being in a state of leprosy; leprous; a leper.
Lepro-ta—leprosy, as a subject; the leprosy.

Lepton—*Gr.*, a small coin; a mite.
Lepton-ta—a mite; it is a mite.
Lo—sounds as *Eng.* 'lo'!
Lot -*pr.n.*, Lot.
Lotúmba—belonging to Lot.
Luka—*Gr. pr.n.*, Luke.
Luka-úmba—belonging to Luke.
Luthania--*pr.n.*, Lysanias.

M

Ma- *imp.*, do (a challenge).
-ma—an auxil. particle denoting the *perf. past aorist*, did; done
-ma korien—did not; not done.
Mabogun—a widow.
Mabogun koba—belonging to a widow; a widow's.
Magdala-kälín—(*fem.*), a woman of Magdala; Magdalene.
Mai—sounds as *Eng.* 'my.'
Maiya—a snake; a serpent (the genus).
Makoro-ban—one who fishes; a fisherman.
Makoro—fish (the genus).
Makoró—fish, as an agent.
Makoró birug—away from fish; a piece of a fish.
Makorrin—from fish, as a cause; on account of fish.
Malma—lightning.
Mamuya—a ghost, the spirit of a departed person; not the spirit of a living person, which is marai; *cf.* Marai (*not* mamuya) Yirri-yirri 'the Holy Ghost.'
Man—sounds as *Eng.*, 'man.'
-man—as a particle, denotes *the present tense* of the verb causative.
Mankilli-ġél—the place of taking *or* receiving, as the counter of a shop; the bank; the treasury.

Mankilli-kan—one who takes in hand; a doer; a servant.
Mankilliko—to take in hand; to do; to receive.
Mankilli kolaġ—about to take in hand.
Mankillin—now taking; holding; doing; receiving.
Manki-ye—one who is a habitual taker; a thief.
Mankiye-ko—to (against) a thief.
Mankiye nukuġ-ka—a taker of women; a woman stealer; an adulterer.
Manki yikorn—*prohib. imp.*, do not steal; do not take.
Man korien—*neg.*, did not take.
Mankulla—have taken in hand; did take; took.
Man pa—*privative of effect*, unable to take; could not accomplish the taking hold of.
Mantala—did take, at some former period.
Mantan—does take hold of.
Mantilléa—*imp.*, take it.
Mantilliko—to take; to receive.
Mantillin—now receiving.
Mantillinún wal—will certainly take; it shall be taken.
Mantoara—that which is taken, received *or* held; the deposit; the theft.
Manumbilla — *imp.*, permit to take; let take.
Manumbilliko—to allow to take; to let take.
Manún—*fut.*, will take.
Manún wal—will certainly take; shall take.
Mara—*imp.*, take; do take; take hold; receive.
Marai—spirit; soul of a living being not a ghost; which is mamuya.
Marai-kan—one who is a spirit; having a spirit.

Marai-kan-to —one possessing a spirit, acting as an agent.
Marai koba—belonging to the spirit or soul; of the spirit.
Marai-marai—actively engaged doing something; busy; busily employed.
Marai nurúnba—spirits belonging to you; your spirits; your souls.
Marai-to—the spirit, as an agent.
Marai yirri-yirri—the spirit sacred; the Holy Spirit.
Marallía—*imp.*, continue to take; receive.
Marátha—*pr. n.*, Martha.
Mara-uwil—*opt.*, that...... may take.
Mara-uwil koa—*subj.*, in order that...might take or receive.
Mari—*pr. n.*, Mary.
Maro—an indigenous thorn; a thorny bush; a bramble.
Mata-ye—one habitually given to greediness; a glutton. Also, Matayei.
Mataye-koa-katéa-kún—lest any greediness (gluttony, surfeiting) should be.
Máttara—the hand.
Máttárrin—from (on account) of the hand; by the hand, as an instrument.
Máttáró—the hand, as the agent; with the hand.
Máttároa — with (accompanied with or through) the hand, as an instrument.
Matti—*dual*, acts together; did together.
-mau—rhymes with *Eng.* 'cow.'
-ma-u—the causative particle in the optative and subjunctive form of the verb.
Meapa—recently cultivated or planted.

Meapala—*aor. def.*, planted, at some certain time past.
Meapulla—planted; did plant.
Meapullía — *imp.*, plant; do plant.
Meapulliko—to plant, set, cultivate.
Me—sounds as in *Eng.* 'may.'
Mentha—*Lat.*, mint.
Mi—is sounded as *Eng.* 'me.'
Mikan—presence; fronting; in the face of; before.
Mikan-ta—the presence.
Mikan tako—in the presence of; before.
Mimá—did cause to stay.
Mimulliko —to detain; to urge to stay.
Mín—sounds as *Eng.* 'mien.'
Minn—sounds as in *Eng.* 'mint.'
Mina—*Gr.*, a pound.
Minariġ?—what?
Minariġ-bo?—what very thing?
Minarigbo—any selfsame thing; anything.
Minariġ-ke?—what is? what are?
Minariġ tin?—what from, as a cause? wherefore? from what cause? why?
Minbilliko—to crush; to grind.
Minbinún—will grind.
Minbinún wal—will certainly crush or grind; shall grind.
Minka—*imp.*, wait.
Minkéa—remained; waited.
Minki — any mental or moral feeling; the feeling of sympathy; sorrow; compassion; penitence; patience; repentance; pondering.
Minki kabiruġ—from (out of) such a feeling.
Minki kakilliela—was sympathising.
Minki kakillilela—was and continued to sympathise or feel penitent, &c.

Minki kakilliko—to be in a state of inward feeling; to sympathise; to sorrow; to mourn; to be penitent.
Minki kakulla — sympathised; have sympathised.
Minki-kan—one who sympathises or feels sorry and repents.
Minki-kanne—sympathy; any inward feeling; repentance.
Minki-kanne-ta—sympathy it is; the sympathy.
Minki kanán—will sympathise (sorrow, repent).
Minki kátan—sympathises; repents.
Minki korien—without feeling.
Minki-lag — sympathises; feels sorrow; repents.
Minkilliko—to wait (stay, dwell)
Minkin—waits; dwells; delays.
Minnán!—what are actually present? how many? how much?
Minnug?—what things, as the object?
Minnug-ban?—what thing now about (I, we, you, &c.)
Minnug-banún? — what will... do? what will be done?
Minnug-banún-kan?—what now will some one do?
Minnug-banún wal?—what will ...certainly do? what shall be done?
Minnugbo or minnambo—something; anything; somewhat.
Minnugbo - minnugbo — many things; everything; all things.
Minnug-bulliela?—what was going on? what was doing?
Minnug-bulliko—(an interrogative form of the verb) what is doing? what is going on?
Minnug-bulli kolag—about to do something.
Minnug-bullinún?—what will be going on or doing.

Mipparai—honeycomb.
Mipparai kabirug—from (out of) honeycomb.
Mirka—perhaps; i.q. murka.
Mirka-ta—perhaps it is.
Mirkín—virginity; purity.
Mirkun—pure; clean.
Mirobunbillía—imper. and permissive, permit to continue to take care of or save.
Miromá — took care of; did keep; did save.
Miroma-bunbilla—imp., permit to take care of or save.
Miromanún—will take care of; will save; will occupy.
Miroma pa—privative, did (not) take care of; without care of.
Miromulla—imp., take charge of, if necessary.
Miromullía—imp., continue to take care of; save and continue to save.
Miromulli-kan—one who takes charge of (watches over, saves from harm); a saviour.
Miromulliko—to take charge of; to take care of; to watch over; to keep; to save from harm.
Mirrál—desolate; unproductive; barren; poor.
Mirrálla, murulla— a maid; having no husband; barren; poor.
Mirrál kaiko—for the miserable.
Mirrál-lo—the poor and destitute, as agents.
Mirrál-mirrál-kan—one who is in a miserable state; poor; destitute.
Mirrigil — ready; prepared to remove or to go a journey.
Mirro-mirromá—rubbed and continued to rub.
Mirromulliko—to rub.
Mirug—the shoulder.
Mirug ka—on the shoulder.
Mita—a sore.

Mita-mitag—sores ; full of sores.
Mittéa—waited ; did wait.
Mitti—small ; little ; a little one ; the youngest child.
Mitti—the youngest son.
Mitti-ko—the youngest son, as the agent.
Mittilliela — waited and continued to wait ; was waiting ; waited ; stayed ; remained.
Mittilliko—to wait or remain.
Mittillin—now waiting.
Miyá—hindered ; prevented.
Miyelliko—to hinder.
Moiya—cool.
Moiya koa—in order to cool ; that...might cool. [fare.
Mokál—arms ; weapons of war.
Money—*Eng.*, money.
Moni-gél—money-place ; a purse ; a bank.
Moni-ko—money, as the agent.
Morig—a particle ; a very small bit ; a mote ; dust.
Moroko—the sky ; the visible heavens ; heaven.
Moroko kaba—is in heaven.
Moroko kabirug — from (away from) the sky ; from heaven.
Moroko kako—in or to heaven.
Moroko koba—belonging to the sky or heaven.
Moroko lin—from (on account) of heaven, as a cause ; from heaven ; of heaven.
Moron—life.
Moron-ba—lives ; is alive.
Moron-ba-katéa-kánún—will be alive again ; will live again.
Moron kakilliko—to be in a living state ; to be alive ; to live.
Moron-kan ta—they (he) who are alive ; the living.
Moron kánún—will be alive ; will live.
Moron kátan— is in the state of living ; is alive ; lives.

Moron ko—for life.
Moron koa katéa-kún — lest ... should be alive again ; lest ...should be saved alive.
Moron-ta katéa-kánún—life will be again ; the life is to be again. [life.
Moron tin—from (on account of)
Moron tin kátan—from (on account of) being alive.
Mot—sounds as *Eng.* 'mote.'
Mothé—*pr.n.*, Moses.
Mothé-ko—Moses, as the agent.
Mothé-to—Moses, as the agent.
Mothé-to noa—Moses he, as the agent.
Mothé-úmba— belonging to M
Motilliela — did smite on the breast.
Motilliko—to smite the breast.
Mu—sounds as in *Eng.* 'moon.'
Mug—rhymes with *Eng.* 'bung.'
Mugga-má—did wrap up.
Mugga-ma-toara—that which is wrapped up or swaddled.
Muggamulliko--to cause to be covered ; to wrap up in soft 'ti'-tree bark as clothing ; to swaddle ; to swathe.
Mukkaka — the noise which a bird utters ; to cackle ; to crow.
Mukkakaka tibbinto—the crow of a cock.
Mukkin—the form of address to a young female ; maid !
Muláréa-kan—one wounded by an instrument ; one caused to become wounded by an instrument.
Mulug—close by ; nigh at hand.
Mulug kakilliela—was and continued to be close by.
Mulug kakilliko—to be near.
Mum— for its sound *cf.* *.
Mumbilla—*imp.*, lend ; do lend.
Mumbillan—does lend.
Mumbilléin—lent ; did lend.

Mumbilliko—to lend.
Mumbinún—will lend.
Mumbitoara—that which is lent; the loan; the debt.
Mupai— fast, shut, silent, dumb.
Mupai kakilliko—to be fast, as the mouth; to be silent or dumb; to hold your peace.
Mupai kakillinún—will be fast or dumb; will be silent.
Mupai kakulla—was fast; was silent; held their peace.
Mupai umulliko—to cause to be silent or dumb.
Múr—sounds as *mur* in *Eng.* 'murder,' but the *r* is rougher.
Mur—sounds as *Eng.* 'moor'; *cf.* *
Marka—*see* mirka.
Murkun—pure; clean; free of superfluity; *cf.* mirkun.
Muron—ointment.
Murrá--ran; did run.
Murra—to run; to flee away.
Murrabunbilliko—to let run.
Murrabunbilla—*imp.*, let run.
Murrái—good; well; patient; in a general sense; *cf.* murroi *and* murráráġ.
Murrái-kakillikanne—the thing which is in a state of well-being; happy, if in prosperity; patient, if in adversity.
Murrái-kakilliko — to be good; to be well pleased; to be happy.
Murrakin — a young female; maiden; virgin; *cf.* mukkin.
Murrakin-to—a young female, as the agent.
Murrapatoara—that which is run out; anything numbered.
Murrapullikanne—the taxation; the thing that counts *or* numbers.
Murrapulliko—to run out; to number; to tax each one.
Murráráġ—good; right; just; proper.

Murrá-murráráġ *intens.*, very good; excellent.
Murráráġ kakilli-kan—one who is and continues to be in a good state; one who is righteous; a righteous one.
Murráráġ kakillikanne — anything that is good *or* righteous; righteousness.
Murráráġ kakilliko—to be in a good state; to be well off *or* happy.
Murráráġ koiyelliela — worshipped.
Murráráġ koiyelliko—to be good, in manner; to worship.
Murráráġ-tai—the good, indefinitely; the just; the righteous.
Murráráġ-ta—a good thing.
Murrárog-tara—good things.
Murráráġ wiyelliela—was saying good; was praising.
Murráráġ wiyelliko—to speak good; to praise.
Murrariġ—within; into; inside.
Murriṅg—forward; onward.
Murriṅg kolaġ—about to go forward.
Murrin — the body; *cf.* marai —the soul; the spirit.
Murrinauwai—a floating vessel; canoe; boat; ship; the ark.
Murrin kiloa—like a body.
Murrin ko—for the body.
Murrin tin—from (on account of) the body, as an instrumental cause.
Murrin-murrin—frequent; very often; often-times.
Murroġ-kai—a sort of wild dog, like a fox.
Murroi—peaceful; at his ease; in peace; *i.q.* murrái; *cf.* also murráráġ.
Murrulliko—to run away; to flee.
Murruġ—within; in; *locally.*

Murruġ ka—is within; is inside.
Murruġ ka temple la—is inside or within the temple.
Murruġ-ka-má—pressed upon.
Murruġ-kámulliko—to cause to let be overcome, as water runs within and overcomes; to let be choked or drowned.

Murruġ-ká-ma—was caused to let be overcome or smothered; was choked.
Murruġ kolaġ—about to go in.
Muta-mután—powder; dust.
Mutard—*Eng.*, mustard.
Mutuġ—a crumb; a small piece; a bit; a mote.

NOTE.—*This Lexicon is incomplete; the author was working on it at the time of his death.*—ED.

PART IV.

THE APPENDIX.

APPENDIX.

(A.)

A SHORT
GRAMMAR AND VOCABULARY
OF THE
DIALECT SPOKEN BY THE MINYUG PEOPLE,
on the north-east coast of New South Wales.
(By the Rev. H. Livingstone, Wimmera, Victoria.*)

I. THE GRAMMAR.

The Minyuġ dialect is spoken at Byron Bay and on the Brunswick River. The natives on the Richmond River have a sister dialect called the Nyuġ; those on the Tweed call their own Gando *or* Gandowāl, but the Minyuġ they call Gendo. The words minyuġ and nyuġ mean 'what'? or 'something,' for they are used either interrogatively or assertively. Similarly, the words ġando and ġendo mean 'who'? or 'somebody.' These three dialects are so closely related that they may be regarded as one language; it is understood from the Clarence River in New South Wales northward to the Logan in Queensland. For this language the aborigines have no general name.

It is well known that the Australian dialects are agglutinative, everything in the nature of inflection being obtained by suffixes. To this, the Minyuġ is no exception; so that, if I give an account of its suffixes, that is nearly equivalent to giving an exposition of its grammar. It will, therefore, be convenient to take, first, such suffixes as are used with the noun and its equivalents, and, afterwards, those that may be regarded as verbal suffixes. The words that take what may be called the noun-suffixes are (1) Nouns, (2) Adjectives, and (3) Pronouns.

NOUNS and ADJECTIVES.

As the same general principles apply to both nouns and adjectives, these may be examined together as to (1) Classification, (2) Number, (3) Gender, (4) Suffixes.

---

*Written for this volume at my request.—Ed.

1. CLASSIFICATION.

Nouns in Minyuġ may be arranged thus :—

Life-nouns.

(1.) Persons (*masc.*); all proper and common names of males.
(2.) Persons (*fem.*); all proper and common names of females.
(3.) Animals; all other living creatures.

Non-life nouns.
(1.) Names of things.   (2.) Names of places.

I divide them into *life-nouns* or nouns denoting living beings, and *non-life nouns* or names of things and places, because the former often join the suffixes to lengthened forms of the nouns, while the non-life nouns have the suffixes attached to the simple nominative form. Again, subordinate divisions of both of these classes is necessary, because the adjectives and pronouns often vary in form according as they are used to qualify names of human beings, or animals, or things.

A few examples will make this plainer. If a man who speaks Minyuġ is asked what is the native word for 'big' or 'large,' he replies, kumai. This kumai is the plain or vocabulary form, which may be used on all occasions to qualify any kind of word. But if a native is speaking of a 'large spear,' he will usually say kuminna ćuan. Either kumai *or* kuminna will suit, but the longer form is more common; kuminna is used only to qualify such things as spears, canoes, and logs, and never to qualify persons and places. If a native is speaking of a 'big man,' while he might say kumai paigál, the usual form is kumai-bin, which is then a noun; but since all nouns can also be used as adjectives, the longer form kumai-bin paigál is also correct. To express, in Minyuġ, 'that boy is big,' we might say either kully kumai-bin ćubbo, *or* ćubbo kumai. The feminine form of kumai is kumai-na-gun, which is only the suffix -gun added to the form in -na; like kumai-bin, this is either a noun, when it means 'a big woman,' or an adjective used to qualify a feminine noun. The suffix -gun is sometimes added to the plain form; as, mobi, 'blind,' mobi-gun, *fem.*; sometimes to the masculine form; as, baliġ-gál, 'new,' 'young,' baliġ-gál-gun, *fem.*; and sometimes to the form in -na; as, kumai-na-gun. Some adjectives have only two forms, while others have three, four, and even five. In some cases different words are used, instead of different forms of the same word. The principal suffixes used for the masculine are, -bin, -gin, -jára, -rim, -ri, -li, -gári, -gál. The table given below, for ordinary adjectives, adjective pronouns, and numerals, illustrates these uses. Forms rarely used have a † after them.

THE MINYUNG DIALECT.

EXAMPLES of the SUFFIXES of ADJECTIVES.

Plain form, qualifying any noun.	Masculine form or masculine noun.	Feminine form or feminine noun.	Form qualifying animals and places.	Form in -n or -na qualifying things.
1.	2.	3.	4.	5.
Kunai, 'big, large.'	Kunai-bin.	Kunai-na-gun.	Kunai.	Kunai-nyon.*
Bijug, 'small,' like a point.	Bijug-bin.	Bijug-na-gun.	Bijug-galug.	Bijug-nan.
Korára, 'tall, long.'	Kora-rim.	Kora-na-gun.	Korara.	Kora-na.
Bumbai, 'straight.'	Bumbai-bin.	Bumbai-na-gun.	Bumbai.	Bumbai-na.
Yilyul, 'sick.'	Yilyul-gári.	Yilyul-gár-gun.	Yilyul-gári.	
Kujin, 'red.'	Kuj-árim.	Kuj-ári-gun.	Kuj-ári.	Kujin-na.
Balin, 'new'; 'young.'	Balig-gál.	Balig-gál-gun.	Balig-gál.	Balig-gun-na.
Kurella, 'old.'	Kiéon.	Merrug	Kurella.	Kurella-na.
Mobi, 'blind.'	Mobi.	Mobi-gun.	Mobi; mobi-gári.	*also*
Kugári, 'mad.'	Kugári.	Kugári-gun.		Kumin-na.
Pronouns.				
Kully, kullait, 'this here'; 'he (she, it) here.'	Kully.	Kulla-na-gun.	Kully.	Konno.
Mully, mullait, 'that there'; 'he (she, it) there.'	Mully.	Mulla-na-guní.	Mully.	Monno.
Kaiby, 'another.'	Kaibi-jára.	Kaibi-jára-gun.	Kaiby.	Kaibi-na.
Numerals.				
Yahúru, 'one.'	Yaburu-gin.	Yaburu-gin-gun.	Yaburu.	Yabunon.
Bula, bulait, 'two.'	Buláiry†.	Buláiri-gun†.	Bula.	Bula-na.

The adjective dukkai, 'dead,' takes numerous forms; thus :—
2. dukkai, dukkai-bin†; 3. touara-gun, dukkai-gun†, dukkai-bin-gun†, dukkai-gun-bin†; 4. dukkai, dukkai-bin†.

2. NUMBER.

Nouns and adjectives do not change their form to denote number. The word paigàl may mean one 'man,' or any number of 'men.' With regard to the pronouns, some of them are singular, some dual, some plural, and some of them indefinite so far as number is concerned. The number of a noun is generally known by the use in the same sentence, or in the context, of a singular, dual, or plural pronoun, or by the scope of the sentence or other surrounding circumstances.

3. GENDER.

There are two ways by which the feminine is distinguished from the masculine—either by a different word or by adding the termination -gùn, of which the *u* is always short; as :—

Masculine.	*Feminine.*
Mobi, 'a blind man.'	Mobi-gun, 'a blind woman.'
Yérubilgin, 'a male singer.'	Yérubilgin-gun, 'a female singer.'
Kićom, 'old man.'	Merruġ, 'old woman.'
Ċubbo, 'boy.'	Yagàri, 'girl.'
Koroman, male 'kangaroo.'	Imarra, female 'kangaroo.'

PRONOUNS.

These are :—(1) Personal pronouns, (2) Demonstratives, (3) Indefinite pronouns, (4) Numerals, and 5) Interrogatives.

Personal pronouns.

Singular. Gai, 'I.'   Wé, 'thou.'   Nyuly, 'he'; nyan, 'she.'
Plural. Gully, 'we.'   Buly, 'you.'   Cannàby, 'they.'

The Minyuġ has no simple dual, although there are compound terms and phrases denoting the dual number; such as, gulliwé, gullibula, 'we two'; wé ġerriġ, 'you two,' 'you and another.' The personal forms of bula are sometimes used as dual pronouns; as, bulaily, 'they two,' *masc.*, and bulaili-gun, 'they two, *fem.*; and even such phrases as wé ġerriġ bulaily and wé ġerriġ bulaili-gun, 'you two,' are used.

Demonstratives.

Besides these, there is a peculiar class of words, which may be called demonstratives. When used as predicates, they have the general meaning of 'here,' 'there,' *or* 'yonder.' They are often used as demonstrative adjectives, and then mean 'this,' 'that 'these,' 'those.' As such, they usually agree in form with the nouns which they qualify, that is, they take similar suffixes. Often, however, the noun is omitted, and then they become true personal pronouns, retaining whatever suffix they would have if the noun were used. For example, the word kully, used as a predicate, means 'here'; as, paigál kully, 'a man is here'; but paigál kully yilyul means 'this man is sick'; and, omitting paigál, kully yilyul means 'he is sick'; kully thus means 'here'; 'this'; 'the'; 'he here'; 'she here'; and 'it here.'

Such words are real demonstratives, and must be carefully distinguished from ordinary adverbs of place; for, often an adverb of place is, as it were, promoted to the rank of a demonstrative, and in this way it may come to take the place of a personal pronoun. This may account for the fact that the third personal pronouns are so numerous, and have little or no etymological connection in Australian dialects. These demonstratives are kully, mully, killy, kunde, kanyo, mún, kam, kaka, ka, and kaba. As these are sometimes doubled or reduplicated and have some other variations in form, the following scheme may be convenient :—

Singular.   Plural.

I.—Kully, kú-kully, 'this'; 'the';
   'he (she, it) here'; 'this here.'
II.—Kulla-na-gun, 'this'; 'she here.'   Múnyo;
III.—Konno, ko-konno, 'this'; 'it here,'   sometimes
IV.—Kúlly, kú-kully; kúkai;   mún.
   kullai, kú-kullai; 'here.'

I.—Mully mú-mully, 'that'; 'the';
   'he (she, it) there.'
II.—Mulla-na-gun, 'that'; 'she there.'   Kámo, ka-kámo;
III.—Monno, 'it there.'   sometimes
IV.—Mully, mú-mully;   kám,
   mullai, mú-mullai; 'there.'

I.—Killy, ki-killy, 'yon'; 'he';
   'he (she, it) yonder.'
II.—Killa-na-gun, 'yon'; 'she yonder.'
III.—Kundy, 'it there'; 'it.'   Kaka.
   Kanyo, ka-kanyo, 'this'; 'it near.'
IV.—Kanyo, ka-kanyo, 'here.'

I. is the common masculine form used as an adjective or pronoun. II. is the feminine form so used. III. is the neuter form so used. IV. is used as a predicate for masculine, feminine, and neuter.

Demonstratives used either as singular or plural are—ka, 'it'; plu., 'they in that place there'; kaba, 'it'; plu., 'they there.'

The Nyuġ dialect, instead of kully and mully, has muġga and kuġga; thus:—

	Singular.		Plural.
Masculine.	Feminine.		
Muġga.	Muġgun.		Maka.
Kuġga.	Kuġgun.		Kaka.

Kaka is thus a recent addition to the Minyuġ dialect. It is at present almost exclusively used instead of ćannaby. Maka is sometimes used for mully, but always as a singular. Kuġga is used in the sense of 'he out there.' So it is evident that ka is the root form of all the demonstratives beginning with k, and ma of those beginning with m. Most of the plural demonstratives are formed from ka and ma; thus, kama consists of ka+ma, maka of ma+ka, and kaka of ka+ka; yet there are many doubled forms that are singular. Ma, however, is used, but not as a demonstrative. Ka, ma, ly, ba, and nyo are all root-forms.

Indefinite pronouns.

There are four indefinite pronouns:—Kurrálbo, 'all'; kaiby, 'another'; undúru, unduru-gun, unduru-na, 'some'; and ġerriġ, 'both'; to these may be added the adjective kumai, which is sometimes used in the sense of 'much' *or* 'many.'

Kurrálbo has but one form, viz., kurrál, but it is never used without the addition of the ornamental particles, -bo *or* -juġ. The four forms of kaiby have been given already. Gerriġ has but one form.

Numerals.

Strictly speaking, the language has only two words, yaburu and bula, that can be called numerals. Yet, by doubling and repeating these, counting can be carried on to a limited extent; as,

Yabúru, 'one.'	Bula-bula, 'four.'
Bula, 'two.'	Bula-bulai-yaburu, 'five.'
Bulai-yaburu, 'three.'	Bula-bula-bula, 'six'; &c.

Yabúrugin, and yaburu-gin-gun are sometimes used for the singular personal pronouns, and bulaily and bulaili-gun for the dual. Other uses of these numerals may be seen in—yaburugin yùnbully, 'go alone' (said to a male); yaburugingun yùnbully, 'go alone' (said to a female); yaburu-min-ba, 'at once,' *or* 'with one blow,' 'with one act'; bula-nden, 'halves'; bula-ndai, bula-ndai-gun, 'twins.'

Interrogatives.

In Minyuġ, the difference between an interrogative sentence and an assertive one consists, not in any different arrangement of the words, but simply in the tone of the voice. Therefore the words which we call interrogatives have also assertive meanings. For example, the expression ġen kuġgallen, taken as an assertive, means 'somebody calling,' but, as an interrogation, 'who is calling'? thus, ġen represents 'who'? *or* 'somebody'; it is used like the life-nouns and personal pronouns. In the same way, minya, minyuġ, minyuġbo, mean 'what'? or 'something.' There is also inji, winjit, which means 'where'? or 'somewhere.' Another word of the same kind is yilly, 'in what place'? and 'in some place.' Such words are the connecting links between the nouns and the verbs.

4 (*a*). SUFFIXES TO NOUNS.

The suffixes used with nouns are the following:—

1. -o.

This is usually said to be the sign of the agent-nominative case, but it also denotes an instrumental case; *e.g.*, human ġaio wanye murrunduġgo, 'I will beat you *with-a-club*.' Here the words for *I* and for the *club* both have this suffix. Yogům ġai yuġgan bumbumbo, 'I cannot go *with-swollen-feet*.' Here the word, '*swollen feet*,' has this form.

2. -nye, -ne, -e, -ġe.

This may be called the accusative suffix. It usually follows the use of such transitive verbs as buma, 'beat'; na, 'see'; iġga, 'bite'; wia, 'give to'; bura, 'take out.' As a general rule, only life-nouns and personal pronouns take this suffix. Non-life nouns retain their plain nominative form. Since adjectives and adjective pronouns agree in form with the nouns they qualify, it follows that they have a twofold declension. The accusative form of 'that man' is mullanye paiġännye; of 'that tomahawk,' the accusative is mully bundan.

Examples of its use are :—Mullaio ġunye yilyulman, 'he will make me sick.' Wanye yilyulman mullaio, 'he will make thee sick.' Gaio mullanye yilyulman, 'I will make him sick.'

Sometimes either the form in -o or in -nye is omitted.

3. -na, -a.

This is used to denote the genitives; as, paiġanna koġgara, 'a man's head'; taiéumma jennuġ, 'a boy's foot.' This form in -na belongs only to life-nouns and words connected with them. It is the same that is used with adjectives qualifying things; so that unduruna éuan may mean either 'some spear' or 'somebody's spear.' There are also other forms to denote possession. When followed by this case, the interrogative minyuġ takes the sense of 'how many'? as, minyuġbo kittomma nogům? 'how many dogs has the old man'?

4. -go, -go-by, -gai.

The meaning of these is 'to, of, for.' The by may be taken as a variation of bo, and, like bo, very little more than an ornament of speech. Go is suffixed to all kinds of nouns to denote 'to,' -go-by and sometimes -go to non-life nouns, in the sense of 'for,' and gai to life-nouns, in the same sense.

Examples of its use are:—Yilly ćubbulgun killagóby kundalgóby, 'where is the paddle of that canoe'? Gaio kindan junaġ bundango, 'I will make a handle for the tomahawk.' Gaio ćuan kinan ćubbogai biaġgai ġerriġgai, 'I will make spears for both the boy and the father.'

5. -gál, -jil, -gál-lo, -na-gál, -na jil.

The suffixes -go and -gál correspond to one another in the sense of 'to' and 'from.' Inji-go wé means 'where are you going to'? inji-gál wé is 'where are you coming from'? ġai kamgál, 'I come from there.' Jil is a variant-form seldom used. The life-nouns add -gál *or* -jil to the form in -na; as, paigánna-gál, 'from the man.' Sometimes -gál takes the form gál-lo, and then has the meaning, of 'in coming' *or* 'when coming.' This is apparently the agent-nominative added to a strengthened form in -gál.

6. -ba.

Ba is simply a locative form. Probably there is some connection between it and -bo and -by, which may be regarded as little more than ornaments. It is sometimes found as a termination to names of places. Its principal use as a noun-suffix is to strengthen the simple forms of life-nouns, and thus form a new base for the addition of the suffixes.

7. -ma, -bai-ma.

Ma is rarely used as a noun-suffix, but, when so used, it has the meaning of 'in'; *e.g.*, walo dulbaġga ballunma, 'you jump in the river'; the longer form is used with life-nouns; as, warré paigál-baima konno, 'carry this with the man.'

8. -a, -bai-a.

This takes the meaning of 'from,' 'out of.' Examples of its use:— bura junaġ bundanda, 'pull the handle out of the tomahawk'; bura monno ćuan pagálbaia, 'pull that spear out of the man.' It often denotes possession; as, ġaiabaia ćuan, 'I have a spear.'

9. -e, -ai, -ji, -bai

This is the converse of the particle -a; it means 'into.' Ji is used with nouns ending in -in; as, umbin-ji, 'in the house.' Ba-i has the *i* added to the strengthening suffix *ba*; as, pagálbai, 'in the man.'

10. -no, -ba-no.

This is used after certain verbs of motion; as, koroally wè bon-no, 'go round the camp'; but koroally paigál-bano, 'go round the man.' It is also used in such sentences as kaġga kúg ballunno, 'carry water from the river.' Its meaning may be given as 'from,' 'around,' 'apart,' and the like.

11. -urrugan.

This means 'with.' It may be regarded as a kind of possessive; *e.g.*, yilly nogùm-urrugan paigál may be translated, 'where is the dog's master'? *or* 'where is the man with the dog'? There is a phrase waluġàra, 'you also,' which has some connection with this; the ġ is intrusive between vowels to prevent hiatus.

12. -jùm.

Jùm means 'without.' Yilly nogùm jùm paigál? 'where is the dog without a master'? This is one of the verbal suffixes.

13. -gerry.

The peculiarity of this suffix is that, whilst it follows the rules of the noun-suffixes, it has a verbal meaning. For instance, kwáġ-gerry ġai, 'I wish it would rain'; nyan minyuġ-gerry kúg, 'she wants some water'; ġai killa-gerry umbin-gerry, 'I would like to have that house'; yogùm gai mulla-gerry ćulgun-gerry, 'I do not like that woman.'

Many of these are merely additions to the simple nominative case, and are not used for inflection. To these may be added the suffix -bil, which is used to turn some nouns into adjectives; as, woram, 'sleep,' woram-bil, 'sleepy.' All terms for relatives are usually strengthened by -jàra and -jàr-gun; *e.g.*,

Yirabúġ } a 'malecousin.' Yirabúġ-gun } a 'female cousin.'
Yirabúġ-jàra   Yirabúġ-jàr-gun

Adjectives generally agree in termination with the nouns they qualify; but it should be noticed they do not follow any hard and fast rule. The suffix may be dropped from the adjective; more frequently it is dropped from the noun and retained with the adjective; and rarely, when the sentence can be understood without it, it is dropped from them both. On the other hand, this rule is carried out to an extent that surprises us. For instance, nubuġ and nubuġ-gun mean 'husband' and 'wife,' but the longer form of nubuġ-gun is nubuġ-jàr-gun. Now, Kibbinbaia means 'Kibbin has,' and to say 'Kibbin has a wife,' would usually be Kibbinbaiagun nubuġjàrgun. Again, bura jin ġaiabaia mia would mean 'take the speck out of my eye'; where ġaiabaia and mia agree in termination, yet mia has the shorter non-life form and ġaiabaia has the longer life form.

Suffixes as Verbal Interrogatives.

The interrogatives seem to be the connecting link between the nouns and the verbs. This arises from the fact that they take both the noun and the verbal suffixes. For instance, while inji 'when'? takes, at times, the forms inji-go and inji-gàl, it also becomes inji-gun and inji-gun-ga, and these last terminations are verbal suffixes. The word minyuġ 'what'? may also take such forms as these:—minyuġallela? 'what are you doing'? minyuġen? 'what is the matter'? minyuġoro? 'what is done'? In form, there is really no distinction between interrogative and assertive sentences; hence any interrogative may have also an assertive meaning; minyuġallela ġai, therefore, may mean 'I am doing something.' In this dialect, there is a grammatical distinction between the imperative, the affirmative, and the negative forms of speech; but all these forms may be made interrogative by the tone of the voice.

Suffix-postpositions used with Nouns and Pronouns.

It may be as well to ask, at this stage, if there are any prepositions in Minyuġ. There is a large number of words denoting place; most of them are simple adverbs, and some of them demonstratives, and some occasionally have such a relationship to the noun that they can only be regarded as fulfilling the office of prepositions. They are not always placed before the noun, the Minyuġ having the greatest freedom with respect to the collocation of words. The word kam, which is among the demonstratives, may also be regarded at times as a preposition. When a native says walo kam kubbàl kyua, which is, literally, 'you to scrub go,' why should not kam be called a preposition? In the same way, kaġga kubbàl means 'out to the scrub.'

There are a few words of this kind that have a limited inflection; *e.g.*, balli *or* ballia means 'under'; juy, jua, junno are 'down,' 'into'; bundagàl, bundagàlly, bundagàlla, 'near.' Of these, the particular form used is that which agrees in termination with the noun qualified.

Every word in Minyuġ ends either with a vowel or a liquid, and there are certain euphonic rules to be followed in connecting the suffixes with each kind of ending. In the following tables examples will be given of each kind. In Table I., all the inflecting suffixes will be joined to mully. In Table II. will be found the singular personal pronouns, which contain some irregularities, and a life-noun ending in *l, m, n, ng, ra,* or *o*. It will, however, be unnecessary to give in full the declension of these.

In Table III., four non-life nouns are chosen, ending in *-l, -n, -in,* and *-ra,* and the terminations given are those numbered 1, 8, 9, From these examples, all other forms can be understood.

EXAMPLES of the USE of SUFFIXES.

TABLE I.

	Suffixes as used		General meaning.	Suffixes as joined to -mully	
	With life nouns.	With non-life nouns.		With life-nouns.	With non life-nouns.
1.	O.	O.	Action.	Mullai-o.	Mullai-o.
2.	Nye, ne, ge, &c.	Same as *Nom.* 1.	Accusative.	Mulla-nye.	Mully.
3.	Na, a.	Not in use.	Genitive.	Mulla-na.	....
4.	Gai, go.	Go, go-by.	'For; to; of.'	Mulla-gai.	Mulla-go, -goly.
5.	Na-gal, na-jil.	Gal, gal-lot.	'From.'	Mulla-na-gal.	Mulla-gal.
6.	Ba.	Ba.	'At; with.'	Mulla-ba.	Mulla-la.
7.	Bai-ma.	Ma.	'In.'	Mulla-bai-ma.	Mulla-ma.
8.	Ba-ia.	A, ba-iat.	'From; out of.'	Mulla-ba-ia.	Mulla.
9.	Bai.	E, ai, ji.	'Into; in; to.'	Mulla-bai.	Mully.
10.	Ba-no.	No.	Indefinite.	Mulla-bano.	Mulla-no.
11.	Urrugan.	Urrugan.	'With.'	Mull-urrugan.	Mull-urrugan.
12.	Jum.	Jum.	'Without.'	Mulla-jum.	Mulla-jum.
13.	Gerry.	Gerry.	Verbal; 'wish or like.'	Mulla-gerry.	Mulla-gerry.

EXAMPLES of the DECLENSION of NOUNS and PRONOUNS by the USE of SUFFIXES.

TABLE II.

Case.	Ngai, 'I.'	Wé, 'thou.'	Nyuly, 'he.'	Paigal, 'a man.'	Nogum, 'a dog.'	Kibbin, 'a man's name.'	Biang. 'a father.'	Kéra, 'a cockatoo.'	Chubbo, 'a boy.'
Nom. 1.	Ngai.	Wé.	Nyuly.	Paigal.	Nogum.	Kibbin.	Biang.	Kéra.	Chubbo.
2.	Ngaiot.	Wálo.	Nyulaio.	Paigallo.	Nogumbo.	Kibbindo.	Bianggo.	Kéro.	Chubboio.
Acc.	Nganye.	Wanye.	Nyulanye.	Paiganye.	Nogumme.	Kibbinye.	Biangge.	Kenne.	Chubbonge.
Gen.	Nganna.	Wangga.	Nyulangga.	Paiganna.	Nogumma.	Kibbinna.	Biangga.	Kenna.	Chubbonga.
Dat. 1.	Ngaia.	Wia.	Nyulangai.	Paigalgai.	Nogumgai.	Kibbingai.	Bianggai.	Kéragai.	Chubbogai.
Abl.	Nguiabáno.	Wiabano*.	Nyulabano.	Paigalbano.	Nogumbano.	Kibbinbano.	Biangbano.	Kérabano.	Chubbobano.

* *Or* Wanggabano.

TABLE III.

Case.	Kundal, 'a canoe.'	Bundan, 'a tomahawk.'	Umbin, 'a house.'	Wébara, 'a fire-stick.'
Nom. 1.	Kundal.	Bundan.	Umbin.	Wébara.
2.	Kundallot.	Bundando.	Umbinjo.	Wébaro.
Dat. 2.	Kundálle.	Bundande.	Umbinje.	Wébare.
Abl.	Kundálno.	Bundanno.	Umbinnyo.	Wébanna.
Abl. 2.	Kundálla.	Bundanda.	Umbinja.	Wébara.

VERBS.

4 (b). Suffixes to Verbs.

Imperative and Affirmative Forms.

The imperative, in the Minyuġ dialect, is the simplest form of the verb; it will therefore be quoted as the stem of the verb. In true verbs, it ends in *-a* or *-e*; as, kulga, 'cut,' buġge, 'fall.' If the *-a* or *-e* is cut off, there remains the root of the verb, and to it the verbal suffixes are attached. These are very numerous, and appear, at first sight, to be very complicated; but the whole may be simplified by taking them in the following order :—(1) Final suffixes; (2) Internal strengthening particles or letters; and (3) Separable demonstrative particles. The usual final suffixes are :—

1. *-a, -e,* used in giving a command or in expressing a wish.
2. *-ala, -ela,* denoting present action.
3. *-an,* denoting future action.
4. *-anne, -inne, -unne,* denoting unfinished past action.
5. *-oro,* denoting finished action.
6. *-en,* the historical past tense; often an aorist participle.
7. *-inna,* used, but rarely, as a participle.
8. *-ian,* past time; with passive sense, when required.
9. *-ia, -ē, -aia,* when used with a leading verb, has a future meaning, but it is generally the infinitive or noun form to express verbal action.
10. *-ai,* may be called the subjunctive, but the verb does not take this form in all positions where we might expect a subjunctive to be used.
11. *-enden, -unden, -anden,* is probably derived from *kinda,* the sixth form of which is *kinden.* It adds the idea of 'made' or 'did' to the root idea of the verb. It is sometimes equivalent to the passive, and at times it becomes the foundation of another verb, so that there are such forms *-endene, -endeloro,* &c. It sometimes takes, between it and the root, the strengthening particles of the next paragraph.
12. The internal strengthening particles are (1) *le, l, r, re,* (2) *g, ng-g, ing-g,* and (3) *b.* These are inserted between the root and and the final suffix, and are sometimes compounded together, so that there are such form as *galle* and *balle.* These particles add but little to the meaning. It may be that *le* or *re* gives a sense of continuance to the action, so that while *ala* is a simple present, while *alela* may be a progressive present. This, however, is very doubtful. In fact, it may be stated, once for all, that while there is an abundance of forms, the aborigines do not seem to make very exact distinctions in meaning between one form and another.

If it is desired to give emphasis to the idea that the action is continuative, a separate word is used to denote this. Thus *alen*, which is the strengthened form of *en*, is purely a participle without distinction of time. The forms in *r*, *re* are simple variations of *le*, and seldom used. The forms in *g*, *ng-g*, are from **ga**, 'to go on,' and those in *b* from **ba**, 'to make,' 'cause to be.' The following table will show the various possible forms in which a verb may be found. The separable demonstrative particles inserted in the table are:—*be*, *bo*†, *yun*, *de*, *ji*. *Bo* and *be* seem to add nothing to the meaning; *yun* means 'there'; *di* or *ji* means 'to' or 'at.'

The Suffixes as attached to the root-form of Verbs.

To the forms in italics, the *separable* demonstrative particles are added.

	Simple		Compound		
*1. -a, -e, -ade.	-alé. -elé. -errat†.	-ga. -gga.	-galé. -ggale.	-ballé.	
2. -ala. -ela.	-alela. -elela. -erralat†.	-gala. -ggala.	-galela. -ggalela.	-bulela.	
3. -an. -anbe. -anji.	-lan. -rant†.	-gan. -ggan.			
4. -anne. -inne. -unne.	-alinne.	-gàune. -ggàune.	-galinne. -ggalinne.	-bulenne.	
5. -oro.	-aloro. -eloro. -*aloroby.*		-galoro. -ggalore. -*galoroby.*		
6. -en. -*enyun.*	-allen. -arent†. -*allenji.*	-gen. -ggen. -*genji.*	-gallen. -ggallen. -*gallenji.*	-bulen. -*bulenji.* -*bulenyun.*	

7. -inna; 8. -ian; 9. -ia, -aia, -ē; compound, -alia; 10. -ai; compound, -bai; 11. -enden; compound, -genden, -ggenden; -bunden.

*The numbers indicate the Moods and Tenses; thus, 1 is *the Imperative Mood*; 2, *The Present Tense*; 3, *The Future Tense*; 4, *The Past (unfinished)*; 5, *The Past (finished)*; 6, *A Participle form (often past)*; 7, *A Participle form (generally present)*; 8, *A Participle form (often passive)*; 9, *A Noun form of Verbal action (the infinitive)*; 10, *The Subjunctive*, i.e., *the form which the verb takes when compounded with Auxiliary Verbs*; 11, *A Participle form (generally passive.)* 2, 3, 4, and 5 are of the Indicative Mood.

Besides these, there are some other compound verbal suffixes which are formed from *inda* and *ma*, and from *b* and *ba*, as shown below. These are sometimes attached, not to the simple stem-form of the verb, but to specially lengthened forms.

Kinda, 'make.'

This, as a principal verb, has all the forms of the simple suffixes except No. 11, and many of the compound ones; as, kinda-bulela, kinda-galoroby, &c. It sometimes takes the form, though rarely, of kiġge, and, as such, enters into composition with other verbs; but the usual method of compounding it with verbs is to omit the *k*, and use only the terminations; as, bo-alé, 'be great,' bo-indalé, 'be made great.' In the Minyuġ dialect, when two words are brought together, it is common for the second to lose its initial consonant. *Kinda* itself is a derivative from *da*, which is in use to turn nouns and adjectives into verbs; as, umbin, 'a house,' umbin-da, 'make a house.'

Ba, 'cause to be.'

Ba, as a locative, is also a noun-suffix, but, like *da*, it helps to convert other words into verbs; as, kirriba, 'awake.' As already noticed, it enters into composition with verbs, lengthening their forms, at times, without adding to or altering their meaning. As part of a principal verb, it generally has the meaning of 'cause to be'; as, nyarry, 'a name,' nyarri-ba, 'give a name' *or* 'cause to have a name.' It is also attached to the past tense, and is often used when a secondary verb is in a sentence; *e.g.*, monno wébáro kunjillinneban nobo, 'that fire will be lighted' (made to burn) to-morrow.'

Ma, 'make,' 'cause to be there,' 'cause' generally.

This is one of the most important verbal suffixes in the language. As a noun-suffix, it has the sense of 'in,' and many of its derivative words have the idea of 'rest in a place,' and not of causation. *Maia* means 'in a place,' while *kaia* means 'go to a place.' Waimaia means 'it is above'; waikaia, 'go above.' It is evident that *ma* originally meant both 'there' and 'cause to be' generally. But, after all, there is nothing strange in this. Even now, with all the variation of forms, a good deal of the meaning of a speaker depends upon the tone of the voice or the gesture of the hand. We can conceive of a demonstrative as meaning (1) 'there,' (2) 'go there,' (3) 'be there,' (4) 'cause to be there,' according to the tone of voice and the subject of conversation. Any adjective can take this suffix; as, yilyúl, 'sick,' yilyúl-ma, 'cause to be sick'; dukkai, 'dead,' dukai-ma, 'to kill.' It enters into composition with adverbs of place as well; as, with wai, 'above,' and kully, kundy, *q.v.*, it gives waikálkullima, 'put crosswise,' waikundima, 'put on.'

It sometimes follows adjectives; as, bunyarra-ma yerrúbil, 'make a good song'; and sometimes pronouns; as, kaibi-ma junaġ, 'make another handle.' With verbs, it is sometimes attached to the imperative form; as, kory, 'run,' kori-ma, 'make to run'; sometimes it takes the particle bin between it and the root form or the imperative form; as, duġbin-ma, 'cause to lie down.' Very often it is attached to a form in -illi; as, duġgilli-ma, 'make to cry,' minjilli-ma, 'make to laugh.' Sometimes it is attached to two words; as, bunyarra-ma warrim-ma, 'to make well by doctoring,' and each of these can take all the forms in agreement; as, (*future*) bunyarraman warrimman; (*past*) bunyarramunne warrimmunne.

Gerry, 'wish,' 'like to.'

This was placed amongst the noun-suffixes, because, although it has a verbal meaning, it follows the rules of the noun-suffixes. It also has a place as a verbal-suffix. It never changes its form, and is always the final suffix. It is generally attached to the subjunctive; as, yunai-gerry ġai, 'I should like to lie down'; often to the form in -bai; as, yunbai-gerry ġai, 'I should like to go on'; and sometimes it is attached to the form in -illi; as, kunjilli-gerry, 'desire to burn.'

Negation.—*Jum*, 'without.'

Jum is another of the noun-suffixes, and is used in negative sentences. It is often attached to the imperative form, sometimes to the simple subjunctive form, and sometimes to the subjunctive form in -*bai*. It is the negative of the present. Wanye kunlela ġai means 'I know you'; but wanye kunlejum ġai, 'I do not know you,' *or* 'I am without knowledge of you.' Na is 'look'; naijum ġai *or* nabaijum ġai is 'I do not see.'

Yogum is another negative. It is a word distinct from jum, and its use turns any sentence into a negation. Yogum and jum, when both are used, do not cancel one another; on the contrary, they strengthen the negation. Wana is the negative of the imperative. It means 'leave it alone'; *e.g.*, wana yunbai, 'do not go.' It has all the usual forms of a verb; as, ġai wanalen, 'I left it alone.' Kingilga, 'that will do,' kingilanna, 'go away, numoé, 'stop,' also help to form negations.

Some Idioms in the Minyung Dialect.

The following sentences show some of the aboriginal idioms:—

1. *Rest in a place.*

Kukully ġai, 'I am here'; mumully wé, 'you are there'; kukaibo, 'stay here'; kokonno, 'it is here'; yilly nyan? 'where is she'; mully nyan, 'she is there'; killy Kibbin, 'there is Kibbin'; webena killy wai, 'the camp is above'; killy juy webena 'the camp is below.'

These sentences illustrate the use of the demonstratives as predicates. We can either say that they are used without the verb 'to be' as a copula, or that they themselves are used as neuter verbs in the present tense. The latter view is more in accordance with the idiom of the language. There is, however, in the language, a general absence of connecting words; there is no word for 'and,' the nearest word to it being urru or urrugan, 'with,' which is sometimes attached to words used as personal pronouns in the sense of 'also'; as, mullagurru, 'he also.' There are no relative pronouns, and we may almost say there is no verb 'to be,' used as a copula.

2. *Adjectives as predicates.*

Adjectives follow the same rules as demonstratives; for instance, yilyul ġai, 'I am sick'; killy dukkai, 'he over there is dead'; monno bundan bunyarra, 'this tomahawk is good.'

3. *The use of* yùna.

But we can say kùkulliyen ġai, for 'I was here'; and killy dukkaien, 'he was dead.' We can also say dukkaiánna, 'may you die,' or 'may you go to death'; dukkaiyuġgan ġai, 'I will kill myself,' or 'I will go to death.' These endings are from the verb yùna, which means 'to go.' The rule may be expressed thus:— Any word which is an adjective may be used in its plain form as a predicate in the present tense, and may, by adding the forms of the verb yùna, be turned into a true verb with all the tense-forms of a verb. The y of yùna is often omitted, and the forms ungan, unna are used; also en or yen, as if the original root was ya. Yuna means not only 'to go,' but 'to live,' 'to move,' and 'to be.' The language has three verbs closely allied in form, yùna 'to go,' yùna 'to lie down,' and yana 'to sit down.' The first of these has the derived forms yuġga, yùnbalé; the second, yúnalé; and the third, yangalé.

4. *Verbs of Motion and Adverbs of Place.*

Verbs of motion are very numerous, and so are adverbs of place; thus, speakers of the Minyuġ can be very exact in directing others to go here or there. Bukkora goa, 'go past'; bundagal boa, 'go near'; duloa, 'go down'; wande, 'go up'; kaie, 'go in'; wombin kwé, 'come here'; kaga, 'come down'; dukkan kyua, 'go over'; kankyua junimba, 'keep to the right'; kankyua worrembil, 'keep to the left.'

5. *Time.*

The language can be very exact in the expression of time. Numgerry is 'daylight'; karamba, 'mid-day'; yán, 'sunset'; nobo, 'yesterday' or 'to-morrow.' The particles -bo and -juġ are also used to distinguish former time from latter; so that nobo-bo is 'yesterday,' and nobo-juġ 'to-morrow.'

6. *Manner.*

There is a class of words that fulfil the duty of qualifying action as adverbs of manner, but they have the forms of verbs; so that they may be called qualifying verbs. They agree in final termination with the verbs they qualify. Karaia *or* karoé is 'to do anything in a great manner.' In the participal form it is used thus:—gibbum karandallen, 'full moon'; karandallen kwoġ, 'heavy rain'; karandallen wibára, 'the fire is hot'; karaġgen wurriġ, 'very cold.' With verbs it is used in a different form; as, wemully karaielly, 'speak loudly.'

Gumoé is 'in a small way'; as, ġumundallen gibbúm, 'little moon'; wemully ġumoelly, 'speak gently.' Magoé means 'to continue'; as, magoalé wemully, 'continue speaking.' Boé is 'to speak by oneself'; as, boelly wemully, 'speak by yourself,' *or* 'speak alone.' Others are,—karaharai-elly duġga, 'cry very loudly'; nunnoelly duġga, 'cry very gently'; nuġummanna duġga, 'cry quickly'; niġanna duġga 'stop crying.'

7. *Affections of the mind.*

'Doubt' is expressed by wunye, which sometimes takes the form of bunye. Gaio wanye buman, nobo wunye, 'I will beat you, perhaps to-morrow.' 'Hope' is expressed by jùn; as, mullaijún kulgai wibára, 'it is hoped that he will cut wood.' 'Fear' is expressed by the word twin; as, ġaio twiġgalla wébára kulgai, 'I am afraid to cut wood.' 'Pity' and 'sympathy' are often expressed by idioms meaning literally, 'smelling a bad *or* a good smell'; *e.g.*, ġai mullagai kunlunny bogon, 'I for him smell a bad smell,' *or* 'I pity him.'

8. *The use of* bunyarra.

Bunyarra, 'good,' means not only 'good,' but anything 'great.' It sometimes means 'very'; as bunyarra juġ, 'very bad.'

9. *The use of* karaban.

Reciprocal action is expressed by karaban; *e.g.*, ġully karaban bummallé, 'let us paint one another.'

10. *Comparison.*

Gai koren karaialen, wunnanden wanye, 'I run fast, you slowly'; that is, 'I am faster than you'; ġai wanye ġuluġ paigál, 'I am a man before you'; that is, 'I am older than you.' The pronoun (wanye or any other) is always in the accusative.

11. *Government of Verbs.*

Sometimes the infinitive form in -*ia*, and sometimes the form in -*bai* or -*ai*, which may be called the subjunctive, is used to show dependence on another verb; but often the two verbs agree in having the same final suffix. Examples are:—wana yúnbai, *or* wana yúna, 'do not go'; wana ćabbai, 'do not eat'; wana mullanye ćubbinmai, 'do not feed him'; yúna ġully ćullum kaġgale means 'let us go to catch fish'; *lit.*, 'let us go, let us catch fish'; both verbs are in the imperative. Kia mullanye bumalia, 'ask him to fight'; this is the more common form; but walo kia mullanye wébára kundia, *or* walo mullanye kia wébára kunjeba, 'you ask him to light a fire'; here the endings of the verbs will agree in all the tenses; as, (*imper.*) kia kunjeba; (*past*) kianne kunjebunne; (*fut.*) kian kunjebau.

EXAMPLES OF THE FORMATION OF THE TENSES OF VERBS.

The numbers here are the Tenses as on page 16 of this Appendix.

Buma, 'to fight, beat, kill.'

1. Buma, bumalé, bumga, bumgalé; 2. Bumala, bumalela, bumgala, bumgalela; 3. Buman, bumgan; 4. Bumanne, bumalinne, bumgánne, buminne; 5. Bumaloro, bumgaloro, bumaloroby; 6. Bumen, bumallen, bumgallen; 7. Buminna; 8. Bumian, bumalian; 9. Bumalia; 10. Bumai; 11. Bumenden. *Compound forms are:*—
Bumaigerry, 'wish to fight'; bumejúm (*imper. neg.*), 'fight not'; karaban bumalé (*imper. reciprocal*), 'fight one another'; bumille-ma, 'cause to fight,' which also, as above, may change ma into -mala, -malela, -man; -munne, -men; -ma-ia, &c.

Kinda, 'make.'

1. Kinda, kindabalé; 2. Kindalela, kindabulela; 3. Kindan; 4. Kindinne; 5. Kindaloro, kindabuloro; 6. Kinden, kindabulen, &c. Kinda does not take the forms in -ga; nor buma those in ba.

TABLE OF RELATIONSHIPS IN MINYUG.

(1.)

	Native words.	Equivalents.
A black† calls a *father's brother*..	biaġ*...	*pater, patruus.*
„ is called in return....	moiùm .	*illius fili-us, -a;*
		hujus nepos.‡
A black† calls a *mother's sister*...	waijuġ .	*mater, matertera.*
„ is called in return ...	moiùm .	*illius fili-us, -a;*
		hujus nepos.‡
A black† calls a *mother's brother*	káoġ ...	*avunculus.*
„ is called in return....	burrijuġ	*ejus nepos.*‡
A black† calls a *father's sister* ..	narrún .	*amita.*
„ is called in return	nyógon .	*ejus nepos.*‡

* Biaġ also means 'father,' and waijuġ 'mother.'

The child of biaġ or of waijuġ is 'brother (sister)' to moiùm; and a child of kaġ or narrún is cousin to burrijuġ and nyogon.

† Male or female.   ‡ For brevity, I make *nepos=nephew, niece*.—ED.

(2.)

	Native words.	Equivalents.
A man calls an *elder brother* ...	kagoġ ...	elder brother.
,, is called in return	bunam ..	younger brother.
A man calls a *younger brother*..	bunam ..	,,
,, is called in return	kagoġ ...	elder brother.
A man calls any *sister*.	nunnaġ..	sister.
,, is called in return	bunam ..	brother.
A woman calls any *brother*	bunam ..	brother.
,, is called in return ...	nunnaġ..	sister.
A woman calls an *elder sister*...	nunnaġ..	elder sister.
,, is called in return ...	yirgaġ...	younger sister.
A woman calls a *younger sister* .	yirgaġ...	,,
,, is called in return ...	nunnaġ..	elder sister.

A black† calls a *male* cousin .. yirabúġ *or* kújáruġ. ⎫
  ,,   ,, a *female* ,, .. yirabúġ-gun *or* kújáruġ-gun. ⎬ cousin.
she is called in return ..... yirabúġ-gun *or* kújáruġ-gun. ⎪
he ,,   ,, ... yirabúġ *or* kújáruġ. ⎭

(3.)

Grand relationships.

A grandchild† calls a *grandfather*, and is called by him naijoġ.
  ,,   ,, *father's mother*, ,, ,, her kummi.
  ,,   ,, *mother's* ,, ,, ,, ,, bailuġ.

† Whether male or female.

(4.)

A man calls his *wife*, his *wife's sister*, and some others . nubuġgun.
  ,, is called by them in return .... nubuġ.
A man calls his *wife's father* .... wómen.
  ,, calls his *wife's mother* .... bogai.
  ,, is called by them in return .... wómen.

Other terms for relations-in-law are—weoġ, ćumbuġ, yambúru. Such relationships are very complicated, and require to be specially investigated.

(5.)

When there is no specific term for a relationship, the terms for 'brother' and 'sister' are used ; for instance—a *great-grandfather* is called kagoġ, 'elder brother,' and in reply to a male he says bunam, 'younger brother.'

II. THE VOCABULARY.

Words, Phrases, and Sentences used by the Minyung Tribe.

1. Words and Phrases.

(The verbs are given in their shortest form, the imperative.)

Berrin—the south, the south people; *e.g.*, berrinba—to the south; *cf.* kokin—the north, the north people; *e.g.*, kokingal—from the north. The aborigines on the Richmond River call the Clarence River 'Berrin,' and the Tweed 'Kokin'; but, to those on the Tweed River, the Richmond is 'Berrin,' and the Logan is 'Kokin.'

Binnug—an ear; *e.g.*, binnugma—make to hear; tell; answer.

Birra—to cast through.

Birré—fly away; *e.g.*, birryalen garrig—crossed over.

Bugge—fall; it is sometimes equivalent to 'gone away' or 'disappeared'; as, inji buggeloro mibin kurralbo wairabo? 'where have all the blacks been this long time'? If the imperative ends in *a* (as bugga), the word means 'kick,' 'stamp,' 'leave a mark,' as a foot-print. In the Pirripai dialect, spoken by the natives on the Hastings River, buggen means 'killed,' for they say bunno butan buggen, 'he killed a black snake.' In Minyug, nyugga bukkoyen means 'the sun has risen,' nyugga buggen, 'the sun has set'; but with this compare the Brisbane dialect, which says piki bog, 'the sun is dead.'

Buggo—(1) a native shield; (2) the tree from which it is made.

Bujabuyai—a swallow. Bujarebin—a daisy. Bujagun—a quiet girl. Bujaro—quiet; *e.g.*, yiran bujaro, 'whip-snakes (are) harmless.'

Bujará, Bujárabo—morning.

Bujáre, Bujáro-bujáro—this morning, just before daybreak.

Buji, bujin—a little piece; bujigan—into little pieces.

Buma *or* bumga—strike, beat, fight, kill by fighting.

This is probably a derivative from bugge, just as wag, the noun for 'work,' becomes wamma, the verb 'to work.'

Burre—the top of a tree; with this compare culle, 'the barrel' *or* 'trunk' of a tree; waian, 'the root'; cerrug, 'the branches'; kunyal, 'the leaves.' Culle is also a general name for a 'tree.' It often means 'logs' lying down, and 'firewood'; *e.g.*, kulga culle webáragai, 'cut wood for the fire.' Cerrug, besides, is 'the open palm of the hand,' 'a bird's claw,' *or* 'the paw of an animal,' and it is the name of a constellation. Kunyal, 'leaf,' may be allied to with kuggal, 'an arm' *or* 'wing.' Waian also means 'a road.' When a tree is cut down, the stump is called gunun.

Dukkai—dead; a dead man; 'a dead woman' is touaragun. The word tabullen is often used to mean 'dead,' instead of dukkai and touaragun. It is a participle from some verb not at present used. In some dialects, duggai, probably the same word, means a kind of 'fish'; in the Turrubul dialect it means 'man.' This may have given rise to the idea that some of the aborigines believe that, when they die, they become fishes.

Duggerrigai—white man; duggerrigaigun—white woman. Perhaps this word comes from dukkai, 'dead,' but it does not mean 'ghost' or 'spirit.' For 'spirit,' there are two terms, ġuru and wágai. After a man dies, he is spoken of as ġuru wanden, 'a spirit up above.' All the ġuru go to waijoġ (from wai, 'above'), where they live on murrabil, a kind of celestial food. Murrabil is from the Kamilaroi word murraba, 'good.' Guru in some dialects means 'dark' or 'night,' and a word derived from it means 'emu.' Dawson, in his "Australian Aborigines" (page 51), states, that, if a native "is to die from the bite of a snake, he sees his wraith in the sun; but, in this case, it takes the form of an emu." Wágai means 'shadow,' and has a more superstitious use than ġuru. When a person is ill, the warrima, 'wizard,' is sent for to throw on him a good spell, called bunyarama warrima. The warrima takes something like a rope out of his stomach (!), and climbs up to waijog to have an interview with the wágai. On his return, if the man is to recover, he says, 'Your wágai has come back and you will soon be well'; but if he is to die, he says, 'I could not get your wágai.' The sick man is sure to die then. The wágai are also the spirits consulted, when anyone dies suddenly, to discover by whose means the death was brought about. Yiralle is another name used by the Nyuġ people for 'white man'; it means, the 'one who has come.'

Garre—dance; cf., yerrube—sing.

Guluġ, ġuluġbo—first; before; e.g., ġai minjen ġuluġbo, 'I laughed first,' i.e., before you. Gnluġ-gerry is 'immediately'; nyuġga bukkoyen ġuluġ-gerry, 'the sun will be up immediately'; ġuluġga wé, or wé ġuluġga buna means ' 'go thou first'; waire ġurrugin, or waire ġuluġgurrugin are those men in a tribe whom the colonists call 'kings'; each of these gets a brass plate with a suitable inscription, to wear on his breast, as an emblem of his rank.

Gumma—tent. Gummabil—milk.

Kibbára—(1) white or yellow; (2) a half-caste, a yellow man or woman; whence kibbárgun, a half-caste girl; kibbárim, a half-caste male; (3) fig., anything young, small, or light; as, kibbára pailela, which may either mean, 'light rain falling,' or 'young lads fighting'; (4) a stringy-bark tree; this word, in the Kamilaroi dialect, is kuburu, a 'black-box tree'; (5) the ceremony of man-making; possibly the name bora may come from this, by dropping the initial syllable, as uyuġ is for minyuġ; or, bora may be connected with the Minyuġ word bul or bule, 'a ring'; (6) 'a made-man,' that is, one who has passed the kippára; and in this sense it is used in many of the coast dialects. The names given to a male, at different stages of his life, are—taićum, 'a baby'; balun, balungai, 'a 'a boy'; ćubbo, ćubboyil, 'a youth'; murrawon, 'a lad' who is getting whiskers and has all his berruġ or prescribed 'scars on his back'; kumban-gerry, a lad who has received his kumban or 'scars on his breast'; kibbára, 'one who had been made a man'; paigál or mibin, 'a man'; kićom or mobeg, 'an old man.'

Kuji—(1) a bee; (2) honey; (3) red; cf. kujin—red.
Kunle—know, hear, feel, smell; e.g., ġai kunlejům, 'I don't know.'
Moiúm, (1) a child, a son or daughter; (2) the black cockatoo with yellow feathers in its tail. The black cockatoo with red feathers is called ġarerra, and the white cockatoo, kéra.
Nyuġġa—(1) the regent bird; (2) the sun. Nyuġġal-gerry—summer; cf. wurrig—cold; wurriġbil—winter.
Ća—eat; e.g., walo éu, ġai yo,' you eat (now), I (will eat) by-and-by.'
Ćubbinma—feed. Ćukka—drink.
Wébára—(1) a fire; (2) firewood; (3) a camp. Examples:—(1) kunji wébára, 'light a fire'; kunji, by itself, would mean 'make it burn' (bobbinda means 'make a light'; ćulloma, 'make smoke,' i.e., 'make a fire'; palloma, 'put out the fire'); (2) kulga wébára, 'cut firewood'; this has the same meaning as kulga ćullo; (3) ġai yûnbulela wébára 'I am going to the camp'; lit., 'I am going to the fire.' The gunyas or 'wind-shelters' are ġumbin; and a large building like a church is called kumai ġumbin, which words, however, may mean, a collection of houses, as a 'town' or 'village.' The blankets which are given to the aborigines on Queen's Birthday are called ġumbin, and so is a rag tied round the foot. A sock is ġumbin, but a boot is bonumbil. In some dialects a 'sheet of bark,' 'a gunya,' and 'a canoe' have the same name, but in the Minyuġ dialect 'a sheet of bark' is bagul, and 'a canoe' is kundal or kulgerry.
Worám—sleep; worámbil—sleepy; e.g., worám búna, 'go to sleep.' A mother will say to her child, worám-worám búna, but to herself, ġai worám yunan, 'I will lie down and sleep.'
Yaraba—marry; e.g., nanna yaraba, 'marry my sister.'
Yerrube—sing; yerrubil—song; yerrubil-gin-gun—a singer (fem.).
Youara (also kirrin and wogoyia)—a 'karábari.'* Youara-ġurrugin—a maker of karábari songs.

---

*This I take to be the correct spelling, not 'corrobboree.'—ED.

2. Sentences.

Minyugalela wé—'what are you doing'? Yogum gai únduru-mullela—'I am doing nothing'. Minyugaloro wé nobo?—'what did you do yesterday'? Gaio kaggaloro ćullúm Nogguggai—'I caught fish for Noggng.'
Gaio wanye bundan wianje, kulga ćully gaia—'I to you a tomahawk will give, (if) you cut down a tree for me ; *or*, cut down a tree for me, (and) I will give you a tomahawk.' Yile bundan? —'where (is) the tomahawk'? Kunde bukkora—'over there.'
Kulga ćulle koranna—'cut down that high tree.' Yile walo kulgajumgerry, wana—"if you do not like to cut it down, leave it alone.' Gaio kulgunne kaba ćulle wia baijúm bibbo —'I cut down that tree before you came.' Gaio wanye naienne kulgabulenne—'I saw you cutting (it).'
Gaio wanye monno wébára gaia kunjilligerry—'I would like you to light that fire for me.' Walo kia mullanye kunjeba —'you ask him to light (it).' Gaio mullanye nobo kianne kunjebunne—'I asked him to light it yesterday.' Munno wébára kunjilloroho—'the fire is lighted.' Munno wébára kunjillinneban nobo—'that fire will be lighted to-morrow.'
Gen kuggalela?—'who is calling'? Kéra kuggalela—'a white cockatoo is calling.' Mully kéra mibin kialela—'that cockatoo speaks like a man.' Paian-jug gún—'it is warm to-day.'
Kubberry gai paian—'I am hungry to-day.' Wia kunlunne bogon gai—'I am sorry for you.' Walo ća, bunyarra-d-unda—'you eat, (you) will be all right.'
Gaio naienne kurrunnebo manne, kenne; gaio buminne úndurrunebyu; úndurr berranne.—'I saw a number of ducks and white cockatoos ; I killed some ; some flew away.'
Loganda, ćannabigy gaio naienne wébárabo. Ćannaby yerrubilloro wébárabo. Yaburugen gaiaba kyuanne. Yaburugen gullawonne, 'injeo wé'? Gaio kiallen 'Brisbane-gobullen.' Gaio naienne nogumme kakaba. Ćannaby bikbullen. Ćannaby kowallen nogumme webanno—'On the Logan, I saw them in the camp (*lit*., at the fire). They were singing in the camp. One came to me. One asked me where I was going. I replied, 'Going to Brisbane.' I saw dogs there. They were barking. They called them into the camp.'

Miscellaneous.

Gaio nan ćuan bowan, 'I will see (one who) will throw a spear.' Gaio nan ćuan bowalen, 'I will see a spear thrown.' Gaio nan ćuan bougunneban nobo, 'I will see (that) a spear shall be thrown to-morrow.' Gaio naienne yúnbulela undurunne poiolgo, 'I saw somebody going up the hill.' Gaio naienne kamy ćuan warre bulenne, 'I saw him carrying spears.'

Gaio kunleoro kamy yerrúbiloroby, 'I heard them singing.' Gaio kunlan kamy mendié, 'I will hear them laughing.' Gaio kunlunne kamy minjenne, 'I heard them laughing'; if the act of laughing is finished, this sentence would be, ġaio kunlunne minjeloroby. Gaio kunlela wemullenyun, 'I hear speaking there.' Gaio naienne korenyun taićumme, 'I saw children running away.' Gaio kunloigerry yerrúbil kamy, 'I like to hear them sing.' Wóġ wia bunyarra, 'working is good for you.' Waġgo wia ġowenyen, 'working is making you tired.' Paigàl wammullen wallenyun, 'the man working is gone.'

3. MYTHOLOGY.

Berruġen korillábo, ġerriġ Mommóm, Yabúróġ.—' Berruġ came long long ago, with Mommóm (and) Yaburóġ.'

Thus begins a Minyung Legend to the following effect:—

Long ago, Berrúġ, with his two brothers, Mommóm and Yaburóġ, came to this land. They came with their wives and children in a great canoe, from an island across the sea. As they came near the shore, a woman on the land made a song that raised a storm which broke the canoe in pieces, but all the occupants, after battling with the waves, managed to swim ashore. This is how ' the men,' the paigàl black race, came to this land. The pieces of the canoe are to be seen to this day. If any one will throw a stone and strike a piece of the canoe, a storm will arise, and the voices of Berrúġ and his boys will be heard calling to one another, amidst the roaring elements. The pieces of the canoe are certain rocks in the sea. At Ballina, Berrúġ looked around and said, nyuġ? and all the paigàl about there say nyuġ to the present day, that is, they speak the Nyuġ dialect. Going north to the Brunswick, he said, minyuġ, and the Brunswick River paigàl say minyuġ to the present day. On the Tweed he said, ġando? and the Tweed paigàl say ġando to the present day. This is how the blacks came to have different dialects. Berrúġ and his brothers came back to the Brunswick River, where he made a fire, and showed the paigàl how to make fire. He taught them their laws about the kippàra, and about marriage and food. After a time, a quarrel arose, and the brothers fought and separated, Mommóm going south, Yaburóġ west, and Berrúġ keeping along the coast. This is how the paigàl were separated into tribes.

NOTE.—Each brother has his own 'karábari,' for there is the youára Berruġna, the girran Mommómna, and the wogoyia Yaburóġna).

(B.)

[ABSTRACT.]

GRAMMAR

OF THE LANGUAGE SPOKEN BY

THE NARRINYERI TRIBE IN S. AUSTRALIA.

(By the late Rev. G. Taplin, Aborigines' Missionary, Point Macleay, South Australia.)

[This Grammar of the Narrinyeri dialect is to be found in a book entitled "The Folklore, Manners, Customs, and Languages of the South Australian Aborigines; Adelaide, 1879." I have re-arranged and condensed the material of the Grammar, and adapted the whole to the system followed in this present volume.—ED.]

THE Narrinyeri aborigines occupy a portion of the coast of South Australia, near Adelaide. Their territory includes the shores of Encounter Bay, Lakes Alexandrina and Albert, and the country to the east of the Murray, for about 20 miles from its mouth. The first attempt to master and commit to writing the grammar of this language was made in 1843 by the Rev. H. E. Meyer, a Lutheran Missionary. His sketch of the grammar is not free from blunders. Nor can the present effort expect to be faultless, but it is approximately correct, being founded on a practical acquaintance with the language.

1. LETTERS.

The Narrinyeri have not the sounds of *f, r, s, z*, but they have the sonant sound of *th* (here written *dh*), as in the English words 'this,' 'thine,' 'breathe,' and the surd *th*, as in 'thin,' 'breath.'

2. GENERAL PRINCIPLES.

There is no article, but the numeral 'one' is used as a sort of indefinite article. Nouns, pronouns, and adjectives are declined by the use of affixes, and have forms for the singular, dual, and plural numbers.

Number is indicated by a change of termination; for example:—

	'Man.'	'Man.'	'Eye.'	'Lip.'	'Ear.'
Sing.	May-u.	Korni.	Min-a.	Mun-a.	Yur-e.
Dual	May-ula.	Korn-egk.	Min-ula.	Mun-agge.	Yur-illa.
Plu.	May-una.	Korn-ar.	Min-una.		

	'Eye.'	'Eyebrow.'	'Trouser.'
Sing.	Pil-i.	Pi-chagge.	Yerkoan-a.
Dual	Pil-agge.	Pi-ko.	Yerkoan-ula.

In the declension of nouns the affixes used as case-endings may be regarded as post-positions. There is no distinction of gender in nouns and adjectives, but, for some words, there is a change of termination to indicate the feminine; as, yúga, 'brother,' yúgáta, 'sister.' This dialect likes to end its words with a vowel, especially the short *i*, which is here represented by *y*.

3. Nouns.

Their Declension.—There are *two* declensions of nouns, the one used for words denoting human relationships, and the other for all nouns else.

(a.) *Common Nouns.*

Their cases.—For common nouns, the case-endings of the singular number are:—

The *Genitive* takes the affix -ald meaning 'of,' but, with placenames, 'at,' 'in,' 'upon.' This affix is also used as a separate word, with the sense of 'belonging to.'

The Dative 1. takes -amby, which may be translated 'for,' 'for the purpose of,' 'for the use of.'

The Dative 2. takes -agk, 'to,' 'by,' and -ágai, 'on,' 'by'; but these two terminations seem to be interchangeable. The English for this case is, 'to,' 'with,' 'by,' 'on,' 'at'—either locative or instrumental.

The Ablative 1. has the affix -il; as, kornil mempir napagk, 'the man struck his wife'; from korni, 'man,' mempin, 'striking,' napy, 'wife'. This case means 'by,' 'through,' 'because of' —either instrumental or causative.

The Ablative 2., if used to signify 'place from,' takes -anmant; as, guk perk-anmant, 'water from the well'; but, when it relates to persons or things, it takes -inend; as, gum-anyir-inend pil-inend, 'from your eye.' The English for this case is 'from.'

Another case-ending in the singular is -anyir; this I shall call *Ablative* 6. It denotes 'from,' expressing a cause and a result; but with pronominal adjectives, it stands for the *Genitive* form.

These are the principal cases, but the number of them may be multiplied indefinitely by the use of any of the following:—

4. Post-Positions.

Amby, 'for.'
Gugkura, 'before.'
Gurn-kwar, 'outside.'
Loru, 'up.'
Mare-muntunt, 'beneath.'
Moru, 'down.'
Taragk, 'between.'
Tepagk, 'close to.'
Tuntagk, 'between two.'
Tunti, 'in the middle.'
Ugul, ugunel, ugunai, 'in front of.'

Some of these, when used as post-positions to nouns, are constant; others vary their form when affixed to the dual or the plural.

PARADIGM OF THE DECLENSION OF COMMON NOUNS.

Korni, 'a man.'

		Singular.	Dual.	Plural.
Nom.	1.*	Korn-i	Korn-egk	Korn-ar
Gen.		Korn-ald	Korn-egk-al	Korn-an
Dat.	2.	Korn-agk		
			Korn-ugegun	Korn-ugar
Acc.		Korn	Korn-egk	Korn-ar
Voc.		Korn-inda	Korn-ula	Korn-una
Abl.	1.	Korn-il	Korn-eggul	Korn-ar
	2.	Korn-anmant	Korn-ugegun	Korn-ugar
	6.	Korn-anyir	Korn-ugegun	Korn-an

Porly, 'a child.'

		Singular.	Dual.	Plural.
Nom.	1.*	Porl-y	Porl-egk	Porl-ar
Gen.		Porl-ald	Porl-egk-al	Porl-an
Dat.	2.	Porl-agk		
		Porl-ugar	Porl-ugegun	Porl-ugar
Acc.		Porl-y	Porl-egk	Porl-ar
Voc.		Porl-inda	Porl-ula	Porl-una
Abl.	1.	Porl-il	Porl-eggul	Porl-ar
	2.	Porl-inend	Porl-(en)eggulánd	Porl-ánánd

(b.) *Nouns of Relationship.*

For nouns of relationship, the case-endings are :—

    Acc., Gen.   —   -yin.†
    Dative 1.   'for'   -yin-amby.
    Dative 2.   'to'   -yin-agk.
    Causative.   'by'   -yin-inda.
    Ablative 6.   'from'   -yin-anyir.

†That is, -in or -an preceded by the euphonic *y*.

For nouns of this kind there are also special terminations to express the nature of the relationship, whether 'mine,' 'yours,' or 'his'; thus :—

    Nag-gai, 'father,' 'my father.'
    Yiko-wally, 'his father.'   Gai-uwy, 'your father.'
    Nag-ku-owy, 'mother,' 'my mother.'
    Nagku-wally, 'his mother.'   Nagku-uwy, 'your mother.'
    Kelan-owy, 'my (elder) brother.'
    Kelan-wally, 'his brother.'   Kelan-uwy, 'your brother.'

---

*See foot note, p. 15 of appendix.

Naggai, 'my father,' is thus declined:—
  Nom. Naggai, 'my father.'
  Gen. Naggai-yin, 'of my father.'
  Dat. 1. Naggai-yin-amby, 'for my father.'
  Dat. 2. Naggai-yin-agk, 'to my father.'
  Acc. Naggai-yin, 'my father.'
  Caus. Naggai-yin-inda, 'by my father.'
  Abl. 6. Naggai-yin-anyir, 'from my father.'

All the other terms of relationship, with their possessive adjuncts, may be declined by adding these case-endings. But sometimes the *Genitive* of relationship puts the -ald of ordinary nouns before its own ending: as, tart-ald-an, 'of my (younger) brother.'

5. Derivatives from Nouns, &c.

Derivatives are formed from nouns by adding to them such terminations as:—

1. -inyeri, 'belonging to'; as, kurl-inyeri, 'a hat,' from kurly, 'head'; turn-inyeri, 'a boot,' from turny, 'foot'; kurr-inyer-egk, 'a pair of trousers,' from kurregk (dual) 'the shins.' Such a derivative word, when declined, is treated as a common noun, and the post-position is added to the adjective termination; as, kurl-inyer-ald, 'of a hat,' kurr-inyer-egkal, 'of a pair of trousers.'

2. -urumi *or* -urmi, which is added to the stem of a verb to denote 'the instrument' with which the action expressed by the verb is done, *or* a thing which is used for some particular purpose; as, tyety-urumi, 'oil, ointment,' from tyetyin, 'anointing'; kunk-urumi, 'pills,' from kunkun, 'swallowing'; mutt-urmi, 'a drink,' from muttun, 'drinking'; kalt-urmi, 'a spade,' from kalt, 'to dig'; drek-urmi, 'a tomahawk,' from drek, 'to cut *or* chip.' Here also the post-position is affixed to the formative for the purposes of declension.

3. -amaldy, which is added to the stem of a verb, to denote the agent or person who does the action; as, pett-amaldy, 'a thief,' from pett, 'to steal'; yelpul-amaldy, 'a liar,' from yelpul, 'to tell a lie.' Here also the post-position is placed at the end of the word.

4. -watyeri means 'full of'; as, plogge-watyeri, 'possessed of sorcery'; tuni-watyeri, 'full of sand.'

5. When yandy, 'old,' 'useless,' is used with a noun, it modifies the form of the noun, and attaches the case-ending to itself; as, yandy orn *(for* korn), 'an old man,' yant-ald orn 'of an old man'; yandy imin *(for* miminy), 'an old woman,' yant-ald min, 'of an old woman.'

6. Pronouns.

(a.) Personal Pronouns.

The personal pronouns have two forms in the *nominative*, the *accusative*, and the *causative* (Abl. 1) cases, as shown in the paradigm below; the second form is used only as an affix to nouns, or in rapid speaking. The third pronoun is of all genders.

Paradigm of the Declension of the Personal Pronouns.

———————————Singular———————————

	1st.	2nd.	3rd.
Nom.	Gape, ap	Ginte, inde, ind	Kitye, itye, atye
Gen.	Gan-auwe*	Gum-auwe	Kin-auwe
Dat. 1.	Gan-amby	Gum-amby	Kin-amby
2.	Gan-aġk	Gum-aġk	Kin-aġk
Acc.	Gan, an	Gum, um	Kin, in, ityanian
Voc.	——	Ginta, inda	——
Abl. 1.	Gaty, atty†	Ginte, inde	Kil, il
6.	Gan-anyir	Gum-anyir	Kin-anyir

———————————Dual———————————

	1st.	2nd.	3rd.
Nom.	Gel, aġel	Gurl, ugurl	Keġk, eġk
Gen.	Lam-auwe*	Lom-auwe	Keġgun-auwe
Dat. 1.	Lam-amby	Lom-amby	Keġgun-amby
2.	Lam-aġk	Lom-aġk	Keġgun-aġk
Acc.	Lam, alam	Lom, olom	Keġ-gún, eg-gún
Voc.	——	Gurla, ula	——
Abl. 1.	Gel, aġel†	Gurl, ugurl	Keġk, eġk
6.	Lam-anyir	Lom-anyir	Keġgun-anyir

———————————Plural———————————

	1st.	2nd.	3rd.
Nom.	Gurn, arn	Gun, úġún	Kar, ar
Gen.	Nam-auwe*	Nom-auwe	Kan-auwe
Dat. 1.	Nam-amby	Nom-amby	Kan-amby
2.	Nam-aġk	Nom-aġk	Kan-aġk
Acc.	Nam, anam	Nom, onom	Kan, an
Voc.	——	Guna, una	——
Abl. 1.	Gurn, arn†	Gun, úġún	Kar, ar
6.	Nam-anyir	Nom-anyir	Kan-anyir

*A variant for the *genitive* form in -auwe is -auwurle.

† This is the case which our author calls the *Causative-Ablative*; I have entered it in the paradigms as Abl. 1.; it is equivalent to Threlkeld's *Agent-Nominative* (*Nom.* 2), for which see page 11.—Ed.

THE NARRINYERI DIALECT.

An adjective or a possessive pronoun, when used as an attribute to a noun, is declined with the noun, and has its own case-endings; thus :—

Wundi kinauwe, '*his spear.*' Wundi nung-gari, '*good spear.*'

Singular.

Nom. Wundi kin-auwe (nuġġári)
Gen. Wund-ald kin-anyir-ald (nuġġär-ald).
Dat. 2. Wund-áġk kin-anyir-aġk (nuġġär-uġar).
Acc. Wund kin-auwe (nuġġäri).
Abl. 1. Wund-il kin-anyir-il (nuġġär-il).
  2. Wund-inend kin-anyir-inend.

Dual.

Nom. Wund-eġk keġgun-auwurle (nuġġär-eġk).
Gen. Wund-eġgal keġġun-anyir-ald (nuġġär-eġkal).
Dat. 2. Wund-uġeġun keġgun-anyir-aġk (nuġġär-uġeġun).
Acc. Wund-eġk keġgun-auwe (nuġġär-eġk).
Abl. 1. Wund-eġgul keġgun-anyir-il (nuġġär-uġeġul).
  2. Wund-uġeġun keġgun-anyir-inend.

Plural.

Nom. Wund-ar kan-auwe (nuġġär-ar).
Gen. Wund-an kan-anyir-ald (nuġġär-an).
Dat. 2. Wund-uġar kan-anyir-eġgun (nuġġär-uġar).
Acc. Wund-ar kan-auwe (nuġġär-ar).
Abl. 1. Wund-ar kan-anyir-il (nuġġär-ar).
  2. Wund-uġar kan-anyir-inend.

Kornar ngruwar, '*many men.*'

Plural.

Nom. Korn-ar ġruwar.
Gen. Korn-an ġrunt-uġar.
Dat. Korn-uġar ġrunt-uġar.
Acc. Korn-ar ġruwar
Voc. Korn-una ġrúwún.
Abl. 1. Korn-ar ġrunt-ar.
  2. Korn-uġar ġrunt-inend.

Peculiarities in the syntax of the pronouns are shown in such sentences as :—ġaty mempir kin-anyir-aġk (*not* kin-auwe) kurly, 'I struck his head'; here apparently the object of a transitive verb is in the *dative* case; kil pleppin keġgun-auwe, pilar, 'he touched the eyes of these two'; but here the *accusative* case is used.

c

(b.) Demonstrative and Interrogative Pronouns.

The demonstrative pronouns are :—hik-kai, hik-ke, 'this'; hitye-katye, 'this one' (emphatic); and nai-ye, 'that.' They are thus declined :—

	Instant.	Proximate.	Remote.
		—Singular—	
Nom.	Hikkai	Hitye-katye	Naiye
Gen.			Orn-auwe
Dat.			Orn-aġk
Acc.	Hin	Hityene katye	Orne
Abl.	Hil		
		—Dual—	
Nom.	Heġgeġk	Heġgene-keġk	Nakak
Acc.	Heġgun		
Abl.	Heġgul		
		—Plural—	
Nom.	Harar	Harnakar	Narar
Acc.	Haran		Narar
Abl.	Harar		

The interrogative pronouns are ġaġke, 'who'? minye, 'what'? They are thus declined :—

	Ngang-ke, '*who*'?		Minye, '*what*'?
Nom.	Gaġke		Minye
Gen.	Nauwe, nauwurle		Mek
Dat.	1. Namby		Mekimby
	2. Nak *(sing.)*		
	Nak-an-aġk *(plu.)*		
Abl.	1. Gande		Mengye, 'how'?

Other forms of the interrogative minye are :—minyandai, 'how often' (*lit.*, 'what times'?) minyurti, 'what sort'? minyai or minyarai, 'what number'? minde, 'why? for what reason'? murel, 'with what intention'?

7. Verbs.

In the Narrinyeri dialect, the form of the verb is often participial, and is closely allied to the adjective.

If we take the root-form lak, 'to spear,' as the example of a transitive verb, the moods and tenses with their meanings may be shown thus :—

Indicative Mood.

Tense.	Meaning.
1. *Present tense,*	I spear him.
2. *Past tense,*	I speared him.
3. *Remote past tense,*	I did spear him.
4. *First (simple) future,*	I will spear him.
5. *Second (intention) future,*	I will (*i.e.*, intend to) spear him.
6. *Third (predictive) future,*	I will spear him.
7. *Repetitive tense.*	I spear again.

Reflexive Mood.
I speared myself.

Reciprocal Mood.
Let us two spear each other.

Imperative Mood.

1. *Simple imperative,*	Do thou spear.
2. *Prohibitive imperative,*	Spear not.
3. *Compulsory imperative.*	Thou must spear.

Optative Mood.

1. *Present optative,*	I may spear him.
2. *Imperfect optative.*	I could *or* would spear him.

Infinitive Mood.
To spear.

Participles.
Spearing ; speared.

Passive Voice.
I am speared.

DECLENSION of the VERBS.

In the declension of the moods and tenses of the Transitive and Intransitive Verbs, five sets of modified forms of Personal Pronouns are used as the subjects to the verb. They are :—

	Singular	
I.	*Thou.*	*He.*
With Transitive Verbs.		
1. Gate (*or* gaty)	kile	ginte
2. Atte (*or* atty)	il	inde
With Intransitive Verbs.		
3. Ap	inde	itye
4. Ap	inde	itye
5. Gap	gint	kity

	—Dual—	
We (two).	*You (two).*	*They (two).*
	With Transitive Verbs.	
1. Gel	ġurl	koġgul
2. Aġel	uġurl	eġul
	With Intransitive Verbs.	
3. Gel	uġurl	eġk
4. Aġel	uġurl	eġk
5. Gel	gurl	keġk

	—Plural—	
We.	*You.*	*They.*
	With Transitive Verbs.	
1. Gurn	ġun	kar
2. Uġurn	uġun	ar
	With Intransitive Verbs.	
3. Uġurn	uġune	ar
4. Arn	uġune	ar
5. Gurn	ġun	kar

DECLENSION OF A TRANSITIVE VERB.

'Lak, 'to spear.'

Example of the Declension of a Transitive Verb in the Present Tense of the Indicative Mood.

Any Tense may be declined in full in the same manner.

T. 1. *Sing.*	Gate*	yan lakkin		I spear him.
	Ginte	,,	,,	Thou spearest him.
	Kile	,,	,,	He spears him.
Dual.	Gel	,,	,,	We two spear him.
	Gurl	,,	,,	You two spear him.
	Keġgul	,,	,,	They two spear him.
Plu.	Gurn	,,	,,	We spear him.
	Gun	,,	,,	You spear him.
	Kar	,,	,,	They spear him.

[*NOTE.—Yan, 'him,' is for ityan, an accusative form of the pronoun itye, kitye, 'he.' Instead of yan, any pronoun or noun in the accusative case may be used as the direct object of the transitive verb; and to decline the tenses of the Indicative and other Moods, five sets of pronouns are used, as shown above; the particular set which ought to be used with each tense is indicated by the 'superior' numeral put after the subject in the following paradigm of declension. Also, *T*. 1, 2, 3, &c. indicates the Tenses as shown on the previous page.—ED.]

Indicative Mood.

T. 1. Gate¹ yan lakkin.   T. 4. Gate¹ yan lak-kani.
2. Gate¹ yan lakkir.   5. Gate¹ lak-el ityan.
3. Gate¹ yan lak-emb.   6. Lakkin-el atte² ityan.
T. 7. Gate lak-uġanye.

Other forms of the future are :—

Ginte el our ityan lak,   'thou must spear him.'
Lak amb el ityan,   'shall I spear him'?
Tarno lak amb ityan,   'shall I not spear him'?

Reflexive.

T. 2. Gap⁵ anaġk laġgelir.

Reciprocal.

T. 1. Gel⁵ anaġk laġgel-amb.

Optative or Potential Mood.

T. 1. Gate¹ in-anyura lakkin   T. 2. Lak-ilde atte² ityan

Imperative Mood.

Singular.   *Dual and Plural.*
T. 1. Lak war ind   Gel¹ war lakkin
      Il war lak   Gurn¹ war lakkin
T. 2. Lak ó (ityan, 'him.')   Tauo lak ityan.
T. 3. Laggel-el our (*or* war) ap³.

Infinitive Mood.

Lak, 'to spear'; lak uramb, 'for the purpose of spearing.'

Participles.

Laggelin, 'spearing'; laggelir, 'speared.

Passive Voice.

Indicative Mood.

	Singular.	*Dual.*	*Plural.*
T. 1.	Gan lakkir	Lam lakkir	Nam lakkir
	Gum lakkir	Lom lakkir	Nom lakkir
	Kin lakkir	Keġgun lakkir	Kan lakkir

[Note.—This is not a real Passive Voice, but only a substitute for it; see page 33 of this volume. The pronoun forms used with **lakkir** show this, for they are in the accusative.—Ed.]

DECLENSION OF AN INTRANSITIVE VERB.

Ngai, 'to come.'

Indicative Mood.

T. 1. Gai-in ap³.   T. 2. Puntir ap¹.   T. 3. Gai-el ap¹.

IMPERATIVE MOOD.

Koh, 'come'; ġai war, 'do come'; ġai akhi, 'come here.'

OPTATIVE OR POTENTIAL MOOD.

T. 1. Gap⁵ inanye ġai.

INFINITIVE MOOD.

Gai, 'to come.'

PARTICIPLES.

Puntin, 'coming'; puntani, 'about to come.'

8. OBSERVATIONS ON THE USE OF THE VERBS.

1. Lakkin properly signifies 'piercing'; gate lakkin itye koye means 'I make a basket,' *lit.*, 'I pierce that basket,' by piercing through and through the rushes of which it is made; but the word is mostly used to mean the casting of any missile, as a spear, a dart, a stone.

2. The intransitive verbs take the simple nominative form of the pronouns as their subject; the transitive verbs take the causative form.

3. There appear to be two conjugations for verbs in the Narrinyeri language:—(1.) those in which the form for the present indicative is the same as the present participle; as, merippin, 'cutting,' ġate yan merippin, 'I cut it'; (2.) those that have another form for the present participle; as, dretulun, 'chipping,' ġate yan drekin, 'I chip it.' Of the former class are mempin, 'striking'; pempin, 'giving'; morokkin, 'seizing.' To the latter belong pornun, 'die,' pornelin, 'dying'; nampulum, 'hide,' nampundelin, 'hiding'; nyrippin, 'wash,' nyribbelin, 'washing.'

4. Some intransitive verbs become transitive by changing the sonant *g* into the surd *k*, or by adding -undun to the root; as, piġkin ap, 'I fall,' piġgen atte ityan, 'I throw it down'; yelkulum ap, 'I move,' yelkundun atte ityan, 'I move it'; nampulun ap, 'I hide,' nampundun atte ityan, 'I hide it.'

5. A causative meaning is given to verbal adjectives by adding -mindin to them; as, ġuldamulun, 'tired,' ġuldamulmindin, 'causing to be tired,' 'making tired.'

6. The most common auxiliary verbs are wallin, 'being,' and warin, 'making' *or* 'causing.' Examples of these are:—nuġgari, 'good', nuġga-wallin, 'being good,' nunga-warin, making good'; pilteġi, 'strong,' pilteġ-wallin, 'being strong,' pilteġ-warin, 'making strong'; wirraġ-wallin, 'being bad" wirraġ-warin, 'making bad.'

7. Verbs may therefore be arranged in four classes:—(1.) the simple verbs as, mempin, 'striking'; takin, 'eating'; ġoppun, 'walking'; lulun, 'breaking'; mampulun, 'hiding'; (2.) verbs ending in -wallin, 'existing'; as, tunku-wallin, 'play-

ing'; yuntu-wallin, 'crowding; (3.) verbs ending in -warin, 'causing,' 'making'; as, nunku-warin, 'doing right'; wirraġ-warin, 'doing wrong'; wurtu-warin, 'saturating with water'; (4.) verbs ending in -mindin; as, kildei-mindin, 'fetching.'

8. The word ellin means 'being,' 'state of being,' and sometimes 'doing'; but ennin is the proper word for 'doing'; el appears to mean 'intention or tendency towards'; as, luk ap atye ellir, 'thus I it did,' 'I did so'; ġate yan ellani, 'I (emphatic) will do it'; ġate yan ennani, 'I will do it'; en al yan, 'do with it,' i.e., 'do it'; kunitye ellir, 'enough he has been,' i.e., 'he is dead.' The following are the meanings which belong to ellin and ennin:—ellin, 'doing'; ellir, 'done'; ellani, 'about to do'; ellin, 'having'; ellin, 'being'; ellir, 'has been'; ennin, 'doing'; ennir, 'done'; ennani, 'will do.'

9. The stem of the word warin is used with the imperatives and interrogations; as, kuġ war, 'do hear'; nak war, 'do see'; ġai war, 'do come'; ġinte wara, 'get out of the way,' lit., 'do thou'; ġint war,' do thou '(sc., it); mant war, 'do slowly'; murrumil war, 'make haste'; yelkul war, 'do more'; mint war, 'give me a bit,' lit., 'do to me thou'; kåkin wara, 'put it here'; yaġ wari, 'where do you go.'

10. There are idiomatic expressions in which the words 'go' and 'come' are omitted; as, loldu el itye, or loru el itye, 'up will he,' i.e., 'he will go'; mare el itye, 'down will he,' i.e., 'he will come'; loldan an, 'up it,' i.e., 'fetch it'; moru an, 'down him,' i.e., 'he has gone down'; mare itye, 'down he,' i.e., 'he has come'; moru el ap, 'down will I,' i.e., 'I will go down.'

Loru and loldu both mean 'up'; mare and moru, 'down.'

9. ADJECTIVES.

(1) Simple adjectives are nuġġari, 'good'; wirraġi, bad'; and others; some of these are declined like nouns. (2) Verbal adjectives; as, talin, 'heavy'; balpin, 'white'; kinemin, 'dirty'; kinpin, 'sweet'; prittyin, 'strong.' Some adjectives have both forms; as, balpe, balpin, 'white.'

The mode of declining adjectives has already been shown in connection with the nouns.

Adjectives have no degrees of comparison, but the diminutive particle -ol—used both with adjectives and nouns—is sometimes added to the positive; as, murralappi, 'small'; murralappi-ol, 'very small.'

The numeral adjectives are:—yammalai or yammalaitye, 'one'; niġġeġk, 'two', neppaldar, 'three'; beyond that, all numbers else are ġruwar, 'many.' Gunkar means 'first.' Some adjectives are formed from adverbs; as, karlo-inyeri, 'of to-day,' 'new,' from karlo,' to-day'; kaldan-inyeri, 'old,' from kaldan, 'a. long time'; koġk-inyeri, 'alone,' ' by itself,' from koġk, 'away.'

10. Adverbs.

There are numerous adverbs in the language, but the most common are:—

Adverbs of Time.

Grekkald, 'to-morrow.'
Gurintand, 'often.'
Hik, 'now.'
Kaldau, 'a long time.'
Karlo, 'to-day.'

Palli, 'while,' 'by-and-by.'
Rauwul, 'a long time ago.'
Uġunuk, 'when' (relative).
Wataġgrau, 'yesterday.'
Yaral, 'when' (interrogative).

Yun, 'by-and-by.'

Adverbs of Negation.

Nowaiye, 'none.'
Nowaiye ellin, 'no more.'
Tarnalin, 'not yet.'

Tarnalo, 'no more'; 'never.'
Tarno, 'no'; 'not.'
Tano, 'don't' (imperative).

Tarno el, 'don't' (do it).

Adverbs of Place.

Aiau, 'by (at) that place.'
Akhi, alye, alyikke, 'here.'
Alyenik, 'this place here.'
Kiuau, 'where' (relative).
Ku-un, 'far off.'
Ondu, 'over there.'

Yak, yauo, 'where to.'
Yaġi, 'where'?
Yaġalli, 'where is he'?
Yarnd, 'whence'?
Yarnd inde, 'whence thou'?
Yarnd ande, 'whither thou'?

Examples of the use of Adverbs.

Yak al inde tantani, 'where will you sleep'; ġurluġ aiau, 'at-the-place-where the hill' (is); manti kiuau tantani ap, 'the hut where I shall sleep'; ġap taġulun ku-un, 'I stand far off'; keġk taġulun ku-u, 'they two stand far off'; kar taġulun kuar-un, 'they stand far off.'

The word wunye, 'then,' usually coalesces with the pronoun or verb-sign which follows it; as, wunyap, 'then I'; wunyar, 'then they'; wunyel itye, 'then will he.'

The words uk, ukke, luk, lun, 'so,' 'thus,' denote *resemblance*; as, luk u *or* lun u, 'so,' 'thus'; luk itye yarnin, 'thus he speaks'; lun ellin, 'so being,' *i.e.*, 'like'; luk uġge, 'like this one'; hikkai ukke, 'this way'; hil amb uk, 'for this way,' *i.e.*, 'because'; lun uk, 'thus'; ġo uk ap, 'I go so.'

The word amby may be translated either 'instead of' (preposition) or 'because' (conjunction); as, kaldau amb, 'for a long time'; hil amb uk, 'because'; pinyatowe ald amb anai pelberri means 'sugar for my tea.'

11. Notes on Syntax.

1. The form of the verb is constant in its mood and tenses; only the pronoun-subjects vary.

2. The postpositional suffixes to pronouns are always attached to the accusative case; as, kan-aġk, 'to them.'

3. Pronominal adjectives are always declined with their nouns; as, kin-anyir-aġk taldumand-aġk, 'to his house'; and so also hikkai korn, 'this man,' harnakar kornar, 'these men'; ornaġk nuġgugai, 'in that day.'

4. The diminutive is placed after the case-ending of the noun; as, porl-ald-ol, 'of a little child'; porl-ar-ol, 'of little children.'

5. When an adjective and its noun are declined together, the case-ending is attached only to the adjective; nuġgar-ald korn, 'of a good man.'

6. The post-position -uramb, 'for the purpose of,' is always attached to any verb which is put in the infinitive by another verb; as, pempir il anaġk nakkari tak-uramb, 'he gave me a duck to eat.'

12. Formation of Words.

This is effected by adding on various terminations, some of which have already been noticed:—

(1) -wallin, 'being'; as, pilgeru-wallin, 'greedy.'

(2) -warin, 'making'; as, koġk-u-warin, 'sending away from,' from koġk, 'apart'; anaġk-warin, 'preparing,' 'getting ready' (*lit.*, 'making towards it'), from anaġk, kanaġk, ityanaġk, the dative of the pronoun itye.

(3) -atyeri, 'belonging to'; as, lamm-atyeri, 'wood for a fire,' from lammin, 'carrying on the back.'

13. List of Prepositions, Adverbs, &c.

The prepositions are used as post-positions; those words which in this list are preceded by a hyphen are used as affixes.

Above—kerau, kiath.
After—uġ.
Again—kaġulandai.
    muġanyi.
    -uġanyi.
Agent— -urmi, -amaldy.
Ago, long time—kaldau, klauo.
Ah!—yakkai! takaná!
Almost—ġak.
Alone—naityi, -knotycrai.
Also—inye, -inyin.
Always—kaldau-amp.
Apart—yinbaikulun.
As—luk.
At—warre.

Away from here— -andek.
  ,, from anywhere— -koġk.
  ,, apart—koġkinyeri.
Be off—loru, lolden, ġópwar.
Because—marnd, hil-amb-uk.
Before (of time)—uġunai, uġul.
  ,, (in front of)—ġuġuraġk.
  ,, —ġunkura. [wan.
Behind—yarewar, waiaġ, karlo-
Below—moru.
Beneath—maremuntunt.
Between—taraġk.
Besides—karnanye, -anye.
By itself—koġkinyeri.
By—il, ile.

By-and-by—yun, palli, yuwunuk.
Can— -inyúra.
Close by thee—nungṅ-gai.
Close (near to)—tapagk.
Day, 'this day'—hikkai nugge.
„ after—kinagkurnugk.
Day before yesterday—kagulun nugge.
Down (in)—moru, loldu.
Don't—tano.
Down—wald, muggau.
Eh !—ke ! keh !
Enough—kunye, yikkowun.
Ever—kaldau-amp.
Far off—ku-utyun.
Fast (quickly)—tiwi-warin.
First—kagulandai.
Five—kuk-kuk-ki, keyakki.
For— -amby, arámi, -urumi.
„ -urumi (for-to).
„ them—an -anyiril.
Formerly—kaldau.
For—kuk, kuko.
From, out of— -nend.
„ (because)—mare, marnd.
„ (place)— -anmant.
„ (causative)— -anyir.
Gently—mant.
Go away—thrugkun, taiyin.
Go (imper.)—gowalwar.
Half—galluk, narluk, mirimp.
Hark !—kugwar.
Hence— -andi, -nend. [hi.
Here—kalyan, alye, alyalle, ak-
Here (this here)—alyenik, hikkai alye.
Here (that here)—anailyalye.
„ (close by)—ak-in-ik.
Hereafter—pallai, yun.
How ?—megye, yarild ?
How often ?—minyandai ?
How many ?—minyai, minyárai ?
If—ugun.
Immediately—hikkai, hik, karlo.
In— -ugai.
In that—muggan.

In there—muggar.
Into—agk.
Is—el.
It, that is it—anailyalye. [lo.
Just now—yikkigge, hikkai, kar-
Like—(similar) luk, lun.
„ (similar to) glalin
Long time ago—rande, ranwul.
Long ago—gulli. [war.
Make haste—murrunmil, tyiwe-
Many times—gurintand,
Many (too many)—multu-warin.
May (optative)—ur.
„ (verbal affix), -inanyúra.
„ (postfix)— -urmi, -uramb.
Might (postfix)— -ant.
Morrow (to-) —grekkald.
Much—gruwar.
Much more—gruinyerar.
Much (too much)—multu-warin.
Must— -war or -our.
Near—muggau.
Near thee—tapagk.
Near me—hik alye(-nik), hikak.
Never—tarnalo.
No—tarno.
No (imper. neg.)—tano.
Not—tarno, tano, nowaiye.
Once more—kagulandai.
One more—yammalel.
One—yammalaitye.
Only— -on, -ai.
On the other side—laremmtunt.
Out of the way—nent-wara.
Outside—gurukwar.
Over there—wara.
Perhaps— -ant.
Quick—murrunmilin, tyiwewar.
Round about—laldilald.
Second—wyag, karlowan.
Single—yammalaitye, -ai.
So—lun.
Still (adv.)—thortuld.
Thanks—au-ugune.
That there—naiye uwe.
That way—gauwok.
Then—wanye, wunye.

Then one—iuna.
Then two—yikkuk.
There (being down)—oldau.
„ (up there)—walde, warre.
„ (over there)—naiyuwe.
„ (from there)—ondu.
„ (in there)—muggar.
„ —naiye uwe, muggau.
This way (road)—hikkai-yarluk.
„ (manner)—hikkai-ukke.
Three—neppaldar.
Thus—luku.
Time, a long time ago—kaldau.
„ a short time ago—karlo.
To (into)—agk.
„ (towards)—ugai.
To-day—hikkai nugge.
To-morrow—grekkald.
Too far in—tumutyun.

Together—yunt.
Truly—katyil.
Two—nigkaiegk, pullatye.
Up above—kerau.
Up—loru, war, mari.
Up there—erouke, uaiyewarre.
Upside down—laremuntunt.
Very—pek.
Very near—gake.
Well—golde, gulde.
While—pallai.
Whither—yauo ande. [anyir.
Why?—megye, mind, mindin-
With (a material)—ugai, ugar.
„ (instrument)—in agk ai.
With—ald, al, ugai.
Within—maremuntunt.
Without—indau.
Yes (truly)—katyil.

THE DIYERI DIALECT.

The Diyéri tribe occupies the region about Cooper's Creek, in the heart of South Australia, about 630 miles north of Adelaide. For comparison, their system of pronouns may be given here, as furnished by the Rev. E. Homann, Lutheran Missionary:—

PERSONAL PRONOUNS.

		Singular		
	1st	2nd	3rd	
			Masc.	Fem.
Nom. 1.	Nani	Yidni	Nanya	Nania
2.	Nato	Yundru	Nulia	Nandruya
Gen.	Nakani	Yinkani	Nunkani	Nankani
Dat.	Nakagu	Yinkagu	Nunkagu	Nankagu
Acc.	Nana	Yidnana	Nanya	Nania
Voc.		Perlaia		

		Dual	
Nom. 1.	Nali, naliena	Yudla	Pudlaia
2.	Naldra	Yudla	Pudlali
Gen.	Nalina, naldrani	Yudlani	Pudlani
Dat.	Naliga, naldragu	Yudlagu	Pudlagu
Acc.	Nalina, naldrana	Yudlana	Pudlanaia
Voc.		Yudla	Pudlaia

	⎯⎯⎯⎯⎯⎯Plural⎯⎯⎯⎯⎯⎯		
Nom. 1.	Naiana, naiani	Yura	Tanana
2.	Naiani	Yura	Tanali
Gen.	Naianana	Yurani	Tanani
Dat.	Naianagu	Yuragu	Tanagu
Acc.	Naianana	Yurana	Tananaia
Voc.		Yura	Tanani

The possessive pronouns, which are the personal pronouns of the genitive case, are declined also like substantives; thus:— *Nom.* 1.—Nakani, 'my'; *Nom.* 2.—Nakanali; *Gen.*—Nakanaia; *Dat.*—Nakanani; *Acc.*—Nakani; *Voc.*—Nakanaia.

Mr. Gason, who is well acquainted with another portion of the Diyéri tribe, gives their pronouns thus:—

PERSONAL PRONOUNS.

First Pronoun.		Second Pronoun.	
Singular.		*Singular.*	
Nom. 1.	Althu		
2.	Athu	*Nom.* 2.	Yondru
Gen.	Ni		
Dat.	Akúga		
Acc.	Ani	*Acc.*	Ninna

Plural.		*Plural.*	
Nom. 1.	Janana, uldra	*Nom.* 1.	Yini
Gen.	Janani, uldrani	*Gen.*	Yinkani
Acc.	Ali		

Third Pronoun.

	⎯⎯⎯⎯Singular.⎯⎯⎯⎯			
	Masc.	Fem.	Neut.	*Plural.*
Nom. 1. 2.	Nulia	Naniya, nundroya	Ninna	Thana
Gen.	Núnkani	Nankani		Thanani
Dat.				Wirri, wurra.
Acc.	Nulu	Nania, nandrúya		Thaniya, gúndru

Other pronouns are:—Ninna, ninnea, 'this'; ninna, 'that'; thaniya, gúndru, 'those'; warana, 'who'? wurni, 'whose'? wuroga, 'whom'? whi, wodau, 'what'?

Nouns.

Nouns are declined, as usual, by affixes; after the following manner :—

Kintalo-butu	Apa - n - undru
Dog-with	Water relating-to.
Buću-ali	Kurna - thulka
Blind-of	Man relating-to.
Kurna - undru	Yinkani - ku
Man relating-to.	Yours-to.

The Verb.

The Diyéri verbs, as in other Australian languages, have their tense-forms based on the forms of the imperative and the present participle, as shown in the paradigm below. The numbers indicate the tenses quoted, which are :—1. *Infinitive Present*; 2. *Participle Present*; 3. *Participle Past*; 4. *Participle Reciprocal*; 5. *Indicative, Perfect Definite*; 6. *Indicative, Pluperfect*; 7. *Indicative, Future*; 8. *Imperative, Singular*; 9. *Imperative, Plural*.

	'Grow.'	'Ask.'	'Strike.'
1.		Aćami*	Diami
2.	Búnkuna	Aćana	Diuna
5.	Búnkanaori†	Aćmaori	Dinaori
6.	Búnkanawonthi	Aćanawonthi	Dinawonthi
7.	Búnkanalauni		Dialauni
8.	Búnka	Aćca	
9.			Dimarnu

	'Cover, bury.'	'See.'
1.	Numpani	
2.	Numpuna	Niuna
3.	Numpathuruna	
4.	Numpamulluna	Niamulluna
5.	Numpanaori†	Nianaori
6.	Numpunawonthi	Nianawonthi
7.	Numpalauni	
8.		Nii *or* nihi
9.		Niamaran

*The post-position mi means 'to.' †To decline any tense, prefix the *causative* form of the personal pronouns as the subject.

Some adjectives are participal in their form; as, múnćuruna, 'sick'; mundathuruna, 'lazy'; kukutharkuna, 'unlevel'; kúnkuna, 'lame'; mulluna, 'alike.'

Some adjectives seem to have forms of comparison; as, wordu, 'short,' wordu-murla, 'shorter,' wordu-muthu, 'shortest'; umu, 'good,' umu-murla, 'better'; nuru, 'quick,' nuru-pina, 'very quick'; moa, 'hungry,' moa-pina, 'very hungry.'

(From Dr. Moorhouse's Grammar.)

THE MURUNDI TRIBE.

From Mannum to Overland Corner, on the River Murray, and thirteen miles back from the river on each side; Blanchetown is their head-quarters.

Declension of Nouns.

Nguilpo, 'child.'

		Singular.	Dual.	Plural.
Nom.		Guil-po	Guil-pakul	Guil-pa
Gen.		Guil-yog	Guil-yamakul	Guil-yarago
Dat.	1.	Guil-yanno	Guil-yakullamann	Guil-yarumanno
	2.	Guil-pallarno		
Acc.		Guil-po	Guil-yapakul	Guil-pa
Abl.	2.	Guil-yanmudl	Guil-kakulla mainmudl	Guil-yaramainmudl
	4.		Guil-kulla manno	Guil-yaramanno
	6.	Guil-yanna		

Note.—*Abl.* 2 means 'from'; *Abl.* 4, 'at,' 'with' (a locative form); *Abl.* 6 is the *Causative*, and may be translated 'by.'

Declension of the Personal Pronouns.

	Singular		
	1st.	2nd.	3rd.
Nom.	Gape	Gurru	Ninni
Gen.	Gaiyo	Gurrogo	Nunnago
Dat.	Ganne	Gurrunno	Ninnanno
Acc.	Gape	Gurru	Ninni
Abl. 6.	Ganna	Gurra	Ninna

	Dual		
Nom.	Gedlu	Gupal	Dlano
Gen.	Gedlago	Gupalago	Dlanogo
Dat.	Gedlunno	Gupalanno	Dlanunno

	Plural		
Nom.	Gennu	Gunnu	Nana
Gen.	Gennago	Gunnago	Nanago
Dat.	Genunno	Gununno	Nanunno

Note.—There are no abbreviated forms of the pronouns, and no gender forms.

Declension of the Verb.

The verbs parldkun, 'strike' and terrin, 'stand,' may be taken as examples; in form, both of these are Present Participles.

1. *Present.*	Parldkun	Terrin
2. *Aorist* 1.	Parldka	Terra
3. *Aorist* 2.	Parldkul	
4. *Future*	Parldla	Terridla
5. *Imperative*	Parlka	Terra
6. *Conditional*	Parldkunna	Terrinna
7. *Prohibitive*	Parldkumoi	Terrinni
8. *Preventive*	Parldkulmun-nainmudl	Terrulmun-nainmudl
9. *Optative*	Parldla	Terridla
10. *Infinitive*	Parldlappa	Terrilappa
11. *Past Participle*	Parldkulmugko	Terrulmugko

NOTE.—The meanings are:—No. 2, 'did strike'; No. 3, 'struck'; No. 6, 'would strike'; No. 7, 'strike not'; No. 8, 'that...may not strike'; No. 9, 'may strike'; No. 10, 'for-to strike'; No. 11, 'having struck.' And similarly for the verb terrin.

THE MAROURA TRIBE.

System of kinship found amongst the Maroura tribe.

The Maroura inhabit the country at the junction of the River Darling with the River Murray, and a considerable distance up the Darling.

In the names for relationship, there are different terminations for those that are 'mine,' 'yours,' 'hers'; *e.g.*,

Kambiya, 'my father.' Gammugiyi, 'my mother.'
Kambiyanna, 'your father.' Gammugammu, 'your mother.'
Kambiyanna, 'his father.' Kittha gammu, 'his mother.'

These Mauroras are the tribe which descended the Darling between the years 1831 and 1836 (*cf.* "Mitchell's Expedition"). The Narrinyeri have a tradition that they came down the Darling and then across the desert to the head of Lake Albert.

SOUTH AUSTRALIAN DIALECTS.

English.	1.*	2.	3.	4.
I	Gaii	gapu	gap	gapo
We two	Gadli	gel	ganal	geli
We	Gadlu	gun	nagan	nagano
Thou	Ninna	ginte	gint	gint
You two	Niwa	gul	gul	gulo
You *(plu.)*	Na	gun	gunnu	gun
He, she, it	Pa, padlo	kitye	kitye	kitye
They two	Purla	kegge	kegge	kegge
They	Purna	kar	kar	kar

*NOTE.—The numbers indicate the localities where the words are used; 1. is the Adelaide dialect, 2. is Encounter Bay, 3. is Pomunda, 4. is the dialect spoken to the west of Lake Alexandrina.

	1.	2.	3.
Head	Mukarta	kuli	kuli
Two heads	Mukartilla	kuleġ	kuleġ
Heads	Mukartanna	kular	kular
One	Kunna	yammuli	yammalaityo
Two	Purlaityo	nciġeġ	nciġegi
Three	Mankutyo	maalda	maalda
Four	{ Purlaityo-pur-laityo	} kukar-kukar	{ kiġgaruġ or kukar-kar

(C.)

[ABSTRACT.]

GRAMMAR

OF THE LANGUAGE SPOKEN BY

THE ABORIGINES OF WESTERN AUSTRALIA.

[This short sketch of the Grammar of the language of Western Australia is the only one that I can find anywhere. It is in "The Western Australian Almanac for 1842," and is printed there as an appendix, 'compiled by Chas. Symmons, Protector of the Aborigines, from material furnished by Mr. Francis F. Armstrong, the native interpreter.' Some portions of it are taken 'from the preface to Captain (Sir George) Grey's vocabulary.' I have abridged the material of the Grammar, and adapted it to present uses.—ED.]

1. NOUNS.

The cases are indicated by inflections, thus :—

The Genitive takes the suffix -ák, which means 'of' or 'belonging to'; some districts say -á ġ instead of -ák. *Examples :*—Kalla, 'fire,' kalla-r-ák, 'hot'; miki, 'moon,' mik-áġ, 'moonlight'; dta, 'mouth,' dta-láġ, 'tongue'; gabbi, 'water,' gabbi-láġ, 'belonging to water'; budjor, 'ground,' budjor-láġ, 'belonging to the ground'; mammarápák gidji, 'a man's spear'; yagoák boka, 'a woman's cloak.'

The Dative; its sign is -ál, sometimes -ák; as, ġadjo allija ġulaġ-ál yoġaga, 'I gave it to the child'; Perth-ák bardin, 'going to Perth.'

The Accusative ends in -in; as, ġadjo yan-gorin ġan-gau bru, 'I do not see the kangaroo.'

The Ablative affixes -ál to the nominative case; as, ġadjo boat-ál Perth-ák bardáġa, 'I went in a boat to Perth'; galata kaibra-ál watto bardáġa, 'we went away in a ship'; balgun-ál bumaga, 'she was killed by a gun'; durda cart-ál barduk bardáġa, 'the dog went away with the cart.'

The Plural number is indicated by adding the numerals, but all beyond three are bula, 'much,' 'many.' The words for human beings add -mán, *or* -árra, *or* -gárra to form the plural; mán is an abbreviated form of mán-da, 'altogether,' 'collectively.' Words ending with a vowel take -mán; those ending with a consonant take -gárra; as, kardo, 'a husband *or* wife,' *plu.*, kardo-mán; yago, 'a woman,' *plu.*, yago-mán; djuko, 'sister,' *plu.*, djuko-mán; mammul, 'son,' *plu.*, mammul-gárra; ġulaġ, 'a child,' *plu.*, ġulaġ-gárra.

Declension of a Noun.

Yago, 'a woman.'

	Singular.	Plural.
Nom.	Yago	Yago-mán
Gen.	Yago-ák	Yago-mán-ák
Dat.	Yag-ol *or* Yago-ál	Yago-mán-ál
Acc.	Yago-in	Yago-mán-in
Abl.	Yago-ál	Yago-mán-ál

The Ablative means 'with,' 'by means of.'

Examples:—Yago maiak-ál yugau bardága, 'a woman came to the house'; n'yagga yago-ák wanna, 'that is a woman's staff'; ġadjo marain yago-ál yoġága, 'I gave flour to a woman'; ġadjo yago-in djinnáġ-ga, 'I saw a woman'; budjor yago-ál bianága, 'the ground was dug by a woman.'

The commonest and most useful nouns are:—

Time, Weather, &c.

Cloud—mar-gabbi.
Comet (meteor)—binnar.
Darkness—maiart.
Dawn—waulu.
Daylight—birait.
Lightning—babbáġ-win.
Mid-day—malyárák.
Moon—miki.
Moonlight—mikáġ.
Rain—gabbi; moko.
Sky—gudjait.
Stars—ġan-gar.
Sun—ġan-ga.
Sunshine—monak.
Thunder—málgar.
To-day—aiyi.
To-morrow—morogoto; bináġ.
Yesterday—mairh-ruk.

Elements.

Air (wind)—mar.
Earth—budjor.
Fire—kalla.
Water—gabbi.

Seasons.

Spring—jilba.
Summer—birok.
Autumn—burnuro.
Winter—mág-goro.

Individuals.

A man—mammaráp.
An old man—windo.
A young man—gulambiddi.
A woman—yago.
An old woman—windo.
A young woman—mándiggára.

d

A child—ġulaġ.
An infant—gudja.

Relations.

Ancestors—n'yettin-ġal.
Aunt—man-gat.
Brother—ġundu.
" (eldest)—ġuban; boran.
" (middle)—kardijit.
" (youngest)—guloain.
" -in-law—deni.
Daughter—gwoairat.
Father—mamman.
" -in-law—kan-gun.
Husband, wife—kardo.
Mother—ġan-gan.
" -in-law—man-gat.
Nephew—maiur.
Niece—ġambart.
Sister—djuko.
" (eldest)—jindam.
" (middle)—kauat.
" (youngest)—guloain.
" (married)—mairak.
" -in-law—deni.
Son—mammal.
Uncle—kan-gun.

Parts of the body.

Arm (upper)—wan-go.
" (lower)—marga.
" (right)—ġunman.
" (left)—d'yu-ro.
Back—bogal.
Beard—ġan-ga.
Blood—ġubo.
Bone—kotye.
Bowels—konáġ.
Breast (male)—mingo.
" (female)—bibi.
Chin—ġan-ga.
Countenance—dtamel; minait.
Ear—ton-ka.
Elbow—nogait.
Excrement—konáġ.
Eye—mel.
" -brow—mimbat.

Eye-lash—mel-kambar.
" -lids—mel-nalyak.
Flesh—ilain.
Foot—jina.
Forehead—bigaić.
Hair of head—kattamangarra.
Hand—marbra.
Head—katta.
Heel—ġardo.
Knee—bonnit.
Leg—matta.
Liver—maierri.
Mouth—dta.
Neck—wardo.
Nose—mulya.
Side—ġarril.
Stomach—kobbálo.
Tear—mingalya.
Teeth—nalgo.
" (upper)—ġardák-yugauin.
" (lower)—ira-yugauin.
Temples—yaba.
Thumb—marhra-ġan-gan.
Tongue—dtalaġ.

Animals, Birds, &c.

Bat—bambi.
Bird (a)—jida.
Crow—wardaġ.
Dog—durda.
Flea, louse—kolo.
Fly—nurdo.
Lizard—jina-ara.
Pig—maggoroġ.
Snake—wan-ġal.

Miscellaneous.

Bark (of tree)—mabo.
Egg—nurdo.
Food (of all sorts)—daḋja.
Grass—bobo.
Grave (a)—bogol.
Hill (a)—katta.
House (a)—maia.
Lake (large)—mulur.
" (small)—ġu-ra.
River—bilo.

Rock, stone—buyi.
Sand—goyarra.
Sea—odern.
Stick (wood)—garba.
,, (fire-)—kalla-matta.

Tree—burnu.
Water—gabbi.
Water (fresh)—gabbi dji-kŭp.
,, (stream)—gabbi gurjait.
Young (animal)—noba.

2. ADJECTIVES.

The adjectives most commonly in use are:—

Alive—won-gin, dordăk.
Angry—gărrag̈.
Arm (left)—n'yardo.
,, (right)—g̈un-man.
Bad—djul.
Big—g̈omon.
Bitter—djallăm.
Black—moàn.
Clear (as water)—karrail.
Cold—nagga.
Dead—wonnaga.
Dry (not wet)—ilar.
Far away—urar.
Fat—boain-gadăk.
Fresh—milgar.
Good—gwabba.
Green—gerip-gerip.
Hard—murdoen.
Health (in)—barra-barra.
High—iragàn.

Hot—kallag̈.
Like (similar)—mogin.
Little—n'yu-map.
Long, length—walaiadi.
Low—g̈ar-dăk.
Narrow—nulu.
Near—barduk.
Old—windo.
Red—wilgilăg̈.
Short—gorad (-da).
Sick—mendaik.
Slow—dăbbăk.
Soft—g̈unyăk.
Sweet—mulyit.
Tall—urri.
Thin—kotyelarra.
True—bundo.
Wet—balyan.
White—wilbun.
Wild—waii-waii.

A substantive acquires an adjective meaning by taking such suffixes as -gadăk, 'having, possessing,' -bru, 'without,' which corresponds to the English suffix 'less'; as, jig̈ala-gadăk, 'having horns,' 'a cow'; kardo-gadăk, 'having a husband *or* wife,' 'married'; boka-bru, 'cloak-less'; gabbi-bru, 'without water.'

Comparison of Adjectives.

Some adjectives add jin for the comparative; as, from dăbbăk, 'slow,' dăbbăk-jin, 'slower'; gwidjir, 'sharp,' gwidjir-jin 'sharper'; yerrăk, ' high,' yerrak-jin, 'higher.' But usually a reduplication makes the comparative, and -jil is added to the base for the superlative; as, gwabba, 'good,' gwabba-gwabba, 'better'; gwabba-jil, 'best.' This intensive particle -jil, equivalent to 'verily,' may be added to other parts of speech; as, kardo-jil, 'one who is in the direct line for marrying with another'; dadja-jil, 'it is certainly meat'; kannah-jil, 'is it indeed so'? The English 'very' is rendered by a reduplication; as, mulyit-mulyit, 'very sweet.'

Numerals.

'One,' gain; 'two,' gudjal; 'three,' warh-raġ; 'four,' gudjal-gudjal; 'five' is marh-jin baga, 'half the hands'; 'ten' is belli-belli-marhjin baga, 'the hand on either side.'

In reckoning time the natives say 'sleeps' for days, and 'summers and winters' for years. There is no *Article*.

3. PRONOUNS.

The pronouns must be carefully used, for a very slight change in the termination of any one of them will alter altogether the force and meaning of a sentence.

The *personal pronouns* are :—

Singular.	Plural.
Gadjo or ġanya, 'I.'	Gala-ta, 'we.'
N'yundo or ġinni, 'thou.'	N'yuraġ, 'ye.'
Bal, 'he, she, it.'	Balgun, 'they.'

They are thus declined :—

Singular.

	1st.	2nd.	3rd.
Nom.	Gadjo / Ganya	N'yundo / Ginni	Bal
Gen.	Gannalák	Nyunnolák	Balák
Dat.	Gama	N'yunno	Balák
Accu.	Ganyain	Ginnin	Balin
Abl.			Balál

Plural.

Nom.	Galata	N'yuraġ	Balgun
Gen.	Gannilák	N'yuraġak	Balgunák
Dat.	Gannilák	N'yuraġál	Balgunák
Acc.	Gannil (-in)	N'yuraġin	Balgunin
Abl.	Gannilál	N'yuraġál	Balgunál

There are thus two forms for the *Sing. Nom.* of the first and second pronouns; ġadjo and n'yundo seem to be used with an active sense of the verb, but ġanya and ġinni with a passive sense; for there is no passive *form* of the verb, and there is no verb 'to be'; ġanya and ġinni are always used with a participle or an adjective; ġadjo and n'yundo are never so used. *Examples of their use :—*Gadjo djinnaġ, 'I see,' but ġanya bardin, 'I am going'; ġadjo dtan, 'I pierce,' but ġanya gannauin, 'I am eating.'; ġadjo burno dendaġaga, 'I climbed a tree,' but ġanya waugálál bukkanaga, 'I was bitten by a snake'; ġanya windo, 'I am old'; ġanya ġárraġ, 'I am angry.' Similarly for the second pronouns; as, n'yundo kattidj, 'do you understand'? but yan ġinni wan-gauin, 'what are

THE DIALECT OF W. AUSTRALIA. 53

you talking about'? n'yundo naitjȧk gabbi ġanna gaġau-
bru, 'why do you not fetch me water'? but ġinni naitjȧk
balin bumawin, 'why are you beating me'?; ġinni djul,
'you are wicked'; ġinni goradda, 'you are short.'

		—————Dual—————	
	1st.	2nd.	3rd.
Nom. 1.	Galli	Nubal	Bula
2.	Galla	Nubal	Bulala
3.	Gannik	Nubin	Bulen.

Another form of ġannik is ġannana.

The forms marked *nom.* 1 are used by brothers and sisters *or*
two friends closely related; *nom.* 2., by parent and child *or* by
nephew and uncle; *nom.* 3., by husband and wife *or* by two
persons of different sexes affectionately attached, *or* (ġannana)
by two brothers-in-law.

The *Possessive Pronouns* are :—
Ganna, 'my,' ġannalȧk, 'mine'; n'yunna, 'thy,' n'yun-
nalȧk, n'yunnalȧġ, 'thine'; balȧk, balalȧk, 'his, her, its,'
ġannilȧk, 'our *or* ours'; n'yuraġȧk, 'your *or* yours'; balgunȧk,
' their *or* theirs.' The *Demonstrative Pronouns* are :—N'yagga,
'that,' 'those'; nidja, ' this,' 'these.' The *Interrogative Pronouns*
are:—Ganni, ' who '? *i.e.*, ' who are you '? ġando, ' who '? *i.e.*,
' who did that '? ġannoġ, ' whose '?

4. VERBS.

The verbs in most common use are :—

Arise—irabin
Beat—buma
Become—abbin
Bite—bȧkkan
Break—takkan
Bring; carry off; take
   away—bȧrraġ
  Marry—kardo barraġ
Burn (fire)—burrarȧp
Bury—bianan
Carry—gaġau
Cook—dukun
Cry—miraġ
Cry out—mirau
Dig—bian
Eat, drink —ġanno ; nalgo.
Fear—waien

Fight—bakadju
Fly—bȧrdaġ
Go—bardo; watto
Go away—kolbardo
Hear—kattidj
Pain—bȧkkan
Pierce—dtan
See—djinnaġ; ġan-gau
Sit—ġinnau
Speak—wan-gau
Spear—gidjil
Stand—yugau
Take—gaġau
Tear—jeran
Throw—gwardo
Tie—yutarn
Understand—kattidj
  Walk—gannau.

Imperatives are:—

Come here—kowa-kowa, yual	Leave it alone—bal *or* wanja
Go on—ġatti	Listen—näh-näh
Get up—irap	Take care—garrodjin
Go away—watto	Stay, remain—nannäp

Tenses.

1. *Indic. present.*—For this, use either the infinitive or the form of the present participle; as, ġadjo djinnäġ, 'I see'; but ġanya bumawin, 'I am beating.'
2. *Indic. preterite.*—Use the past participle, *or* add -ga to the infinitive; the relative distance of the past periods of time is indicated by prefixing to the tense the words gori, 'just now,' karamb, 'a short time since,' gorah, 'a long time ago.'
3. *Indic. future.*—Here the first and second personal pronouns singular become ġadjul and n'yundul, 'I will,' 'you will.' The distance of the future time is indicated by placing before the verb the adverbs burda, 'presently,' and mila for any more remote time.
4. *Imperative mood.*—Lay emphasis on the last vowel of the present indicative.
5. *Participle present.*—Add -in or -win to the infinitive.
    ,,   *past.*—Add -ga to the infinitive.
6. *Passive voice.*—Here the form of the sentence is elliptical; therefore ġanya, ġinni are used with the past participle and the ablative of the instrument or cause.

DECLENSION OF A TRANSITIVE VERB.

Buma, 'to beat,' 'kill,' 'blow as a flower.'

Infinite—Buma.   *Part. pres.*—Bumawin.
    Part. past.—Bumäga.
Tense 1. *bumawin. *T.* 2. *gori bumäga. *T.* 3. †burda buma.
    T. 4. buma.
These numbers indicate the Tenses as shown above.

*The pronouns to be used here are:—*Sing.* ġanya, ġinni, bal; *Plur.* ġalata, n'yuraġ, balgun; but instead of ġanya and ġinni, *T.* 2. takes gadjo and nyundo; †there use the forms ġadjul, n'yundul.

Passive Voice.—For the passive voice, use the same tense-forms as in the active voice, that is, buma for the *pres.* and the *fut.*, and bumäga for the *past*, but prefix to them the *accusative* cases of the personal pronouns; thus, ġanya-in gori bumäga, 'I was beaten lately'; *lit.*, '(some one) beat me lately.' But the ablative of the cause or instrument may also be used to form a passive voice; thus, ġanya gidjial dtannaga, 'I am pierced by a spear.'

The substantive verb.—There does not appear to be any copula; it is certainly not used in such sentences as ġanya yulap, 'I am hungry'; ġinni kotyelara, 'thou art thin'; bal windo, 'he is old'; ġalata gwabba, 'we are good'; n'yuraġ djul, 'you are wicked'; balgun mindait, 'they are sick.'

5. Adverbs.

The adverb is placed before the verb; useful adverbs are:—

After (behind)—ġolan-ga
Again—garro
Already—gori
Always—dowir
Before (in front)—gwaićaġat
Close to; near—barduk
Continually—kalyagal
Enough—belak
Formerly—karamb
Here—n'yal
How many—namman
Immediately—gwaić; ilak
Thus—wanno-ić
More—ġatti-ġatti

Never—yuatjil
No—yuada
Not—bart; bru; yuada
Now—yaii
Perhaps—gabbain
So—winnirak
So many—winnir
That way—wunno
Then—garro
There (*prox.*)—yellinya
„ (*remote*)—boko; bokoja
Where—winji; winjal; yan
Yes—qua
Yonder—bokoja

6. Prepositions.

These are few in number:—

After (*dat.*)—ġolaġ
Among (*partitive*)—manda
„ (mixed with)—kardagor
By (affix)—-al
In (within)—bura
Of—-ak

On (upon)—ġadja
To—-ak *or* -al
With (in company with)—
„ gambarn (takes the *acc.*);
„ barduk (takes the *dat.*)
Without—bru

In use, they are all *post-positions*, and are always placed *after* the noun or pronoun. Gadja is used of one thing lying on another, but never of anything lying on the ground.

7. Interrogation, Affirmation, Negation.

A question is asked by putting kannah at the end of the sentence; as, n'yundo tonka, kannah, 'do you hear'? An answer may be given by qua, 'yes,' or by affixing -bak to the word used in reply; as, yallanait, 'what is that'? burnu-bak, 'it is a tree.' If the reply is negative, put bart *or* bru after verbs, and yuada after adjectives.

8. Conjunctions.

Gudjir, 'and'; minnig, 'if'; ka, 'or.' There is no word for 'when,' but minnig and ka are used in its stead; for instance, 'when I see you to-morrow' will be expressed by 'if I see you to-morrow'; and 'when did you come to Perth'? will be 'did you come to Perth to-day or yesterday'?

9. Interjections.

Nah—ah! so! (to indicate that a person is listening to what is related), and n'yón—'alas'!

(D.)

GRAMMAR AND VOCABULARY

OF THE ABORIGINAL DIALECT CALLED

THE WIRRADHURI.

[The Wirradhuri dialect, or, as I call it, the Wirádhari, covers the whole heart of N. S. Wales; its limits are shown on the map of the native tribes. I consider myself fortunate in having secured the publication of the Grammar and Vocabulary of so important a tribe. The following manuscript was written about fifty years ago by the late Archdeacon Günther, and is specially reliable because of its author's character and experience, and because, at that time, the tribe had not yet begun to decay, and its language was entire. He was educated for the Ministry at Basle, in Switzerland, attending lectures there at the University and the Missionary College; subsequently he prosecuted his studies at the C. M. Society's College, Islington, London.

In 1837, he commenced his missionary work among the aborigines of the Wirádhari tribe at "Wellington Valley," now Wellington, in New South Wales. Here he compiled this Grammar and Vocabulary; he also translated the Gospel by St. Luke and portions of the Prayer Book for the use of the tribes on the Macquarie River and the neighbouring country. His efforts and those of the mission party, in ameliorating the condition of the natives and teaching them, met with considerable success. After the mission was abandoned by the authorities, he was induced by Bishop Broughton to accept the parish of Mudgee, where he laboured for many years, and died in December, 1879.

These MSS. are the property of the late Mr. Günther's son, the present Archdeacon of Camden, New South Wales, who has kindly lent them to me for this purpose. In editing them, I have retained the author's mode of spelling the native words, and have made only some slight alterations in the form of the matter of the Grammar and the Vocabulary, with the view of securing greater symmetry throughout.—Ed.]

1. THE GRAMMAR.

1. The Declension of Nouns.

There is, properly speaking, only one primary declension, but the principle of assimilation, to which the language has a strong tendency, sometimes produces slight variations of the terminations of the nouns before the case-endings; similarly, when the last letter but one of the stem is *i*.

In order to cover all these variations, the number of the declensions will amount to eight. It must, however, be observed that here the formation of cases differs materially from the modes used in other languages, at least from that of the Latin and Greek. The simple or nominative form undergoes no alteration, but, to form the cases, it takes additions by means of postfixes. The only apparent exception to this rule is that where the letter *i* is cast out. The number of cases cannot easily be fixed, since almost every relation in which a noun may be placed is signified by some postfix or other; those given in the examples below include the most common and essential relations.

A strange peculiarity of this language is the existence of two nominative-forms—the one the *simple nominative* or nominative-declarative, corresponding to the question 'who *or* what is it'? and the other the *nominative active*, when the thing or person spoken of is considered as an agent; this answers to the question, 'who *or* what does it'? The *genitive* and the *dative* are alike; the *accusative* is the same as the simple nominative; the *vocative* is known by the exclamatory word 'ya' put before the simple nominative, or by its termination, which is like that of the genitive.

The case-endings and their meanings may be shown thus :—

Case.	Terminations.	Meaning.
1. *Nominative*		the simple form.
2. *Nom. agent.*	-du, -dyu, -gu, lu, -ru	the agent form.
3. *Genitive*	-gu	'of'; 'belonging to.'
4. *Dative*	-gu	'to,' 'for,' 'towards.'
5. *Accusative*	the same as *nom.* 1.	the direct object.
6. *Vocative*	prefixes *ya* to *nom.* 1.	
7. *Locomotive*	-dyi, -li, -ri	place from which.
8. *Conjunctive*	-durai *or* -durei	'together with.'
9. *Locative*	-da, -dya, -ya, -la, -ra	'in,' 'on,' 'at.'
10. *Instrumental*	-durada	'by means of.'

The numbering of the cases corresponds with that shown on the Paradigm.

The same word is both singular and plural without change; only when the idea of plurality is to be conveyed, the noun adds the word galaġ and is then declined like wallaġ of the paradigm.

58   AN AUSTRALIAN LANGUAGE.

PARADIGM OF THE DECLENSION OF NOUNS.

Cases.	1st. Maddan 'wool'	2nd. Burai 'boy'	3rd. Giwaldain 'cook'	4th. Balli 'baby'	5th. Bulbin 'whirlwind'	6th. Ugal 'young man'	7th. Inar 'woman'	8th. Wallang 'stone'
1. Maddan		Burai	Giwaldain	Balli	Bulbin*	Ugal	Inar	Wallang
2. Maddandu		Buradu	Giwaldandu	Ballidyu	Bulbindyu	Ugallu	Inarru	Wallanggu
3.&4. Maddangu		Buraigu	Giwaldaingu	Balligu	Bulbingu	Ugalgu	Inargu	Wallanggu
5. Maddan		Burai	Giwaldain	Balli	Bulbin	Ugal	Inar	Wallang
6. Ya maddan		— the vocative prefixes ya to the simple nominative —						
7. Maddandi		Buraidyi	Giwaldaindyi	Ballidyi	Bulbindyi	Ugalli	Inarri	Wallandi
8. Maddandurai			Giwaldaindurai	Ballidurai	Bulbindurai	Ugaldurai	Inardurai	Wallandurai
9. Maddanda		Burada		Ballidya	Bulbindya	Ugalla	Inarra	Wallangga
10. Maddandurada		Buraidurada	Giwaldaindurada	Ballidurada	Bulbindurada	Ugaldurada	Inardurada	Wallandurada

*Thus also is declined ng final, even when preceded by the vowel i; as, kaling, 'water,' nom. ag., kalindyu, &c., &c.

NOTE.—By using other postfixes, additional cases may be formed; e.g., birandi and biranga, added to the proper name Bidarai, give Bidarai-birandi and Bidarai-biranga, 'from ('at') Bidarai's place.'

☞ These words are shown here in all the principal cases only for the sake of example.

The examples given above show that the variations in declension arise from assimilation. Thus, when *r* or *l* is the last sound of the word, these letters assimilate the initial consonant of the postfix. If the vowel of the last syllable is *i*, either ending the word or syllable or followed by *n*, euphony adds the sound of *y* to the *a* of the postfix; thus, dya, dyu, dyi appear instead of da, du, di. When *i* is ejected, this rule does not apply. The ejection of *i* preceded by *a* takes place in the *Nom.* 2 and in the *Locative*.

If the possessive pronoun is put before its noun, it is declined with the same termination as the noun. But the more common practice is to put the pronoun behind it in an abbreviated form as a postfix; as, buraigundi, 'to my boy'; buraigunu, 'to your boy'; buraigugula, 'to his boy.' 'To my boy,' with the possessive pronoun detached, would be ġaddigu buraigu.

2. THE COMPARISON OF ADJECTIVES.

There is no comparative form of the adjective, nor, properly speaking, a superlative, though certain terminations, such as baġ 'very,' bambilaġ 'exceedingly,' express a superlative or a very high quality of the thing. Hence the comparisons on things are expressed in an indistinct manner. To say, 'this is better than that,' would be ġinna maroġ, wirai ġannalla; *lit.*, 'this is good, not that'; nila ġarambaġ, ġainguagual, *lit.*, 'this very good, that also.' But to say, 'this is the best of all,' would be nila maroġbangan, wirai iġianna ġinnallal; *lit.*, 'this is good indeed, these are not like it.' Adjectives may be declined like nouns, but in syntax they are not always declined.

3. THE VERB.

The study of the verb is attended with some difficulty on account of its many tenses and modifications; it is, however, conjugated in a very regular manner, and, excepting the imperative, it is non-inflexional throughout all its tenses, all the persons, both singular and plural, having the same form. The conjugations may be reduced to about five, nor do these vary much, and, so far as they do vary, they follow strict rules according to the termination of the last syllable and the vowel preceding it.

The verbs, then, are arranged in conjugations according to the terminations of the present tense of the indicative; thus :—

Terminations of Conjugations.

1. -ánna *or* -āna; 2. -unna; 3. -inga; 4. -arra; 5. -irra.

The vowel of the penultimate syllable may be said to terminate the radical part of the verb, which is retained in all the tenses and modifications, whilst the remainder is liable to be thrown off. Those tenses where *a* becomes *ai* are only apparent exceptions to the rule.

In the formation of the tenses and modifications, the letter *r* is changed into its relative liquid *l*, and *n*, for the sake of euphony, is changed into *m* by assimilation. Euphony also requires an *a* terminating the root to be modified into the diphthong *ai*; and *nd*, on account of the influence of the preceding *i*, becomes *ndy*.

THE TENSES.

There are no fewer than ten tenses in the language; besides those common to most languages, some are peculiar tenses which have an adverbial signification.

The following shows the conjugation of a simple verb:—

Buma, 'beat.'
INDICATIVE MOOD.

T. 1. (*Present Tense*).

Sing. 1. Gaddu* bumarra   I beat.
       2. Gindu* bumarra   Thou beatest.
       3. Guin* bumarra   He, she, beats.

Dual.   Galli bumarra   We (two) beat.
          Galligu bumarra   He and I beat.

Plu. 1. Geanni bumarra   We beat.
      2. Gindugir bumarra   You beat.
      3. Guaingulia bumarra   They beat.

T. 2. Gaddu bumalgarrin   *T*. 6. Gaddu bumalinni
    3. Gaddu bumalgurranni   7. Gaddu bumalgirri
    4. Gaddu bumae   8. Gaddu bumalgurriawagirri
    5. Gaddu bumalguan   9. Gaddu bumalgarrigirri
       T. 10. (*Fut.-perf.*) Gaddu bumalyigirri.

The *T*. numbers here indicate the Tenses as on page 26 of this volume.

INFINITIVE.
Bumalli, 'to beat.'
IMPERATIVE.

Sing. 1. Bumallidyu, 'let me beat.'
       2. Bumalla (†buma), 'beat thou.'
       3. Bumallaguin barri, 'let him beat.'‡

Dual   Galli bumalli, 'let us two beat.'
         Gulagalligunna bumalli, 'let him and me beat.'

Plu. 1. Bumalli geanni, 'let us beat.'
     2. Gindugir bumalla (†buma), 'beat you.'
     3. Bumalla guaingulia barri, 'let them beat.'

* For emphasis use here—*Sing.* 1. yallu *or* baládu, *or* yalludu; 2. balundu; 3. balaguin. † This abbreviated form is often used. ‡ The verbs ending in -ana *or* -anna differ from this in *Imp. sing.* 1, 2, 3.

THE WIRADHARI DIALECT. 61

VERBAL NOUN.

Bumalgidyal (bumagidyal), 'beating.'
This form, being a verbal noun, can never be used as a participle. In the Greek language and the German, the infinitive serves as a verbal noun; so also the Latin *supine* and *gerundive*.

The forms which supply our participles are classed with the modifications of the verb. The subjunctive is formed with mallaġ, the optative with baġ; for there are no real subjunctive or potential forms. Sentences of that description are expressed by a kind of auxiliary, such as garra or mallaġ; or by the future tense, with the conditional conjunction yandu attached :—

Yandundu dalgirri, 'if I should eat.'
Gaddu garra dalgirri, 'I can *or* would eat.'
Gaddu mallaġ dé, 'I would *or* should eat' (*or* have eaten).
Yandundu mallaġ dé, 'if you did eat' (*or* would eat).
Mallaġ here is not a verb but a mere subjunctive particle.

Nor is there a form for the passive. A kind of passive is sometimes expressed by putting the subject in the accusative, along with the active form of the verb; but the source whence comes the action is not named, for that can only be put in the *agent-nominative case*. Hence, it must be that this is not in reality a passive, but an active sentence; only, for the sake of laying more emphasis on the action done, the agent is omitted.

TABLE OF CONJUGATIONS, PRINCIPAL TENSES, AND MOODS.

	Present.	*Imperfect.*	*Perfect.*
1.	Yannanna	Yanné	Yan-nān (*i.e.*, -naán)
	Guna	Guné	Gaguain
2.	Yunna	Yunné	Yunnān
3.	Gumbiga	Gumbinna	Gumbinnān
4.	Baddarra	Baddae	Baddalguān
5.	Gaddambirra	Gaddambie	Gaddambilguān

	Future.	*Infinitive.*	*Imperative.*
1.	Yannagirri	Yannagi	Yannada*
	Gagirri	Gagi	Gaga
2.	Yungirri	Yungi	Yunga
3.	Gumbigirri	Gumbigi	Gumbidya
4.	Badalgirri	Badalli	Badalla
5.	Gaddambilgirri	Gaddambilli	Gaddambia

This table contains all the principal tenses—those in which different conjugations vary. The other tenses of each conjugation follow the model given for the verb bumarra. Of course, not every verb is used in all the tenses; thus, yunné, the imperfect, is not used. The numbers indicate the conjugations.

* The imperative is often shortened; as, nada, na; galla, ga; malla, ma.

The conjugations of certain letters may occasionally, but rarely, cause the general rules to be violated for the sake of euphony; thus, the verb mugāna has in the perfect tense mugaiguān, not, as might be expected, mugaguan, no doubt, on account of two 'g's' being so near each other.

4. Modifications of the Verb.

A characteristic feature and peculiarity of this aboriginal dialect is the use of numerous postfixes. By means of these, the noun shows an unusual number of cases, which supply in a certain measure the absence of our prepositions. In a similar manner, the verb takes additions or changes of its form, by which new forms it expresses its modified significations according to the various relations in which the simple verb may be placed. These tend to enrich the language considerably, since the modified ideas implied in them often produce quite a new kind of word or signification. As new verbs, they may be adjusted to some one or other of the examples already given, agreeably to their terminations. Hence they can never be supposed to be merely conjugations.

For the sake of convenience, I shall carry one verb through the modifications, though it cannot be expected that all verbs are used or needed in every modification. I will take the root-form buma, 'beat,' as the chief example of these modifications, but another suitable one will be always added.

Some of the postfixes in those examples have doubtless lost or changed their original signification in certain verbs.

Examples of the use of Suffixes to modify the meaning of Verbs.

1. Bianna, 'a constancy of action'; as, bumal-bianna, 'to be always beating'; ġa-bianna, 'to be always looking.

2. Gunnanna, 'a present continuance of action'; as, bumal-gunnanna, 'to be now beating'; ġa-gunnanna, 'now looking on.'

Both of these are used for our participle, but in a definite and indicative way; but as, like other verbs, they are conjugated, and never employed as adjectives, they cannot be considered as participial forms, but only as modifications of the verbs.

3. Awaigunnanna, 'a long continuance'; as, bumal-awaigunnanna, 'to be beating a long time'; ġagawaigunnanna, 'to be looking on long.' This does not much differ from No. 2.

4. Garrimāna, 'a continuance of all day long'; bumal-garrimāna, 'to be beating all day long'; bunba-gar̩rimāna, 'to run about all day long.'

5. Guabianna, 'a continuance for the night'; bumallai-guabianna, 'to beat (fight) all the night'; winai-guabianna, 'to sit up all night.'

6. Dillinga (*reflexive*); as, bumangi-dillinga, 'to beat one's self'; mirama-dillinga, 'to defend one's self.'

7. Lanna (*reciprocal*); as, bumal-lanna,'to beat each other,' 'to fight'; nurungamil-lanna, 'to love each other.'

8. Alinga (*reiterative*); as, bumal-alinga, 'to beat again'; yannai-alinga, 'to go again.'

9. Numinga implies that an action is to last for a little time only before another; as, bumal-numinga, 'to beat previously'; ganuminga, 'to see beforehand.'

10. Mambirra is causative and permissive; as, bumali-mambirra, 'to let beat'; yal-mambirra, 'to cause one to speak,' 'to teach.'

11. Gambirra, instrumental; meaning that a thing has been done by means of an instrument, tool, *or* weapon; as, bumalgambirra (not used); bangal-gambirra, 'to break by throwing at (or hitting) with something.'

12. Billinga, submissive; expressive of obedience to a command; as, buma-billinga, 'to beat when told *or* ordered'; yanna-billinga, 'to go when ordered off.'

13. Eilinga implies a vicarious action—an action done on behalf of, or instead of, another; as, bum-eilinga, 'to beat instead of another'; barram-eilinga, 'to get or provide for another.'

14. Duringa seems to intimate a change of action, the turning of one's attention from one thing to another, or to do a thing well and thoroughly; as, bumal-duringa, 'to leave of the present act of beating'; winnanga-duringa, 'to forget,' 'to think of something else'; 'to reflect.'

15. Wanna probably signifies an aim at *or* a purpose to do a thing; or rather, to act in a kind of series of doings, one after another, going all round, or to be just in the act of doing; as, bumalla-wanna, 'to beat one after another'; yannaia-wanna, 'to walk away,' 'to walk from one place to another.'

16. Danna means the resuming of an action after having taken refreshment; as, bumal-danna, 'to beat again' after eating; bumba-danna, 'to run off again' after a little refreshment.

17. Gilanna indicates a kind of dual action; as, bumalugilanna, 'two to beat together at once'; bumban-gilanna, 'two to run together.'

18. Yarra is the verb 'to speak'; it can be put or joined to any verb as a postfix, and is then expressive of a command; 'ba' is put between as a uniting syllable; thus, yanna-ba-yarra, 'to order to go', 'to send away'; bumal-ba-garra, 'to tell to beat.'

19. Birra, nirra, dirra, banirra, bamarra, bunmarra; these particles, when joined to a neuter or an intransitive verb, give it a transitive and causative signification; thus, from gannarra, 'to burn,' is formed gannal-birra, 'to set on fire'; ballunna, 'to die' gives ballubunirra, 'to kill'; banganna,

to break' (of itself), banga-dirra, 'to chop, smash'; yannanna 'to go,' yannabanirra, 'to make go,' 'to drive,' and yanna-bunmarra, 'to cause to go away'; from mabbinga, 'to stay, stop' comes mabbi-bamarra, 'to make one stay.' Bunmarra is a verb by itself signifiying 'to make, to do.'

20. Maranna implies a reference to a previous action, on which the action of the verb is dependent; as, bumal-maranna, 'to beat after' having caught one; dal-maranna, 'to eat after' having picked it up.

21. Nāna implies the adverb 'after'; as, bumal-nāna, 'to beat after another'; bunban-nāna, 'to run after another'; ġan-nāna, 'look after one.'

22. Einga implies 'precedent, before'; as, bumal-einga, 'to beat first,' *i.e.*, before another; ġolleng-einga, 'to return first.'

23. Naringa, joined to a few verbs, implies that the action is done by 'falling'; also figuratively, it is expressive of a rest after moving; as, (1.) banga-naringa, 'to break by falling'; dalba-naringa, 'to be dashed by falling'; (2.) wi-naringa, 'to settle down'; warran-naringa, 'to make a call and stay a little.'

24. Bilāna *or* balāna is always preceded by *m* even after *l.* It implies the idea of 'moving on' *or* going along, and gradually getting into, whilst engaged in an action; as, ya-mbilāna, 'to cry whilst going along'; dé-mbilāna, 'to eat whilst walking'; ġu-mbilāna, 'to become *or* get gradually.'

25. Buoanna implies both coming back and giving back; as, buogal-buoanna, 'to come back'; yanna-mbuoanna, 'to go back'; ġu-mbuoanna, 'to give back'; nanna-mbuoanna,' to throw back.'

There are also some words that attach themselves to verbs as auxiliaries; as,—

1. Garra, 'to be,' used only with the present indicative. Its abbreviation, ga, is used interrogatively.

2. Warré goes with present and future time. Its abbreviation is wa—also used interrogatively.

3. Bala, 'to be,' *or* ba, is more affirmative; in its shorter form, ba, it strengthens pronouns; as, baladu, 'I am.'

4. Yamma is an interrogative word, like the English 'do'; it is most commonly joined to pronouns. None of these auxiliaries has any effect on the structure of the sentence.

In the passive use of the verb, the subject is merely put in the accusative, and the verb remains unaltered.

5. Formation of Words.

Derivatives are formed from the roots of verbs by adding various terminations. Thus, -dain denotes the agent who does the action expressed by the verb; as, birbára, 'to bake,' birba dain, 'a baker.' The word -gidyal forms participial nouns; as, kabinga, 'to begin,' kabin-gidyal, 'a beginning'; winanganna, 'to know,' winan-gidyal, 'the knowing,' 'knowledge.' The terminations -mubaġ and -múgu denote the absence of some quality; as, uda, 'ear,' uda-múgu, 'deaf'; marong, 'good' marom-mubang, 'bad,' *lit.*, 'good-less.' Adjectives are formed from nouns by reduplication, or by suffixes; as, wallang, 'stone,' walla-wallang, 'stony'; win, 'fire,' wi-win, 'hot'; ngarru, 'honey,' ngarru-ngarru, 'sweet.' Terminatives are, -durai; as, wallan-durai, 'having stone,' 'stony'; -bang; as, win-munnilbang 'hollow firewood,' from munnil, 'a hole'; -bang also signifies increase or multitude and thus has a collective force; as, gibbir, 'man,' gibbir-bang, 'many men,' 'mankind'; ingel, 'ill,' ingelbang, 'very ill.' Durai, as a suffix to a verb-stem, implies ability to perform the action of the verb; as, bambinga, 'to swim,' bambi-durai, 'able to swim'; yanna, 'to walk,' yannaidurai, 'able to walk'; with nouns it also denotes the possession of the thing; as, yamandu daluban-durai, 'have you a soul,' *lit.*, 'are you soul-having *or* soul-with?'

Marra, 'to do,' 'to make,' joined to another verb, or, oftener, to nouns and adjectives, answers exactly to the Latin *facio*; as, giwai, 'sharp,' giwai-marra, 'to sharpen'; giwa, 'wet, moist,' giwa-marra, 'to moisten'; gullai, 'net,' gullai-marra, 'to net, to make a net.' Hence the natives join -marra to English verbs; as, grind-marra, 'to grind'; ring-marra, 'to ring the bell.'

6. Conjunctions and Adverbs.

Wargu, widdyua, 'what for,' 'why'? widdyung, 'which way'? widdyuġġnor, 'which side (direction)'? widdyuġgu, 'when'? widdyuġgaga, 'I don't know when'; minyangan, 'how many'? minyanganga, 'I don't know how many'; minyanganda, 'how many times'? minyangandaga, 'I don't know how many times'; warban (used with yammagarra), 'how much'?

Da (the *d* being sounded very soft) signifies locality; as, dága, 'where'? dagu, 'of what place'? dagú, 'to what place'? dagannibangalla, 'in what place'? dadibaġgalli, dadilabaġgalli, 'whence'? dadiurruinbaġgalli, 'through what place'? dadibaġgallinġirriage, 'by what place did he come'? Each of these by the addition of -ga may become an answer, equivalent to 'I don't know where,' &c. Other adverbs of place are:—dain, 'this way,' 'hither'; yain, 'that way,' 'thither'; ngidyi, 'here'; nganniain, 'over there.'

7. Numerals.

Ngunbai, 'one'; bula, 'two'; bulangunbai, 'three'; bungu, 'four' *or* 'many'; murrugai, 'first'; umbai, 'last.'

c

EXAMPLES of THE DECLENSION of VERBS and PRONOUNS.

1. The Verb.

Dara, 'to eat.'

The Tense numbers here are the same as on page 26 of this volume.

INDICATIVE MOOD.

1. Dara
2. Dé
3. Dalgurranni
4.
5. Dalguáan

6. Déinni
7. Dalgirri
8. Wari dalgarriawagirri
9. Dalgarrigirri
10. (*Fut.-Perf.*) Dégirri

IMPERATIVE MOOD.

Singular.

Dalla, 'eat thou' Dallidyu, 'let me eat'
Dallaguin barri, 'let him eat.'

Dual.

Gullaligunnanna barri dalla, *or* ngaguala dalla barri, *or* gulangalligunna dalli, 'let him and me eat together.'
Gula barri dalla bulagu, *or* dalla guain bulagu barri, 'let them two eat together.'
Ngallibul dalla, *or* ngindu bula dalla, 'you two eat.'

Plural.

Dalla ngéanni, 'let us eat.' Ngindugir dalla, 'eat you.'
Dalla guaingulia barri, 'let them eat.'
Gulagalangundugir dalla, 'let me and many eat together.'

SUBJUNCTIVE AND POTENTIAL MOODS.

These moods are frequently expressed by the future tense with yandundu, 'if,' 'when,' added; by the auxiliary verb garra, and especially by the word mallang; see page 61 of this appendix.

PARTICIPLES.

These are declined like verbs in all the tenses and moods. There are two participles; the one ends in -biauna, and the other in -gunnanna; the former seems to imply a longer continuance of time than the other.

INDICATIVE.

1. Dalgunnana (*or* dalbianna), 'I am eating.'
2. Dalgunnani, 'I was eating.'
5. Dalguain, 'I have been eating.'

THE WIRADHARI DIALECT.

Reflexive Mood.

1. Dalgydyillinga
2. Dalgidyillingarrinni
3. Dalgidyillingurranni
4. Dalgidyillinyi
5. Dalgidyillin
6. Déingidyillin
7. Dalligidyilligirri [girri.
8. Wari dalligidyillingarriawa-
9. Wari dalligidyillingarri
10. Wari déingidyillingirri

By using other verbs from the Wiradhari Vocabulary, additional examples of the formation of tenses in the Indicative are:—

Pres. Dara—Yanna. *Perf.* Bumalguáan—Yannáan.
Imperf. Ngunné—Yunné. *Pluperf.* Mindallanni—Yannanni.
Incep. fut. Widyalgirri—Yannigirri.
Indef. fut. Yalgarrigirri—Yanngarrigirri.
Fut. Perf. Gurragamegirri—Yannegirri.
Def. past (a). Badalgurranni—Yangurranni.
  „   (b). Giwalgarrin—Yangarrin.
Def. fut. Bangamalgarriawagirri—Yangarriawagirri.

2. *The Pronouns.*

The numbering of the cases here is the same as for the nouns.

Singular. *Plural.*

2. Gaddu, 'I' 1. & 2. Géanni
3. Gaddi *or* gaddigu 3.
   4. Géannigingu†
4. Gannunda‡ Géannigingunnaga‡
5. Gannal 5. Géanninginguuna
7. Gaddidyi 7. Géannigindyi
8. Gannundurai 8. Géannigindurai
9. Gannunda milanda, ('near') 9. Géannigindya milanda
  Gannundi, ('from') Géanniginbai

2. Gindu, 'thou' 1. & 2. Gindugir
3. Ginnu 3. Ginnugir
4. Ginyunda‡ 4. Ginnundugir
5. Ginyal 5. Ginyalgir
Plu. 8. Ginnundigirdurai *Plu.* 9. Ginnundugira milanda

2. Guin, gu, 'he' 1. & 2. Guin- (*or* -guain) gulia
3. Guggula *or* 3. Guinguliagu *or*
  Guaguwan Guingulialla
4. Guan, gagguan 4. Gaggu-lia (*or* -lialla)†
   Gannigu-lia (*or* -lialla)‡
5. Ginyal 5. Gannaiagulialla
Plu. 7. Gannain-gulialla *Plu.* 8. Gannigulialladurai

* This portion of Mr. Günther's manuscript is so imperfect that I cannot say that the cases of these pronouns are all correct.—Ed.
† An ethical dative, as in 'give to me.' ‡ A sort of locative, as in 'come to me.'

Dual pronouns are:—

Nom.—(1) Ngalli, 'thou and I'; (2) ngéan-ngalligunna, 'he and I'; (3) ngindubula, 'you two'; (4) ngainbula, 'they two'; (5) bulagual, 'the other two'; (6) nginna bula, 'these two'; (7) ngilla bula, 'those two'; (8) ngalliguyunganba, 'our two selves.'

Of these, the inflexions of (3) are:—*gen.*, ngindubulagu; *dat.* (*local*), nginyunda bulagu; of (4):—*gen.* and *dat.*, ngagguwanbulagu; *acc.*, ngannainbula; *ablatives*, ngainbulabar, ('about'); ngaddainbuladi ('from'); ngannainbulaga, ('in'); the inflexions of (8) are:—*gen.*, guyunganġalliġinbul; *dat.*, ngalliġingunnabul; *acc.*, ngallibulguyungan; *abl.*, ngalliġingunnabuli ('from').

Reflexive pronouns are:—

Ngadduguyunganbul,'I myself'; nginduguyunganbul, 'thou thyself'; gúlaguingnyunganbul, 'he himself'; ngalliguyunganbul, 'we (two) ourselves'; ngéanniginyangagul, 'we ourselves.'

Possessive Pronouns are:—

Ngaddiguyungan, 'my own'; nginnuguyungan, 'thy own'; gulaguinguyungan, 'his own'; ngéannigirnindinguyungan, 'our own'; nginnugirninguyungan, 'your own'; ngaggualanindin, 'their own.'

Demonstratives are:—

Nginna, nganna, ngunnalla, nilla, dilla, 'this here'; ngaggualla, 'that one'; ngaggu, 'that.' The declension is:— *nom.*, nginna; *gen.*, nginnagu, nginnalagu, 'belonging to this'; *dat.* (*local*), nginni, 'to this place'; *acc.*, nginna, 'this'; *ablatives*, ngirinal-la (-da), 'at this,' nginnal-li (-di), 'from this'; nginnadurai, 'with this.'

Indefinite pronouns are:—

Ngunbaimarrang, 'some'; gulbir, 'part of, 'some'; ngunbai, 'one'; ngunbaigual, 'another'; -gual (*a postfix*) 'other'; biambul, 'all,' 'the whole'; bianggallambul, 'all,' 'everybody'; minyam-minyambul, 'everything'; bulagual, 'the other two'; murrimurrri, 'each.' .

All the pronouns on this page are declined like nouns.

Interrogatives are:—

Nom. 1., ngandi, 'who (is)'? *nom.* 2., ngandu 'who (does)'? *gen.*, ngangu, 'whose'? *dat.*, ngandigu, 'to *or* for whom'? nganngun (*local*); *ablatives*, nganġundi, 'from whom'? nganġundi birandi, 'away from whom'? ngangundidurai, 'with whom'? ngangundila, 'from whom'? ngangurgu, 'towards whom'?

Nom. 1. Minyanganna, minyaġgarranna, 'what (is it)'? *nom.* 2., minyallu, 'what (does it)'? *gen.*, minyanġu *or* minyaġguba, 'belonging to what'? *dat.*, minyaġgu, 'to *or* for what'? *acc.*, minyang, 'what'? *ablatives*, minyaġgurgu, 'towards what'? minyalla, 'in *or* on what'? minyalalla, 'on what'? minyalli, 'from what'? minyandurada, 'with what'? minyaġguliadhi, 'like what'? minyaġguor, minyaġgarra, 'in what place' 'where'?

II. THE VOCABULARY.

Words, Phrases, and Sentences in the Wirádhari dialect.

1. WORDS AND PHRASES.

[In this Vocabulary, dy=j; ng=either the nasal g *or* n-g in separate syllables; -nga final of the verbals, if preceded by *i*, may be pronounced -nya from the influence of the *i*; *p* and *t* are so like *b* and *d* in sound that the author has not given a separate place to them. Words marked with † have come in from other dialects. The verbs are given in the *present Indicative*; to form the *Infinitive*, gu, 'to,' is added on after the verb-stem. There are probably some mistakes still in this Vocabulary, although much labour has been spent in getting its contents made fit for the press.—ED.]

B

Ba—frost; a cold winter.
Babang—winter.
Babannirra—to make *or* to be very hot.
Babbildain—a singer.
Babbilla—a wild cat.
Babbimubang—fatherless.
Babbin—father.
Bábbir—large.
Babbirbambarra–to sing a song.
Babbirbang—slender.
Babbirra—to sing.
Bábin—a nettle.
Badanin—the gum of the 'kurrajong' tree.
Badda—a bite.
Badda—the bank of the river.
Baddabaddambul—very soon.
Baddabaddarra—to scrape and then use the teeth like a dog.

Baddabaddaġijillinga—to gnash the teeth together.
Baddal—a kind of hair plaiting; the hair made into a bunch.
Báddambirra—to catch fish.
Baddan—sooner, before, ere.
Baddang—a cloak, a blanket.
Baddangal--a long-married man
Baddanni—the gum of a tree.
Baddarbaddar—a native bird.
Báddarra—to bite.
†Baddawal—the native weapon known as the 'bumarang'; *cf.* 'bargan.'
Baddawar—a weapon like the 'bargan,' but with a knob at one end.
Baddawaral—a dry plain.
Baddiang—nonsense.
Badding—an edible root.

Baddul—a little bird.
Badin—grandmother; a relative.
Badinbadin—water weeds.
Badyan—the little finger.
Badyar—a black ant.
Baggabin—a beautiful bluish flower, like a hyacinth.
Baggadirrar—very thin.
Baggai—a shell; a spoon.
Baggaidyarrar—anything that is thin *or* light; a little stone.
Baggaigang—a small shell.
Baggaimarra—to take out of a pod, as peas.
Baggal—a venomous snake.
Baggandar; bawadar—a shoe.
Baggandar—a sore which has the skin off.
Baggar—meat.
Baggaraibang—restored, comforted, healthy, comfortable.
Baggarbuawarra—to stand on a dangerous precipice.
Baggarran—a dry well.
Baggin—a bad spirit; it enters into the natives, but may be driven out by their doctors.
Baggin—a wound, a sore.
Baggirngan—an uncle; a cousin.
Baggirngun—a female who has become a mother.
Bagguang—water weeds. [arm.
Baggur—the back part of the
Baggurain — refreshed after a faint; strengthened by food; strong for work, industrious.
Baggurainbang — one that is industrious.
Baggurbannia — a string tied round the arm.
Baggurgan—a young man in the second stage of initiation.
Bagurra—blossom of the 'yammagang' tree, *q.v.*
Bai—a footmark left.
Baiamai—a great god; he lives in the east.
Baibadi—venereal.

Baibian—twin.
Baien—semen animalis.
Baigur—ear ornaments.
Baigurbaigur—water weeds.
Baimur—any kind of female.
Bainbain—empty.
Bainbanna—unable to reach.
Baingarra—to hold to the wind, as in winnowing wheat.
Bainguang—stupid, bad.
Bairgain—leeches.
Baiyai—a meeting place of two parties; a tryst.
Ba-la *or simply* ba—to be; is always joined to pronouns.
Balbu—a kind of 'kangaroo-rat.'
Balburranna—to tumble; to fall down headlong.
Balgabalgar—chief, ruler, king.
Balgagang—barren, desolate.
Balgal—sound, noise.
Balgang—barren. [as fleas.
Balganna—to kill on the nails,
Balgar—noon.
Balgargal—sunlight; the glory where Baiamai *(q.v.)* lives.
Balgarra—to emit sparks.
Balguranna—to slip (roll down).
Balgurei—little spots of clouds.
Ballaballamauna—to move, lift softly *or* slowly. [to slap.
Ballaballanirra—to beat a little,
Ballaballayallanna—to whisper; to talk in each other's ear.
Ballaballelinga—to whisper.
Balladi—a saw; *adj.*, serrated.
Ballagirin—an old opossum (*m.*)
Ballagun—an old woman.
Ballanda—long ago; at the first; in the beginning.
Ballandallabadin—a kind of reed.
Ballandunnang—thick-head; a term of reproach.
Ballang—the head. [flower.
Ballaggarang—the top bud of a
Ballangimarra—to wring anything by squeezing and pressing at one end.

Ballanguan—a pillow
Ballanguang—a mizzling rain.
Ballarra—the hooks at the end of the spear.
Ballaurong—a cap.
Ballawaggur—a kind of lizard.
Balleballea—silence of night.
Balli—a very young baby.
Ballima—very far off, distant.
Ballinballin—a whip.
Ballnuronna—to take to flight.
Balluballungin—almost dead.
Ballubangarra—to extinguish; *also* ballubiarra.
Ballubundambirra—to cause to be dead, to kill. [teeth.
Ballubundarra—to kill with the
Ballubungabillanna—*recip.*, to kill each other.
Bállubúnildáin—a murderer.
Ballubunirra—to kill, murder.
Ballubunningidyillinga—to kill one's self.
Ballubuolin—dead altogether.
Ballubuyarra—to tell to die.
Ballumballang—a native flower.
Ballumbambal—the dead ones; the ancients.
Balludai—cold.
Balludarra—to feel cold.
Balluga—fire gone out; dark.
Ballugan—that which lives in the fields; beasts.
Ballugirbang—the dead ones.
Ballun—dead.
Ballúnna—to die. [very feeble.
Ballunginbar—almost a-dying;
Ballunumminga—to die before.
Balluolinga—to be pregnant.
Balmang—empty.
Balmang—soft, smooth.
Balwándára—to swim, to float.
Bambangang—a wish, a desire.
Bambawanna—to be busy with, to be industrious.
Bambinga—to swim.
Bambung—the little toe.
Bamirman—a long water-hole.

Bammal—a relation by marriage.
Banbal—the place where the native men meet first in the morning; a place of assembly.
Bánbán—little waves raised by the wind; the motion of the water when anything is thrown into it.
Bandaibarna—to climb a tree by putting the toes into the cuts; to climb.
Bandain—the band around the loins; a girdle.
Bandal—a species of grub.
Bandalong—joining, junction.
Bandánbandán—a bundle.
Bándar—a kangaroo.
Bandarra—to tie.
Bandhé—ill; thin.
Bandung—a large blood-sucking fly; its bite is very sharp.
Bandung—soot, vegetable black.
Bandyabandya—pain. [pain.
Bandyabandyabirra—to cause
Bandyabanjirra—sore, painful.
Bangabilbangabil — a cutting instrument.
Bangabildain—a cutter.
Bangabirra—to cut, shear.
Bangadirra—to cut, split, chop.
Bangaduolinga—to stop raining.
Bangaduringa—to finish and to leave off when finished. [ing.
Bangadarra—to destroy by bit-
Bangainbangain—broken, torn, ragged.
Bangaiyelinga—to interfere, to dissuade, to intercede.
Bangal—time, (or rather) place.
Bangalbuorei—the country all over; the whole earth.
Bangalgnalbang—belonging to another place.
Bang-galgambirra—to break off *or* cut; to maim by throwing.
Bángal-gára-gára—every place; all over the world.

Bangalla—a low hill.
Bangamallanna—to part among.
Bangamanna—to ward off.
Bangamarra—to break.
Bangalmu—square.
Bángăn—*an assertive particle*; it is so; indeed; truly.
Banganálbirra—to burn.
Banganarinbirra—to break timber with the hand without an instrument.
Banganna—to break; to break into rain.
Bangarra—to make fire.
Bangawadillinga—to be tired.
Banganaringa — to break by falling.
Banganbilang—broken in pieces
Bangawarra—to break anything by trampling on it.
Bangayadillinga—to dislike; to be disinclined; to be offended.
Bangayalinga—to break again.
Bangayarra—to dissuade from fighting; to reconcile.
Banggil—a crack, a split.
Banggo—a kind of root.
Bangin—a kind of berry.
Bangolong—the autumn; *lit.*, the fore-part of the winter.
Bangu—a kind of squirrel.
Banna—verily, truly; *i.q.* banyan
Bannambannang—to lend or exchange wives.
Bannang—lean flesh.
Banne—an *inter. particle*; like *Lat.* 'an,' 'anne.'
Bannirra—to beat two stones together to make fire.
Bárá—a step; *v.*, to tread upon.
Bararwarra—to tear.
Barbai—a small kangaroo.
Barbar—deep.
Bardain—a black rat (mouse).
Bardang—bitter; nasty in smell or taste; *s.*, a bug.
Bargan—a native weapon; the 'bumarang.'

Barganbargan—the moon when forming a sickle.
Barguranna—to fall, slip down.
Bári—long, tall.
Barinma—attendants and messengers of the monster Wawe.
Barla—a footstep.
Bárlabáral—poison.
Barrabal—the dark middle part of the eye.
Barrabarra—to crackle.
Barrabarra—very white.
Barrabarrai!—quick! *emphatic.*
Barrabarrama—a handle; anything to lay hold of.
Barrabarrandin — old (said of clothes), ragged, worn out.
Barrabirra—to strike against, as little splinters when wood is chopped.
Barraburrun—a kind of quail.
Barradambang—a bright star.
Barrăggăná—to get out of the way.
Barrai!—quick! make haste!
Barraibirra—to accelerate.
Barraiawanna—to get up.
Barrain—'schambedeckung.'
Barraiyalinga — to rise again; said of the resurrection.
Barramai—the thumb.
Barramallang—cohabitation.
Bárramárra—to take, lay hold of.
Barramalbillinga—to fetch or take when bidden.
Barramalinga—convalescent.
Barrambamarra—to rouse up, to make get up.
Barrambarang—a mushroom.
Barrámbiyarra—to tell to get up; to awaken.
Barramelinga—to get, provide, procure for another.
Barraminga—to recover.
Barrandang—a native monkey.
Barrandarra—to gnaw.
Barrăndirra—to cut.
Barrang—white.

Barranganna—to make a noise as by sounding the letter *r-r*.
Barraggára—to rise, to get up.
Bárranmárra—to tear.
Barranna—to fly.
Barranna—to roast.
Barrarbarrar—a rushing noise; *v.*, to make a rushing noise.
Barrawarrainbirra—to be full-fledged; said of birds.
Barrawidyain—one that always wanders about; a hunter.
Barrawinga—to hunt; to camp.
Barruomanna—to run fast, to gallop.
Bárre—no!
Barreidyal—a bird like a robin.
Barrima—a musket.
Barrimarra—to get fire by rubbing two pieces of wood.
Barrinan—a little shrub.
Barrigngia—let it alone! never mind!
Barru—a rabbit-like rat.
Barrudang—a juice from a tree; 'manna.'
Bawalganna—to hatch.
Bawamarra—to relate news; to communicate.
Báwán—a white stone, said to belong to Wandong, *q.v.*
Báwan!—no, no! by no means!
Bawar—a prepared skin; leather
Bawarnguor—inside.
Bi—the fore part of the arm.
Biagga—often, many times.
Bial—*emph. particle*; up, high.
Bialbial—very high, a-top.
Bialgambirra—to hang; *trans.*
Bialganna—to hang; *intrans.*
Biambul—all.
Biamburruwallanna—to govern, to rule over.
Biang—many.
Biangarra—to take out, dig out, as from a hole.
Biangulalinga—to dig out again, *e.g.*, when buried.

Bibanna—to crouch down; to be in a sitting position.
Bibarra—to tease.
Bibbidya—a kind of fish-hawk.
Biddirbung—a challenge word; as much as to say 'I am not afraid of you.'
Bidyaidya—a mother's sister.
Bidyaingarra—to poke the fire.
Bidyar—any male.
Bidyur—pointing up, very high.
Biembai—a hook, a fish-hook.
Biggun—a water-mole.
Bildur—'fat-hen,' an edible herb.
Bilinmarra—to strip long pieces of bark.
Bílunmarra—to split.
Billa—a river.
Billabang—the Milky Way.
Billadurra—a water-mole.
Billagal—down a mountain towards a river.
Billar—a river 'swamp-oak.'
Billawir—a hoe.
Billili—herbage like dock-leaf.
Billimarra—to push near to.
Billinbalgambirra—to recede, to go back; try to escape, avoid.
Billinga—to go backwards.
Billingarra—to take care.
Billingaya—going backwards.
Billir—a black cockatoo.
Ballirán—the silence of night, when all are asleep.
Billuán—a kind of parrot.
Bilundarra—to chap the skin, as frost does.
Bimbai—a spot where the grass has been burnt. [fire.
Bímbarra—to set the grass on
Bimbil—a kind of tree.
Bimbin—a native bird.
Bimirr—an end *or* point.
Bín—high, tall.
Binbin—silent.
Binbin—the belly.
Bindugai—a small shell.
Bindugan—shellfish.

Bindurgarra—to move along, as children before they can walk.
Bindyabindyalganna—an itch.
Bindyarra—to crack.
Bindyilduringa—to cut into a tree to get opossums out.
Bindyinga—to stumble.
Bindyirra—to dig with a hoe.
Bindyulbarra—to sink under the feet, as the ground.
Bindyurmai—very warm.
Bingal—a needle.
Bingumbarra—to hear a fall.
Binnal—the eldest.
Binnalbang—the greatest, the highest; a name applied to some heavenly being.
Binnalbirra—to light.
Binya; binna—to dig, to cut.
Binyalbarra—to make fire.
Binyalbirra—to make a light.
Binyalgarna—lumpy.
Biran—a boy; *cf.* birrain.
Biranbiran—steep, downhill.
Birandi—from.
Biraggal—a step's distance.
Birbaldain—a baker.
Birbarra—to bake.
Birbi—a flea.
Birbir—extremely cold.
Birdaebirdae—downhill.
Birdain—ironbark-tree blossom
Birdi—a cut.
Birdirra—to cut.
Birdyulong—an old scar.
Birgainbarra—to kick against.
Birgananna—to carve meat.
Birgánbirra—to plough.
Birgang—a ground-grub.
Birganna—to scratch.
Birgilli; birgillibang—scorched by fire.
Birgu—shrubs, thickets.
Birgun—a bird like a duck; its appearance portends rain.
Biring—the breast.
Biringa—a scar; a scratch; *v.* to make a scar.

Birombailinga—to take and go away with.
Biromballanna—to throw at each other.
Birombanirra—to drive away.
Birombanna—to go away to a distance. [tance.
Birombarra—to throw to a dis-
Birong—far-distant; high.
Birra—tired, fatigued.
Birrabang—up, above, outside.
Birrabirra—to be tired.
Birrabuadillinga—to be tired.
Birrabiang—poor, thin.
Birra-bildain; -bidyan—poor.
Birrabinabirra—to move gently; to whisper.
Birrabirrawainbul—downhill.
Birrabuoanna—to come back.
Birradan—the straight scars on the back.
Birragumbil—back bent, as in old age; reclining.
Birrag-guor—behind.
Birramal—the bush.
Birrain—the navel.
Birrain—a young male.
Birraindyong—a little boy.
Birramammau—long-backed.
Birrambang—a 'kangaroo-rat.'
Birrau—stiff, cold; as in death.
Birrawanna—to descend.
Birrenelinga—to run away with.
Birrha—the back.
Birri—the 'box-tree.'
Birrian—a grub found in trees.
Birribirrimarra—to meet.
Birrimannar—sitting in a circle; walking in a row.
Birrinallai—'box-tree' blossom.
Birrindaimarra—to meet each other.
Birrirra—to scratch.
Bomarra—to take away.
-bu—and, also; a *postfix*.
Buabuowanna—a lump.
Buadambirra—to overfill the mouth.

Buadarra—to fill the mouth.
Buarbang—tame, quiet, orderly.
Buardang—scabby.
Bubaibunnanna—to get small, to lessen ; to boil in.
†Bubal—a boy.
Bubbadagúng—a little fellow.
Bubbadang—anything little.
Bubbai—little.
Bubbaidyong—very little.
Bubbil—a wing ; feathers.
Bubu—that august being who is said to preside at the 'burbandigána' and there 'makes' the young men. He is said to be as big as a rock or mountain.
Buddabarra—to smoke.
Buddainbuddain—a species of mint, 'pennyroyal.'
Buddang—dark in colour, black.
Buddanna—to smell.   [other.
Buddarballanna—to kiss each
Buddarbanna—to kiss.
Buddarong—a 'flying-squirrel.'
Buddawaral—a dry place where no water is.
Buddé—a small narrow passage; a small island.
Buddi—a corner.
Buddima—inside in the house.
Buddin—a sunbeam.
Buddu—stars.
Buddulbuddul—far off ; high; the bluish air at a distance.
Buddumbuddain — a fragrant water herb.
Buddurbuddur—a smell.
Budyabudya—moth, butterfly.
Bugang—beads ; a necklace.
Bugga—meat when tainted.
Buggabanna—to be struck by flies, as meat.
Buggabugga—black.
Buggal—a plant with an edible root and grass-like seeds.
Buggamin—eatables that have improved by keeping.
Buggang—the 'gum-tree' flower.

Buggaran—a dry well.
Buggarnan—a bad smell.
Bugguainbang—fruitful.
Buggulong—a native shrub.
Buggiunbarrhúl—the time after sunset; twilight.
Buguin—grass.
Bula—two.
Bula-bial-yallaigunnanna — two to speak together and a third interfering.
Bulabinga—to be in couples.
Bulabulamanna — to pace together ; said of two.
Bulami—having two wives.
Bula-ngunbai—three.
Bulbaggurain—a native bird.
Bulbin—a whirlwind.
Balduraidurai—a kind of owl.
Bulinbulin—bald-headed ; any part of animals bare of hair.
Bullambullang—a wave.
Bulliang—a 'kangaroo-rat'; *fig.*, a bad run-about female.
Bullinbullin—a water bird.
Bulludyan—a rag.
Bullun—a large bird.
Bumadillinga—to row.
Bumalláua—*recip.*, to beat each other ; to fight.   [self.
Bumangidyillinga—to beat one's
Bumanna—to move the wings.
Bumarra—to beat, to strike.
Bumbain—a bunch.
Bumbanna—to smoke; *intrans.*
Bumbanumminga—to outrun, to run before.
Bumbarramanna—to rush into.
Bumbinna—to smoke; *trans.*
Bumbir—greasy.
Bumburgalbian — a shrub resembling the 'swamp-oak.'
Bumcilinga—to run to another for assistance.
Bummabumarra—to knock.
Bummalbummal—a stick used as a hammer; a hammer stick.
Bammalgal—the right hand.

Bunbabillinga—to escape; to run away when beaten.
Bunbaimarranna—to long for, to wish for; to be anxious.
Bunbabanirra—to set a running
Bunbambirra—to cause to run; to roll; to move a wheel.
Bunbangarrimanna—to bustle about.
Bunbanna—to run.
Bunbananna—to run after.
Bunbea—a grasshopper.
Bunbinga—to sit down, to rest; to be tired; tired of.
Bundalganna—to suspend; to be hanging.
Bunbun—a locust, grasshopper.
Bunburribal—ground; *cf.* dagun.
Bundadillinga—to expectorate freely.
Bundalganna—to lean to one side.
Bundalinga—to hang; to hang with the hands *or* arms slung round something.
Bundambirra—to fasten.
Bundang—a kind of grub.
Búndang—a blackish butterfly.
Bundanna—to draw. [freeze.
Bundarra—to feel very cold, to
Bundi—a war-weapon; a cudgel with a thick knob at its end.
Bundibanirra—to knock down.
Bundibumarra—to cause to fall.
Bundibundinga—to tumble, to stumble.
Bundibundingin—ready to fall; (of a plan) dangerous, unsafe.
Bundilauna—to fall over each other.
Bundin—the hair-bands hanging down the neck.
Bundimambirra—to let fall.
Bundinga—to fall.
Bungadillinga—to be pleased.
Bungain—a gift, a present.
Bungalbungal — a broom, anything to sweep with.

Bungambirra—to make smooth *or* soften; to iron; to sweep.
Bungany—the knee.
Bungannabanna—to comb the hair.
Bung-arra, -ambirra—to sweep.
Bungimarra—to wag the tail.
Bungirra—to swing.
Bungu—four; many; an indefinite number.
Bungubungu—every thing; a great many.
Bungul—short; *s.*, a little man.
Bungulgal—short.
Bunbia—a 'wild-oak' tree.
Búnin; búninganna—to breathe.
Bunmabunmarra—to assist.
Bunnanna—to burn.
Bunnabunnanga—abundance of food; *adj.*, sumptuous.
Bun-ngàn—made by another.
Bunmarra—to make.
Bunnallauna—to take another man's wife.
Bunnan—ashes.
Búnnarra; *imperf.*, bunnai—to take away; to take back.
Bunnebunne, *or* bungebunge—warm; oppressively hot winds.
Bunnidyillinga—to beat.
Bunninganna—to breathe.
Bunnumeilinga—to go from one place to another, to remove.
Buobarra—to be like the parent.
Buoda—a kind of opossum (*f.*); often used as a nickname.
Buogain—an edible root.
Buogalbumarra—to drive out.
Buogalbuonanna—to return.
Buogan-anna, -arra—to follow.
Buoganumminga—to be before.
Buogarra—to come.
Buonung—some grass-seeds.
Buorgarra—to pull up.
Buowaibannanna—to boil.
Buoyabialngidyal—a command, a law; betrayal, exposure.
Buoyal—a mother-in-law.

Buoyarra—to bid *or* advise; to to tell to do; to instigate.
Burai—a child, a boy.
Buralgang—a large native bird called Native's Companion.
Burambabirra—to divide, to distribute. [arms.
Burambirra—to stretch out the
Burambungambirra—to be dry; *trans.*, to make dry.
Burambunganna—to get dry.
Buramburambang—very dry.
Buran—a tendril; *v.*, to twine.
Burang—drought.
Burang—dry branches *or* leaves.
Burbandiganna—to initiate the young men of the tribe.
Burbang—round; a round heap, a circle.
Burbirra—to beat the time and sing, like the women beating on their bundled cloaks.
Burbirra—to do carpenter work.
Burbirra—to scrape, to scratch; to smooth; make smooth, as the carpenter does the wood.
Burdón—large, wide.
Burguin—a hatchet, tomahawk.
Burguinmudil—a blacksmith.
Burimbirra—to empty, to wring out, drink all.
Burrabanna—to make one ill, as Wandong does; to be ill; to have a swelling. [fire.
Burrabannalbirra—to light a
Burraburrabána—to have sores *or* wounds. [wounds.
Burraburrabul—full of sores *or*
Burraddar—the pine tree.
Burradirra—to cut down.
Burragambirra—to knock down.
Burragallanna—to leap all together in play.
Burrain—a fragment.
Burral—a bed.
Burramagang—the shoulders, together with the upper part of the back.

Búrrambal—a native game of jumping over the rope.
Burrambian—a term applied to the god Baiamai, *q.v.*
Burrambin—a term first applied to white people by the blacks.
Burrambin—eternal.
Burrambinga—to be eternal.
Burramarra—to loosen *or* take off. [in a row.
Burrar—a row; a line of things
Burrawi—a tree on fire.
Burrawirra—to set fire to a tree.
Burrè—breaking wind.
Burrigal—a kind of wood.
Burriinal—a fly.
Burru—bottom; the testicles.
Burruarra—to make a stir with the feet; to fly, as dust.
Burrubinga—to jump, to leap.
Burrubialinga—to jump again.
Burrudarra—the dim appearance of a distant object.
Burruganna—to rub against, to touch.
Burrugurra—a tuberous plant.
Burrumbal—round, like a globe.
Burrunbi—inside.
Burundäng—dark, very dark.
Burrundi—black (inside).
Burrunmarra—to pick, choose.
Burruira—the sap of the 'apple-tree.'
Burrurgian—a large black bird.
Burrunganna—to thunder.
Buyabarra—to give orders.
Buyabialdain—one who gives orders, a commandant, a magistrate, a governor.
Buyabianna—to speak good of; to praise, flatter; to please.
Buyabiyarra—to give orders.
Buyamaldain—a beggar.
Buyamanna—to beg, to pray.
Buyamarra—to beg.
Búyu—the thigh, the leg.
Buyuma—the foot of a hill.
Buyuwari—long-legged.

D

Dabal—a bone.
Dabbarmallang—mob of natives
Dábbugárra—to bury; to plant.
Dabbungung—a father.
Dabburang—pipe-clay.
Dabbuyarra murou—to give or bestow life.
Dabuan—a small kind of leeches.
Daddirra—to be filled, to have enough, to be satisfied.
Daddur—curdled, as milk.
Dagagualbirang—belonging to another place; a stranger.
Daggal—the cheeks.
Daggalbuddi—bushy whiskers.
Daggàn—sticking fast, like bark when not splitting well.
Daggarang—a wood-worm.
Dagu—dung, dirt.
Dagui—a shadow.
Dagun—ground, soil.
Dagun—when?
Dagunbil—a dirty fellow.
Dagunbilmarra—to make dirty.
Dagundu—where to?
Dagunmar—a grave.
Daiangun—forward.
Daiba—voluptuous.
Daimarra—to dispute.
Daimiangarra—to dash in, as rain driven by wind.
Dainbunninga—to come back after being driven off.
Daindu—here!
Daingamallanna—to outdo, to excel. [ing.
Daingamarra—to vie in throw-
Dalaimbang—sharp, as a tomahawk.
Dálain—the tongue.
Dalaingaldain—one that doubts; an unbeliever.
Dalaingarra—to misbelieve, to doubt.
Dalalinga—to eat again.
Dalára—snow.

Dalbadambirra—to crush to atoms, to grind.
Dalbagarra—to tear asunder, to put apart, to open.
Dalban-dalbannirra—to bruise, to pound.
Dalbanna—to be bruised.
Dalbar—the shoulder bone.
Dalbarra—to be wet.
Dalbinga—to turn upside down.
Dalbirra—to strike the time with the 'bargan,' as the native men do in singing.
Dalga—gum in the eye.
Dalgang—very crooked; *subst.*, a bent bough.
Dalia—a species of iguana.
Dallabadarra—to split.
Dallabadirra—to split with an instrument.
Dallabalga—'schambedeckung.'
Dallabalganna—to part; as the parting of the hair.
Dallabauna—to go to ruin; to destroy.
Dallabumarra—to destroy, to break in pieces.
Dalladallabunna—to split.
Dallagarra—to avoid; to try to escape.
Dallai—angry.
Dallaimarra—to be angry with.
Dalläin—root of the 'pear-tree.'
Dallamarra—to break, break in pieces; to destroy.
Dállambul—very soon.
Dállan—soon.
Dallangir—fresh, new.
Dallawang—an 'apple-tree.'
Dallunarong—a young man still growing.
Dallungal—a fine fellow.
Dalmambirra—to feed (a baby).
Dalman—a place of plenty.
Dalgi—transgression. [long.
Dalgarrimanna—to eat all day.
Dalnumminga—to eat before.
Damalien—sweet, pleasant.

Dámbadámba—soft; very soft.
Dambai—a kind of wiry grass.
Dambulbang—late in the night.
Damburdambur—a curl, a fold; like a snake when curled.
Damburmadillinga—to wrap all round close from the cold, as with a cloak.
Damburmarra—to wrap round, to fold up.
Damburra—to put into, wrap up.
Dammal—the wrist; the inside of the fore part of the arm.
Dammín—a venomous snake.
Dăn—too many orders at once; confusion.
Danba—ripe.
Danbang—green, alive (said of plants); fresh, strong. [rat.'
Danbur—a kind of 'kangaroo-
Dandámbirra—to feel cold, to be freezing.
Dandain—a frog.
Dandalla—a hailstone.
Dandan—scattered all about in confusion.
Dandang—cold; s., a cold wind.
Dandar—pretty, nice.
Dandarang—very cold.
Dandarbang—very pretty.
Dandarra—to be cold.
Dandu—wet.
Dandudarra—to be wet.
Dăng—long edible roots.
Dangai—rain water; old water.
Dangal—a shelter, a covering.
Dángang—the heel.
Dangang—bread made by the natives from seeds.
Dangarin—shellfish.
Dangarumanna—to dance.
Dangung—bread, food.
Dangur—a species of fish.
Dánna—to net *or* knit.
Danna-danna—small-pox.
Dannal—the fist.
Dannamai—a corpse.
Dannamandan—a knot in string.
Dannambandanna-to be knotty.
Daunaing—fore-arm; the wrist.
Dannaggang—a wart.
Danni—gum, honeycomb, wax.
Dara—to eat.
Darga—honeycomb.
Dargimbirra—to lay across.
Dargin—across.
Dargin—a kind of meal made of 'gullu' grass seeds.
Darimumbinga—to be a whore; to give one's self up.
Darnan—very tough, not breakable.
Darngidyal—one who begets; a progenitor; a father.
Darrabang—having many wives
Darrabanna—to sit cross-legged *or* with the knees flat.
Darrabunda—maggots in meat.
Darradabal—bones.
Darraiwarra—to struggle with death; to be dying.
Darrálangauna—to be restless, to move about.
Darrambal—foot-marks, a roadway.
Darrambalgarra—to take by surprise; to frighten.
Dárrambin—a little bird.
Darrambirra—to frighten.
Darramial—a shallow place like a basin.
Darranderang—an avenger.
Darrandurai—a corner.
Darrang—the thigh.
Darrang—a little creek.
Darrangagain — walking with the knees much bent.
Darrangarbanna—to walk to and fro.
Darrar—a rib.
Darrawarrambirra — to throw away; to throw the 'bargan' along the ground.
Darrawarranna—to lie with the knees bending upwards.
Darrawildung—thin-legged.

Darri—old stumps of grass.
Darrial—a bed.
Darribal—the return of the 'bargan' when thrown.
Darribun—a queen bee.
Darrilanna—to cohabit.
Darrawirgal—the name of one of the native gods; he lives down the river; he sent the small-pox.
Darruan—tough.
Darrubanna—to leap over.
Darrúbarra—to rush on and tear up the ground, as water does.
Darruin—a handle.
Dawa—very fat.
Dawai—the lair of the sorcerer or of his 'wandong,' *q.v.*
Dawarang—a native dog.
Dawin—a hatchet.
Dhin—this, that.
Dibanna—to hiss, accompanied with clapping of the hands.
Dibbillain—birds.
Dibbin—a bird.
Dibbindibbin—the hollow part underneath the breastbone.
Dibbong—nails, spikes.
Diggal—a fishbone.
Diggar—a sneezing.
Diggarra—to sneeze.
Diggu—the small 'blackwood.'
Digún—top-knot of a cockatoo.
Dilbaimananna—to come slyly upon one.
Dilbána—to tread softly, to walk on the toes.
Dilgaindilgain—the hair combed.
Dilganna—to comb the hair.
Dilgar—a splinter of wood.
Dilman—silent, quiet.
Dillabirra—to scatter, to sow.
Dillabirra—to draw.
Dilladillabirra—to throw about, to cause confusion.
Dilladillan-garra—to shake.
Dillagar—a native berry-fruit.
Dillaggarra—to shake.

Dilläng—a brother.
Dilledille—rotten.
Dillidilli—small wood.
Dillirbunia—*imp.*, smash, dash against; *i.q.* dillirbunnarrabin
Dimbanna—to make a whizzing noise, as greenwood in the fire.
Din—meat, flesh.
Din—the inner rind of the 'yam-magang'; the natives suck it.
Dinbain—any sharp and pointed steel instrument fit to make native weapons, especially the 'bargan.'
Dinbana—to buzz (like flies).
Dinbuorin—a native lark.
Dindabarra—to take the rough-ness off, as a carpenter does.
Dindadinda—work left rough.
Dindar—bald-headed.
Dindarra—to bite off, make ill, as Wandong does.
Dindima—the Pleiades.
Dingai—a walking stick.
Dingandingan—flat, even.
Dinganna—to walk with a stick.
Dingarra—to sweep, to pull up.
Dingelinga—to make smooth.
Dingurbarra—to sharpen.
Dinmanna—to pick the nose.
Dinmé—war, battle.
Dinmirr—an eyebrow.
Dinna—honeycomb, wax.
Dinnang—the foot.
Dinnawan—an emu.
Diragambirra—to raise.
Diramadillinga—to be proud.
Dirámarra—to speak well of, to praise.
Diran—a mountain *or* hill.
Diranbang—noon; when the sun is in the zenith.
Diraugalbang—high, exalted; entrusted with authority.
Diran-ġaran-ġaran—many hills *or* mountains.
Diránna—to rise, like the dough.
Diren-direng—red.

Dironbirong—the red streams of clouds in the evening; *adj.*, red, said of white men.
Dirradambinga—to dress the hair.
Dirradirrawarra—to shoot up like mushrooms.
Dirradirrawanna—an herb.
Dirragarra—to dig deep.
Dirraggalbang—haughty; *also* dirangal-bang.
Dirraibang—a brother.
Dirraiawanna—to get up.
Dirrainamgarra—to disarrange; to move about everything in seeking for a thing.
Dirral—a little bird.
Dirramai—an edible herb.
Dirramananna—to boil over.
Dirramarra—to the left.
Dirramarra—to lift, to take off, to lift off (as from the fire).
Dirrangal—one that is superior to work; a lazy gentleman.
Dirrawan—uneven, clumsy.
Dirri—grey hair.
Dirribang—an old man.
Dirridirri—a little bird.
Dirrige—gorse; a prickly and stinging stuff inside the native 'munga,' *q.v.*
Dirril—a bulrush.
Dirrinan—an edible plant.
Dirru—a 'kangaroo-rat.'
Diwil—any collection of small particles; as sawdust, siftings.
Diwingil—a spark.
Diyan—soft, loose.
Dombar—the mist that precedes rain; the sight of rain far off.
†Dombock—sheep.
Dŏn—tail (*etiam sig.* penis).
Dondo-mirin-mirinmal—a snail.
Dondu—a swan.
Duaduamirra—to have fancies; to be delirious, talk nonsense.
Duambian—a little plant with a pink flower, and edible root.

Dubbi—a grub with wings; a butterfly.
Dubbu—a kind of frog *or* toad.
Dubo—a net cap.
Duddarra—to suck.
Duddu—the female breast; as a call to infants.
Dudduwarranna—to rush down, as water.
Duganna—to draw water.
Duggeillinga—to fetch for another.
Duggin—shade.
Dugginga—to hang (like fruits on the tree).
Dugguaibalbinga—to be on a dying bed; beyond recovery.
Dugguaibul-altogether, wholly.
Dugguarra—to overtake.
Duggumbirra—to be not greedy, generous.
Duggumi—glad, fond of.
Dugguwai-buoanna — to come back; to reach home.
Dugguwarra—to overtake.
Duguinbirra—to give always, to give freely, to be generous.
Dulba—a drop.
Dulbagal—a monstrous birth.
Dulbaganbirra—to crack.
Dulbamanna—to drop.
Dulbibalganna—to hang down the head.
Dulbibannirra—to bow down; to turn upside down; to be reclined.
Dulbinbirra—to lie prone on the belly.
Dulbinga—to bend low; to worship. [bends.
Dulbunbunmaldain — one that
Dulbunbunmarra—to bend, bow
Dullaidullai—staggering from exhaustion.
Dullar—a red bird.
Dullin—a kind of lizard.
Dullondullong — sinking, exhausted, ready to tumble.

f

Dullu—a spear.
Dullubang—the soul.
Dullubauna—to split.
Dullubi—marrow.
Dullubi—a little shrub.
Dullubin—very straight.
Dullubul—straight.
Dulludullu—big logs of wood.
Dullugal—the north wind.
Dúllugang—a little spear.
Dullugarra—to find guilty; to be convicted.
Dullugudanna—to spear.
Dulluwarai—straight.
Dulmarra—to press together, to squeeze.
Dulwarra—to press out water or juice. [mony.
Dumbal—proof, evidence, testi-
Dumbaldain—one that shows, a director.
Dumbalmai—a witness, testifier.
Dumbalmaldain—one that gives proof *or* testimony.
Dumbalmarra—to bear witness *or* indict; to accuse, betray.
Dumbangidyal—a pointing out.
Dumbanna—to point, to show.
Dumbi—a blush.
Dumbirra—to spit.
Dummirra—to carry.
Dunban—little ants.
Dunbur—some kind of wood.
Dundilai—walking in single file.
Dundilaimallanna—to walk in a row *or* line one after another.
Dunduma—the 'badawal,' *q.v.*
Dundumbirra—to suck out, as marrow from a bone.
Dung—mud, dirt.
Dungain—a kind of parrot.
Dungal—a post, pillar, support.
Dungardungar—tall, long.
Dungin—a sleeping ground between two fires.
Dungindain—a kind of water-mole. [gularly.
Dunguwarranna—to stand irre-

Dunma—a bow, an arch.
Dunna—to spear; to write.
Dunnai—a tall, long fellow.
Dunnang—a knot.
Dural—a hollow tree set on fire at the bottom and smoke coming out at the top.
Dúrang—the bark.
Durbarra—to chip *or* smooth, as with the 'dinbain.'
Durdain—a writer.
Durgung—a cuckoo.
Durgunnanna—to pick.
Durian—news; a message.
Duriangarra—to deliver a message.
Duriduringa—to be ill.
Durilgai—fruitful.
Durimambirra—to make ill; to cause to be ill; as Wandong does.
Durin—wound.
Durinda—to spear, to prick.
During—a snake.
Durmanbirra—to aim at.
Duronggargar—a glow-worm, a common worm.
Dururbuolin—always, ever.
Dururdururbuolin—ever, *emph*.
Durrabarra—to drive the bad spirit away by blowing.
Durrain—a long white cloud.
Durraggarang—a bee.
Durraumé—sorcery, a sorcerer.
Durrawal—the piece of bark used as a bier.
Durri—birth.
Durri—alluvial soil, rubbish.
Durribil—muddy. [forth.
Durrirra—to be born; to bring
Durrubanna—to tear up soil, as water does.
Durrudurrugarra—to follow.
Durrugarra—to track, to trace.
Durrui—ants.
Durruibil—full of ants.
Durrulbarra—to burst.
Durrulgarra—to hide.

Durrumang—a young snake.
Durrumbal—some water weeds.
Durrumbin—a caterpillar.
Duyon—fat; *subst.*, fat meat.
Duyul—a hill; *adj.*, hilly, uneven, rough.

G

Gabban—a father-in-law; a relative in general.
Gabbargabbar—green; *s.*, grass.
Gabbilga—a head-band made of a native dog's tail.
Gabbuga—an egg; brains.
Gabbung—a species of moths *or* butterflies.
Gabburgabbur—anything rotten *or* broken.
Gabirra—to eat with the mouth hanging over the vessel, to eat in a nasty way.
Gabura—a cap of white down.
Gádarra—to erase; to rinse.
Gadda—supposing; perhaps.
Gaddagadda *or* gaddawirra—a bad woman, a prostitute.
Gaddagadda—heard it myself; an eye-witness.
Gaddagadda—a swollen sore.
Gaddai—the throat.
Gaddal—smoke, tobacco.
Gaddalbar—the smoke-like appearance of rain at a distance.
Gaddaldurai—a young man.
Gaddalumarra—to be annoyed by smoke.
Gaddambidyillinga — to wash one's self.
Gaddambillannininga—to wash again.
Gaddambinga—to wash.
Gaddambirra—to rinse.
Gaddäng—glad, happy.
Gaddang—a little lizard.
Gaddangeillinga—to be pleased with; to rejoice over one.
Gaddangillinga—to please.

Gaddar—the back of the thigh.
Gaddaraibunninga — to overcome, humble, frighten.
Gaddawirra—to be mischievous.
Gadderai — frightened, sorry, penitent; the disposition not to do evil again after having suffered for evil-doing.
Gaddi—a snake.
Gaddirbarra—to make a creaking noise, as new shoes.
Gaddirbuodalin—a creaking.
Gaddul—congealed blood.
Gaddun—raw, uncooked.
Gadyal—hollow.
Gagamin—a younger brother.
Gagāmanna—to lead astray, to seduce.
Gágang—the eldest brother.
Gai!—ah!
Gain—like, similar.
Gairgair—meat which smells.
Gäl—string; any tie.
Galbar—little, some, not all.
Galdang—a rushing noise.
Galga—empty; hungry.
Galgan—the husk.
Galgang—a shrub.
Galge—seeds.
Galgura—a little bird.
Gallabarra—to halve.
Gallaganbarra—to wipe.
Gallaggabang—very many.
Gallar-barra, -banna—to rattle, to make a noise.
Galliainbal—uphill.
Galliarbang—glad, pleased.
Gallua—a kind of lizard.
Gamambirra—to draw out, to fetch out.
Gambái—yesterday.
Gambain—a white head-band.
Gambal—a wild turkey.
Gámban—weak, thin.
Gambang—a brother. [thing.
Gambilána—to carry *or* hold a
Gambu—the groin.
Gambuananna—to bring back.

Gambungang—thin, little, small
Gamé—to seduce; *s.*, strong voluptuous desires and practices
Gamma—a kind of spear.
Gammagamma—a kind of bird.
Gammandi—a pillow.
Gammang—unwilling to work; lazy; sticking fast, as bark when not stripping well.
Gámmar—a storm, a tempest.
Gammarra—to awaken.
Gammayan—from behind.
Gánanna—to burn, to smoke.
Ganarra—to smoke, as when the smoke descends.
Ganaurda—fainting, exhausted.
Ganbannna—to wipe; *cf.* murru.
Ganbánná—to blot out.
Ganda—the bend of the leg under the knee.
Gandaiwarra—to grow long.
Gandalgandal—to be of unequal length; unlike.
Gandalmambirra—to drive a spear through, to cut through.
Gandamai—hard, difficult.
Gandarra—to pass by.
Gandarra—to push *or* roll along the ground.
Gandiaggulang—a mountain.
Gangàn—surface, top.
Gangar—a spider.
Gánggar—a little shadow; the small thread of a spider's web.
Ganginmarra—to tell a lie.
Gangul—sloping, steep.
†Gàni—a tree on fire.
Gánna—to bring, to carry.
Gánna—the shoulder.
Gannabarra—to carry on the shoulder; *also*, gannabunna.
Gannagallanbial—shoulder, all over the shoulder.
Gannai—a woman's stick.
Gannalduringa—to burn a hole into a tree so as to drive out the opossum.
Gannal-birra, -dirra—to burn.

Gannambang—the palm of the hand; the sole of the foot.
Gannambaldain—one that is intrusive, troublesome.
Gannambarra—to do the work for another.
Gannang—warm.
Gannanna—to burn.
Gannandu—near, at hand.
Gannardang—very hungry.
Gannawardarra—to want food, to feel hungry.
Ganne—*a particle*; I suppose.
Gannung—the liver.
Gannur—the red kangaroo.
Gánur—a kind of 'kangaroo-rat.'
Garabuoangarra—to have abundance of water.
Gárai—stern, grave in aspect.
Garándarra—to eat forbidden food.
Garang—liberal, generous.
Garba—the waist.
Garbangaudu—stout, large.
Gardagarda—having cramp in the limbs, stiff.
Gardar—stiff, as in death.
Gargumarra—to embrace.
Garibawallanna—to run over.
Gariwan—a black wood, much used for making weapons.
Gariwang—a cold east wind.
Garngan—very strong.
Garwal—withered.
-garra—to be; *a postfix.*
Gárra—to cough.
Garrabarál—very thirsty.
Garragé—another, not the one intended.
Garrage—yes. it is so!
Garraigal—palm of the hand.
Garrain—raw, underdone.
Garrainjang—a survivor, in reference to another brother.
Garraiwarra—to seek, look out.
Garraiyarra—to slander; to speak ill of any one.

Gárràn—a little hook to take out grubs with.
Garran—horn.
Garrăng—the gum of the pine tree, used for binding spears.
Garrangarran—a thorn.
Garro—a marsh. [cut.
Garrúmarra—to break down, to
Garrunmanna—to slip, to slip out of the hands.
Gaumaran—an emu.
Gaunang—moonlight.
Gaundirra—to call; to appoint.
Gaurandu—a green beetle.
Gaurei—the down of birds.
Gawa—continued a long time.
Gawai—come here!
Gawaimbanna—to welcome, to tell to come.
Gawal—a plat, a valley
Gawalla—a road.
Gawalma—sloping, not steep.
Gáwàn—white ; a white man.
Gawang—a fit; apoplexy.
Gawan-gawang—stupid, foolish.
Gawier—a hut, a house.
Gawimarra—to gather, pick up.
Gawir—podex ; *cf.* muggun.
Gayamian—foam, saliva.
Gayamian—any thick kind of fluid, as paste ; *adj.*, sticky.
Gayang—gristle.
Gayir—a bad smell, as of flesh when tainted.
Gayuwal—after a long time.
Gedur—a kind of wood.
Gial—shame ; *adj.*, ashamed.
Gialang—saliva.
Gialdain—one that is frightened, a coward.
Gialdungiaya—to be ashamed.
Gialgigijillinga—to be ashamed of one's self.
Gialmambirra—to frighten.
Gialombuolin—saliva.
Gialong—a suffix to name of a native tribe; as, Dubo-gialog, the 'Dubbo tribe.'

Gialwambirra—to threaten.
Gialwarra—to be chaste.
Giandadelang—an escape.
Giarra—to be afraid.
Gibainbirra—to barter, to buy, to exchange.
Gibba—a white crystal which, as the natives believe, comes from Wandong, who puts it in their body to make them ill.
Gibban *or* gibbain—retribution, revenge.
Gibainnirra—to punish.
Gibbir—man.
Gibbirbang—mankind.
Gibbirgin—the Pleiades.
Gidya—a little tree.
Gidyaggijang—a kind of crane.
Gidyang—hair of animals, wool.
Gidyanguor—outside; the hairy side of the opossum skin.
Gidyar—a kind of lobster.
Gidyauruin—very much afraid, overcome with fear.
Gidyubarra—to tickle.
Gidyumbang—skin very hairy.
Gién—an adulterer, adulteress ; a run-away wife.
Giengé—the thin skin cast off by snakes.
Gigé—eaten enough.
Giggal—an itching disease.
Gíl—gall.
Gilgaldain—a nurse.
Gilgarra—to nurse.
Gilgil—a species of butterfly.
Gilgín—arm-pit; the hair under the arm ; the fins of fish.
Gílinga—to make water.
Gilluban—to poke the fire.
Gillubarra—to pick *or* get out, as the marrow from bones.
Gillun—sharp-edged.
Gillunbang—sharp-pointed.
Gillungillun—a dangerous place to pass.
Ginang—a 'kangaroo-rat.'
Gimarra—to milk.

Gilmami—a spot in the eye, caused by an injury.
Gimmang—a species of 'kangaroo-rat.'
Gimbir—spring, well, fountain.
Gin—the heart.
Gin; gén—a kind of gum-tree.
Ginanna—to melt.
Ginarginar—light, not heavy.
Ginbayanna—to be anxious for; to desire much.
Ginbinginbin—scabby.
Ginbirra—to itch; bite as fleas.
Gindadalla — a kind of large beads, made of water reeds.
Gindyal—griping in the bowels.
Gindyang—a state of diarrhœa.
Gindyarra—to have the bowels relaxed.
Gindyarra—to drink water like dogs, to lap.
Gindyirén—cramp.
Gindyung—marrow.
Ginma—a caterpillar.
Ginnan—*subst.*, a sudden surprise; *adj.*, astonished.
Ginnar—tough; strong. [self.
Ginnemadilinga—to lead one's
Ginnemaldain—a leader.
Ginne-manna, -marra—to lead.
Ginnirmarra—to scrape a fish, to scrape the scales off.
Gion—a centipede.
Giraggan—the red appearance of the sky at sunset.
Giralang—the stars.
Girambanna—to feel the fire, to feel too hot. [warm.
Girambannanna—to cause to be
Girambirra—to be ill.
Giräng—a leaf.
Girang—a native club.
Girangiran—poorly; ill.
Girar—wind.
Girarumarra—to blow, as wind.
Girgungan—a mushroom.
Giring-giring—froth, sweat.
Girinya—to play.

Girinyallanna—to converse together.
Girong—perspiration.
Girragirra—well, healthy, happy, merry, lively.
Girragirrabang — happy, comfortable. [burnt.
Girramanna—to feel hot, to be
Girrambayarra—to have nothing to offer in excuse; to stand convicted.
Girrambiyarra—to scold, speak with anger.
Girraran—pipeclay.
Girrawarra—to take unawares.
Girredambirra—to make secure; to lock.
Girrenil—a door-lock.
Girring-girring—luke-warm.
Girrugal—hungry.
Girrugalbang—very hungry.
Girua—a long-tailed iguana.
Girwarra—to disturb, to drive away, to frighten off.
Giwá—moist, soft, as the ground after rain.
Giwai—a sharpening stone; a grindstone.
Giwaldain—a cook.
Giwáimarra—to sharpen. [wet.
Giwamarra—to make moist *or*
Giwambang—moonlight.
Giwámmaldain—a bad woman; *adj.*, saucy, wicked.
Giwang—the moon.
Giwangabbung—a kind of grub.
Giwarra—to roast, to cook.
Godth—a kind of shield.
Gön—flint.
Gonín—very old.
Gonnguor—sultry dull weather.
Gonnu — implies dislike; as, gonnu *or* wiraidu gonnu—I don't like it.
-guabianna—*a postfix*; lasting all night; as, yubannai-guabianna—to rain all the night.
Guabin—cool.

THE WIRADHARI DIALECT.

Guabinga—to rest, to sit.
Guaiman—a native herb.
Guainbalgarra—to fetch blood;
  also, guainbummanna.
Guainginma—a black fly.
Gual—a shadow.
Gúan—blood.
Guanbilau—the menses.
Guandang—a native berry.
Guandubang—reddish.
Guang—mist, fog.
Guarián—a cockatoo, a parrot.
Guarra—to fetch, to fetch back.
Guarraguarra—eye blood-shot.
Guayo—after some time, afterwards, by-and-by.
Gubbagubbarra—to imitate.
Gubbaimanna—to wish to be with one, to follow.
Gubbalduringa—to drive off the enemy; to conquer.
Gúbbar—red stone, red paint.
Gubbarduringa—to follow; *also* gulbalduringa.
Gubbargubbarbirra — to make red; to paint red.
Gubbarra—to run after.
Gubbir—a kind of fish.
Gúdarra—to shine like metals or polish.
Gúdarra—*s.*, a current of wind.
Gudarra—*v.*, to feel cold; to feel a draught; to refresh.
Guddagudda—brightness; *adj.*, shining; *s.*, a noisy nightʃ 'bird. [very soft.
Guddalguddal—even, smooth;
Guddawirra — to be glad; to boast; to be showy. [songs.
Guddingan — a composer of
Guddiyarra—to be silent.
Guddu—the cracking of the joints of the fingers.
Gudin—a dead man.
Gudyugang—a kind of tassel.
Gudyuru—a small club thrown.
Gudyurumarra—to throw along the ground.

Guggabang—anything cooked.
Gugga-barra, -banna—to boil.
Guggaidyalaug—an infant that begins to crawl about.
Guggan—a kind of caterpillar.
Guggangugggamillanna—to walk with the back bent.
Gugganna—to creep, to crawl.
Guggé—any kind of vessel.
Guggin—near, at hand.
Guggingu—near.
Guggubal—a kind of codfish.
Gugguma—a stump.
Guggun—lame, unable to walk.
Gúggur—the knee.
Guggurmin—a very dark place in the Milky Way, supposed by natives to be like an emu.
Gúgu—water.
Guibanbirra—to spread to dry.
Guibanna—to be warm.
Guibarra—to roast.
Guin—*pron.*, he.
Guingal—a stone used by the natives to cut with.
Guingunnungal — a kind of grasshopper.
Guinguyung—himself, self.
Gulagallang *or* gallang—a good many.
Gulamiang—sought in vain, nothing found, disappointment.
Gúlar—a belt round the loins; the thread or worsted is spun by the natives.
Gulbal—a kernel *or* little bladder inside a fish.
Gulbaldain—one that understands well; *adj.*, intelligent.
Gulballanna—to be at peace; to have no fighting.
Gulbarra—to understand.
Gulbi—smoke *or* mist in the air
Gulbigulbir—partly.
Gulbir—some, part of.
Gulbirmarra—to make parts, to divide. [place).
Gulgandowa—before (of time *or*

Gulgarra—to bark.
Gulgog-gulgog—marks or scars, such as are left by small-pox.
Gulgong—the top of the head.
Gulgong—a little hole, a pit.
†Gulgoug—a ditch or gully; a gap in a mountain range.
Gulgurringa— to sing with a low voice.
-gulia—like, similar (a postfix).
Gullá—a net.
Gullabirra—to refuse, reject.
Gulladarra—to taste.
Gullai—a crossing-place, bridge.
Gullai—netting; a net bag.
Gullaigan—the second.
Gullaingain—the second child.
Gullaimarra—to net.
Gullainan—younger, born later.
Gullamarra—to open.
Gullamillanna—to be alone.
Guilaminga—to be or pass over, to delay; to be detained.
Gullamirra—to seek in vain.
Gullu—herb-seeds ground by the natives to make bread of.
Gulluin—distant, far off.
Gulluman—a wood for making a dish; the dish itself.
Gullun—lice. [together.
Gullun yananna—to go away al-
Gullung—a native badger.
Gullungirrin—lice, fleas; any kind of troublesome insect.
Gulmain—a younger brother.
Gumba—raw, not done enough.
Gumba—not ripe, green.
Gumba—a native fruit.
Gumbadda—metal.
Gumbal—a brother.
Gumbalang—a kind of seeds.
Gumban—a kind of herbage on which horses and cattle graze.
Gumbíl—uneven, not straight; bunchy, hump-backed.
Gumbilbirra—to walk with a bowing or bent back.
Gumbinbirra—to sprinkle.

Gumbinga—to wash, to bathe.
Gumbu—the crown of the head.
Gumbugal—honey-dew, found on the leaves of trees.
Gúmil—a belt, a girdle.
Gummiġ-gulgong—a thistle.
Gummil—thread from opossum wool.
Gunanna—to have the bowels relieved.
Gunargunar—a white butterfly.
Gundádeyannallinga—to go or come from behind.
Gundai—behind.
Gúndai—a 'stringy-bark' tree.
Gundai—a shelter, as when hid behind something.
Gundaibian—the blossom of the 'stringy-bark' tree.
Gundaimadillinga—to shelter one's self. [tect.
Gundaimarra—to shelter, pro-
Gundain—this one; this way.
Gundalla—someone, somebody.
Gundiwai—shade.
Gunduringa—to give a daughter away.
Gundyar—a fictitious deity that makes natives die; he sees and knows everything.
Gungalang—a frog.
Gúngámbirra — to harrow or plough.
Gun-ngang—little streams; i.e., traces of small water-courses.
Gungan—a running stream.
Guġgan—a flood.
Gungarra—to comb.
Gungil—dew.
Gunguari—a halo, a circle round the moon.
Gungun—a piece of bark that serves for a dish.
Gunnabunbinga—to sit down tired; to take rest.
Gunnaġgunnaġ—yellow ochre.
Gunnaġgalong—a long way off, distant.

Gunnama—hailstones.
Gunnama—a black ant.
Gunnamain—a kind of quail.
Gunnambarra—to depend on another either for work or for food; to be troublesome *or* intruding.
Gunnang — another, besides, else.
Gunnawi—the side of the body.
Gunné—a mother.
Gunnigalang—plain ground.
Gunnigal—a plain; a valley.
Gunnigalgarral—a plain where there are no trees.
Gunnigalla—plain, flat; a valley.
Gunnilmarranna—to groan, as under a heavy burden.
Gunnimar—hooks at the end of spears.
Gunnimbang—a mother.
Gunnin—thumb; *lit.*, mother.
Gunnindyang—motherless.
Gunnirra—to exert one's self *or* labour with groaning.
Gunnirra—to squeeze.
Gunno—tired, lazy.
Gunnog-gunnong—a cough.
Gunnubiyarra—to be loath to speak.
Gunnug-gulang—very distant.
Gunnuggurràn—a rainbow.
Gunnugilanna—to be tired of; to dislike; *cf.* gonnu.
Gunnundurai — a constellation of three stars, one of which is very bright in the eastern horizon soon after sunset.
Gunnungadillinga—to excuse one's self.   [denies.
Gunnungaldain—a liar, one that
Gunnungarra—to deny.
Gúrai—fat.
Gurai—a voice, a groan.
Guraimarrabirra—to sigh.
Guralong—the liver.
Gurawin—a flower.
Gúrba—the fork in a tree.

Gurbigang—a grub in the yam.
Gurda—cool; *subst.*, the cool of the evening.
Gurgagurga—a joint.
Gurgur—very deaf.
Gurian—a lake *or* large lagoon.
Guril—a smooth bluish stone somewhat resembling flint.
Gúrilgang — marks, as on an opossum-cloak.
Gurilmarra—to mark the skin.
Gurin—charcoal.
Guringurin—soot; *adj.*, sooty.
Gurou—foolish, stupid.
Gurra—a plate, a dish.
Gurrabang—the knee-cap.
Gurragadàn—finished, all done.
Gurragalang—bitter; medicine.
Gurragalgambirra—to finish.
Gurragalgarra—to finish.
Gurragallagali—a son of Baiamai, *q.v.*
Gurragamanna—to do fully, to finish; to go all away.
Gurragang—the knee-cap.
Gurragurragang—the knee.
Gurraggarang—a kind of frog; said to indicate rain.
Gurrai—refreshment; change.
Gurrai — dimly visible, indistinct, small.
Gurraibunminga—to see indistinctly.
Gurraibunmirra—to be weaksighted.
Gurraimuggumuggu — in distress; suffering.
Gurraingumminyu—to be dim, without light enough to discern.
Gurramarra—to push.
Gurriabal—tired of a place.
Gurriabarra—to be tired of a place.
Gurriban—a noisy night bird.
Gurrigurriabal—wretched.
Gurril—flint.
Gurrubar—reddish; a red stone

Gurrugadarra—to eat all, finish eating.
Gurrugamarra—to finish.
Gurrugambirra—to cover over; *also,* gumburgambirra.
Gurrugandyillinga — to cover one's self.
Gurruganna—to cover, put on, to dress.
Gurruganna—to cover; to hang all over. [ing.
Gurrugayarra—to finish speaking.
Gurruggarra—to butt. [cow.
Gurrugonbulong—bullock and
Gurrugurru—the rump *or* loins just above the podex.
Gurrúlgán—the fictitious being that causes thunder.
Gurruman—a shadow.
Gurrumarra—to draw the fire together.
Gurrumbaldain—a mimic.
Gurrumbarra—to mimic, to repeat, to imitate.
Gurrumbinga—to turn aside, to go out of the way, to go back.
Gurrunbirra—to make a noise indicating disgust *or* dislike.
Gurrundar—a wrinkle on the face.
Gurrundirra—to lean upon each other, like things in a row.
Gurruwai—night time.
Gurruwir—sad news.
Gúrumbirra—to make sport of.
Gurung—the claw of animals, as of the lobster
Gurúngulumbinga — to delay; to stop long.
Gurwaldain—deliverer, saviour.
Gurwarra—to deliver, to save.
Guwa—the taking shelter under a tree.
Guya—fish. [man.
Guyabadambildain — a fisher-
Guyabadambirra—to fish.
Guyal—dry.
Guyang—fire.

Guyo-ngammadillin—myself.
Guyulgang—very strong, enduring.
Guyungan—of himself, itself; spontaneously.

G.

Nga : ngadáu—here then! very well! have it! you may!
Ngabinbirra — to measure by spanning; *i.q.* ngabin-dirra, -binga.
Ngabinga—to try, attempt, examine.
Ngabin-gidyal—examination.
Ngadarra—to taste. [hair.
Ngaddangaddung — dishevelled
Ngaddéguor—on the other side.
Ngaddigallila—belonging to me.
Ngaddiwal—up here.
Ngaddu—I.
Ngadigallilabul—a long time.
Ngadin-balgaddilin—belonging to myself; my property.
Ngaduringa—to tend, care for.
Ngadyang—water.
Ngagarra—to ask.
Ngaguaingual—altogether.
Ngai—*particle of emphasis;* but, however.
Ngaiwari—used to.
Ngäl—a large hollow in a tree where one can stand upright.
Ngalan—light. [light.
Ngalanbamarra — to make a
Ngalar—clear, clean, white.
Ngalgambirra—to try the 'bargan' by throwing it.
Ngalgarra—to shine, give light.
Ngag-guaiwala—above.
Ngál-gal-marra—to feel loathing, like a sick stomach.
Ngalguamma—on high, above.
Ngalla—the underneath part of a tree *or* leg *or* pillar; the thick end of a thing.
Ngallaiman—very near, almost.

Ngalláin—a kind of white crystal quartz.
Ngallanbamirra—to kindle.
Ngallanbirra—to make a light.
Ngallanguranna — to give a bright light.
Ngalliman—nearly, almost.
Ngalluai—perspiration.
Ngalluġgan—a little mouse.
Ngama—indeed! ah! [for.
Ngamangamarra—to feel about
Ngamaġilla—to be sure! it is so!
Ngamanna—to feel, to touch.
Ngamarra—to feel, to touch.
Ngamarranána—to feel the loss of a wife.
Ngambaingarra—to gape.
Ngambalngambal—giddy, ready to tumble, intoxicated.
Ngambar—curious, inquisitive, wanting to know everything.
Ngambarang—a little boy.
Ngambarġána—to be covetous.
Ngameiligan—a hole where the tortoise lays its eggs.
Ngaminya—to be able to see.
Ngamma—a lump; *adj.*, swollen.
Ngammáia—an edible root.
Ngamon—milk.
Ngamonna—to suck.
Ngamondurai—a marriageable woman.
Ngamor—a daughter.
Ngamorgang—the breast.
Nga-mubang—blind.
Ngan—the brim.
Ngàn—the mouth.
Nganbinga—to lean, lean upon.
Nganbirra—to lean upon; *trans.*
Ngandabirra—to be dry, thirsty.
Ngandargang—the epiglottis.
Ngandi?—who?
Ngandir—deep.
Nganduġual?—who else?
Nganġána—to look after; to regard, care for.
Ngangijillinga—to see one's self.
Ngan-ġirra—to meet, assemble.

Ngánna—to see.
Nganna—there.
Ngannabul—over there, behind.
Ngannadar—down, underneath.
Ngannadarnġnra—underneath.
Ngannadarrain—downwards.
Ngannadwallain—upwards.
Ngannagan—one that steals a wife, not being a near relative to the husband.
Ngannaġunnuġgualla—the day after to-morrow.
Ngannaigurai—sorry, distressed, thoughtful.
Ngannaingarri—there; here.
Ngannaingulia—they.
Ngannaiwal—up, above.
Ngannal—me.
Ngannalla—that one.
Nganna-ngannadar—low.
Ngannanguor—behind there.
Ngannanguorma—behind.
Ngannawal—up above (in the sky).
Nganniain—all about, all over.
Ngannidyarġuor—underneath.
Ngannigunnuġ-guala—another time. [foot.
Ngannudarġuor—the sole of the
Ngannuġuor—the other side.
Ngaradan—a bat.
Ngaraimbang—sharp.
Ngarġundurei—to be with child; *adj.*, pregnant.
Ngararbang—a poor fellow; *adj.*, piteous.
Ngararbarra—to pity.
Ngargan—break of day. [dog.
Ngariugaribarra—to pant like a
Ngarra—the corners of the mouth.
Ngarradan—a bat.
Ngarrai—steep.
Ngarraingarri—an edible berry resembling the gooseberry.
Ngarrama—the loins, the rump.
Ngarran—hungry.
Ngarrang—a species of iguana.

Ngarranga—after.
Ngarrangarambang — arriving too late.
Ngarran-garran-garang—a fine blue-bell flower.
Ngarrangbain—the little finger.
Ngarrannarra—to pity.
Ngorrar—sorry.
Ngarrarmadillinga—to distress one's self; to feel sorry; *also* ngarrargijillinga.
Ngarrarmarra—to feel sorry, to be penitent; to pity.
Ngarré-ngarré—out of breath.
Ngarridyumarra—to look sideways; to view slyly.
Ngarriman—the native 'manna.'
Ngarringarri—breathing hard, resting, languishing.
Ngarringurribalgianna — panting for water, as a dog.
Ngarrogayamil—a star seen by the natives, as they say, in the zenith in the day time.
Ngarru—honey; sweet; a bee.
Ngarrung—decayed.
Ngarrungarra—sweet.
Ngarruriau—a white hawk.
Ngaumbin-gidyal—showing, demonstration, proof.
Ngaumbirra—to show.
Ngawa—yes.
Ngawang—a little shrub.
Ngawar—the marsupial bag of kangaroos and opossums.
Ngawarra—to tread upon.
Ngawillan—very high.
Ngayamadain—one that asks; an examiner, a judge.
Ngayalduringa—to be asked; to examine closely.
Ngayamanna—to ask, examine, try.
Ngayangijillinga—to ask one's self; to examine one's self.
Ngayur—warm.
Ngéanni—we; *also* ngianni.
Ngelidyain—greedy.

Ngelinga—to take part in, to interfere; to keep in possession.
Ngellengal—a face-likeness to some one.
Ngiabinya—to do again.
Ngiadyanna—to get *or* catch (a disease); to be afflicted with.
Ngiag-garang—speech, address.
Ngiag-garang—the beginning of conversation in the morning to awaken others.
Ngiaggir—clever, wise.
Ngiaginga—to revive.
Ngiambalgananna—to converse together.
Ngiambalgarra—to speak together, to converse, to reply.
Ngiambanang—braggadocio.
Ngiambangan—truth; a fact.
Ngiamildain—an overseer.
Ngiamirra—to supervise.
Ngiamugga—deaf, speechless.
Ngiang—a word.
Ngiangarra—to look upward.
Ngiawaigunnanna-to be (exist) always.
Ngiar—an eyebrow.
Ngiarau—a black-swan.
Ngidye—here; there.
Ngidyegallila—here; *emph.*
Ngidyigallila—this day, to-day.
Ngidyignor—on this side.
Ngimambirra—to wait for.
Ngimbilanna—to make progress or get into gradually.
Nginalla—these (*plu.*).
Ngindi—implies want (neither declined nor conjugated).
Ngindu—thou.
Ngindugir—you, ye.
Nginga—to be.
Ngingarimage—all day long.
Ngingurain—yesterday.
Ngolong—the forehead *or* face.
Ngologgaibuoanna— to return, to come back.
Ngologgairin—a red head-band.

THE WIRADHARI DIALECT. 93

Ngologgambilanna— to be returning home.
Ngologganna—to return.
Ngologgurrundar — distorted features.
Ngōng—a rut; a mark left.
Nguan; ngualla—that one.
Nguanda—a long time ago.
Ngubān—a husband.
Nguggog—a kind of cuckoo-owl.
Nguiyar (gibba)—the white crystal which, as the natives believe, comes from Wandog; he or some bad native sends it into another man's belly to make him ill; the native doctors pretend to draw it out.
Ngulluai—meeting each other.
Ngullarimarra—to do quickly.
Ngulburnan—a waterhole.
Ngullubal—the evening place of assembly.
Ngulluman—a large waterhole; a watercourse down-hill.
Ngullumuggu—the end, edge, border; the outside of a thing.
Ngúmambinga—to trust to for help.
Ngumambirra—to send.
Ngumbangillanna—to hold up the hands pretending to fight (said of two persons).
Ngumbanna—to be ready to hit.
Ngumbarrang—a bug.
Ngumbuoanna—to give back.
Ngumbuor—closed, wrapped up.
Ngumburbarra—to howl, as the wind. [away.
Ngummalgang—refuse thrown
Ngummambillanna—to borrow.
Ngunanna—to scorch.
Ngunba—sometimes.
Ngunbadal—union.
Ngunbadalngillanna—united.
Ngunbai—one.
Ngunbaidyil—in one place, all together.
Ngunbaigual—another.

Ngunbaimarrang—some.
Ngunbai-ngunbai—few.
Ngunbarra—to shut the door.
Ngundaigal—generous, liberal.
†Ngundanni—any.
Ngundan-ngillanna—to distribute to all, to be generous.
Ngungandain—a little farther.
Ngungiladanna—to give to another.
Ngungilanna—to give to each other, to exchange.
Ngungiyarra—to make a promise, to agree to.
Ngunmal—a fence.
Ngunna—the elbow.
Ngunna—to give.
Ngunnadar-guor — underneath the earth.
Ngunnagan—a friend.
Ngunnamilbarda—one related by marriage; a brother-in-law.
Ngunnuinguor—beyond, on the other side.
Ngunnuminga—to lend.
-nguor—side; towards (*postfix*).
Ngurambal—deep.
Ngurambalgal— high, chief.
Ngurambalbang—very deep.
Ngurangbang—country.
Nguragganna—to roll about on the ground.
Ngurain—an emu.
Ngurambirang—a friend.
Ngurang—camp, nest.
Nguranguräng—nobody at the camp; a deserted camp.
Ngurbirra—to kill by frost.
Nguringurian—an edible berry.
Ngurombang—evening, night.
Nguroggal—morning (early).
Nguroggalangal—very early in the morning. [dark.
Ngurog-ginga—to be getting
Ngurragaundil—a small beetle.
Ngurrambirrang—a hole used as a sleeping place (warmed by a previous fire).

Ngurrawang—a nest like that of some birds, or of an opossum.
Ngurrigal—surprise, wonder.
Ngurrigelang—vain, proud; s., showy dress.
Ngurru—water weeds.
Ngurrnai—choice, fancy.
Ngurruarra—to claim as one's own.
Ngurruigarra—to see new or strange things; to wonder, to be surprised.
Ngurrulganna—to snore.
Ngurrumirgang—blue, as the sky.
Ngurrumurdin—very dark.
Ngurrurganna—to snore.
Ngurui—the belly.
Nguruin-dinnag-garag — emu's feet; Baiamai (q.v.) has such feet.
Ngurumbi—winter; frost.
Nguyargir—a native doctor.
Nguyog-guyamilag—beautiful.

I

Ibbai—an eagle-hawk.
Ibbir-ibbir—little marks.
Ibbuga—a nephew; a relative.
Ibirnaanna—to paint, ornament.
Iddangin-gidyillinga—to hurt one's self.
Iddarra—to hurt, to injure.
Idya—the little finger.
Igge—ripe.
Iggebirra—to get ripe.
Iggebuananna—to make ripe.
Illi—dry, withered; like brown withered leaves.
Illigidyang—of a faded colour.
Illibirra—to wither, to dry.
Illilbamarra—to make a rattling noise.
Ilware—little hailstones.
Inar—a woman, a female.
Inarginbidyal—one that is fond of women.
Inargung—a girl.
Inarmubang—without a wife.
Indyamarra—to be gentle, polite; to honour, respect; to do slowly.
Indyambildain—a childish man.
Indyambirra—to act childishly, to be silly.
Indyang—slow, soft; slowly.
Ingamarra—to unloose, take off.
Ingang—a species of locust.
Inganna—to give way; to slip; as the ground.
Ingar—a lobster or crayfish.
Ingel—ill, sick.
Ingelbang—very ill.
Ingian—like, similar.
Ingiananna—to resemble.
Ingianbirra—to make similar.
Ira—the gills.
Iraddu—day.
Iraga—spring.
Iragunnanna—to pick the teeth.
Iragŭr—bitter, unpleasant to the taste; sour; said of unripe fruits.
Iraidurai—the morning star.
Iramangamanna—to pick the teeth.
Irambang—steep, mountainous, dangerous; a big mountain.
Irambang—seeds of herbs.
Irambarranna—to grin, to show the teeth.
Irambannang—toothless.
Irambin—kangaroo teeth.
Iramir—a precipice, a steep bank at the river.
Iramir-ngarang — precipitous; also irangarang.
Iramuggu—not sharp, blunt; without teeth.
Iramurrun—a tallish boy.
Irang—teeth.
Iraroarala—red-hot, very hot; unquenchable.

Irawari—a large thick cloud, a thunder cloud.
Irbadarra—to eat *or* drink all; to consume, exhaust, finish.
Irbagarra—to emtpy, to take all.
Irbaamnna—to go away, leave; to go to the bush. [all.
Irbamarra—to empty, draw out
Iré—the sun.
Irebang—summer.
Ircirimbananna—to feel comfortable (well, happy).
Ircirimbang—happy, comforted
Iremillan—the dawning of day, cockcrow.
Ireu—skin attached to bones.
Irgarra—to be empty; to be exhausted; to cease.
Iribadarra—to tremble. [hole.
Irimbauna—to peep through a
Irin—trembling.
Irin—the scales of a fish.
Irin—clear; *s.*, the light of day.
Iringa—to tremble.
Irinirin—a cold west wind.
Irinmarra—to cause to tremble.
Irribin—a swallow.
Irubar—deep, high, steep.

K

Kábbibáda—limestone.
Kabingidyal—a beginning.
Kabin-ya, -birra; kabinkabinga—to begin fighting; to begin.
Kaiya—a spade.
Kaiyai—lustful.
Kaiyaibirra—to be lustful.
Kaiyang—sinew, a thread.
Kaldigar—a kind of tree; *also* the white people.
Kaliaibalgambirra—to drive up.
Kaliainbal—an uphill ascent.
Kaliambirra—to let go up.
Kalianna—to ascend, climb up.
Kalianummiga—to get up again; to make sport of one.

Kalimbang—rainy weather.
Kaling—water.
Kalig-balgag-balgag—an insect.
Kaliggal—a knife.
Kalindyi—an island.
Kalindyuor—wet.
Kalinginbanga—a dry desert; a place without water.
Kalinkaling—wet.
Kallaganbauna—to rub off dirt from *or* wipe the feet.
Kallagang—an edible root.
Kalléibumarra—to draw up.
Kallindulein—a black snake.
Kalmaldain—a composer, a poet.
Kálmarra—to compose (songs).
Kalmarra—to fasten.
Kannãn—shallow, not deep.
Karamarra—water.
Karba (bula)—a fork.
Karbabandain—a girdle, a belt.
Karbarra—to sew.
Karbumma—a fork, a gallows.
Karí—truth.
Karia—*neg. interj.*, do not!
†Kariadal—no! by no means!
Kariadúl—no! do not say so! no! hope not! is it possible?
†Karigarra—to be true.
Kariggarra—to pour out, spill.
Karinbul—not yet! wait a bit!
Karingale—a native dog.
Karingun—a granddaughter.
Kariwang—a leaf.
Karrai—land.
Kárraimárra—to turn round in the hand, as the 'bargan.'
Karraingarra—to send.
Karraiwarra—to seek, to find.
Karraiyarbarra—to cry aloud.
Karralgarra—to pour out.
Karrámaldain—a thief.
Kárrámánna—to sneak away.
Karrámarra—to steal. [other.
Karrameilinga—to steal for another.
Karrandarang—a paper, a book.
Karrãng — poisonous wax-like stuff on the point of spears.

Karrari—a net. [work.
Karrariwibirra—to make net-
Karri-karri-darra — extremely cold, frosty.
Kárrindubálunbil — a beetle found in wood.
Karro—a magpie.
Kindai—play ; *adj.*, playful.
Kindaiawanna—to laugh, smile.
Kindaigallanna—to laugh at each other. [another.
Kindaigarra—to make sport of
Kindaiguldauna—to make sport of any one. [sister.
Kindaimaldain—a playmate, a
Kindaimanna—to play.
Kindaimarra—to make laugh.
Kindaimilanna—to laugh whilst walking along.
Kindain—a ring-tailed opossum
Kindaiwaruar—always laughing.
Kindanna—to laugh.
Kinnambang—very kind.
Kinnau—kind, gracious.

M

Mabbinbirra—to cause one to stay.
Mabbinga—to stop, to wait.
Mabbirra—to spill ; to pour out.
Mabbon—a messenger.
Mabbnorda—the cracking noise of crossing branches on trees caused by the wind.
Mabi—a wild cat.
Maddamadda—narrow.
Madarra—to suck, to chew.
Maddan—wood ; tree.
Maddang—lying down, sick.
Maddang—thick ; thick-headed, obstinate ; *cf.* ballamaddang.
Maddeilinga—to chew for another. [self.
Maddilinga—to chew for one's
Maddo—heavy, strong.
Maddu—one that intends to fight ; an enemy.

Maganna—to refuse to do a thing when ordered ; to disobey.
Magarra—to be bright, to look pretty.
Maggadalla—red soil. [cup.
Maggambirra—to have the hic-
Magganna—to drown, to choke.
Maggar—'iron-bark' wood.
Magge—all the day.
Magguar—happy.
Maggumanna—to sit with the knees erect.
Maibal—a 'grass-tree.'
Maibanmarra—to bore through, as a gimlet.
Maigang—a widow.
Mailgan—death.
Main—a native.
Maindaldain—a man-eater.
Maingarra—to paint red.
Maingualbang—a stranger.
Maingulia—native-like.
Malbillinga—to do when bidden
Malburdung—one that turns the feet inwards in walking.
Maldain—a maker.
Maldanna—to get ; to provide.
Maldhan—workmanship, work.
Malduringa—to dig roots.
Malgian—barren.
Malgianna—to dig out roots.
Mallaiar—friend, acquaintance.
Mallaidyin—feeble, infirm, ill.
Mallanggun—a little girl.
Mallu—lazy.
Mallungan—a young woman ; a female.
Mamarra—to paste on, to make sticky.
Mambar—a native fruit.
Mambarra—a native tree-fruit.
Mambuar—very hot, oppressed with heat, exhausted.
Mambuar—poorly, unwell.
Mammabba—a grandfather, an uncle.
Mammadin—a husband *or* wife

Mammaibanirra—to cause to cleave together; *also*, mammaibamarra.
Mammaibumarra—to hold down, subdue.
Mammal—a mixture. [with.
Mammalbamarra — to mingle
Mammallanna—to pay a visit, as when strangers arrive.
Mammandarra—not to know exactly; to forget.
Mam-marra, -manna—to cleave to, to be sticky, to adhere.
Mammurrain—a native root.
Manär—underdone.
Mandai—the rind; thin bark.
Mandang—a sort of wood.
Mandang—thankful, happy.
Mandarra—to be closed up; to have no air.
Mandiabba—an opossum.
Mandirra—to hit (strike, beat) sufficiently so as to break it.
Mandu—else; besides.
Mandumbillanna—to refuse to come when sent for.
Mandur—quiet *or* undisturbed, not meddled with.
Mangai—sore.
Mangamangan—a wind-shelter of boughs at the camp.
Mangar—a sling.
Mänginga—to lean against.
Mannanbil—muddy.
Mannang—dirt, ground, soil.
Mannanna—to be half-raw.
Mannara—wide.
Mannargauna—to be wide.
Mannargirang—very wide.
Mannarra—to spread; to make wide.
Mannarwirrimbirra—to spread.
Manngar—a wound, a sore.
Mannirra—to be too heavy to be carried.
Mannung—a kind of spear.
Mar—the small of the back.
Marambang—very good.

Marambagbillang—exceedingly good; *cf.* marang.
Marambir—better.
Marammubang—bad.
Marang—good; *also* marong.
Maragnginga—to be good.
Marbarmarbar—marked with diverse colours, striped.
Marbildain—a 'flogger.
Marbilduringa—to beat out, to beat thoroughly.
Marbirra—to flog.
Marga—a native shield.
Margamanna—to shield, defend.
Margon—the ankles.
Marinmarra—to clear off.
Marombungé—refreshment.
Maronirra—to make good *or* well.
Marra—the hand.
Marra—to do, to make.
Marrabadambirra—to be scattered about. [hands.
Marrabinga—to stretch out the
Marradir—a very large rock.
Marradul—a long time ago; long since.
Marragarra—to hold fast.
Marragayamirra—to shield the eyes against the sun with the hand.
Marragir—naked; *s.*, a widower.
Marragungang—a widow.
Marraibirang—very old.
Marraldirra—to frighten.
Marramaldain—an artificer.
Marremanna—to make haste.
Marramarrang—haste, hurry.
Marrambirra—to hasten.
Marramin—a kind of lobster.
Marramurgang—the fist.
Marran—a lung.
Marrang—little ants.
Marrangarra—to be convicted of murder.
Marrangungan—a large spider.
Marranmarran—raw, not done enough, not ripe.

g

Marrar—a tarantula spider.
Marrawir—to go to the bush without wives.
Marrayagal—very old.
Marria—a relation by marriage.
Marrin—the body. [rect.
Marrombul—good, right, cor-
Marrommanna—to be bright.
Marrommarra—to do, to create, to make.
Marruanna—to make, to form.
Marunbunmirra—to be kind to, to love.
Mawambul—all met together.
Mawang—altogether.
Mawarrar—a pod of grass seed.
Mayal—some kind of weeds.
Mayol—a wild blackfellow.
Memmang—very short; a short fellow.
Menar—very hot.
Mennu—lice.
Merri—a native dog.
Merribinga—to be very greedy.
Merrimborainga—very angry.
Merrimerrimal—a kind of grasshopper.
Merrin—angry.
Merringan—dog-like, thievish, wicked.
Merringin-gin—a bellyful.
Mian—one that provides and cares for another.
Miadyambarra—to look sharp.
Mibar—a butterfly when in its cocoon.
Middang—alone, one, single.
Midyur—sharp, pointed.
Migganma—an arch, a bow.
Migganmiggan—edge, corner.
Migge—lightning.
Miggé—a marriageable young woman.
Miggemána—to flash, to lighten.
Mil—the eye.
Milbang—snot from the nose.
Milbarra—to beat softly and regularly, like a watch.

Milbi—a hole; a well.
Milbomgarra—to stare, wonder, be astonished; *also* milbommanna.
Milbuun—dimness of the eyes.
Mildong—a handle, as of the 'marga,' *q.v.*
Milgain—openly; face to face.
Milge—large drops of rain.
Milgurai—a dim sight.
Millalmillal—awake; wakeful.
Millang—the hip.
Millangul—very near.
Millángún—sidewards.
Milwarranna—to open the eyes.
Millawelang—a native shrub.
Millumarra—to wink.
Mimarra—to pull, to pull from or back, to hold fast.
Minbanna—to beg, to pray.
Mindyambinga—to stretch.
Mindyarra—to be fast; fixed.
Mindyui—a needle; *cf.* bingal.
Mingan—the eldest sister.
Minganna—to prop, as a pillar.
Mingarra—to be wrong, mistaken.
Minngar—an edible root.
Minni—a sister.
Minyambal—something.
Minyambung—a bad dream.
Minyang—what?
Minyagga—what is it?=I know not what (as a reply).
Minyangan—how many?
Mirga—the woman's shield.
Mirganna—to protect with the 'mirga,' as the women do.
Micilmiril—nostrils.
Mirol—pipeclay.
Mirra—the left hand.
Mirra—left; *s.*, the left arm.
Mirral-birra—to be afraid; *s.*, apprehension.
Mirrhal—greedy.
Mirrimbulbul—dejected, dull.
Mirrimirringarra—to be very down-hearted.

THE WIRADHARI DIALECT.

Mirrinmarra—to drag along the ground.
Moildain—a backbiter.
Mombal—a native shrub.
Mombanna—to cry; especially the cry of mourning.
Mondarra—to pick.
Mondu—the upper lip.
Mondudiranna—to look stern.
Monnubang—lousy-headed.
-mubang—destitute of, without; *a postfix*; *cf. Eng.* -less.
Muddai—content, satisfied.
Muddaingindanna—to be satisfied.
Muddamuddaġ—an acacia-tree.
Muddirra—to beat out, to gather (fruit); to thrash.
Múge—an owl.
Muggaindyal—worn out, old.
Muggamarru—to make a knot.
Mugganna—to pick up.
Muggén—a mosquito.
Muggi—a species of eaglehawk.
Muggin—blind.
Mugginga—to close the eyes.
Muggomma—inside (the hut).
Muggommagga—the palate; the inside of the mouth.
Muggon—podex.
Muggu—void of, without (as a *postfix*); *v.*, to stop up.
Muggúar—quiet, silent.
Mugguarbang—quiet, peaceful.
Muggaigawanna—to go to sleep.
Muggugalúrgarra—to conceal, to keep secret.
Mugguinbabbirra—to give anything readily so as to avoid being teased longer.
Muggulun—a grub in wood.
Muggumandan—a knot caused by tying.
Muggumnoa—in; internally.
Muin—swampy black soil.
Muin—a kind of ground-spider.
Mulba—very short; a little man;
Mulgabirra—to give all.

Mulgamarra—to span.
Mulgamarra—to take hold of to grasp, to lay hold of bodily
Mulgunmadillinga—to wrap u one's self.
Mulgunmarra—to wrap up *or* roll round.
Mullaġdirra—to be sick, vomit.
Mullaimirra—to lie in wait, to watch for.
Mullamullang—very sick.
Mullan—part of.
Mullang—sick.
Mullangual—another part.
Mullanna—sick, ready to vomit.
Mullarmullar—slippery.
Mullawar—'opossum-grass.'
Mullen—a little bird.
Mullian—an eagle hawk.
Mulludin—the moustache.
Mulludyin—a kind of whiskers round a fish called 'dangur.'
Mullunma—inside, within.
Mumang—short; *cf.* bergul.
Mumarra—to rub between the hands.
Mumbir—a mark; a scar.
Mumbirmarra—to mark.
Mumbuar—a thoughtful *or* distressed look; quiet, unassuming, humble.
Mundubang—a hatchet.
Mundyambarra—to smack the lips when eating.
Munga—a native fruit.
Munga—a little infant.
Múngallána—to get the mastery of, to conquer.
Mungar—a kidney.
Mungimanna—to rub the eyes.
Mungo—the calf of the leg.
Munguma—a lump, a piece.
Mungur—straight, stiff. [leg.
Mungurmarra—to break one's
Munil—a hole.
Munilbunmara—to make a hole.
Munirgallanna—to scold, find fault with.

Muogamarra—to keep in reserve for future use.
Muogan—a younger sister.
Muogelang—a species of wood.
Muomadi—a term of reproach.
Muoyarra—to tell behind the back; to speak secretly.
Mural—anything (as dust, sand, dirt) that gets into the eye.
Murannanna—to make or feel warm.
Múrgambanna—to craunch, as in biting a hard crust. [sort.
Murigual—different; of another
Muro—the entrails of a grub.
Munmanna—to stifle the cough; to hold the hand before the mouth while coughing.
Munnaingubildain—deceitful.
Munnaigubirra—to make sport of, to disappoint, to tantalise.
Munnalwé—greedy, voracious.
Munnarra—an afternoon visit.
Munnirganna—to be jealous.
Munnuin—a sharp end or point; the point of a spear.
Munnun—big, much. [tree.'
Muogalambin—a kind of 'box-
Muogallan—a kind of tree.
Murrabialinga—to get worse or sick again, to have a relapse; also, murrabinga. [asleep.
Murrabinda—to be ill, to be fast
Murrabirra—to throw down.
Murradambirra—to make fast.
Murradirra—to hit, to kick.
Murra-gan-gan—having many fingers or legs, like spiders.
Murrai—soft.
Murraidyung—very soft.
Murrain—the white cockatoo.
Murralmurral—slippery.
Murral—something in the eye.
Murramirra—to stare or look at with surprise.
Murramurrabirra—to part for ever, never to see again; to neglect, to forsake.

Murranal—blind.
Murraudan—a little rat.
Murrang—mud.
Murranillanna—to fight much.
Murrawal—much, great.
Murrawalgiran—a stout, large man.
Murrawarra—to stand fast.
Murrayallalinga—to raise the voice.
Murrayarra—to speak out, to speak loud.
Murredyang—curious, strange.
Murrhum-murrhung— smiling, ready to laugh.
Murri—a sort, a kind.
Múrri—a stranger.
Murriang—the place where the ocean ceases at the end of the world; there Baiamai lives.
Murrigual—another sort.
Murrigualbang—different ones, strangers.
Murrimurri—each, of each sort.
Murrin—no.
Murróg-garra—to leap, as in dancing.
Murron—life; adj., alive.
Murrongialinga — to come to life again, to revive.
Murronginga—to live.
Murru—a road.
Murru—nose.
Murrua—the west wind.
Murruban—the first.
Murruberai—thunder.
Murruberaigarra—to thunder.
Murrudadain—a native bird.
Murrudalain—thorns.
Murrudinolinga—to turn up the nose at; to treat with contempt.
Murrudirra—to speak through the nose.
Murrudirran—a protuberance; projecting and hanging over.
Murrugai—first.
Murrugal—to read.

THE WIRADHARI DIALECT. 101

Murrugian—the bone worn in the nose.
Murrumarra—to hold fast, to sift seeds in a piece of bark, to rub between the hands.
Murrumbain—the firstborn.
Murrumbir—sky, firmament.
Murrumbirrhe—a loud sound heard in the air by the natives.
Murrumurrung—laughable; s., one that is always laughing.
Murrung—a kind of grasshopper.
Murrungayarra—to say always.
Murrungelinga—to surround, to encompass, to inclose.
Muruġ-gamirra-to like or fancy a thing.
Muruidarra—to make a noise when eating.

N

Nammunmanna—to hold the hand to the mouth.
Nammundambinga—to shut up; to tie up, as clothes.
Nan—the neck.
Nanan—quick, fast-running.
Nandirang—bent, like a hook.
Nangan—putrified meat.
Nangundarra—to trespass by eating things forbidden.
Nangunmarra—to trespass, intrude, to do wrong.
Nannaibirra—to be in a hurry; to be very eager.
Nannaibungarra—to waste.
Nannaigan—poor, miserable.
†Nannaigur—poorly, unwell.
Nannaigure—miserable, uncomfortable.
Nannainia—very steep.
Nannaimarra—to spill, to waste.
Nannainannaibina—to be very lucky.
Naranmarra—to strip off.

Narbang—a woman's bag; the pouch of an animal.
Narguaima—round.
Narrannanangerang—a flower.
Narrarwarra—to slip backwards
Narrawai—the smoky appearance of the air caused by great heat.
Narriar—hot.
Narrin—the hip-bone.
Narro—a man's bag.
Narruldirra—to escape.
Narrundirra—to kick.
Naruin—fresh skin.
Narwarra—to slip.
Nigganagga—very hot, oppressive; said of the sun.
Nilla—he, she, it (pron.).
Nimmadillinga—to pinch one'sself; also nimma-ġidyillinga.
Nimuggang—a little rat.
Nin—one's own.
Ninganna—to come begging in a sly manner.
Ninirwara—to search minutely.
Nirgian—sulky, peevish.
Nirin—an edge.
Nirmarra—to break one's arm.
Nuggadang—reddish gum from the 'gum-tree.'
Nugganirra—to beat regularly; as the heart.
Nuggur—loathing food; not inclined for eating.
Nulang—mist ascending.
Nulang—the mist-like appearance of the atmosphere in summer indicative of great heat; Germ., höhenrauch.
Nullabang—many.
Nullari—hurry, haste.
Nulluimarra—to turn upside down, to tilt.
Nulluimbinga—to be folded upwards.
Nulluinbibaddi—folded up.
Nulluin-marra,-manna—to spill
Numbanna—to blow the nose

Nunnumarra—to take away from.
Nurra-nurra-bul—always, constantly.
Nurrurdarra—to suck, as the juice out of a bone.

U

U—anything airy or open, such as a pipe.
Uba—a native rat.
Ubbuginga—to go under the water, to dive.
Ubbur—full, swollen; s., a lump
Ubu—a kind of frog-stool.
Uda—an ear.
Udabarrambang—the thick end (knob) of the 'bundi' cudgel.
Udadurai—clever, intelligent.
Udagarbinga—to listen.
Udagual—a different purpose; lit., another ear.
Udag-garag-garra—to know a great deal, to be intelligent.
Udamugga—deaf; lit., ear-shut.
Uddagarragarra—whirling as a leaf in falling.
Ugal—a young man.
Uganguang—rotten, decayed; s., corruption (in the grave).
Ugil—heat, warmth, hot wind.
Ulbundarra—to draw out, as a native doctor draws out a charm-stone from the belly of a sick person, as they say.
Ulbundinga—to pull off, cause to fall off.
Ulbunmalalinga—to pull again.
Uldumbarra—to get unfastened; disunited.
Ulinga—to fly.
Ulinga—to lie down, go to sleep.
Ulla—voice, sound; a call.
Ullabarra—to have a rolling noise inside the bowels.
Ullanna—to call.

Ullawaranna—to howl, shriek.
Ulleilinga—to call for some one.
Ullui—rubbish.
Ullunma—the calf of the leg.
Umbai (ú)—the last. [off.
Umbanna—to get loose, to come
Umirra—to peep. [light.
Undirra—to stand in one's own
Uran—hair.
Uranbai—very hairy.
Urganba—a thing to open with, a key.
Urganna—anything that is inside; as maggots in meat.
Urgarra—to put in.
Uriabare—never mind!
Urimbirra—to take care of, to keep, preserve.
Urong—leafless.
Urommarra—to take out, to take from underneath.
Urra—weak, feeble; very thin.
Urragarra—to make a noise.
Urranna—to enter.
Urrembillinga—to come in when told.
Urraurramarra—to feel acute pain.
Urrubirra—to swallow.
Urrugan—a fastening, a tie.
Urrugarban—unable to breathe well, hoarse, unable to talk.
Urrugurrai—hoarse; s., a sore throat.
Urrungillanna—to encompass.
Urrúnmarra—to pull, to draw; to open like a beast when slaughtered; also ulbutmarra.
Urrur—full; v., to be satisfied.
Urrurbanna—to rush upon; to bluster.
Urrurbáuna—to be full, to be satisfied.
Urrurgirrín—a very bad sore.
Urrurubil—the throat.
Uru—the neck.
Urumbanninga—to get through underneath.

Urumbumarra—to push through or into.
Urung—a bow, a branch.
Urungambirra—to put on (into)

W

Wabba—a wild pigeon.
Wabban—a spy.
Wadda—the ashes of a burnt [tree.
Waddag̈-gallanna—to talk together, to dispute, to scold.
Waddag̈ganna—to be angry; to scold, to use bad language; to grumble, to be dissatisfied.
Waddagung—a wild rabbit-rat.
Waddanganna—to be angry or provoked.
Waddawadda—the ankle bone; an edge; *adj.*, uneven.
Wadyargal—the hinder part of the back of a fish.
Waerawi—any fancy, a dream.
Waggawagga—reeling, like a drunken man.
Waggadain—a dancer.
Wag̈gai—a little child.
Waggambirra—to play, to dance about.
Wúg̈gan—a black crow.
Wagganna—to dance.
Waggara—a spade.
Wag̈gé—a species of ants.
Waggura—a crow; a different sort from 'wágan.'
Waibar—to the left.
Waibarma—the left hand.
Waiyamarra—to turn over, to turn round.
Waiyarang—teachable, clever.
Waiyuberai—bent, crooked.
Walaullon—a kind of limestone.
Walbai—crooked.
Walbang—thin bark, rind.
Walgar—the projecting bone in the upper front part of the arm; the collar-bone.

Walgawalga—marks, as on the trees near a native grave.
Walgun—anything crosswise; confusion.
Walgunwalgun—going to and fro (once crosswise).
Wallagai—the bare part of a tree where the bark has been stripped off.
Wallag̈agag̈—not strong, weak.
Wallagarra—to strip. [skin.
Wallagur—scars burnt on the
Wallamannayalinga — to take care of till strong; to train a child.
Wallan—strong.
Wallanbang—very strong.
Wallanbaungan—strong, mighty, possessed of authority.
Wallang—a stone.
Wallanmarra—to make strong.
Wallar—a waterhole in rocks
Wallar—flat, even, smooth.
Wallaru—a small kangaroo.
Wallawallang—stony.
Walliwalli—crooked; *cf.* bargan
Wallui *or* walluigang—a young man.
Walluin—good, well, healthy.
Wallumarra—to be a guardian, to protect.
Wallunmanna — to sit still as unwilling to go.
Wallun-g̈inga—to be good.
Wallunbuoyarra—to forbid to tell a thing.
Walgun—ignorant, barbarous.
Wamarra—to skin.
Wambad—a badger.
Wambadar—the lights next the liver.
Wambalwamballa—hilly, rugged
Wambinga—to support.
Wambong—a constellation.
Wambuainbang—a duck; *also* the name of a constellation.
Wambuan—mixture.
Wambuanbunmarra—to mix.

Wambun—*subst.*, covetousness; *adj.*, covetous.
Wambunbunmaldain—a covetous person.
Wambunbunmarra—to make or be covetous *or* greedy.
Wammal—a native weapon, *i.e.*, a little sharp-pointed stick.
Wammang—wrong, not right; not straight, out of the road.
Wammar—the hand-stick with which the spear is thrown; the 'wommara.'
Wammarra—to build.
Wámu—fat.
Wanarra—to mark a skin.
Wanbang—the mound of earth on a grave.
Wanbuan—a kind of kangaroo.
Wandaiyalle—a porcupine.
Wándong—the bad spirit.
Wandyu—a crow; *i.q.* wágan.
Wangaduringa—to be lost.
Wángai—a large species of ant.
Wangaidyung—astray, lost.
Wangal—hair matted together.
Wangan—clotted.
Wanganna—to lose.
Wangar—idle, lazy.
Wangarra—to cry like a crow.
Wangi—a night-owl. [the fire.
Wangian—to sit at the back of
Wannabanna—to leave behind, to forsake.
Wannaggarra—to throw away; *also* wannag-gilarra.
Wannaggilgan—single, *i.e.*, unmarried.
Wannamambilána—to separate from each other, to part.
Wannamindyarra—to neglect, to be careless; to care for no longer; to forgive.
Waunangijillinga—to abandon one's self; to despair.
Wannanna—to throw.
Wannarra—to dig with a stick, as native women do.

Wannál—one that is under the restriction of tribal law with respect to food; a lad not yet fully initiated.
Wannamarra—to do, to finish.
Wannamarradanna—to leave alone; not to meddle with.
Wannawanna—to scratch.
Wannunduringa—to cease, to discontinue, to throw away.
Wanyanna—to scratch.
Wanyannadillinga—to scratch one's self.
Wanyarra—to mark.
Warbanna—to blow hard; as when wind unroofs houses; to destroy.
Wargu—wherefore? why?
Warngandarra—to be troublesome, quarrelsome.
Warngangi—tiresome, troublesome, quarrelsome, bad.
Warnganna—to disturb.
Wawé—a monstrous water animal.
Wárra—the edge *or* hemming; the end; the brim.
Warrabamarra—to stop, to impede; to cause to cease.
Warrabarra—to make a noise.
Warrabinga—to look about, to seek for what is lost.
Wárradagang—a yellow stone; *adj.*, yellow.
Warradannang—quarrelsome, warlike, wicked.
Warraga—under there, downwards.
Warragianna—to stand over *or* before the fire, to warm one's self.
Warrágu—limestone.
Warrai—a kind of iguana.
Warraingarra—to hurry away, to lead astray, to lead into temptation.
Warral—stiff, unbending.
Warralag—a long brown snake.

Warralginga—to stretch one's self.
Warramba—a turtle. [again.
Warrambilalinga—to put down
Warrambinga—to put on (a cap).
Warrambirra—to put down.
Warrandhain—a peevish, crying fellow. [foreign.
Warrangan—difficult, strange,
Warranna—to stand.
Warrarang—oppressively hot.
Warraur—string, a band.
Wárrawánagé!—let us go! get ready!
Warrawarra—to shout.
Warrawarrada—standing as if ready to go.
Warrhul—an echo; a loud sound sometimes heard by the natives as an intimation of death.
Warriwarri (diran)-a long chain of hills.
Warria—a pup; the little toe.
Warrian—a kind of 'kangaroo-rat'; wirŏng is another kind.
Warro—a kind of small fly.
Warrubalbal—a large hornet.
Warrugaldain—a helper.
Warrugang—red.
Warrugarra—to help.
Warrul—honey.
Warruyarra—to count, number.
Waur—steam.
Wawai—a large water-snake.
Wawal—barren.
Wawalgang—a kind of tassel.
Wawina—to move the wings, fly.
Wawirra—to clean.
Wayadan—a relative.
Wayal—a kangaroo skin.
Wayambinga—to turn round.
Wayamilbuoanna—to look back.
Wayamirra—to look back.
Wayan—out of sight, lost.
Wayandi—all round.
Wayangarra—to turn round, to go round the corner; to stir, as food in the pot.

Wayanmarra—to get out of sight, to be lost to view.
Wayarang — possessing much property; rich.
Wayawayambinga—to revolve, to turn round; *also* wirbunba.
Wayawayanga—encompassing.
Wayunmarra—to wind up, to wring out.
Wayuwaynanbinga—to swing, to turn to and fro.
Weddingán—a man that has left his brother.
Wiang—the part of the forehead just behind the temples.
Wiargualin—fog. [detain.
Wibaiyarra—to tell to stay, to
Wibianna—to sit down.
Wibirra—to spin.
Widyalang—a child not yet walking.
Widyua—what for? what?
Widyunga—when?
Widyugguor—which way?
Widyulainmallang—victory.
Widyung—which way?
Wigawanna—to sit watching.
Wiggé—bread, vegetable.
Wiggilgil—worms in wood.
Wiggarrinil—one that sits all day. [night.
Wigurabianna—to sit up all
Wilban—a cave.
Wilbanna—to whistle.
Wilbur—a branch, a twig.
Willaidul—curious, strange.
Willáimarra—to do mischief.
Willaiyarra—to use bad words.
Willei—an opossum.
Willidya—standing *or* lying in the way; *s.*, an obstacle.
Willigain—the firstborn.
Willima—middle, midst.
Willin—the under lip.
Willinga-willinga—part of the beard close to the under lip.
Willurain—fluid honey.
Willurding—slender, small.

Willurci—very sweet. [self.
Wiman-gijilliga—to rub one's
Wim-anna, -arra—to anoint.
Win—fire, fuel, wood.
Winbangarra—to make a fire.
Winbangelinga—to make a fire for another.
Windil—grease, gravy, fat.
Windimanna—to wait for, to be meddlesome, to trouble.
Winga—to sit down, to live.
Wingaddan—a woman that has become a mother. [egg.
Wingambang—the yolk of an
Wingarang—a poor man, *i.e.*, one having no wife, *lit.*, 'no fire.'
Winingarra—to pick out.
Winnaggabillinga—to believe.
Winnaggadillinga — to know one's self; to feel.
Winnagaduringa — to know (*emph.*); to reflect, meditate.
Winnangadain—a clever man; *adj.*, intelligent.
Winnaggalang—clever.
Winnanga-gi-gillanna—to care for each other.
Winnanga-garra-garra—knowing everything.
Winnagganna—to know, think.
Winnaggarra—to hear.
Winnangibillang — clever, intelligent.
Winnawinnang—an insect.
Winnummiawanna—to stay a short time.
Winnumminga—to sit down again, to wait. [water.
Winyu—a waterhole without
Wir—the air, heaven, sky.
Wirai—no. [all!
Wiraibul—by no means! not at
Wiraigualman—nothing more.
Wirain—not level, sloping up, oblique.
Wirbingal—a very tall man.
Wirbunba—lame.

Wirbunba—a flame of fire bursting forth.
Wirgain—in the air.
Wirgal—the tree, in the form of a rainbow, which grows out of Darrawirgal's thigh.
Wirgaldain—a carpenter.
Wirganna—to be lame, to halt.
Wirgarang—weeds.
Wirgarra—to make smooth, to scrape off.
Wirrhan—sloping. [care of.
Wirimbirra—to preserve, take
Wirong—the north wind.
Wirradil—a nail.
Wirradirra—to nail.
Wirragal—poisonous black wax put on the points of spears.
Wirriaganna—*see* wirringanna.
Wirriawannag—to lie down, to go to sleep.
Wirribang—destitute of vegetation.
Wirrimbildána—to leave a portion, as of food.
Wirrimbirra—to lay up, keep, preserve.
Wirrindanna—to roast.
Wirringa—to lie down to sleep.
Wirringanna—to sing as the natives do at 'karábaris' with the strong sound of *r-r*.
Wirringillanna—to cohabit.
Wirrirmarra—to detain.
Wirurngar—meat when tainted and smelling badly.
Wiwin—hot.
Wiyé—the hinder part *or* back; little sticks.
Wuye—shavings of wood.
Wuyŏng—a bird like the crow.

Y

Ya—*exclam.*, oh!
Yabba—a diamond snake.
Yabbaibang—all round.

THE WIRADHARI DIALECT.

Yabbaibang—voluptuous.
Yabbain—a prize for which two or more contest.
Yabbang—behind.
Yabbang—vestiges; a footpath.
Yadarra—to be too narrow.
Yaddang—well, right; because.
Yaddár—a dream.
Yadillinga—to be ready to go.
Yaddu—I; *for* ngaddu.
Yaggailia—a term of reproach.
Yaggar—an edible lettuce-like grass eaten by the natives.
Yain—that way! so!
Yaindyibul—all round.
Yaingalmallabul—that's all.
Yaingalman—so many; the person showing the number with the hands.
Yaingambirra—to assist.
Yaingayaingarra—to help.
Yake!—*exclamation* of pain.
Yála—that way!
Yalaiyarrhagillanna—to speak well of one, to praise.
Yalbillinga—to speak when bidden; to learn.
Yalduringa—to confess.
Yalgar—hard, dried up.
Yalgarbunbirra—to make dry.
Yalgu—dry; *s.*, a leafless tree.
Yallabal — generous always; liberal.
Yallabarra (birrbaga)—to carry on the back.
Yalu—yes, that will do!
Yalladanna—to scold.
Yallai-yallai—a flap; hanging down, like a dog's ears.
Yallalinga—to speak again.
Yallanna—to speak to one another; to scold each other.
Yallaradang—gum oozing from trees.
Yallaraingarra—to let go down.
Yallaranna—to hiss, as a snake.
Yallar-anna, -ambirra—to fall down headlong; to let down.
Yallé—the soft part between the rib and hip.
Yallul—always.
Yalmambirra—to teach.
Yama—*interrog.*, as much as; joined to pronouns.
Yamaiamaldain—a helper.
Yamandirra—to carry fire.
Yambadarra—to shrink from.
Yambinya—to stay *or* live with, as a man with a woman.
Yambiyambidyal—one that can get no husband, an old maid.
Yambiyambinga—to imitate, to do like another.
Yambiyambinga—to help, assist.
Yambuan—any *or* every thing.
Yambul—nothing, nonsense, a lie, mere talk.
Yambulgarrambin — anything that roams about, but is not seen.   [pear' tree.
Yamma; yammagang—the 'wild
Yammadain—a companion.
Yammadi—a dog; *fig.*, a sensualist.
Yammaiamarra—to help, assist.
Yammanna—to go along with.
Yamoa—why? what for?
Yanbarra—to exchange wives.
Yandammulla—the name of one of the two wives of Baiamai.
Yandandu—if, when.
Yandambullan — Darrawirgal's partner.
Yandangarang—a false beard, a mask.
Yandarra—to mess together.
Yandayanbarra—to eat for the sake of company.
Yandiandirra—to laugh after another.
Yandu—yet, at that time, then.
Yandul—now, at the present.
Yandulabul—at one and the same time.
Yandyima—all over, all round.
Yangan—common property.

Yan-ganma,-garra—*see* yunganna
Yangarra—to grind seeds in the native way; to rub on a stone; to clean by rubbing, as knives.
Yange—drought. [woman.
Yangerang—a run-about, a bad
Yangerang—all along, all about.
Yangerangbuolia—all round.
Yanguainbanna—to stumble, to stammer.
Yangumbi—always, a long time.
Yangumbinga—to leap over.
Yannabayarra—to send, to tell to go.
Yannabillinga—to go when told.
Yannabuoananna—to go with exertion. [wanderer.
Yannadarrambal—a stroller, a
Yannagagi—a walk, *v.* and *s.*
Yannaidurai—an infant beginning to walk; any walker.
Yannamambirra—to let go.
Yannamanna—to pursue.
Yannamarra—to go quickly.
Yannambabirra—to come for something to eat.
Yannangarimanna—to go about all day long.
Yannanna—to go, to walk.
Yannanuwal—go on!
Yánnarra—a long fishing spear.
Yannaurar — smooth, nicely finished.
Yannemaingarrin—having gone in vain.
Yanniyanirra—to come to one's assistance.
Yannulabul—at the same time.
Yannumbilanna—to walk.
Yara—a 'gum-tree.'
Yaran—the chin; the beard.
Yarbarra—to dig, scrape with the spade.
Yarbimma—round.
Yariwan—as sensual as a brute.
Yarmanna—to seek all about.
Yarmarra—to move about and scratch *or* bite, like fleas.

Yarngun—the root of a tree.
Yarra—to speak.
Yarradamarra—to dream.
Yarradunna — to beat on the 'bargan,' *q.v.*
Yarraga—spring.
Yarraibarra—to make a hissing noise, like the 'bargan' when thrown.
Yarrain—a native shrub.
Yarrainbadanna—to gnash the teeth together.
Yarraiyannanna—to go about.
Yarraman—a horse.
Yarrān—a kind of grub.
Yarrān—a grub found in trees.
Yarrandang—a dream.
Yarrang—splinters.
Yarranna—to make an angry noise, like dogs when ready to seize on an object.
Yarrarbai—creaking, as shoes.
Yarrarbarra—to creak.
Yarrawullai—the blossom of the 'gum-tree.'
Yarre—raw, underdone.
Yarridyundain—strong, as raw hide.
Yarringan—clear, transparent, like clear water.
Yarriwan—voracious.
Yarrudag-ginga—to dream.
Yarruwalla—very strong, very mighty.
Yaryan-buolia—everywhere.
Yaung—a small shadow.
Yawai; yungi—stones used for grinding *or* sharpening.
Yawaima—round; *subst.*, a ring.
Yawaingar—a cockroach.
Yawaldain—one that watches, a watchman.
Yawallanna—to watch one another.
Yawandyillinga—to take care of one's self.
Yawannayallinga—to care for, as a mother a child.

Yawarra—to watch *or* take care.
Yawarrang—a kind of fish.
Yawillawillawil--cooling breeze.
Yayallanna—to assist to talk.
Yelinga—to reprove, find fault with.
Yuambanna—to frighten away evil spirits by a hissing noise.
Yuar—hungry.
Yuar—a kind of 'gum-tree.'
Yuarbin—the blossom of 'yuar.'
Yubanirra—to cause to rain.
Yubarra—to rain.
Yuddillanna—to touch.
Yuddinga—to hit against, to touch; *also* yudirra.
Yuganna—to move. [self.
Yuggan-gijillinga—to stir one's
Yuggawai—a sleeping place.
Yuggawanna—to select a place where to sleep.
Yugongbirra—to turn back.
Yuggé—a fierce native dog.
Yuggubul—this one, this fellow.
Yugguggirra—to look from underneath, to peep.
Yuggui—having no water, dry.
Yuin—a name.
Yuinballai—one who is respected, famous.
Yuinbarra—to tell the name.
Yuinbir—this way!
Yulain—skin.
Yulung; yulumban—a kind of milk-thistle.
Yulla—nails on fingers and toes.
Yullai-yullai—shaking, staggering.
Yullang—a little shrub.
Yullawanna—to stretch out the arms; to lie straight.
Yullawarra—to stretch.
Yullubirgen—a rainbow.
Yullugayan-anna—to go on the toes.
Yullugur—a part of the throat.
Yulluma—a kind of kangaroo.
Yumambirra—to cause to cry.

Yumarradinga—to cry whilst walking.
Yumbalgarra — to pass from playing into crying.
Yumbanidyillinga—to be sorry for having made one cry.
Yumbanirra—to cause to cry.
Yumbi—a species of pine.
Yumbiyumbidyang—a servant, an assistant.
Yumbul—that way!
Yung—scars.
Yungaddain—a stroller.
Yungaibarra—to cry out, shout.
Yunganna—to groan, to cry, to make much a-do at work.
Yungarang —illegal cohabitation.
Yungbunmarra—to push back
Yungerang—very noisy.
Yungir—a crier.
Yungun—backwards.
Yurai—sleep; *adj.*, sleepy.
Yuranna—to grow.
Yurbai—a kind of seed.
Yurbarra—to nod in sleep, to be sleepy.
Yurbayurba—sleepy.
Yuren—a scratch, scar, sore.
Yuron—convalescent.
Yurong—a cloud.
Yurraibulbul—very sleepy.
Yurrubang—very tall and big.
Yurruga—the sun.
Yurrugai—thistle.
Yurrugaidyurai—name of the mountain near my home.
Yurrumbamarra—to rear, to bring up.
Yurrumbannayalinga—to take care of another's child.
Yurumbawal—an old man who has seen much; one who has seen his children's children; a very old man.
Yurummulló – a dull sultry day.
Yuyui—no water: a dry plain.
Yuyung—backwards.

2. Sentences.

[The spelling and the word-forms here should be received with caution. I have corrected some errors; but all our Australian Vocabularies need critical examination before they can be declared thoroughly reliable.—Ed.]

Gula dain yannabiye—he told him to come here.
Ngaddunu dilmangu wibaiye—I tell you to be quiet.
Widyunga main dain buogalgirri?—when do the men* come here?
Biambul main yannáan dirangu—all the men went to the hills.
Ngandunu nilla karrandarang ngunné?—who gave you the paper?
Baimbul main bunbangarrimanna diranda—all the natives are running about on the mountains the whole day.
Main ngolonggai-buoanna dirandi—now the natives are coming back from the mountains.
Indyangga yanna!—walk slowly! Barrai yanna—go quickly.
Minyandu (or minyang ngindu) yarra?—what do you say?
Yama ngindu (or yamandu) balludarra?—do you feel cold?
Yálu, wari—yes, it is so. Iradu ngalgarra—the sun shines.
Maindyu dain gaán—a native brought it.
Guin ngurandi wirrigirri—he will sleep at the camp.
Yamanu babbiá murou ginya?—is your father alive?
Ngindu durgunnanna nurranurrabul—you are always writing
Karia durriladda—do not spear one another
Karbaga bundinya yawanna—to commit adultery.
Wirai nurranurrabul, ngunbangunbadda—not always, sometimes.
Guin ngurongga mallang dunni—he was to spear him that night.
Ngolong burrabadde—he sunk the hatchet in his face.
Yamandu ngannal winnanggauna?—do you know me?
Wargundu ngannal dallaimarra?—why are you angry with me?
Yamandu ngannal ngannumminye?—have you seen me before?
Bainba ngaddu—I cannot reach it.
Birramalgu yannáan—gone to the bush.
Ngundunu nilla ngunné?—who gave you that?
Dagundu yannanna?—where are you going?
Ganggunnanna giwaldaindu—the cook fetches things.
Dagunnu ngurambang?—where is your country?
Daindu dain buogé?—where did you come from?
Guin kalianna madandi—he is climbing up the tree.
Guin dullugdurada dunné—he killed with the spear.
Guin bargundurada bindye—he killed with the hatchet.
Ngaddu wime gurindyurada maingulia—I made a man's likeness with charcoal.
Ngaddu winai-guabianna—I was sitting up all night.
Ngindu yallabul wibiagirri—you shall sit down always.
Ngaddu ngabinbilgirri—I will try.

---

* In these sentences, the word main means 'men,' 'natives,' 'blackfellows.'

THE WIRADHARI DIALECT.

Wiraidu malgirri—I shall not do it.
Kaliug ngindi baidyu—I want water.
Wirai-du girugal—I am not hungry. Girugal-du—I am hungry.
Karia bumalladda—do not fight.
Wiraidu winnanganna—don't know.
Ngannal girambannanna iradu—the sun makes me very warm.
Ngannal murrawal balludarra—I feel very cold.
Wiraidu giarra—I am not afraid.
Gialngingidyillidya—be ashamed of yourself.
Ngunna guindu, yaddandi guin yalmambi—I give it to him because he taught me.
Wirai durrambaranna—the bark will not strip.
Wiraidyi gaddal—I have no tobacco.
Karia warraba—do not make a noise.
Minyanduradundu bumé?—what did you kill him with?
Widyunggandu wannabaan Dubo?—when did you leave Dubbo?
Widyunggandu yannagirri Dubogu?—when will you go to Dubbo?
Widyungga inar dain yanáan?—when did the women come up?
Ngunbai wibian—a single man or woman.
Uda yarbidya (or uda warrambia)—listen.
Dullu yalla—speak right (true); kari yalla—speak the truth.
Karia yumbul yalla—do not tell me a lie.
Minyandu dalgunnanna?—what are you eating?
Wirai dinnu ngungirri, ngaddu yannagirri—if you do not give me meat, I shall go away.
Yamandu dallai ngingé marradal?—have you been angry with him a long time?
Mainguala karrámé inargung—other men took his wife away.
Nilia inar Badaraigu—this is Badarai's wife.
Nilla merringan—this is a saucy fellow; *lit.*, 'he (is) dog-like.'
Nilla dallaibulbul—this is a very angry fellow.
Wiraidu karidyi winnangganna—I do not believe what you say.
Gammarru bangamé maddan—the storm broke a tree down.
Indyanga yalla—speak slowly.
Karia mallu nginga—do not be so lazy.
Yamandu gurragammé gaddambingidyal—have you done washing?
Ngabba bundinyc dagunda, wirai idde—baby fell down, not hurt.
Yaudundu ballubunilgirri, nginya ballubuailgirri—if you kill, you must be killed.
Yàla nginge gawan—that is the way the white men do.
Nurra-nurra ngindu dalbianna—you are always eating.
Yurai wirridya; dambulbang nginne—go to sleep; it is very late.
Dulludi ngunga, yaludu gibainbilgirri—if you give me your spear, I will give you another.
Yannagi ngéanni Patriggu—let us go to Bathurst.
Dullubang ngaligin muron wigirri, yandundu ballungirri—our souls will live, when we are dead.

Yandulli ballungirri ngaunaiawalla, ngali wibiagirri dururdurur-buolin—when we die, we shall always live above.
Yandundu walluin ugingirri, Godda ngéanni yannbigirri yallabal wibigiagirri dururdururbuolin—if we are good, we shall go to God and always live with Him.
Ballungidyala, dullubang marong kalliagirri (wirgu) murrubirgu—in death, good souls will ascend to heaven.
Biambul main yannáan birramalgu; bula wiganna—all the men have gone to the bush; two are staying.
Wiraidyu nguranggu yannagirri dallan—I cannot go to the camp to-day.
Ngaddu barrangarrigirri nguronggalongal—I shall rise very early to-morrow.
Birradu nginya bunmangidyala—I am tired through work.
Giwanggu marrommanna—the moon shines brightly.
Gaddandi ballunne biambul—all my friends are dead.
Girarru kaling gánnagirri—the wind will bring rain.
Nilla gaddal ngindi murrawal ngindi—he is very fond of smoking.
Ngaddieu ngindi ladu—I want (or like) that one.
Ngaddi bariggia—let it belong to me.
Ngunbadda giwangga wigirri—I shall stay one moon.
Karia burai yummambia—do not make (or let) the child cry.
Yammada nganmunda!—go with me!
Ngali yannagé (bula)—we two go together.
Maingalang ngolonganne birramalle—all the men are returned from the bush.
Minyang ngindi wandu (or gandu)?—what do you want?
Dullubul yalla!—speak plainly (or distinctly)!
Yamandu ingelbang?—are you very poorly?
Báladu birrabang—I am very tired.
Yamandu gulbarra Wiradhari?—do you understand Wiradhari?
Gaddal-di ngunga—give me tobacco.
Guin urai winye—he was asleep.
Ngindu ngannal ngannumingáan—you have seen me before.
Wargundu burai bumé?—why did you beat the child?
Yamagu urai winaigunne widyunga ngindu ngin bumé?—was he asleep when you beat him?
Biang main buogé—many natives have come.
Ngandunu nginyal bunmé?—who has made you?
Ngindu windya bundigirri—you will fall into the fire?
Ngaddu buogalgirri ngangigu nginyal—I will come to see you.
Wargu guin burai ngaddi bumé?—why did he beat my boy?
Guin barramé inar ngaddi birong—he took my wife far off.
Ngindu yé ngannal buma main—you told me to strike the native.
Ngágadi (or nga) ngannal!—look at me!
Nilla buyu bangadinye—he has broken his leg.
Dallanbul ire úrongirri—the sun will soon set.

Yalladi minyamminyambul—tell me all about it.
Murrawal murruberai buogalgirri—a great storm is coming on.
Minyandu dalguabien?—what did you eat yesterday?
Minyangan main ingel?—how many natives are ill?
Ngunba-ngunbai main ballunna—very few natives are dying.
Yamandu winnaugganna dagundu ballungidyala (*or* yandundu ballungiri) dullubaug yannagiri?—do you know where your souls are going to when you die?
Murrawaldu giring—I am perspiring very much.
Ngandi nginmundi kindain?—who laughed at you?
Minyandu wirai buddang buoge?—why did you not come sooner?
Buddunbulandu wirai buogé?—why did you not come sooner?
Minyang dalgarriawagirri?—what will you eat to-morrow?
Wiraigual main ngigagarrigirri—there will soon be no more blacks
Maingalang bumallanné murrawal (*or* maingalang murranil-lanné)—the natives have had a great fight.
Ngaggualla durrur bummalbianna—that one is always fighting.
Ngunguda nilla burauu ngaddunu; minyamminyambul ngumbiagirri—give me that child and I will give you plenty to eat.
Minyangguandu yannauné?—what have you come for?
Wirai buguin warranna gunnigalli—no grass on the plain.
Ngarrangga buguin buogunagirri yundu kaling bangaduoligirri—after rain the grass will grow.
Yuronggelang buddang—the clouds are dark.
Wirai babbinnu yungingindi—your father wants you not to cry.
Gunninu bamir babbianu bungul—mother is taller than father.
Dullu warradda—stand upright.
Kaling indyunga yunnanna—the rain is coming very slowly.
Yurai wiridya wannumaragirri—go to bed when you are done.
Dallanbuldu ngolonggagirri?—will you return soon?
Ngurombang mawambul ngéanni ngangillagirri—we shall meet together this evening.
Minyandu bummalgirri dallan?—what will you do to-day?
Ngindyalla karra buongarra!—there is water!
Ngaddu winnanguana udagual—I have changed my mind; *lit.*, I think with another ear.
Widyunggandu nyingunanna?—what are you doing?
Ngandiga ngiu?—who is dead?
Minyangandu ngamme buraigelag?—how many boys did you see?
Yama nilla marrung?—is that good?
Wiraibudu ingiang ngindi la—I do not like that at all.
Ngindu nilla?—are you there?
Ngunbadul ngagguaiwala marrammarra—only he who is above can make everything.
Widyundu yuin ngolong?—what is your name?
Baiamai yallabul wiawaigun naggirri—Baiamai lives for ever.

h

Ngindu ngaddi ngamor, ngaddunu babbin—you are my daughter and I your father.
Nilla ware magannu billaga—he was drowned in the river.
Ngaddu birrammalli wangarrarre—I lost myself in the bush.
Ngaddi uran bumbir—my hair is greasy.
Bulabulgundubula yannagirri?—are you two going together?
Yama ngali bulabul yannagirri birammalgu—shall we two go together to the bush?
Yama ngannaia bula yannagirri Ngannimagu?—are these two going together to Ngannima?
Gunyo gandu ngagunain?—did you watch him a long time?
Widyunggarranyal ngolong durinye dinnundi?—how did you hurt your foot?
Kalinggu nginya yamma girrar murrawal barranna?—do you think this high wind will bring rain?
Karia dinnang yuddia—do not touch my foot.
Gibbannilgirri gualdu—I will repay you (revenge myself).
Walgunwalgun yannanna—to go to and fro and crossways.
Dinnandinyal durrinye—my foot was hurt.
Wirai walluin nginye yandungia murron nginye—he has been a bad fellow all his lifetime.
Yamaddu yandul gaddambilli?—shall I wash it now?
Widyunga nginalla nginye?—what is the matter with him?
Wirai gannanda ballu—death is not near.
Wiraidu nidge ngindilu bungalli ngindi—I do not like this place.
Minnang ngindi gannung wanden?—what else do you want?
Ngaddu dugguwe nginyal—I'll catch you.
Dibbanggu durriguain dinnandi—a nail has gone into my foot.
Widyundu ngoling yé?—which way (*i.e.*, what) say you?
Warguinyal gunedyunu bume?—why did your mother beat you?
Ngaddubullinyal yalgirri kariabul malle—do it not till I bid you.
Ngaddunyal ngunne burramballi burrubingidyal—I saw you jumping over the rope.
Wiraidyu karidyi winnangabilligirri—I don't credit what you say.
Waluin warrambilalidyn—put things in order (right) again.
Ngannal karinga yandundu ngingirri gindi—send me, if you like.
Wiraibu ngéanni bumarra—we never fight.
Willaidul baiware nginna nginye—that was curious.
Yaladu nginnal gunnambai—I depend on (expect from) you.
Barri ngingulia ngiya—I will not have that.
Wingarri maggidyu—I was sitting down all day.
Buramburambang dagun nginga yundul—there is a drought now.
Budyabudya barrambillana wirra—moths are flying in the air.
Goddu dulubang marong gangirri murrubirra—God will take good souls to heaven.
Yambulnal guin buoye—he told me a lie.
Guin birrhaga dilbán—he came slyly from behind.

THE WIRADHARI DIALECT.

Warga baggagu ngin bumé?—why did he beat him?
Ngidyi (ngaddi) ngullumuggu—here (there) is an end.
Wargu bagandu wiggi karrame?—why did you steal the bread?
Gangadain ngindu—fetch it yourself.
Ngaddu nginnal bumalgirri, ngannalgual ngindu wargu bumé—
    I shall beat you because you did beat me.
Ngindu ballamaddáng wibillinya—you are obstinate to go.
Ngali yannagirri—we two will go together.
Ngaddu ballaga irradu ngingirri ngolonggai ngarrigirri bialdu—
    I shall return after two days.
Ngundi ngallana dain yannanna?—who is coming there?
Ngaddu ngannal bumallé?—who will dare to beat me?
Wiraiayu maindyi giarra—I am afraid of nobody.
Wirai gilandu ngannal bumalawagirri—you can not beat me.
Ngindu dallaimaldain—you are a troublesome fellow.
Windurai maddan gunga—bring me a firestick.
Widyungala gannaldu gayaligirri?—when shall I see you again?
Minyalla vaddu dalli? girugaldu—what can I eat? I am hungry
Karia ngal warnganda—do not disturb me.
Ngaddu nginnunda yammagi?—shall I go with you?
Karia gurondu yalla—do not speak long.
Karia wirain ganga—do not carry it aslope.
Ngaddu yanáan birong dallan—I have gone a long way to-day.
Windyu marradi gunnanne—the fire burnt my hand.
Kalindyu darrube ngulluman—the water did make a hole.
Wargundu wirai yurai wininya?—why do you not sleep?
Yamandu winnanganna daga nilla?—do you know where he is?
Yamandu winnanganna dagu main yanáan?—do you know where
    the natives are gone?
Wargundu wirai yannabillinga yandundunyu ye?—why don't
    you come when I tell you?
Karia ngunga wangagirri guin—do not give it him, he will lose it.
Ngaddu mallang diranggu yumманne, yandu mallandu wirai ingel
    nginye—I should go to the mountains, if I were not ill.
Karidyidin maindyu winnangabilligi—you will not make me
    believe that.
Ngabba darrar banganna—the baby is sobbing.
Nilla yannangalang billána—there are two walking along.
Ngannagula yannanna bulagualia dain ngolong—there are three
    coming yonder this way.
Yalu gilla—yes, it is so. Ngameingilla—I believe so.
Karia nilla yala yanna, ballanggun ngindu bundigirri—do not go
    that way, lest you fall down headlong.
Gai! barranmallawan—ah! you have torn it.
Ngaddu bai wirai yala mé—I wish I had not done it.
Karia buma; guyungan ballunna—don't kill it; it will die of itself.
Murrawal iradu dunna—the heat of the sun is very powerful.

Ngannal gumbil, bundarra—I am crooked, frozen.
Ngannaguor maggalla ngin diranda—he is behind the hills.
Ngaddu wannanni udagu—I have forgiven it; *lit.*, I have thrown it away with the ear.
Wiraidu winnangayalinya—I forgive it; *lit.*, I think not of it again.
Yamandu mabbiggirri yanagirri wandu?—will you stay or go?
Yamandu dullubandurai?—have you got a soul?
Ngaddan gadda main warraigunnein—I thought a native was standing there.
Yamandu bambidurai?—can you swim?
Wirai ngaddu indyama ye—I did not speak slowly.
Guayo Baiamai yalmambigirri maingu—by-and-by I shall teach the natives about Baiamai.
Guayodu wirai wanmambu yalgirri—by-and-by I shall no more speak incorrectly.
Karia indyama yalla—do not speak so slowly.
Widyunga main ngolongaigarrigirri?—when will the men return?
Ngaddu winnange main ulla—I knew him by his voice.
Dumbog dandan ngunbai-ngunbai warrana—the sheep are scattered all over.
Buradu dumbog mawang burruarra—the boy collects the sheep.
Gaddanngeilinya ngaddu nginundi—I delight in thee.
Kari ngaddu yalguain—I have spoken truth.
Ngaddu gubbaimadain ngingi ngindi—I want to be a comrade.
Barigngia wiggo wirai ngindidyu—I do not care about bread.
Ngaddangadandu ngiunalla gubbalgirri—I thought he would run after her.
Bamirgal iradu duggin, bungarra urrangidyala—the shadow gets long, when the sun sets.
Iradu gannanna, ngannalla dugguda warranna—(when) the sun burns, he stands in the shade.
Ngurang ngannawalla bimbanna; baddang ngannanal guanagirri inaru wambilngarria; wirai yama gannaan, yannáan; birong yuma yannangarria, wiraiya baddunbuogalgirri; win bungia ballabunia, baddang guannagirri narbangbu—the camp over there is on fire; also those cloaks which the women have left will burn. I do not think they took them when they went. I suppose they have gone far, and I daresay will not come back soon. Take branches and extinguish the fire, (for) the cloaks and bags will burn.
Karia win munnilbang wambia, duralu burana ballubunilgirri—do not put hollow fuel on, else the smoke will kill the child.
Mandura wirigieya—let it alone, *or* do not meddle with it.
Mandura windimaiya—let him at rest, *or* do not disturb him.
Dagurandu ngolong yannaigunnain ngingunnane?—where have you been
Minyalligandu gullaminye?—what has delayed you?

Dagarnu baddang ngadunu ngungurain?—where is the cloak I gave you?
Ngaddu gulbarra widyungolong—I know how, *i.e.*, how to do it.
Ngindu bunmang ngadualligunnanna—you look all about.
Wiraingaddu walluin gaddambirra yain ngindu—I cannot wash as well as you.
Ngaddu yannáan gulgunggu kaling ngagigu, wirai kaling wirrinya—I went to the well to see(k) water, but found none.
Bullockdu burrué kaling mannamannambil—the bullocks have made the water dirty.
Warrangillaġgabianna—stand looking at.
Dagandu din mé ngannadunu ngunne? dé wandu yama? ngunne wandu?—what have you done with the meat (which) I gave you? did you eat it? (or) did you give it away?
Ngannalla yambul yalgunnannu gula udagu—the fellow speaks deceitfully to obtain information, *or* plays the spy.
Dinbinya udagu ngannalla—the fellow spies out information; *lit.*, listens to the ear.
Wirai bamir iré ngingarimāna, badanbul urruyawanna—the sun does not shine long, (but) goes down soon.
Minyangundu yuggu yannáan?—what you come here for?
Gāne bagandu wirai ngubannu?—why not bring your wife?
Maingalang birramalla gurrun gulaminya—the natives delay long in the bush.
Goddu ngéannigin ngangarri māna; yalabul ngabianna dagun ngarrangarang, main; ngarrangarra yandulbu ngaru, ngurungga yandubule wirinya—God sees us all the day long; He always is beholding the earth everywhere, (as well as all) the people; even now He sees us, (whilst) we are lying down in the night.
Ngagguaiwalaman dagunbu maruanne, diranbu, buguinbu dagundi buogarra, irébu, giwambu, gira lumbu wirai warrangá; maddanbu, kalimbu, wallanbu, karraibu; wimbu guyabu billaga warranna. Wirai ngéanni ngénga minyambul dé, wirai ngannaiwalla wingidyal. Mandambial ngéannigin Goddu minyam-minyambul ngunne. Yain ngéanni dalgunnagi murron widyai gunnagi—He who is above has made the earth and the mountains, the grass also, which springs from the ground, and sun, and moon, and stars, which are fixed in the heavens; and trees, and water, and stones and sand; and the fire, and the fish which are in the river. We should not have anything to eat, were it not for Him who dwells above. We are indeed thankful that God has given us everything. Thus we can eat and may live.
Gulbarragualdu yalu—I understand that full well.
Karia wannammindya ngannanduyan—do not break a promise.
Ngaddugual wirai giarradu—neither am I afraid.

Nguigargirra buyu maingu mammaibamalguain—the doctor has
   set a man's leg.
Duggualli baddabaddan ngannalla bunbannāna—he runs after to
   overtake him soon.
Guyungundu udaga—that's my own device.
Millang guarra—to walk closely by one's side so as to push him.
Bunnan burruarra—the dust flies.
Dagua ngannalla wigge gila dunnu nginne? Dédyu—where is
   the bread I gave you? I have eaten it.
Ngéanni billagal yannanna—we are going down the valley.
Ngali duyulli kaliaimarranna—we two are ascending the hill.
Burai gié durulgangidyillin—the boy was frightened and hid
   himself.
Wirai marong ngaminya—it does not look well.
Minyangu ngindu barramalmambic inarnu?—why did you allow
   your wife to be taken away?
Yama ugil burruarra gubundidyu?—does that cap make you warm?
Guddibaidyu duggumi—I like that song.
Urgaya nginyundal—keep it to yourself.
Ngaddu yurai murrabinyc—I was fast asleep.
Yandulabulgual nilla urronne, yandugual ngaddu windinye—he
   came in whilst I was there.
Windinye mallang ngaddu nginga wirai mallang nginya nilla
   bumé—had I been there, he would not have been beaten.
Ngaddu winnangán ngaddanga kalindyu yubalgirri—I thought
   it would rain.
Ngaddangandu ngaddila kalin dugan; ngaddi gunnung garragal
   —I thought you did (fetch) draw water there; from that
   other place over there.
Goddu ngunbadu dalangir gin bunmalgicri—God alone can make
   the heart new.
Wirai gamanna dagun kalindyu—the rain has not gone through.
Ngainbuldu warrambi guggidya kalindurai—I have filled the
   vessel with water.
Kalin karringa guggidyi—empty the vessel of the water.
Minyangganna meridyu gulgannaiguabianna ngiuga?—what is
   the dog barking about all the night?
Wargundu giarra nilla deribandyi dallaimangidyalli?—what you
   care about the old man scolding you?
Minyangundu nguyamanna?—what you ask for?
Widyuggarra golog main gingirri?—what are men about to do?
Yandunu dullubang irimbaggingirri ngindu wari babbindyanu
   yannagirri, yandundu ballungirri—if your soul is holy, you
   will go to your Father when you die.
Guyungandi yawarradu—I mind my own business.
Darawirgal ngéannigin winnanganna—D. knows us (see *s. v.*
   Wirgal).

THE WIRADHARI DIALECT. 119

3. THE CREED.

Ngaddu winnangabillinya Godda Babbindya, Yarruwalla, Marromaldain murrubirgu dagungubu :
Urrumandalabu ngunbai Jethu Chrit Dirangalbanga ngiannigin, Burambinye Gundyarri Irimbang, Durrie Maridyu darngidyalmubandi, Gibbainbinye Pontidyi Pilatdi, Maddandi wirradi, Ballunne dabbugé, Birrawanne helgu, Bullaga ngoronga dabbugain murron, Barraialinye balludi Kalianne murrubirgu, Wibiannabu bummalgala Goddugu Babbingu ; Yarruwallagu agaddigallila buogalaligirri ngabbinbilligu murron ballabu.
Winnangabillinyabu ngaddu Gundyarra Irimbang; Irimbangabu'Kattolika Churcha ; Ngunbadala mawanga Irimbangu ; Uddagu wannangidyala naugunmalngidyalgu, Barraialingidyala marrindyi, Murrona yallabul. Amen.

4. THE TEN COMMANDMENTS.

1. Ngaddu bala Dirangalbang God nginnu ngunbai; Ngannunda nginda nginya wirai gualmán God nginda.
2. Karia nginnunda maingulia bumma, wirai ingianna minyambul ngannaiwal murrubirra, wirai ingianna dagunda birrabangga, wirai ingianna ngannadaruguora kalindya. Karia ngualla bunganga warradda, wirai buoyamadda : Ngaddubial Diranggalbang Godnu bala munnirgadain God, ngaddubu gibainbilgirri naugumalngidyal babbindyila, buraigelang thirdgu fourthgubu generationgu yandungannalla dallaimalgirri ngannal, ngaddu binnalbang ngingirri thousandgu yandu ngannalla murungamilbilgirri ngannal, ngaddibu ngiang malbillirgirri.
3. Karia nannai yalla yuinga Godgu wiraibial Dirangalbanggu : bangayalgirri ngannalla nannai yarra yuingulagu.
4. Winnangaddu Sabbatha irimbang widya. Bullaga-bullagabullaga irada minyambul malla, bummallabu minyaminyambul nginnunda bala bummalligu ; seventhabial irada bala Sabbath Dirangalbangu Godgunginnu. Gaddialla wirai minyambulbial bunmalla, wirai ngindu, wirai urrumannu, wirai ngamornu, wirai servantgalang nginnu gibbir inarbu, wirai cattle nginnu, wirai maingualbang ngannalla nginmudurai winya. Sixdabial irada Dirangalbangu murrubir, dagunbu, murriangbu, minyaminyambulbu nginalla nginya bunmae, guabinyebial seventha irada. Nilla irada seventh bangan Diraugalbangu walluin yae, bunmaibu irimbang.
5. Indyamalla babbingunu gunnigunubu ; yala ngindu guayo wiawaigunnagirri ngurambangga, ngannalla Goddu ngungirri.
6. Karia ballubunia.   7. Karia garbaga bundidya.
8. Karia karrama.   9. Karia maindya dumbalma yambul.
10. Karia gurai nginga milmagu maingualbiranga, karia gurai nginga inargu maingualbiranga, wiraibu gibbir servant, inar servantbu, wiraibu ox, wiraibu ass, wiraibu ngaguari ngannallagung.

5. THE LORD'S PRAYER.

Ngiannigin Babbin, ngindu murrubirra ginya (*or* murrubirra nginya). Yuinnu walluin yalla barri. Ngurambanganu barri buogalla. Gurai nginnu (*or* guranu) ngia barri nginni yain dagunda, ingian wari murrubirra. Nginni irada yallabul wiggo nginnigingunna ngungunadda. Karia ngiannigin naugumalngidal winnanga yalidya, ingian ngianni wirai wari winnangayalinya ngaggnallabu nangumarra ngiannigingunna. Karia ngiannigingunna gagamambia; Gurwabiallu ngiannigingunna maromubandi; Nginnu bala ngurambang, wallanbamba; ngalgarambu, durrurdurrurbuolin. Amen.

(E.)
PRAYERS
IN THE
AWABAKAL DIALECT.

[I have left the spelling just as I found it in the manuscript. The reader, however, will recognise the syntax of the words by comparing them with those in the Gospel. The title in the manuscript runs thus:— "A selection of prayers for the morning, from the service of the Church of England, intended for the introduction of public worship amongst the aborigines of Australia; by the Venerable W. G. Broughton, A.M., Archdeacon of New South Wales and its dependencies. Translated into the Northumberland dialect by L. E. Threlkeld; 1835."—ED.]

Wiyella Ta Yirriyirri Ta Ngorokan Ka Ko.

WEYENNUN ngeen ba, keawai yarakai korien geen ba, nakoiyan ngaiya ngeen bo; wonto ba ngeen wiyennun ba yarakai ta ngearun ba, Murrorong ko tuloa ko Eloi-to warikulliko yarakai umulli ta ngearun ba, ngatun murrorong kakilli ko ngearun yarakai umulli ta birung.

A! Eloi kaiyukan, Biyung-bai ngearun ba Piriwul koba, Jesu koba Krist koba, ngintoa ta umulli kan yantin koba, ngintoa ta wiyelli kan to Piriwullo yantin kore koba ko; wiyan ngeen ngatun minki lan kuttan ngeen ngearun ba kowwul lin yarakai tin, ngatun yarakai umulli tin ngeen yantin ta birung purreung ka birung, kauwullan yarakai umalala kotulli kannei to, ngatun wiyelli kan nei to, ngatun umulli kan nei to ngearun ba ko; ngiroung Pirriwul yirriyirri kan kin bukka pai ya bien kowwul ngeen kakilli ko ngiroung kauwa yuna bota kakilli ko minki ngeen katan kauwul ngali tin yarakai umulli tin ngearun ba tin, ngatun yarakai ta kotalli ko ngearun ba ko umulli ta yarakai Kamunbilla ngearun, Kamunbilla ngearun, ngintoa Biyungbai to murrorong tai ko, Yinal lin ngiroumba tin ngearun ba tin Pirriwullin Jesu tin Krist tin, warikulla yantin tara umatoara yura ki kal, ngatun kamunbilla yaraki ta birung ngurrauwil koa ngeen niroung, ngatun pital umauwil koa ngiroung yanti ko tia, Morron ta bungai kulla kauwil koa ngiroumba yitirra murrorong wiyelli ko, ngatun killabinbin kakilli ko ngali tin Jesu kin, Krist tin Pirriwullin ngearun ba kin. Amen.

A! Pirriwul Biyungbai ngearun ba, Moroko ka ba, Eloi kaiyu kan ta yanti ka tai, Ngintoa ta ngearun miroma ngorokan ta unti ta purreung. Ngolomulla bi ngearun unti purriung ka ngiroemba ko kaiyu kan ta ko kowwul lan ta ko, ngatun kamunbilla, yanoa wal umai yi kora yarakai ngeen, murra yikora yarakai kolang. Wonto ba kauwil koa ngearun ba yantin umulli ta kakilli ko ngiroumba wiyelli ta birung murrorong umulli ko mikan ta giroung kin ngali tin Jesu kin Krist kin, Piriwul lin ngearun ba kin. Amen.

Biyung-bai ngearun ba wokko ka ba moroko ka ba kuttan, kummunbilla ngiroung yitirra yirri-yirri kakilli ko. Paipibunbilla ngiroumba Pirriwul koba. Ngurrurbunbilla ngiroumba wiyelli kannei yanti moroko ka ba ngatun yanti purrai ta ba. Nguwa ngearun purreung ka yanti katai takilli ko, Ngatun warekulla ngearun ba yarakai umatoara; yanti ta ngeen warika yantin to wiyapaiyeen ngearun ba; ngatun yuti yikora ngearun yarakai umulli kan kolang; miromulla ngearun yarakai ta birung kulla ta ngiroumba Pirriwul kannei, ngatun kaiyu kan, ngatun killibinbin yanti katai. Amen.

A! Pirriwul potokullea bi willing ngearun ba wiyelli ko ngatun wiyennun wal kurraka ko ngearun ba ko murrorong ngiroumba.

Kauwa killabinbin kakilli ko gikoung Biyungbai ko, ngatun ngikoung yinal ko, ngatun ngikoung Marai yirri-yirri kan ko.

Yanti kakulla ta kurri-kurri ka, yanti katan yakita, ngatun kunnun wal yanti ka tai kakilli ko, yanti katai purrai wirran korien. Amen.

Eloi kaiyu kan Biyungbai yantin ko ba murrorong ko ba, Wirrobullikan ngeen ngiroumba, murrorong korien ta, wiyan ngeen murrorong tuloa ngiroung yantin tin murrorong ngiroumba kin, ngatun murrorong pittul umulli tin ngearun ngatun barun yantin ko kore ko. Wiyan murrorong ngiroung ngeen ngali tin umatoarin ngearun ba tin, ngali tin ngolomatoarin ngearun ba tin, ngatun yantin tin murrorong umulli tin, ngali koba tin unti morron tin, ngatun wiyan murrorong kowwul lan ngeen ngiroung ngali tin, pittul tin ngiroumba tin ko kowwul tin ngali tin Burungbungngulli tin yantin kore tin ngikoung kin pirriwullin ngearun ba kin Jesu kin Krist tin; ngatun ngali tin kaiyu kan tin, pittul kakilli koba tin, ngatun ngali tin kotelli tin killibinbin kakilli koba tin. Ngatun wiyellan ngeen bin kotelli ko ngearun kotauwil koa ngeen tuloa yantin ta murrorong umulli tin ngiroumba tin

ngatun kauwil koa búlbúl ngearun ba murrorong wiyelliko;
ngatun túngunbiuwil koa ngeen ngiroúmba murrorong wiyelli ta,
yanoa wal willing kabirung ngearun ba ka ta birung ngatun tantoa bota wal, wonto ba morron ngearunba kin birung; ngukilinnun ngeen ngearun ngiroung kakilli ko ngiroumba ko; ngatun
kakillinnun mikan ta ngiroung kin yirri-yirri ka, ngatun murrorong ka yantin ta purreung ka ngearun ba ngali tin Jesu tin
Krist tin, Pirriwullin ngearun ba tin; kauwa ngikoung kakilli ko
ngatun ngiroung, ngatun Marai ta ko yirriyirri kan ta ko kakilli ko yantin murrorong wiyelli ko, ngatun killibinbin kakilli ko
yanti ka tai purrai wirran korien. Amen.

Eloi Kaiyu kan to ke, ngintoa ngearun ngukulla kaiyukan kakilli ko yaki ta ko wakol bota wal upulli ko wiyelli kanne ngearun
ba ngiroung, ngatun bi wiya buloara nga ngoro kautilinnun ba
yitirrin ngiroung ka ta ngunun ngaiya wal bi barun unnoa tara
bara wiyennun; kauwa yanti yakita Pirriwullo kotatilli kanne
ngatun wiyelli kanne ngiroúmba wirrobulli kan ko ba, yanti murrorong kauwil barun kin ko; ngukilli ta ngearun kin ko unti ta
purrai ta, ngurrulli ko ngiroumba wiyelli kanne tuloa ko, ngatun
unta ta tarai ta purrai ta morron kakilli ko yanti ka tai. Amen.

Kauwa ngearun kin ko murrorong umullita Pirriwul koba
ngearun ba Jesu koba Krist koba, ngatun pittul mulli ta Eloi
koba, ngatun kakilli ta Marai koba yirri-yirri kan koba kakilli ko
ngearun katoa yantin toa ko. Amen.

Wiya ta Yirri-Yirri Ta Yarea Kako.

Eloi-to noa pitul ma kowwul kore ngukulla ta noa wakol bo
ta yinal ngikoemba ngali ko yantien to ba ngurran ngikoung kin,
keawai wal bara tatti kunnun kulla wal yanti morron katai barunba kako binnun.

Murrorong ta bara minki kan marai kan kulla barun ba, katan
pirriwal koba moroko ko ba.

Murrorong ta bara kapirri kan ngatun tambun kan murrorong
ko; kulla bara wara punnun.

Murrorong ta bara murrorong kan búlbúl kan; kulla bara
nanun wal bon Eloi nung.

Murrong ta bara pitul umullikan; kulla barun wiyennun, wonnai tara Eloi koba.

Murrorong ta bara warikan yarakai umatoara barun ba, ngatun
wutea kan yarakai umatoara barun ba.

Murrorong ta kore wiya-yemma korien bon noa ba ba Pirriwul
lo yarakai umatoara.

Wiyan bang ngiroung yarakai umatoara emmeomba, ngatun keawai wal bang yuro pa korien emmoemba yarakai. Wiya bang
niakai wiyennun bang yarakai umatoara emmoemba Pirriwolla;
ngatun bi warika yarakai umalli ta birung emmoumba.

Eloi, gintoa kaiyukan, &c., &c.

A! Eloi, ngala koba yanti ka tai murrorong umulli kan nei ngatun warekulli kan nei, ngurrulla bi wiyelli kan nei karra kannei ngearun ba, ngatun ngeen ba ngiratoara katan tipung ko yarakai umatoara koba, ngearun ba; kummunbilla minki ko kowwollo ngiroumba ko burungbungulla ngaiya ngearun, ngali tin murrorong tin Jesu koba tin Krist tin, ngearun ba wokkol bo ta Kamulli kan ngatun Wiyellikan. Amen.

A! Eloi kaiyu kan ngatun murrorong umullikan wiyalan ngeen ngiroung ngali tin ngiroemba tin murrorong kowwol lin miromulli ko ngearun, yantin ta birung yarakai umulli ta birung ngearun; kingngereen kowwil koa ngeen buloara bo kurrabung ngatun marai, pitul kowwil koa umulli kolang ngeen unnoa tara yantin wiyatoara ngiroemba umulli ko ngali tin Jesu tin Krist tin ngearunba Pirriwul lin. Amen.

A! Mirromulli kan to kore ko ba, wirea ngearun tulling kabilli ko ngatun ngiroung ko yirriyirri ko ngiroemba ko; a! Pirriwul, pirriral man bien ngeen kara man mirromulli ko ngearun ngatun umulli ko ngearun.

Kauwa killibienbien kakilli ko, &c., &c,

Biyungbai ngearúnba wokka kaba, moroko kaba katan, &c., &c.

Eloi kaiyukan Biyungbai yantin koba murrorong koba, &c., &c.

Kauwa Pitul ko Eloi koba, kowwol ke ngurra korien, mirromulla ngearun ba búlbúl ngatun marai ngurrulli ta ngatun pitulmulli ta Eloi koba, ngatun yinal ko ba ngikoemba Jesu koba Krist koba ngearun ba Pirriwol koba; ngatun kowwa murrorong umulli kannei Eloi koba, Kaiyu kan koba, Biyungbai koba, Yinal koba, ngatun Marai koba yirri-yirri kan koba, kakilli ko ngearun kin ngatun munkilliko ngearun kin yanti katai. Amen.

Responses after the Commandments, if intended.

Pirriwol, Kamunbila ngearun ngatun, kakilia búlbúl ngearun ba ugurrur ko unni ta wiyalli kan nei.

At the last one.

Pirriwol, Kamunbila ngearun, ngatun upala yantin unnitara wiyalikan nei ngiroumba búlbúl la ngearun ba, wiyan ngeen ngiroung.

Eloi, Kaiyu kan to ke, Ngintoa natan yantin búlbúl, ngintoa ngurran yantin kotali kan nei keawai bo yuropa ngiroung kin birung. Kakilia be ngearun ba kotali kanne búlbúl (koba); murrorong kakili ko; pitul maowwil koa ngeen ngiroug tuloa, ngatun wiyaowwil murrorong koa ngeen ngiroemba yitirra yirri yirri kan, ngali tin Jesu kin, Krist tin, Pirriwol lin ngearun ba. Amen.

Wiya noa Eloi to unni tara wiyali kannei ngatun wiyaliala Ngatoa ta Pirriwol katan ngiroung ba Eloi, yutea banung purrai ta birung Egypt ta birung, kokira birung umali ta birung.

1. Yanoa wal bi tarai Eloi kaki yikora ngiroemba kakilli ko mikan ta emmoung kin.

2. Yanoa wal uma yikora bi ngiroung tarai umatoara, nga tarai kiloa ta yantin kiloa wokko ka ba ba moroko ka ba, nga yantin kiloa purrai toa barra koa, nga yantin kiloa kokoin toa barra koa purrai toa:

Yanoa wal bi upalinnun barran warrong bung ko barun kin, nga yanoa ngurra yikora barun: kulla wal bang Pirriwol ta Eloi ngiroung ba purrei kan ta katan, koyul mankilan yarakai umatoara barun ba biyungbai ta koba, barun wonnai ta willung-ngéil ngoro ta, ngatun warran ta barun ba bukka kan tia katan; ngatun murrorong umaullan barun kowwol kowwol, la pitul kan tia katan, ngatún ngurran wiyali kan nei emmoemba.

3. Yanoa bi wiya yikora wonkullo yitarra pirriwoi ko ba Eloi ngiroemba ko ba; kulla noa Pirriwollo keawai noa kotunnun bon yarakai korean wiyali kan wunkullo yitirra ngikoemba.

4. Kota la purreung ta Sabbat ta yirriyirri kakilli ko. Six ka purreung ka umunnun wal bi, ngatun umunnun yantin umatoara ngiroemba: wonto ba seven ta purreung ka Sabbat katan ta Pirriwol ko ba ngiroemba koba Eloi koba, unti ta purreung ka yanoa uma yikora tarai umali kanne; ngintoa, nga wonnai to ngiroumba, nga yinalkun to ngiroemba ko, koreko umalikan to ngiroemba ko, nga napal lo umalikan to ngiroemba ko, nga butti-kang ko ngiroemba ko, nga ngowi to ngiroumba ko ngiroung kin ba purrai ta ba; kulla six ta purreung ka noa Pirriwollo uma moroko, ngatun parrai, ngatun wombul, ngatun yantin katan yantun ta ba, ngatun korea purreung ka seven ta; yaki tin Pirriwol pitulma purreung Sabbat ta, ngatun uma yirriyirri kakili ko.

5. Ngurrulla biyungbai ngiroemba ngatun tunkan ngiroemba, kowwil koa purreung ngiroemba kowwol kowwol kakilli ko purrai ta ngatun noa Pirriwol lo ngikoemba ka Eloi to ngiroung.

6. Yanoa wal be bunki yikora.

7. Ya noa wal be manki yikora nukung tarai koba.

8. Ya noa wal be manki yikora tarai koba.

9. Ya noa wal be wiyayamma yikora ngakoiya yikora ngiro-emba koti ta ka.

10. Yanoa wal be willai kora kokira koti ta koba ngiroemba koba, yanoa wal be willai yikora nukung koti ta koba ngiroemba, koba, ngatun keawai kore mankilli kan ngikoemba, ngatun keawai napal mankilli kan ngikoemba, ngatun keawai buttikang, ngatun keawai tarai kan yantin ngiroemba ko ba koti ta ko ba.

Alla, Eloi Biyungbai moroko kaba, ngurraramulla bi tia, mirrul bang kuttan, yarakai bang kuttan.

Alla, Jesu, Yinal Eloi koba, ngupaiyi ko yantin kore koba kummara ngiroumba ko, ngurrara mulla bi tia mirrul bang kut-tan, yarakai bang kuttan.

Alla, Marai yirriyirri kan, ngurrara mulla bi tia, mirrul bang kuttan, yarakai bang kuttan.

Jesu, Pirriwul, kotá yikora bi unni ta yarakai umulli ta emmoumba, turokon bi yikora bi tia ngali tin yarakai umulli tin emmoumba tin, wommunbilla bi tia waita wokka kolang moroko kolang tetti kunnun bang ba; yanoa bukka ban kora bi tia, ngurrara-mulla bi tia, kulla bang kinta lang kauwul yakita; Jesu mara bi marai emmoumba.

A! Jesu, Pirriwul ta moroko koba, yantin purrai koba, yantin kore koba, kamulla bi tia, warikulla bi yarakai umulli ta emmobmba, yanoa wal yuti yikora bi tia koiyung kolang baran kolang tetti bunnun ngaiya bang ba, yutilla bi tia murron kolang ngiroung kai kolang moroko ka wokka ka yanti ka tai. Amen kauwa.

A! Jesu, Pirriwul emmoumba nauwa bi tia, kulla bang kinta lang kauwal kata yakita, ngali tin tetti tin, wommunbilla bi tia waita koa bang wauwil moroko kolang ngiroung kai kolang wokka kolang, Jesu wokka ka ba mara bi tia marai emmoumba tetti bunnun ngaiya bang ba. Amen; kauwa.

A! Jesu, Puntimai ta bi, moroko kabirung wokka ko birung, ngurrulla bi tia wiyelli ta emmoumba, yakita kauwul lang bang yarakai uma; yanoa bukka ban kora bi tia, yanoa niuwarra yikora bi tia, warikulla bi yarakai kauwal kauwal umulli ta emmoumba, umulla bi tia murrorong kakilli ko pittul kauwil koa bi emmoung yellawauwil koa bang ngiroug kai wokka ka moroko ka yanti ka tai tetti kunnun bang ba. Amen.

Kamunbilla ngearun, kamunbilla ngearun, ngintoa Biyung bai to murrorong tai ko, yinal-lin ngiroumba tin ngearun ba tin Pirri wullin Jesu kin Krist tin, warikulla yantin tara umulli ta yarakai yuraki kal, ngatun kamunbilla yarakai ta birung, ngurrauwil koa ngeen ngiroung, ngatun pitul umauwil koa ngiroung yanti ka tai; mórón ta bunyai kal kulla kauwil koa ngiroumba yitirra murrorong wiyelli ko ngatun killibinbin kakilli ko, ngali Jesu kin Pirriwul lin. Amen.

THE LORD'S PRAYER.

Biyungbai ngearun ba wokka kaba moroko kaba, kuttan kummunbilla ngiroumba yitirra yirriyirri kakulli ko; paipibunbilla ngiroumba Pirriwul koba; ngurrur bunbilla ngiroumba wiyelli ta, yanti moroko kaba ngatun yanti purrai ta ba; nguwa ngearun purreung ka yanti katai takilliko ngatun warikulla ngearun ba yarakai umulli ta; yanti ta ngeen warika yantin to wiyapaiyeen ngearun ba; ngatun yuti yikora ngearun yarakai umulli kan kolang, miromulla ngearun yarakai ta birung; kulla ta ngiroumba Pirriwul kan ne ngatun kaiyu kan, ngatun killibinbin yanti ka tai. Amen.

A! Pirriwul, potokullea bi willing emmoumba wiyelli ko, ngatun wiyennun wal kurraka ko emmoumba ko murrorong ngiroumba.

Eloi to noa pitul noa kowwol kore ngukulla ta noa wakol bota yinal ngikoumba ngaliko yantin to ba, ngurran ngikoung kin, keawai wal bara tetti kunnun kulla wal yanti katai morón barun ba kakillinun.

Murrorong ta bara minki kan marai kakulla barun ba kuttan Pirriwul kaba moroko koba.

Murrorong ta bara wari kan yarakai umulli ta barun ba.

Wiyan bang ngiroung, Jesu nung, yarakai umulli ta emmoumba ngatun keawai wal bang yuropa korien emmoumba yarakai; ngiakai wal bang wiyennun yarakai umulli ta emmoumba Pirriwulla; ngatún bi warika yarakai umulli ta birung emmoumba.

Wiyennun ngeen ba, keawai wal yarakai korien ngeen ba, nakoiyan ngaiya ngeen bo. Wonto ba ngeen wiyennun ba yarakai ta ngearun ba, murrorong ko tuloa ko Eloi to warikulli ko yarakai umulli ta ngearun ba, ngatun murrorong kakili ko ngearun

A! Eloi kaiyu kan, Biyungbai ngearun ba Pirriwul koba Jesu koba, ngintoa umullikan yantin koba, ngintoa ta wiyelli kan to Pirriwullo yantin kore koba ko; wiyan ngeen ngatun minki lang kuttan ngeen ngali tin ngearun ba kauwullin yarakai tin, ngatun yarakai umulli tin ngeen yantin ta birung purreung ka birung, kauwullan yarakai umullalla kotulli ta, ngatun wiyelli ta, ngatun umulli ta ngearun ba ko, ngiroung Pirriwul yirriyirri kan kin bukka-pai-ya bin kauwul ngeen kakilli ko ngiroung kauwa yuna bo ta kakilli ko, minki kauwal kuttan ngeen, ngali tin yarakai umuili tin ngearun ba tin, ngatun yarakai kotelli tin ngearun ba tin.

Ella Jesu, ngurrulla bi tia yarakai bang kuttan yakita kinta lang bang kuttan, ngali tin ngiroung kin; bukka ban kora bi tia, warikulla bi yantin yarakai umullita emmoumba; wommunbi yikora bi tia koiyun kolang, mara bi tia marai emmoumba tetti bungngunnun ngiya bang ba; waita wauwil koa bang mikan kolang ngiroung kai kolang moroko kolang wokka kolang; minki bo ta wal bang, kauwa, yuna bo ta, ngali tin kauwul kauwul yarakai tin umulli tin emmoumba tin, umulla bi tia murrong kakilli ko pittul kauwil koa bi tia yarakai kan, warikulla bi yantin yarakai umulli ta emmoumba. Jesu wiyella binung Biyungbai nung ngearun ba moroko ko ba bukka katea kun koa noa tia tetti bungngunnun ngiya bang ba; ngintoa, Jesu, Pirriwul ta yantin ko ba kore koba, umulla bi tia wirrobulli kan kakilli ko ngiroumba ko; ngurrulla bi tia wiyeli ta emmoumba, yakita kulla bi murrorong ta kuttan.

Biyung bai ngearun ba moroko ka la wokka koba ngurrurrurmulla bi tia, bukka ban kora bi tia ngiroumba kin yinallin Jesu tin naki yikora bi tia yantin yarakai umulli ta kauwul emmoumba.

Ella Jesu, Pirriwul kore koba, ngurrulla bi tia wiyelli ta emmoumba yakita, kamulla bi tia murrorong mikan kai kolang ngiroumba tetti bungngunnun ngiya bang ba. Yuti yikora bi tia koiyung kolang. Yutilla bi tia mikan kai kolang ngiroung kai kolang tetti bungngunnun ngaiya bang ba.

Jesu ngurrurrurmulla bi tia, kinta lang bang kuttan, mirul bang kulla warikulla bi yantin yarakai umulli ta emmoumba, mara bi tia marai emmoumba yakita.

(F.)

GURRE KAMILAROI—'KAMILAROI SAYINGS.'

[This is the primer referred to on the second page of my Introduction. It was printed in 1856, and was intended for the use of the blacks on Liverpool Plains, among whom Mr. Ridley laboured for a short time as a missionary. The sentences are English thoughts expressed in simple Kamalarai words. The dotted *g* for the nasal *ng* is the only change I have introduced.—ED.]

1. Baiame gír* yarai, gille, mirri, taon ellibu, gimobi.
God verily sun, moon, stars, earth also made.

2. Baiame yalwuga murruba; Baiame minnaminnabul gummilda, minnaminnabul winugulda.
God always is good; God everything sees, everything hears.

3. Baiame gir kánugo kubba, kúnial, maian, tulu, yindal, be] ran, boiyoi, gimobi.
God verily every hill, plain, watercourse, tree, grass, beran (an herb), pennyroyal made.

4. Baiame gír yaráman, búrumo, bundar, múte, dúli, dínoun, buralga, bilocla, millimumul, gulamboli, kobado, mullion, guiya, núrai, gundoba, burulu, mugin, kánugo di gimobi.
God verily horse, dog, kangaroo, opossum, 'guanna, emu, native companion, cockatoo, swallow, pelican, parrot, eagle, fish, brown-snake, deadly-black-snake, flies, mosquitos, all animals made.

5. Baiame gír giwír gimobi; mal giwír Adam. Baiame goë: 'Kamil murruba giwír gandil guddelago; gaia giwírgo ínar gimbille.' Ila baiame ínar gimobi; mal ínar ív; ív gulír Adamu.
God verily man made; first man Adam. God said, 'Not good man alone for to dwell; I for man woman will make.' Then God woman made; first woman Eve; Eve wife of Adam.

* In the Wiradhari dialect, this word, gir, is used as an intensive and a pluralising particle; *cf.* gindu-*gir*, 'you,' niang-*gir*, 'clever,' &c., in the Vocabulary.—ED.

6. Adam buba murrigu, buba wundagu, buba kánugo; ív gumba murrigu, gumba wundagu, gumba kánugo.

Adam is father of the blackfellows, father of the whites, father of all; Eve the mother of blacks, mother of whites, mother of all.

7. Adam, ív ellibu, warawara yanani. Kánugo giwír, kánugo ínar, warawara; yanani, kánugo kagil ginyi. Baiame yili ginyi; goë : 'Kánugo giwír, kánugo ínar, warawara yanani, kánugo kagil ginyi, gaia gárma bálu bumále.' Immanuel, wurume Baiamegu, goë: 'Kamil; kamil ginda garma bumala; ginda gunna bumala; gaia balugi; giwír inar moron gigigo.'

Adam, Eve also, astray went. All men, all women, astray went; all bad became. God angry became; he said: 'All men, all women, astray are gone; all bad have become. I them dead will smite.' Immanuel, Son of God, said: 'Not so; not thou them smite; thou me smite; I will die; man, woman, alive for to be."

8. Immanuel geanekúnda Baiame; germa Baiame giwír ginyi. Murruba Immanuel; kamil garagedúl murruba yealokwai germa.

Immanuel with us God; he God man became. Good is Immanuel; not another is good like him.

9. Ilambo Immanuel taongo taiyanani; giwír ginyi. Germa gír burula wíbil murruba gimobi, burula múga murruba gimobi, burula múga-binna murruba gimobi.

Long ago Immanuel to earth came; man he became. He verily many sick well made, many blind well made, many deaf well made.

10. Giwír kair Laváru. Gergu bular boádi, Mári, Máta. Layáru wibil ginyi. Bular boádi gurre wáala Immanuelgo, goaldendai: 'Gai daidadi, ginnu Layáru, wíbil.' Kamil yanani Immanuel. Yerála Layáru balúni. Bularbularo bábine balún taonda. Ila Immanuel taiyanani. Mári, Máta ellibu, yugillona. Immanuel goë : 'Ginnu daiadi yealo moron gigi.' Burula giwír, burula ínar, yugillona. Immanuel daonmago yanani. Yárul daonma kundawi. Immanuel goë : 'Gindai yárul diomulla.' Garma gír yárul diome. Immanuel kákúldono: 'Layáru, taiyanuga.' Ila Layáru moron ginyi; taiyanani. Bular boádi burul guiyé.

A man name Lazarus. Belonging to him two sisters, Mary, Martha. Lazarus sick became. The two sisters word sent to Immanuel, saying : 'My brother, Thy Lazarus, is sick.' Not went Immanuel. By and by Lazarus died. Four days he lay dead in the ground. Then Immanuel came. Mary, Martha also, were weeping. Immanuel said : 'Your brother again alive shall be.' Many men, many women, were weeping. Immanuel to the grave went; a stone the grave covered. Immanuel said : 'Ye the stone take away.' They the stone lifted up. Immanuel cried aloud : 'Lazarus, come forth.' Then Lazarus alive became; he came forth. The two sisters were very glad.

11. Garagedúli, miédúl wíbil ginyi; gumba boiyoi wune; kamil miédúl murruba ginyi; murru ginyi wíbil, gullimun balúni. Buba yanani Immanuel gummillego ; gír gummi; goë : 'Inda barai taiyanuga ; murruba gimbildi gai miédúl ; gai miédúl burul wíbil gullimun balúni; inda taiyanuga gai kúndigo.' Immanuel goë : 'Gulle yanoai kúndigo.' Ila yanani bular kúndigo. Gumba duri; yugillona; goë : 'Gii! gii! gai miédúl balúni.' Burula ínar

SENTENCES IN THE KAMALARAI DIALECT.   129

yugillona; goë: 'Gii! miédúl balúni.' Immanuel goë: 'Kurria yúga; kamil miédúl balúni; yeal babillona.' Burulabu giudami; garma gir balundai winugi. Immanuel murra kawáni miédúl; goë: 'Miédúl, waria.' Ila miédúl moron ginyi; warine; gurre goë. Gumba, buba ellibu, burul guiye.

At another time, a little girl sick became; the mother pennyroyal gave; not the little girl well became; much she grew sick, almost dead. The father went Immanuel to see; truly he found Him; he said: 'Thou quickly come; well make my little girl. My little girl is very sick, almost dead; you come to my house.' Immanuel said: 'We two will go to the house.' Then went the two to the house. The mother came; she wept; said: 'Alas! alas! my little girl is dead.' Many women were weeping, said: 'Alas! the little girl is dead.' Immanuel said: 'Cease weeping; not the girl is dead; only she is asleep.' All of them laughed; they verily her to-be-dead knew. Immanuel by hand took the girl; said: 'Damsel, arise'. Then the girl alive became; arose; words spoke. The mother, father also, very glad.

12. Garageduli, bular giwír múga guddelona turrubulda. Immanuel aro yanani. Bular múga winugi; kákúldone: 'Immanuel, Dúrunmi, Wurume Davidu, gummilla! gurrága geane.' Burula giwír goë: 'Kurria! kurria giudai kakúllego.' Giwír múga yealo kákúldone: 'Durunmi, Wurume Davidu, gummilla! gurraga geane.' Ila Immanuel warine; goë: 'Minna gindai goalle? minna gaia murramulle'? Garma goë: 'Durunmi, wuna geane gummildai.' Ila Immanuel garma mil támúlda; baianbu garma murru gummillego.

Another time, two men blind sat by the way. Immanuel there came. The two blind heard; they cried aloud: 'Immanuel, King, Son of David, look! pity us.' Many people said: 'Have done! cease ye to cry aloud.' The men blind again cried aloud: 'King, Son of David, look! pity us'! Then Immanuel stood still; said: 'What you will say? What I shall do'? They said: 'King, grant us to see.' Then Immanuel them eyes touches; instantly they are able to see.

13. Burula kagil giwír Immanuel kunmulta. Garma kaogo bindéa yulalle. Garma gír tulu wimi; garagedul tulu ganbir wimi; garma gír Immanuel wimi; murra biru-dún; idinna birudúni; tuluí wirri. Garma tulu tiome, Immanuel tuluí pindelundai. Yerála Immanuel balúni. Yerála, giwír pilari turrur duni; gue dulirri.

Many bad men Immanuel seized. They on his head thorns bound. They indeed a log laid; another log across they laid; they indeed Immanuel laid down; hands they pierced; feet they pierced; on cross fastened. They the cross raised, Immanuel on the cross hanging. Soon Immanuel died. Soon after, a man with a spear his side pierced; blood flowed.

14. Bullului, garma gír Immanuel taonda wimi, kundawi. Immanuel gúru bábine balún taonda; yealo malo bábine balún taonda; yealo garagedul guru bábine balún taonda; garagedul guruko moron ginyi, warine. Yerála gúnagullago yanani. Yeladu Immanuel gunagullada guddela; germa kánugo gummilda; kánugo winugulda.

In evening, they verily Immanuel in ground laid, covered. Immanuel the night lay dead in ground; also one day he lay dead in ground; also

i

another night he lay dead in ground ; next morning alive he became, arose. Soon after to heaven he went. Now Immanuel in heaven dwells ; he all sees ; all knows.

15. Murruba Immanuel ; kamil garagedul murruba yealokwai germa. Yerála Immanuel yealo taongo taiyanillo ; geane kánugo gummillo. Immanuel kaia goalle ; ila kánugo balún, giwír, ínar, kaigal kánugo moron gigi. Immanuel goalle : 'Minna inda gimobi ? minna inda gimobi ? inda murruba gimobi ? inda gununda taiyanuga gunagullago ; inda kagil gimobi ? inda biru yanuga, urribú yanuga.'

Good is Immanuel ; not another is good like Him. Hereafter Immanuel again to earth will come ; we all shall see. Immanuel aloud will speak ; then all the dead, men, women, and children, all alive shall become. Immanuel will say : 'What hast thou done? what hast thou done ? thou good hast done ? thou to me come to heaven ; thou evil hast done ? thou far go, very far go away.'

16. Giru ginda kagil ginyi ; inda warawara yanani ; giru Baiamo yili ginyi. Baiamo yalwuga murruba ; geane kánugo warawara yanani. Winugulla : kamil gaia yal goalda ; giru gaia goalda. Immanuel girribatai yarine, gúnagulladi taongo. Kánugo giwír kagil ginyi ; Immanuel gandil murruba ; Immanuel balúni, giwír moron gigigo.

Truly thou bad hast become ; thou astray hast gone ; truly God angry is. God always is good ; we all astray have gone. Hearken : not I lies tell ; truth I tell. Immanuel from above came down, from heaven to earth. All men bad are become ; Immanuel only is good ; Immanuel died, men alive for to be.

17. Yeladu Baiamo goalda : 'Gindai, kánugo giwír, kurria kagil gigile, berúdi warraia ; geane murru gurrile ; kamil gaia yili gigila ; murruba Immanuel balúni.' Yeladu Immanuel goalda : 'Taiyanuga gununda, kánugo gindai iggil, ila gaia gindai tubbiamulle.' Inda taiyanuga Immanuelgo.

Now God saith : 'Ye, all men, cease bad to be, turn ye ; we will be reconciled. Not I angry am. Good Immanuel died.' Now Immanuel saith : 'Come unto me, all ye weary, then I you will cause to rest." You come to Immanuel.

18. Giwír guddelona Littraga ; bain dinna tuggór, gurribu bain ge bain ; kamil yanelina. Paul, Barnaba ellibu, aro yanani. Paul goaldone ; baindúl germa winúgailone. Paul kaia gummildone ; kákúldone : 'Waria gurriba dinnaga.' Tuggórdúl parine, yanani ellibu.

A man dwelt at Lystra : with sick foot diseased, very ill indeed ; not he could walk. Paul, Barnabas also, there came. Paul was speaking ; the lame man him was hearing. Paul earnestly looked ; he cried aloud : 'Stand upright on feet.' The lame man leapt, walked also.

19. Burulabu giwír gummi ; goë 'gipai'! kákúldone : 'Baiamo bular yarine yealokwai giwír.' Paul, Barnaba ellibu, bunnagunne, kákúldone : 'Kurria ! kamil geane Baiamo ; geane giwír yealokwai gindai ; geane guiye duri ; geane budda ginyi ; geane yili ginyi ; yealo geane murru gurrigillone ; geane murru goalda burulabu ; kurria gindai yealo kagil gigile ; berúdi warraia, gum-

milla Baiame moron; Baiame gír gúnagulla, taon, burul kolle, kánugo minnaminnabul gimobi; Baiame yalwuga Baiame.'
All the people saw; they wondered; they cried aloud: 'Gods two, are come down like men.' Paul, Barnabas also ran, cried aloud: 'Have done! not we gods; we men like you. We glad become, we sorry become, we angry become, again we are reconciled. We good tell to all; cease ye any more evil to be; turn ye, look to God the living. God verily heaven, earth, the great water, all, everything made. God always is God, (the same ever).

(G.)

SPECIMENS OF A DIALECT

OF THE

ABORIGINES OF NEW SOUTH WALES;

BEING THE FIRST ATTEMPT TO FORM THEIR SPEECH INTO A WRITTEN LANGUAGE.

[I print this, because it is the earliest attempt to exhibit the structure of the aboriginal languages. The date is 1827. I have omitted the numbering of the sentences, the accents, and the table of sounds, referred to in the Author's preface. Naturally, there are some errors in such a first attempt as this. Such of these errors as were likely to mislead a reader, I have removed or altered; in other respects I have left the pamphlet very much as I found it. But, from its early date and its use of the English system of pronunciation, it cannot be quoted as an authority.
I print also the Author's Preface to this pamphlet.—ED.]

IN submitting a specimen of a dialect of the aborigines of New South Wales, no speculative arrangement of grammar is attempted. Out of upwards of fifteen hundred sentences, the most satisfactory ones are selected. The English is in a separate column on the right side of the page, and underneath the aboriginal sentences is placed, word for word, the English meaning, without regard to English arrangement or grammar, in order to show the idiom of the aboriginal tongue. The sentences are numbered for easy reference, should any friend wish to make any remark tending to simplify the present adopted mode. As one of my objects in applying to the language is to pave the way for the rendering into this tongue the sacred

Scriptures, every friendly hint will be most thankfully received. The accents are not marked for want of type, but the last arrangement of the verb will, it is hoped, be a sufficient guide. A table of the sounds, being an epitome of the plan pursued in the orthography of the language, will also be sufficient, it is presumed, to show the nature of the syllables; it would have increased the work to an inconvenient size had it been further explained. To ascertain the ellipsis with which the language abounds is the best means to obtain satisfaction in the use of the particles, and without the knowledge of this it appears very often a mere jargon. Ma-ko-ro to-a, 'fish to me,' is all they say for 'give me some fish'; but no possible mistake can arise, as in the English, using the nouns in a verbal sense. A double use of the preposition 'from' puzzled me exceedingly; but one day when the signal for a vessel was hoisted up at the signal-post, the remarks of a black man proved that it was from, on account of the vessel, the ball was hoisted from that cause. The cutting down a tree in the woods similarly showed from what part the log was to be chopped. I would also remark that we often think there is a difference in the language because the names of substantives differ; *e.g.*, a man was asked one day what he had got; 'ta-ra-kul,' was the reply—*i.e.*, peaches. But they had no peaches formerly; whence came the new name?—from a word 'to set the teeth on edge!' Now, at the Hawkesbury, the natives may call it by a name meaning rough skin, or any other quality. At the Hawkesbury, the English say that 'kob-ba-ra' is what the natives call 'head,' but the blacks told me to say 'wol-lung,' and it was only by an anatomical drawing my black teacher showed that by 'kob-ba-ra' he understood the 'skull bone.' No doubt there are provincialisms, but perhaps the language is radically the same. In presenting a copy to those in this colony who are connected with other societies, I beg to assure them that whatever knowledge I may obtain of the aboriginal tongue shall be always available to them with cheerful readiness, the noble principles of Christianity forbidding the indulgence of any selfish motive or party feeling in those who profess to be the promulgators of its precepts. An anxiety to satisfy the friends of humanity that our employment is not altogether without hope, as it respects attaining the language of the blacks, and that success may ultimately be expected, with the Divine aid, have suggested and urged the putting of these imperfect specimens to the press.

Eighteen months less interrupted than the time past will, it is hoped, enable me to make known salvation to the aborigines in their own tongue. To attempt instruction before I can argue with them as men would be injurious, because Christianity does not make its votaries mere machines, but teaches them how to give an answer to every one that asketh a reason of their hope. My time, therefore, must be devoted wholly to that single object until I am competent; and whatever may be the expenses, or whatever may be the privations of individuals to reclaim sinners, whether black or white, the remembrance of it will be no more, or, if it exist, it will excite only a song of praise when we shall behold the great multitude which no man could number, of all nations, and kindreds, and people, and tongues standing before the Lamb, clothed with white robes, and palms in their hands, saying, "Thou hast redeemed us to God by Thy blood, out of every kindred and tongue and people and nation, and hast made us unto our God kings and priests for ever. Amen."

Doctor Johnson observes that the orthography of a new language formed by a synod of grammarians upon principles of science would be to proportion the number of letters to that of sounds, that every sound may have its own character, and every character a single sound. Doctor Lowth's rule hath been attended to in syllabication—namely, "Divide the syllables in spelling, as they are naturally divided in a right pronunciation," so that, to use the words of another author, "Syllabication shall be the picture of actual pronunciation."

The English alphabet is used with little variation of sound, The table (an abridgement) shews the fixed sounds of the letters and syllables agreeably to the English examples, leaving nothing arbitrary.

The attempt to form the aboriginal speech into a written language with perspicuity is made on the above principles; time only can decide on its practicability.

L. E. THRELKELD.

ABORIGINAL SENTENCES VERBALLY RENDERED INTO ENGLISH UNDERNEATH THE RESPECTIVE WORDS.

1. Nga-to-a.—The pronoun *I* in answer to a question, as, *it is I*; it is used also in a relative sense, *it is I who*. The pronunciation of the *ng* is very soft, but exactly the same as *ng* in *hang, bang*. The pronoun *I*, when forming the simple subject to the verb, is *bang, I*.

Nganke un-nung? ngatoa un-ne; *m*., who is there? it is I
  Who   (is)   there   I   this.
Ngatoa man-nun; man-nun bang; *m*., it is I who will take.
  I   take-will; take-will   I.
Ngatoa un-te ka-tan; un-te bang ka-tan; *m*., I am
  I   at this place am. at this place I   am.   here.
Ngatoa woya-leyn; wean bang; *m*., I am speaking; I
  I   speak-ing; speak I.   speak.

Ngatoa uma-kaan unne, ngorokan; *m.*, it is I who made
I   made-have   this, thismorning. this, this morning.
Unne bang uma-kaan, ngorokan; *m.*, I have made this,
This I made-have, this morning. this morning.
Ngatoa wa-leyn un-ta-ring; wa-leyn bang un-te-ring.
I move-ing to that place; move-ing I to this place.
  m., I am going to that place; I am coming to this place.
Ngatoa bo wal wea bounnoun; *m.*, I myself spoke to her.
I myself spoke her.
Ngatoa bo wal bounnoun bun-ka-leyn; *m.*, I myself am
I myself her striking. beating her.
Ngatoa bo wa-le-a-la wa-kol; *m.*, I myself went alone.
I went one.

  2. Ngin-to-a—the pronoun *thou* in answer to a question,
    it is thou who. The pronoun used to the verb in simple
    form is be, *thou*.

Ngan-ka be unne? ngintoa-ta unne; *m.*, who art thou now?
Who thou this? thou this. it is thou, *emph.*
Ngeroung koa ban-nu wean ngurra-le-ko.
For thee why I-it speak for to hear.
    m., I speak it in order for thee to hear.
Ngintoa tatte ba-nun; *m.*, it is thou who wilt be dead.
Thou dead be-will.
Ngintoa kinta, ngatoa kaawaran; *m.*, it is thou who fearest,
Thou fear, I not. I do not.
Ngatoa bo wal yaraki, ngintoa kaawaran; *m.*, I myself am
I myself evil, thou not. evil, thou art not.
Ngintoa kinta; kinta be; *m.*, it is thou who fearest; thou
Thou fear; fear thou. fearest.
Ngintoa kinta ka-nun; kinta be ka-nun.
Thou fear be-will; fear thou be-will.
  m., it is thou who wilt fear; thou wilt be afraid.

  3. New-wo-a—the pronoun *he*, in answer to a question, *who
    is it?* The pronoun for the verb is noa, *he* or *it*.

Newwoa kinder; kinder noa; *m.*, it is he who laughs; he
He laugh; laugh he. laughs.
Newwoa wal kore yarai; *m.*, it is he who is a bad man.
He man bad.
Newwoa warekul nowwi ta ba; *m.*, the dog is in the canoe.
He the dog canoe. in.
Newwoa-bo keyn kokon ta ba; *m.*, it is he himself in the
He being water in. water.

  4. Bo-un-to-a—the feminine pronoun, *she*.

Unne bountoa Patty ammoung kin-ba; *m.*, this is Patty
This she Patty me with. with me.

Ammoung katoa bountoa wa-nun; *m.*, she will go with me.
  Me   with   she   move-will.
Wonni bountoa tea unnung tatto ammoun-ba;
  Child   she to me there dead   mine.
         m., my child, there is dead.
Ngan-ke bountoa unne? unnoa? unnung? *m.*, who is she?
  Who   she this?   that?   there?   (here, there)?

5. Nga—the pronoun *it* or *it is*, in answer to a question.

Wea, unnoa boat kowwol? nga-ba unnang kowwol-an.
  Say, that boat large? it is that large-being.
    m., is that a large boat? it is a large boat.
Wea, unnoa murrorong? nga-ba unnoa murrorong.
  Say, that good? it is that good.
    m., is that good? it is it that is good.
Ngan-to bon bun-ka-la? nga-le noa bon bun-kala.
  Who him struck? this he him strike-did.
    m., who struck him? it is he that struck him.
Nga-la noa bon bunkala; nga-la noa   *ya.
  That he him struck; that he there close at hand.
    m., it was he that struck him; it was he there.
Won-nung? nga-la noa wea-leyn unnung.*
  Where? that he speak-ing there.
    m., where? it was he speaking there.

6. Nga-an—the plural pronoun, *we*.

Ka-bo! ngaan wa-nun; *m.*, stop, we will go presently.
  Stop! we move-will.
Ka-i! wita ngaan; *m.*, come, we depart, *i.e.*, let us go.
  Ho! depart we.
Ka-i! be yan-ta, ta-nan, wita ngaan; *m.*, come thou hither;
  Ho! thou hither, approach, depart we. approach, we depart.
Ka-bo, ka-bo, wa-ow-wil koa ngaan ngeroung katoa.
  Be still, be still, move may that we you with.
    m., stop, stop, that we may go too with you.
Wita ngaan nowwi-ta wing-ow-wil; *m.*, we depart to row
  Depart we canoe may row. the canoe.
Wita-lang ngaan; wita wal ngaan; *m.*, we do depart; we
  Depart we; depart shall we. are about to depart.
Ya-ko-un-ta ka ngaan wa-nun Kuttai kolang?
    When   we move will Sydney towards?
    m., when shall we depart for Sydney?
Ya-ko-un-ta kan ngaan†; *m.*, we do not know when.
  When being we.
Ya-ko-un-ta ngatong†; *m.*, when is it to be? (a negative.)
  When   that?

---

*Note—Unnung, 'there,' means at a greater distance than ya, 'there.'
† In this collection of sentences, the † shows that the phrase is an idiom.

7. Nu-rur—the plural pronoun *ye*. The *r* as in *rogue*.

Wea, nu-rur wa-nun Mulubinba ko-lang; *m.*, will ye go to
Say, ye move-will Newcastle to. Newcastle.
Wea-la nurur, ngatoa wita; *m.*, do ye talk and I will go.
Speak ye, I depart.
Kari nurur ta-kaan ngoro-kan-ta; *m.*, ye have eaten kan-
Kangaroo ye eaten-have this morning. garoo this morning.

8. Ba-rur—the plural pronoun, *they*.

Ngan-bo barur uwah? ngan-bo kan†; barur napal.
Who they moved? who being; they woman.
  m., who are they gone? I don't know; they are women.
Wea-lang barur; wea-leyn barur; *m.*, they talk; they are
Speak they; speak-ing they. talking.
Wita ka-ba barur; *m.*, they are in the act of departing.
Depart in they.

9. Ba-le—dual pronoun *thou* and *I*, *we two*.

Wita ba-le wah-ow-wil ya-ka-ta; *m.*, thou and I will go
Depart we-two move to at this time. now.
Min-na-ring ko-lang ba-le bon wea-la?
  What towards we-two him speak?
  m., art thou and I to speak to him? about what art, &c.
Wea bula tanan wa-nun? a-a, wa-nun bale?
Say, ye-two approach move-will? yes, move-will we-two.
  m., will ye two come? yes, we will come.

10. Bu-la—dual pronoun, *ye two* or *the two*.

A-la! bula; ka-bo! won-ta ko-lang bula?
Hallo! ye two; be still! whither for ye two?
  m., hallo! ye two; stop; whither are ye two going?

11. Bu-la bu-lo-a-ra—dual pronoun, *they two*.

Won-ta ko-lang bula unnung buloara? *m.*, whither are
Whither the two there two? they two going?

12. Min? (an interrogative) *m.*, *what*?

Min-na-ring unne? minnaring kan.†
  What this? What being?
  m, what is this? I don't know, *lit.*, what (is it) being?
Minnaring unnoa? minnaring ngatong?
  What that? what the thing
  m., what is that? I don't know.
Minnaring tin ba unnoa? murrenowwa tin unnoa
  What from that ship because of that.
  m, what is that for? on account of the ship that.
Minnaring tin bounton unnung tun-ka-leyn?
  What from she there cry-ing?
  m., why does she cry there?

FIRST SPECIMEN OF THE AWABAKAL DIALECT.

Minnaring tin kan? mamuya tin bountoa tunkaleyn?
What from being? corpse from she cry-ing.
m., I don't know ; on account of the corpse she is crying.

Minnaring ka unnoa-nung? minnaring kan be wean?
What that there what being thou speak.
m., what is that there? what dost thou say?

Minnaring ko ka unnoa-nung? m., what is that there for?
What for that - there?

Makoro ko-lang tura-nun bang; m., it is for fish I will spear.
Fish towards spear-will I.

Minnaring be unnoa kurra-leyn? m., what are you carrying?
What thou that carry-ing?

Minnaring ko be unnoa kurra-leyn? m., why art thou
What for thou that carry-ing carrying that?

Minnaring be unnoa petan? kokoin bang unne petan.
What thou that drink? water I this drink.
m., what is that thou drinkest? this is water I drink.

Minnaring be unnoa ta-ka-leyn? m., what is that thou art
What thou that eat-ing? eating?

Kari bang unne takaleyn; m., this is kangaroo I am eating.
Kangaroo I this eat-ing

Minnaring berung uma unnoa? m., what is that made of?
What from made that

Koli berung; brass berung ta unne; m., of wood; of brass,
Wood from; brass from this. this.

Minnaring berung kan? m., what can it be made of?
What from being.

Minnaring tin be ka-ka-la buk-ka? m., on what account
What from thou wast furious? was't thou so angry?

Minnaring tin ngatong†; ngukung tin bang bukka.
What from nothing; wife from I furious.
m., from no cause; on account of wife I (am) furious.

Minnaring-ko bonoun tura? kota-ro, ware-ko, bibi-to.
What her pierced? waddy, spear, axe.
m., what didst thou pierce her with? with a waddy, spear, axe.

Minnaring tin be-noun tura? m., from what cause didst
What from thou-her pierced? thou spear her?

New-wara-kan-to bang tura bounnoun; m., through anger
Angry being I pierced her. I speared her.

Minn-an beyn wonni? wonni korean.
How-many to thee child? child not.
m., how many children hast thou? none.

Minn-an beyn terrakul ngeroamba? kowwol-kowwolo.
How many to thee peaches thine much much.
m., how many peaches hast thou with thee? a great many.

Minn-an kol-bun-te-nun? wa-ra-a kol-bun-te-la.
How-much cut-will? little cut do
m., how much is to be cut? let a little be cut.

Kowwol-kowwol kolbunte-a; minn-an kant?
Much   much   cut;   how many being.
  m., a great quantity is cut; I don't know (how much).
Min-nung banun be bungi? *m.*, what wilt thou be about
What   will-do thou to-day?   to-day?
Min-nung banun boyn bungi? *m.*, what will be done to
What   will-do to thee to-day?   you to-day?
Min-nung ba-nun bul bungi noa-ya be-loa?
What   do-will   to-day   he thee-with.
  m., what will become of thee to-day?
Min-nunt kan? wonkul be ka-nun; *m.*, I don't know;
What   being; stupid thou be-wilt.   thou wilt be a fool.
Min-nung-ba boyn unnoa mattara? *m.*, what is the matter
What   to thee that hand?   with thy hand?
Teir-nung-a; kun a; kulla-ba; *m.*, it is broken; it is
Broken;   burnt; cut (it is.)   burnt; it is cut.
Min-nung u-pa-loyn be unnoa? *m.*, what is that thou art
What   do-ing thou that?   doing?
Mirre-loyn bang ware; ka-a-wi, yalla-wa-loyn bang.
Sharpen-ing I spear;   no,   resting   I.
  m., I am sharpening a spear; no, I am sitting still.
Min-nung ba-nun be bungi? *m.*, what wilt thou make
What   do-will thou present time?   to-day?
U-pa-nun bang ware bungi; *m.*, I will make a spear
Will make I spear present time.   to-day.
U-pa wal bang ware bungi; *m.*, certainly, I shall make a
Make shall I spear to-day.   spear to-day.
Min-na-ring ko makoro? ta-ke-le-ko; *m.*, what is fish for?
What   for fish?   eat-for.   to be eaten.
Minnaring unne bungi ka-tau? *m.*, what is to-day?
What   this to-day   is?
Minnaring ko unnung upaa? (*or* wu-pe-a).
What   for there put?
  m., what is (it) put there for? (two balls as a signal.)
Ya-re, upaa murrenowwi ko buloara ko.
Truly, put   ship   for   two   for.
  m., it has been put for two ships (as a signal).
Minnaring be unnoa tatan? *m.*, what is that thou eatest?
What   thou that eatest?
Makoro unne bang ta-tan; won; *m.*, fish is what I eat;
Fish   this I eat; where?   where?
Won-ta tin koa horse? Sydney tin.
Where from why horse? Sydney from.
  m., from what place is the horse? from Sydney.
Won-ta ko-lang unne (*sc.*, uwan)? *m.*, whither does this go?
Where towards this   (move)?
Won-ta ko-lang unnoa nowwi wa-leyn?
Where towards that canoe move-ing?
  m., whither does the canoe go?

Won-ta-ring noa uwa? koeyong bountoa unnam-bo.
Where he moved? camp she that.
m., whither is he gone? she is at the camp.

Won-ta ko-lang be? Sydney ko-lang bang.
Where towards thou? Sydney towards I
m., whither art thou (going)? to Sydney I am (going).

Won-ta-ring ngurur uwa? un-te-ko ngaan uwa.
Where ye moved? this-place for we moved.
m., where have you moved to? to here.

Won-ta-ring we-reyn wibbe ko? pa-ki tin wibbe.
Where blowing wind for? southward from wind.
m., whither is the wind blowing? from the southward is the wind.

Won-ta berung be? nowwi-ta berung bang.
Where from thou? canoe from I.
m., where hast thou come from? from the canoe.

Won-ta-ko ka bang unne kur-reyn; *m.*, whither am I
Where for I this carry-ing. carrying this?

Un-to-a ko yong; koke-ra ko; *m.*, to that place there; to
That place for there: house for. the house.

Won-ta tin unnoa? wokka tin; *m.*, whence that? from up.
Where from that? up from.

Won-nung ka beyn kari? unne-bo; *m.*, where is thy kan-
Where at to thee kangaroo? this. garoo? this is (it).

Won-nung ka beyn ngukung? unne-bo bountoa.
Where at to thee wife? this she.
m., where is thy wife? this is she.

Won-ta tin-to bang Sydney na-nun? *m.*, at what place can
Where from I Sydney shall see? see Sydney?

Wou-nong kowwol? unne kowwol; *m.*, which is big;
Where big? this big (or much). this is big.

Unnoa ba-ta kowwol; *m.*, that is the biggest.
That certainly big.

Won-ta-ring bountoa uwan? *m.*, whither does she go?
Where she move?

Un-ta-ring; Mulubinba ko-lang; *m.*, to that place; to New-
Thither; Newcastle towards. castle.

Won-nung ka Bun-umba kokera katan? *m.*, where is Bun's
Where Bun's house is? house?

Won-nung toa katan boat ammoamba? *m.*, where is my
Where to me is boat mine? boat?

Won-nung bountoa unnung? *m.*, which is she there?
Where she there?

Won-nung be man-nun, unne? unnoa ta uman bang.
Where thou take-will, this? that take I.
m., which wilt thou take, this? I take that.

Won-nung be a? unne bang; *m.*, where art thou, ay?
Where thou ay? this I. here I am.

Won-nayn unnoa yeterra? Trelkeld ye-terra-bul bang.
Which way   he   named?   ,,   named   I.
   m., which way is he named? I am named Threlkeld.
Won-nayn be bereke-a? ngeakai bang bereke-a.
Which-way thou sleep (about to)? here   I   about to sleep.
   m., where wilt thou sleep? I shall sleep here.
Won-nayn noa uwa? ngaa noa uwa; won-naynt kan?
Which way he moved? forward he moved; which way.
   m., which way is he gone? forward he is gone; I don't know.
Won-nayn bang unne wean yeterra? *m.*, which way am I to
Which way   I   this speak named?   call this?
Won-nayn unne purri yeterra? Pami-kan; *m.*, what is this
Which way this land named?   Pahmi.   land called?
Won-nayn ngaan wa-la? ngea-ka-i ngaan wa-la.
Which way   we   move-do?   here   we   move-do.
   m., which way shall we go? this way we shall go.
Won-nayn bale wa-la? ngea-ka; *m.*, which way shalt thou
Which way we two move-do? this way.   and I go? this way.
Won-ta-kaleen unnoa napal? *m.*, where does that woman
Of what place   that   woman?   belong to?
Won-ta tin unnoa man-tan? *m.*, where is that taken from?
Where from   that   take?
Won-ta nurur bun-ke-lang? *m.*, where do ye fight?
Where   ye   fight-now-do?
Un-te ngaan bun-ke-lang un-te; *m.*, here we fight.
Here   we   fight-now-do   here.
Wonnung beyn bun-ka-la? *m.*, what part of thee was
Where   to thee   struck?   struck?
Unne tea bun-ka-la wollung; *m.*, this, my head was
This to me   struck   head.   struck.
Won-ta be unnoa man-ka-la? *m.*, where was it thou
Where thou that   tookest?   didst catch that?
Mulubinbakaleen bountoa; *m.*, she belongs to Newcastle.
Woman-of-Newcastle   she.
Unne bountoa Irelandkaleen; *m.*, she is an Irishwoman.
This   she   woman-of-Ireland.
Won-ta ko-lang? korung ko-lang; *m.*, whither? to the bush.
Where towards the bush towards.
Wonnam bountoa? unambo bountoa; *m.*, whereat is she?
Whereat   she?   at that   she.   at that place she is.
Wonnam bara? unambo Sydney; *m.*, where are they at; at
Whereat they? at that Sydney.   Sydney they are.
Wonnam bountoa (noa, kore, napal)? *m.*, where is she at
Whereat   she   (he, man, woman)? (he, man, woman)?

13. Ngan? (an interrogative) *who? who is?*

Ala! ngan be yeterra? ngan unnung?
Hallo! who thou named? who   there?
    m., hallo! what is thy name? who is there?

FIRST SPECIMEN OF THE AWABAKAL DIALECT.   141

Ngan unnang? ngan† ngatong? ngatoa Beraban.
Who at this place? who   then?   I   Eaglehawk.
    m., who is that? don't know; it is I, Eaglehawk.
Patty bountoa; kaaran Patty korean; *m.*, it is Patty; no,
Patty she;   no,   Patty   not   it is not Patty.
Ngan noa unne (unnoa, unnang, unnung)?
Who he this (that, at this place, there)?
    m., who is this here (that, at this place, there)?
Ngan bula uwa? Dismal bula Jem; *m.*, which two went?
Who the two moved? Dismal the two Jem.   Dismal and Jem.
Ngan noa unnung? murcung (korung) kolang?
Who he there?   the sea   (the bush) towards?
    m., who is he there? towards the sea? the bush?
Ngan-to tura bounnoun? nga-le noa; *m.*, who has speared
Who pierced   her?   this   he   her? he has.
Nga-le noa ya; nga-la noa yong; *m.*, it is he here; it is he
This   he here; that   he there;   there.
Ngan-to unne uma? ma, u-ma-la; *m.*, who has done
Who   this done? do (thou) do.   this? do thou it.
Ngan-to beyn uma koparo? ngatoa uma-laan.
Who to thee done red ochre?   I   done.
    m., who has colored thee with red ochre? it is I have done it.
Ngannung-ka uma-nun bang? unnoa bon uma-la.
Whom   do-will   I?   that   him   do.
    m., whom shall I do? do him.
Ngan-to man-nun kurre-kurre? *m.*, who will catch the first
Who take-will the-very-first?   (in fishing)?
Nga-la noa ma-nun; *m.*, that is he who will have (it).
,, That he take-will
Kaawaran be man-nun; newwoa man-nun.
Not   thou take-will; he   take-will.
    m., it is not thou wilt take; it is he will.
Ngan-bo perewol un-te? ngintoa; *m.*, who is the chief
Who   chief   this   thou.   here? it is thou.
Kaawaran bang perewol korean; *m.*, I am not chief.
Not   I   chief   not.
Unne noa? a-a, unnoa-ta noa; *m.*, this he? yes, that is he.
This he? yes,   that   he.
Nga unnoa ngeroamba? kaawi; nga-le ko ba bon.
Is it that   thine?   no.   this belonging to him.
    m., is it thine that? no; it belongs to him.
Ngan-umba ka warekul? ammoamba-ta unnoa.
Whose   dog?   mine   that.
    m., whose is the dog? it is mine, that.
Bumburukan-um-ba warekul? ngan-umba-kan†?
B.'s   dog?   whose?
    m., Bumburukan's dog? I don't know.

NOTE.—Ngale noa, 'this is he who'; ngala noa, 'that is he who.'

Ngan-um-ba-ka unnoa napal? *m.*, whose is that woman?
   Whose   that   woman?
Ngan kin-berung be unnoa man-ka-la? *m.*, from whom didst
  Whom   from   thou that   tookest?   thou take that?
Mr. Brooks kin-berung; Mulubinba ka-berung.
  Mr. Brooks   from;   Newcastle   from.
         m., from Mr. Brooks; from Newcastle.
Ngannung be wean? ngeroung bang wean.
  Whom thou speakest? thee   I   speak.
        m., to whom speakest thou? to thee I speak.
Ammoung be wean? kaawi; nge-ko-ung bang wean.
   Me thou speakest? no;   him   I   speak.
     m., is it to me you speak? no; to him I speak.
Ngan-bo wingun-nun nowwi-ta? *m.*, who will paddle the
   Who   paddle-will canoe?   canoe?

14. Ya-ko-un-ta? *m., when? at what time?*

Ya-ko-un-ta be noun na-kala Patty-nung? *m.*, when didst
    When   thou her see-did   Patty?   thou see Patty?
Yaketa, bungi, bang nakala; buloara-ka-la; korowarung.
  Now, to-day, I saw;   two at;   a long time since.
   m., I saw her just now, to-day; two (days) past; long ago.
Yurake bang-nung na-ka-la; *m.*, some time ago I saw (her).
Some time ago I-her see did.
Korowarung ka-ta-a-la; yuraki ta ka-ta-a-la.
     m., it was a long time back; it was formerly.
Ya-ko-unta kurre be wan-nun tanan? *m.*, when wilt thou
   When   first thou move-will approach?   come again?
Kumba be ba-la wan-nun unte-ko; *m.*, to-morrow thou
To-morrow thou must move-will here-for.   must come here.
A-la! tanan, wea-wil koa bang-nu; *m.*, hallo! come that
Hallo! approach, speak-may that   I-it.   I may tell it.
A-la! wa-mun-billa tea; *m.*, hallo! let me go.
Hallo! move-let   me.
Ya-ko-un-ta ka be makoro ko-lang? *m.*, when dost thou
   When   at thou fish towards?   fish?
Kumba koa bang wa-kayn; *m.*, why, to-morrow I am coming.
To-morrow, why, I move-ing.
Yura-ke-ta-o; yura-ke-ta bang; korowarung ka bang.
   Long ago;   a long time since I; long while at I.
m., a long while; I shall be a long while; a long time since I have.
Ya-ko-un-ta ka be yan-tara (yante) uma-nun?
   When   at thou like as that (like as this) make-will?
     m., when wilt thou make like that? like this?
Ya-ke-ta bang uma-nun; *m.*, I will make it now.
  Now   I   make-will.
Yakounta be-nu na-kala, Bun-nung?
   When thou-him see-did,   Bun?
        m., when didst thou see Bun.

Kora koa be wa-ba unambo kumba? ko-ra ko-a?
Not   why thou was   at this yesterday?   not   why?
  m., why wast thou not at this place yesterday?
Kora koa be tatan untoa-kal? m., why dost thou not eat
Not   why thou eat   there-of?   some of that?
Kora koa be tea wea-ya-loyn? m., why dost thou not
Not   why thou me speaking?   answer me?
Wonkul kora be; wea-ya-la tea; m., do not be a fool; answer
 Fool not thou; speak to me.   me.
Kora koa be tea wean? m., why dost thou not speak to me?
Not why thou me speak?
Kora koa be ammoung katoa uwan? m., why dost thou not
Not why thou me   with   move?   come with me?
Kora koa be tea ban tea kan? ma! ba-la, wea-la.
Not   why thou me strike me again? do! come! speak.
 m., why dost thou not strike me again? do! speak you must.
Kora koa be tanan uwan? kora koa be wita uwan?
Not why thou approach move?   not why thou depart move?
 m., why dost thou not draw nigh? why dost thou not depart?
Kora koa be man-tan makoro? m., why dost thou not catch
Not why thou take   fish?   fish?
Kaawi bon bang bunuba; m., I did not strike him.
Not   him I   struck.

15. We-a (used interrogatively); m., *do, speak, say, tell;*
    wea is the imperative of the verb 'to speak.'

Wea, be unte-kal makoro man-nun? a-a, man-nun bang.
Say, thou here-of   fish   take-will? yes, take-will I.
 m., wilt thou take some of the fish here? yes, I will take some.
Wea, be unte-kal ta-ow-wa? a-a, ta-nun bang untoa-kal.
Say, thou here-of eat?   yes, eat-will I   that of.
 m., wilt thou take some of this here? yes, I will eat of that.
Wea, be unte yalla-wa-nun? yalla-wa-nun bang unte.
Say, thou here rest   will?   to rest-move-will I   here.
 m., wilt thou rest here? I will rest here.
Yalla-wan bang unte; unte bang unte yalla-wan.
To rest-move I   here; here I here to rest-move.
 m., I rest here; here I rest.
Wea, be untoa bereke-nun? m., wilt thou sleep on that place?
Say, thou that sleep-will?
Kaawi bang untoa; unte-bo bang bereke-nun.
Not   I   that; here   I   sleep-will.
 m., no, not at that place; here is where I will sleep.
Wea, be unnoa peta-nun? ta-nun? m., wilt thou drink
Say, thou that drink-will? eat-will;   that? eat?
Wea, be tanan wa-nun unte-bo? m., wilt thou come here; to
Say, thou approach move-will here?   this place?
Wea, ngaau Mulubinba ko-lang wa-nun? m., shall we go to
Say, we   Newcastle towards move-will? Newcastle?

Wea, be unne man-nun? man-nun bang; *m.*, wilt thou take
 Say, thou this take-will? take-will I. this? I will take.
Kaaran bang man-nun; *m.*, I will not take.
 Not I take-will.
Wea, unne murrong? murrorong-ta unnoa; *m.*, is this good?
 Say, this good? good that. that is good.
Wea, unne murron warekul? murron-ta unnoa.
 Say, this tame dog. tame that.
  m., is this a tame dog? that is tame.
Wea, unne buk-ka? buk-ka-ta unnoa; *m.*, is this savage?
 Say, this savage? savage that. that is savage.
Wea, unte-wan-ta pibelo? unn-am-bo-ta.
 Say, here there pipe? there.
  m., is the pipe here? it is, at this place.
Wea, ba-le wa-la? won-ta-ring? Sydney ko-ba.
 Say, thou-I move-do? where? Sydney to.
  m., shall thou and I go? where? to Sydney.
Wea, unnoa porol? porol-ta unnoa; *m.*, is that heavy? it is
 Say, that heavy? heavy this. heavy this.
Kaawi; wir-wir-ran-ta unne; *m.*, it is not (heavy); it is light
 No; light this. this.
Wea, tea be ngu-nun? *m.*, (what) wilt thou give me?
 Say, to me thou give-will?
Ngu-nun bang-nu ngeroung; *m.*, I will give it thee.
 Give-will I-it for-thee.
Wea, bula tanan wa-la? wea, ngaan tanan wa-la?
 Say, ye two approach move-do? say, we approach move-do?
  m., will ye two come? shall we come?
Wea, be wa-nun ammoung katoa? *m.*, wilt thou go with me?
 Say, thou move-will me with?
Wea, bountoa wa-nun* ngeroung katoa? *m.*, will she go
 Say, she move-will thee with? with thee?
Wea, bountoa unnung ka-nun ngeroung kin?
 Say she there be-will thee with.
  m., will she live with thee?

16. Ka-i; Ka-bo; *m., come; stop, remain, be still, halt.*

Ka-i! unte-ko tanan wa-la; *m.*, be thou here, approach,
 Come! here-to approach move-do. move.
Ka-bo! unnambo yallawa-la unnoa; *m.*, be thou where thou
 Stop! there rest there art; rest thou there.
Yanoa! be bunke yekora; kaaran bang bun korean.
 Let be! thou strike not; not I strike not.
  m., let it be; do not thou strike; I am not about to strike.
Yanoa, be bunke yekora bounnoun; *m.*, let be; do not
 Let be, thou strike not her. thou strike her.

*It is not yet exactly decided whether wa-nun or waw-nun or wan-nun. Wa is a verb of motion. Hence it means 'to come or to go.' The verbs tanan, 'to approach,' and wita, 'to depart,' determine 'the sense.'

Kaarau! kaawi ko-lang bang-nu bun-tan; *m.*, no! I am not
   No!   not   towards I - it   strike.   going to strike it.
Wita koa, bang memi yekora; *m.*, do not detain, for I depart.
 Depart why, I   detain not.
Ma! kipulla; yanoa, kipi yekora; tunke yekora, yanoa.
 Do! call out; let be, call   not;   cry   not,   let be.
   m., do call out; do not call out; do not weep, leave off.
Yuring, be wala, minke yekora kare be.
 Away, thou move do, stay   not   first thou.
     m., away with thee, go, stay not; be first.
Bun-nun bang ba-la unne warekul; bun-nun bon bang.
 Beat-will I   must this   dog;   beat-will him   I.
     m., I must beat this dog; I will beat him.
Yanoa, tea bunke yekora; *m.*, let be, do not strike me.
 Let be, me strike   not.
Kinta-lang bang bunkele tin; *m.*, I do fear being struck.
 Fearful   I   strike at.
Tanan ka-i; na-ow-wil koa unne; *m.*, draw nigh; come to
 Approach come; see-may that this.   see this.
Boung-ka-lea nakele-ko; na-ow-wa! na-ow-wa nurur.
 Stand   to see for ;   see !   see ?   ye !
   m., stand up to see *or* stand up and look ; look ye !
Boung-ka-lea ngur-row-wil; *m*, stand up (that) (you) may see.
 Stand (thou)   hear-may that.
Wea-la, tea ngurrow-wil koa bang-nu; *m.*, tell me that I
 Speak, me hear - may that I - it.   may know it.
Tura-la be-nu; be-bounnoun; ammoung be tura-la.
 Spear thou-it ;   thou-her.   me   thou   spear.
     m., spear thou him ; spear her ; spear thou me.
Ka-i! unte-ko yalla wa-ow-wil koa be; murra yekora.
 Come! here-to rest move-may that thou; run not.
m., come hither in order that thou mayest rest ; run ; do not run.
Wea-la be-nu unnung tanan ; *m.*, tell him there to come.
 Speak thou-it there   approach.
Ngan-nuug-ka? yeterra-bul-nung; *m.*, to whom? to such
 Whom to?   such a one there (to).   a one.
Kai! unne ta-ow-wil; ta-o-wa kirun ; *m.*, come to eat this;
 Come ! this eat-may-that ;   eat   all.   eat it all.
Ma! bu-wi tea ya-ke-ta; bu-a be-tea; kinterye kora.
 Do! strike me   now;   strike thou me; laugh not.
    m., go on! strike me now ; strike me ; do not laugh.
Wute-lea wal be; wutea bang; *m.*, thou art covered; I am.
 Covered shalt thou ; covered   I.
Ammoung be wea-la; wea-la be tea; *m.*, speak to me;
  Me   thou   speak;   speak thou me.   do tell me.

17. Mun-billi, the *permissive* verbal.

Ta-mun-billa tea; wa-mun-billa tea; man-mun-billa tea.
 Eat-let   me ;   move-let me ;   take-let   me.
   m., let me eat ; let me go ; let me take.

Tura-mun billa tea; wita tea wa-mun-billa.
Pierce-let   me;   depart me   move-let.
       m., let me spear; let me depart.
Bereke-bun-billa tea; yalla-wa-bun-billa tea.
Sleep-let   me;   rest   move-let   me.
       m., let me sleep; let me go to rest
Wea-bun-billa tea; ngurrur-bun-billa tea.
Speak-let   me;   hear-let   me.
       m., let me speak; let me hear.
Tanan tea wa-mun-billa koeyung kako.
Approach me   move-let   fire   to.
       m., let me draw nigh to the fire.
Tatte-ba bun-billa tea; *m.*, let me die.
Dead   let me.
Yan-te kore murrong, tatte-ba bun-billa tea.
Like-as man   good,   dead   let   me.
       m., let me die, like as a good man.
Yuring ba-la bula wa-la; *m.*, away ye two must go.
Away   must ye-two move.
Bu-wa bon kore unne; buwa noun napal unnoa.
Beat   him man   this;   beat   her woman   that.
       m., beat this man; beat that woman.
Bu-wa be-nu warekul unnung; kai! wa-la, wa-la, wa-la.
Beat   thou   it   dog   there;   come! move,   move,   move.
       m., beat thou the dog there; come move, make haste.
Ka-bo yarai ka; *m.*, stop till the evening.
Stop   evening to.
Yanoa! take yekora be; yai! take kora, yanoa.
Let be!   eat   not   thou; let be!   eat   not   let be.
       m., thou shalt not eat; let it be; on no account eat; let it be.

18. Ya-no-ow, *m.*, *I remain; I will not.*

Man-ke yekora; bunke yekora; peta yekora; peta-la.
Take   not;   smite   not;   drink   not!   drink-do.
       m., do not steal; do not kill; do not drink; drink.
Yake! beyn petayeka; *m.*, serve thee right if thou art drunk.
Let be! to thee drunken.
Ya ke! beyn murrayeka; *m.*, serve thee right if thou wilt run.
Be as it is! to thee a runner.
Wea, be tanan; unte bang ka-tan; *m.*, wilt thou draw nigh?
Say, thou approach; here   I   am.
Wita korean bang; kaawi bang nga-le ko; nga-la ko.
Depart   not   I;   not   I   this   for;   that   for.
       m., I depart not; I am not for this; for that.
Kabo, kabo! me-tela tea; yanoa! me-te yekora.
Stop!   wait   me;   let be!   wait   do not.
       m., stop, stop! wait for me; never mind; do not wait.
Kakul-ba-ta unne; kakul koreannan unne; *m.*, this is nice;
Nice   this;   nice   not   this.   this is not.

Kooyung tea marao; yake-ta koa uma-la.
Fire   me bring (take); now   why   do.
    m., bring some fire to me; why! do it immediately.

Yan-to ko-lang uwan; yan-to barur-ba uwan.
Thus towards move;   thus   they   move.
    m., to this it moves; thus they move.

Yan-te-ta ngeroamba; yan-to unne-ba.
Thus   thine;   thus   this.
    m., to this it is like thine; it is like this.

Yan-to-bo kore ko-ba wean; *m.*, let it be thus, as a black
Thus   man belonging-to speak.   man speaks.

Yan-to-bo tea ngu-wa; yan-te wan-ta wea be.
Thus   me give;   thus as   say thou.
    m., just as it is, give it to me; just so as thou sayest.

Yupa-la unnoa yan-te; *m.*, do it like this.
Do, do   that thus as.

Upan noa yante unnoa-ba; uma-la unnoa yan-to.
Does he thus-as that;   make that thus as.
    m., it is done like that; make it like this.

Uma noa yante-ta; *m.*, he made it as this.
Made he thus as.

Ngu-ke-la nurur yan-toyn ko; kulla-ba-lea kote.
Give   ye   alike   for;   cut   own.
    m., give equally to all; cut thine own.

Bun-nun noa tea ba, tura-la be-nu; *m.*, if he strikes me,
Strike-will he me if, spear thou him. do thou spear him.

Purrul beyn ngora; purrul-lea purrul.
White to-thee face; whitened white.
    m., whiten thy face; it is whitened.

An—the sign of the present tense; as, we-an bang, 'I speak.'

Man-tan be, 'thou takest'; kow-wol, to be 'great,' or 'much,' or 'large'; kow-wol-lan unnoa, 'that is large'; kur-kur, 'cold'; kur-kur-ran bang, 'I am cold'; ta kur-rara, 'it is cold.' The consonants are doubled, in order to preserve their full sound, and to divide the syllables for pronouncing.

Eyn—forms the present participle; as, wa-leyn, 'moving'; tu-ra-leyn, 'spearing'; wa-leyn bang nar-ra-bo ka ko, 'I am getting to sleep,' *lit.*, 'I am moving for-to sleep'; bun-keyn noa, 'he being to be beaten.'

A—the sign of the past tense; as, wea bon bang, 'I told him'; na-ka-la bang, 'I saw' *or* 'did see'; bun-ka-la noa, 'he smote,' or 'struck,' or 'fought.'

An—the sign of the perfect; as, ta-ka-an bang, 'I have eaten'; ta-ka-an wal bang, 'I have just eaten'; wi-ta wa-la-an ngaan, 'we have departed'; ta-nan wa-la-an wal ba-rur, 'they have just arrived.'

Nun—forms the future; as, bun-nun bon bang, 'I will beat him'; kum-ba-bo wita bang wa-nun, 'I shall depart to-morrow'; wita wal bang wa-nun, 'I am about to depart.' wita wal bang pa-la wa-nun, 'I must depart.'

La—forms the active imperative; as, wea-la, 'speak'; ngurra-la, 'do hear': bu-mun-bil-la tea, 'let me smite'; ngur-ra-bun-bil-la toa bon, 'let him hear me.'

Wa—imperative of motion; as, bu-wa toa-be, 'smite thou me'; na-ow-wa, 'look.'

Ra—as in ra, imperatively used. Thus, kai bo, 'be thou here'; kabo bo, 'be thou where thou art,' 'stand still,' 'be still,' 'wait,' 'halt.' The bo reflects the verb on itself.

Ya—appears to be the imperative passive 'to be'; as, yanoa; weayo kora, 'let it be as it is'; 'do not speak.' This is often used with the negative imperative, yai, 'do not trouble me'; 'let me be as I am.'

Wil or ow-wil—this, whenever used, expresses a wish or desire; as, bu-wil bang goro-ung, 'I wish to beat thee'; pe-re-ke-wil bo, 'thou wishest to sleep'; pe-ta-ow-wil noa, 'he wishes to drink.'

Ko-a—has the same force; thus, bu-wil koa bang, 'in order that I may beat'; pe-re-ke-wil koa be, 'in order that thou mightest sleep'; pe-ta-ow-wil koa noa, 'in order that he may drink'; we-a-ow-wil koa bang, 'that I may speak.'

Ke-le-ko or le-ko—this forms the infinitive; thus, unne uma ammoung ta-ke-le-ko, 'this is made for me to eat'; tura-le-ko, 'to spear.' The idiom requires ko to form the infinitive; as, murrorong ta ta-ke-le-ko, 'it is good for-to eat.'

Eyn or Ke-leyn—this forms the present participle; as, ta-ke-leyn, 'to be eating'; tat-te-ba-leyn, 'to be dying.'